Human Resource Development

Human Resource Development

David M. Harris
Rhode Island College

Randy L. DeSimone
Rhode Island College

The Dryden Press
Harcourt Brace College Publishers
Fort Worth   Philadelphia   San Diego   New York   Orlando   Austin   San Antonio
Toronto   Montreal   London   Sydney   Tokyo

Acquisitions Editor	**Ruth Rominger**
Developmental Editor	**Traci Keller**
Project Editor	**Joan Harlan/Charlie Dierker**
Production Manager	**Mandy Manzano**
Art Director	**Beverly Baker**
Literary Permissions Editor	**Shirley Webster**
Publisher	**Liz Widdicombe**
Director of Editing, Design, & Production	**Diane Southworth**

Copy Editor	**Jennifer Moorhouse/Ann Helming**
Indexer	**Maggie Jarpey**
Compositor	**Typo•Graphics, Inc.**
Text Type	**10/12 Janson**

Address for Editorial Correspondence
The Dryden Press, 301 Commerce Street, Suite 3700, Fort Worth, TX 76102

Address for Orders
The Dryden Press, 6277 Sea Harbor Drive, Orlando, FL 32887
1-800-782-4479, or 1-800-433-0001 (in Florida)

ISBN: 0-03-055758-5

Library of Congress Catalog Number: 93-72077

Printed in the United States of America

3 4 5 6 7 8 9 0 1 2   016   9 8 7 6 5 4 3 2 1

The Dryden Press
Harcourt Brace College Publishers

The Dryden Press Series in Management

Anthony, Perrewe, and Kacmar
Strategic Human Resource Management

Bartlett
Cases in Strategic Management for Business

Bedeian
Management
Third Edition

Bedeian and Zammuto
Organizations: Theory and Design

Bereman and Lengnick-Hall
Compensation Decision Making: A Computer-Based Approach

Boone and Kurtz
Contemporary Business
Seventh Edition

Bowman and Branchaw
Business Report Writing
Second Edition

Bracker, Montanari, and Morgan
Cases in Strategic Management

Calvasina and Barton
Chopstick Company: A Business Simulation

Costin
Readings in Total Quality Management

Czinkota, Ronkainen, and Moffett
International Business
Third Edition

Daft
Management
Third Edition

Eckert, Ryan, and Ray
Small Business: An Entrepreneur's Plan
Third Edition

Etienne-Hamilton
Operations Strategies for Competitive Advantage: Text Cases

Foegen
Business Planning Guide
Revised Edition

Gaither
Production and Operations Management
Sixth Edition

Gatewood and Feild
Human Resource Selection
Third Edition

Gold
Exploring Organizational Behavior: Cases, Readings, Experiences

Greenhaus and Callanan
Career Management
Second Edition

Harris and DeSimone
Human Resource Development

Higgins and Vincze
Strategic Management: Text and Cases
Fifth Edition

Hills, Bergmann, and Scarpello
Compensation Decision Making
Second Edition

Hodgetts
Management: Theory, Process, and Practice

Hodgetts
Modern Human Relations at Work
Fifth Edition

Hodgetts amd Kroeck
Personnel and Human Resource Management

Hodgetts and Kuratko
Effective Small Business Management
Fourth Edition

Hodgetts and Kuratko
Management
Third Edition

Holley and Jennings
The Labor Relations Process
Fifth Edition

Huseman, Lahiff, and Penrose
Business Communication: Strategies and Skills
Fourth Edition

Jauch and Coltrin
The Managerial Experience: Cases and Exercises
Sixth Edition

Kemper
Experiencing Strategic Management

Kuehl and Lambing
Small Business: Planning and Management
Third Edition

Kuratko and Hodgetts
Entrepreneurship: A Contemporary Approach
Second Edition

Kuratko and Welsch
Entrepreneurial Strategy: Text and Cases

Lewis
Io Enterprises Simulation

Luthans and Hodgetts
Business
Second Edition

McMullen and Long
Developing New Ventures: The Entrepreneurial Option

Matsuura
International Business: A New Era

Mauser
American Business: An Introduction
Sixth Edition

Montanari, Morgan, and Bracker
Strategic Management: A Choice Approach

Northcraft and Neale
Organizational Behavior: A Management Challenge
Second Edition

Penderghast
Entrepreneurial Simulation Progam

Sandburg
Career Design Software

Sawyer
Business Policy and Strategic Management: Planning, Strategy, and Action

Schoderbeck
Management
Second Edition

Schwartz
Introduciton to Management: Principles, Practices, and Processes
Second Edition

Varner
Contemporary Business Report Writing
Second Edition

Vecchio
Organizational Behavior
Second Edition

Walton
Corporate Encounters: Law, Ethics, and the Business Environment

Wolford and Vanneman
Business Communication

Wolters and Holley
Labor Relations: An Experiential and Case Approach

Zikmund
Business Research Methods
Fourth Edition

The Harcourt Brace College Outline Series

Pentico
Management Science

Sigband
Business Communication

Pierson
**Introduction to Business Information
Systems**

An organization's success is determined as much by the skill and motivation of its members as by almost any other factor. While this has always been true, the pace and volume of modern change is focusing attention on ways human resource development (HRD) activities can be used to ensure organization members have what it takes to successfully meet their challenges. Yet while we know that HRD works, it is not a "magic bullet." The challenges many organizations face are complex, and new dimensions, such as an increasingly diverse workforce, make it more difficult to ensure HRD efforts will succeed. Unless those responsible for training and developing make informed choices about the content and methods of delivering the developmental experience, the results of many HRD efforts will fail to meet expectations.

Fortunately, there is a rich and growing base of theory, research, and practical experience in HRD efforts. We wrote this book to help students, HRD professionals, and managers at all levels take advantage of this knowledge and experience. We firmly believe that if they do so, they will increase their effectiveness along with that of individuals with whom they work and with the organizations of which they are a part.

Intended Audience

We wrote *Human Resource Development* to serve primarily as a comprehensive text for undergraduate and graduate courses in business, management, public administration, educational administration, and other fields that prepare students to train and develop other people. As such, the book:

- covers the entire field of HRD (as defined by the American Society for Training and Development's competency study), from orientation and skills training, to career development and organizational development.

- provides a clear understanding of the concepts, processes, and practices that form the basis of successful HRD.
- shows how concepts and theory can and have been put into practice in a variety of organizations.
- focuses on the shared role of line management and the human resource specialists in HRD.
- reflects the current state of the field, blending real-world practices and up-to-date research.

In addition to being an appropriate text for academic courses, this book is an excellent resource for HRD professionals. It can also serve as a comprehensive introduction for managers and supervisors who have had limited (or no) course work or experience with HRD. Not only can they become better trainers and developers, they will become more informed consumers of the HRD efforts offered by their organizations.

Pedagogical Features

We have included a number of pedagogical aids in the text to enhance student learning and interest. These aids include:

- **learning objectives** at the beginning of each chapter.
- an **opening case** in each chapter that places the contents into a meaningful context.
- **illustrations, examples,** and **references** throughout the chapter to help students better assimilate the information.
- a **return to the opening case** to provide closure and show how the chapter contents may be used to address the issues in the case.
- a list of **key terms** and **concepts** at the end of each chapter.
- **end of chapter questions** intended to stimulate thought and provide students with an opportunity to use the information.

In addition, numerous examples from organizations, along with perspectives offered by organization leaders and HRD professionals, are used to reinforce concepts and demonstrate the importance of effective HRD to organizational success.

Organization of the Text

The text is organized to ensure the reader builds a base of foundational concepts prior to exploring the HRD process and the various ways that HRD is practiced in organizations. Chapters 1 through 3 present the foundational material. Chapter 1 presents an overview of HRD, including its history and the current view of the field encompassing three major focuses: training and development, career development, and organizational development. Because all HRD efforts involve trying to bring about changes in behavior, it is important that the reader understand why people in the workplace behave the way they do and how people learn. These issues are the focus of Chapters 2 and 3. Chapter 2 explores the major factors that affect workplace behavior, while Chapter 3 focuses on how people learn, the factors that affect learning, and ways to maximize learning.

Chapters 4 through 6 describe the HRD and training process, focusing on three sets of activities common to all HRD efforts: needs assessment, design and implementation, and evaluation. These chapters are anchored by a model that shows the relationships among these three critical phases of the HRD process. Chapter 4 details the importance of assessing the need for HRD and the approaches that can be used to perform a needs assessment. Chapter 5 focuses on designing and implementing HRD programs based on the information obtained from a needs assessment. Activities discussed in this chapter include establishing program objectives and content, selecting the trainer, HRD methods and media, and the practical issues involved in delivering the program. Chapter 6 completes discussion of the HRD process by explaining the importance of evaluating HRD efforts and ways that evaluation can be done to ensure decisions made about HRD programs are based on meaningful, accurate information.

Chapters 7 through 11 focus on employee development processes and programs, from orientation to career development. Chapter 7 discusses the socialization process, its importance to employee and organizational effectiveness, and how orientation programs can be used to facilitate successful socialization. Chapter 8 describes skills training programs, including approaches used to ensure employees possess the specific skills, such as literacy, computation, and interpersonal skills, they need to perform effectively and contribute to the organization's success. Chapter 9 discusses the importance of coaching as an employee development process, and explains how supervisors and line managers can successfully fulfill their critical coaching responsibilities. Chapter 10 provides a comprehensive overview of employee counseling as a way to ensure employees can overcome personal and other problems (such as, substance abuse or stress) to remain effective in the workplace. Finally, Chapter 11 focuses on career development as a way to ensure organization members can be prepared to meet their own and the organization's needs over the course of their working lives. In particular, career development issues and approaches are discussed.

The final three chapters in the book focus on more macro issues in HRD. Chapter 12 discusses how individuals can be developed to fulfill the multifaceted challenge of becoming effective managers. Chapter 13 explores how HRD can be used to prepare organizations for change, including ways to diagnose organizational problems and how to create and implement intervention strategies to improve individual, group, and organizational effectiveness. Chapter 14 closes the book with a discussion of the challenges organizations face as the workforce becomes increasingly diverse, and the role HRD can play in meeting these challenges and achieving the goal of multiculturalism.

Acknowledgements

One of the most rewarding aspects of writing this book has been the opportunity to work with a team of professionals as supportive, knowledgeable, and dedicated as the folks at The Dryden Press. We are particularly grateful to Butch

Gemin, who provided valuable support, guidance, and gentle prodding during the early stages of developing the manuscript. We also thank Ruth Rominger for her support and suggestions in developing the manuscript down the home stretch. Traci Keller also earned our thanks for her contribution in developing the manuscript and coordinating the review process. Joni Harlan and Charlie Dierker were invaluable in taking the completed manuscript and transforming it into a book of which we are proud. We would also like to thank Jennifer Johnson and Ann Helming for expert copyediting, Shirley Webster for pursuing permissions, and Beverly Baker for the design of the book. We feel truly fortunate to have worked with such a fine team.

We would also like to acknowledge our colleagues who provided expert advice, reviews, and suggestion for changes that made this book significantly better. They are Brien N. Smith, Ball State University; John F. Binning, Illinois State University; Alan Cabelly, Portland State University; Harry W. Hennessey, Jr., University of Hawaii–Hilo; Debra J. Cohen, George Washington University; Margaret E. Holt, University of Georgia; Raymond A. Noe, University of Minnesota; and Michael H. Korzeniowski, LaSalle University.

Our students and colleagues at Rhode Island College deserve thanks for their genuine support and enthusiasm for this project, especially for being understanding when either of us said, "Well I'd have gotten that to you sooner, but I was working on an important part of the book." Our HRD students over the past several years also provided valuable comments and suggestions on earlier versions of the manuscript.

David Harris would like to acknowledge his family and friends for their support during the project. To my sister Ginny, whose love, guidance, support, and sacrifice, particularly during my early life, will always be remembered. To my children, David and Kien, whose continued love and respect have made parenting a joy. Finally, my special thanks to Patricia Morgan whose assistance, encouragement, and selflessness since the inception of this book helped me to overcome many frustrating days. Her continued love, friendship, and caring have made this all possible.

Randy DeSimone would like to thank his family and friends for their support and encouragement during this project. In particular, I am grateful to my parents, Mary and Carmen DeSimone, for their love and encouragement throughout my life and career. John Fiore deserves special thanks for listening and for helping me keep the tough times in perspective. Acknowledgement is also due to the I/O Psychology faculty (especially Ralph Alexander, Bob Lord, and Gerald Barrett) and my fellow graduate students at the University of Akron during my graduate training, for their help in shaping my critical capacities and approach to the field. Finally, and most importantly, I would like to thank my wife and best friend, Taina, for her continued love, support, and counsel, and especially for her faith in me at times when I wasn't so sure myself. Thank you, Taina.

Finally, we would like the reader to know that creating this book was truly a team effort, and that this book would not be what it is without the important contributions of each author. While it is true that one author must be listed first, the order of authorship of this text is not intended to indicate the authors' relative contribution to the work.

BRIEF TABLE OF CONTENTS

Preface   viii

Chapter 1
Introduction to Human Resource Development   1

Chapter 2
Influences on Employee Behavior   23

Chapter 3
Learning and HRD   53

Chapter 4
**The Training and HRD Process and the Assessment
of HRD Needs**   87

Chapter 5
Designing and Implementing Training Programs   123

Chapter 6
Evaluating HRD Programs   165

Chapter 7
Employee Orientation   203

Chapter 8
Skills and Technical Training   235

Chapter 9
Coaching

263

Chapter 10
Employee Counseling Services

287

Chapter 11
Career Development

323

Chapter 12
Management Development

369

Chapter 13
Organizational Development and Change

413

Chapter 14
HRD in a Multicultural Environment

451

References   483

Name Index   535

Subject Index   543

Preface   viii

Chapter 1
Introduction to Human Resource Development   1

Introduction   2
The Evolution of Human Resource Development   3
   Early Apprenticeship Training Programs   3
   Early Vocational Education Programs   3
   Early Factory Schools   4
   Early Training Programs for Semiskilled and
      Unskilled Workers   4
   The Human Relations Movement   5
   The Establishment of the Training Profession   5
The Relationship between Human Resource
  Management and HRD   6
   Primary HRM Functions   6
   Secondary HRM Functions   7
   Line versus Staff Authority   8
Human Resource Development Structure and
  Functions   8
   Training and Development (T&D)   10
   Organization Development   10
   Career Development   11
   The Supervisor's Role in HRD   11
   Organizational Structure of HRD   11
Roles of an HRD Professional   11
   The HRD Executive/Manager   13
   Other HRD Roles and Outputs   14

HRD Competencies   14
   Certification and Education for HRD Professionals   16
   HRD Education: Developing Closer Ties to
      Academia   17
Challenges to HRD Practitioners   18
   Changing Work Force Demographics   18
   Competing in a Global Economy   18
   Eliminating the Skills Gap   19
   The Need for Lifelong Learning   19
Summary   20

Chapter 2
Influences on Employee Behavior   23

Introduction   24
Model of Employee Behavior   25
Motivation: An Internal Influence on Employee
  Behavior   26
   Need-based Theories of Motivation   26
   Cognitive Theories of Motivation   29
   Reinforcement Theory: A Non-Cognitive Theory
      of Motivation   38
   Summary of Motivation   39
Other Internal Factors that Influence Employee
  Behavior   39
   Attitudes   40
   Knowledge, Skills, and Abilities (KSAs)   41
Environmental Influences on Employee Behavior   43
   Outcomes   43
   The Supervisor   45
   The Organization   46
   Co-Workers   47
Summary   49

Chapter 3
Learning and HRD   53

Introduction   54
Learning and Instruction   54
   The Search for Basic Learning Principles   55
   Limits of Learning Principles in Improving
      Training Design   56
   Instructional Psychology: Incorporating the
      Situation in Learning   56

Maximizing Learning   57
     Trainee Characteristics   57
     Training Design   60
     Retention of What Is Learned   62
     Transfer of Training   63
Individual Differences in the Learning Process   66
     Rate of Progress   67
     Attribute-Treatment Interaction (ATI)   68
     Training the Older Worker   68
Learning Strategies and Styles   73
     Kolb's Learning Styles   73
     Learning Strategies   76
     Perceptual Preferences   77
Emerging Perspectives from Instructional Psychology   78
     The ACT* Approach to Learning Procedural Skills   78
     Learning to Regulate One's Own Behavior   79
     The Gagné-Briggs Instructional Theory   79
Summary   82

Chapter 4
The Training and HRD Process and the Assessment of HRD Needs   87

Creating an HRD Program   88
     Needs Assessment Phase   88
     Design/Implementation Phase   89
     Evaluation Phase   90
Needs Assessment   91
     Definition and Purposes of Needs Assessment   91
     What Is a Training Need?   92
     Level of Needs Analysis   94
Organizational Analysis   95
     Components of an Organizational Needs Analysis   95
     Advantages of Conducting and Organizational Analysis   96
     Organizational Analysis Methods   97
Task Analysis   99
     The Task Analysis Process   100
     An Example of a Task Analysis   108
     Summary of Task Analysis   110
Person Analysis   110
     Components of Person Analysis   110
     Performance Appraisal in the Person Analysis Process   111
     Developmental Needs   115

Employees as a Source of Needs Assessment
Information   115
The "Benchmarks" Specialized Person Analysis
Instrument   116
Prioritizing HRD Needs   119
Participation in the Prioritization Process   119
The HRD Advisory Committee   119
Summary   121

Chapter 5
Designing and Implementing Training Programs   123

Introduction   124
Defining Program Objectives   126
Purchasing HRD Programs   128
Selecting the Trainer   130
Train-the-Trainer Programs   131
Preparing a Lesson Plan   132
Selecting Training Methods   133
On-the-Job Training (OJT) Methods   133
Job Instruction Training (JIT)   138
Job Rotation   139
Classroom Training Methods   140
The Lecture Method   141
The Discussion Method   142
Audiovisual Methods   142
Experiential Methods   148
Computer-Based Training Methods   152
Selecting Appropriate Training Methods   155
Preparing Training Materials   156
Program Announcements   156
Program Outlines   156
Training Manuals or Textbooks   157
Scheduling the Training Program   157
Scheduling during Work Hours   157
Scheduling after Work Hours   158
Implementing the Training Program   159
Arranging the Physical Environment   159
Getting Started   160
Summary   162

Chapter 6
Evaluating HRD Programs   165

Introduction   166
The Purpose of HRD Evaluation   167

How Often Are HRD Programs Evaluated? 168
Pre-purchase Evaluation of Training and HRD
    Programs 169
Evolution of Evaluation Efforts 169
Models of Evaluation 170
Kirkpatrick's Model 170
Other Models of Evaluation 172
Comparing Evaluation Models 173
Data Collection for HRD Evaluation 174
Data Collection Methods 174
Choosing Data Collection Methods 177
Types of Data 179
Limits of Self-Report Data 179
Research Design 180
Research Design Validity 180
Nonexperimental Designs 181
Experimental Designs 183
Quasi-Experimental Designs 186
Selecting a Research Design 188
Ethical Issues of Evaluation Research 188
Confidentiality 189
Informed Consent 189
Withholding Training 189
Use of Deception 190
Pressure to Produce Positive Results 190
Assessing the Impact of HRD Programs in Dollar
Terms 190
Evaluation of Training Costs 191
Utility Analysis 195
A Closing Comment on HRD Evaluation 197
Summary 199

Chapter 7
Employee Orientation 203

Introduction 204
Socialization: The Process of Becoming an Insider 205
The Fundamental Concepts of Socialization 205
Content of Socialization 208
Outcomes of Socialization 209
Stage Models of the Socialization Process 210
People Processing Tactics and Strategies 213
What Do Newcomers Need? 216
The Realistic Job Preview 217
How RJPs Are Used 219
Are RJPs Effective? 221

Employee Orientation Programs   222
    Orientation Program Content   222
    Orientation Roles   223
    Problems with Orientation Programs   227
    Designing an Employee Orientation Program   228
    Orientation Program Effectiveness   229
Summary   231

Chapter 8
Skills and Technical Training

Skills and Technical Training   235

Introduction   236
Basic Workplace Competencies   237
Basic Skills/Literacy Programs   238
    Addressing Illiteracy in the Workplace   239
    Designing an In-House Basic Skills/Literacy
        Program   240
    Federal Support for Basic Skills Training   241
Technical Training   243
    Apprenticeship Training Programs   243
    Computer Training Programs   245
    Technical Skills/Knowledge Training   246
    Safety Training   247
    Quality Training   248
Nontechnical Training   251
    Communication/Interpersonal Skills Training   251
    Sales Training   252
    Customer Relations/Service Training   252
    Team Building/Training   254
Professional Development and Education   255
    Continuing Education at Colleges and Universities 255
    Continuing Education by Professional Associations 256
    Continuing Education Programs Offered On-Site   257
    HRD Department's Role in Continuing Education   257
Summary   259

Chapter 9
Coaching

Coaching   263

The Need for Coaching   264
    Coaching: A Positive Approach to Managing
        Performance   265
Definition of Coaching   266
    Role of Supervisor and Manager in Coaching   267
    The HRD Professional's Role in Coaching   267

Coaching to Improve Poor Performance ... 268
    Defining Poor Performance ... 268
    Responding to Poor Performance ... 269
    Conducting the Coaching Analysis ... 271
    The Coaching Discussion ... 274
Maintaining Effective Performance and Encouraging
    Superior Performance ... 277
Skills Necessary for Effective Coaching ... 278
The Effectiveness of Coaching ... 281
    Employee Participation in Discussion ... 281
    Being Supportive ... 281
    Using Constructive Criticism ... 282
    Setting Performance Goals During Discussion ... 282
    Training and the Supervisor's Credibility ... 282
    Closing Comment ... 283
Summary ... 284

Chapter 10

Employee Counseling Services ... 287

The Need for Employee Counseling Programs ... 288
    Employee Counseling as an HRD Activity ... 289
An Overview of Employee Counseling Programs ... 290
    Components of the Typical Program ... 290
    Who Provides the Service? ... 291
    Characteristics of Effective Employee Counseling
        Programs ... 292
Employee Assistance Programs ... 292
    Substance Abuse ... 293
    Mental Health ... 294
    The EAP Approach ... 295
    Effectiveness of EAPs ... 299
Stress Management Interventions ... 301
    Defining Stress ... 302
    A Model of SMIs ... 303
    The Effectiveness of SMIs ... 305
Health Promotion Programs ... 305
    Exercise and Fitness Interventions ... 309
    Smoking Cessation ... 310
    Nutrition and Weight-Control Interventions ... 311
    Control of Hypertension ... 311
Issues in Employee Counseling ... 312
    Effectiveness of Employee Counseling Interventions ... 312
    Legal Issues in Employee Counseling Programs ... 314
    Whose Responsibility Is Employee Counseling? ... 315
    Ethical Issues in Employee Counseling ... 316

    Unintended Negative Outcomes of Employee
        Counseling Programs   317
    Closing Comment   318
Summary   319

Chapter 11
Career Development   323

Introduction   324
Defining Career Concepts   325
    What Is a Career?   325
    Relationship of Career to Nonwork Activities   326
    Career Development   326
    Career Planning and Career Management   327
Stages of Career Development   328
    Stage Views of Adult Development   329
    A Model of Career Development   334
    Life Stage and Career Stage Models as Conceptual
        Base for Career Development   336
The Process of Career Management   337
The Supervisor's Role in Career Management   338
Career Development Practices and Activities   340
    Self-Assessment Tools and Activities   341
    Individual Career Counseling   346
    Internal Labor Market Information/Job Placement
        Exchanges   347
    Organization Potential Assessments   349
    Developmental Programs   350
Issues in Career Development   353
    Developing Career Motivation   354
    The Career Plateau   354
    Career Development for Nonexempt Employees   357
    Enrichment: Career Development without
        Advancement   358
    Career Development and the Baby Boom
        Generation   359
Delivering Effective Career Development Systems   360
Summary   365

Chapter 12
Management Development   369

Introduction   370
    Extent of Management Development Activities   372

Organization of the Chapter   372
**Describing the Manager's Job: Management Roles
and Competencies**   373
Approaches to Understanding the Job of Managing   374
Importance of Needs Assessment in Determining
Managerial Competencies   380
The Globally Competent Manager   382
Management Education   387
Bachelor's or Master's Degree Programs in Business
Administration   387
Executive M.B.A. Programs   388
Short Courses in Management   389
Management Training and Experiences   390
Company-designed Courses   391
Company Academies or "Colleges"   391
On-the-Job Experiences   392
Examples of Approaches Used to Develop Managers   396
Leadership Training   396
Performance Rater Training   403
Behavior Modeling Training   405
Designing Management Development Programs   408
Summary   409

Chapter 13
Organizational Development and Change   413

Organization Development (OD) Defined   414
Organization Development Theories and Concepts   415
Change Process Theory   415
Implementation Theory   416
Lack of Fundamental OD Research   419
Model of Planned Change   420
Designing an Intervention Strategy   422
Specific Roles   423
Designing the Intervention Strategy   425
Role of HRD Practitioners in Design of OD
Interventions   427
The Role of Labor Unions in Design of OD
Interventions   428
Types of Interventions: Human and Processual   428
Survey Feedback   428
Team Building   429
Effectiveness of Human Processual Interventions   430
Types of Interventions: Technostructural   430
Job Design/Enlargement   431

Job Enrichment   431
Alternative Work Schedules   432
Effectiveness of Technostructural Interventions   432
Types of Interventions: Sociotechnical Systems   433
Quality Circles   434
Total Quality Management   435
Self-Directed Teams   437
Differences Between TQM and SDT   439
HRD Programs as Sociotechnical Intervention
    Techniques   440
Types of Interventions: Large Systems Change   440
Cultural Interventions   442
Strategic Changes   442
Effectiveness of Large Systems Change Strategies   444
Roles of HRD Practitioners in Design of Large
    Systems Change   445
Summary   447

Chapter 14
HRD in a Multicultural Environment   451

Introduction   452
Organizational Culture   452
Organizational Culture Defined   453
**Effects of Labor-Market Changes on Organizational
Culture**   454
Women and Organizational Culture   455
The "Glass Ceiling"   456
Lack of Role Models and Mentors   457
Department of Labor Study   458
Challenges to Human Resource Development   459
Minorities and Organizational Culture   459
Access Discrimination   460
Treatment Discrimination   460
Impact of Recent Immigration Patterns   461
Challenges to Human Resource Development   463
Adapting to Demographic Changes   463
Affirmative Action Programs   464
Valuing Differences   466
Managing Diversity   467
Potential Roadblocks to Multiculturalism   468
**Introducing Multiculturalism through Change
Strategy**   470
Determining Readiness of the Organization to
    Accept Change   470
Developing a Commitment Plan   470

Developing Change Strategy   471
Evaluating Results   472
Multicultural Education and Training Programs   473
    Potential Problems with Diversity Education
       and Training   476
Human Resource Development Programs Needed
  for Multiculturalism   477
    Socialization, Orientation, and Career Development   477
    Career Development   478
    Other Human Resource Management Programs
       and Processes   479
    Closing Comment   479
Summary   480

References   483

Name Index   535

Subject Index   543

Human Resource Development

1

Introduction to Human Resource Development

Learning Objectives

1. *Define human resource development (HRD).*
2. *Identify and briefly describe each of the HRD functions.*
3. *Relate the major historical events leading up to the establishment of HRD.*
4. *Recognize the importance of HRD roles and competencies.*
5. *Cite four challenges currently faced by HRD professionals.*

OPENING CASE

When Arthur Andersen founded his famous accounting and consulting firm over 80 years ago, he used part-time accountants to perform tax and audit work. However, he quickly became convinced that his employees would be more productive if they participated in training programs and worked full-time. This commitment to job training, or human resource development (HRD), has helped make Arthur Andersen & Company (AA) the third-largest accounting and consulting firm in the world today. For example, in 1992, AA invested over $300 million (approximately 5.5 percent of that year's $5.6 billion revenues) in HRD efforts, while devoting an average of 138 hours to the training of each employee. This commitment reflects how AA has continued the corporate philosophy of its founder.

The main hub of HRD activity at AA is the Center for Professional Education (CPE). The CPE is responsible for a wide range of HRD programs and services throughout the company that include training design and development, curriculum planning, and training support. The CPE provides approximately 6 million hours of training a year with a variety of formats, including classroom training and multimedia programs at computer workstations.

In 1989, AA expanded its traditional accounting operations so that it could also provide its customers with management consulting services. The new division, Andersen Consulting, sought to expand its share of the market for helping clients utilize information-based technology on their desktop computers by linking them to client/server networks. However, many of the Andersen Consulting employees were trained on larger mainframe computers and knew little about desktop computing and client/server networks. It was obvious that Andersen Consulting employees would need considerable training to take advantage of this lucrative opportunity.

Faced with this challenge, and a tight project schedule, the CPE staff began the task of designing and developing this critical HRD program.

Introduction

It is often said that an organization is only as good as its people. Organizations of all types and sizes, including schools, retail stores, government agencies, restaurants, and manufacturers, have one thing in common: they share the common challenge to employ competent and motivated workers. Today, the need is becoming even more acute for employees with the knowledge and skills necessary for their organizations to compete in a global economy. It has been estimated that education and training programs account for as much as 26 percent of the increase in U.S. production capacity between 1929 through 1982 (Carnevale & Gainer, 1989).

Human resource development (HRD) can be defined as a set of systematic and planned activities designed by an organization to provide its members with the necessary skills to meet current and future job demands. HRD activities should begin when an employee joins an organization and continue throughout his or her career, regardless of whether that employee is an executive or a semiskilled line worker. HRD programs must respond to job changes and integrate the long-term plans and strategies of the organization in order to ensure the efficient and effective use of resources.

This chapter provides a brief history of the significant events contributing to contemporary thought within the HRD field. We will briefly discuss human resource management and the HRD structure and functions, detailing roles and outputs. Then we will briefly discuss HRD competencies and their role in the establishment of professional standards. Finally, we will cite several critical challenges facing HRD professionals today.

The Evolution of Human Resource Development

Human Resource Development is a relatively new term, but not a new concept. To understand its modern definition, it is helpful to recount the history of this important professional field.

Early Apprenticeship Training Programs

The origins of HRD can be traced directly to early apprenticeship training programs in the eighteenth century. During this time, small shops operated by skilled artisans produced virtually all household goods, such as furniture, clothing, and shoes. To meet a growing demand for their products, craft shop owners had to employ additional workers. Without vocational or technical schools, the shopkeepers had to educate and train their own workers. For little or no wages, these trainees, or apprentices, learned the craft of their master, usually working in the shop for several years until they became proficient in their trade. Not limited to the skilled trades, the apprenticeship model was also followed in the training of physicians, educators, and attorneys. Even as late as the 1920s, a person apprenticing in a law office could practice law after passing a state supervised exam (Steinmetz, 1976).

Apprentices who mastered all of the necessary skills were considered "yeomen," and could leave their master and establish their own craft shops. However, most remained with their masters because they could not afford to buy the necessary tools and equipment to start their own craft shops. To address a growing number of yeomen, master craftsmen formed a network of private "franchises" so they could regulate such things as product quality, wages, hours, and apprentice testing procedures (Hodges & Ziegler, 1963; Miller, 1987). These craft guilds grew to become powerful political and social forces within their communities, making it even more difficult for yeomen to establish independent craft shops. By forming separate guilds called "yeomanries," the yeomen counterbalanced the powerful craft guilds and created a collective voice in negotiating higher wages and better working conditions (Miller, 1987). Yeomanries were the forerunners of modern labor unions.

Early Vocational Education Programs

In 1809, DeWitt Clinton founded the first recognized privately funded vocational school, also referred to as a manual school, in New York City (Nadler & Nadler, 1989). The purpose of the manual schools was to provide occupational training to unskilled young people who were unemployed or had criminal records. Manual schools grew in popularity, particularly in the midwestern states, because they were a public solution to a social problem: what to do with misdirected youths. Regardless of their intent, these early forms of occupational training established a prototype for vocational education.

In 1917, Congress passed the Smith-Hughes Act, which recognized the value of vocational education by granting funds (initially $7 million annually) targeted for state programs in agricultural trades, home economics, industry, and teacher training (Steinmetz, 1976). Today, vocational instruction is an important part of each state's public education system.

Early Factory Schools

With the advent of the industrial revolution during the late 1800s, machines began to replace the hand tools of the artisans. "Scientific" management principles recognized the significant role of machines in better and more efficient production systems. Specifically, the design of machines operated by semiskilled workers could produce more than the products of skilled workers in a small craft shop. This marked the beginning of factories as we know them today.

Factories made it possible to increase production by using machines and unskilled workers, but they also created a significant demand for the engineers, machinists, and skilled mechanics needed to design, build, and repair the machines. Fueled by the rapid increase in the number of factories, the demand for skilled workers soon outstripped the supply of vocational school graduates. In order to meet this demand, factories created mechanical and machinist training programs, which were referred to as "factory schools" (Pace, Smith, and Mills, 1991).

The first documented factory school, in 1872, was located at Hoe and Company, a New York manufacturer of printing presses. This was soon followed by Westinghouse in 1888, General Electric and Baldwin Locomotive in 1901, International Harvester in 1907, and then Ford, Western Electric, Goodyear, and National Cash Register (Steinmetz, 1976). Factory schools differed from early apprenticeship programs in that they tended to be shorter in duration and had a narrower focus on the skills needed in a particular job.

Early Training Programs for Semiskilled and Unskilled Workers

While both apprenticeship programs and factory schools provided training for skilled workers, very few companies during this time offered training programs for the unskilled or semiskilled workers. This changed with the advent of two significant historical events. The first was the introduction of the Model T by Ford in 1913. The Model T was the first car to be mass-produced using an assembly line, in which production only required the training of semiskilled workers to perform several tasks.

The new assembly lines cut production costs significantly and Ford lowered its prices, making the Model T affordable to a much larger segment of the public. With the increased demand for the Model T, Ford had to design more assembly lines and thus provide more training opportunities. Most of the other automobile manufacturers who entered the market copied Ford's production design, resulting in a proliferation of semiskilled training programs.

Another significant historical event was the outbreak of World War I. To meet a huge demand for military equipment, many factories that produced nonmilitary goods had to retool their machinery and retrain their workers, including the semiskilled. For instance, the U.S. Shipping Board was responsible for coordinating the training of shipbuilders to build warships. To facilitate the training process, Charles Allen, Director of Training, instituted a four-step instructional method referred to as "show, tell, do, and check" for all of the training programs offered by the Shipping Board (Miller, 1987). This technique was later named job instruction training (JIT) and is still being used today for training workers on the job.

The Human Relations Movement

One of the by-products of the factory system was the abuse of unskilled workers, including children, who were subjected to unhealthy working conditions, long hours, and low pay. The appalling conditions spurred a national anti-factory campaign. Led by Mary Parker Follett and Lillian Gilbreth, the campaign gave rise to the "human relations" movement advocating more humane working conditions. Among other things, the human relations movement provided a more complex and realistic understanding of workers as people instead of "cogs" in a factory machine.

The human relations movement broadened the scope of inquiry to the importance of human behavior on the job. This was addressed by Chester Barnard, the president of New Jersey Bell Telephone, in his book entitled *The Functions of the Executive*. Barnard (1938) described the organization as a social structure integrating traditional management and behavioral science applications.

The movement continued into the 1940s, with World War II as a backdrop. Abraham Maslow (1943) published his theory on human needs, stating that people can be motivated by noneconomic incentives. He proposed that human needs are arranged in terms of lesser to greater potency (strength), and, under conditions of equal deprivation, the prepotent needs are the most urgent and persistent. Maslow also distinguished between lower order (basic survival) and higher order (psychological) needs. Theories like Maslow's serve to reinforce the notion that the varied needs and desires of workers can become important sources of motivation in the workplace.

The Establishment of the Training Profession

With the outbreak of World War II, the industrial sector was once again asked to retool its factories in order to support the war effort. As had happened in World War I, this initiative led to the establishment of new training programs within larger organizations and unions. The federal government established the Training Within Industry (TWI) Service to coordinate training programs across defense-related industries. TWI also trained company instructors to teach their programs at each plant. By the end of the war, the TWI had trained over 23,000 instructors, awarding over 2 million certificates to supervisors from 16,000 plants, unions, and services (Miller, 1987).

Many defense-related companies established their own training departments with instructors trained by TWI. These departments designed, organized, and coordinated training across the organization. In 1942, the American Society for Training Directors (ASTD) was formed to establish some standards within this emerging profession (Nadler & Nadler, 1989). The requirements for full membership in ASTD included a college or university degree plus two years of experience in training or a related field, or five years of experience in training. A person working in a training function or attending college qualified for associate membership.

During the 1960s and 1970s, professional trainers realized that their role extended beyond the training room. The move toward employee involvement in many organizations required trainers to coach and counsel employees. Training and development (T&D) competencies also expanded to include interpersonal skills, such as coaching, group process facilitation, and problem solving. This additional emphasis on employee development provoked the ASTD to professionally designate themselves the American Society for Training and Development.

The 1980s saw even greater changes affecting the T&D field. At several ASTD national conferences held in the late 1970s and early 1980s, discussions centered around this rapidly expanding profession. As a result of these discussions, the ASTD approved the term *human resource development* to encompass this growth and change.

The Relationship between Human Resource Management and HRD

In most organizations, human resource development is part of a larger human resource management department. **Human resource management** (HRM) is defined as the effective utilization of employees in order to achieve the goals and strategies of the organization. The responsibility for HRM is shared between human resource specialists and line management. How the HRM function is carried out varies from organization to organization. Some organizations have a centralized HRM department with highly specialized staff, while in other organizations the HRM function is decentralized and effected throughout the organization.

The most comprehensive way to present the HRM function is to examine the activities carried out by a large department, such as the HRM division headed by a vice president depicted in Figure 1-1. HRM can be divided into primary and secondary functions. **Primary functions** are directly involved with obtaining, maintaining, and developing employees. **Secondary functions** either provide support for general management activities or are involved in determining or changing the structure of the organization. These functions are detailed below.

Primary HRM Functions

- **Recruiting and selection** activities are designed for the timely identification of potential applicants for current and future openings and for screening applicants in order to make a selection and placement decision.

- **Compensation and benefits** administration is responsible for establishing and maintaining an equitable internal wage structure and a competitive benefits package.

- **Employee (labor) relations** activities include developing a communications system through which employees can address their

FIGURE 1-1	ORGANIZATIONAL CHART OF A LARGE HRM DIVISION

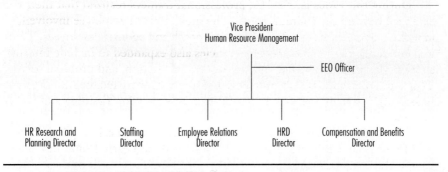

problems and grievances. In a union shop, labor relations will include developing working relations with each labor union, and contract negotiations and administration.

- **Human resource planning** activities are used to predict how changes in management strategy will impact future human resource needs. These activities are becoming increasingly important with the rapid changes in external market demands. HR planners must continually chart the course for future plans, programs, and actions.

- **Equal employment opportunity** activities are intended to satisfy both legal and moral responsibilities of the organization through the prevention of discriminatory policies, procedures, and practices, particularly when making employment decisions.

- **Human resource development** activities are intended to ensure that organizational members have the competencies to meet current and future job demands. This will be the focus of this textbook.

Secondary HRM Functions

The other functions that may be shared between HRM units include the following:

- **Organization/job design** activities are concerned with interdepartmental relations and the organization and definition of jobs.

- **Performance management systems** are used for establishing and maintaining accountability throughout the organization.

- **Research and information systems** are necessary to make enlightened human resource decisions.

Line versus Staff Authority

One of the primary components of organization structure is the authority delegated to a manager or unit to make decisions and utilize resources. **Line authority** is given to managers and organizational units who are directly responsible for the production of goods and services. **Staff authority** is given to organizational units who advise and consult line units. Traditionally, HRM functional units, including HRD, have staff authority. Generally speaking, line authority supersedes staff authority in matters pertaining to the production of goods and services. For example, suppose several trainees miss training sessions because their supervisor assigned them to duties away from the job site. Can the HRD manager or trainer intervene and force the supervisor to reassign these employees so that they can meet their training responsibilities? The short answer is no. The long answer is that HRD managers and staff must exert as much influence as possible to ensure that organizational members have the competencies to meet current and future job demands. At times this may require some type of intervention (such as organization development) to achieve a greater amount of understanding of the values and goals of HRD programs and processes.

An important dimension of authority, whether it is line or staff, is its scope. The scope of authority refers to the limitations placed on decision making and the use of resources. Many organizations specify scope in official documents like job descriptions, employment contracts, procedures, and work rules. The scope of authority is particularly important in the area of expenditures. For example, an HRD director may have the authority to issue contracts up to a maximum of $5,000, while larger amounts must be approved by the vice president of administration.

Human Resource Development Structure and Functions

Human resource development, as we discussed, is one of the primary functions within the human resource management (HRM) department. The structure of the HRD function and its scope has been shaped by the challenges faced by organizations. During the late 1980s, the ASTD sponsored a two-year study to explore emerging models and to identify the HRD roles and competencies needed for an effective HRD function. The study documented a shift in HRD models from the more traditional training and development function to include career development and organization development functions. The study identified four trends affecting modern HRD:

1. The work force of the 1990s will be more diverse.

2. In the 1990s more people will do knowledge work, which requires judgment, flexibility, and personal commitment rather than submission to procedures.

3. People in the 1990s will expect meaningful work and involvement.

4. A shift is occurring in the nature of the contract between organizations and their employees. (McLagan, 1989, pp. 50–51)

The relationship between HRM and HRD functions can be depicted as a "human resource wheel" (see Figure 1-2). The HR wheel identifies three primary HRD functions: (1) training and development, (2) organization development, and (3) career development (McLagan, 1989). We will now discuss each of these functions in greater detail.

FIGURE 1-2 **HUMAN RESOURCE WHEEL**

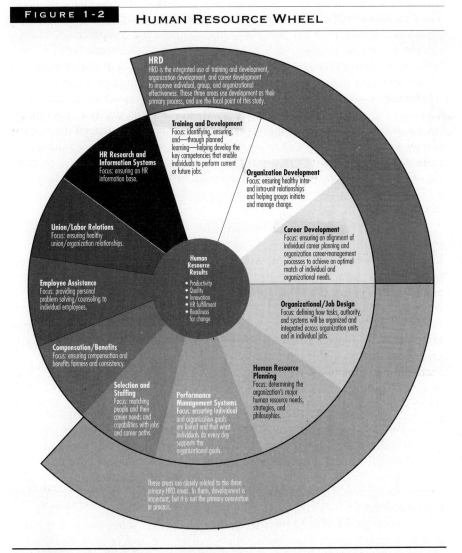

SOURCE: From McLagan, P. A. (1989) "Models for HRD practice," *Training and Development Journal, 41,* p. 53.

Training and Development (T&D)

Training and development focus on the improvement of the knowledge, skills, and abilities (KSAs) of individuals. **Training** involves a process of providing KSAs specific to a particular task or job. **Developmental** activities, in contrast, have a long-term focus on preparing for future responsibilities while increasing the capacities of employees to perform their current jobs.

T&D activities begin when a new employee enters the organization, usually in the form of employee orientation and skills training. **Employee orientation** is a formal process in which new employees learn important organizational values and norms, establish working relationships, and learn how to function within their jobs. The HRD staff and the hiring supervisor generally share the responsibility for designing the orientation process, conducting general orientation sessions, and beginning the initial skills training. **Skills and technical training** programs then narrow in scope to teach the new employee a particular skill or area of knowledge.

Once new employees have become proficient in their jobs, HRD activities should focus on development—specifically, coaching and counseling. In the **coaching** process, individuals are encouraged to accept responsibility for their actions, to address any work-related problems, and to achieve and to sustain superior performance. Coaching involves treating employees as partners in working toward personal and organizational goals. **Counseling** techniques are used to help employees deal with personal problems that may interfere with the achievement of these goals. Counseling programs may address such issues as substance abuse, stress management, smoking cessation, and fitness, nutrition, and weight control.

HRD departments are also responsible for coordinating **management training and development** programs to ensure that managers and supervisors have the knowledge and skills necessary to be effective in their positions. These programs may include supervisory training, job rotation, seminars, and college and university courses.

Organization Development

Organization development (OD) is defined as the process of enhancing the effectiveness of an organization and the well-being of its members through planned interventions that apply behavioral science concepts (Beckhard, 1969; Alderfer, 1977; Beer & Walton, 1990). OD emphasizes both macro and micro organizational changes: macro changes are intent on ultimately improving the effectiveness of the organization, while micro changes are directed at small groups and individuals. For example, many organizations have sought to improve organization effectiveness by introducing employee involvement programs that require fundamental changes in work expectations, reward systems, and reporting procedures.

The role of the HRD professional involved in OD intervention is to function as a change agent. Facilitating change often requires consulting with and advising line managers on strategies that can be used to effect the desired change. The HRD professional may also become directly involved in carrying out the intervention strategy, such as facilitating a meeting of the employees responsible for planning and implementing the actual change process.

Career Development

Career development can be defined as "an ongoing process by which individuals progress through a series of stages, each of which is characterized by a relatively unique set of issues, themes, and tasks" (Greenhaus, 1987, p. 9). Career development involves two distinct processes: career planning and career management. Career planning involves activities performed by an individual, with the assistance of counselors and others, to assess his or her skills and abilities in order to establish a realistic career plan. Career management involves taking the necessary steps to achieve that plan.

There is a strong relationship between career development and T&D activities. Career plans can be implemented, at least in part, through the organization's training programs.

The Supervisor's Role in HRD

There is also a strong relationship between the design of HRD programs and processes and their implementation through the responsibilities of the supervisor. As we will emphasize throughout this textbook, many organizations rely on the line supervisor to implement HRD programs and processes that include orientation, training, coaching, and career development.

Organizational Structure of HRD

HRD structure and function, like that of HRM, should be designed to support the organization's strategy. Using the chart from Figure 1-1, Figure 1-3 further delineates how the HRD function may be organized in the HRM department. Alternatively, Figure 1-4 depicts how the HRD function may be organized in a multiregional sales organization. In this example, the training activities, except for management/executive development, are decentralized and other HRD activities are centralized.

Roles of an HRD Professional

An HRD professional must perform a wide variety of functional roles. A functional role is a specific set of tasks and expected outputs that may be included in a given job. McLagan (1989) identified 11 HRD functional roles, which are listed in Table 1-1. These roles are briefly discussed below.

The HRD Executive/Manager

The HRD executive/manager has primary responsibility over all HRD activities. This person must integrate the HRD programs with the goals and strategies of

FIGURE 1-3	ORGANIZATIONAL CHART OF A LARGE HRD DEPARTMENT

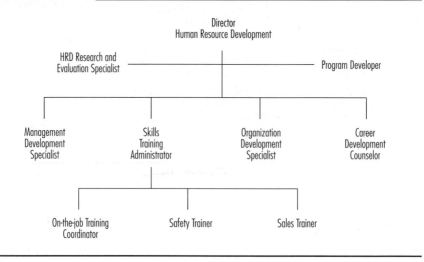

FIGURE 1-4	ORGANIZATIONAL CHART OF AN HRD DEPARTMENT IN A MULTIREGIONAL SALES ORGANIZATION

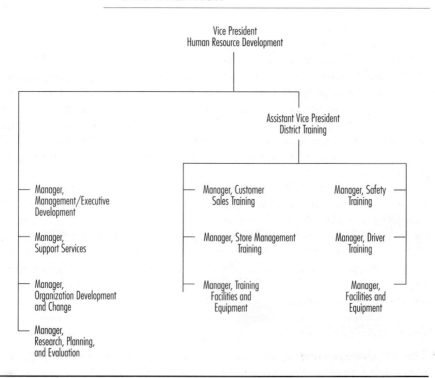

TABLE 1-1	HRD ROLES

1. HRD Executive/Manager
2. HRD Administrator
3. Evaluator
4. HRD Materials Developer
5. Career Development Counselor
6. Instructor or Facilitator
7. Marketer
8. Needs Analyst
9. Organization Change Agent
10. Program Designer
11. Researcher

SOURCE: McLagan, P. A. (1989). "Models for HRD practice." *Training and Development Journal, 41*, pp. 54–55.

the organization, and normally assumes a leadership role in the executive development program. The HRD executive also serves as an advisor to the CEO and other executives. The outputs of this role include long-range plans and strategies, policies, and budget allocation schedules.

One of the important tasks of the HRD executive is to promote the value of HRD as a means of ensuring that organizational members have the competencies to meet current and future job demands. If senior managers do not understand the value of HRD, it will be difficult for the HRD executive to get their commitment to HRD efforts, and to justify the expenditure of funds during tough times. Historically, during financial difficulties HRD programs have been a major target of cost-cutting efforts with the emphasis on the "bottom line." Unless the HRD executive establishes a clear relationship between HRD expenditures and organizational effectiveness (including profits), HRD programs will not receive the support they need. But how does an HRD executive who wants to offer a program on stress management compete with a line manager who wants to purchase a new piece of equipment? The answer is clear: the executive must demonstrate the benefit the organization receives by offering the program. Evaluation data are vital to the HRD executive when presenting a case (evaluation will be discussed in Chapter 6).

The role of the HRD executive has become more important and visible as organizations make the necessary transition to a global economy. The immediate challenge during these difficult times is in continuing to advise top management on HRD issues. According to Allan Cox, "the HRD director is viewed today as a counselor by the chief executive officer and other key executives" (Bove, 1985, p. 81). As a counselor, the HRD executive is in an excellent position to establish the credibility of HRD programs and processes as a tool for managing in today's challenging business environment.

Other HRD Roles and Outputs

The *HRD administrator* coordinates and supervises at least one of the HRD activities or sub-functions. The outputs of this position include facility and equipment selection, schedules, staffing assignments, record preparation and maintenance, and performance reviews of HRD staff.

The *evaluator* must determine the overall effectiveness of HRD programs and processes. Outputs would include research/evaluation designs, instruments, evaluation reports, and data archives.

The *HRD materials developer* prepares the materials used in delivering HRD programs and processes. Outputs would include forms, lesson plans, instructional handouts, overhead transparencies, videos, manuals, and software.

The *career development counselor* assists individual employees in assessing their strengths and weaknesses so that they can develop realistic career plans. Outputs would include individual assessment sessions, workshop facilitation, and career guidance.

The *instructor or facilitator* effects the delivery of the HRD programs, including organizing a learning environment, presenting information, and managing discussion. Outputs would include the selection of appropriate instructional methods and techniques and the actual HRD program itself.

The *marketer* promotes and "sells" the HRD products and services to both internal and external clients. Outputs would include promotional materials, contracts or agreements of services, and presentations.

The *needs analyst* determines the individual needs of the members or employees for various HRD programs and processes. Outputs would include tools to measure performance deficiencies and changes in job requirements if necessary.

The *organization change agent* facilitates change through advising line management, building client relationships, and developing intervention strategies. Outputs would include more efficient work teams, quality management, intervention strategy, implementation, and change reports.

The *program designer* designs HRD programs and processes, including training programs. Outputs would include program objectives, lesson plans, and intervention strategies.

The *researcher* tests new theories, concepts, and program designs to improve the effectiveness of HRD programs and processes. Outputs would include research designs, research findings and recommendations, and reports.

In summary, the HRD functional roles show the level of specialization present in those organizations participating in the McLagan study. Each role can stand alone as a full-time job, or several can be combined in one position. For example, in progressive organizations like Arthur Andersen, HRD employees specialize in positions as program designers and instructors. In smaller organizations, with less developed HRD functions, one HRD professional may assume all 11 of the roles listed in Table 1-1.

HRD Competencies

The term **competency** refers to the knowledge, skills, and abilities needed to perform a particular task. The 11 HRD functional roles described require a broad range of competencies. McLagan (1989) analyzed these roles and developed a list of 35 HRD competencies, dividing them into four categories: technical, business, interpersonal, and intellectual (see Table 1-2). **Technical** competencies refer to the knowledge and skills needed to design HRD programs.

Business competencies help the HRD professional to understand the broader business practices and the environment in which the organization operates. **Interpersonal** competencies are necessary in a number of situations in which the HRD professional must relate to people both inside and outside the organization. **Intellectual** competencies include the thinking, reasoning, and creative skills needed to be an effective HRD professional. Table 1-2 defines each of the 35 individual competencies.

TABLE 1-2	HRD COMPETENCIES	
Category	**Competency**	**Description**
Technical	1. Adult learning theory	Knowledge of how adults learn and acquire new skills
	2. Career development theories and practices	Knowledge and application of different career management models.
	3. Competency-identification	Knowledge of how to assess individual KSAs
	4. Computer	Ability to operate and apply different software tools
	5. Instructional technology	Ability to operate and apply different electronic equipment (such as computer-based training)
	6. Facility management	Ability to manage the use and logistics of facilities
	7. Writing program objectives	Ability to write clear program objective statements
	8. Performance observation	Ability to observe job behaviors and prepare reports
	9. Subject matter knowledge	Broad knowledge of a specific job function and skills for training purposes
	10. Training methods and techniques	Knowledge and appropriate use of different training methods and techniques
	11. Research methods	Knowledge of research methodology including research design, data collection, and analysis
Business	12. Business management	Knowledge of how businesses operate and how managers make decisions
	13. Cost-benefit analysis	Assessing the cost of different approaches compared to the benefits derived

Continued

TABLE 1-2	HRD COMPETENCIES (CONTINUED)
14. Delegation	Ability to assign responsibility and accountability for a specific task
15. Industry understanding	Knowledge of how a specific industry operates, including critical issues, trends, and markets
16. Organization behavior theory	Knowledge of motivation theory and group dynamics, and different applications
17. Organization development	Knowledge and appropriate uses of methods used to facilitate planned change
18. Organization theory	Knowledge and appropriate uses of methods to structure organizations
19. Project management	Ability to facilitate problem solving by organizing project teams
20. Records management	Ability to store and retrieve information

Interpersonal

21. Coaching	Ability to help individuals understand their strengths and weaknesses in order to achieve job and personal goals
22. Constructive feedback	Ability to communicate observations in a manner that is constructive and useful to that person
23. Group process	Ability to assess group dynamics in order to improve group effectiveness
24. Negotiation	Ability to understand and communicate differences in position in order to achieve acceptable outcomes
25. Presentation	Ability to prepare and present material orally
26. Questioning	Ability to collect data through interviewing, questionnaires, and other probing techniques
27 Building relationships	Ability to establish work relationships that are vital to the HRD goals and objectives
28. Writing	Preparing written material using acceptable rules of style and form appropriate to a specific audience

Intellectual	29. Data-reduction	Ability to analyze material and draw conclusions
	30. Literature review	Ability to review, summarize, and report on printed material using appropriate sources
	31. Objective analysis	Ability to generate ideas, options, and solutions to a specific problem or issue without undue influence from personal bias
	32. Model building	Ability to conceptualize and construct theoretical frameworks to describe complex events
	33. Observation	Ability to recognize and define individual behavioral trends and group dynamics
	34. Self-knowledge	Knowledge of one's own personal values, beliefs, attitudes, and needs that affect individual perceptions
	35. Forecasting	Ability to identify business trends and predict future events

SOURCE: From "Models for HRD practice" by P. A. McLagan, *Training and Development Journal, 43*, pp. 56–57. Adapted by permission.

Certification and Education for HRD Professionals

One indication of the growth of the HRD field is the strong push to develop a professional certification process. According to a survey of over 1,500 trainers, approximately 60 percent expressed a preference for some form of certification (Lee, 1986). This response was probably based on an increasing desire to enhance the credibility of the broadening HRD field. Thus, to determine a set of agreed upon standards or competencies, upon which most professional certification programs are based, the ASTD sponsored the McLagan competency base study outlined in Table 1-2.

HRD Education: Developing Closer Ties to Academia

Over the past ten years the HRD profession has also become more involved with the academic community. Three recent developments illustrate this relationship: (1) the ASTD now produces the *Human Resource Development Quarterly* of academic research on HRD issues; (2) the ASTD changed its governance structure to include a Professor's Network and an Academic Relations Committee; and (3) the ASTD published "Academic Directory of Programs in HRD" in 1993, which lists undergraduate, graduate, and continuing education programs.

HRD programs at colleges and universities are typically found in one of three academic departments: business/management, psychology, and education. The content and philosophy of these programs tend to reflect the founding professors (Gerber, 1987). Certain schools of business (or management) offer majors or minors in HRD, with courses in training and development, organization development, and career development. Some psychology departments offer degree programs and courses in industrial and organizational psychology and personnel psychology with specific courses in HRD. In addition to HRD classes, schools of education may also offer degrees and courses in fields related to HRD, such as educational technology, curriculum development, and adult education.

Challenges to HRD Practitioners

Looking toward the next century, there are a number of challenges facing HRD practitioners. These challenges include (1) changing work force demographics, (2) competing in a global economy, (3) eliminating the skills gap, and (4) the need for lifelong learning. Each of these challenges and their potential impact on HRD will be briefly discussed below and further amplified in future chapters.

Changing Work Force Demographics

In 1986, based on a study of demographic changes, the Hudson Institute published a significant report entitled *Workforce 2000: Work and Workers for the 21st Century*. Among other things, the report predicted that women and minorities would represent approximately 85 percent of all *new workers* entering the work force between 1988 and 2000 (Johnston & Packer, 1987). This trend highlights several important challenges, including (1) reconciling work/family issues; (2) integrating black and Latino workers into the economy; and (3) improving educational opportunities for all workers. The report, although controversial, forced many organizations to re-think their organizational policies and programs and to begin to make necessary changes. As a result, organizations are introducing or refining family-leave policies, child-care programs, EEO/affirmative action efforts, and sexual harassment programs. In addition, some organizations have tried to help employees become more sensitive to cultural differences by introducing valuing difference, managing diversity, and cross-cultural training programs. These programs will be discussed in more detail in Chapter 14.

Competing in a Global Economy

As U.S. companies prepare to compete in a global economy, many are introducing new technologies that require more educated and trained workers. In fact, it is predicted that by the year 2000, over one-half of the jobs in the United States will require education beyond high school. Thus, successful organizations will have to hire employees with the knowledge to compete in an increasingly sophisticated market.

Competing in the global economy will require more than educating and training workers to meet new challenges. In addition to retraining the work force, successful companies will institute quality improvement processes and introduce change programs (e.g., involvement programs). The work force must learn to become culturally sensitive in order to communicate and conduct business in foreign countries. Above all, employers must change the way they manage. Approaches to managing change will be discussed in Chapter 13.

Eliminating the Skills Gap

As we discussed, for companies to compete successfully in a global economy, they must hire *educated* workers. However, the U.S. public education system is in desperate need of reform. Almost 30 percent of today's high school students fail to graduate, and employers must confront the fact that many young adults entering the work force are unable to meet current job requirements. Even though the United States has one of the highest standards of living in the world, a large number of American workers—between 20 and 30 percent according to the Office of Technology Assessment—lack basic writing, reading, and computational skills (Stone, 1991).

This skills gap poses serious consequences for American companies. For example, how can trainees learn how to operate new equipment if they cannot read and comprehend operating manuals? Furthermore, how can new employees be taught to manipulate computer-controlled machines if they do not understand basic math? Obviously, the business community has a vested interest in education reform. There are some encouraging signs, however. The Los Angeles public school system is offering a guarantee to employers, stating that if any high school graduate is found to be deficient in basic skills, such as computation and writing, the school system will retrain the graduate at no cost to the employer.

Other industrialized nations have made systematic changes in order to bridge the skills gap. For example, Japan and Germany, two of the United States' biggest competitors, have educational systems that do a better job of teaching students the basic skills needed by most employers. Among other things, Germany emphasizes vocational education and school-to-work transition programs so that school-age children can begin apprenticeship programs as part of their formal education. These and other approaches to public education will be discussed in more detail in Chapter 8.

The Need for Lifelong Learning

Given the rapid changes that all organizations face, it is clear that employees must continue the learning process throughout their careers in order to meet these challenges. This need for lifelong learning will require organizations to make an ongoing investment in HRD.

Lifelong learning can mean different things to different employees. For example, for semiskilled workers, it may involve more rudimentary skills training to help them to build their competencies. To professional employees, this learning may mean taking advantage of continuing education opportunities. This is particularly important for certified professionals who are required to complete a certain number of continuing education courses in order to maintain their certificates. To managers, lifelong learning may include attending management seminars that address new management approaches.

The challenge to HRD is to provide a full range of learning opportunities for all kinds of employees. One way that some organizations are meeting this challenge is by establishing multimedia learning centers. These centers offer a variety of instructional technologies that can be matched to each trainee's unique learning needs. Individual assessments can determine academic deficiencies in employees while also pointing out their preferred learning styles. For instance, self-motivated employees found to be deficient in arithmetic might be trained in an interactive video program allowing them to set their own pace. A multimedia learning center could also provide teleconferencing facilities for technical and professional employees to participate in a seminar that is being conducted thousands of miles away. These and other different approaches to learning will also be discussed in future chapters. What remains clear, however, is that whether they use multimedia or other training approaches, organizations must find a way to provide lifelong learning opportunities to all of their employees.

Summary

This chapter traced several historical events that contributed to the establishment of human resource development. Much of the earlier training programs

RETURN TO OPENING CASE

Arthur Andersen's Center for Professional Education (CPE) faced the challenge of equipping the professionals in the new Andersen Consulting Division with the skills needed to assist customers using client/server networks with their desktop computers. The CPE staff was given a tight schedule in which to design and deliver the training. The CPE staff responded by planning and implementing their first client/server training in just five months. As of 1992, more than 3,000 professionals have been trained in client/server technology, and it is expected that an additional 6,000 people will need to be trained by 1993. Herbert W. Desch, head of the professional education division, predicts that "the company will have as many as 24,000 consulting professionals skilled in client/server solutions by the end of 1994." This kind of response to a need for change was one reason why Arthur Andersen became the eighth company recognized with the ASTD Award for Excellence. (Other companies awarded include Xerox, Motorola, IBM, Ford Motor Company, Dayton-Hudson, Aetna, and Federal Express.) Arthur Andersen & Company provides an excellent example of utilizing HRD to gain a strategic advantage.[1]

[1]From "Training Keeps the Cutting Edge Sharp for the Andersen Companies" by P. Galagan, 1993, *Training and Development Journal, 47*(1), pp. 30–35. Adapted by permission.

(such as apprenticeship) focused on skilled training. At the turn of the century, more emphasis was placed on training semiskilled workers in response to the industrial revolution. It was during World War II that training departments as we know them today were introduced in many large companies. The establishment of the professional trainer led to the formation of a professional society (the ASTD). This culminated in the 1980s when the ASTD, in partnership with the academic community, officially recognized the professional designation of human resource development.

HRD, part of a larger human resource management system, includes training and development, career development, and organization development programs and processes. HRD managers and staff must establish working relationships with line managers in order to coordinate HRD programs and processes throughout the organization. To be effective, HRD professionals must be able to serve in a number of roles and possess certain competencies. These competencies will help the HRD professional to meet the challenges facing organizations in the 1990s and beyond. These challenges include changing work force demographics, competing in a global economy, eliminating the skills gap, and the need for lifelong learning.

Key Terms and Concepts

Americans with Disabilities Act
apprenticeship training
ASTD
behavioral science
career development
coaching
competencies
craft guilds
employee counseling
evaluator
human relations
human resource development (HRD)
human resource management (HRM)
management development

motivational programs
multicultural environment
needs analyst
orientation programs
organization change agent
organization development
participation rate
professional development
researcher
restructuring
roles
skills training
technological change
training and development

Questions for Discussion

1. Do supervisors have HRD responsibilities? If so, how do they coordinate these with HRD professionals?

2. What HRD competencies are needed by an HRD manager? How are these competencies learned?

3. What qualities do you think an HRD professional must possess to be effective in a small organization of approximately 1,000 employees? Support your answers.

4. Briefly describe an HRD effort in a familiar organization. Was it successful? If so, why? If not, what contributed to its failure?

5. Which challenges to HRD professionals discussed in this chapter will directly affect your present or future working environment? What additional challenges do you foresee affecting HRD?

Influences on Employee Behavior

Learning Objectives

1. *Identify the major factors that influence employee behavior.*
2. *Define motivation and describe the main approaches to understanding motivation.*
3. *Explain how ability and attitudes influence behavior.*
4. *Describe two types of outcomes that may result from behavior and tell how they may influence future behavior.*
5. *State how a supervisor's leadership and expectations for employees may affect behavior.*
6. *Recognize the impact co-workers and the organization itself have on employee behavior.*

OPENING CASE

Prior to the court-ordered break-up of AT&T, the more than 370,000 employees who worked within the Bell System tended to view layoffs as something that happened to other people. After all, the company's history of taking care of its employees was part of the reason employees referred to the company as Ma Bell. All that changed in 1984 when a federal judge ordered that AT&T be divided into smaller units. Not only would these new entities be competing in the open marketplace for the first time, the company would have to lay off over 100,000 employees in order to be competitive.

The layoff process helped protect the company's interests, but it was hard on its employees, both to those who lost their jobs as well as those who remained. The laid-off employees left the company feeling scared, angry, hurt, and insecure about their futures. Their last days and weeks on the job were generally unproductive, and their negative feelings were often communicated to others, including potential customers or employees. Furthermore, the employees who survived the layoffs began to question not only the company's commitment to them, but their own commitment to the company as well.

Management recognized that this was a serious problem. Diminishing employee commitment increased the likelihood of a mass exodus of employees—including many of the top performers. Since both the employees and the organization stood to lose if things remained the same, management began to look for ways to protect the employees while at the same time meeting the company's goals.

Management decided that one way to address this problem was to help the employees scheduled for layoffs to acquire skills to enhance their careers, both during their stay at AT&T and after the layoff. Such an approach would address the company's needs to remain competitive by maintaining morale during downsizing and improving employee skills and knowledge, while at the same time satisfying the employees' needs to take control of their lives and careers in the face of uncertainty. But how can employees who are so worried about their futures be motivated to focus and act upon improving their current skills and performance?

Introduction

Ultimately, all HRD programs are efforts to change employee behavior. In order to change any behavior, however, we must first understand the factors that cause employees to behave the way that they do. Armed with this knowledge, we can more accurately diagnose performance problems, understand what makes effective performance possible, and design HRD programs to create the behavior we want.

Identifying the causes of employee behavior is not as easy as it might appear. The factors contributing to any behavior are numerous, complex, and difficult to ascertain. However difficult, a thorough understanding of employee behavior and its causes is critical for any HRD program to be effective. The purpose of this chapter is to introduce readers to the factors influencing employee behavior and their implications for HRD. For students with backgrounds in organizational behavior or applied psychology, this chapter provides an important review and an opportunity to reinforce the significance of these topics to HRD.

Model of Employee Behavior

The model of employee behavior shown in Figure 2-1 presents what we consider to be the key factors affecting employee behavior and their corresponding relationships. It includes two categories of forces: (1) those within the employee, including motivation, attitudes, and KSAs (knowledge, skills, and abilities); and (2) those found in the environment, including the supervisor, the organization, co-workers, and the outcomes of performance (such as praise). The model assumes that internal and environmental forces interact and combine to produce a given behavior. While it may be possible to trace the cause of a behavior to one or two dominant forces in some cases, we believe that overall patterns of behavior can be best explained by the combination of many factors.

The model is relatively simple for purposes of clarity and relevance to HRD. Our goal is not to cover all the possible causes for employee behavior, but to include only those most critical to designing, delivering, and using HRD programs. Additional relevant concepts will be presented in later chapters. The remainder of this chapter will focus on the elements contained within the model.

FIGURE 2-1	MODEL OF EMPLOYEE BEHAVIOR

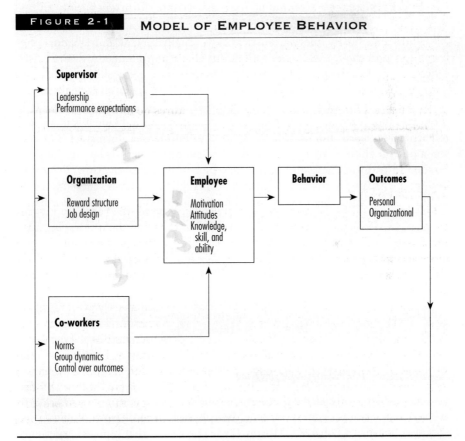

Motivation: An Internal Influence on Employee Behavior

Motivation is one of the most basic elements of human behavior. Motivational theories attempt to explain how effort is generated and channeled. Mitchell (1982, p. 81) synthesized many definitions of work motivation as "the psychological processes that cause the arousal, direction, and persistence of voluntary actions that are goal directed."

This definition makes several important points. First, work motivation pertains to the causes of *voluntary* behavior—the nature of nearly all behaviors performed in the workplace. Even in situations where employees feel they do not have a choice, their behavior reflects their consideration of the perceived consequences of their actions.

Second, motivation focuses on several processes affecting behavior.

- **Arousal or energizing**   The generation or mobilization of effort

- **Direction**   Applying effort to one behavior over another

- **Persistence**   Continuing (or ceasing) to perform a behavior

Third, and finally, motivation at work is usually seen as an individual phenomenon (Mitchell, 1982), since all people have unique needs, desires, attitudes, and goals. Most motivational theories recognize these differences, and often include components that describe how they affect the motivational process.

Understanding motivation is critical to HRD. The success of many HRD programs and processes depends in part on whether the individual is motivated to participate, learn, and use what is learned to improve performance. The reason a person chooses to attend a training class but then fails to use the skills learned in training back on the job may be rooted in motivation. Programs designed with an eye toward motivation can explicitly address these issues. In addition, motivation theories are useful in diagnosing the cause of performance problems, and often serve as the basis for designing or choosing HRD programs to remedy those problems.

There is no shortage of work motivation theories. Although some theories share common processes and constructs (Evans, 1986; Ilgen & Klein, 1988), there is still no single, inclusive, and widely accepted explanation of work motivation (Katzell & Thompson, 1990; Pinder, 1984). In general, approaches to explaining motivation can be grouped into the three categories displayed in Table 2-1: need-based, cognitive, and non-cognitive.

Need-based Theories of Motivation

Several popular motivational theories are rooted in the concept of needs. **Needs** are deficiency states or imbalances, either physiological or psychological, that energize and direct behavior. Murray (1938) proposed that humans experience a large number of needs, such as aggression, affiliation, autonomy, and achieve-

TABLE 2-1	APPROACHES TO EXPLAINING MOTIVATION

Approach	Theories
Need Based Underlying needs, such as the needs for safety or power, drive motivation.	Maslow's Need Hierarchy Alderfer's Existence, Relatedness, and Growth (ERG) Theory Herzberg's Two Factory Theory
Cognitive Motivation is a process controlled by conscious thoughts, beliefs, and judgments.	Expectancy Theory Equity Theory Goal-Setting Theory Cognitive Evaluation Theory Social Learning Theory Attribution Theory
Non-cognitive Motivation is explained as an interaction between behavior and external events without appealing to internal thoughts or needs.	Reinforcement Theory

ment. Although needs are internal states, they can be influenced by forces in the environment. The opening case, for example, suggests that a poor economy and the potential for layoffs within an organization may heighten an employee's need for security.

Needs are said to drive behavior through the combination of need activation and need satisfaction, a process depicted in Figure 2-2. A need becomes activated when a person lacks something necessary for maintaining psychological or physiological equilibrium. The activated need is felt as tension. The tension may be a recognizable feeling such as loneliness, or may be more general, such as anxiety. Because tension is unpleasant, the person will look for ways (perform behaviors) to reduce the tension by eliminating the deficiency that is causing it. That person will continue to perform different behaviors until one is found to effectively reduce the tension and, thus, satisfy the need.

Only activated needs can be motivational, because only an activated need produces the tension the person is motivated to eliminate. Once the need is satisfied, the tension is gone and the need is no longer felt.

Two widely cited need-based theories of motivation, **Maslow's need hierarchy theory** (Maslow, 1943, 1954, 1968) and Alderfer's **existence, relatedness, and growth (ERG) theory** (Alderfer, 1969, 1972), suggest that needs are arranged in a hierarchy. They propose that needs emerge in a particular pattern, in which certain groups of needs (those important to physical survival) emerge first and must be satisfied before other needs (psychological and social needs like affiliation and esteem) can emerge and affect behavior. Once the currently activated needs are satisfied, the next most powerful group of needs are felt and thus will drive behavior.

FIGURE 2-2   THE NEED ACTIVATION–NEED SATISFACTION PROCESS

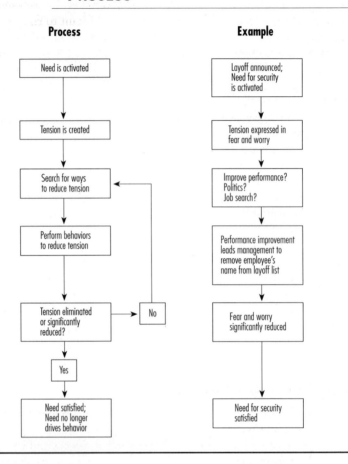

Maslow's need hierarchy lists five categories or levels of needs: physiological, safety and security, love, status and esteem, and self-actualization. Alderfer's ERG theory reduces Maslow's hierarchy to only three levels of needs: existence, relatedness, and growth. More importantly, ERG theory proposes that if a person becomes frustrated trying to satisfy the currently activated needs, this frustration will cause previously satisfied needs to be activated and drive behavior.

Another widely discussed need-based theory is Herzberg's (1966) **two factor theory.** Herzberg claimed that people have two sets of basic needs, one focusing on survival and another focusing on personal growth. He argued that factors in the workplace that satisfy survival needs, or **hygiene factors,** cannot of themselves provide job satisfaction—they only prevent dissatisfaction. Alternatively, **motivator** factors, which satisfy the growth needs, can create feelings of job satisfaction, but their absence will not lead to dissatisfaction. Following the two factor theory, workers can be motivated by ensuring that hygiene factors are present, thereby preventing dissatisfaction, and then adding motivator factors to create job satisfaction. This strategy is referred to as **job enrichment.**

Need-hierarchy theories have become popular with managers and students in part because they are easy to understand and are intuitively appealing. They seem to make sense. But it is unclear whether these theories are valid explanations of motivation. Need-hierarchy theories are difficult to rigorously test, in that they require measuring internal states that people find difficult to accurately identify and explain. While most of the studies of Maslow's theory have failed to support it (Wahba & Bridwell, 1976), much of this research has not been conducted properly (Mitchell & Moudgill, 1976). Although some research has been conducted to test the ERG theory (Alderfer, 1972), there is insufficient evidence to support or reject the theory. Needs do exist, but a generalizable hierarchy explaining the relationships among them is not yet available.

Similar problems exist with Two Factor theory. Herzberg's initial studies (Herzberg, Mausner, & Snyderman, 1959) supported the notion that there are two separate sets of factors that affect job satisfaction differently. But other researchers could not replicate Herzberg's results using other methods. The theory became embroiled in controversy (see Bockman, 1971, and Pinder, 1984, for summaries of the controversy). While there is some support for job enrichment as a way to motivate employees, it is still unclear whether Two Factor theory is valid.

So while need-based theories of motivation do provide some insight into one category of possible forces that drive behavior, they have proven difficult to test and apply and are insufficient as a complete explanation of motivation. Even so, HRD programs based on need-based theories, such as job enrichment and achievement motivation training, have been used in organizations with some success.

Cognitive Theories of Motivation

Few of us would deny that our conscious thoughts play a role in how we behave. A second group of motivation theories, called cognitive theories, recognizes this and argues that motivation is based on a person's thoughts and beliefs (cognitions). These theories are sometimes referred to as process theories because they attempt to explain the sequence of thoughts and decisions that energize, direct, and control behavior.

Cognitive motivation theories have direct relevance to HRD. Most HRD programs include attempts to change employee behavior by influencing their thoughts, beliefs, and attitudes. Learning, which lies at the heart of HRD, is often seen as a cognitive process (learning will be discussed in Chapter 3). We can do a better job of designing and implementing HRD programs if we understand how employees' thoughts and beliefs affect their behavior.

In the section below, we will briefly review six cognitive theories of motivation: expectancy theory, equity theory, goal-setting theory, cognitive evaluation theory, social learning theory, and attribution theory. Each theory has some significance for the practice of HRD.

Expectancy Theory **Expectancy theory** (e.g., Vroom, 1964) assumes that motivation is a conscious choice process. According to this theory, people choose to put their effort into activities they believe they can perform and that will produce desired outcomes. Expectancy theory argues that decisions about which activities to engage in are based on the combination of three sets of beliefs: expectancy, instrumentality, and valence.

Expectancy beliefs represent the individual's judgment about whether applying (or increasing) effort to a task will result in its successful accomplishment. Stated another way, a person with a high expectancy believes that increased effort will lead to better performance, while someone with a low expectancy does not believe their efforts, no matter how great, will affect their performance. All other things being equal, people should engage in tasks about which they have high expectancy beliefs.

The second belief, called **instrumentality,** is a judgment about the connection the individual perceives (if any) between task performance and possible outcomes. Making instrumentality judgments is like asking the question "If I perform this task successfully, is it likely to get me something I want (or something I don't want)?" Instrumentality ranges from strongly positive (the individual is certain that performing a task will lead to a particular outcome), through zero (the individual is certain there is no relationship between performing the task and the occurrence of a particular outcome), to strongly negative (the individual is certain that performing a certain task will prevent a particular outcome from occurring).

The third belief important to expectancy theory is called **valence.** Valence refers to the value the person places on a particular outcome. Valence judgments range from strongly positive (for highly valued outcomes), through zero (for outcomes the person doesn't care about), to strongly negative (for outcomes the person finds aversive).

Expectancy theory states that employees will make these three sets of judgments when deciding which behaviors and tasks to engage in. Specifically, the theory predicts that employees will choose to put effort into behaviors they

- believe they can perform successfully (high expectancy) **and**

- believe are connected (high instrumentality) to outcomes they desire (high valence) or

- believe will prevent (negative instrumentality) outcomes they want to avoid (negative valence)

Figure 2-3 graphically depicts this process. For example, suppose the manager of a bus company tries to motivate bus drivers to drive more safely by offering safe drivers additional vacation days. Whether this will motivate a driver to drive more safely depends on whether:

1. She thinks she can improve her safety record to the level desired by the manager (expectancy);

2. She believes the manager will give her more vacation days if she does improve her safety record to the desired level (instrumentality);

3. She values having more vacation days (valence).

FIGURE 2-3   A GRAPHIC REPRESENTATION OF
EXPECTANCY THEORY

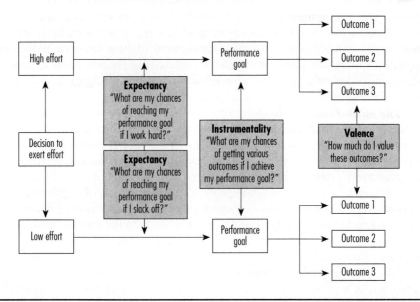

SOURCE: From *Organizational Behavior*, 2d ed. (p. 213), by R. Kreitner and A. Kinicki, 1992, Homewood, IL: Irwin. Reprinted by permission.

Do people behave in the way expectancy theory predicts? Empirical studies testing the theory have shown some support for its prediction (Mitchell, 1974; Wanous, Keon, & Latack (1983). However, several writers (Behling & Stark, 1973; Mitchell, 1974) have pointed out that methodological problems in some of these studies may have led to underestimates of the theory's predictive ability.

While more research is needed to understand whether the theory accurately represents the behavioral choices we make (see Landy & Becker, 1987, for a summary of recent research), expectancy theory is clearly relevant to HRD. It offers a way to diagnose performance problems and then suggests how these problems can be overcome. In addition, expectancy theory has implications for the design and effectiveness of HRD programs. For example, according to expectancy theory, employees will not be motivated to attend HRD programs and try to learn from them unless they believe:

1. They can learn the new skills or information presented in the program;

2. Attending the program and learning new skills will increase their job performance; and

3. Doing so will help them obtain desired outcomes or prevent unwanted outcomes.

Viewing employee behavior from an expectancy theory perspective, supervisors and HRD professionals can market and design programs in ways to ensure that employees make the appropriate judgments, and as a result will be motivated to attend, learn, and apply what they have learned back on the job. Ways to do this include offering incentives such as holding HRD programs in attractive locations (such as resorts), offering paid time off from work to attend, designing the program to be interesting and/or enjoyable, and making success in the program a prerequisite for promotion and other desirable outcomes.

Equity Theory   A second cognitive theory of motivation, called **equity theory,** suggests that motivation is strongly influenced by the desire to be treated fairly and people's perceptions about whether they have been treated fairly. The theory as it has been applied to work motivation (Adams, 1963) is based on three key assumptions (Carrell & Dittrich, 1978):

1. People develop beliefs about what is fair for them to receive in exchange for the contributions they make to the organization.

2. People determine fairness by comparing their relevant returns and contributions to those of others.

3. People who believe they have been treated unfairly (called inequity) will experience tension, and they will be motivated to find ways to reduce it.

Equity theory predicts that employees who believe they are being treated fairly (a judgment called equity) will be motivated to continue their present performance and behavior patterns. On the other hand, employees who believe they are victims of inequity will search for ways to reduce their feelings of unfairness. Theorists (Campbell and Pritchard, 1976) have suggested at least five ways in which individuals reduce their feelings of inequity:

1. Cognitively **distorting** views of the contributions or rewards ("She must be smarter than I thought")

2. Influencing **the perceived rival to change** their contributions or rewards (convincing the person to be less productive)

3. **Changing** one's own contributions or rewards (either working harder or contributing less)

4. **Comparing** one's self to a different person

5. **Lea ing** the situation (requesting a transfer or quitting)

According to Downs (1963), people will choose the way to reduce inequity that appears to be the least costly. Figure 2-4 depicts this process.

FIGURE 2-4 A GRAPHIC REPRESENTATION OF EQUITY THEORY

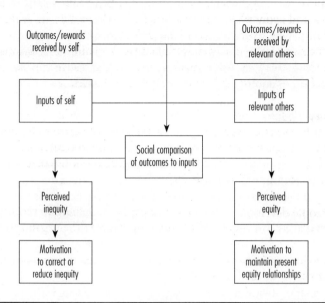

Are the predictions made by equity theory supported by research? In general, there is research support for the predictions equity theory makes about what people do when they believe they are under-rewarded (Campbell & Pritchard, 1976; Pinder, 1984), but there is less support for predictions about what people do when they believe they are over-rewarded (Mowday, 1979). However, mistakes and problems in early research studies prevent firm conclusions about the validity of equity theory (see Pinder, 1984). Recent research that rectifies some of these problems is being conducted (such as Huseman, Hatfield, & Miles, 1987). However, equity theory clearly has implications for HRD, particularly in understanding how employees perceive HRD programs and their response to them.

In some organizations participation in HRD programs is used (or perceived) as a reward for good performance or punishment for poor performance. Also, the decisions about which employees to include in HRD programs are not without consequences. Equity theory suggests, for example, that employees who consider themselves unjustly left out of an HRD program (such as a management development seminar) will experience inequity. As a result, those employees may attempt to reduce the inequity by lowering their job performance or becoming less committed to the organization. The employee may even leave the organization for someplace where they feel their talents will be more appreciated. To prevent this from occurring, managers should make the selection criteria for attending HRD programs clear, and also provide employees with feedback so they can see that participation judgments are made fairly.

Equity theory can also help us determine whether employees will use the skills or knowledge they have learned in an HRD program back on the job. For example, if the employees view the application of their new skills or knowledge as an input in their exchange with the employer, they may expect the organization to provide them with certain outcomes in return. If the employees see other employees who lack the newly acquired skills receiving the same outcomes as themselves, they may choose not to use the new skills on the job as a way to restore a feeling of equity.

Goal-Setting Theory   A third cognitive theory of motivation that has relevance to HRD is **goal-setting theory.** Goal-setting theory, as articulated by Locke (1968), states that performance goals play a key role in motivation. The theory proposes that the presence of performance goals can mobilize employee effort, direct their attention, increase their persistence, and affect the strategy they will use to accomplish a task (Locke, 1968; Locke, Shaw, Saari, & Latham, 1981). According to Locke, goals influence the individual's *intentions*, which are defined as the "cognitive representations of goals to which the person is committed" (Katzell & Thompson, 1990, p. 145). This commitment will continue to direct employee behavior until the goal is achieved, or until a decision is made to change or reject the goal.

Writers on motivation generally agree that goal setting is the best supported theory of work motivation (Pinder, 1984), and one of the best supported theories in management (Miner, 1984). Research convincingly shows that goals that are specific, difficult, and accepted by employees will lead to higher levels of performance than easy, vague goals (such as "do your best") or no goals at all. This research also demonstrates that the presence of feedback enhances the effectiveness of goal setting (Locke, et al., 1981; Mento, Steel, & Karren, 1987). Still further research is needed to understand how and under what conditions goal setting works best.

Goal setting has become an integral part of many HRD programs, particularly in helping participants understand the desired result of each program and to motivate them to achieve these results. Goals can then be discussed with their supervisors back on the job to ensure that the employees use what they have learned during the HRD program to improve their performance. For example, a key component of the career development process (and many career development programs) is setting career goals (Greenhaus, 1987). According to goal setting theory, an employee who establishes career goals is more likely to advance his or her career, especially if the goals set are specific, challenging, and accompanied by regular feedback on progress toward the goals. The career development program should ensure that employees set such goals and help employees and the organization establish mechanisms for regular feedback.

Cognitive Evaluation Theory   A fourth cognitive theory of motivation, **cognitive evaluation theory** (Deci, 1975; Deci & Porac, 1978), explains why incentives and rewards don't always increase motivation and performance. According to this theory, the key factor in whether rewards will be beneficial is the individual's perception of the reward. Cognitive evaluation theory states that rewards have two aspects, informational and control. When employees perceive a reward as providing **information** about their performance, the reward increases the employees' feelings of control over their own actions. This in turn enhances intrinsic (internal) motivation, which will ensure that performance will continue. On the other hand, when employees perceive the reward as something being used by others to **control** their behavior, the reward increases the employees' feelings that they are being manipulated by the reward giver. This in turn decreases intrinsic motivation, which may lead the employees to decrease their performance or perform the particular behavior only when the reward is present. A diagram of this process is shown in Figure 2-5.

Research support for cognitive evaluation theory has been mixed. While research conducted in laboratory settings has offered some proof of the validity of cognitive evaluation theory, but this support has not been replicated in field settings (Boal & Cummings, 1981; Guzzo, 1979; Pittman & Heller, 1987). In addition, the theory has been criticized for failing to specify the conditions under which a person will perceive a reward as either controlling or informational (Guzzo, 1979). So, while the theory is valuable in that it suggests why rewards and incentives sometimes fail to increase motivation, it is unclear whether its predictions hold true within organizations.

And yet, cognitive evaluation theory does have implications for HRD, particularly in the areas of learning during training and the transfer of training

| FIGURE 2-5 | A GRAPHIC REPRESENTATION OF COGNITIVE EVALUATION THEORY |

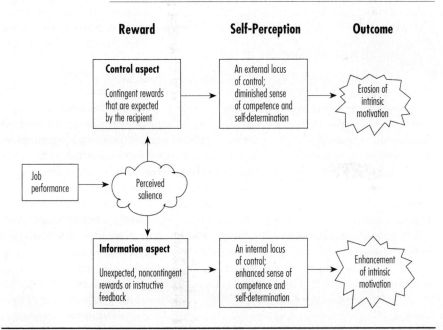

SOURCE: From *Organizational Behavior* (p. 241) by R. Kreitner and A. Kinicki, 1989, Homewood, IL: Irwin. Adapted by permission.

back to the job. For example, many trainers are taught to praise learners as a way to motivate them to learn. According to cognitive evaluation theory, if the trainer provides praise and recognition in a way that is perceived as controlling rather than informational, they may be unwittingly reducing the employee's intrinsic motivation to learn. Similarly, supervisors who use praise and recognition inappropriately may be reducing the employee's motivation to use what they have learned in an HRD program back on the job.

One way to deal with this possibility, based on cognitive evaluation theory, is to create ways for employees to gauge their own progress and reward themselves during and after training (through self-tests and selecting their own rewards), rather than relying solely on trainers and supervisors to provide feedback and rewards. Doing so will increase the likelihood that the rewards will be perceived as informational and thereby increase the employee's intrinsic motivation to learn and use what they have learned.

Social Learning Theory   A fifth cognitive theory of motivation, **social learning theory** (Bandura, 1977), proposes that self-efficacy and outcome expectations affect individual performance. A **self-efficacy** expectation is the belief in oneself to successfully perform a given behavior; an **outcome** expectation (similar to instrumentality) is a person's belief that performing a given behavior will lead to a given outcome (Bandura, 1977). Self-efficacy beliefs are malleable, and can be influenced by one's accomplishments, observing others, verbal persuasion, and physiological states (Bandura, 1977).

The major prediction of the social learning theory is that a person's self-efficacy expectations will determine:

1.   Whether a behavior will be performed;

2.   How much effort will be spent; and

3.   How long the person will continue to perform the behavior.

Bandura argues that people who believe they have high self-efficacy for a particular task will focus their attention on the challenges of the situation and use greater effort in mastering them, thus increasing the chances of successful task performance. Conversely, the theory states that people who believe they have low self-efficacy for a particular task will focus their thoughts on obstacles and shortcomings, and as a result, reduce their chances of successful task performance.

Research conducted by Bandura and others (Bandura & Cervone, 1983, 1987; Brief & Hollenbeck, 1985; Frayne & Latham, 1987; Locke, Frederick, Lee, & Bobko, 1984) shows that self-efficacy is strongly related to task performance. (A more detailed discussion of the implications of self-efficacy for work behavior is provided by Gist [1987]).

Clearly, self-efficacy has direct relevance for success in HRD. If an employee has low self-efficacy expectations, it is unlikely they will attempt to improve performance. If they do try to improve performance, they will not put forth the same effort as persons with high self-efficacy expectations. Therefore, trainers and supervisors should behave in ways that increase the trainees' judgments of their self-efficacy.

Of particular relevance to HRD, social learning theory also proposes that most behavior is learned by observing others, a process called **modeling.** Research suggests that through observing the behavior and its consequences in others, individuals can learn new behaviors and make decisions about whether to perform a particular behavior themselves. Modeling is a key component of mentoring, a development technique we will discuss in Chapter 11.

Modeling has also been applied to HRD with great success in a training approach known as **behavior modeling** (Decker & Nathan, 1985; Goldstein & Sorcher, 1972). In behavior modeling training, the trainee is told the components of the behavior to be learned (for instance, firing a poor performer) and shown a film or videotape in which an actor (the model) demonstrates how to perform the behavior. Then the trainee practices the behavior with feedback from others, and finally receives social reinforcement for performing the behavior. This technique will be discussed at greater length in the management development discussion in Chapter 12.

Attribution Theory   The sixth and final cognitive motivation theory we will discuss is **attribution theory** (Kelley, 1973; Weiner, 1971, 1980). Attribution theory attempts to explain how people assign causes to their own behavior and the behavior of others. Kelley's model of the attribution process suggests that individuals seek to identify causes for certain events or behaviors. This **causal attribution** then significantly influences the attitudes, behavior, and expectations of the individuals regarding the event or behavior they are trying to explain. As an example, suppose a supervisor requires an employee to attend a training program without telling the employee why. According to attribution theory, the employee will attempt to find a cause for the supervisor making them attend the program (either they are performing poorly or they have shown potential for advancement). When the employee identifies a cause (say, the supervisor thinks the employee has potential for advancement), the employee will adjust or reinforce his or her attitudes and expectations (this training can lead to a promotion or raise; the supervisor respects me) and probably behave accordingly (thus willingly attend the program and work hard to learn). While Kelley (1973) suggests that attributions affect a person's behavior directly, other research has shown that attributions first influence the individual's expectancies (McMahan, 1973).

Attributions appear to affect an individual's judgments of self-efficacy. Research has shown that if an employee attributes past successes to personal causes (such as their own abilities or efforts), self-efficacy will be increased; but if the employee attributes past successes to environmental causes (such as task simplicity or luck), self-efficacy may be decreased. Further, when successes are attributed to personal causes, people report higher levels of job satisfaction, a greater desire for achievement, and more ambitious performance goals (Chacko & McElroy, 1983; Diener & Dweck, 1988; Norris & Niebuhr, 1984; Weiner, Heckhausen, Meyer, & Cook, 1972). On the other hand, attributing past *failures* to personal causes can lead to decreased self-efficacy judgments, while linking failures to environmental causes can increase self-efficacy judgments.

In HRD, the attributions of trainers and trainees may have a significant impact on the success of a training program. A recent model offered by Steiner, Dobbins, and Trahan (1991) predicts that trainers will vary their behavior, such as the pace of instruction or the use of punishment, depending on the attributions they make about trainee performance. For example, suppose during a training program a trainer asks "Are there any questions?" and gets no response from the trainees. The trainer who attributes that lack of response to laziness may criticize the trainees' effort and seriousness about learning. However, the trainer attributing the silence to the trainees' fears of making a mistake or looking foolish may try to reassure them that there is no such thing as a foolish question.

The Steiner, Dobbins, and Trahan (1991) model also suggests that trainees' performance and emotional responses to a training program will be affected by their attributions about their own success and failure. For example, suppose a trainee attempting to learn to rope cattle fails to get the rope around the cow's neck after several tries. If the trainee attributes the failure to the difficulty of the task of roping, he or she will likely try again. If, however, the failure is attributed to a lack of ability ("this proves I'm uncoordinated"), the trainee will likely become frustrated and may be reluctant to try again.

Thus, it is clearly important that trainers and trainees make accurate attributions during an HRD program. If their attributions are incorrect, trainers and trainees may behave inappropriately, thereby undermining the success of the program. Steiner, Dobbins, and Trahan (1991) suggest that it may be useful to teach trainers to avoid attributional errors and biases, and to construct training programs to ensure that trainees attribute their successes to their efforts and abilities, which can increase their confidence, self-efficacy, and performance. While these suggestions seem reasonable, the model awaits further testing.

Reinforcement Theory: A Non-Cognitive Theory of Motivation

The last motivation theory we will discuss, **reinforcement theory** (Skinner, 1953, 1974), is rooted in behaviorism (Watson, 1913), which attempts to explain behavior without referring to unobservable internal forces such as needs or thoughts. Behaviorists try to explain behavior by focusing only on things that can be directly observed: the behavior itself and environmental events that precede and follow the behavior. In short, reinforcement theory argues that behavior is a function of its consequences. This is based on the **law of effect** (Thorndike, 1913), which states that behavior that is followed by a pleasurable consequence will occur more frequently (a process called reinforcement) and behavior that is followed by an aversive consequence will occur less frequently. According to reinforcement theory, a manager or trainer can control an employee's behavior by controlling the consequences that follow the employee's behavior.

Reinforcement theory can be applied by using a set of techniques known as **behavior modification.** Behavior modification suggests four choices for controlling an employee's behavior:

1. **Positive reinforcement** refers to increasing the frequency of a behavior by following the behavior with a pleasurable consequence.

2. **Negative reinforcement** increases the frequency of a behavior by removing an aversive consequence.

3. **Extinction** seeks to decrease the frequency of a behavior by removing the consequence that is reinforcing it.

4. **Punishment** seeks to decrease the frequency of a behavior by introducing an aversive consequence immediately after the behavior.

In addition to the type of consequence that follows a behavior, the way consequences are paired with behaviors, called a schedule of reinforcement, is an important part of how behavior modification can be effectively applied.

Reinforcement theory and behavior modification have been strongly supported by voluminous research and have helped increase our understanding of work-related behavior (see Campbell, 1971; Dunnette, 1976). Reinforcement theory has also had an influence on HRD. Methods of instruction, such as programmed instruction and some approaches to computer-based training, draw heavily from reinforcement theory (we will discuss these and other training methods in Chapter 5). Trainers and managers can also motivate employees to learn and use what they have learned back on the job by using behavior modification techniques. A more complete discussion of how reinforcement theory has been applied to HRD can be found in Latham (1989).

Summary of Motivation

As we have seen, there are many approaches to explaining and understanding motivation. Each theory we have discussed enhances our understanding of employee behavior and has at least some research support (with the strongest support going to goal setting, reinforcement theory, and social learning theory). In addition, each approach offers valuable insight to the design and implementation of HRD programs.

This brief discussion of ten approaches to work motivation is not exhaustive, nor does it explain the complexity and interrelationships among the theories. Some theories, such as expectancy theory and reinforcement theory, make many similar predictions (Vecchio, 1991). In addition, researchers have attempted to integrate several theories into a larger, more inclusive model (the Porter-Lawler model combines expectancy and equity theories). We hope that this discussion encourages the reader to appreciate both the importance of motivation in determining employee behavior, as well as the richness of potential applications that motivation theories have for HRD.

Other Internal Factors that Influence Employee Behavior

Attitudes and knowledge, skills, and abilities (KSAs), like motivation, are also internal factors that influence employee behavior. Each of these factors is discussed below.

Attitudes

Attitudes are the second major internal influence depicted in our model of work behavior (Figure 2-1). Attitudes add to our understanding of employee behavior by showing another way thoughts can influence behavior. Many HRD programs and processes, including training evaluation, management development, and organizational development, either focus on modifying employee attitudes or use attitudes as a central component. For example, one way HRD programs are evaluated is by means of assessing employee attitudes toward the program and its content.

What is an attitude? An attitude "represents a person's general feeling of favorableness or unfavorableness toward some stimulus object" (Fishbein & Ajzen, 1975, p. 216). Attitudes are always held with respect to a particular object—whether the object is a person, place, event, or idea—and indicate one's feelings or affect toward that object. Attitudes also tend to be stable over time and are difficult to change (e.g., Staw & Ross, 1985).

Of particular interest to HRD is the nature of the relationship between attitudes and behavior. While common sense tells us that attitudes often cause behavior, the reality is often more complex. If attitudes did directly affect our behavior, without any other intervening factors, our behavior should be consistent with those attitudes. Unfortunately, this is not always the case. Attitudes can be used to predict behavior, but the predictions are at best only moderately accurate. Researchers attempting to prove a direct relationship between attitudes and behavior have been met with considerable frustration.

Research conducted over the past 20 years suggests that the relationship between attitudes and behavior is not simple or direct. One widely discussed model that explains this relationship is the behavioral intentions model (Ajzen and Fishbein, 1977, 1980; Fishbein & Ajzen, 1975). This model states that attitudes are combined with perceived social pressure to behave in a given way (called subjective norms) to influence an individual's intentions. These intentions, in turn, more directly influence behavior (see Figure 2-6). When attitudes and subjective norms conflict, the stronger of the two plays the dominant role in determining what the individual's intentions will be. According to the behavioral intentions model, then, attitudes appear to affect behavior only to the extent that they influence one's intentions.

The behavioral intentions model of attitudes influences HRD when measuring the effectiveness of its programs (a topic discussed in Chapter 6). Relying solely on measuring attitudes to determine whether employees will apply what they have learned in an HRD program will likely produce only moderately accurate results. The behavioral intentions model suggests that it may be more useful to measure trainees' *intentions* to use what they have learned, since intentions incorporate attitudes and more directly influence behavior. While this is no substitute for assessing an actual change in job behavior, the behavioral intentions model implies that intentions, rather than attitudes alone may be a better indicator of program effectiveness.

However, attitudes are an important factor in HRD programs. Noe (1986) proposed that two types of attitudes, reaction to skills assessment feedback and career/job attitudes, can have a direct effect on the motivation to learn. Noe's

| FIGURE 2-6 | A GRAPHIC REPRESENTATION OF THE BEHAVIORAL INTENTIONS MODEL |

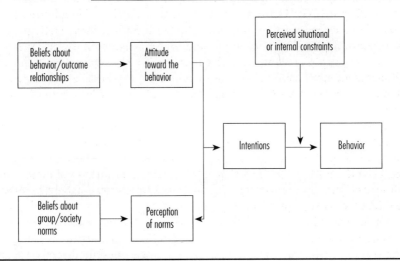

SOURCE: From *Organizational Behavior* (5th ed.) (p. 51) by D. Helriegel, J. W. Slocum, Jr., and R. W. Wood-man, 1989, St. Paul, MN: West. Adapted by permission.

model of the effect of attitudes on training is shown in Figure 2-7. An empirical test of the model (Noe & Schmitt, 1986) suggested that these factors do in fact influence motivation and learning in a training program. Based on these results, Noe and Schmitt modified the original model. The modified model (shown in Figure 2-8) suggests that job involvement and career planning can have a signif-icant impact on pre-training motivation and motivation to learn. We believe that explicitly considering and understanding the effects trainee attitudes can have on training effectiveness, as Noe and Schmitt have done, is a promising avenue of research—one that will likely yield new insights into ways HRD programs can be made more effective.

Knowledge, Skills, and Abilities (KSAs)

The third and final internal factor included in our model of employee behavior (Figure 2-1) is the employee's knowledge, skills, and abilities (KSAs). It is clear that KSAs have a significant impact on employee performance. All other things being equal, if employees lack the KSAs to perform a task or behavior, they will likely fail. Almost all HRD programs focus on improving or renewing the KSAs of employees.

Despite the ubiquitous nature of KSAs in HRD, these factors can be difficult to define with precision. Definitions differ according to the person defining them. Edwin Fleishman, a leading researcher of human abilities, defines **abilities** as general capacities related to the performance of a set of tasks (1972). Abilities develop over time through the interaction of heredity and experience, and are

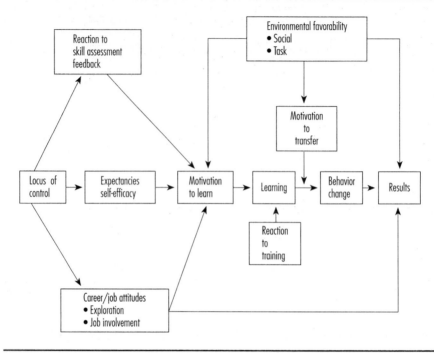

FIGURE 2-7

MODEL OF MOTIVATIONAL AND ATTITUDINAL
INFLUENCES ON TRAINING EFFECTIVENESS

SOURCE: From "Trainee's Attributes and Attitudes: Neglected Influences on Training Effectiveness" by R. A. Noe, 1986, *Academy of Management Review, 11*, p. 738. Adapted by permission.

long-lasting. **Skills** are similar to abilities, but differ in that they combine abilities with capabilities that are developed as a result of training and experience (Dunnette, 1976b). Skills are often categorized as psychomotor activities (while abilities tend to be more cognitive) and are typically measured in terms of the ease and precision evident in the performance of some task (Goldstein, 1991). Finally, **knowledge** is defined as an understanding of factors or principles related to a particular subject.

Over 100 different types of abilities have been identified (see Guilford, 1967; Dunnette, 1976; Fleishman, 1975), including general intelligence, verbal comprehension, numerical ability, and inductive reasoning. Some types of abilities, like general strength, have even been partitioned into subcategories (including explosive, dynamic, and static) (Fleishman & Mumford, 1989).

Researchers have attempted to develop taxonomies to describe the abilities needed to perform particular tasks. Taxonomies help HRD professionals to select and assign employees to training, choose appropriate learning strategies for individuals of differing skill levels, and specify training needs and content when designing training programs. Fleishman and his colleagues (Fleishman, 1967, 1972; Fleishman & Quaintance, 1984) have developed one such taxon-

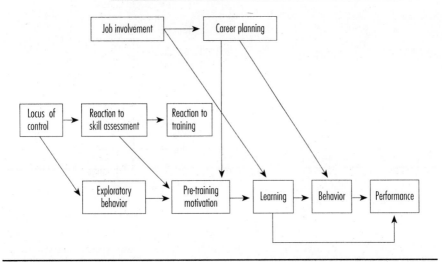

FIGURE 2-8 REVISED MODEL OF MOTIVATIONAL AND ATTITUDINAL INFLUENCES ON TRAINING EFFECTIVENESS

SOURCE: From "The Influence of Trainee Attitudes on Training Effectiveness" by R.A. Noe and N. Schmitt, 1986, *Personnel Psychology, 39*, p. 515.

omy that has been applied to HRD (see Fleishman & Mumford, 1989, for a description of the system and its development and application). We will discuss needs assessment in Chapter 4.

It should be clear from the preceding discussion that motivation, attitudes, and ability are critical to explaining employee behavior and to understanding and applying HRD. Next, our attention turns to external influences affecting employee behavior.

Environmental Influences on Employee Behavior

While forces within an employee play a strong role in determining employee behavior, situational factors play an important role as well. Our model (Figure 2-1) includes four sets of environmental forces that can affect employee behavior: outcomes, the supervisor, the organization itself, and co-workers. Table 2-2 presents a list of these forces and some of the issues found in each.

Outcomes

Outcomes occur as a result of a given employee behavior. There are two categories of outcomes: personal and organizational. Personal outcomes are those that have value to the individual, such as pay, recognition, and emotions. Organizational outcomes are things valued by the organization, such as team work, productivity, and product quality. The word value in this context should not imply that outcomes will always be positive or desirable. Behavior can also result

| TABLE 2-2 | ENVIRONMENTAL INFLUENCES ON EMPLOYEE BEHAVIOR |

Factor	Issues
Outcomes	Types Effect on motivation
Supervisor	Expectations Leadership
Organization	Reward structure Job design
Co-workers	Control of outcomes Norms Group dynamics

in outcomes the employee fears or dislikes. Embarrassment, disciplinary actions, transfers, loss of pay or privileges, and ostracism are all possible unpleasant outcomes of employee behavior.

Several of the motivation theories we discussed earlier propose that employee perceptions of outcomes are important determinants of behavior. Consider two examples:

1. **Expectancy theory** states that people will perform behaviors that they perceive will bring valued outcomes. If employees fulfill certain obligations to the organization, but do not receive promised outcomes (such as promotions or pay raises), the employees may lower their instrumentality judgments and choose to behave differently. Further, if outcomes are not as rewarding as anticipated, the employees may revise their valence judgments and perform different behaviors.

2. **Equity theory** states that outcomes are evaluated by comparing them to others. If an inequity is perceived, performance and/or cognitions may be changed to reduce the inequity. In addition, outcomes can serve as a form of feedback to the employee. Bonuses and recognition, for example, let employees know whether they have performed appropriately and whether their performance is valued by the organization.

Outcomes are important to HRD. If employees do not believe attending a training program will lead to valued outcomes, they may choose not to attend the program, or devote little effort to learning and using the skills being taught. If an employee perceives that company training will require increased individual effort with no resulting personal outcomes, relative to others, the training may be seen as unfair. As a result the employee may resist participating in the program.

On the other hand, it is often the outcomes of performance or behavior (such as embarrassment or a poor evaluation) that act as attention-getters and convince an employee that training or development is needed. If a nurse who treats patients rudely never experiences any unpleasant outcomes as a result, (in the form of complaints to the supervisor or disciplinary actions), it is unlikely that the nurse will perceive any need to change this behavior. Similarly, if college professors who have not kept current in their field continue to receive support and recognition for their work in the classroom, they may perceive that their behavior is acceptable and thus see no reason for them to attend professional seminars.

Thus, it is important that supervisors and managers remain aware of the outcomes of their subordinates' performance, as well as how their subordinates view these outcomes. This knowledge can be useful in detecting needs for training, motivating employees to participate in training, and in ensuring that what employees do learn is applied to their jobs.

The Supervisor

The immediate supervisor plays an important role in the employee's work life, delegating tasks and responsibilities, setting expectations, evaluating performance, and providing (or failing to provide) feedback, rewards, and discipline. While the influences supervisors have on subordinates are numerous and sometimes complex, two factors deserve comment.

First, research on **self-fulfilling prophecy,** or the Pygmalion effect (Eden, 1984), has shown how the expectations a supervisor establishes can influence the subordinate's behavior. First demonstrated in classroom settings, self-fulfilling prophecy states that expectations of performance can become reality because people strive to behave consistently with their perceptions of reality. If supervisors (or trainers) expect good performance, their behavior may aid and encourage their subordinates to raise their own self-expectations, increase their efforts, and ultimately perform well. The opposite would happen if the supervisors expected poor performance (Eden, 1984).

Eden and his colleagues (Eden & Ravid, 1982; Eden & Shanni, 1982) have demonstrated in a variety of work settings that raising manager's performance expectations does in fact result in higher levels of performance in their employees. The implications for supervisors and HRD professionals who conduct training programs is clear: all must be aware of their own expectations and what they communicate to others, while taking advantage of the benefits resulting from high but realistic expectations. In addition, supervisory expectations play a key role in the coaching process, which will be discussed in greater detail in Chapter 9.

The supervisor's approach to leadership may have an influence on an employee's performance as well. **Leadership** is the use of non-coercive influence to direct and coordinate the activities of a group toward accomplishing a goal (Jago, 1982). There are almost as many definitions of and theories about leadership as there are leadership researchers. Two examples serve to demonstrate the effect a supervisor's or manager's leadership may have on employee behavior.

First, House (1971) argued in his path-goal theory that a leader's role is to identify goals and clarify the paths employees may take to reach the goals. If this is done effectively (according to the theory, by applying one of four possible leader styles, depending on employee characteristics and environmental factors), then motivation, job satisfaction, and the job performance of subordinates are all predicted to increase. Subsequent research has provided some support for the theory's predictions regarding job satisfaction (Al-Gattan, 1985; Schriesheim & DeNisi, 1981).

Graen's vertical-dyad linkage model of leadership (Dansereau, Graen, & Haga, 1975) observes that supervisors treat each of their employees differently, including some in a favored "in-group," while relegating others to a less favored "out-group." In-group members have relationships with their supervisors characterized by respect, liking, mutual trust, and influence; the opposite is true of out-group member relationships. Research (Vecchio & Godbel, 1984) has shown that in-group members have higher performance and satisfaction than out-group members, and that the theory can be used to predict turnover (Ferris, 1985) and career outcomes (Wakabayashi & Graen, 1984).

These and other leadership theories further highlight the effect the immediate supervisor can have on employee behavior. Subordinates look to their managers and supervisors for cues about appropriate and inappropriate behavior. If a manager or supervisor speaks and behaves in ways that indicate training and development are unimportant, employees will likely have little enthusiasm for these activities. Alternatively, if managers and supervisors take these activities seriously and reward employees for learning and using new skills, techniques, and attitudes, HRD efforts will be more effective, and ultimately the employee, manager, and organization will benefit. Leadership is also a key aspect of management development. Many organizations use management development programs (discussed in Chapter 12) as a way to improve the leadership skills of managerial employees.

The Organization

The organization itself can influence employee behavior through its reward structure and job design. **Reward structure** focuses on:

- The **types** of rewards an organization uses (material, social);

- How rewards are **distributed** (equally to all, relevant to each individual's contribution, or on the basis of need); and

- The **criteria** for reward distribution (results, behavior, or nonperformance issues, such as tenure). (Pearce & Peters, 1985; Von Glinow, 1985)

Rewards include not only tangible things, such as financial bonuses and plaques, but also intangible things, such as recognition and acceptance.

Motivation theories are used as the foundation for many organizational reward systems. They can also help to explain why reward systems sometimes fail. As expectancy theory and reinforcement theory suggest, employees tend to do what they are rewarded for. If management does not carefully design and implement the reward system, then it may unintentionally reinforce undesirable behavior in employees (such as lack of initiative, acceptance of the status quo, and low participation rates in HRD programs). Also, recall that cognitive evaluation theory suggests that rewards perceived as control mechanisms may reduce motivation and performance.

Therefore, it is important for supervisors and HRD professionals to understand what the organization's reward system is intended to do, how it is put into practice, and how employees respond to it. Solving some performance problems may be solved simply by adjusting the reward system. It must also be understood that one of the primary reasons employees become involved in HRD programs is to obtain valued rewards, such as promotions, pay increases, and more desirable assignments. As mentioned earlier, some organizations choose to highlight the linkages between desired rewards and HRD as a way to pique employee interest in them. Rewards and their effective distribution can also be a topic of training, particularly in supervisory and management development programs.

Job design is the development and alteration of the components of a job (such as the tasks and their configuration, and the scope of responsibilities) to improve productivity and the quality of the employee's work life. To the extent a job contains the factors that can satisfy personal growth needs (Herzberg's two factor theory), or provides elements that generate feelings of responsibility, meaningfulness, and knowledge of results (Hackman & Oldham's [1980] job characteristics approach), the employee will be more satisfied and more productive. Job design has received a great deal of attention and research support (Loher, Noe, Moeller, & Fitzgerald, 1985).

The implication of job design for HRD is twofold. First, the way an organization chooses to construct its jobs can affect an employee's behavior and attitudes. Second, to improve an employee's performance and affect (or reduce excessive stress), the focus can be on altering the job rather than the employee. Job design will receive more attention in the Chapter 13 discussion of organizational development.

Co-Workers

Co-workers can exert a strong influence on an employee's behavior in at least three ways. First, co-workers control some of the outcomes an employee values and may use those outcomes to influence the employee's behavior. For example, if the employee behaves in a way co-workers value, they may reward or reinforce that behavior by offering friendship and recognition. Similarly, co-workers may choose to react to behavior they disapprove of by withholding desired outcomes or punishing the employee through insults, ostracism, or threats.

Second, **norms,** or informal rules for appropriate behavior established within work groups, can serve as guidelines for appropriate behavior, if the employee chooses to comply (Feldman, 1984). Norms send a clear message about what behavior is expected and may lead employees to behave in ways that differ from typical patterns. (Norms will be discussed further in Chapter 7.)

Third, because HRD programs are often administered in groups and employees must perform newly learned behaviors in group settings, HRD professionals need to understand the effect of group dynamics on group behavior. **Group dynamics** influence the way an employee may behave when interacting in a group. Dynamics such as groupthink (Janis, 1982) and social loafing (Latane, Williams, & Harkins, 1979) show that performance of individuals within groups can differ from their behavior alone. *Groupthink*, occurs when group members are primarily concerned with unanimity, making poor decisions by failing to realistically assess alternatives (Janis, 1982). *Social loafing* is the tendency for group members to reduce their effort as group size increases (Latane et al., 1979).

The implication of dynamics such as social loafing and groupthink is that employees sometimes behave differently in groups than when alone. Because many HRD programs involve group settings and activities, care should be taken when designing and implementing HRD programs to ensure group dynamics do not undermine the learning process. Similarly, group dynamics should be taken into account when planning actions designed to ensure what is learned is transferred back to the job. Supervisors can monitor potentially destructive dynamics and act to address them to maximize the chances what employees learn in training and development activities will be used. Involving co-workers in the learning process, as participants or trainers, can increase acceptance of using newly learned skills. Similarly, managers and supervisors should pay attention to the attitudes of employees in a unit or division toward training and using new methods and skills.

RETURN TO OPENING CASE

AT&T's answer to the dilemma of improving employee skills, performance, and morale during downsizing—while at the same time encouraging employees to focus on career development should they be laid off—was a unique HRD program called **safe landing.** One of the main goals of safe landing was to assist employees in obtaining another position that continued their career progress, either within AT&T or elsewhere.

One AT&T division that successfully implemented safe landing was the National Personnel Services Organization (NPSO), which went from 901 to 376 employees between 1989 and 1991. From the beginning, the company was honest with employees about the plans for reductions and reorganizations, changes in levels of funding, and the potential for layoffs.

This honesty provided a foundation for the rest of the program. The safe landing approach was a partnership between the company and the employee. The company offered assistance in providing opportunities for employees to develop their careers; the employees were ultimately responsible for taking control of their futures. Assistance provided by the company included arranging for employees to exchange positions for a period of time to gain some experience and try out new things (for instance, allowing an employee with a goal in HRM to spend several weeks in a position dealing with compensation issues). In addition, managers and supervisors held regular meetings with individual employees to evaluate their progress and identify additional ways to help.

From both the employees' and the company's points of view, the safe landing program was a success. Of the 514 NPSO employees whose positions were declared to be surplus during the program, 512 were able to make "safe landings" either elsewhere within AT&T or outside the company (by finding other jobs or retiring early). Further, employees within the program showed evidence of shifting their focus from fear of the future to safe landing issues such as skills improvement and improving customer satisfaction.

Through a combination of honesty, tangible support, real opportunities to develop skills, and making employees believe that the company cared about their future, AT&T found a way to motivate employees to improve performance and take control of their careers.[1]

Summary

Because HRD programs are attempts to change employee behavior, it is important to understand the factors that influence employee behavior. This chapter presented a number of such factors that have direct relevance to HRD, using a simple model of employee behavior to guide the discussion. The model contains two sets of factors that interact to influence employee behavior: (1) internal factors, including motivation, ability, and attitudes, and (2) environmental factors, including outcomes, the supervisor, the organization, and co-workers.

Motivation is one of the key internal factors that influence employee behavior. Motivation is defined as the psychological processes that cause energizing, direction, and persistence of voluntary behavior. Theories of motivation use different sources to explain behavior, including needs (Maslow's need hierarchy, Alderfer's ERG theory, and Herzberg's two factor theory), cognitions (expectancy theory, equity theory, goal-setting theory, social learning theory, cognitive evaluation theory, and attribution theory), and the consequences of behavior (reinforcement theory). Each of these theories have implications for developing and conducting HRD programs.

---

[1]From "Safe Landings for Outplaced Employees at AT&T" by W. J. Barkley, Jr., and T. B. Green, 1992, *Personnel Journal*, 71 (6), pp. 144–147. Adapted by permission.

Attitudes and the employee's knowledge, skills, and abilities (KSAs) are also important internal factors of behavior. Without ability (the capability one has to perform a set of tasks) a person will be unable to perform a given behavior, regardless of motivation. Attitudes, which are made up of beliefs, feelings, and behavioral tendencies, affect behavior indirectly through intentions. According to the behavior intentions model, attitudes combine with the perception of social pressure to form intentions, which in turn directly affect behavior. Research has shown that both employee attitudes and ability play a role in the effectiveness of HRD programs.

Outcomes—the results of performing a behavior in a particular way—are an external influence on employee behavior. Both personal (relevant to the individual, like pay or recognition) and organizational (relevant to the organization, like productivity or profits) outcomes can be used to diagnose and motivate employees to attend, learn, and apply what they have learned in HRD programs. Theories of motivation, such as equity theory, expectancy theory, and reinforcement theory, attempt to explain whether and how outcomes affect employee behavior.

Supervisors, through their leadership and expectations, also influence employee behavior. A supervisor can use leadership (non-coercive influence) to affect a subordinate's performance, attitudes, and motivation. According to the vertical dyad linkage theory, employees who are treated by their supervisor with trust, respect, and friendship are more satisfied and perform better than those who are not. Research on self-fulfilling prophecy has shown that a supervisor's expectations of an employee can affect the way the supervisor interacts with the employee, with the employee's performance tending to live up or down to those expectations.

Two additional environmental factors influencing employee behavior are co-workers and the organization itself. Co-workers provide influence through group norms, group dynamics, and by controlling valued outcomes. The organization can also affect employee behavior in several ways, including its reward structure and the way it designs the employee's job.

HRD professionals, as well as supervisors and managers, are in the business of understanding and influencing employee behavior. As the sampling of concepts and theories in this chapter shows, there are many possible explanations but few unequivocal facts. The techniques we will discuss in the chapters that follow draw upon the foundation that researchers of work behavior have laid, but applying them to a given situation often requires judgment and modifications. In this sense, designing and delivering HRD programs is an art as well as a science.

Key Terms and Concepts

ability	expectancy
attitudes	expectancy theory
attribution theory	goal-setting theory
behavioral intentions model	group dynamics
causal attribution	instrumentality
cognitive evaluation theory	job design

equity
equity theory
leadership
motivation
needs
norms
outcomes
reinforcement theory

job satisfaction
law of effect
rewards
self-efficacy
self-fulfilling prophecy
social learning theory
valence

Questions for Discussion

1. Suppose that you are the recruitment manager for a medium-sized bank. One of your best recruiters appears to be unmotivated lately. The number of recruits she brings in is normally above the average for effective performance, but she has fallen below the standard for the past two weeks. What might expectancy theory suggest is causing the drop in her performance? What might equity theory suggest? Based on your knowledge of equity and expectancy theories, develop two recommendations for helping her improve her performance.

2. Suppose you are the HRD manager for a large electric utility company. The quarterly report shows a 25 percent decrease in participation in management development programs over the same quarter last year. The number of managers employed by the company has not changed, and the company's profits have remained stable. You already hold these programs in desirable locations off-site (local hotels and conference centers) and participating in these programs counts toward the employees' annual performance evaluation. Using your knowledge of motivation theory, suggest three possible reasons that could explain why participation rates are down. If after investigation those reasons turned out to be the true causes, what might you be able to do to improve participation rates?

3. Compare and contrast the need-based and cognitive-based approaches to understanding motivation.

4. The HRD manager for a chicken processing plant has come to you for advice. Even though all employees in the plant recently completed a safety training program, the accident rate has not improved. In particular, the manager has found that employees are not wearing safety gear (goggles, shoes with non-skid soles) consistently and are not following safe procedures. Using your knowledge of attitudes and supervisory expectations, develop two possible

reasons to explain the employees' behavior. If your hypotheses are true, how could the HRD manager improve the situation?

5. Why do people with low self-efficacy perform more poorly in training programs than those with high self-efficacy?

6. Briefly describe three ways that co-workers can affect an employee's behavior at work.

7. Recall a time at work or school where you found it difficult to motivate yourself to complete a required task (like start a report or study for an exam). Using two different motivation theories, explain why this lack of motivation may have occurred.

8. Select a familiar problem encountered in the workplace. Use the model of employee behavior presented in this chapter to explain why this problem exists. Be specific.

3

Learning and HRD

Learning Objectives

1. *Define learning and list three learning principles.*
2. *Identify several personal characteristics that affect trainee learning.*
3. *Describe the training design issues that can be used to maximize learning.*
4. *Explain the factors that affect learning retention and the transfer of training.*
5. *Tell how individual differences between trainees affect the learning process.*
6. *Describe the role that learning strategies play in learning.*
7. *Cite three emerging perspectives from instructional psychology that have importance for HRD in the future.*

OPENING CASE

How do you train employees to operate equipment in a manufacturing system that is still being designed? Several years ago, management at Planters LifeSavers Company (PLC) (a division of RJR-Nabisco Corporation) faced this problem at its Franklin Park, Illinois, candy manufacturing plant. PLC was introducing new equipment and knew employees would have to be trained to operate and to maintain it. However, because the manufacturing system was still being designed, it was unclear what job tasks the new equipment would require. As a result, neither job analysis nor traditional training could be done.

Faced with this challenge, PLC management chose an approach that would not only prepare supervisors and hourly workers to work with the new equipment and manufacturing system, but would also prepare them for other changes that were likely to affect the work environment. They decided to develop a program about learning how to learn.

Introduction

Learning is an important part of all HRD efforts. Whether you are training a carpenter's apprentice to use a nail gun, conducting a workshop to teach managers to use discipline more effectively, or trying to get meat packers to understand and follow new safety procedures, your goal is to change behavior, knowledge, or attitudes through learning. Supervisors and HRD professionals who understand the learning process and how to create an environment that facilitates learning can design and implement more effective HRD programs.

The purpose of this chapter is to define learning and present the learning-related issues important to HRD. The topics we will cover include the relationship between learning and instruction, maximizing learning, and individual differences in the learning process.

Learning and Instruction

Learning is defined as a relatively permanent change in behavior or cognition that occurs as a result of one's interaction with the environment. Several aspects of this definition are important. First, the focus of learning is change, either by acquiring something new (like skill in conducting meetings) or modifying something that already exists (like achieving greater accuracy in shooting a pistol). Second, the change must be long lasting before we can say learning has really occurred. If a word processing operator can recall the commands needed to format a paragraph on the second day of a training course, but cannot remember them four days later back on the job, learning has not occurred. Third, the focus of learning can include either behavior or cognitions, or both. Learning outcomes can be physical skills (climbing a utility pole), procedures (applying for a grant), or attitudes (becoming more safety conscious). Finally, learning results from the individual's interaction with the environment. Learning does not include behavior changes attributable to maturation or a temporary condition (such as fatigue or drugs).

Researchers have studied learning from a variety of perspectives, such as behaviorism and cognitivism, using both humans and animals in their experiments. Progress has followed two main approaches. One approach is to study how people learn simple tasks, such as identifying symbols and associating pairs of meaningless syllables (such as *bix*, *rik*, and *moc*). The goal of this line of research is to identify basic principles that apply to learning any kind of content. The other approach focuses on how people learn complex tasks, including school subjects such as reading and math. While some researchers who use this approach seek generalizable principles, many believe that learning cannot be separated from what is being learned, and therefore different principles may apply to different learning outcomes (Gagné & Glaser, 1987).

The Search for Basic Learning Principles

Over the past 100 years, research has yielded a number of principles considered to govern learning. The concept of association is the cornerstone of learning theory (Gagné & Glaser, 1987). **Association** is the process by which two cognitions become paired together (e.g., "dozen" and "twelve items") so that thinking about one evokes thoughts about the other (Anderson & Bower, 1973). Three principles that govern the learning of associations include:

1. **Contiguity**   Objects that are experienced together tend to become associated with each other (James, 1890). For example, learning vocabulary in a foreign language usually involves pairing a new word with an object or picture of an object (like the French word *chat* and a picture of a cat).

2. **The Law of Effect**   As we discussed in Chapter 2, the law of effect states that a behavior followed by a pleasurable consequence is likely to be repeated (Thorndike, 1913). For example, when a police officer who values recognition is complimented by her superior for the way she handled a difficult arrest, she associates the compliment with the arrest method, and will likely use that method to make difficult arrests in the future.

3. **Practice**   Repeating the events in an association will increase the strength of the association. For example, the more times a soldier rappels down a cliff or wall, the more adept he or she becomes at rappelling. But practice alone is not enough to guarantee a stronger association. The effect of practice is strengthened with reinforcement, such as a pleasurable consequence (Gagné & Glaser, 1987).

An alternative to the association view of learning was offered by a group of researchers known as Gestalt psychologists. These researchers (including Kohler, 1927, and Wertheimer, 1959) proposed that learning does not occur by trial and error or by associating facts and ideas, but rather happens suddenly in the form of an insight. Insight is seen as a sudden reconceptualization of one's experiences that results in a new idea or discovering the solution to a problem. For example, learning to solve a puzzle like Rubik's cube may occur in the form of a series of "sudden flashes" in which new ideas bring one closer and closer to getting all sides of the cube to be the same color.

Insight as a mechanism for learning has received some criticism. Gagné (1985) states that some critics explain insight by saying the person has simply transferred what they have learned in one set of situations to another. If this is true, insight may not be a particularly useful model for how people learn. While some learning may occur through insights, many of the behaviors of interest to HRD programs (such as learning a new set of regulations or procedures) are likely to be learned in other ways.

Limits of Learning Principles in Improving Training Design

Unfortunately, when it comes to improving training design, these general principles are not as helpful as one might expect. Much of the research that demonstrated these principles was conducted in tightly controlled laboratory settings using artificial tasks, which limits the applicability of the findings to real-world training settings.

The limited benefit of using learning principles to improve training effectiveness was convincingly stated by Robert Gagné (1962) in a landmark article, "Military Training and Principles of Learning." Gagné showed that practice and reinforcement failed to improve performance of three representative tasks: gunnery (a motor skill), turning on a radar set (a procedural task), and diagnosing malfunctions in complex electronic equipment (troubleshooting). Rather than relying on the prevailing learning principles, Gagné argued that training can be improved by using three principles:

1. **Task Analysis** Any task can be analyzed into a set of distinct component tasks.

2. **Component Task Achievement** Each component task must be fully achieved before the entire task may be performed correctly.

3. **Task Sequencing** The learning situation should be arranged so that each of the component tasks is learned in the appropriate order before the total task is attempted. (Gagné, 1962)

Instructional Psychology: Incorporating the Situation in Learning

In the 1960s, based on the work of Gagné and others, the field of **instructional psychology** was developed and has since become an active field of theory and research on how the learning environment may be structured to maximize learning. Whereas traditional learning theorists focused on describing what happens in learning situations, instructional theorists focus on what must be done before learning can take place (Bruner, 1966). Glaser (1982) characterized instructional psychology as "focusing on the acquisition of human competence" (p. 299) with the following four components:

1. Describing the **learning goal** to be obtained;

2. Analyzing the **initial state** of the learner (what the learner knows or can perform prior to learning);

3. Identifying the **conditions** (instructional techniques, procedures, and materials) that allow the learner to gain competence; and

4. **Assessing and monitoring** the learning process to determine progress and whether alternative techniques should be used.

Glaser further identified five principles that guide researchers investigating instructional issues. These include (a) attention to performance and learning, (b) a focus on specific knowledge domains (such as learning to diagnose medical conditions) rather than artificial laboratory tasks, (c) a prescriptive approach that explains how competence can be achieved, (d) theory oriented to the individual, and (e) an approach recognizing that learning is a dynamic process and that performance levels change during instruction, possibly requiring a corresponding change in the instructional technique. This stands in sharp contrast to the way traditional learning theorists studied learning.

Since the late 1970s instructional psychology has been heavily influenced by developments in cognitive psychology (Resnick, 1981), adopting the language, methods, and models that portray humans as information processors. In this view, mental processes such as attention, perception, encoding, memory, and retrieval are considered the building blocks of thought and behavior. Much of the current research focuses on complex thought processes, including problem solving, reasoning, and language comprehension (for recent reviews see Gagné & Dick, 1983; Glaser & Bassok, 1989; and Pintrich, Cross, Kozma, and McKeachie, 1986).

Instructional psychology holds much promise for maximizing learning in the design and implementation of HRD programs. As the nature of work continues to shift from manual skill to more complex mental processes, the findings from instructional psychology will help pave the way for effective HRD efforts in the years to come. A recent paper by Howell and Cooke (1989) shows how information processing models and instructional psychology concepts and research can be applied to training. We will briefly consider some of these applications at the end of this chapter.

Maximizing Learning

The definition of learning makes it clear that people acquire and develop skills, knowledge, and behavior as a result of an interaction between forces within the learner and in the environment. In this section of the chapter, we present factors that have been shown to affect learning and discuss their outcomes. We will focus on maximizing learning by discussing trainee characteristics, training design, and the transfer of training (see Table 3-1).

Trainee Characteristics

It is logical to expect that a trainee's personal characteristics will have an effect on how he or she learns new tasks and new information. Three such characteristics are trainability, personality, and attitudes.

Trainability Trainability is concerned with the readiness to learn, combining trainees' levels of ability and motivation (Maier, 1973) with their perceptions of the work environment (Noe, 1986).

Trainability = f (Motivation × Ability × Perceptions of the Work Environment)

TABLE 3-1	ISSUES INVOLVED IN MAXIMIZING LEARNING

Trainee Characteristics

Trainability
Personality and Attitudes

Training Design

Conditions of Practice
    Active practice
    Massed versus spaced practice sessions
    Whole versus part learning
    Overlearning
    Knowledge of results (feedback)
    Task sequencing
Retention of What Is Learned
    Meaningfulness of material
    Degree of original learning
    Interference

Transfer of Training

Identical elements
General principles
Stimulus variability
Support in the work environment

The formula above illustrates that a trainee must have both the motivation and the ability to learn; if either is lacking, learning will not occur. The equation also shows that a very high level of one cannot completely overcome a very low level of the other (Maier, 1973). In addition, if employees perceive little support in the work environment (including supervisors and co-workers) for learning new knowledge or skills, they will be less likely to learn and use them (Noe, 1986).

Trainability is an important factor in HRD. Placing employees in programs they are not motivated to attend or are not prepared to do well in can waste time and resources. Trainees with less ability take longer to learn, which can increase the length of the training period and the expense involved in conducting training. In fact it is possible that these trainees will not learn at all.

To illustrate the effect trainability can have on learning, suppose a service technician for an office equipment company is in a training program designed to teach selling skills for the equipment being serviced. Selling requires skills in oral communication and interpersonal relations. If the technician lacks either skill, it is likely that learning to sell effectively will prove to be very difficult. The technician may want to learn, and try very hard to do so, but this low level of ability will hinder learning. Similarly, if the technician has excellent communication skills but sees selling as unpleasant or distasteful, or does not think learning to sell will help to achieve personal goals, no effort may be made to learn the sales skills.

A number of studies have shown ability affects learning (Downs, 1970; Gordon, 1955; Gordon & Klieman, 1976; McGehee, 1948; Neel & Dunn, 1960; Taylor, 1952; Taylor & Tajen, 1948). The same is true for motivation (Eden & Ravid, 1982; Eden & Shani, 1982; Hicks & Klimoski, 1987; Komaki, Heinzemann, & Lawson, 1980; Reber & Wallin, 1984; Wexley & Baldwin, 1986), and for perceptions of the work environment (e.g., Peters, O'Connor, & Elbers, 1985).

Trainability testing is one approach that can be used to ensure that trainees have the motivation and ability to learn. This approach focuses on measuring the motivation and/or relevant abilities of candidates for training and selecting for training only those who show a sufficient level of trainability. For example, Tubiana and Ben-Shakhar (1982) developed a questionnaire that measured motivational and personality factors to predict success in combat training. The questionnaire measured such things as independence, sociability, and motivation to serve in a combat unit. The combination of questionnaire responses and other predictors proved to be highly correlated with training success.

Another approach to trainee testing is to allow candidates to complete part of the training program and use their performance on that section as a predictor of how well they will perform throughout the remainder of training (Robertson & Downs, 1979). Siegel (1983) described a method called "miniature training and evaluation testing," in which U.S. Navy recruits were trained on a sample of important tasks and tested on their ability to perform these tasks. Using 11 training and evaluation modules or situations, the approach yielded better predictions of success for several jobs than the test normally conducted by the Navy. Trainability testing has also been effective in predicting the training success of older workers (Robertson & Downs, 1979). Robertson and Downs (1989) also conducted a meta-analysis of research studies examining the use of work sample tests of trainability and concluded that such tests do predict success in training and job performance for untrained job applicants.

Personality and Attitudes   Although not explicitly mentioned in the definition of trainability, a trainee's personality and attitudes can also have an effect on learning (see Chapter 2). Noe (1986) suggested that an employee's attitudes toward career exploration and job involvement have an effect on both learning and its applications to the job. Other research has shown that job involvement, course expectations, and confidence are all related to success in training (Noe and Schmitt, 1986; Ryman and Biersner, 1975).

Personality is the stable set of personal characteristics that account for consistent patterns of behavior. Personality traits that are related to employee learning include locus of control and the need for achievement (Baumgartel, Reynolds, & Pathan, 1984), and activity, independence, and sociability (Tubiana & Ben-Shakhar, 1982). Barrick and Mount (1991) report that the results of a meta-analysis show that two personality dimensions—extraversion and openness to experience—are valid predictors of success in training. As further research is conducted on the relationship of personality characteristics and success in training, it may be useful to include measures of relevant traits in the selection process for attendance at expensive or lengthy training and other HRD programs.

To summarize, assessing employee's relevant abilities, motivation, and personality prior to HRD programs can be important in maximizing the chances learning will occur. This approach to maximizing learning fits with Glaser's (1984) notion that knowing the initial state of the learner is an important part of effective training.

Training Design

Training design involves adapting the learning environment to maximize learning. Training design issues (listed in Table 3-2) include (a) the conditions of practice that affect learning, and (b) the factors that affect retention of what is learned.

Although much of the research on these issues was conducted before 1970, new programs of research in instructional psychology have revived interest. While the information presented below can be helpful in designing an effective training program, not all the findings will work in all situations. Recall Gagné's (1962) arguments about traditional learning principles. There is no substitute for conducting a thorough task analysis and clearly specifying what is to be learned (task analysis will be discussed in Chapter 4).

Conditions of Practice   At least six issues have been studied that relate to practice and learning. They include active practice; massed versus spaced practice sessions; whole versus part learning; overlearning; knowledge of results; and task sequencing (see Table 3-2).

Active Practice suggests that learners should be given an opportunity to repeatedly perform the task or use the knowledge being learned. For example, if a paramedic is learning how to operate the "jaws of life," a machine used to extract passengers from vehicles damaged in accidents, the training sessions should include multiple opportunities for the paramedic to operate the "jaws."

Massed versus Spaced Practice Sessions concern whether to conduct the training in one session or divide it into segments separated by some period of

---

TABLE 3-2	**TRAINING DESIGN ISSUES INVOLVED IN MAXIMIZING LEARNING**

Conditions of Practice

1. Active Practice
2. Massed versus Spaced Practice Sessions
3. Whole versus Part Learning
4. Overlearning
5. Knowledge of Results
6. Task Sequencing

Retention of What Is Learned

1. Meaningfulness of Material
2. Degree of Original Learning
3. Interference

time. For example, is it better to study for an exam over a period of several days (spaced practice) or in one cram session (massed practice)?

In general, information and skills can be learned either way, but spaced practice sessions with a reasonable rest period between them lead to better performance and longer retention of what is learned than a massed practice session (Briggs & Naylor, 1962; Naylor & Briggs, 1963). Holding (1965) suggests that for difficult, complex tasks, an initial massed session followed by spaced practice sessions leads to improved performance.

Using massed rather than spaced practice sessions is often a matter of practicality winning out over science. Time and resource constraints may lead some organizations to schedule a single training sessions even though a series of spaced sessions would be more effective. However, HRD professionals should realize that under these conditions retention may suffer. It may be necessary to schedule follow-up sessions to boost retention.

Whole versus part learning concerns the size of the unit to be learned. Should trainees practice an entire task or study certain material as a whole, or should the task or material be learned in separate parts? Gagné (1962) argues that procedural material (material organized into a series of steps) should be analyzed and divided into the subunits, with the trainees mastering each subunit before performing the entire procedure.

Actually, the answer to which method is most effective depends on the nature of the task to be learned. When the subtasks are relatively easy to perform and are well organized (interrelated), the *whole* method is superior; otherwise, the *part* method has proven to be more effective (Blum & Naylor, 1968; Naylor & Briggs, 1963). For example, operating a chain saw involves adding fuel, holding it properly, starting it, making various cuts, and turning it off. Given that these subtasks are interrelated, it makes sense that they be learned together. On the other hand, the task of supervising others includes subtasks such as scheduling, evaluating employee performance, discipline, planning, and delegating work. These subtasks are less closely related and would best be learned by focusing on each subtask separately.

Overlearning is defined as practice beyond the point the material or task is mastered (McGehee & Thayer, 1961). For example, an instructor teaching cardiopulmonary resuscitation (CPR) in a first aid course would be using overlearning if trainees were required to repeatedly practice the CPR procedure even after they had successfully "revived" the training dummy.

The rationale for overlearning is threefold. First, overlearning may improve performance in a variety of different situations. By developing stronger associations between the parts of a task or unit of knowledge, it is less likely that situational changes will interfere with learning (McGehee & Thayer, 1961). Second, overlearning provides additional practice in using the skill or knowledge when there is little opportunity for doing so in the job setting (Goldstein, 1986). For example, overlearning the procedure to handle an engine flameout would be useful in airline pilot training, because pilots don't often face this situation when flying. Third, overlearning is thought to make what is learned more automatic, thereby improving performance in stressful or emergency situations (Fitts, 1965). For instance, U.S. and coalition soldiers in the Persian Gulf War of 1991 practiced their maneuvers and tasks (including set-up and firing procedures for Patriot missile batteries, troop movements, and using chemical warfare gear) repeatedly, so that when the orders came to attack these tasks would be "second nature" to the soldiers and they could perform them quickly and correctly.

Thus, research indicates that overlearning does in fact increase retention of what is learned (Atwater, 1953; Hagman & Rose, 1983; Mandler, 1954; Schendel & Hagman, 1982). Its major drawback, however, is that overlearning can increase training time and expense.

Knowledge of results, or feedback, provides objective information regarding the adequacy of one's performance, and it can come from observers, the performer, or the task itself. The relationship of feedback to learning and retention has been studied since the 1920s (Thorndike, 1927), with research showing that feedback enhances learning and retention (including Komaki, Heinzemann, & Lawson, 1980; and Wexley and Thornton, 1972). Trainers and educators often agree that feedback improves learning.

Researchers suggest that feedback is both *informational*—when it helps learners determine whether they've performed something correctly, and *motivational*—when it is valued by the learner or indicates valued outcomes (Ilgen, Fisher, & Taylor, 1979).

The effectiveness of feedback depends on how it is provided, especially in regards to timing and specificity. To ensure that the learner clearly understands the relationship between the feedback and the behavior, it should be provided as soon as possible after the trainee's behavior occurs (Wexley & Thornton, 1972). Blum & Naylor (1968) suggest that general feedback is most beneficial early and late in the learning process, and specific feedback is appropriate during intermediate stages of learning; however, empirical evidence to support this claim is lacking (Baldwin & Ford, 1988). For a more complete discussion of feedback and how it affects performance, see Taylor, Fisher, and Ilgen (1984).

Task sequencing, as proposed by Gagné (1962), suggests that tasks and knowledge can be learned more effectively if what is to be learned is divided into subtasks that are arranged and taught in an appropriate sequence. Gagné, Briggs, & Wager (1988) also provide guidelines for how task sequencing can help in learning intellectual skills, motor skills, and attitudes. Clancey's (1984) success with an intelligent medical diagnosis tutoring program called GUIDON offers some support for this approach, as does Decker's (1980, 1982) research on behavior modeling training. However, there is insufficient evidence to make any definitive conclusions about the effectiveness of task sequencing.

To summarize, research on the various conditions of practice does offer some guidelines for designing more effective training programs. In general, overlearning, feedback, and practice sessions spaced over time can all help to improve the learning process for trainees.

Retention of What Is Learned

The goal of training goes beyond ensuring the trainee learns the task or material being presented. It is equally important that newly learned material is retained. Three additional issues bear directly on what can be done to maximize retention are the meaningfulness of material, the degree of original learning, and interference.

The **meaningfulness of material** is the extent to which it is rich in associations for the individual learner. A new way of soldering circuits might be quite significant to an electronics enthusiast but absolutely meaningless to a professional athlete.

Research shows that the more meaningful factual material is, the easier it is to learn and remember (McGehee & Thayer, 1961). Thus, training can be designed to be more meaningful to employees to encourage learning retention. Overviews of learning topics presented at the beginning of training sessions can help trainees understand the course content as a whole. Using examples and terminology familiar to trainees and mnemonic devices (such as creating a word out of the first letters of items in a list) will also increase meaningfulness by providing more associations (Wexley & Latham, 1981).

The **degree of original learning** also influences learning retention. The better information is learned initially, the more likely it will be retained—after all, you can't retain something you never had to begin with. While this is not surprising, it does reinforce the research on overlearning, massed versus spaced practice, and whole versus part learning as ways to ensure initial learning.

Interference can also affect the extent to which learning is retained. There are two types of interference (Bourne & Ekstrand, 1973). First, material or skills learned **before** the training session can inhibit recall of the newly learned material. For example, an accountant who is an expert on the rules and tax code for New York may have difficulty remembering recent instruction regarding the tax code and procedures for Florida. Her prior knowledge is so well learned that she may automatically follow New York procedures when helping a client who must file in Florida.

Second, information learned **after** a training session may also interfere with retention. For example, a firefighter trained to operate the power ladder on the city's old fire truck may have difficulty retaining that knowledge if a different sequence of steps must be learned for the same operation on a newer fire truck.

Both types of interference are similar in that the learner is required to make different responses to the same situation. The more responses one learns, the greater the chance is for interference in learning.

Transfer of Training

Transfer of training is a recurring theme in HRD literature, and for good reason. The goal of HRD is to ensure that employees perform their jobs effectively. In addition to learning and retaining new material, the employee must also use it on the job to improve performance. The transfer of training to the job situation is critically important to the success of HRD efforts.

Transfer can take one of three forms. **Positive transfer** occurs when job performance is improved as a result of training. **Zero transfer** occurs when there is no change in job performance as a result of training. **Negative transfer** occurs when job performance is worse as a result of training. While negative transfer may seem an unlikely possibility at first, recall the detrimental effect interference can have on learning and performance. Tennis players may actually find their tennis shots become less accurate after learning how to play racquetball. Although the two sports seem very similar, an accurate tennis shot requires a locked wrist, while racquetball players use their wrists during the swing. Therefore, the player's tennis stroke may become more "wristy" after learning racquetball, leading to less accurate shots and low scores in tennis.

Baldwin and Ford (1988) developed a model that offers an explanation of the training transfer process (see Figure 3-1). The model suggests that training inputs—including trainee characteristics, training design, and the work environment—affect learning, retention, and transfer, with trainee characteristics and the work environment affecting transfer directly. However, Baldwin and Ford have concluded that the lack of a clear theoretical framework and the limited number of research studies limit the generalizability of the training transfer findings to organizational settings.

Despite this pessimistic conclusion, several training design principles offer some relevance to maximizing transfer of training. These include the use of iden-

---

FIGURE 3-1   **BALDWIN & FORD'S (1988) TRANSFER OF TRAINING MODEL**

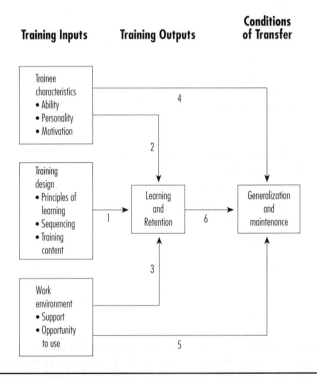

SOURCE: From "Transfer of Training: A Review and Directions for Future Research" by T. T. Baldwin and J. K. Ford, 1988, *Personnel Psychology, 41*, p. 65. Reprinted by permission.

tical elements, general principles, stimulus variability, and the degree of support for transfer in the work environment.

Identical Elements   The principle of **identical elements,** proposed by Thorndike and Woodworth (1901), suggests that the more similar the training and the performance situations are in terms of the stimuli present and responses required, the more likely it is that transfer of training will occur. For example, if customer service representatives are expected to handle complaints from angry, impatient customers, practice with such customers (possibly by using role playing) can improve transfer of training. But if the only examples used in training are customers who are polite, reasonable, and patient, transfer of training to the job is less likely.

Similarity is seen as having two dimensions, physical fidelity and psychological fidelity. **Physical fidelity** is the extent to which the conditions of the training program, such as equipment, tasks, and surroundings, are the same as in the performance situation. Building a highly realistic airline cockpit simulator, with the same controls, appearance, and physical sensations as experienced in true flight, would be an attempt to achieve a high level of physical fidelity. **Psychological fidelity** is the extent to which trainees attach similar meanings to both the training and performance situations. Psychological fidelity would be encouraged in a learning experience that imposes time limits on training tasks that are similar to those that exist back on the job. According to Berkowitz and Donnerstein (1982), there is some evidence that psychological fidelity is more important to transfer than physical fidelity, but Baldwin and Ford (1988) call for more research to support this theory.

The principle of identical elements is particularly relevant to simulation training, such as a case study, a business game, role play, or a machine. However, increasing fidelity often involves increasing complexity and costs, which can strain a limited HRD budget.

General Principles   Rather than focusing on identical elements, the **general principles** theory suggests that learning the fundamental elements of a task will ensure transfer from training. Hendrickson and Schroeder (1941) demonstrated this theory by teaching trainees to accurately hit an underwater target by learning the principle of refraction of light. Because light bends when crossing the air-water boundary, the target is not exactly where it visually appears to be. Understanding this principle allowed trainees to correctly judge where the target really was and adjust their aim accordingly.

However, it is often difficult to identify and include in training those principles that maximize positive transfer. It is still not clear whether training programs that apply the general principles theory to a certain group of tasks will actually result in skilled performance on those tasks (Goldstein, 1986).

Stimulus Variability   Ellis (1965) suggested that transfer can be enhanced when training contains a variety of stimuli, such as using multiple examples of a concept or involving the trainee in several different practice situations (Kazdin, 1975). For example, stimulus variability is increased when clothier trainees are required to practice making button holes in a variety of fabrics, rather than in only one or two types of fabric. Research has shown stimulus variability to be effective in increasing transfer (Baldwin, 1987; Shore & Sechrest, 1961).

Support in the Work Environment   The extent to which the trainee perceives support for using newly learned behavior or knowledge on the job may also affect transfer of training. For example, if a supervisor who is trying to become more participative is ridiculed by peers and receives the cold shoulder from subordinates, it seems unlikely that this person will continue to use these new found skills.

Supervisory support is an important aspect of work environment support (Baldwin & Ford, 1988). Supervisory support is a multidimensional concept, with components such as encouragement to attend training, goal-setting, reinforcement, and behavior modeling all having shown to increase transfer (Baumgartel, et al., 1984; Huczynski & Lewis, 1980; Sims & Manz, 1982; Wexley & Baldwin, 1986). Further research is needed to determine which of these and other dimensions of support are most effective in maximizing transfer (Baldwin & Ford, 1988).

Marx (1982) proposed a model of improving training transfer based on counseling techniques used to prevent relapse in substance abusers. The approach teaches trainees and supervisors to anticipate and prevent regressions to old behavior patterns. By developing strategies to cope with and overcome foreseen obstacles, the trainee will feel a greater sense of control and self-efficacy, thereby reducing the chances of relapse.

Supervisory support can also help to increase transfer by clarifying the manager's and trainee's expectations prior to training, and making managers aware of their role in the transfer process so they can develop ways to encourage transfer (Leifer and Newstrom, 1980; Michalak, 1981).

Research on transfer of training offers a number of suggestions for designing training and HRD programs, six of which are listed in Table 3-3.

TABLE 3-3	SUGGESTIONS FOR INCREASING THE CHANCES TRAINING WILL TRANSFER BACK TO THE JOB

1. Maximize the similarity between the training situation and the job situation.
2. Provide ample opportunity during training to practice the task.
3. Use a variety of situations and examples.
4. Identify and label important features of a task.
5. Make sure trainees understand general principles.
6. Provide support back in the work environment.

SOURCE: Based on "Transfer of Training: A Review and Directions for Future Research" by T. T. Baldwin and J. K. Ford, 1988, *Personnel Psychology, 41,* and *The Transfer of Learning* by H. C. Ellis, 1965, New York: Macmillan.

Individual Differences in the Learning Process

As we discussed earlier, trainee characteristics can play a role in the learning, retention, and transfer of skills and factual material. We will now identify three additional factors that account for differences in individual learning processes: rates of trainee progress, interactions between attributes and treatment, and the training of older workers.

Rate of Progress

People learn at different rates. Some people progress more quickly than others, and individual learners may even progress at different rates during the same training program. For example, a new employee learning how to operate a punch press may show little progress at first, making many mistakes, and then suddenly master the procedure and quickly progress to competence.

A useful way to show rates of learning is by drawing **learning curves.** A learning curve is plotted on a graph with learning proficiency indicated vertically on the *y*-axis and elapsed time indicated horizontally on the *x*-axis. Five types of learning curves are shown in Figure 3-2.

The learning curve for Trainee 1 shows a very fast rate of learning, taking little time to achieve high performance. The curve for Trainee 2 shows a slower rate of learning, with training ending at a lower level of final performance than Trainee 1. Trainee 3 reaches a moderate level of performance quickly but then makes little further progress despite continued practice. This contrasts to the progress of Trainee 4, who learns slowly at first but steadily improves to a high level of performance. Finally, the S-shaped learning curve for Trainee 5 shows rapid progress at first, followed by a period of little progress during the middle of training, and then rapid progress in the latter part of training.

Learning curves can provide useful feedback to both trainer and trainee. For instance, if a trainer notices a plateau (the flat part of a curve indicating no progress is being made), a different approach, encouragement, or some other intervention may be needed for the trainee to improve. When implementing a new HRD program, plotting learning curves can be used as a baseline for communicating expectations of progress to future trainees and trainers, and as aids in scheduling and planning future training sessions.

Attribute-Treatment Interaction (ATI)

Interest in the effect of trainee intelligence on learning has led some instructional psychology researchers to hypothesize that the effectiveness of training methods may be influenced by various trainee characteristics. Stated simply, some methods of training may be better suited to certain types of people. Thus, attribute-treatment interactions (ATI) research has sought to develop training systems that can be adapted to individual learner differences (Cronbach, 1967; Cronbach and Snow, 1977). Further research is needed, however, to identify those attributes that moderate training design effectiveness in organizational settings.

| FIGURE 3-2 | TYPES OF LEARNING CURVES |

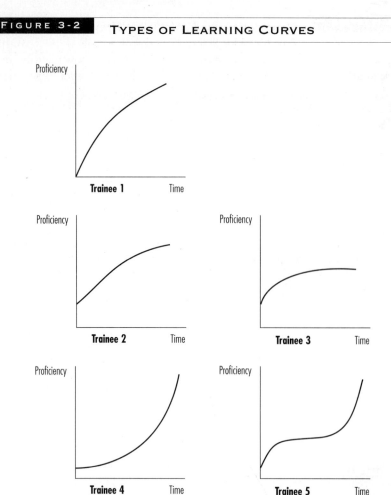

Training the Older Worker

Given the graying of the work force and the rate at which jobs have been changing, some have questioned whether training older workers requires a different approach than training younger people. This subject has been approached from two directions: andragogy and gerontology.

Andragogy Some researchers (such as Knowles, 1970) have noted that many principles of learning and instructional methods have been developed with and for children, and argue that teaching adults may require using a different set of techniques. Proponents call this adult-oriented approach **andragogy,** in response to pedagogy, the label assigned to child-oriented instructional techniques. Table 3-4 lists the differences between a pedagogical and andragogical approach to learning.

TABLE 3-4	COMPARISON OF PEDAGOGY AND ANDRAGOGY ON SEVEN ISSUES	
Characteristic	**Pedagogy** *Children oriented*	**Andragogy** *adult oriented*
Structure	Based on aging process Rigid format Subject/curriculum-centered Rules procedures, laws	Flexible, open, broad Responsive Interdisciplinary Developmental
Atmosphere	Authority-oriented Formal, low trust Competitive Win-lose	Relaxed, trusting, mutually respectful Informal, warm Collaborative, supportive Win-win

Leadership	Teacher dominant
	High task, low relationship
	Controlling
	Does not value experience
	Assumes student immaturity
	   and dependency
	Low risk
		Innovative, creative
		High task, high relationship
		Interdependent, mature
		   relationship
		Mentoring, modeling
		Experiential
		High risk

Planning	Administration and teacher
	
	Emphasizes rationale, legal
	   mechanisms
	Policies, plans and decisions
	Highly political
		Administration, faculty, and
		   students
		Mutual assessment
		Collaborative needs assessment
		Mutual negotiation
		Problem centered

Motivation	External rewards and
	   punishments
		Internal incentives
		   (curiosity)
		Self-directed
		Learning contracts

Communication	One-way downward Transmittal techniques Feelings repressed	Two-way Mutually respectful Feelings expressed Supportive
Evaluation	Teacher Norm-referenced (curve) Grades Subjective	Criterion-based Objective and subjective Jointly chosen standards by students, peers, and teachers

SOURCE: From *"Adult Learning and Organizations,"* by N. Dailey, 1984, *Training and Development Journal, 38*, pp. 66, 68. Adapted by permission.

   Andragogy is based on four assumptions about the differences between adults and children:

1.   Adults are **self-directed.**

2.   Adults have acquired a large amount of **knowledge and experience** that can be tapped as a resource for learning.

3. Adults show a greater **readiness to learn tasks that are relevant** to the roles they have assumed in life.

4. Adults are **motivated to learn** in order to solve problems or address needs, and **expect to immediately apply** what they learn to these problems and needs (based on Knowles, 1970).

Andragogical instructional techniques are designed with these factors in mind. These techniques include joint planning, self-diagnosis, formulation of learning objectives, a collaborative teaching process, and involvement of students in the evaluation of success (Knowles and associates, 1984).

Two examples can help illustrate how the andragogical approach can be applied. First, Daloisio and Firestone (1983) describe a management development program offered by the American Management Association called "The Competency Program," which is built around the assumptions of the andragogical approach. The program is geared toward developing participants' capabilities in 18 competency areas, including spontaneity, developing others, managing group processes, use of socialized power, and logical thought. Table 3-5 describes how 15 issues in the design and delivery of the Competency Program were addressed using andragogical ideas.

While Daloisio and Firestone consider the program effective, several problems were noted. For example, motivation of participants was reported to be highest after the feedback week (in which participants receive feedback on their competency levels and progress before going back to their jobs), but then tended to decrease over time.

Sommer describes another andragogical approach in a program used to teach writing to adults (1989). Sommer designed the writing program using 15 strategies based upon writing and andragogy theories. Of particular note are the following:

- Consider the audience (for instance, conduct a needs assessment)

- Remember that adults need to be self-determining

- Use peer collaboration

- Include assessment to enhance course content

- Find clear applications for writing

- Rely on students' experiences

- Include students in evaluation writing

While andragogy has strong intuitive appeal, it has been criticized (Davenport and Davenport, 1985). Critics argue that separating the learning process into two stages—child and adult learning—makes little sense. Rather, they see learning as a continuous process. In addition, Newstrom and Lengnick-Hall

TABLE 3-5	AN ANDRAGOGICAL APPROACH TO MANAGEMENT DEVELOPMENT: THE COMPETENCY PROGRAM
1. Learner Motivation	Grades and time limits not used; rely instead on awareness between self and idea of an excellent manager, development of a social support network, and increased self-esteem.
2. Learning Climate	Relaxed, informal, comfortable
3. Learning Plan	Participants select preferred areas from alternatives generated by the leader (trainer)
4. Discussion of Conceptual Material	Preliminary review of concepts and theories
5. Diagnosing Learner Needs	Input from participant, training group members, and program leader
6. Establishing Learning Objectives	Decided by learners themselves
7. Learning Activities	Active learning (independent study, experiential exercises)
8. Evaluation of Learning Activities	Integrated into learning process; seen as taking stock of what has happened, including appraisal of objectives and evaluation process
9. Designing Developmental Plans	Self-designed learning contract
10. Learning Climate	Group learning contract established early, with issues of confidentiality and guidelines for feedback discussed openly
11. Planning Learning	Program leaders do initial plans; learners assist in interim plans
12. Didactics	Competencies are explored behaviorally and interactively, with the leader asking process questions and the learners relating material to their own experiences
13. Diagnosing Learner Needs	Participants compare their own managerial competencies to a model of an effective manager, including self-evaluation, feedback from group members, a faculty advisor, and a battery of tests
14. Designing Developmental Plans	Created through group discussion
15. Field-based Learning	Learning activities carried out in the job setting; regular contact with faculty advisor for feedback and support (six-month intervals)

SOURCE: Based on "A Case Study in Applying Adult Learning Theory in Developing Managers" by T. Daloisio and M. Firestone, 1983, *Training and Development Journal, 37*, pp. 73–78. Adapted by permission.

(1991) cite significant problems and weaknesses of the andragogical approach, questioning the rigidity of the paradigm, the extent to which an individual is either a child or an adult as far as their approach to learning, its lack of recognition of the differences among adult learners, and the reluctance of others to criticize the approach because it presents a socially desirable view of adults as learners.

While Knowles has moderated some of his original claims, he still maintains andragogical techniques can be used to teach adults and traditional students (Knowles, 1980; Knowles and Associates, 1984).

Some researchers have tried to move beyond andragogy by offering a more complex (and more realistic) view of adults as learners than that offered by either pedagogy or andragogy. **Newstrom and Lengnick-Hall's** (1991) contingency model of adults as learners assumes that "adult learners are a heterogeneous group requiring different approaches to training and development depending on individual differences across important characteristics" (p. 46). Based on this approach, trainee differences should be considered in designing HRD programs, leading to programs adapted to fit the characteristics of the participants. Newstrom and Legnick-Hall propose groups be assessed on ten dimensions, including attention span, self-confidence, and locus of control (see Table 3-6).

This contingency approach to adult learning shares some similarities with

---

TABLE 3-6   **A CONTINGENCY APPROACH TO ADULT LEARNING: DIMENSIONS FOR ASSESSING THE TRAINEE**

1. **Instrumentality** Degree to which the trainee is concerned with the immediate applicability of the concepts and skills being taught.

2. **Skepticism** Degree to which the trainee exhibits a questioning attitude and demands logic, evidence, and examples.

3. **Resistance to Change** Degree to which the trainee fears the process of moving to the unknown, or the personal effects of that process.

4. **Attention Span** Length of time the trainee can focus attention before substantial attentiveness is diminished.

5. **Expectation Level** Level of quality (process) and quantity (content) that the trainee requires from the trainer or the training.

6. **Dominant Needs** Range of intrinsic and extrinsic individual needs that currently drive the trainee.

7. **Absorption Level** Pace at which the trainee expects and can accept new information.

8. **Topical Interest** Degree to which the trainee can be expected to have personal (job-relevant) interest in the topic.

9. **Self-confidence** Degree of trainee's independence and positive self-regard, thus requiring high or low levels of feedback, reinforcement, and success experiences.

10. **Locus of control** Degree to which the trainee perceives that training can be implemented successfully back on the job with or without organizational support.

SOURCE: From "One Size Does Not Fit All" by J. W. Newstrom and M. L. Lengnick-Hall, 1991, *Training and Development Journal, 45* (6), p. 46. Adapted by permission.

the notion of ATIs discussed earlier, but while it has intuitive appeal (as did andragogy), research has yet to determine its superiority to other adult learning approaches.

Gerontology   A second answer to the question of whether older adults need to be trained differently is rooted in gerontology and industrial gerontology. Sterns and Doverspike (1988, 1989; Sterns, 1986) have written several articles outlining the learning differences found in older adults. Their results challenge the stereotype some managers (and trainers) hold about older adults' ability to learn. Their most consistent finding is that although older adults do take longer to learn new knowledge and skills and tend to make more errors during learning, they can and do attain performance levels equal to those achieved by younger adults. In addition, research shows that individuals' expertise can be maintained throughout their lives.

Sterns and Doverspike (1988, p. 108) offer five principles that should be used to ensure effective training and development of older adults:

1. Older workers can and do develop.

2. Supervisors need to realize that they may consciously or unconsciously exclude older workers from training opportunities due to unwarranted negative attitudes.

3. For a training program to be effective for older workers, attention must be paid to motivation, structure, familiarity, organization, and time.

4. The organizational climate must reward entry into training and transfer of skills back to the job.

5. Training must be considered within an integrated career perspective.

With respect to motivation, older adults may need more encouragement to attend training programs because of the negative attitudes others have about their ability to learn. Because older adults tend to take longer to reach proficiency, sufficient time should be scheduled to allow them to do so. And, because older adults may have a fear of failure or competition, and may feel alienated in traditional training settings, active participation in the training program should be encouraged (Sterns & Doverspike, 1989).

Learning Strategies and Styles

Another perspective on the learning process and how to maximize learning examines what people do when they learn. Research on learning styles and strategies can be important factors in determining learning outcomes. In this section, we will briefly relate a sampling of ideas from the research studies regarding this aspect of learning.

Kolb's Learning Styles

David Kolb, a leading theorist on experiential learning, argues that the learning process is not the same for all people. Because of the complex nature of the learning process, there are opportunities for individual differences and preferences to emerge. A **learning style** represents how individual choices made during the learning process affect what information is selected and how it is processed. Kolb illustrates the notion of learning styles by observing how people learn to play pool:

> Some people just step up and hit the ball without bothering to look very carefully at where their shot went unless it went in the pocket. Others seem to go through a great deal of analysis and measurement but seem a bit hesitant on the execution. Thus, there seem to be distinctive styles or strategies for learning and playing the game (1984, p. 66).

Differences in learning styles can explain why some individuals are more comfortable and successful with some training approaches (such as role playing, lectures, and videotapes) than others. Similarly, learning style differences among trainers can also contribute to their preferences for certain training approaches over others.

Kolb theorizes that an individual's learning style is based on their preferred modes of learning. A **mode of learning** is the individual's orientation toward gathering and processing information during learning. Kolb (1984) proposed four basic modes of experiential learning:

1. **Concrete experience (CE)** An intuitive preference for learning through direct experience, emphasing interpersonal relations and **feeling** as opposed to thinking. For example, someone using this mode to learn about job politics would personally use various political tactics in different group situations to get a sense of how each one feels, while also gauging others' responses during each interaction.

2. **Abstract conceptualization (AC)** A preference for learning by **thinking** about an issue in theoretical terms. For example, a person using this mode to learn about job politics would analyze political tactics and their implications, perhaps consulting or constructing a model that includes abstract representations of the components of political activities.

3. **Reflective observation (RO)** A preference to learn by **watching** and examining different points of view to achieve an understanding. For example, people using the RO mode to learn about job politics would most likely observe others involved in political activities and reflect on what they've seen from a variety of perspectives.

4. **Active experimentation (AE)** A preference for learning something by actually **doing** it and judging its practical value. For exam-

ple, someone using this mode to learn about job politics might experiment with various political tactics, determining their effectiveness by the amount of influence they had on other people.

Kolb argues that an individual's learning style often combines two modes of learning, such as abstract conceptualization and active experimentation (thinking and doing). Each learning style emphasizes some learning abilities and deemphasizes others. Based on his own work and the work of earlier theorists (including Lewin, Dewey, and Piaget), Kolb identified four learning styles (1984):

1. **Convergent**   A combination of abstract conceptualization and active experimentation **(thinking and doing),** with a focus on problem-solving, decision making, and the practical application of ideas.

2. **Divergent**   A combination of concrete experience and reflective observation **(feeling and watching),** emphasizing imagination, an awareness of values, and the ability to generate alternative courses of action.

3. **Assimilation**   A combination of abstract conceptualization and reflective observation **(thinking and watching)** that stresses inductive reasoning, the integration of disparate observations into an explanation, and the creation of theoretical models.

4. **Accommodative**   A combination of concrete experience and active experimentation **(feeling and doing),** this style is usually demonstrated by accomplishment, executing plans, and involvement in new experiences.

Kolb theorizes that learning styles are developed as a result of life experiences, both past and present, and hereditary influences. He also notes that while individuals may have a dominant learning style, they may also use other learning styles in particular situations.

To help individuals identify their learning style, Kolb developed a self-descriptive questionnaire called the **Learning Style Inventory (LSI).** The LSI, which is currently marketed by the consulting firm of McBer and Company, assesses the individual's orientation toward the four modes of the learning process (CE, RO, AC, and AE). Its scores also reflect the individual's tendencies toward abstractness over concreteness and action over reflection.

Kolb's theory and the LSI can help HRD professionals, supervisors, and employees to identify and appreciate the number of different approaches to learning. As a result, training and development programs can be tailored to individual learner preferences in both traditional HRD programs and in those using computerized instruction. For example, a research team at the University of Colorado at Colorado Springs is developing a prototype of a computer-based tutoring system that can assess an individual's learning style, using Kolb's theory, and adjust its presentation accordingly (Eurich, 1990).

Learning Strategies

Similar to Kolb's modes of learning, **learning strategies** represent the "behavior and thoughts a learner engages in during learning" (Weinstein & Mayer, 1986, p. 315). Learning strategies are the techniques used by the learner to rehearse, elaborate, organize, and/or comprehend new material, as well as influence self-motivation and feelings.

Weinstein and Mayer grouped learning strategies into the following eight categories (examples of each are listed in parentheses):

1. **Rehearsal strategies for basic learning tasks** (repeating items in a list)

2. **Rehearsal strategies for complex learning tasks** (underlining text in an article; copying notes)

3. **Elaboration strategies for basic learning tasks** (forming a mental image)

4. **Elaboration strategies for complex learning tasks** (taking notes; paraphrasing or summarizing new material)

5. **Organizational strategies for basic tasks** (grouping or ordering information to be learned)

6. **Organizational strategies for complex tasks** (outlining an article; creating a hierarchy of material)

7. **Comprehension monitoring strategies** (self questioning)

8. **Affective strategies** (increasing alertness; relaxation; finding ways to reduce test anxiety)

HRD efforts have applied learning strategies in "learning to learn" programs, which try to provide learners with the skills necessary to learn effectively in any learning situation. Given the dynamic nature of organizations and the environment, as described in Chapter 1, there is now a greater pressure on individuals to learn continuously throughout their lives. Learning to learn programs are aimed at enhancing the learning process and making individuals more independent. The programs emphasize the skill of selecting those learning strategies needed to cope effectively with the nature of the material and the demands of the learning situation.

In addition to the formal learning strategies, Carnevale, Gainer, and Meltzer (1990) list four strategies a learner can use to enhance learning effectiveness in unstructured learning situations:

1. Identify the assumptions underlying interpretations and conclusions;

2. Test the assumptions for validity;

3. Generate and test alternative assumptions; and

4. Develop an orientation that decreases the likelihood of errors (such as seeing errors as opportunities for learning).

Clearly, if employees can acquire and become skilled in applying a variety of learning strategies, they will likely benefit more from both formal (a training program) and informal (a problem-solving meeting) learning opportunities.

Perceptual Preferences

Just as individuals have preferences about the types of information they seek out in learning situations and how they process it, they also have preferences for the sensory channels they use to acquire information (Carnevale, et al., 1990). For example, if someone asks you for directions, they may request that you either write the directions out, draw a map, explain them verbally, or use some combination of the three.

Research conducted by James and Galbraith (1985) suggests that there are seven primary perceptual preferences:

1. **Print** (reading and writing)

2. **Visual** (such as graphs and charts)

3. **Aural** (listening)

4. **Interactive** (discussing, asking questions)

5. **Tactile/manipulative** (hands-on approaches, such as touching)

6. **Kinesthetic/psychomotor** (role playing, physical activities)

7. **Olfactory** (association of ideas with smell or taste)

These authors report that the vast majority of adults are considered to have a preference for visual material. Further, some have argued that those growing up watching television and movies and playing interactive computer games may have different perceptual preferences than previous generations.

Perceptual preferences imply that trainers should, if possible, tailor their material and training techniques to match the preferences of the trainees. Further, it would be desirable to train learners to increase their learning efficiencies by taking advantage of other perceptual channels.

Emerging Perspectives from Instructional Psychology

As we discussed earlier, instructional psychology focuses on identifying instructional principles and techniques that maximize learning. Progress in this field—in particular, the three promising initiatives that we will now present—should yield applications that can help make HRD efforts more effective. We feel it is useful to give the reader a sense of what is on the horizon.

The ACT Approach to Learning Procedural Skills*

John Anderson and his colleagues at Carnegie-Mellon University have developed instructional computer programs that have been effective in teaching students how to perform complex procedural skills, such as solving algebraic equations (Lewis, Milson, & Anderson, 1988) and programming using the computer language LISP (Anderson, Farrel, & Sauers, 1984). The underlying theory is called **ACT* theory,** which assumes the learning process is the same regardless of the material being learned. ACT* theory (Anderson, 1983, 1993) focuses on the changes that occur as the learner proceeds from knowing what to do (called declarative knowledge) to knowing how to do it (procedural knowledge).

Progressing from declarative to procedural knowledge is important to successful performance. For example, just because a person understands the steps involved does not mean they can actually make an effective sales presentation. It is one thing to learn what must be done to make a failing company succeed, and another thing to accomplish it.

An instructional technique called **model tracing** is used in developing a computer tutoring program. This approach starts with the assumption that there is an ideal way to solve problems in the content area being learned. This is identified, along with the types of mistakes that may be made. A **learning model** is then developed that contains all the correct and incorrect rules for performing the task, and includes a set of assumptions about how the student's knowledge changes after each step in the process.

Through problem solving, trainees learn by doing. The tutoring program helps the learner identify problems and corrects their errors immediately. The tutor reduces the burden placed on the learner's memory by displaying the goals to be reached and helping to fill in some of the details. The tutor in effect guides the student through the learning process.

As seen above, the ACT* approach features an intelligent computer-assisted instruction program. One example of an industry using this approach can be found in the Campbell Soup Company's computer-based Cooker Maintenance Advisor (Eurich, 1990). Campbell's food processing plants use a huge cooker to sterilize processed food. Cooker breakdowns are expensive, since they disrupt all other operations in the plant. And because cookers are such complex systems, training engineers and mechanics to install, operate, and maintain them is not easy. When the engineer who knew the system best was nearing retirement, the company developed an intelligent tutoring personal computer software program that captured much of the knowledge he had acquired over 44 years on the job.

The Cooker Maintenance Advisor is an interactive system, using a question and answer format similar to the LISP tutor developed by Anderson. Engineers and maintenance technicians now use the system in training and as a job aid. Use of the Cooker Maintenance Advisor has resulted in both cost and time savings, and employees throughout the company can benefit from the expert's advice and experience.

The ACT* approach is limited to the acquisition of procedural skills, but many of the skills used in organizations are procedural. Thus, this technique may prove useful in developing effective computer-assisted HRD training programs.

Learning to Regulate One's Own Behavior

What is it that makes experts able to perform more quickly and at higher levels than novices? Research suggests that experts develop **self-regulation and control strategies** through experience. These strategies enable them to monitor their performance by quickly checking their work, accurately judging how difficult a problem is, allocating their time, assessing progress, and predicting the results of their efforts (Brown, 1978; Chi, Glaser, & Rees, 1982; Larkin, McDermott, Simon & Simon, 1980; Miyake & Norman, 1979; Simon & Simon, 1978).

The development of expertise is an important goal of HRD efforts, and this line of research suggests that one way to reach this goal is to teach trainees these self-regulatory and control skills. Brown and Palinscar (1984, 1988) have developed a program for teaching reading comprehension based on a technique called reciprocal teaching, in which students learn strategies they can use to monitor their performance. By individually applying learning techniques such as questioning, clarifying, summarizing, and predicting, with the teacher serving as a coach, in a supportive climate, the group shares responsibility for their own learning.

While this research has been conducted using schoolchildren, it is likely that such an approach will work well in group training courses within organizations. HRD approaches such as behavior modeling (which will be discussed in Chapter 12) already use components of this strategy. For example, when trainees in a behavior modeling session practice the behaviors they are learning, they receive feedback and coaching from one another on the adequacy of their performance and on ways it can be improved.

Similar programs have also been developed with the goal to improve general problem-solving and thinking skills as a way to improve learning (Nickerson, Perkins, & Smith, 1985; Sternberg, 1986). Glaser and Bassok (1989) conclude their review of these techniques by calling for additional research on their effectiveness and the processes upon which they are based.

The Gagné-Briggs Instructional Theory

The Gagné-Briggs theory of instruction (Gagné, 1972, 1984; Gagné & Briggs, 1979) focuses on the kinds of things people learn and how they learn them. The theory argues that fundamentally different learning outcomes are learned in different ways; in other words, there is no one way to learn everything.

The two main components of the theory are a taxonomy of learning outcomes (what is being learned) and the techniques needed to teach them. Gagné proposed that human performance can be divided into five distinguishable categories, each of which requires a different set of conditions for maximizing learning, retention, and transfer. The five categories are as follows:

1. **Intellectual skills,** sometimes called procedural knowledge, are the rules, concepts and procedures that we follow to accomplish tasks. Intellectual skills may be simple or complex. English grammar is an example of an intellectual skill.

2. **Verbal information,** or declarative knowledge, involves the ability to state or declare something, such as a fact or an idea. Reciting the Bill of Rights or an article of the tax code are examples of verbal information.

3. **Cognitive strategies,** or strategic knowledge, are the skills that we use to control learning, thinking, and remembering. Cognitive strategies allow us to determine what procedural knowledge and verbal information we need to perform a task. For example, an I.R.S. representative uses a cognitive strategy when selecting the auditing approach to take for a particular tax audit.

4. **Motor skills** involve using our bodies to manipulate something. Writing, icing a cake, and balancing a tray of dishes are examples of motor skills. Motor skills are learned by practicing the movement, and in doing so the quality of the movement is improved.

5. **Attitudes** are internal states of mind that can influence which of several behaviors we may choose (recall our discussion of attitudes in Chapter 2). Attitudes are not learned simply by hearing facts from others. (For instance, is it likely your attitude toward nuclear power is going to change just because someone tells you it is good or bad?) Something additional, such as reinforcement or personal experience regarding the object of the attitude, is needed for learning to occur. Even so, attitudes are highly resistant to change.

According to Gagné (1984), these five categories exist because

they differ, first as human performances, second, because the requirements for their learning are different despite the pervasiveness of such general conditions as contiguity and reinforcement, and third because the effects of learning, the continued learning, appear also to differ from each other (p. 384).

Gagné and Briggs argue that successful performance on any given task requires learning in one or more of these categories.

Gagné and others are researching which techniques are best suited to teaching each kind of outcome. Table 3-7 presents a summary of this work. The

TABLE 3-7

INSTRUCTIONAL EVENTS AND THE CONDITIONS OF LEARNING THEY IMPLY FOR FIVE TYPES OF LEARNED CAPABILITIES

Instructional Event	Type of Capability				
	Intellectual Skill	Cognitive Strategy	Information	Attitude	Motor Skill
1. Gaining Attention	Introduce stimulus change; variations in sensory mode				
2. Informing learner of objective	Provide description and example of the performance to be expected	Clarify the general nature of the solution expected	Indicate the kind of verbal question to be answered	Provide example of the kind of action choice aimed for	Provide a demonstration of the performance to be expected
3. Stimulating recall of prerequisites	Stimulate recall of subordinate concepts and rules	Stimulate recall of task strategies and associated intellectual skills	Stimulate recall of context of organized information	Stimulate recall of relevant information, skills, and human model identification	Stimulate recall of executive sub-routine and part-skills
4. Presenting the stimulus material	Present examples of concept or rule	Present novel problems	Present information in propositional form	Present human model, demonstrating choice of personal action	Provide external stimuli for performance, including tools or implements
5. Providing learning guidance	Provide verbal cues to proper combining sequence	Provide prompts and hints to novel solution	Provide verbal links to a larger meaningful context	Provide for observation of model's choice of action, and of reinforcement received by model	Provide practice with feedback of performance achievement
6. Eliciting the performance	Ask learner to apply rule or concept to new examples	Ask for problem solution	Ask for information in paraphrase, or in learner's own words	Ask learner to indicate choices of action in real or simulated situations	Ask for execution of the performance
7. Providing feedback	Confirm correctness of rule or concept application	Confirm originality of problem solution	Confirm correctness of statement of information	Provide direct or vicarious reinforcement of action choice	Provide feedback on degree of accuracy and timing of performance
8. Assessing performance	Learner demonstrates application of concept or rule	Learner originates a novel solution	Learner restates information in paraphrased form	Learner makes desired choice of personal action in real or simulated situation	Learner executes performance of total skill
9. Enhancing retention and transfer	Provide spaced reviews including a variety of examples	Provide occasions for a variety of novel problem solutions	Provide verbal links to additional complexes of information	Provide additional varied situations for selected choice of action	Learner continues skill practice

SOURCE: From *Principles of Instructional Design* by R. M. Gagné and L. J. Briggs. Copyright 1979 by CBS College Publishing Company, Inc. Reprinted by permission of Holt, Rinehart and Winston.

events listed in the left column of the table are the nine steps, or instructional events, Gagné believes should be used in instructional design. Corresponding entries in the table list the actions that should be taken to implement each of these steps for each of the five categories of learning outcomes.

The Gagné-Briggs theory is the best developed and most researched of the current initiatives in instructional psychology. It provides a good source of ideas for HRD professionals who are looking for ways to enhance the effectiveness of their training programs.

Summary

Understanding the learning process and how learning can be maximized are critical issues in designing and implementing HRD programs. Learning is defined as a relatively permanent change in behavior or cognitions that occurs as a result of one's interaction with the environment. Traditional research on the learning

RETURN TO OPENING CASE

Planters LifeSavers Company (PLC) decided that the way to prepare supervisors and hourly workers for a new, unfinished manufacturing system was to teach them generic learning-to-learn skills. The goal of the program was to enable employees to anticipate and adapt to the technological changes they would face both with the new manufacturing system and in future challenges. This initial program expanded into a week-long course called Learning Management.

Learning Management is a highly interactive course conducted on company time, usually attended by 10 to 12 employees. The course teaches participants how to get the most out of a learning situation, including:

- Assessing each participant's learning style

- Discussing how individuals with different styles learn

- The experiential learning process (based on Kolb's work)

- Learning how to analyze an event to determine what happened and why (done in groups)

- Practice in planning for learning by analyzing non-work tasks and the different ways they can be learned, and discussing the merits of each approach

- Experiential exercises to explore the benefits and limitations of collaborative learning

- Learning and practicing various learning strategies (like note-taking)

- Gaining an understanding of the importance of the environment to learning and the readiness to learnIn addition, each participant has a chance to identify his or her individual developmental needs.

In addition, each participant has a chance to identify his or her individual developmental needs.

PLC evaluates the Learning Management course through interviews conducted at the end of the program and during the subsequent three months, and examining production data. Evaluation so far has shown a reduction in downtime as the most significant change following the program.[1]

process has identified three principles of learning: contiguity, the law of effect, and practice. While these principles enhance our understanding of the learning process, they are not sufficient for designing programs to maximize learning.

Trainee characteristics play a significant role in the learning process. Three trainee characteristics that affect the extent to which trainees learn are trainability, personality, and attitudes. Trainability is a combination of motivation and ability. The higher the level of trainability, the more likely it is the trainee will learn. Several personality traits, such as locus of control and the trainee's attitudes, have also been shown to affect learning.

Knowledge of training design issues—in particular, the conditions of practice—can be used to maximize learning. These conditions include active practice, massed versus spaced practice sessions, whole versus part learning, overlearning, knowledge of results, and task sequencing. In general, trainee learning, can be improved by overlearning, feedback, and practice sessions spaced over time with sufficient rest periods between them.

The information or skills an employee learns are of little value to the organization if the employee does not retain or use them back on the job. Retention of what is learned is influenced by the meaningfulness of material, the degree of original learning, and interference. Factors that affect learning transfer to the work situation include identical elements, general principles, stimulus variability, and support in the work environment.

Obviously, not all trainees are alike. Individual differences among trainees affect the learning process. First of all, different people learn at different rates, a fact that should be considered in designing training programs. Second, it is possible that people with different characteristics (such as intelligence levels) may learn best using different training approaches. And third, contrary to the stereotype, older adults can learn as well as younger adults, but they do learn differently.

---

[1]From *Workplace Basics: The Essential Skills Employers Want* by A. P. Carnevale. L. J. Gainer, and A. S. Meltzer, 1990, pp. 60-62. Adapted by permission.

Finally, several emerging perspectives from research in instructional psychology demonstrate significantly the future of HRD. The ACT* approach, reciprocal teaching, and the Gagné-Briggs theory all offer promise in suggesting ways to designing training approaches that maximize learning.

Key Terms and Concepts

andragogy	learning strategy
aptitude-treatment interaction	learning style
association	pedagogy
contiguity	practice
identical elements	psychological fidelity
instructional psychology	overlearning
interference	task analysis
law of effect	task sequencing
learning	trainability
learning curve	transfer of training

Questions for Discussion

1. Compare and contrast the pedagogical and andragogical approaches to instruction. Suppose the president of a local hospital asks you to design a program to increase employee awareness of sexual harassment and train participants in ways to deal with harassment complaints. Which andragogical principles do you feel might be useful? Support your choices.

2. Explain the role that trainability plays in the effectiveness of an HRD program. Briefly describe the options available to assess the trainability of employees.

3. Robert Gagné and others have argued that traditional principles of learning (such as contiguity and association) are not sufficient for designing effective training programs. State the reasoning for this argument. What does research in instructional psychology offer as a resolution to this problem? Do you agree with this solution? Support your answer.

4. Few would disagree that practice plays an important role in learning and retention. Using your knowledge of the conditions of practice, what sort of practice do you think would be most effective for training mechanics in a new installation procedure for an automobile air conditioner? For training supervisors on the main points of and how to comply with a new law, such as the Americans with Disabilities Act of 1990?

5. Identify and discuss the factors that can affect whether training transfers back to the job. Which two factors do you feel are the most important to ensure transfer? Support your choices.

6. A common stereotype about older workers is that they are unable to learn or find learning difficult. Does research from the field of gerontology support or disprove this stereotype? Explain. What two findings or recommendations do you feel supervisors should follow to ensure effective training experiences for older workers?

7. Research by Kolb and others suggests individuals have different learning styles. How would a manager who has a convergent learning style and a manager who has a divergent learning style differ in their approach to learning? Suppose you are going to conduct training sessions designed to teach managers how to give feedback to subordinates. These two managers are scheduled to participate. What might you do (if anything), to handle the style differences between them to ensure they will both learn the material you present?

8. Learning strategies are used by learners to rehearse, organize, elaborate, and comprehend new material. From the learning strategies discussed in this chapter, select two that you have used. For each one, identify how you applied it and how it helped you learn more effectively.

9. Supervisors and co-workers are often asked to serve as trainers. While they may be experts on the material they are teaching others, many times they are novices when it comes to understanding how others learn. Based on the material presented in this chapter, what three things do you think supervisors and co-workers who train others should know about learning? Describe each one, and explain why you feel it is important.

4

The Training and HRD Process and the Assessment of HRD Needs

Learning Objectives

1. *Identify the three phases of the training and HRD process.*
2. *Discuss the purpose and advantages of conducting a needs analysis.*
3. *State the purpose of conducting an organizational analysis, and describe the four issues it is intended to address.*
4. *Discuss five approaches that can be used to conduct a task analysis.*
5. *Explain the importance of identifying individuals' performance deficiencies and developmental needs in planning and developing training and HRD programs.*
6. *Explain the importance of prioritizing training and HRD needs.*

OPENING CASE

HRD programs can often be a key component of an organization's efforts to revitalize the management team and address internal problems. No one knows this better than the management team at Scott Worldwide Foodservice (SWF), a division of the Philadelphia-based Scott Paper Company that manufactures food service products such as paper cups and containers.

When it acquired the facilities that became SWF, Scott Paper realized it faced significant problems in its new division, many of which seemed to be rooted in poor employee morale. According to Sharon Robbins, vice president and head of SWF, "People were downtrodden after years of difficult business conditions and downsizing; an autocratic style of management prevailed; people didn't understand their jobs; and layers of management had been stripped out of the company, creating broader and less-manageable spans of control." Scott Paper decided that in order to turn the division around, they needed a new approach to management that, according to Robbins, "linked constant improvement of products and services to the continual growth of individual employees."

The centerpiece of this effort was a succession planning system and management development program that identified and developed managers who could make the new approach work. And work it did. In just four years, the company had made a dramatic turnaround, with such critical improvements as a reduction in product defects to less than 1 percent, an increase in on-time delivery rate to 98 percent, and an expansion in plant manufacturing capacity by 35 percent. Scott management believes that HRD efforts played a key role in achieving these impressive results.

How did Scott Paper create such successful HRD programs? Part of the answer lies in their thorough approach to an important and often ignored component of the HRD process: needs assessment.

Creating an HRD Program

HRD programs can be used to address a wide range of issues and problems in an organization. As discussed in Chapter 1, HRD programs are used to orient and socialize new employees into the organization, provide skills and knowledge, and help individuals and groups become more effective. To ensure that these goals are achieved, care must be taken when designing and delivering HRD programs.

Designing HRD programs involves a sequence of steps that can be grouped into three phases: **needs assessment, design/implementation,** and **evaluation** (see Figure 4-1).

Needs Assessment Phase

HRD programs are used to address some need within the organization. A need can either be a current deficiency, such as poor employee performance, or a new challenge that demands a change in the way the organization operates (new legislation or increased competition). For example, in 1989, when the number of fatal accidents in the U.S. Navy increased dramatically, the Navy responded with a two-day stand down (alert for inspection) throughout the entire fleet in order to provide additional safety training. Similarly, in the early 1980s it became obvious to the Ford Motor Company that the poor quality of their cars and trucks was a major reason they were losing market share to foreign competitors.

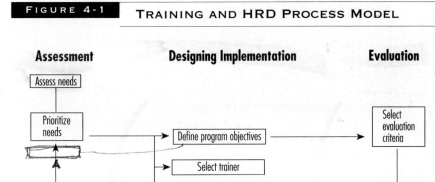

FIGURE 4-1   TRAINING AND HRD PROCESS MODEL

In response, Ford boosted spending on HRD programs to train employees in quality improvement and problem-solving techniques.

Identifying needs involves examining the organization, its environment, job tasks, and employee performance. This information can be used to:

- Establish priorities for expending HRD efforts;

- Define specific training and HRD objectives; and

- Establish evaluation criteria.

The needs assessment process will be discussed in detail later in this chapter.

Design/Implementation Phase

The second phase of the training and HRD process involves designing and implementing the HRD program. This phase may include the following activities:

- Selecting the person to deliver the program

- Selecting and developing the content of the program

- Scheduling the program

- Implementing or delivering the program

Selecting the person to deliver the HRD program is an important decision, and it can be difficult, depending on the resources available. If the organization employs a group of full-time HRD professionals, the choice will depend largely on the expertise and work schedules of those professionals. However, if the organization does not have an HRD staff, they will have to rely on other people, including managers, supervisors, co-workers, or outside consultants. Using such individuals raises a host of issues, including their willingness, ability, availability, and cost.

The planning process also involves selecting and developing the content of the program. This means choosing the most appropriate setting for the program (on-the-job, a classroom, and so on), the techniques used to facilitate learning (such as lecture, discussion, role play, simulation), and the materials to be used in delivering the program (such as workbooks, job aids, films and videos). Inherent in these decisions is the issue of whether to develop the program in-house or purchase it (or parts of it) from an outside vendor.

Scheduling the program may not be as easy as it appears. Issues to be resolved include lead time for notification of potential participants, program length and location, covering participants' regular job duties, and potential conflicts (such as vacations, busy periods, and facility availability).

Finally, delivery of the program also presents its own challenges, such as executing the program as planned, creating an environment that enhances learning, and resolving problems that may arise (missing equipment, conflicts between participants, and so on). These issues and many others involved in designing and implementing an HRD program will be discussed in detail in Chapter 5.

Evaluation Phase

Program evaluation is the final phase in the training and HRD process, during which the effectiveness of the HRD program is measured. This is an important but often ignored activity. Careful evaluation provides information on participant reaction to the program, how much they learned, whether they use what they learned back on the job, and whether the program improved the organization's effectiveness. This information allows managers to make better decisions about various aspects of the HRD effort, such as:

- Continuing to use a particular technique or vendor in future programs

- Offering a particular program in the future

- Budgeting and resource allocation

- Using some other HR or managerial approach (like employee selection or changing work rules) to solve the problem

It is important that HRD professionals provide proof that HRD programs improve individual and organizational effectiveness. Armed with this information, HRD managers can better compete with managers from other areas of the organization when discussing the effectiveness of their actions and competing for resources. The issues and methods involved in evaluating HRD programs will be discussed in detail in Chapter 6.

Needs Assessment

Ultimately, the goal of HRD is to improve the organization's effectiveness by:

1. Solving current problems (like an increase in customer complaints);

2. Preventing anticipated problems (such as a shortage of skilled technicians); and

3. Including as participants those individuals and units that can benefit most.

In short, HRD is effective if it successfully addresses some organizational need. How are those needs identified? The answer is through conducting needs assessments.

Definition and Purposes of Needs Assessment

Needs assessment is a process by which an organization's HRD needs are identified and articulated. It is the starting point of the HRD and training process. A needs assessment is a study that can be used to identify:

- The organization's goals and its effectiveness in reaching these goals

- Discrepancies between employees' skills and the skills required for effective job performance

- Discrepancies between current skills and the skills needed to perform the job successfully in the future

- The conditions under which the HRD activity will occur

With this information, HRD professionals learn where and what kind of programs are needed, who needs to be included in the programs, whether there are currently any roadblocks to the program's effectiveness, and establish the criteria to guide program evaluation. It is obvious, then, that needs analysis forms the foundation for an effective HRD effort.

Despite its importance, many organizations do not perform needs analysis as frequently or as thoroughly as they might. There are a number of reasons for their unwillingness, including the following:

1. **Needs assessment can be a difficult, time-consuming process.** A complete needs analysis involves measuring a variety of factors at multiple levels of the organization.

2. **Action is valued over research.** Managers often decide to use their limited resources to develop, acquire, and deliver HRD programs rather than to conduct an activity they see as a preliminary study.

3. **The incorrect conclusion that needs assessment is unnecessary since available information already specifies what an organization's needs are.** Factors such as fads, demands from senior managers, and the temptation to copy the HRD programs of widely admired organizations or competitors often leads to such conclusions. (See Table 4-1 for some vivid examples of this kind of rationale.)

4. **Lack of support for needs assessment.** This can be caused by either lack of bottom line justification or the HRD professional's inability to sell needs assessment to management. Documenting the assessment and its benefits, and using analogies from respected fields (e.g., medical diagnosis, engineering scoping) are two ways that may build support for doing needs assessment (Rossett, 1990).

These factors should be considered when promoting needs assessment. While it is possible to improve the organization's effectiveness without accurate needs assessment information, the results are by no means guaranteed. If the limited resources available are spent on programs that don't solve the organization's problems, the effort is a failure and the resources are wasted. And the original problems still demand solutions.

Before discussing the approaches to needs analysis, it is useful to examine what is meant by the term "need."

What Is a Training Need?

The concept of **need** typically refers to a discrepancy between what the organization expects to happen and what actually occurs. For example, a discrepancy exists if a supervisor has been charged to maintain an average turnaround time of 24 hours for shipping customer orders, and it is actually taking an average of 36 hours. A similar inconsistency is demonstrated when a police officer is

TABLE 4-1	RATIONALES EXPRESSED BY TRAINING DIRECTORS FOR ADOPTING MANAGEMENT DEVELOPMENT PROGRAMS

1. **Follow the Leader** "Look at all the big companies who use this program. It's got to be right for us."

2. **The Bandwagon** "Here are some new subjects that many big firms are starting to include in their programs. We should, too."

3. **The Consensus** "We researched dozens of management programs. These are the subjects that are common to most of them."

4. **Star Gazing** "We're going to get Professors A, B, and C to do our program. Everybody's talking about how great they are."

5. **Did You Ever See a Dream Walking?** "Our program includes all the things that textbooks say managers should do."

6. **Tell Me Your Dream . . .** "We asked senior managers to give us a list of the subjects they felt should be in the program. About a third responded, and we've included everything they suggested."

7. **. . . And I'll Tell You Mine** "We sat down and thought of all the things our managers should do better."

8. **Bingo!** "We sent out a 20-item subject list to a sample of senior managers and this is what they chose. They confirm the need for subjects we had recently identified as critical."

9. **Let's Go Smell the Flowers** "All we really have to do is upgrade the program we've been using, give it a new title, and move it to a nice conference center."

10. **A Burger, Fries, and Coffee to Go** "The Midwestern division has to have some management training in two weeks. I've found a firm that can do it."

11. **Mrs. Winslow's Soothing Syrup** "We've had a consulting firm come in to talk to our senior management and they recommend a program they've successfully presented for years now."

12. **Just for You** "The consulting firm did a survey and the results show we need their All-Inclusive Management Program, but with a lot of tailoring to our environment. It's expensive, but they guarantee results."

13. **Why Bother?** "The more we thought about it, the more sure we became that we don't need a program designed especially for us. Let's use one of the institutional programs."

SOURCE: From "Wanted: Professional Management Training Needs Analysis" by W. S. Mitchell, Jr., 1984, *Training and Development Journal, 38*(10), p. 68.

expected to use minimum force to apprehend suspects, but the department receives documented complaints of police brutality about this officer. These discrepancies may become the foundation of a training or HRD need.

Identified needs in this sense focus on correcting substandard performance. In some cases, an HRD intervention such as coaching or skill training may be necessary to correct the discrepancy. However, sometimes another HRM strategy (such as improving compensation or changing selection and recruiting practices), or management action (like replacing machinery or negotiating new work rules with the union) may be more appropriate solutions.

Brinkerhoff (1986) suggested that focusing only on performance discrepancies in needs analysis is too restrictive, and proposed three other possible ways of looking at training needs (see Table 4-2). These include democratic needs, diagnostic needs, and analytic needs.

Democratic needs are options for HRD that are preferred, selected, or voted for by employees and/or managers. Programs that address these needs are likely to be accepted and desired by organization members. Therefore, democratic needs can be used to build support for HRD programs. **Diagnostic needs** focus on the factors that lead to effective performance and prevent performance problems, rather than concentrating on existing problems. Diagnostic needs are identified by examining the relationships among factors that may affect performance in order to determine how effective performance is obtained. **Analytic needs** identify new, better ways to perform tasks. These needs are discovered by intuition, insight, or expert consideration.

Brinkerhoff's categorization of needs reinforces the notion that HRD should be proactive and future oriented. Addressing needs from an analytic or diagnostic perspective is proactive in its emphasis on preventing problems and enhancing performance and productivity. This contrasts with the reactive approach of using only performance discrepancies as the basis for training and HRD needs, in which a problem must already exist before a need can be identified. Clearly the organization can be better served if HRD efforts consider all four types of needs, focusing on ways to maintain effective performance and make it even better, as well as fixing what is done poorly.

Levels of Needs Analysis

Needs can exist at any of at least three levels, considering the organization, the job, and the individual. To ensure an effective HRD effort, needs must be measured on each level. As a result, three types of assessments must be conducted: organizational analysis, task analysis, and person analysis (McGehee & Thayer, 1961). Each level of assessment measures different aspects of needs assessment (see Table 4-3). **Organizational analysis** suggests where in the organization training is needed and under what conditions it will occur. **Task analysis**

TABLE 4-2	FOUR TYPES OF HRD NEEDS
Type of Need	**Description**
Performance Deficiency	Gaps between current and effective performance
Democratic	Employee preferences for HRD programs or topics
Diagnostic	Factors and conditions that create and ensure effective performance
Analytic	New and better ways to perform tasks

SOURCE: From "Expanding Needs Analysis" by R. O. Brinkerhoff, 1986, *Training and Development Journal, 40*, pp. 64–65.

TABLE 4-3	LEVELS OF NEEDS ASSESSMENT

Level	What Is Measured
Organization	Where training is needed and the conditions in which training will be conducted
Task	What must be done to perform the job effectively
Person	Who should be trained and what kind of training they need

explains what must be done to perform a job successfully. **Person analysis** reveals who needs to be trained, and what kind of training they need.

Organizational Analysis

Needs assessment at the organization level is usually conducted by performing an organizational analysis. Organizational analysis is a process used to better understand the characteristics of the organization to determine where training and HRD efforts are needed and the conditions within which they will be conducted.

Components of an Organizational Needs Analysis

This type of analysis requires a broad view of the organization and what it is trying to accomplish. The organizational characteristics studied may include goals and objectives, reward systems, planning systems, delegation and control systems, and communication systems.

According to Goldstein (1986), an organizational analysis should identify:

1. Organizational goals;

2. Organizational resources;

3. Climate for training; and

4. Constraints in the environment.

Each of these factors provides important information for planning and developing HRD programs and deserves further comment.

Organizational Goals   Understanding the organization's goals provides a starting point in identifying the effectiveness of the organization. Areas where the organization is meeting its goals probably don't require training efforts, but should be monitored to ensure that potential problems are identified early. Effective areas may also be used as models and as a source of ideas for how things can be done even more effectively. Areas where goals are not being met should be examined further and targeted for HRD or other appropriate HR or management efforts.

Organizational Resources   An awareness of the organization's resources is particularly useful in establishing HRD needs. Obviously, the amount of money available is an important determinant of HRD efforts. In addition, knowledge of resources such as facilities, materials on hand, and the expertise within the organization also influence how HRD is conducted. Resource availability can dictate some of the options to be considered when designing and implementing HRD programs, and can influence the priorities given to HRD needs. For example, if there are no classroom or conference room facilities within the organization, scheduling and location of an HRD program that requires such facilities can become more difficult or expensive. In this case, using an off-site location, such as a conference center or hotel, or scheduling the program in the company cafeteria after working hours, may be necessary.

Organizational Climate   The climate within the organization is an important factor in HRD success. If the climate is not conducive to HRD, designing and implementing a program will be difficult. For example, if managers and employees do not trust one another, employees may not participate fully and freely in a training program. As a result, their skills will probably not improve. Similarly, if problems exist between senior and middle management, as has happened in many organizations during the recent economic recession, middle managers may resist or not fully cooperate in the training effort, seriously reducing training effectiveness.

Environmental Constraints   Environmental constraints include legal, social, political, and economic issues faced by the organization. Demand for certain types of HRD programs can be effected by these constraints. For example, in late 1991, the charges of sexual harassment made by Anita Hill during the Senate confirmation hearing for Supreme Court Justice Clarence Thomas heightened awareness of this volatile social issue. Many organizations responded by offering workshops to educate managers and employees on what sexual harassment is and how it should be addressed.

Knowledge of the legal issues can ensure the HRD effort is in compliance and will not itself be a source of problems. For example, equal employment opportunity goals should be considered when determining how people will be assigned to a training program, especially if the program is a prerequisite for entry into a particular job. Similarly, economic issues, such as a recession, can also have an impact on HRD programs. If the organization decides to reduce staff as a part of a cost-cutting program, training may be necessary to ensure the employees who remain will be able to perform the tasks that were performed by the laid-off workers.

Advantages of Conducting an Organizational Analysis

As discussed earlier, organizational analysis reveals where HRD is needed and the environmental conditions that may affect the HRD effort. Knowledge of these issues ensures that the HRD programs are tied to the organization's strategy and mission, which is crucial to its success. Communicating the link between

HRD activities and the organization's strategic plan to operating managers and employees makes the importance of HRD programs clear. This may also generate support for HRD efforts and increase the motivation of those being trained.

One way to establish this connection is to link organizational analysis with the strategic planning process, especially since much of the same information is obtained in both procedures. The strategic plan can be a valuable source of information for the organizational analysis, while HRD efforts can become a major component of carrying out the strategic plan. For example, if an insurance company decides as part of its strategic plan to expand the services it offers to clients (for instance, pension management), it is likely that the current employees will require training in the new service area to ensure successful implementation of the plan. Carnevale, Gainer, and Villet (1990) provide a list of questions that can be included in an organizational analysis to assess strategic issues. A sampling of these questions is provided in Table 4-4.

Organizational Analysis Methods

Organizational analysis methods depend on the particular organization. Moore and Dutton (1978) reviewed the literature on needs analysis and compiled a list of the data sources available for determining training and HRD needs (see in Table 4-5). The list includes manpower inventory, skills inventory, organizational climate, and efficiency indexes. Some of these sources, such as efficiency indexes, are continuously monitored by many organizations as part of the normal control procedures and the data is readily available. Other sources, such as organizational climate, may have to be measured specifically for the organizational analysis.

Goldstein (1986; Goldstein, Macey, & Prien, 1981) provides a list of questions to ask during an organization needs analysis, that also summarize some important issues:

1. Are there any unspecified organizational goals that should be translated into training objectives or criteria?

2. Are the various levels in the organization committed to the training objectives?

3. Have the various levels and/or interacting units in the organization participated in the development program beginning at the end assessment?

4. Are key personnel ready both to accept the behavior of the trainees and to serve as models of the appropriate behavior?

5. Will trainees be rewarded on the job for the appropriate learned behavior?

6. Is training being utilized as a way of overcoming other organizational problems or conflicts that require other types of solutions?

TABLE 4-4	QUESTIONS TO ASK TO OBTAIN STRATEGIC INFORMATION IN AN ORGANIZATION ANALYSIS

Broad Strategic Issues

1. Is the organization's industry evolving or stable? What do the growth trends of competitors look like? Who are the main foreign and domestic competitors, and what is the organization's main advantage over these competitors?

2. Why has the organization been successful in the past?

3. What technology does the organization plan to use? If new technology is being planned, when will it come on line?

4. Are innovations anticipated that could change the competitive playing field?

5. What new management philosophies or procedures will be instituted by the organization? When?

6. Are there any regulatory issues—current, pending, or anticipated—that could influence strategic considerations?

7. What functional strategies will be employed by the various divisions or operating units to effect the overarching strategy? Why? How?

Human Resource Issues

1. What are the current strengths and weaknesses of the workforce?

2. What changes, if any, must occur in the job(s), organizational culture, and skill levels of the workforce?

3. Is the organization's overall strategy likely to result in layoffs and turnover? How much is anticipated?

4. How will union contracts be affected? What is the strategic role of the union?

5. What HRM policies should be reviewed in light of the organization's strategic effort?

6. What are the training implications of the overarching strategy? How could training help the organization reach any or all of its strategic goals?

7. What kind of specific training and HRD programs are needed? Does the organization have in-house capability to implement the necessary programs? Are there outside experts who can assist? Who are they?

8. How has training been regarded by: the workforce in the past? By management? How credible are the programs and trainers?

9. What delivery mechanisms are the most cost-effective and practical for each program?

10. What kind of training evaluation process is currently being used? Does it provide information on return on investment (ROI)? If not, would such a process contribute to a strategic flow?

11. Is there a formal procedure to ascertain if current training is appropriate in light of a new strategy, or, alternatively, to identify training needs that will be dictated by the new strategy?

12. Do HRM functions other than training and HRD need to be reviewed? Should they be modified?

SOURCE: From Training in America (pp. 203–205) by A. P. Carnevale, L. J. Gainer, and J. Villet, 1990, San Francisco: Jossey-Bass. Adapted by permission.

7. Is top management willing to commit the necessary resources to maintain work organizations while individuals are being trained? (Goldstein, 1986, p. 36)

As we have suggested, organizational analysis can be a critical component to an effective HRD effort. While it would be optimal to conduct a complete organizational analysis on a regular basis, resource and time limitations can make this difficult. At the very least, HRD managers and professionals should continuously monitor the organization's environment, goals, and effectiveness by taking advantage of information already collected by the organization. This responsibility is increasingly expected of all managers and supervisors, and many employees, as the environment becomes increasingly turbulent and competition more fierce.

Task Analysis

Task analysis (sometimes called operations analysis) is a systematic collection of data about a specific job or group of jobs to determine what an employee should be taught to achieve optimum performance (Moore & Dutton, 1978). Results of a task analysis typically include standards of performance, how tasks should be performed to meet these standards, and the knowledge, skills, and abilities (KSAs) and other characteristics employees need to meet the standards.

Table 4-6 lists a variety of data sources available for a task analysis identified by Moore and Dutton (1978), including job descriptions, observing the job, asking questions about the job, and reviewing literature about the job.

While there is general agreement on what the purpose of task analysis is, there are differing views of how it should be accomplished. Table 4-7 (page 103) shows the basic steps in task analysis offered by five sets of researchers (Campbell, 1988; Goldstein, 1986; Goldstein et al., 1981; McGehee & Thayer, 1961; Wexley & Latham, 1981). Each of these approaches contains common elements, which can be combined into the following five-step process:

1. Develop an overall job description

2. Task identification
   a. Describe what should be done in task
   b. Describe what is actually done in task

3. Describe KSAs needed to perform the job

4. Identify areas that can benefit from training

5. Prioritize areas that can benefit from training

While this reformulation is by no means radical, it does include the main elements from the various ways to conduct task analysis. It also presents these steps in an order that will facilitate our following discussion.

TABLE 4-5	SOURCES OF DATA FOR ORGANIZATIONAL NEEDS ANALYSIS

Data Source Recommended	Training Need Implications
1. Organizational Goals and Objectives	Where training emphasis can and should be placed. These provide normative standards of both direction and expected impact which can highlight deviations from objectives and performance problems.
2. Manpower Inventory	Where training is needed to fill gaps caused by retirement, turnover, age, etc. This provides an important demographic data base regarding possible scope of training needs.
3. Skills Inventory	Number of employees in each skill group, knowledge and skill levels, training time per job; etc. This provides an estimate of the magnitude of specific training needs. Useful in cost benefit analysis of training projects.
4. Organizational Climate Indexes	These "quality of working life" indicators at the organization level may help focus on problems that have training components.
Labor-Management data— strikes, lockouts, etc. Grievances	All of these items related to either work participation or productivity are useful both in discrepancy analysis and in helping management set a value on the behaviors it wishes improved through training
Turnover	once training has been established as a relevant solution.
Absenteeism Suggestions Productivity Accidents Short-term sickness Observation of employee behavior	

The Task Analysis Process

Step 1: Overall Job Description   The first step in the process is to develop an overall description of the job or jobs being analyzed. A **job description** is a narrative statement of the major activities involved in performing the job and the conditions under which these activities are performed. In some organizations, job descriptions are readily available and are updated regularly so that they accurately reflect the job as it is performed. If this is the case, the HRD professional should

Data Source Recommended	Training Need Implications
Attitude surveys	Good for locating discrepancies between organizational expectations and perceived results.
Customer complaints	Valuable feedback; look especially for patterns and repeat complaints.
5. Analysis of Efficiency Indexes	Cost accounting concepts may represent ratio between actual performance and desired or standard performance.
Costs of labor Costs of materials Quality of product Equipment utilization Costs of distribution Waste Down time Late deliveries Repairs	
6. Changes in System or Subsystem	New or changed equipment may present training problem.
7. Management Requests or Management Interrogation	One of most common techniques of training needs determination.
8. Exit Interviews	Often information not otherwise available can be obtained in these. Problem areas and supervisory training needs especially.
9. MBO or Work Planning and Review Systems	Provides performance review, potential review, and long-term business objectives. Provides actual performance data on a recurring basis so that base-line measurements may be known and subsequent improvement or deterioration of performance can be identified and analyzed.

SOURCE: From "Training Needs Analysis: Review and Critique" by M. L. Moore and P. Dutton, 1978, *Academy of Management Review*, 3, pp. 534–535. Reprinted by permission.

obtain and review the description. Without accurate job descriptions, however, it may be necessary to conduct a job analysis.

   Job analysis is a systematic study of a job to identify its major components. The job analysis process (described in detail in Gael, 1988; and Gatewood & Field, 1990) generally involves observing the job being performed; asking job incumbents and supervisors questions about the job, tasks, working conditions, and KSAs; examining the outcomes of the job; and reviewing relevant literature about the job.

| TABLE 4-6 | SOURCES OF DATA FOR TASK NEEDS ANALYSIS |

Technique for Obtaining Job Data	**Training Need Implications**
1. Job Descriptions	Outlines the job in terms of typical duties and responsibilities but is not meant to be all-inclusive. Helps define performance discrepancies.
2. Job Specifications or Task Analysis	List specified tasks required for each job. More specific than job descriptions. Specifications may extend to judgments of knowledge and skills required of job incumbents.
3. Performance Standards	Objectives of the tasks of job and standards by which they are judged. This may include base-line data as well.
4. Perform the Job	Most effective way of determining specific tasks but has serious limitations the higher the level of the job in that performance requirements typically have longer gaps between performance and resulting outcomes.
5. Observe Job—Work Sampling	
6. Review Literature Concerning the Job Research in other industries Professional journals Documents Government sources Ph.D. theses	Possibly useful in comparison analyses of job structures but far removed from either unique aspects of the job structure within any *specific* organization or specific performance requirements.
7. Ask Questions about the Job Of the job holder Of the supervisor Of higher management	
8. Training Committees or Conferences	Inputs from several viewpoints can often reveal training needs or training desires.
9. Analysis of Operating Problems Down time reports Waste Repairs Late deliveries Quality control	Indications of task interference, environmental factors, etc.
10. Card Sort	Utilized in training conferences. "How to" statements sorted by training importance.

SOURCE: From "Training Needs Analysis: Review and Critique" by M. L. Moore and P. Dutton, 1978, *Academy of Management Review, 3*, pp. 537–538. Reprinted by permission.

TABLE 4-7	FIVE APPROACHES TO CONDUCTING TASK NEEDS ANALYSIS
Authors	**Steps**
Wexley & Latham (1981)	Job Description Task Identification Course Objectives
Campbell (1988)	Identify components of effective performance Identify components that could be improved by training Identify what employees should do Identify what employees actually do
McGehee & Thayer (1961)	Identify standards of performance Identify tasks Identify how each task must be performed Identify skills, knowledge, and attitudes needed to perform each task
Goldstein, Macey, & Prien (1981)	Overview of the job Interview job experts and determine tasks and KSAs needed to perform tasks Rate tasks and KSAs Determine which tasks should be trained and which should be emphasized
Goldstein (1986)	Task description Develop task statements Determine relevant task dimensions Develop KSA statements

Even if a current job description is already available, it is valuable to observe the job as it is performed—a sort of reality test that can give the HRD professional a clearer idea about the tasks and the conditions employees face.

Step 2: Task Identification Task identification focuses on the behaviors performed within the job. In task identification, the following information about the job is determined and clearly described:

- The major tasks within the job

- How each task should be performed (performance standards)

- The variability of performance (how the tasks are actually performed in day-to-day operations).

Both performance standards and performance variability are critical to an effective needs analysis. While the standards describe **what should be done,** information about the variability of performance shows **what is done.** This allows the HRD professional to identify discrepancies that should be remedied and what the trainees should be able to do at the conclusion of training. Both of these are important in developing training objectives.

Five methods for identifying and describing the major tasks that comprise a job include:

1.   Stimulus → Response → Feedback

2.   Time Sampling

3.   Critical Incident Technique

4.   Job Inventories

5.   Job-Duty-Task Method

The **Stimulus-Response-Feedback method,** developed by Miller (1962), breaks down each task into three components. The first component is the stimulus, or cue, that lets the employee know it is time to perform a particular behavior. The second component is the response or behavior itself the employee is to perform. The third component is the feedback the employee receives about how well the behavior was performed. For example, a fast-food worker may have to respond to a buzzer (the stimulus) signaling that the french fries are done cooking by lifting the basket of fries out of the cooking oil and hanging it on a rack to drain (the behavior). Whether the basket stays in place or falls is the feedback on how well the behavior was performed.

Deterline (1968; cited in Mills, Pace, & Peterson, 1988) developed a similar approach to task analysis focusing on the stimulus and response aspects of the task. (See Figure 4-2 for an example of this approach involving the HRD professional and the task of conducting a task analysis.)

This task identification method results in a list of the cues, behaviors, and feedback that make up each task involved in the job. It is well suited for jobs with relatively simple tasks that can be directly observed (Wexley & Latham, 1981), and can be done by a supervisor, the job incumbent, or a trained analyst.

Time sampling, the second task identification method, involves having a trained observer watch and note the nature and frequency of an employee's activities. By observing at random intervals over a period of time, a clearer picture of the job is understood and recorded.

The **critical incident technique (CIT)** developed by Flanagan (1954) may also be used for task identification. The CIT involves having those familiar with the job record incidents of effective and ineffective behavior they have seen on the job over a period of time (like one year). This can be done by individuals or in groups. For each incident, the observer is asked to describe the circumstances and the specific behaviors involved, and suggest reasons why the behavior was effective or ineffective. The CIT results in an understanding of what is considered both good and poor performance.

FIGURE 4-2	EXAMPLE OF THE STIMULUS-RESPONSE METHOD OF TASK ANALYSIS

Job Title: HRD Professional

Task: Task Analysis

Stimulus	**Response**
1. Need a title to describe job and responsibilities	List the job title
2. Need a classification and title for first duty	Classify it and title the specific duty
3. Need an action verb and noun to label first duty	List the first task
4. Need an action verb and noun to label first subtask	List the first subtask
5. Need to know what is required to perform this subtask	Study and list the knowledge one needs to perform activity

SOURCE: From *Analysis in Human Resource Training and Organizational Development* (p. 57) by G. E. Mills, R. W. Pace, and B. D. Peterson, 1988, Reading, MA: Addison-Wesley. Reprinted by permission.

Using a **job inventory questionnaire** is another approach to task analysis. The questionnaire is developed by asking people familiar with the job to identify all of its tasks. This list is then given to supervisors and job incumbents to evaluate each task in terms of its importance and the time spent performing it. This method allows for input from many people and gives numerical information about each task that can be used to compute indexes and be analyzed with statistics.

Finally, the fifth approach to task analysis is the **job-duty-task method.** In this method, the job is divided up into its subparts, providing a comprehensive list that identifies the job title; each of its duties (and the tasks and subtasks that make up that duty); and, finally, the knowledge, ability, or skill required to perform each subtask. A blank form that can be used to record the results of a job-duty-task analysis is shown in Figure 4-3, and Figure 4-4 shows the same form completed for part of an HRD professional's job.

Each of these five methods use either job experts (incumbents or supervisors) or trained observers to provide and evaluate job information. It is desirable to use more than one method, depending on the nature of the job being studied and the time and resources available, to obtain a more complete view of the job. Methods that involve a range of organization members (supervisors, managers, and employees), such as the CIT and task inventory, have the advantage of building commitment and accountability to the overall HRD effort (Campbell, 1988; Cureton, Newton, & Tesolowski, 1986). This can help ease the progress of the HRD program down the line.

FIGURE 4-3	FORM FOR RECORDING TASK ANALYSIS RESULTS USING THE JOB-DUTY-TASK METHOD

Job title: _____   Specific duty: _____

Tasks	Subtasks	Knowledge and Skills Required
1._____	1._____	_____
		_____
	2._____	_____
		_____
	3._____	_____
		_____
2._____	1._____	_____
		_____
	2._____	_____
		_____
	3._____	_____
		_____
3._____	1._____	_____
		_____
	2._____	_____

SOURCE: From *Analysis in Human Resource Training and Organizational Development* (p. 57) by G. E. Mills, R. W. Pace, and B. D. Peterson, 1988, Reading, MA: Addison-Wesley. Reprinted by permission.

According to Goldstein et al. (1981), task statements should be evaluated in terms of their importance for job performance, the frequency with which the tasks are performed, and how difficult it is to become proficient at the tasks. Armed with this information, the next step in the task needs analysis process is to identify the characteristics it takes to perform the tasks.

Step 3: Identifying What It Takes to Do the Job   Successful task performance requires that employees possess the KSAs to perform the task. The HRD professional must specify the KSAs, because it is these competencies (reviewed in Table 4-8) that employees must develop or acquire during the training program.

A thorough job analysis will contain this information in the job specification section. If this information is not available or current, the HRD professional can determine these factors by questioning supervisors, job incumbents, and other experts, and by reviewing relevant literature. Clear KSA statements should be written and then evaluated as to their importance to job performance, learning difficulty, and the opportunity to acquire them on the job (Goldstein et al., 1981).

Information on KSAs required to perform a job is valuable in determining the focus of an HRD program. Some KSAs, such as oral and written communication skills or knowledge of safety procedures, are necessary for effective performance in many jobs. If this indeed is the case, it may be possible to develop

FIGURE 4-4	APPLYING THE JOB-DUTY-TASK METHOD OF TASK ANALYSIS TO THE JOB OF HRD PROFESSIONAL

Job title: HRD Professional   Specific duty: Task Analysis

Tasks	Subtasks	Knowledge and Skills Required
1. List tasks	1. Observe behavior	List four characteristics of behavior Classify behavior
	2. Select verb	Knowledge of action verbs Grammatical skills
	3. Record behavior	State so understood by others Recorded neatly
2. List subtasks	1. Observe behavior	List all remaining acts Classify behavior
	2. Select verb	State correctly Grammatical skill
	3. Record behavior	Neat and understood by others
3. List knowledge	1. State what must be known	Classify all information
	2. Determine complexity of skill	Determine if skill represents a series of acts that must be learned in a sequence.

SOURCE: From *Analysis in Human Resource Training and Organizational Development* (p. 57) by G. E. Mills, R. W. Pace, and B. D. Peterson, 1988, Reading, MA: Addison-Wesley. Reprinted by permission.

TABLE 4-8	DEFINITIONS OF SKILL, KNOWLEDGE, ABILITY, AND OTHER CHARACTERISTICS

Skill	The ability to perform acts with ease and precision
Knowledge	An understanding of factors or principles related to a particular subject or subject area
Ability	The power to perform a physical or mental function
Other Characteristics	Includes attitudes, personality, and interest factors

SOURCE: From "Needs Assessment Approaching for Training Development" by I. L. Goldstein, W. H. Macey, and E. P. Prien, 1981, in H. Meltzer and W. R. Nord (Eds.), *Making organizations more humane and productive: A handbook for practitioners* (p. 46) New York: Wiley-Interscience.

and conduct an HRD program that can be offered to employees in a wide range of jobs.

Step 4: Identify the Areas That Can Benefit from Training or HRD   In this step, the focus is on determining which tasks and capabilities should be included in HRD programs. Ratings of tasks on importance, time spent, and ease of acquisition, and ratings of KSAs on importance, difficulty to learn, and opportunity to acquire them on the job should be examined. The tasks and KSAs receiving the highest ratings should be considered candidates for inclusion in HRD programs.

Care must be taken to balance the concerns raised by these ratings. For example, a high rating on time spent and ease of learning may indicate that a particular task should be included in training. However, if that same task is also rated low in importance to successful job performance, it may not be worth the time and effort involved in training (or perhaps less expensive training methods can be used). It is also important to remember that not all problems are appropriately dealt with through HRD programs—other HR or management approaches may be better suited for particular issues and situations.

Step 5: Prioritizing Training Needs   At the end of Step 4, it should be clear which tasks and KSAs could benefit from training. Now, these tasks and KSAs should be prioritized to determine which ones should be addressed first. Again, inspection of the ratings provided in Steps 2 and 3 can facilitate the prioritization process. (More will be said about prioritizing training needs at the end of this chapter.)

An Example of a Task Analysis

A task analysis performed to develop a train-the-trainer program at Texas Instruments Corporation (TI) provides a good illustration of the ideas included in our discussion of the task needs analysis process (Wircenski, Sullivan, & Moore, 1989).

The training staff at TI was faced with finding a way to analyze training needs and deliver an inexpensive program to quickly train expert engineers to instruct new engineers. Outside consultants began the needs analysis process by meeting with branch managers, department heads, and employees from five TI branches to determine:

- The mission of the department

- Perceived training needs

- Current and previous efforts in staff development

- Roles, responsibilities, and team arrangements within the different branches

This organizational analysis enlightened the training team about the significant issues involved, and they used this information in persuading the top managers to commit to a five-step approach to task analysis:

1. List of typical tasks

2. Staff survey

3. Classroom observation

4. Structured interviews

5. Final report

The **list of tasks** was developed by examining literature on training delivery, including company technical reports and the American Society for Training and Development's *Models For Excellence* study. The initial list of tasks was reviewed by TI managers, who added several tasks and reworded other task statements. The list was then organized into five areas of responsibility and was given to employees to review and supplement. This ensured that all the professionals had input into defining their jobs from their perspectives. This step resulted in a 117-item list of tasks that trainers would typically be expected to perform.

For the **staff survey,** all members of the department received a questionnaire listing the tasks and asking them to rate each task according to (a) its importance to their job, and (b) their interest in receiving more training related to that task. Each item was given a mean rating score on importance and interest. The results were examined to determine whether differences existed for the five branches (they did not).

Classroom observations of experienced and new TI trainers in the department were conducted to provide additional information on instructional delivery. Teams of two observers viewed instructors for one hour and met with each instructor to provide feedback.

Individuals from each branch participated in **structured interviews** to maintain consistency between the survey findings and the classroom observations. This allowed the training team to gather more information about each branch and to "validate" the data gathered earlier. The authors reported the interview results were consistent with data from the other sources.

The final step was preparation of the **final report.** This consisted of examining the results and developing an executive summary outlining strengths and recommendations for training in each of the five areas of the task list, along with data for each of the data collection methods.

Wircenski et al. (1989) reported the needs analysis was a success because it allowed input and participation at all levels of the department, ensuring cooperation and comprehensiveness. As a result, the training team was able to identify and rank training needs based on sound information rather than relying on intuition.

This example reinforces several important points about task analysis:

1. Input from managers, supervisors, and employees can ensure support for needs analysis and pave the way for support for training.

2. Multiple methods not only provide unique information, but also enable the analyst to confirm findings and identify and resolve discrepancies.

3. Ratings of tasks allow for quantitative analysis of which tasks may benefit from training and which should be addressed.

4. Viewing needs from a broad perspective, rather than focusing on performance deficiencies results in a better understanding of training needs and can build support for training programs.

Summary of Task Analysis

Task analysis focuses on the job, rather than the individual doing the job. Information from task analysis and organizational analysis give a clear picture of the organization and the jobs that are performed within it, and together form a sound foundation for planning and developing training efforts. However, one final question remains. Who needs training and what kind of training do they need? The answer lies in person analysis.

Person Analysis

Person analysis is directed at determining the training needs of the individual employee. The focus is typically on how well each employee is performing key job tasks, but may identify a wide range of both common and unique HRD needs. Person analysis is best performed by someone with the opportunity to observe the employee's performance regularly—typically the employee and the employee's immediate supervisor.

Immediate supervisors play a particularly important role in person analysis. Not only are they in an ideal position to observe employee performance, but it is their responsibility to do so. Many methods of person assessment require an effective supervisor to implement them properly.

Moore and Dutton (1978) list performance evaluation data, direct observation, tests, questionnaires, specially designed situations, and critical incidents as sources of information available for person assessment (see Table 4-9).

Components of Person Analysis

McGehee and Thayer (1961) proposed that person analysis is made up of two components: summary person analysis and diagnostic person analysis. **Summary person analysis** involves determining the overall success of individual employee performance. **Diagnostic person analysis** tries to discover the reasons for the employee's performance. Effective performers may be the source for ideas on how to improve or guarantee employee performance, while analysis of ineffective performers can identify what interventions (HRD or otherwise) are needed to improve performance. Table 4-10 lists and describes these two components of person analysis.

Recall from our discussion of needs that current performance deficiencies make up only one type of need. Therefore, an effective person analysis should also identify future developmental needs.

Performance Appraisal in the Person Analysis Process

As we mentioned, performance appraisal can be a valuable tool for collecting person analysis data. While it may be tempting to believe that performance appraisal itself can be the bulk of person analysis, this view is shortsighted. In reality, using performance appraisal in needs analysis requires a manager to "have access to a variety of different pieces of information and make a number of complex decisions," (Herbert and Doverspike, 1990, p. 253). Herbert and Doverspike's model of performance appraisal in the person analysis process begins with the following steps (see Figure 4-5):

1. Perform or have access to a complete, accurate performance appraisal.

2. Identify discrepancies between the employee's behavior and/or traits and those required for effective performance.

3. Identify the source of the discrepancies.

4. Select the intervention appropriate to resolve the discrepancies.

Two steps in this process bear further comment. First, one should not take the completeness or accuracy of a performance appraisal on faith. Many performance appraisals are flawed by either poor appraisal processes or errors committed during the appraisal. Examination of the organization's appraisal process and practices can help assess the quality of the appraisal. Second, there are a variety of possible sources for a performance or skill discrepancy. Recalling our discussion of employee behavior in Chapter 2, the cause could be either within the employee (like motivation or attitudes) or in the environment (such as a lack of support, outdated equipment, or obstructive work rules). Therefore, identifying the source of the discrepancies will likely involve integrating information from organizational analysis, task or job analysis, and any individual skill or ability testing completed by the employee (Herbert & Doverspike, 1990).

However, Herbert and Doverspike (1990, p. 255) point out that conditions for conducting performance appraisal and person analysis are often less than ideal, and have identified the following as potential problems:

1. There can be enormous costs and complexity when considered at an organization-wide level.

TABLE 4-9	DATA SOURCES AVAILABLE FOR PERSON NEEDS ASSESSMENT

Technique or Data Obtained	Training Need Implications
1. Performance Data or Appraisals as Indicators of "Sickness"	Include weaknesses and area of improvement as well as strong points. Easy to analyze and quantify for purposes of determining subjects and kinds of training needed. These data can be used to *identify* performance discrepancies.

Productivity
    Absenteeism or Tardiness
    Accidents
    Short-term sickness
    Grievances
    Waste
    Late deliveries
    Product Quality
    Down time
    Repairs
    Equipment utilization
    Customer complaints	

2. Observation—Work Sampling	More subjective technique but provides both employee behavior and results of the behavior.
3. Interviews	Individual is only one who knows what he (she) believes he (she) needs to learn. Involvement in need analysis can also motivate employees to make an effort to learn.
4. Questionnaires	Same approach as the interview. Easily tailored to specific characteristics of the organization. May produce bias through the necessity of pre-structure categories.
5. Tests	Can be tailor-made or standardized. Care must be taken so that they measure job-related qualities.

Job knowledge
    Skills
    Achievement	

6. Attitude Surveys	On the individual basis, useful in determining morale, motivation or satisfaction of each employee.

2. The ability of the manager to make veridical judgments is questionable given evidence of rating errors and causal attributional biases.

3. The behavior rating system must include all areas of required performance that can be identified.

Technique or Data Obtained	Training Need Implications
7. Checklists or Training Progress Charts	Up-to-date listing of each employee's skills. Indicates future training requirements for each job.
8. Rating Scales	Care must be taken to ensure relevant, reliable, and objective employee ratings.
9. Critical Incidents	Observed actions which are critical to the successful or unsuccessful performance of the job.
10. Diaries	Individual employee records details of his (her) job.

11. Devised Situations
 	
    Role play
    Case study
    Conference leadership training
       sessions
    Business games
    In-baskets
	Certain knowledge, skills and attitudes are demonstrated in these techniques.

12. Diagnostic Rating	Check lists are factor analyzed to yield diagnostic ratings.
13. Assessment Centers	Combination of several of the above techniques into an intensive assessment program.
14. Coaching	Similar to interview—one-to-one.
15. MBO or Work Planning and Review Systems	Provides actual performance data on a recurring basis related to organizational (and individually or group-negotiated standards) so that base-line measurements may be known and subsequent improvement or deterioration of performance may be identified and analyzed. This performance review and potential review is keyed to larger organization goals and objectives.

SOURCE: From "Training Needs Analysis: Review and Critique" by M. L. Moore and P. Dutton, 1978, *Academy of Management Review*, 3, pp. 539–540. Reprinted by permission.

4. Intentions to use performance appraisal data for needs analysis must be specified **before** the system is developed, operationalized, and implemented.

5. Raters must be motivated to make accurate performance ratings.

TABLE 4-10	COMPONENTS OF THE PERSON ANALYSIS PROCESS

Summary Person Analysis

Global analysis; overall evaluation of individual employee's performance; classification of individual as successful versus unsuccessful performer.

Diagnostic Person Analysis

Determine why results of individual employee's behavior occur; determine how individual's knowledge, skills, and abilities (KSAs), effort, and environmental factors combine to yield the summary person analysis.

Together the summary and diagnostic person analyses combine to determine **who** is performing successfully/unsuccessfully and **why** the individual is performing successfully/unsuccessfully. This is the **Person Analysis.**

SOURCE: From "Performance Appraisal in the Training Needs Analysis Process: A Review and Critique" by G. R. Herbert and D. Doverspike, 1990, *Public Personnel Management, 19*(3), p. 255. Reprinted by permission.

FIGURE 4-5	A MODEL OF PERFORMANCE APPRAISAL IN THE PERSON ANALYSIS PROCESS

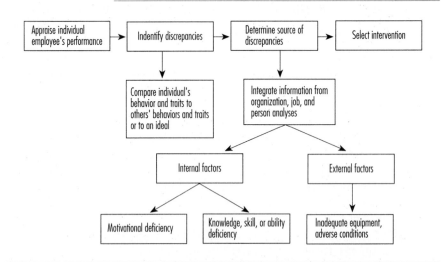

SOURCE: From "Performance Appraisal in the Training Needs Analysis Process: A Review and Critique" by G. R. Herbert and D. Doverspike, 1990, *Public Personnel Management, 19*(3), p. 254. Reprinted by permission.

6.   The manager or training director must be able to match deficiencies identified to specific remedial activities.

Hopefully, future research will address these problems and provide us with better, more accurate means to identify employees' performance deficiencies.

Developmental Needs

Person analysis data is also used to define developmental needs, which can be identified during the periodic performance evaluation. The primary use of developmental data is for maintaining the skills, knowledge, and abilities of each employee. However, the information can also be important to career development by preparing the employee for future job responsibilities, which we will discuss in Chapter 11.

A skills inventory can also help determine a person's need for training. This assesses each employee's KSAs by examining their education, training, experience, certification, performance reviews, and recommendations. Many organizations use a human resource information system (HRIS) to compile this information for easy retrieval. While this type of information is traditionally used to assess the readiness of individuals to take on higher levels of responsibility (a promotion), it can also be used for training needs assessment. Some organizations analyze this information to determine the best strategy for developing its human resources. For instance, if the organization is contemplating future changes that require new skills, the skills inventory may provide necessary information for devising a training program.

Employees as a Source of Needs Assessment Information

One possible source of information for training needs is the employee. Two recent studies (Ford & Noe, 1987; McEnery & McEnery, 1987) provide some useful information regarding the accuracy of employee self-ratings of performance.

McEnery and McEnery (1987) compared self and supervisory ratings of training needs for 200 managers and professionals. They found that while self-ratings were more lenient than supervisory ratings, self-ratings exhibited less halo error (that is, allowing an overall impression to guide the ratings rather than evaluating each item separately). In addition, they found that the two sources of ratings were not significantly related, and that self-ratings discriminated among aspects of performance more than supervisory ratings did. They concluded by stating that self-ratings of training needs may be a useful, valid part of a needs assessment process. Ford and Noe (1987) found that managerial level, function, and attitude toward training usefulness all had a small but significant effect on self-ratings of training needs, concluding that more research is needed to examine this issue.

Taken together, these studies suggest that while self-ratings of training needs may be a useful part of a needs assessment, HRD professionals would be wise to use multiple sources of needs assessment information to ensure validity.

The "Benchmarks" Specialized Person Analysis Instrument

One option in collecting person analysis data is to design an instrument that can be used for a specific population of interest (for instance, clerical workers or supervisors). This can be especially useful if the organization's HRD strategy targets a category of employees for development. The Center for Creative Leadership recently developed "Benchmarks," a specialized person analysis instrument used to identify the development needs of managers (McCauley, Lombardo, & Usher, 1989).

Research conducted at the Center for Creative Leadership on how executives develop, learn, and change over their careers (summarized in McCall, Lombardo, & Morrison, 1988) provided the impetus for Benchmarks. This research identified key developmental events, the lessons learned from these events, and reasons why executives succeeded or did not (Lindsey, et al., 1987; McCall & Lombardo, 1983).

The Benchmarks instrument is divided into two sections (see Table 4-11). Section One, which is based on the lessons executives learn from key developmental events, contains 108 items grouped in 16 scales. Section Two, which is based on the flaws that lead to an executive's "derailment," contains 26 items grouped in six scales (McCauley et al., 1989).

TABLE 4-11	SCALE NAMES, DESCRIPTIONS, AND SAMPLE ITEMS FROM BENCHMARKS, A PERSON ANALYSIS TOOL FOR MANAGEMENT DEVELOPMENT

Section 1 Scales:	**Description of Scale**	**Sample Items**
1A. RESOURCEFUL-NESS	Can think strategically, engage in flexible problem-solving behavior, and work effectively with higher management.	• makes good decisions under pressure with incomplete information • links his/her responsibilities with the mission of the whole organization
1B. DOING WHATEVER IT TAKES	Has perseverance and focus in the face of obstacles.	• faces difficult situations with guts and tenacity • controls his/her own career; does not sit and wait for the company to plan a course to follow
1C. BEING A QUICK STUDY	Quickly masters new technical and business knowledge.	• learns a new skill quickly • quickly masters new vocabulary and operating rules needed to understand how the business works

2A. BUILDING AND MENDING RELA-TIONSHIPS	Knows how to build and maintain working relationships with co-workers and external parties.	• when working with a group over whom he/she has no control, gets things done by finding common ground • relates to all kinds of individuals tactfully, from shop floor to top executives
2B. LEADING SUBOR-DINATES	Delegates to subordinates effectively, broadens their opportunities, and acts with fairness towards them.	• is willing to delegate important tasks, not just things he/she doesn't want to do • relies on persuasion or expertise first; uses the power of the position as a last resort
2C. COMPASSION AND SENSITIVITY	Shows genuine interest in others and sensitivity to subordinates' needs.	• is willing to help an employee with personal problems • is sensitive to signs of overwork in others
3. STRAIGHTFOR-WARDNESS AND COMPOSURE	Is honorable and steadfast.	• relies on style more than substance in dealings with top management • becomes hostile or moody when things are not going his/her way
4. SETTING A DEVELOPMENTAL CLIMATE	Provides a challenging climate to encourage subordinates' development.	• is willing to pitch in and lead subordinates by example • develops subordinates by providing challenge and opportunity
5. CONFRONTING PROBLEM SUBOR-DINATES	Acts decisively and with fairness when dealing with problem subordinates.	• is able to fire loyal but incompetent people without procrastinating • can deal effectively with resistant subordinates
6. TEAM ORIENTA-TION	Accomplishes tasks through managing others.	• acts as if his/her managerial success is built by a team of strong subordinates
7. BALANCE BETWEEN PER-SONAL LIFE AND WORK	Balances work priorities with personal life so that neither is neglected.	• acts as if there is more to life than just having a career • lets job demands cause family problems

Continued

Section 1 Scales:	Description of Scale	Sample Items
8. DECISIVENESS	Prefers quick and approximate actions to slow and precise ones in many management situations.	• displays a real bias for action, calculated risks, and quick decisions • does not hesitate when making decisions
9. SELF-AWARENESS	Has an accurate picture of strengths and weaknesses and is willing to improve.	• sorts out his/her strengths and weaknesses fairly accurately
10. HIRING TALENTED STAFF	Hires talented people for his/her team.	• hires people who are not afraid of responsibility or risks
11. PUTTING PEOPLE AT EASE	Displays warmth and a good sense of humor.	• has a warm personality that puts people at ease
12. ACTING WITH FLEXIBILITY	Can behave in ways that are often seen as opposites.	• is tough and at the same time compassionate • can lead and let others lead

Section 2 Scales:		
1. PROBLEMS WITH INTERPERSONAL RELATIONSHIPS	Difficulties in developing comfortable working relationships with others.	• adopts a bullying style under stress • isolates him/herself from others
2. DIFFICULTY IN MOLDING A STAFF	Difficulties in selecting and building a team.	• chooses an overly narrow subordinate group • is not good at building a team
3. DIFFICULTY IN MAKING STRATEGIC TRANSITIONS	Difficulties in moving from the technical/tactical level to the general/strategic level.	• cannot handle a job requiring the formulation of complex organizational strategies • can't make the mental transition from technical manager to general manager
4. LACK OF FOLLOW-THROUGH	Difficulties in following up on promises, really completing a job, and attention to detail.	• makes a splash and moves on without really completing a job • has left a trail of little problems
5. OVERDEPENDENCE	Relies too much on a boss, powerful advocate, or one's own natural talent.	• has chosen to stay with the same boss too long • might burn out, run out of steam
6. STRATEGIC DIFFERENCES WITH MANAGEMENT	Disagrees with higher management about business strategy.	• disagrees with higher management about how the business should be run

SOURCE: From "Diagnosing Management Development Needs: An Instrument Based on How Managers Develop" by C. D. McCauley, M. M. Lombardo, and C. J. Usher, 1989, *Journal of Management, 15,* pp. 395–396. Reprinted by permission.

A supervisor evaluates the manager using the Benchmarks instrument, resulting in a profile of the manager's strengths and weaknesses that can be used to plan the manager's development. Initial research on the validity and psychometric properties of Benchmarks has been encouraging (McCauley et al., 1989), and further research aimed at understanding and refining this instrument should lead to a valuable tool for making management development efforts more systematic. Efforts like Benchmarks can only improve the effectiveness of HRD by providing an accurate, meaningful base for making program and participant decisions.

Prioritizing HRD Needs

Assuming that a needs analysis reveals multiple needs, management and the HRD staff will have to prioritize these needs. As in any organizational function, there are limited resources available for the HRD effort. Decisions must be made about what resources—including facilities, equipment, materials, skilled personnel, travel, and consultant fees—will be used in the HRD programs.

Participation in the Prioritization Process

The prioritizing of HRD needs should involve individuals throughout the organization. Since HRD programs are intended to serve a specific area or areas of the organization, representatives from those areas should have input in this decision. Some HRD departments regularly solicit ideas from employees, and this information can be used to refine and improve ongoing programs as well to gauge the demand for future programs. With this input, there is a greater likelihood that more employees will perceive the HRD programs as being relevant to the organization and to themselves. By involving others in critical HRD decisions, there is also a greater likelihood that more people in the organization will support the total HRD effort.

The HRD Advisory Committee

One way to continuously reflect the needs of the employees and assist in prioritizing needs is to establish an HRD advisory committee. The role of this committee is to meet regularly and review needs assessment and evaluation data and offer advice on the type and content of HRD programs to be offered.

The advisory committee should be composed of members from a cross-section of the organization. This provides different perspectives on HRD needs and can create a broader level of support from all parts of the organization. The organization should also recognize those employees who volunteer their time to serve on advisory and other committees. This includes the recognition that meeting time may take employees away from their job responsibilities.

As we have discussed, a thorough needs assessment establishes the foundation for an HRD or training program. Next, we will turn our attention to how HRD and training programs are designed and implemented (Chapter 5) and to how such programs can be evaluated to determine their effectiveness (Chapter 6).

RETURN TO OPENING CASE

Management at Scott Paper Company realized early on that their succession planning system and management development program to improve morale at Scott Worldwide Foodservice (SWF) division would succeed only if it was based on a thorough needs assessment. The needs assessment approach they used had five key components:

1. An understanding of the company's organizational objectives and corporate-wide developmental approach;

2. Identifying the specific management jobs that would be included in the program;

3. Creating detailed, results-oriented job descriptions for each job;

4. Creating a list of attributes and core competencies of successful managers in each position; and

5. A one-day individual assessment process that evaluated candidates and provided them with developmental feedback that was tied to the job descriptions and competencies of specific positions.

Scott Paper used both an outside consultant and its own employees to create the system. Groups of Scott Paper managers first created detailed job descriptions for each position and lists of attributes and core competencies. The job descriptions and competencies included detailed statements of what was expected, which incorporated objective measurable results of performance wherever possible. Care was taken to define the relationship of the role competencies to the job, employee relations, and the management philosophy and culture.

The consultants, WMS and Company, Inc., of King of Prussia, Pennsylvania, then developed a variety of tests based on the job descriptions and competencies produced by Scott Paper. Categories of assessment included things such as understanding business and personal attributes (like initiative and interpersonal skills), using devices to measure intellectual ability, problem solving, mathematics, personality, and so on.

The assessment process is designed to give each candidate a clear idea of his or her developmental needs. The emphasis during the assessment feedback discussion is positive, focusing on what the individual can improve. These needs are clearly tied to specific areas of the job description and role competencies for the position the candidate is interested in. This supports the positive approach Scott Paper believes in and helps the candidates see exactly what they must do to reach their goals. Following the assessment, the candidate may then take advantage of the company's training and management development programs to build the skills and competencies he or she needs.

One of the benefits of this effort at Scott Paper, notes one executive, is that the program "has changed the way managers perceive their jobs and their place in the company's future, and already we've seen dramatically changed attitudes among the plant employees they manage." The success of Scott Paper's initiative makes an important point: needs assessment not only provides a foundation for HRD efforts, but the assessment process can play a key role in reinforcing the company's philosophy and culture and in motivating individuals to play an active role in their own development.[1]

Summary

In this chapter we focused on the needs assessment phase of the training process model (design/implementation and evaluation will be emphasized in the following chapters). Needs assessment is performed on three levels: organization, task, and person. The organizational level asks the question, "Where in the organization is there a need for training and under what conditions will it be conducted?" Organization needs analysis focuses on the organization's goals and its effectiveness in achieving those goals, organizational resources, the climate for training, and any environmental constraints. The purpose of organizational analysis is to understand what the organization is trying to accomplish, where training may be needed to enhance effectiveness, and what potential roadblocks to training success exist.

Task analysis level asks the question, "What tasks and KSAs should be included in training?" This analysis involves five steps: (1) describing the job, (2) identifying the tasks within the job, (3) identifying the KSAs needed to perform the job, (4) identifying areas that can benefit from training, and (5) prioritizing the areas that can benefit from training.

Person analysis levels asks the question, "Who needs to be trained and what for?" Individual performance deficiencies and developmental needs can be used to suggest the content of the training program. This information can also serve to identify which employees should participate in the HRD programs.

Because of limited HRD resources it is necessary to prioritize training needs. This ensures that resources have the greatest impact on the organizational goals. Whenever possible, individuals should be encouraged to participate in prioritizing needs.

---

[1]From "Succession Planning Drives Plant Turnaround" by R.J. Sahl, 1992, *Personnel Journal*, 71 (9), pp. 67–70.

Key Terms and Concepts

critical incident technique
job analysis
job description
needs assessment
organizational analysis
person analysis
stimulus-response-feedback
   method

job-duty-task method
job inventory method
need
task analysis
task identification
time sampling method

Questions for Discussion

1. Why is needs assessment information critical to the development and delivery of an effective HRD program?

2. What is the relationship between organizational needs analysis and strategic planning? How can tying HRD programs to an organization's strategic plan make it easier to justify requests for resources to develop and deliver HRD programs?

3. Suppose you have been asked to perform a task analysis for the job of dispatcher in a city police department. Which method(s) of task analysis do you think would be most appropriate for analyzing this job? Support your choice(s).

4. Briefly describe the pros and cons of using performance appraisal information when conducting a person needs analysis. Should an HRD professional use performance appraisals to enhance the value of the information obtained from a person analysis? Support your answer.

5. One important source of person needs assessment information is the potential trainees' own opinions about their developmental needs. What are the advantages and disadvantages of relying on such self-report information as part of a person needs assessment?

6. Why should HRD needs, once identified, be prioritized? What are the benefits, if any, of obtaining the participation of a variety of organization members in the prioritization process?

7. Why is needs assessment so often not performed in many organizations? How could an HRD professional encourage a reluctant manager to approve the time and resources necessary for a needs assessment prior to selecting and implementing an HRD program?

5

Designing and Implementing Training Programs

Learning Objectives

1. Identify outside sources of training programs.
2. List the activities involved in employer-designed training programs.
3. Recognize the difference between a trainer's content skills and training skills.
4. Write training objectives for a specific program.
5. Describe different training methods and the kinds of techniques used in different situations.
6. Compare some different training materials and tell how they are prepared.
7. Point out some of the constraints to scheduling a training program.
8. Explain the activities involved in implementing a training program.

OPENING CASE

One of the most important factors to the success of an HRD program is the trainer. A good trainer can increase the chances of success—a poor one can doom an otherwise sound program. The National Training Service of Alexander Consulting Group (ACG) located in Newburyport, Massachusetts, uses employees who are subject-matter experts (SMEs) to design and implement training courses. ACG uses this strategy for four reasons: (1) most of the training programs involve technical and financial information, (2) ACG felt that SME trainers were more qualified than full-time trainers to teach these courses, (3) they believed that SMEs would be recognized by trainees as having technical credibility, and (4) SMEs would be able to make the courses more job relevant.

In the late 1980s, ACG's course evaluations revealed some shortcomings in the SME approach. The evaluations showed that the training programs were not as job relevant as ACG had expected, and that SME trainers lacked two important KSAs: (1) expertise in designing job relevant training programs and (2) techniques to implement training programs within limited time constraints. The SME trainers' lack of training skills led them to rely more on their own academic experiences, thus following a college-style lecture format that was often inappropriate for some parts of the training.

Even though ACG management was generally pleased with the SME-trainer approach, they felt that it needed to be improved. The training specialists at the National Training Center were given the challenge of finding an efficient approach to increase the SME's knowledge and skills in training program design and implementation.

Introduction

The purpose of this chapter is to discuss the second phase of the training process: designing and implementing training and HRD programs. At this point, an organization following effective HRD practices will have completed Phase I of the training and HRD process—needs assessment—and has needs assessment data that indicates:

1. Where the training or HRD program is needed;

2. What kind of training or HRD program is needed;

3. Who needs to be trained; and

4. The conditions under which training will occur.

In addition, the needs identified will have been prioritized so that senior management and the HRD staff know which programs or issues require attention and resources.

We recognize that in some cases the availability of needs assessment data may be limited. While the HRD practitioner may feel that it will be difficult to design an effective training program, they must improvise and make the best of a suboptimal situation. At the same time, an effort should be made to persuade management of the importance of conducting needs analysis and prioritizing HRD needs, as time and resources allow.

Armed with needs assessment data, the focus now turns to designing and implementing the HRD program. The key activities involved in designing and implementing an HRD program are:

1. Setting objectives;

2. Selecting the trainer or vendor;

3. Developing a lesson plan;

4. Selecting program methods and techniques;

5. Preparing materials;

6. Scheduling the program; and

7. Implementing the program.

Figure 5-1 shows where these activities fit within the training and HRD process model.

Assuming that an important need for training has been identified, the manager or HRD professional must translate that need into a set of program objectives. Objectives define what participants will be expected to learn as a result of

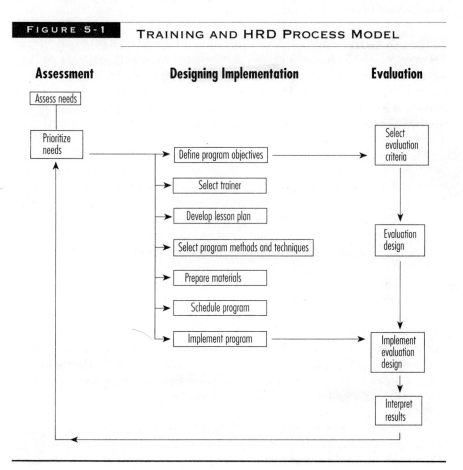

FIGURE 5-1   **TRAINING AND HRD PROCESS MODEL**

participating in the HRD program. However, some managers and HRD professionals may be tempted to make a decision about whether to design the program internally or purchase the program or its key parts—that is, contract a consultant to serve as a trainer, buy program materials, and so on—before establishing objectives. In outside purchases, the organization typically uses the objectives developed by the vendor rather than defining their own. However, the chances of success are greater if the organization identifies the HRD objectives first, before deciding whether to design or purchase the program. How can HRD professionals know what to buy when they haven't clearly defined what they want the program to accomplish?

Statements of HRD needs are often not detailed enough to be used as specific program outcomes. Rather, they state the problem at hand with a diagnosis of the problem's causes. Objectives, in contrast, state the outcome the program is intended to produce, including the specific performance expected, the conditions under which it will be performed, and the criteria to be used to judge whether the objective has been achieved.

Defining Program Objectives

One of the first things a trainer should do is define the program objectives. Mager defines an objective as a "description of a performance you want learners to be able to exhibit before you consider them competent" (1984, p. 3). As such, program objectives describe the intent and the desired result of the HRD program. The results can be achieved in many ways (such as lectures, role-play, and coaching), but this is not specified in the objective. Rather, objectives are used as the basis for determining which methods should be used to achieve the specified outcome.

As we have stated, objectives are essential to a successful training or HRD program. In addition to forming the basis for selecting the program content and methods, objectives are used by the organization to evaluate the program's success, and they also help participants to focus their own attention and efforts during the program (Mager, 1984). In short, objectives tell you where the program is going and how to know when you have gotten there.

Needs assessment data are useful for defining program objectives because they identify the deficiency or challenge to be addressed. For example, suppose the needs analysis data for a brokerage firm show that traders are insensitive to clients' fears and concerns. A training program can be designed that will increase the brokers' sensitivity to and support of their clients. The objectives of this program will be determined by the specific deficiencies, client preferences and concerns, and other factors identified in the needs analysis.

Mager (1984) states that useful objectives describe the **performance** the learners (trainees) should be able to do, the **conditions** under which they must do it, and the **criteria** (how well they must do it) used in judging its success (see Table 5-1).

Some examples of useful program objectives include the following:

- Run one mile in seven minutes or less.

- Identify (by circling) all items in a packing list that have not been included in the shipment.

- Using the standard equipment, draw 10 cc of blood from a patient's arm in two tries (using any member of the class).

- Using the information found on a complete loan application, identify (in writing) whether a client meets the bank's criteria for an acceptable auto loan candidate.

- Accurately recite the company's anti-discrimination policy.

Program objectives that lack the performance, conditions, and criteria are often ambiguous and result in frustration and conflict between those who interpret the objectives differently. Two ways to ensure that objectives are clear are to choose words carefully and have the objectives reviewed by others (like managers and potential participants). If a reviewer is confused, the objectives should be revised.

Writing trainee objectives for behaviors that can be directly observed by others (like giving a patient an injection or performing the Heimlich maneuver to aid a choking victim) can be easier than writing objectives for behaviors that are unobservable (like judging whether a painting is of high quality or determining whether use of deadly force is warranted). It is necessary to specify observable behaviors that indicate an unobservable outcome is achieved (Mager, 1984). Thus, an objective for judging whether a painting is of high quality, can be written as "to be able to judge whether a painting is of high quality by orally listing the characteristics the painting possesses that indicate its quality."

Mager (1984) notes that simply presenting trainees with objectives for learning or performance may be enough to elicit the desired behavior. Many people do not meet performance expectations because they were never clearly told what the expectations were or how they were supposed to meet them. Clear objectives provide this information and represent the organization's expectations, which can play a key role in employee performance.

TABLE 5-1	THE QUALITIES OF USEFUL OBJECTIVES
Performance	An objective always says what a learner is expected to be able to do; the objective sometimes describes the product or result of the doing.
Conditions	An objective always describes the important conditions (if any) under which the performance is to occur.
Criteria	Wherever possible, an objective identifies the criteria of acceptable performance by describing how well the learner must perform in order to be considered acceptable.

SOURCE: From *Preparing Instructional Objectives* (2nd ed., p. 21) by R. F. Mager, 1984, Belmont, CA: Pitman Learning. Reprinted by permission.

Writing objectives is a challenging but essential aspect of effective HRD. Table 5-2 provides a list of the main issues that Mager (1984) argues are essential to consider when writing useful program objectives.

Purchasing HRD Programs

After the supervisor or HRD professional has identified the program objectives, a series of decisions must be made regarding the development and delivery of the program. One of those decisions is whether to design the program internally or purchase it (or portions of it) from other sources. Services available through outside vendors include:

- Assistance with conducting needs analysis

- Guidance for internal staff to design and implement a program

- A program specially designed for the organization

- Supplemental training materials (exercises, workbooks, computer software, videos)

- A previously designed program

- A train-the-trainer program to build instructional skills of internal content experts (Carnevale et al., 1990)

TABLE 5-2	GUIDELINES FOR DEVELOPING USEFUL OBJECTIVES

1. An objective is a collection of words, symbols, and/or pictures describing one of your important intents.

2. An objective will communicate your intent to the degree that you describe: what the learner will be **doing** when demonstrating achievement of the objective, the important conditions of the doing, and the criteria by which achievement will be judged.

3. To prepare a useful objective, continue to modify a draft until these questions are answered:
   - What do I want trainees to be able to do?
   - What are the important conditions or constraints under which I want them to perform?
   - How well must trainees perform for me to be satisfied?

4. Write a separate statement for each important outcome or intent; write as many as you need to communicate your intents.

5. If you give your written objectives to your trainees, you may not have to do much else. Why? Because often employees are already able to do what you are asking them to do and will be happy to demonstrate their ability, now that they know what is wanted of them.

SOURCE: From *Preparing Instructional Objectives* (2nd ed., p. 87) by R. F. Mager, 1984, Belmont, CA: Pitman Learning. Reprinted by permission.

There are many sources of HRD programs, materials, and advice, and their number is growing. Many consulting firms, educational institutions, professional societies, trade unions, publishing houses, governmental agencies, and non-profit community-based organizations offer training programs and information to interested organizations.

Table 5-3 lists a number of factors that should be considered when making a purchase decision. For example, suppose a small manufacturer plans to computerize its billing operation. Given the nature of the training needed, it is likely that the firm's management would contract with an outside vendor because (1) the firm would probably not have the expertise to design the program in-house; (2) management would not likely have the time to design the training program; and (3) it is not likely that the firm has an HRD department.

Other factors that may influence an organization's decisions include personal contacts or past experience with an outside vendor, geographical proximity to the vendor, local economic conditions, and the presence of government incentives to conduct training (Carnevale et al., 1990).

Once an organization decides to purchase a program or part of a program from a vendor, a vendor must be chosen. One rational way to do this is to determine the match between the vendor's product or capability with the organization's needs and objectives. The criteria for these decisions vary among organizations, but in general they include:

TABLE 5-3	FACTORS TO CONSIDER BEFORE A TRAINING PURCHASE
Expertise	When an organization lacks specialized KSAs needed to design and implement a training program.
Timeliness	When it is more timely to hire an agency to facilitate the process.
Number of Trainees	Generally, the larger the number of trainees the greater the likelihood the organization would be willing to design the program itself. Thus, for just a few trainees the HRD department would send them to an outside training agency.
Subject Matter	If the subject matter is sensitive or proprietary the HRD department would conduct the program in-house using employees as trainers.
Cost	The HRD department always considers cost, but only in concert with other factors.
Size of HRD	The size of the HRD department is important for assessing the capacity to design, conduct, and/or implement skills training as opposed to using an outside agency.
"X" Factor	Some other extraneous conditions that would make it preferable that an outside agency be used to conduct the skills training.

SOURCE: From *Training Partnerships: Linking Employers and Providers* (p. 6) by A. P. Carnevale, L. J. Gainer, J. Villet, and S. L. Holland, 1990, Alexandria, VA: American Society for Training and Development. Adapted by permission.

1. **Cost:** Price relative to program content and quality

2. **Credentials:** Including certificates, degrees, and other documentation of expertise

3. **Background:** Number of years in business and experience in the particular content area

4. **Experience:** Vendor's prior clients, success with those clients, references

5. **Philosophy:** Comparison to the organization's philosophy

6. **Delivery Method:** Training methods and techniques used

7. **Content:** Topics included in program or materials

8. **Actual Product:** Including appearance, samples, pilot program available

9. **Results:** Expected outcomes

10. **Support:** Especially in terms of implementation and follow-up

11. **Request for Proposal:** Match between vendors offer and request the organization made for a proposal (Carnevale et al., 1990)

Some of these factors will carry greater weight with particular managers. For example, some managers want to only work with the "best" providers, so they may weigh the vendor's experience and client list more heavily. Other managers may be swayed by "star power," as evidenced by the vendor's identity as a leading expert (like Joseph Juran or W. Edwards Deming for quality improvement) or the presence of a movie or TV star in the vendor's films and videos (actor and former Monty Python member John Cleese appears in a series of widely used training films).

In summary, outside training vendors offer organizations a wide choice of options in designing and developing training and HRD programs. These programs represent viable options when organizations have a small HRD function, a small number of trainees, and when program content has no proprietary value. Even large organizations that have well-respected training functions make regular use of outside vendors for a variety of HRD programs. Large or small, when organizations elect to go outside to purchase training services and programs, they should first conduct a needs assessment so that they can make an informed decision.

Selecting the Trainer

Once the organization has made a decision to design its own training program, a trainer must be selected. Selecting a trainer can be a fairly easy process when an organization has a large, multifaceted training staff with the competencies and subject-matter expertise to train in high demand areas. **Training competency** involves the knowledge and varied skills needed to design and implement a training program. Effective trainers must be able to communicate their knowledge clearly, use various instructional techniques, have good interpersonal skills, and have the ability to motivate others to learn.

Subject-matter expertise refers to the mastery of the subject matter. However, subject-matter expertise alone does not guarantee that an individual will be an effective trainer—many experts (including some college professors, we are sad to say) make poor trainers.

And yet, trainers who lack subject-matter expertise may rely too heavily on a textbook or other training materials, and not be able to explain important concepts and/or how these are applied to the job. Besides contracting with an outside vendor, less qualified trainers can be aided through:

1. **Teaming** skilled trainers with in-house subject-matter experts to form an instructional team.

2. **Train-the-trainer programs,** which involve identifying in-house content experts who lack training skills and training them to become effective trainers.

3. **Using a training technique that does not require a human trainer,** such as programmed instruction or computer-aided instruction programs (this option will be discussed later in the chapter).

Ideally, then, a subject-matter expert (SME) should have the ability to train others. Those who lack the ability to design and implement effective training programs may rely too heavily on a single method of instruction that may be inappropriate to the subject matter (like using a lecture format to train employees in CPR and other first aid techniques) or may lack the interpersonal skills to effectively interact with or motivate participants. To resolve this, organizations have designed train-the-training programs to help SMEs to develop the necessary skills to train others.

Train-the-Trainer Programs

The purpose of train-the-trainer programs is to provide SMEs with the necessary knowledge and skills to design and implement a training program. Train-the-trainer programs are available through local professional associations, colleges, and consultants. These programs range from instruction in a single training technique (e.g., behavior modeling) to a comprehensive program on how to design a training program. The latter would present several training methods and techniques with an emphasis on how each can be used to maximize learning in different situations. Some training providers, such as Development Dimensions International (DDI), conduct train-the-trainer programs in which their client's employees become certified by the consulting firm to present their programs to the organization.

Some organizations elect to design their own train-the-trainer programs, which are desirable when there is a constant demand for skilled or technical trainers, or when employers want to emphasize some training technique. These programs should focus on many of the issues discussed in this chapter, including:

1. Developing trainee objectives and lesson plans;

2. Selecting and preparing training materials;

3. Selecting and using training aids (like videos, overhead projectors, and so on); and

4. Selecting and using different training methods and techniques.

When it is not possible to design a train-the-training program, some organizations have developed training manuals that include these various components of the design and implementation process. Manuals can be valuable when there are insufficient numbers of SMEs to warrant a train-the-training program or when the potential trainers are in different geographical areas.

Thus, the selection of the trainer is an important decision to the HRD effort. A competently designed program that has the potential to address a significant organizational need can be a failure if delivered by an incompetent, unmotivated, or disinterested trainer.

Preparing a Lesson Plan

Program objectives are necessary for pinpointing desired outcomes of a training or HRD program, but these statements alone are insufficient for determining the content of the training program (training methods, techniques, and materials). To translate program objectives into an executable training session, the development of a **lesson plan** is recommended.

A lesson plan is a guide for the actual delivery of the training content. Creating a lesson plan requires the trainer to determine in advance what is to be covered and how much time to devote to each part of the session. Gilley and Eggland (1989) suggest that a lesson plan should specify:

- Content to be covered

- Sequencing of activities

- Selection or design of training media

- Selection and/or development of experiential exercises

- Timing and planning of each activity

- Selection of the method of instruction to be used

- Number and type of evaluation items

Some organizations, as stated in Chapter 1, have program designers whose responsibilities may include defining training objectives and developing lesson plans. This kind of assistance is particularly important for subject-matter experts who have limited training skills. Some organizations include a section on lesson planning in their train-the-trainer programs.

In order to assist trainers, we suggest using a standardized lesson plan form like the one in Figure 5-2. Figure 5-3 shows a completed lesson plan for a training program on the topic of adult learning. As can be seen in the example, the lesson plan serves as a blueprint for conducting the whole training session.

Selecting Training Methods

Up to this point we have discussed some preliminary steps involved in the design and implementation of a training program. The next step in the training process is to select the appropriate training methods. Training methods are numerous and varied, ranging from lectures and role-plays to videos, films, and business games. A 1992 survey conducted by *Training* magazine (see Figure 5-4) revealed that videos were the most often used medium for delivering training materials.

In general, training methods can be grouped into two broad categories: on-the-job methods, which typically occur in the employee's normal work setting, and classroom methods, which typically take place away from the job (such as a conference room or lecture hall). This categorization is not definitive, however—some training methods have multiple uses, such as computer-based training that can be implemented using a computer at the employee's desk or work station, in a company classroom, or even at the employee's home. Table 5-4 (page 138) lists the on-the-job and classroom training methods that we will discuss in this chapter. Other training methods used for particular audiences (such as mentoring for management development) will be discussed in future chapters.

On-the-Job Training (OJT) Methods

On-the-job training (OJT) involves conducting training at the trainee's regular work station (desk, machine, and so on). This is the most common form of training; most employees receive at least some training and coaching on the job. Virtually any type of one-on-one instruction between co-workers or between the employee and supervisor can be classified as OJT. However, much of this training is conducted informally, without advance planning or careful thought.

Formal OJT programs are generally conducted by an assigned trainer who is recognized, rewarded, and trained in correct instructional techniques. Formal OJT has two distinct advantages over classroom training. First, OJT facilitates the transfer of learning to do the job because the trainee has an immediate opportunity to practice the work tasks on the job. Transfer of learning is enhanced because the learning environment is the same as the performance environment

FIGURE 5-2	A LESSON PLAN FORM

Organization: _____ Date: _____

Department: _____ Lesson Plan No. _____

Title of Lesson Plan: _____

Instructor(s): _____ Time Allocation: _____
_____

Trainees: _____

Where: _____

Training Objectives:

Classroom Requirements:

Training Aids and Equipment:

Trainee Supplies:

Trainee Handouts:

References:

  Instructor:

SOURCE: From *Human Resource Development: The New Trainer's Guide* (2nd ed., p. 45) by L. Donaldson and E. E. Scannell, 1986, Reading, MA: Addison-Wesley. Reprinted by permission.

FIGURE 5-3   A COMPLETED LESSON PLAN, PAGE 1

Organization: <u>ASTD Natl. Conference</u>   Date: <u>May 23, 1993</u>

Department: <u>Training Competencies</u>   Lesson Plan No. <u>1</u>

Title of Lesson Plan: <u>"Adult Learning? You've Got to Be Kidding!"</u>

Instructor(s): <u>Edward E. Scannell</u>   Time Allocation: <u>90 minutes</u>

Audience: <u>Relatively New Trainers</u>

Where: <u>Anaheim (CA) Convention Center, Santa Ana Room</u>

Training Objectives:
1. To contrast 3–4 concepts of pedagogy vs. andragogy.
2. To identify at least three theories of adult learning.
3. To demonstrate several applications of learning principles.
4. To differentiate the "All-Star" from the "Falling-Star" Trainer.
5. To list at least six traits of the All-Star Trainer.

Classroom Requirements: 350 chairs (see attached diagram)
          12′ x 16′ raised platform
          lectern

Training Aids and Equipment: Lavalier microphone
           Overhead projector
           16mm
           12′ x 12′ screen
  NOTE: Session will be videotaped by ASTD

Trainee Supplies: Pens and pencils

Trainee Handouts: "What Every Trainer Should Know About Training"
        "All-Star Trainer"
        "Seven Steps to Better Training"

References: <u>Human Resource Development.</u> (Donaldson-Scannell).

     <u>Games Trainers Play.</u> (Newstrom-Scannell).

Continued on next page

SOURCE: From *Human Resource Development: The New Trainer's Guide* (2nd ed., pp. 47–48) by L. Donaldson and E. E. Scannell, 1986, Reading, MA: Addison-Wesley. Reprinted by permission.

Figure 5-3—*Continued*   **TOPIC** _____ **"ADULT LEARNING? . . . " Page 2**

TIME	CONTENT	NOTES	A.V.
3:00 p.m.	I. Speaker Intro	See Data Sheet	
3:02 p.m.	II. Introduction & Overview A. Game Plan B. Objectives 1. Pedagogy vs. Andragogy 2. Theories 3. "All-Star" 4. Practicality	Free Speech Story	Transparency 1
3:05 p.m.	III. Climate Setting A. Your Goals Today B. Learning Can Be Fun C. Quick Group Intros D. Feedback	Group Activity "Why Here?" *Meet 3–4 new people *Call on 2–3 groups	Transparency 2
3:10 p.m.	IV. Adult Learning A. Andragogy-Pedagogy 1. Resentment 2. Experience 3. Readiness 4. Problem-Centered	*Not "Spectator Sport" *Knowles *Not Kids *Fire Truck Story *Real World	Transparency 3
3:15 p.m.	B. Domains 1. Cognitive 2. Psychomotor 3. Affective	*Motivation Story	Transparency 4
3:20 p.m.	C. Levels of Learning 1. Unc. Incmptnt. 2. Con. Incmptnt. 3. Con. Cmptnt. 4. Unc. Cmptnt. D. Laws of Learning 1. Effect	*"Dumb Thing" Anecdote *Dumb but don't know it *Dumb but you know it! *You know that you know *Expert, Habit, etc. **Handout Sheet 1** Introduce Muppet Clip *"People learn best . . . " *Lord Chesterfield *Group Activity (1 minute) *Use of color	Transparency 5 16mm Projector Film Clip 1 (Muppets) (3 min., 20 sec.)
3:55 p.m.	2. Exercise	*John Dewey *Learn by doing *Hand-to-chin exercise	

FIGURE 5-4   PERCENT OF ORGANIZATIONS USING VARIOUS METHODS FOR EMPLOYEE TRAINING

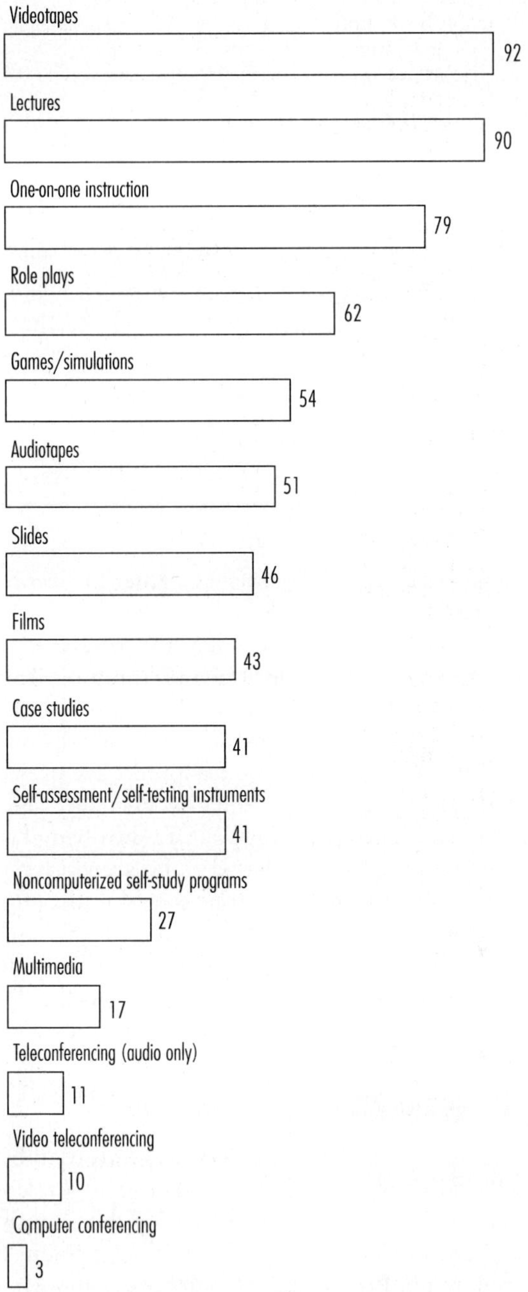

Videotapes

92

Lectures

90

One-on-one instruction

79

Role plays

62

Games/simulations

54

Audiotapes

51

Slides

46

Films

43

Case studies

41

Self-assessment/self-testing instruments

41

Noncomputerized self-study programs

27

Multimedia

17

Teleconferencing (audio only)

11

Video teleconferencing

10

Computer conferencing

3

SOURCE: From "What Employers Teach" by B. Filipczak, 1992, *Training, 29*(10), p. 46. Reprinted by permission.

TABLE 5-4	TRAINING METHODS AND TECHNIQUES

Methods	Techniques
On-the-job training	Job instruction training
	Job rotation
	Coaching
	Mentoring
Classroom	Lecture
	Conference/Discussion
	Audiovisual
	static media (e.g., books)
	dynamic media (e.g., film/video)
	telecommunication (e.g., satellite transmission)
	Experiential techniques
	case study
	business games
	role-play
	behavioral modeling
	Computer-based training
	computer-aided instruction
	intelligent computer-aided instruction

(see our earlier discussion of physical fidelity in Chapter 2). Second, OJT reduces training costs because no training facilities are needed.

There are several limitations to OJT. First, the job site may have physical constraints, noise, and other distractions that could inhibit learning. Many of these cannot be changed because of the nature of the job. Second, using expensive equipment for training can result in costly damage and disruption of the production schedule. Third, using OJT while customers are present may lead to customer inconvenience and a temporary reduction in quality of service while the employee is being trained. Fourth, and finally, OJT involving heavy equipment or chemicals may threaten the safety of others who are working in close proximity. Precautions should be taken by the trainer to minimize the potential for these four problem areas.

There are at least four identifiable OJT techniques including job instruction training (JIT), job rotation, coaching, and mentoring. We will focus on JIT and job rotation now, and discuss coaching and mentoring in later chapters.

Job Instruction Training (JIT)

JIT is defined as a sequence of instructional procedures used by the trainer to train employees while they work in their assigned job. The content of a JIT program is distinguished by its simplicity. Table 5-5 details a simple four-step process that helps the trainer to prepare the worker, present the task, allow practice time, and follow-up. **Preparing the workers** is important because they need to know what to expect. Preparation may include providing a training manual, handouts, or other training aids which can be used as a reference. **Present-**

TABLE 5-5	JOB INSTRUCTION TRAINING

Step 1: Prepare the Worker

a. Put trainee at ease
b. Find out what trainee knows
c. Motivate
d. Set up the task

Step 2: Present the Task

a. Tell
b. Show
c. Explain
d. Demonstrate

Step 3: Practicing

a. Have trainee perform the task(s)
b. Have trainee explain the steps
c. Give feedback on performance
d. Reinforce correct behavior

Step 4: Follow-up

a. Have trainee perform on his or her own
b. Encourage questioning
c. Check performance periodically
d. Gradually taper off training

SOURCE: From *Developing and Training Human Resources in Organizations* (p. 109) by K. N. Wexley and G. P. Latham, 1981, Glenview, IL: Scott, Foresman. Adapted by permission.

ing the task should be carried out in such a way that the trainee understands and can replicate the task. Some trainers demonstrate the task before asking the trainee to repeat the process. **Practice time** is important for the trainee to master a particular set of skills. Finally, the trainer needs to conduct a **follow-up** as a way of ensuring that the trainee is making progress. During this follow-up session the trainer should apply coaching techniques when appropriate (see the discussion on coaching in Chapter 8).

The success of JIT depends on the ability of the trainer to adapt his or her own style to the training process. The trainer, particularly if this person is the trainee's co-worker or supervisor, should have an opportunity to assess the trainee's needs before beginning the training. If the training material is too difficult or too easy, the OJT trainer should adjust the material or techniques to fit the needs of the trainee.

Job Rotation

So far we have discussed techniques that are intended to develop job-related skills. Job rotation is similar in intent, but the trainee is expected to learn more while observing and doing, rather than learning through instruction. Rotation, as the term implies, involves a series of assignments to different positions or departments for a specified period of time. During this assignment, the trainee is supervised by a department employee, usually a supervisor, who is responsible for orienting, training, and evaluating the trainee. Throughout the training cycle, the trainee is expected to learn about how each department functions, including some key roles, policies, and procedures. At the end of the cycle, the accumulated evaluations will be used to determine the preparedness of the trainee and if and where the person will be permanently assigned.

Job rotation is frequently used for first-level management training, particularly for new employees. When this technique is used, it is generally assumed that new managers need to develop a working knowledge of the organization before they can be successful managers. (Chapter 13 will discuss this technique in further detail.)

Two other forms of on-the-job training, coaching and mentoring, also involve one-on-one instruction. Coaching occurs between the employee and their supervisor, and focuses on examining employee performance and taking actions to maintain effective performance and correct performance problems. In mentoring, a senior manager is paired with a more junior employee for the purpose of supporting the employee, helping the employee to learn the ropes, and preparing the employee for increasing responsibility. Each of these techniques will be discussed in later chapters (coaching in Chapter 9 and mentoring in Chapter 11).

Classroom Training Methods

We define classroom training methods as those conducted outside of the work setting. In this sense, a classroom can be any training space set away from the work site, such as the company cafeteria or a meeting room. While many organizations capitalize on whatever usable space they have available to conduct training sessions, some larger organizations (including McDonald's, Motorola, Dunkin' Donuts, and Pillsbury) maintain facilities that serve as freestanding training centers. These training centers operate as a company college (McDonald's refers to its center as "Hamburger U."), with curricula that include courses covering a wide range of skill and content areas.

Conducting training away from the work setting has several advantages over on-the-job training. First, classroom settings permit the use of a variety of training techniques, such as video, lecture, discussion, role playing, and simulation. Second, the environment can be designed and/or controlled to minimize distractions and create a climate conducive to learning. Third, classroom settings can accommodate larger numbers of trainees than the typical on-the-job setting, allowing for more efficient delivery of training. Two potential disadvantages of classroom methods, as a group, include increased costs (such as travel and the rental or purchase and maintenance of rooms and equipment) and dissimilarity to the job setting, making transfer of training more difficult.

Five primary types of classroom training include:

1. Lecture

2. Discussion

3.   Audiovisual methods

4.   Experiential methods

5.   Computer-based training

The Lecture Method

The **lecture** method involves the oral presentation of information by a subject matter expert to a group of listeners. The lecture is one of the most popular training techniques, used in 90 percent of organizations and second only to videos in reported use (Filipczak, 1992). One of the reasons the lecture method is so popular is that it is an efficient way of transmitting factual information to a large audience in a relatively short amount of time. When used in conjunction with visual aids, such as charts, maps, and handouts, the lecture can be an effective way to facilitate the transfer of theories, concepts, procedures, and other factual material.

However, the lecture method has been widely criticized, particularly because the lecture is a one-way communication. Korman (1971) suggests that the lecture method perpetuates the traditional authority structure of organizations, thus promoting negative behavior (such as passivity and boredom), and is poorly suited for facilitating transfer of training and individualizing training. Similarly, Bass and Vaughn (1966) state that while a skilled lecturer could effectively communicate conceptual knowledge to trainees who were prepared to receive it, the lecture had little value in facilitating attitudinal and behavioral change. They imply that the trainee must be motivated to learn, since the method does not allow for eliciting audience responses.

A related disadvantage of the lecture method is the lack of sharing of ideas between and among the trainees. Without dialogue, the trainees may not be able to put things into a common perspective that makes sense to them. Also, many people claim to dislike the lecture method. A survey of training directors conducted by Carroll, Paine, and Ivancevich (1972) showed the lecture was ranked ninth out of nine preferred training methods for acquisition of knowledge. A more recent survey reported only 17 percent of respondents (members of a regional ASTD chapter) believed the lecture method was effective (Cohen, 1990).

Recent research, however, does not support this harsh judgment. For example, a meta-analysis by Burke and Day (1986) found positive learning effects from the lecture method, both alone and in combination with other methods, such as discussion and role playing. In a recent study, Early (1987) found role playing and lecture to be equally effective in a skills training course. Could it be that people just don't like to sit through lectures, even though they can and do learn from them?

The results cited above suggest that research is needed to identify the conditions under which the lecture method is effective as well as ways to improve its effectiveness. In the meantime, two points seem clear. First, it is probably safe to say that interesting lectures are more likely to promote learning than dull lectures. Therefore, trainers should make every effort to make the lectures more interesting. Second, there are likely to be advantages to supplementing the lecture with other methods (including discussion, video, and role playing), particularly when abstract or procedural material is to be presented. These combinations can increase two-way communication and facilitate greater interaction with the material.

The Discussion Method

The **discussion method** involves two-way communication between the trainer and trainees, and among trainees. Because active participation is encouraged, the discussion method offers trainees an opportunity for feedback, clarification, and sharing points of view. Given this dynamic, the discussion technique may overcome some of the limitations of the lecture.

The success of this method is dependent upon the ability of the trainer to initiate and manage class discussion by asking one or more of the following types of questions:

- **Open-ended questions** can be used to challenge the trainees to increase their understanding of a specific topic.

- **Direct questions** can be used to illustrate or produce a very narrow response.

- **Reflective questions** can be used to mirror what someone else has said to make sure the message was received as intended.

Managing discussion goes beyond questioning participants. The trainer must ensure that trainees are reinforced for their responses. The trainer must also act as a gatekeeper, giving everyone an opportunity to express their point of view and not letting the discussion be dominated by a few vocal participants. Managing discussion in large training classes (30 or more trainees) can be difficult. Not only are the opportunities for an individual to participate reduced in a large group, some participants may feel intimidated and be reluctant to get involved. Dividing a large class into smaller discussion groups, which can then share their ideas with other groups, can increase the opportunity for discussion.

There are several limitations of the discussion method. First, a skilled facilitator is needed to manage the discussion process. Second, sufficient time must be available for meaningful discussion to take place. Third, trainees need to have a common reference point for meaningful discussion to occur. Assigning reading material prior to the discussion session can help overcome this obstacle.

Audiovisual Methods

Both the lecture and discussion methods are limited in their ability to adequately portray dynamic and complex events. Audiovisual methods take advantage of various media to illustrate or demonstrate the training material. Audiovisual media can bring complex events to life by showing and describing details that are often difficult to communicate in other ways. For purposes of this chapter (and following Kearsley, 1984), we will categorize audiovisual methods into three groups: static media, dynamic media, and telecommunications.

Static Media Typically involving fixed illustrations that use both words and images, static media include printed materials, slides, and overhead transparencies. **Printed materials,** such as handouts, guides, reference books, and textbooks, allow trainees to keep the material, referring to it before, during, and after the training session. (Some issues involved in selecting and preparing printed materials will be discussed later in this chapter.) **Slides** are often used in ways similar to printed materials, but by projecting a computer or camera-generated image onto a screen, they can serve as a common focus for discussion. Slides can also be synchronized with audiotapes to form a standardized presentation. Such a set-up can be delivered without using a skilled trainer; at a minimum, someone is needed to operate and monitor the equipment (slide projector and tape player). **Overhead transparencies** also allow the trainer to project printed materials or other images on a screen. Transparencies can be more flexible than slides because the trainer can also write on the transparency sheets, turning the screen into a sort of chalkboard. (See Table 5-6 for effective transparencies guidelines.)

Dynamic Media Techniques that present dynamic sequences of events are considered dynamic media and include audiotape and discs, film, videotape, and videodisc. Videos are now the most commonly used training technique. As we saw in Figure 5-4, Filipczak (1992) reports that 92 percent of organizations surveyed use videos for employee training. Films and audiotapes are also widely used (by 44 and 51 percent of organizations surveyed). Organizations as diverse as Taco Bell and New England Mutual Insurance are taking advantage of the ease with which videotaped training programs can be sent to employees around the country. There are literally thousands of commercially produced films and videos

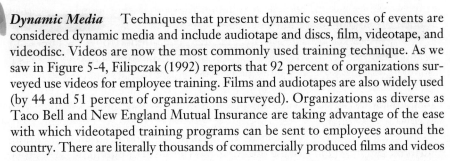

TABLE 5-6	OVERHEAD TRANSPARENCY GUIDELINES

Preparation

1. Present one major idea or concept on each transparency.
2. Use only a few key words or phrases. (Less than 6 words per line and 6 lines per sheet.)
3. Make sure letters and graphics are large and legible.
4. Are your overheads interesting? (Use color, different type styles, and graphics.)

Presentation

5. Start with an outline.
6. Emphasize information by pointing.
7. Control the pace by progressive disclosure.
8. Turn projector off to make a verbal point.
9. Use two projectors for increased effect.
10. Obtain group involvement by writing on a blank transparency.

SOURCE: From *Training and Technology* (p. 19) by G. Kearsley, 1984, Reading, MA: Addison-Wesley Publishing Co. Reprinted by permission.

available to HRD professionals through film libraries, professional societies, and retail outlets. In addition, many organizations are able to produce their own videos at relatively low cost. For example, Southwest Airlines produced a nine minute "rap" music video that introduces employees to work procedures and all aspects of the company's operations, while at the same time conveying the team spirit and fun oriented culture that typifies the company. The Travelers, a Hartford based insurance company, maintains a $20 million education center, which produces videos and transmits satellite broadcasts of training programs throughout the company (Eurich, 1990). Entire training programs can be self-contained within a single film or video presentation.

An effective film or video takes advantage of the capabilities of the medium rather than simply reproducing a printed or static presentation. Unfortunately, many videos are indeed simple reproductions of traditional lectures. However, producing an effective training video is not as simple as owning the equipment and having the desire to be the company's Steven Spielberg. Film and video development involves many activities, including design (like storyboarding), pre-production (including scheduling, casting, crew and equipment selection, prop and set preparation), shooting the film/video, post-production (including editing and sound mixing), and distribution (Kearsley, 1984). The inexperienced HRD staffer would be wise to consult a trained professional to produce (or assist in producing) company films and videos.

Many argue that the baby boom and later generations, who grew up watching films and television, may actually prefer this form of presentation. Yet one potential limitation of this technique is that trainers may rely too much on the film or video and less on the training content. Such reliance can lead to complacency among trainees who view the films and videos as entertainment rather than opportunities to learn.

Videotape is also used as a visual aid for behavior modification by recording actual role plays and then asking the group to critique their experience while they watch the video. For example, a sales training program may include a videotaping segment so that trainees can observe themselves performing an in-class exercise on how to close a sale. This also provides an opportunity for the trainer to reinforce preferred behavior. One potential limitation of this technique is that trainees may feel intimidated by the camera and may even resent the process. To offset this limitation, the trainer must be supportive and create a "safe" environment during the program.

Telecommunication   The transmission of training programs to different locations via telecommunication is now possible with the advent of satellite, microwave, cable (CATV), and fiberoptic networks. Linking several locations together for instructional and conference purposes, known as **instructional television (ITV),** allows entire courses to be televised. For example, eighteen universities collaborated on a program called Mind Extension University that will offer the final two years of a baccalaureate degree "with courses delivered entirely by cable television and satellite" (Watkins, 1991, p. A18). The National Technological University (NTU) network also offers interactive, satellite transmitted continuing-education courses to engineers and computer scientists in companies like IBM, General Electric, and Hewlett Packard (Stackel, 1988).

Telecommunication technology also allows organizations to conduct conferences between remote locations. This technique, known as **teleconferencing**, is being used by organizations such as JCPenney, IBM, AT&T, Domino's Pizza, and Texas Instruments. JCPenney also sells this service to other organizations (Eurich, 1990). Colleges and universities are also taking advantage of this technique, to benefit both their students and their corporate clients. Teleconferencing helps organizations to reduce trainer, travel, and facility costs, and increases the availability of training to remote locations (Lowenthal & Jankowski, 1983; Bove, 1984). The *Training* magazine survey shown in Figure 5-4 also revealed that about 10 percent of organizations use video teleconferencing, 11 percent use audioconferencing, and 3 percent use computer conferencing for employee training (Filipczak, 1992). The North Carolina Office of Day Care Services conducted a study comparing the average cost of traditional classroom training with teleconferencing. They concluded that while teleconferencing cost more for curriculum and materials development, traditional classroom training cost more for trainer, travel, and delivery—but both methods are considered to be equally effective (Berdiansky, 1985). One issue that merits further research concerns the extent to which teleconferencing affects the interaction between the trainer and trainees (Wittock, 1986).

Computer conferencing is currently among the least used training techniques. However, given the availability of personal computers and terminals that are being linked into company communication networks and "public" networks such as INTERNET, this is predicted to change. Also, while most organizations use communication networks primarily for business operations, they have an unlimited potential as training vehicles. Eurich (1990) suggests that computer networks be used to train adults nationwide, although start-up cost of hardware and the low level of reading and writing skills may keep some low income and other potential learners from benefitting from such a system.

Studies have consistently shown that audiovisual training methods like film, television, and teleconferencing are more effective than other methods (primarily lecture) (Schramm, 1962; Chu & Schramm, 1967; Berdiansky, 1985). Table 5-7 lists some of the advantages and disadvantages of various audiovisual methods for training.

Given the choices available, HRD professionals must select the most appropriate audiovisual method for each particular HRD program. Kearsley (1984, p. 145) reviewed a group of models and found that all stress these five directions for media selection:

1. Identify the media attributes required by the conditions, performance or standards of each instructional objective.

2. Identify student characteristics that suggest or preclude particular media.

3. Identify characteristics of the learning environment that favor or preclude particular media.

TABLE 5-7 EVALUATION OF VARIOUS AUDIOVISUAL TRAINING METHODS

		Content	Presentation and Participation	Audience and Scheduling	Cost
Television Broadcast	**Effective uses:**	Uniform material ensures consistent training	Lecture by teacher with other experts Graphics and visuals; informative clips	Unlimited audience; reaches widely scattered employees	
	Limitations:		Presentation static Passive; no interaction	Time limited to viewing schedule	Costs can be high for production and broadcast time
Videotape *Same as television with these differences:*	**Effective uses:**	Can be reviewed in whole or part	Stop and replay	Use at any time with television and videocassette recorder	Cost lowers with reuse and mail distribution
	Limitations:				May be less expensive to produce, but depends on quality
Tutored Video Instruction *Same as video-based instruction with these additions:*	**Effective uses:**	Subject review with tutor, particularly for students with poor language skills	Student interaction Encourages discussion	Adaptable for diverse groups of students Permits flexible scheduling	
	Limitations:		Requires presence of tutor or facilitator and meeting site Group must not be large Not effective for single student		

Videoconference				
Effective uses:	Can use time-sensitive materials; but also many subjects	Lecture or panel discussion Graphics, etc. optional Some interaction allowed via telephone links	Wide distribution	
Limitations:		Interaction limited by group size and time element Rather passive	Broadcast time inflexible	Expensive for small group Requires equipment; if satellite used, receiver sites needed
Audiographic Conference				
Effective uses:	Useful to teach problem solving, also trouble-shooting skills and maintenance procedures	Participants can speak and demonstrate via display screens Complex graphics can be prepared and used interactively	Covers wide geographic area Long-distance telephone data communication	
Limitations:		Small number of persons per session is best	Limited by real-time frame	Equipment expensive: student needs telephone-computer hook-up
Computer Conference				
Effective uses:	Suitable for wide variety of subjects, including problem solving and discussion	Completely interactive via personal computer and telephone; intense interaction common	Serves geographically dispersed persons Crosses national boundaries There is time to consider response Free of time limitations	
Limitations:		No voice or visual contact	Psychological barriers to computers and to working alone May be delay in response	

SOURCE: From *The Learning Industry: Education for Adult Workers* (p. 40) by N.P. Eurich, 1990, Lawrenceville, N.J.: Princeton University Press. Reprinted by permission.

4.   Identify practical considerations that may determine which media are feasible.

5.   Identify economic or organizational factors that may determine which media are feasible.

This list includes both learning-related and practical considerations. Readers who want to know more about these various audiovisual methods and how to select among them would do well to consult Kearsley (1984) and Romiszowski (1988).

Experiential Methods

So far, we have discussed training methods that focus primarily on presentation of training content. In many of these methods, such as video and lecture, the learner is generally assumed to be a passive (or somewhat passive) recipient of information. Experiential learning advocates, such as David Kolb (see Chapter 3), argue that effective learning requires active engagement on the part of the learner. Keys and Wolfe (1988) summarize this point of view as follows:

> Experientialists believe that effective learning is an active experience that challenges the skills, knowledge, and beliefs of participants. This is accomplished by creating a contrived, yet realistic, environment that is both challenging and psychologically safe for the participant to investigate and to employ new concepts, skills, and behaviors. Experiential instructors recognize that learners bring to the learning environment a set of accumulated knowledges and learning methods that are simultaneously functional and/or dysfunctional depending on the learning situation (p. 214).

Experiential training methods commonly used in organizations include case studies, games and simulations, role playing, and behavior modeling. Each of these methods is described below.

The Case Study Method   One way to help trainees learn analytical and problem solving skills is by presenting a story (called a case) about people in an organization who are facing a problem or decision. Cases may be based on actual events involving real people in an organization, or they can be completely fictional. Case studies are typically included in college textbooks in management, public administration, law, and similar subjects.

While cases vary in complexity and detail, trainees should be given enough information to analyze the situation and recommend their own solutions. In solving the problem the trainees are generally required to use a rational problem solving process that includes:

1.   Restating important facts;

2.   Drawing inferences from the facts;

3. Stating the problem(s);

4. Developing alternative solutions and then stating the consequences of each; and

5. Determining and supporting a course of action.

Cases can be studied by individuals or small groups, with the completed analysis and solutions being presented by the trainees to the rest of the class. According to the survey in Figure 5-4, the case study method is used in about 41 percent of organizations for employee and management training (Filipczak, 1992).

Proponents of the case study method argue that this form of problem solving within a management setting offers illustrations of the concepts students are expected to learn and use, improves communication skills, and facilitates the linkage between theory and practice (Osigweh, 1986–1987). Proponents also claim that cases allow students to discuss, share, and debate the merits of different inferences, problems, and alternative courses of action. Such insight can help students to develop better analytical skills and improve their ability to integrate new information.

The case study method also has vigorous critics who argue that it can cause groupthink, focuses too much on the past, limits the teaching role of the trainer, reduces the learner's ability to draw generalizations, reinforces passivity on the part of the learner, and promotes the quantity of interaction among students at the expense of the quality of interaction (Osigweh, 1986–1987). Andrews and Noel (1986) claim that cases lack realistic complexity and a sense of immediacy, and inhibit development of the ability to collect and distill information. In addition, trainees may get caught up in the details of the situation at the expense of focusing on the larger issues and concepts they are trying to learn.

In addition, Argyris (1980) criticizes case studies from the viewpoint that they may undermine the learning process by not leading trainees to question assumptions and positions taken and teaches trainees to be dependent on the instructor. He feels that trainers should create an atmosphere in which trainees are free to confront themselves and each other without defensiveness to allow examination of whether the ideas they claim they believe in are consistent with their actions. Berger (1983) countered Argyris's criticisms by suggesting Argyris did not define the case method and that his study was undermined by methodological flaws.

While there appears to be plenty of rhetoric regarding the advantages and disadvantages of the case study method, there is a lack of empirical evaluation studies to help us determine the facts (Keys & Wolfe, 1988; Osigweh, 1986–1987). The few studies that do exist offer no clear trend from which to draw conclusions.

To overcome these limitations, the trainer should make expectations clear and provide guidance when needed. In addition, the trainer must effectively guide the discussion portion of case study to ensure trainees have an opportunity to explore differing assumptions and positions they have taken and the rationale for what constitutes effective responses to the case. The point in discussing cases is not to find the "right" solution, but to be able to provide a soned and logical rationale for developing a course of action. Variations in the case method have also been proposed (e.g., Argyris, 1986). One such variation, called a living case, has trainees analyze a problem they and their organization are currently facing (Andrews & Noel, 1986).

Osigweh (1986–1987, p. 131) encourages potential users of the case study method to match factors such as:

- Specific instructional objectives

- Objectives of the case approach

- Attributes of the particular incident or case (its content)

- Characteristics of the learner

- Instructional timing

- General prevailing environment (class size, course level, and so on)

- The teacher's own personal and instructional characteristics

Business Games and Simulations   Like the case method, business games are intended to develop or refine problem-solving and decision-making skills. However, this technique emphasizes exclusively business management decisions (such as maximizing profits). The Figure 5-4 survey shows that 54 percent of responding organizations use games or simulations (Filipczak, 1992).

One example is a business game titled "Looking Glass, Inc.," developed by the Center for Creative Leadership (McCall & Lombardo, 1982). The game requires participants to role-play decision makers in a fictitious glass manufacturing company and use realistic organizational data to make a variety of decisions. The three-day Looking Glass training program includes one day for performing the simulation (in which participants operate the company), one day for feedback, and one day to practice the skills focused on during the feedback sessions (Kaplan, Lombardo, & Mazique, 1985). Martin Marietta Inc. uses Looking Glass as a diagnostic and feedback tool in its executive development program (Thornton & Cleveland, 1990). The developers of Looking Glass have reported research that shows the activities of trainees in the simulation are similar to those of managers in the field (McCall & Lombardo, 1982) and suggests the program is effective in the short term (Kaplan et al., 1985).

Business games, particularly computer simulations of organizations and industries, are widely used in business schools. A review of 61 studies (Wolfe, 1985) reported support for the effectiveness of business games in strategic management courses. Whether these results can be generalized to organizational settings is still an open question (Keys & Wolfe, 1988).

Another type of simulation used in management development programs and assessments centers is the **in-basket exercise.** The goal of this technique is to assess the trainee's ability to establish priorities, plan, gather relevant information, and make decisions. The sequence of events involved in a typical in-basket exercise include the following:

1. The trainees are told that they have been promoted to a management position that was suddenly vacated. They are given background information about the organization including personnel, relationships, policies, union contracts, and the like.

2. The trainees then receive the contents of the manager's in-basket. This material includes documents such as telephone messages, notes, memos, letters, and reports.

3. The trainees are then asked to read, organize, prioritize, and make decisions regarding the issues presented by the in-basket material.

4. At the end of the decision period, the trainees' decisions are then evaluated by trained scorers.

The object of this technique is to force the trainees to make decisions in the allotted time period. Since there is usually insufficient time to read each document and respond, the trainees must make quick and accurate decisions. The trainees are evaluated not only on the quality of their decisions, but also whether they were able to deal effectively with all of the critical documents. Research on the in-basket technique has shown it to be successful both in improving trainee effectiveness (Butler & Keys, 1973) and in predicting managerial effectiveness, either alone or in combination with other devices (Thornton & Byham, 1982).

One potential limitation of business games and simulations is that while they can be quite complex, these techniques often lack the realistic complexity and information present in real organizations. Factors such as organizational history and politics, social pressures, risks and consequences of alternatives, and the organization's culture are difficult to replicate in a simulation (Thornton & Cleveland, 1990). This may undermine the extent to which what is learned will transfer back to the job.

In addition, many games and simulations emphasize the use quantitative analysis in making business decisions and underplay the importance of interpersonal issues in managerial effectiveness. It has also been argued that the popularity of simulation techniques is based more on circumstantial evidence rather than rigorous evaluative research (Wexley and Baldwin, 1986), but since simulations are used in conjunction with other techniques, isolating their effect in research is difficult (Keys & Wolfe, 1988).

Role Playing A very popular training technique, role playing is reportedly used in 62 percent of the training programs in the Figure 5-4 survey. In the role playing technique, trainees are presented with an organizational situation, assigned a role or character in the situation, and asked to "act out" the role with one or more fellow trainees. The role play should offer trainees an opportunity for self-discovery and learning. For example, a management development program could include a role play situation emphasizing interpersonal conflicts between a manager and a subordinate. Management trainees would have an opportunity to role-play both the manager and the subordinate in order to better understand some of the dynamics of this situation as well as practice interpersonal skills. The value of this technique is enhanced by conducting a feedback session following the role play in which trainees and the trainer critique the role player's performance. In many organizations, the role episode is videotaped, as discussed earlier, which allows for better feedback and self-observation.

While self-discovery and opportunity to practice interpersonal skills are outcomes of role playing, this method does have some limitations. First, as discussed earlier, some trainees may feel intimidated by having to "act out" a character (and possibly be videotaped doing so). Trainers should take sufficient time in introducing the exercise, explaining the process in detail, and most of all, stress how participation will help each trainee to better understand and apply different interpersonal skills.

A second limitation of the technique is the extent to which the trainees are able to transfer this learning to their job. Some trainees may perceive this role playing as artificial or as fun and games, and not as a legitimate learning tool. Trainees who do not take this technique seriously may interfere with the learning of others. It is important that the trainer manage the process effectively and keep reinforcing the importance of participation.

Behavior Modeling   Social learning theory (see Chapter 2), which suggests that much of our behavioral patterns are learned from observing others, forms the basis for behavior modeling. In organizations, employees learn all kinds of behaviors, some work-related and some not, from observing supervisors, managers, union leaders, and co-workers who serve as role models. Under normal conditions, role models can have a tremendous influence on individual behavior.

In this technique, trainees observe a model performing a target behavior correctly (usually on a film or video). This is followed by a discussion of the key components of the behavior, practicing the target behavior through role playing, and receiving feedback and reinforcement for the behavior they demonstrate. Behavior modeling is widely used for interpersonal skill training and is a common component of management training programs.

Research has shown behavior modeling to be an effective training technique (Burke & Day, 1986), and will be described in greater detail in our discussion of management development (Chapter 12).

Computer-Based Training Methods

Computers have had a significant impact on the delivery of training in organizations. It is estimated that nearly 70 percent of organizations use computers in some way as part of their training effort, with 43 percent using computer-based training (CBT) as a component of their training strategy ("Computers in Training," 1991). Computer-based training involves using the computer as the primary or sole deliverer of the material in the training session or program. One of the biggest influences on the growth of CBT is the advent of microcomputers and the rapid increase in their capabilities. In the early days of CBT, one had to have access to terminals connected to a mainframe computer and software that was time-sharing with other business computing needs. PCs are now in 93 percent of organizations that use computers ("Computers," 1991), and important advances in hardware and software are occurring at a dizzying pace.

The primary advantage CBT has over other methods of training is its interactivity (Kearsley, 1984). The interaction between the learner and the computer in many CBT programs mirrors the one-on-one relationship between student and tutor: questions and responses back and forth, resulting in immediate feedback. Advanced forms of CBT, like intelligent computer-aided instruction, can even analyze the pattern of a student's responses and errors, draw conclusions, and tailor the lesson the learner receives accordingly. Two approaches to CBT include computer-aided instruction (CAI) and intelligent computer-assisted instruction (ICAI).

Computer-Aided Instruction   CAI programs can range from electronic workbooks, using the drill-and-practice approach, to electronic presentation of a traditional training program. CAI software packages are available at relatively low cost for a wide range of material, from teaching basic skills such as reading and typing to highly technical scientific, engineering, and machine maintenance topics. Not only are CAI programs being sold as part of business software programs (like the tutorial programs that come with word processing packages like Microsoft Word), some are sold in retail stores (including *Mavis Beacon's Typing Tutor* and various income tax preparation programs) and have become software best-sellers. Some organizations custom design software from scratch or modify existing programs to meet their unique needs. For example, Manpower, Inc.'s SKILLWARE program was originally developed by the company (the world's largest agency for temporary office workers) but is also used, either as is or with modifications, by some of Manpower's clients, including Xerox and Miller Brewing Company (Hamburg, 1988).

There are several advantages to CAI as compared to other training methods and techniques, especially considering the **interactive** nature of CAI. Based upon the trainee's responses, the computer will present various levels of material until the trainee reaches mastery. A second advantage is CAI's **self-pacing** feature that allows trainees to control the speed of instruction and makes them self-sufficient learners (Ganger, 1990). A third advantage is the **logistics** of CAI that make it more accessible through an internal distribution system (HRD department) or downloaded from a computer mainframe to remote sites to eliminate travel and per diem costs (Schwade, 1985). Finally, CAI offers an **instructional management and reporting system** that automatically "tracks student progress and the allocation and use of instructional resources, including terminals, instructors, and classrooms" (Hillelsohn, 1984, p. 43).

The effectiveness of CAI, like other training methods and techniques, can be measured by changes in productivity and profits. Reinhart (1989) reports that a four-hour CAI program, which trained sales representatives on selling a piece of computer software, resulted in additional revenues of $4.6 million for Xerox. Another measure of effectiveness is a cost/benefit analysis when compared to other techniques. A financial institution in New York, which was paying trainees while they waited for available classroom training programs, switched to CAI and realized enough savings to offset the development cost of the CAI program (Ganger, 1990). Research has also shown that trainees using CAI take less time to learn the same amount of material as conventional methods, with no significant difference in test scores (Wexley, 1984).

However, it does take longer for people to read a computer screen than a printed page (Kruck & Mueire, 1987). Some critics also worry about the loss of personal interaction between a human trainer and the learner, and suggest that reliance on CBT may restrain the development of interpersonal skills (Foegen, 1987). Further, developing a CAI program from scratch can be time consuming and difficult. Eurich (1990) reported that it takes an average of about 200 hours of development time to produce each hour of instruction.

CAI may not always be the appropriate training method. For instance, in training situations that emphasize interpersonal skill building, other techniques (like role playing) may be preferred. Also, traditional training methods might be more suitable for unmotivated trainees who may find it difficult to complete a CAI program without the assistance of a trainer.

Intelligent Computer-Assisted Instruction   ICAI goes beyond CAI in terms of flexibility and the ability to qualitatively evaluate learner performance. Whereas a typical CAI program may allow the learner to select from among several levels of presentation (novice, intermediate, and so on), an ICAI program is able to discern the learner's capability from the learner's response patterns and by analyzing the learner's errors. The goal of ICAI systems is to provide learners with an electronic teacher's assistant that can

> patiently offer advice to individual learners, encourage learner practice and stimulate learners' curiosity through experimentation. This would potentially make the teacher more available for more creative endeavors, or for helping learners to overcome subtle or difficult problems beyond the capability of ICAI (McCalla & Greer, 1977, cited in Eurich, 1990, p. 74).

While the availability of ICAI programs is limited compared to that of CAI, the potential for ICAI is enormous. Some examples of ICAI programs are the Carnegie-Mellon University's LISP computer language tutor and the Navy's STEAMER program, which allows students to learn to operate and repair a ship's complex steam propulsion system (Eurich, 1990). Expert systems, like Campbell Soup's cooker maintenance program "ALDO," which capture the knowledge and experience of experts in a particular field or content area, are also considered ICAI programs.

ICAI programs are based on advances in artificial intelligence, which involves "engineering some aspects of the human thought process" (Eurich, 1990, p. 71) into a computer. Artificial intelligence research is uncovering ways to improve ICAI programs' capability to use natural language to interact with the learner and to understand the learner (by tracking learner responses and learning from them). Given the rate of progress in computer hardware, software, artificial intelligence, and knowledge engineering (designing and organizing information and finding effective ways to present it), it would not be surprising to see ICAI programs become common in training and educational programs in the not-too-distant future.

Selecting Appropriate Training Methods

We have illustrated some of the many options an HRD professional has available when designing a training program. In fact, many HRD programs use several of these methods in order to take advantage of each method's unique strengths. Given such an array of choices, how does the HRD professional go about choosing which is most appropriate for a particular program? Several factors should be considered:

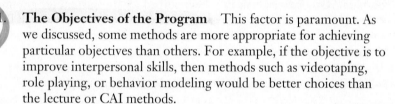

1. **The Objectives of the Program**   This factor is paramount. As we discussed, some methods are more appropriate for achieving particular objectives than others. For example, if the objective is to improve interpersonal skills, then methods such as videotaping, role playing, or behavior modeling would be better choices than the lecture or CAI methods.

2. **Time and Money Available**   In an ideal world, we would have all the time and money we need to accomplish our goals. Unfortunately, in many organizations managers often ask the HRD department to implement programs immediately while spending as little money as possible. Competing needs may also force HRD professionals to select certain methods because of their low cost. For example, when designing a program to train mechanics how to repair a complicated mechanical system an ICAI program might be optimal, but because of its cost, the HRD professional may have to settle for a combination of traditional classes (using lecture, discussion, and reference books) and on-the-job training.

3. **Availability of Other Resources**   Some methods require highly trained trainers and specialized equipment and facilities in order to be delivered effectively. Again, trade-offs are likely to be necessary by choosing alternative methods with less demanding resources.

4. **Trainee Characteristics and Preferences**   The issue here focuses on both trainee readiness and the diversity of the target population. Methods such as CAI require a fairly high level of literacy. If literacy or fluency is a problem, either a less reading- and writing-intensive method (like a video) may be used, or literacy training must be done first. Similarly, because individuals have different learning styles, some training methods may be more appropriate than others.

In the end, selection of the training method(s) to be used requires knowledge of the different techniques and sound judgment on the part of the individual(s) who are designing the program. The HRD professional should investigate all training methods available, and when in doubt, consult experienced colleagues, instructional designers, and consultants.

Preparing Training Materials

After the training methods have been selected, the next logical step is to prepare or purchase the training materials, depending upon whether the program is purchased or designed by the organization. If a training program is purchased from an outside vendor, training materials such as books, handouts, and videos, will usually be part of the package. However, organizationally designed programs will require the preparation of materials. If the program is similar to past training programs, those materials may be modified for the current program.

The kinds of training materials are unlimited. However, we will limit our discussion to only those materials which are relevant to the training methods described earlier. Since we have already discussed audiovisual aides (including slides, transparencies, and so on), we will now focus on program announcements, syllabi or program outlines, training manuals, and textbooks.

Program Announcements

Program announcements are used to inform the target audience about the training program. The announcement should indicate the purpose of the program, when and where it will be held, and how the employee can qualify to participate in the program. Sufficient lead time should be given to employees so that they can adjust their schedules and process the necessary request forms.

Typically, announcements are sent through supervisory channels, union stewards, company newsletters, or even mailed individually to employees. Some organizations designate a bulletin board for announcing training opportunities or make use of electronic mail systems. Some organizations (like the Rhode Island State Department of Administration) publish periodic training bulletins dedicated to providing this information.

Program Outlines

Program outlines (or course syllabi) are documents that communicate the content, goals, and expectations for the program. Typically provided at the beginning of the program, these include such things as course objectives, topical areas to be covered, materials or tools needed, requirements of each trainee, and a tentative schedule of events.

The program outline can also be used to establish behavioral expectations including punctuality, attendance, work habits, speaking in class, and courtesy toward fellow trainees. Such expectations should be clearly explained. For example, some training content is sequenced, so it is important for trainees to be present at all sessions. In this case, the attendance policy should reflect this requirement and explain that if any trainee is absent they may be required to begin a new program from the start.

Training Manuals or Textbooks

Most trainers rely on a training manual or textbook for the basic instructional material, readings, exercises, and self-tests. Some documents are organized into modules that make it easy to organize the training program into sessions. **Textbooks** provide a broad treatment of the subject while training manuals are better known for their brevity. Trainers who decide to use a textbook would normally contact the publisher and determine whether individual modules can be purchased separately, how useful other trainers found the item, and how easily the item can be customized to the needs of the organization (McCullough, 1987). In addition to these factors, the purchase price should be compared with the cost of producing a comparable training manual.

Training manuals can be readily produced by an organization, particularly given the availability of desktop publishing software. The production cost would include staff time for curriculum design and writing, cost of equipment, and printing. The availability of desktop publishing software and laser printers makes it much easier to produce a high-quality training manual in-house. However, unless there is a large demand for the manual, it is usually cheaper in the long run to purchase a commercially produced manual, if one is available.

Scheduling the Training Program

The task of scheduling a training program may seem relatively simple and straightforward when compared to other decisions made by the trainer. This is definitely not the case. Organizations can be very busy, hectic, and unpredictable environments, making scheduling HRD and other support activities very difficult. The goal in scheduling an HRD program is to ensure that the participants (both trainer and learners) are available and have their attention focused on the learning task at hand. In this section, we will discuss some of the issues HRD professionals should consider when scheduling their programs.

Scheduling during Work Hours

One popular option for program scheduling is to run the program during normal working hours. This not only avoids outside conflicts (such as commuting, family, and personal obligations), it also sends a message to employees that learning is an important part of their job. When scheduling a program during normal work hours, the HRD professional should consider factors such as the day of the week, time of day, peak work hours, staff meeting times, and travel requirements.

The **day of the week** becomes an issue because some days, such as Monday, Friday, and the days surrounding a holiday, are favored by employees for time off. Employees often try to extend their weekends and holidays, so these days should be avoided if possible when scheduling training.

Time of day is another factor. Programs scheduled for the start of the work day may face a significant proportion of tardy or tired participants. Scheduling a program for the lunch hour may require building in time for employees to eat during the program, providing lunch, or requiring employees to eat early or go without lunch. Mid-afternoon programs coincide with the time that many people's circadian rhythms are at a low point, resulting in sluggishness and shorter attention spans. To combat this, the program should include active participation, break periods, or the availability of light snacks and beverages (especially caffeinated beverages). In addition, employees attending programs scheduled close to quitting time may be distracted or have to leave early to attend to personal demands. Obviously, a program has to be scheduled sometime, but the wise trainer will note these issues and take steps to deal with them.

In addition to day of the week and time of day, there are other working hour constraints that are unique to particular organizational units or occupational groups. These include peak work hours, staff meeting times, and travel requirements. **Peak work hours** are the times of the day, week, month, or year that departments are the busiest and when scheduling a training program would cause a potential conflict. For example, scheduling a professional development program for accountants and auditors during tax season would likely prevent many potential participants from attending. Managers and supervisors should also be contacted before scheduling programs to determine if participants have any **staff meetings, travel requirements,** or any other special scheduling needs. This information will help the trainer to select the best times and develop contingency plans for any potential conflicts.

Scheduling after Work Hours

Scheduling HRD programs after work and during the weekend to avoid some of the organizational constraints discussed above can create other problems. Extending the work day and week can cause a hardship for some employees, particularly those who have families and other personal commitments. Even when employees know in advance of a scheduled training program, family problems could arise, causing some trainees to miss important training sessions. Another problem is fatigue. Employees may be physically tired from a day's work and may not be mentally alert. For example, in response to employee requests, a supervisory training program at the Electric Boat Division of General Dynamics was held between midnight and 2:00 a.m. for employees working the 2nd shift (4 p.m. to midnight). The training program was poorly attended, and those who did attend experienced fatigue by the second hour of the class. As a result of this experience, the company suspended all future midnight training programs.

Even when after-work and weekend programs do not cause a hardship, many employees are reluctant to give up their leisure time. In this situation, some organizations provide inducements, including overtime pay, compensatory time (equal time off), training as a qualification for promotion, and leisure activities to coincide with the training session (often by conducting it at a resort area).

Implementing the Training Program

The primary responsibility for implementing the training program lies, of course, with the trainer. Up to this point, we have discussed the preparation of training objectives and the lesson plan, followed by the selection of training methods, techniques, and materials, and finally determining the best schedule. During the program, the trainer must put these into practice.

Arranging the Physical Environment

One of the first implementation decisions is arranging the physical environment. The environment is particularly important to on-the-job training, because the trainee must feel comfortable enough to concentrate and learn. If, for instance, the OJT area has a number of distractions (like noise and phone calls) that may interfere with the training process, the trainer must find ways to remove or minimize them. Another common OJT distraction, particularly when the supervisor is the trainer, is interruptions. Interruptions can be avoided by setting aside certain times of the day or a special location for training that is free from distractions. Alternatively, the supervisor can arrange for someone else to handle their calls and inquiries during the time established for training.

In a classroom setting, a number of factors should be considered when arranging the physical environment. These include the seating arrangement, comfort, and physical distractions. **Seating** is important because it establishes a spatial relationship between the trainer and the trainees. For example, a classroom with fixed seats in vertical rows limits what the trainer can do in that setting, but this arrangement may be preferred for the lecture technique because it focuses the participants on the lecturer. In a classroom with movable seats, however, the trainer can arrange the seats to facilitate the program objectives. Arranging the rows on angles (or a chevron-shape) or in a semicircle allows the trainees to view each other during a class discussion. This arrangement can encourage interaction and feedback among the participants. In a large class, the seats can be arranged in small groups to facilitate group discussion.

The physical **comfort level** is also important for successful learning. Extremes in room temperature can inhibit learning. A warm, stuffy room can make participants feel tired. A room that is too cold can distract participants and reduce manual dexterity. One of the authors recalls participating in a management development seminar in a room so cold that trainees spent more time focusing on how uncomfortable they were (and consuming hot beverages) than dealing with the training content.

The third factor that should be considered when arranging the physical environment is the potential for **physical distractions.** These include noise, poor lighting, and physical barriers. Noise, including activity outside the classroom, can often be controlled by closing the door or placing a sign stating "quiet: training in session" outside the area. Inappropriate lighting can make it difficult for participants to take notes, read printed material or overheads, or render projected material unviewable. The trainer should inspect the room in advance if possible to determine whether any physical barriers, such as poles, fixed partitions, and the like, will interfere with the planned activities. If such problems exist, it may be possible to find a more suitable location.

Additional physical factors a trainer may want to consider include wall and floor coverings and colors (carpeted rooms are quieter), the type of chairs, the presence of glare, windows (a view may distract participants), acoustics, and the presence of electrical outlets to run necessary equipment (Finkel, 1986).

Getting Started

Having all of the elements needed to implement a training program—a viable lesson plan, materials and audiovisual equipment on hand, and physical environment ready—the final step is to do it! It is important for the trainer to get the program off to a good start and maintain it. If there are to be multiple sessions, the first session sets the tone for the remainder of the program. As we discussed, a trainer can establish clear expectations by preparing a course outline or syllabus that explains the purpose, objectives, topics, requirements, and establishes class norms for relevant issues (punctuality, participation, participant interaction, and so on). The course outline should be handed out and explained in detail during the first session and, if needed, restated and reinforced periodically throughout the training program.

In addition to establishing expectations, the trainer should try to determine each trainee's capacity and motivation to learn if they have not already done so prior to the session. One way to do this is to conduct an initial exercise or pre-test to assess initial ability. This may be particularly important in one-on-one OJT sessions. Rather than assess participant motivation, it may be more beneficial to include activities to reinforce motivation. Such activities could include asking participants what they'd like to accomplish, illustrating the benefits of achieving the training objectives, explicitly addressing participant fears or concerns, or having participants complete a learning contract.

Many training programs include some sort of ice-breaker exercise to help participants get to know each other and establish rapport with each other and the trainer. This is important for at least two reasons. First, a benefit of many HRD programs is the opportunity for participants to network and get to know their colleagues in other parts of the organization. Second, in HRD programs, as in any group setting, people generally seek social acceptance. For instance, in classes with one or two minority group members (ethnic, racial, gender, and so on), these individuals may feel socially isolated, which affects their ability to perform effectively in that setting. It is important that the trainer be sensitive to the social needs of trainees and respond in ways that enhance their feelings of belonging.

Finally, the trainer should make every effort to build a climate characterized by mutual respect and openness. This in turn will make it easier for trainees to seek help when they need it.

There are many skills involved in effectively running a group meeting and in teaching or facilitating learning. Recall the competencies of an effective HRD professional listed in Chapter 1. The trainer is encouraged to read about the subject and seek out opportunities to build their platform and interpersonal skills.

TABLE 5-8	TIPS FOR TRAINERS

1. Listen and acknowledge ideas.
2. Praise people as they learn.
3. Direct questions back to people.
4. Ask for examples from the trainees' experience.
5. Share your experiences with the trainees.
6. Admit to not knowing the answer—let participants help you.
7. Avoid disputes and making "right" and "wrong" judgments.
8. Show that you enjoy instructing people.
9. Spend additional time with trainees when necessary.
10. Focus on the participants' concerns rather than your own.
11. Express confidence in the trainee.
12. Ask some questions initially that the trainees can answer.
13. Make notes, and follow up on them.
14. Create positive behavior through reinforcement.
15. Use participants' words when writing on the flip chart or board.
16. Put people at ease.

SOURCE: From "16 Tips to Increase Your Effectiveness" by E. C. Fetteroll, 1985, *Training and Development Journal, 39*(6), pp. 68–70. Adapted by permission.

One good source for inexperienced trainers is the book *Human Resource Development: The New Trainer's Guide* by Les Donaldson and Edward Scannell. Professional journals like *Training and Development* and *Training* also include frequent articles on effective training skills. In addition, becoming involved in a local ASTD chapter may also be beneficial. In this spirit, we close this chapter with a list of tips offered by Fetteroll (1985) to increase training effectiveness (see Table 5-8).

RETURN TO OPENING CASE

In the early 1990s, the training specialists at the Alexander Consulting Group (ACG) Training Center were given the challenge of finding a way to build the training and development skills in subject-matter experts (SMEs). After exploring several options, including requiring a conventional train-the-trainer program, the specialists recommended the publication of a trainer's self-directed guide. The *Instructor's Guide* would provide information similar to the three phases of the training process described in this textbook. First, the guide provides techniques on how to construct a needs assessment survey and then analyze that data. Second, the guide helps the SME to translate the analyzed needs assessment data into course objectives, course content, instructional techniques, and selection of visual aids. And third, the guide helps the SME to give feedback to the trainees during and after the training program.

In order to determine whether the guide was effective, ACG measured the results of each training program in terms of its relevance of the training to the trainees' jobs and whether the *Instructor's Guide* was helpful to the SMEs. The relevance to the trainees' jobs was assessed by conducting post-training telephone interviews two weeks after the program and another one or two months after that. The results of the interviews indicated that 50 percent of the trainees could describe at least one significant event (like increased client service) that directly related to the skills or knowledge they gained from the training program. To evaluate the guide's helpfulness, SMEs were given a reaction form at the end of the training program that included questions about the guide. In 1991, 90 percent of all SMEs indicated that they found the *Instructor's Guide* invaluable.[1]

Summary

This chapter described several important activities related to the design and implementation of training and development programs. After an organization identifies a need for training, the next step is to decide whether to purchase the program from an outside vendor or design the program in-house. If the organization decides to stay in-house, the trainer must be selected. If there is a full-time trainer available, with content knowledge, the decision will be an easy one. If not, then a content specialist may need to be identified and sent to a train-the-trainer program.

The trainer then has the responsibility for developing training objectives that define the desired outcomes of the training program. This information should be translated into a lesson plan which provides a guide for the implementation and helps to select the appropriate training methods and techniques. There are three primary training methods: OJT, classroom, and computer-based training. Each method has a number of techniques appropriate for particular situations. The trainer needs to select the best combination of techniques that will maximize trainee learning.

Once the trainer designs the program, the next step is to determine the best schedule while avoiding potential conflicts. The final step is the actual implementation of the program. This includes arranging the physical environment and getting started on a positive note.

Key Terms and Concepts

artificial intelligence (AI)
audiovisual methods
behavior modeling
business games
case study method
classroom training
computer-aided instruction (CAI)
computer-based training (CBT)

discussion method
dynamic media
expert system
intelligent computer-assisted
  instruction
job instruction training (JIT)
job rotation
learning climate

---

[1]From "The Accidental Trainer: Helping Design Instruction" by M. A. Dumas and D. E. Wile, June 1992, *Personnel Journal*, pp. 106–110. Adapted with permission.

lecture

on-the-job training (OJT)

role playing

simulation

static media

telecommunications

train-the-trainer programs

training methods

training objectives

training manual

Questions for Discussion   Answer µek!

1. Compare and contrast behavioral objectives with lesson plans. What role do training objectives play in the design and implementation of training programs?

2. Describe the relative merits of using a trainee's co-workers as a source for selecting a trainer. What should be done to ensure that a co-worker is an effective trainer?

3. What are the advantages of holding a training program off-site?

4. Why do you suppose classroom training is so popular in HRD? Identify two types of training programs a manager might not want to conduct in using a classroom format.

5. State and justify your opinion regarding the effectiveness of the lecture method. What can be done to ensure a lecture is effective?

6. What experiences have you had with role playing in training? Under what conditions might a role-play be effective? Ineffective?

7. What sorts of skills and knowledge do you think computer-aided instruction is well-suited for? Poorly-suited for?

8. How do you feel about attending training sessions or classes scheduled for 8:00 a.m.? What can a trainer do to maximize the chances such a session will be effective?

9. How can the seating arrangement enhance or detract from the success of a training program?

10. Why is it important for trainers and trainees to establish a rapport with each other before a training session?

6

Evaluating HRD Programs

Learning Objectives

1. *Define evaluation and explain its role in HRD.*
2. *List and compare five models of evaluation.*
3. *Discuss the types of evaluation information available and compare six methods of data collection.*
4. *Explain the role of research design in HRD evaluation.*
5. *Describe the various research designs that may be used to evaluate training.*
6. *Identify and explain the choices available for translating evaluation results into dollar terms.*

OPENING CASE

In 1985, Mardee Beckman, the director of employee assistance programs (EAPs) at McDonnell Douglas Corporation, met with the CEO and the president to discuss the aerospace company's commitment to its EAP. The EAP offered treatment to help employees with substance abuse, mental health, and other personal problems to reestablish themselves as productive members of the organization.

During the meeting, the two executives asked Beckman to prove that the EAP could contribute to the organization's bottom line. This was a serious challenge: if Beckman could not demonstrate that the EAP could pay for itself, McDonnell Douglas would terminate the program.

Introduction

In the previous two chapters, we presented the training and HRD model and discussed how to first identify HRD needs and then design and deliver a program to satisfy those needs. The model (shown again in Figure 6-1) illustrates how the evaluation phase relates to needs assessment and planning and implementation in the HRD training process.

In this chapter, we will discuss how to answer the question upon which HRD evaluation is based: Was the HRD program effective? This is a deceptively simple question, which raises a number of concerns, such as:

- What is meant by effectiveness?

- How is effectiveness measured?

- What is the purpose of determining effectiveness? That is, what decisions are made after a program is judged effective or ineffective?

FIGURE 6-1	TRAINING AND HRD PROCESS MODEL

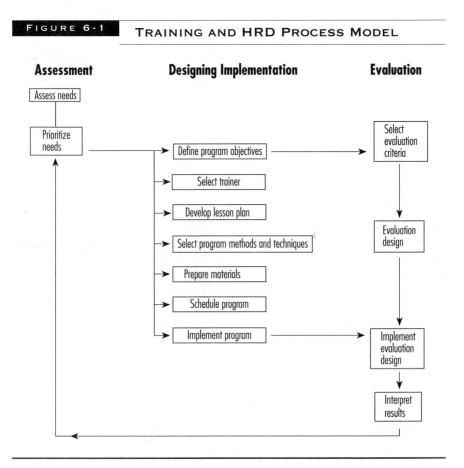

Assessment

Assess needs

Prioritize needs

Designing Implementation

Define program objectives

Select trainer

Develop lesson plan

Select program methods and techniques

Prepare materials

Schedule program

Implement program

Evaluation

Select evaluation criteria

Evaluation design

Implement evaluation design

Interpret results

As we will see in this chapter, the answers to these questions are far from simple.

The term *effectiveness* is relative. Typically, effectiveness is determined with respect to the achievement of a goal or a set of goals. HRD effectiveness must be determined with respect to the goals of the program or programs being examined. Therefore, it makes sense to ask the question of effectiveness more specifically. An HRD or training program can be effective in meeting some goals (like staying within budget or increasing a participant's skills) and be ineffective in meeting others (like improving customer satisfaction).

In this chapter we will define HRD evaluation, describe its purposes and the options available for conducting an evaluation of training and other HRD interventions, and discuss how evaluation findings can be communicated.

The Purpose of HRD Evaluation

HRD evaluation is defined as "the systematic collection of descriptive and judgmental information necessary to make effective training decisions related to the selection, adoption, value, and modification of various instructional activities" (Goldstein, 1980, p. 237). This definition makes several important points. First, when conducting an evaluation, both descriptive and judgmental information may be collected. Descriptive information provides a picture of what is happening or has happened, while judgmental information communicates some opinion or belief about what has happened. For example, the statement "twenty-five percent of first-line supervisors attended a budgeting workshop in the last six months" contains descriptive information; it simply states the facts. However, the statement, "the turnout for the budgeting workshop over the last six months is disappointingly low compared to last year's turnout" provides judgmental information—someone's opinion based on the facts. Both descriptive and judgmental information are needed in HRD evaluation. Some of the judgments are made by those involved in the program, while others are made by those not involved in the program.

Second, evaluation also involves the systematic collection of information according to a predetermined plan or method to ensure that the information is appropriate and useful. Finally, evaluation is conducted to help managers, employees, and HRD professionals make informed decisions about particular programs and methods. For example, if part of a program is ineffective, it may need to be changed or discarded. Or, if a certain program proves valuable, it may be replicated in other parts of the organization.

Evaluation can serve a number of purposes within the organization. According to Phillips (1983), evaluation can help to:

- Determine whether a program is accomplishing its objectives.

- Identify the strengths and weaknesses of HRD programs.

- Determine the cost/benefit ratio of an HRD program.

- Decide who should participate in future HRD programs.

- Identify which participants benefitted the most or least from the program.

- Reinforce major points to be made to the participant.

- Gather data to assist in marketing future programs.

- Determine if the program was appropriate.

- Establish a data base to assist management in making decisions.

Better and more informed decision making, then, is an important benefit of conducting HRD evaluation. But there are other benefits as well. Zenger and Hargis (1982) identified four reasons for conducting HRD evaluation:

1. Training is functional and relevant only when it is evaluated.

2. If HRD staff cannot substantiate its contribution to the organization, its funding and programs may be cut during the budgeting process, especially when the organization faces tough times.

3. Evaluation can build credibility.

4. Senior management often wants to know the benefits of HRD programs.

Building credibility is a key aspect of conducting evaluation. After all, other functions performed within the organization are evaluated to determine their effectiveness. If the HRD department fails to conform to this norm, it may not be taken seriously within the organization.

Thus, evaluation is as important as any other part of the HRD process. It is the only way one can know whether an HRD program has fulfilled its objectives.

How Often Are HRD Programs Evaluated?

Given its importance, one might expect that HRD programs are regularly and carefully evaluated. Unfortunately, this is not the case. A survey of management training and education practices of U.S. companies (Saari, Johnson, McLaughlin, & Zimmerle, 1988) found that while 92 percent of companies surveyed conduct some form of evaluation for company sponsored training, 42 percent conduct no evaluation at all for the executive MBA programs they used. In addition, the survey showed that the most commonly used form of evaluation was participant reaction, which as we will discuss, is useful for only a few of the decisions that must be made about HRD programs.

The results reported by this survey are not atypical. The lack of evaluation of HRD programs has been lamented by a number of HRD researchers (Goldstein,

1980; Latham, 1988; Wexley, 1984). Many articles have been written about the importance of conducting evaluation, but more organizations pay lip service to evaluation than actually do it.

Why isn't evaluation done more frequently? There are several possibilities. First, those associated with HRD programs may be afraid of criticism and program cuts if the evaluation shows that the program was not effective. Second, evaluation is not an easy process. It requires time, resources, and expertise that the HRD staff may not have or may not be willing to expend. Third, many factors beyond the program itself (including the economy, equipment, policies and procedures, other HR efforts, and resource availability) can affect whether employee performance improves, thus making it difficult to evaluate the impact of training.

Yet, the simple fact is that HRD evaluation can and should be done in organizations to ensure effectiveness and accountability. It is our belief that it is the ethical responsibility of HRD professionals to prove to the organization whether or not their programs are indeed beneficial.

Pre-purchase Evaluation of Training and HRD Programs

As we discussed in Chapter 5, many HRD and training programs are purchased by organizations from third parties, such as consultants or other vendors. Some practitioners believe that they fulfill their evaluation responsibility in their pre-purchase decision. Their logic follows that they wouldn't buy a program they didn't think was going to work, so if they have made a wise purchasing decision (or evaluated the program before buying it), then it isn't necessary to conduct any post-program evaluation.

Indeed, supervisors and HRD professionals should be wise consumers of programs and equipment used in their HRD efforts. However, it is equally important to judge the effectiveness of the program or device after it has been put into place. We have all made personal purchases that have not lived up to expectations, even after careful shopping, and it is unreasonable to assume that HRD and training purchases will be any different.

Evolution of Evaluation Efforts

Goldstein (1980) suggests that efforts at training evaluation have evolved through the following four stages since the 1960s:

1. **Stage One** focuses on anecdotal reactions from trainers and program participants. Judging from the Saari et al. (1988) survey, it appears many organizations still operate at this level.

2. **Stage Two** involves borrowing experimental methodology from academic laboratories to use for program evaluation. Organizational constraints (including time, resources, and the inability to randomly select participants or use control groups that receive no

training) make application of these designs difficult, thus discouraging evaluation efforts.

3. **Stage Three** creatively matches experimental methods to organizational constraints (quasi-experimental designs), making program evaluation more feasible.

4. **Stage Four** recognizes that the entire training/HRD process affects the organization, and shifts the focus of evaluation from post-program results to the entire HRD process.

It should be emphasized that it is possible to creatively apply sound research methods to HRD evaluation designs and have useful data for making decisions. Finding ways to perform effective evaluation serves all parties: the organization, the trainer, and the trainees. Before we discuss data collection and research designs, however, we will examine several overall models of evaluation.

Models of Evaluation

A model of evaluation outlines the criteria or focus of the evaluation effort. Since an HRD program can be examined from a number of perspectives, it is important to specify which perspectives will be considered.

Table 6-1 lists five models of HRD evaluation that have been suggested (Brinkerhoff, 1987; Bushnell, 1990; Galvin, 1983; Kirkpatrick, 1967, 1987; Warr, Bird, & Rackham, 1970). The models—most influential of which is Kirkpatrick's —share some features, but they differ in significant ways.

Kirkpatrick's Model

The most popular and influential model of training evaluation was articulated by Kirkpatrick (1967, 1987). Kirkpatrick argues that training efforts can be eval-

---

TABLE 6-1   HRD EVALUATION MODELS

Model	Training Evaluation Criteria
1. Kirkpatrick (1967, 1987)	Four levels: Reaction, Learning, Job Behavior, and Results.
2. CIPP (Galvin, 1983)	Four levels: Context, Input, Process, and Product.
3. CIRO (Warr et al., 1970)	Context, Input, Reaction, and Outcome.
4. Brinkerhoff (1987)	Six stages: Goal Setting, Program Design, Program Implementation, Immediate Outcomes, Intermediate or Usage Outcomes, and Impacts and Worth.
5. Systems approach (Bushnell, 1990)	Four sets of activities: Inputs, Process, Outputs, and Outcomes.

uated according to any or all of four criteria: reaction, learning, job behavior, and results.

1. Reaction   Did the trainees like the program and feel it was useful? At this level, the focus is on the trainee's perceptions about the program and its effectiveness. This is important information. Positive reactions to a training program may make it easier to encourage employees to attend future programs. But, if trainees did not like the program or think they didn't learn anything (even if they did), they may discourage others from attending and may be reluctant to use the skills or knowledge obtained in the program. The main limitation of evaluating HRD programs at the reaction level is that this information cannot indicate whether the program met its objectives beyond ensuring participant satisfaction.

2. Learning   Did the trainees learn what the HRD objectives said they should learn? This is an important criterion, one many in the organization would expect an effective HRD program to satisfy. Measuring whether someone has learned something in training may involve a quiz or test—clearly a different method from assessing their reaction to the program.

3. Job Behavior   Does the trainee use what was learned in training back on the job? (Recall our discussion of transfer of training in Chapter 3.) This is also an important criterion of training success. We all know co-workers who have learned how to do something, but choose not to. If learning does not transfer to the job, the training effort cannot impact the employee's or organization's effectiveness. Measuring whether training has transferred to the job requires observation of the trainee's on-the-job behavior.

4. Results   Has the training or HRD effort improved the organization's effectiveness? Is the organization more efficient, more profitable, or better able to serve its clients or customers as a result of the training program? Meeting this criterion is considered to be the "bottom line" as far as most managers are concerned. It is also the most challenging level to assess, given that many things beyond employee performance can affect organizational performance. Typically at this level, economic and operating data (such as sales waste) are collected and analyzed.

Kirkpatrick's model provides a useful way of looking at the possible consequences of training and reminds us that HRD efforts often have multiple objectives. Implicit in the model is that each succeeding level incorporates the one prior to it, finally culminating in what many consider to be the ultimate contribution of any organizational activity: improving the organization's effectiveness.

Most discussions about training and HRD evaluation are organized around Kirkpatrick's four levels of criteria. However, some researchers argue that its focus is too narrow. Alliger and Janak (1989) question the assumptions of the model and argue that it "may never have been meant to be more than a first, global heuristic for training evaluation" (p. 339). Others complain that the model evaluates only what happens after training, as opposed to the entire training process (Bushnell, 1990).

Other Models of Evaluation

Training researchers have attempted to expand Kirkpatrick's ideas to develop a model that provides a more complete picture of evaluation and encourages practitioners to do a more thorough job of evaluation. Galvin (1983), building upon studies in the education field, suggested the CIPP (Context, Input, Process, Product) model. In this model, evaluation focuses on measuring the *context* for training (needs analysis), *inputs* to training (examining the resources available for training, such as budgets and schedules), the *process* of conducting the training program (for feedback to the implementers), and the *product,* or outcome, of training (success in meeting program objectives). Galvin also reported survey results indicating that American Society of Training and Development members preferred the CIPP model of evaluation over Kirkpatrick's model.

Similarly, the CIRO (Context, Input, Reaction, Outcome) model was offered by Warr et al., (1970). The context, input, and outcome evaluations in this model are essentially the same as the context, input, and product evaluations in CIPP, but CIRO emphasizes trainee *reaction* as a source of information to improve the training program.

Brinkerhoff (1987) extends the training evaluation model to six stages:

1. Goal Setting: What is the need?

2. Program Design: What will work to meet the need?

3. Program Implementation: Is it working, with the focus on the implementation of the program?

4. Immediate Outcomes: Did participants learn?

5. Intermediate or Usage Outcomes: Are the participants using what they learned?

6. Impacts and Worth: Did it make a worthwhile difference to the organization?

Brinkerhoff's model suggests a cycle of overlapping steps, with problems identified in one step possibly caused by things occurring in previous steps.

Finally, Bushnell (1990) suggests a model also based on a systems view of the HRD function (input ⟶ throughput ⟶ output), and contains four stages:

1. Input: What goes into the training effort. This consists of performance indicators such as trainee qualifications, trainer ability, and the like.

2. Process: The planning, design, development, and implementation of the HRD program.

3. Output: Trainee reactions, knowledge or skills gained, and improved job behavior.

4. Outcomes: Effects on the organization, including profits, productivity, and customer satisfaction.

Bushnell states that evaluation measurement can and should occur between each of the stages, and between the four activities in the process stage, to ensure that the program is well designed and meets its objectives.

Comparing Evaluation Models

All of the evaluation models incorporate Kirkpatrick's four levels of evaluation in one way or another, either as explicit steps in the model or as information collected within the steps. In addition, some of the alternatives to Kirkpatrick's model are almost identical. The CIPP and CIRO models differ in only one of the four steps (process and reaction, respectively), and the purpose of third step in both models is the same (improving program delivery).

The other models differ from Kirkpatrick's model in that they bring the first two phases of the training process, needs assessment and planning and implementation, into the evaluation phase. In fact, the first three stages of Brinkerhoff's (1987) model (goal setting, program design, and program implementation) explicitly include these activities.

It can be said that simply merging the rest of the training process into the evaluation model is a trivial improvement to Kirkpatrick's model and adds no new understanding to effective training. On the other hand, there is some merit in helping managers, supervisors, and HRD professionals to realize that evaluation is an ongoing activity, not one that should begin only after implementing the training program. Effective HRD involves many decisions, and having accurate, meaningful information available (through evaluation) throughout the training process can improve the decision-making process and enhance the overall effectiveness of the HRD effort.

And yet, Kirkpatrick's approach is still a useful way to categorize the criteria that an effective HRD program must satisfy. If possible, information assessing all four levels of criteria should be collected at some point (depending on the question being asked that prompts the evaluation study). It is also important to make informed decisions about all aspects of the HRD program. The proper techniques, including those we discussed in Chapters 4 and 5, along with those we will introduce in this chapter, can ensure that such information is available.

In its simplest form, evaluation should address the question of whether the training program achieved its objectives (Campbell, 1988). Basing training objectives on needs assessment information, and then evaluating those objectives (Campbell, 1988; Robinson & Robinson, 1989), is the most parsimonious way of summarizing what training evaluation is all about.

Data Collection for HRD Evaluation

By definition, any evaluation effort requires the collection of data to provide decision makers with facts and judgments upon which they can base their decisions. Three important aspects of providing information for HRD evaluation include data collection methods, types of data, and the use of self-report data.

Data Collection Methods

In Chapter 4, we listed some of the data sources and collection methods that can be used to provide information for needs assessments. The same data collection methods and sources are available when conducting training evaluation. Table 6-2 lists some common methods for collecting evaluation data, including interviews, questionnaires, direct observation tests and simulations, and archival performance data. Questionnaires are most often used in HRD evaluation because they can be completed and analyzed quickly. Figure 6-2 shows an example of a questionnaire that might be used to gather participant feedback (sometimes called a smile sheet), and some guidelines for writing effective questionnaires are listed in Figure 6-3.

Any or all of these methods are appropriate for collecting evaluation data, depending on their relevance to the questions being asked. For example, if the HRD department is interested in assessing trainee reactions to a seminar on pension benefits, interviews or questionnaires might be good choices. Alternatively, if management wanted to know whether the seminar affected interest in the company's pension system, the number of inquiries employees make to the HR department about the pension plan could be tracked through direct observation or archival data. Some advantages and disadvantages of using various data collection methods are listed in Table 6-3.

Ostroff (1991) has recently developed a new method of data collection targeted at measuring whether trainees use what they have learned back on the

TABLE 6-2	DATA COLLECTION METHODS FOR HRD EVALUATION
Method	**Description**
1. Interview	Conversation with one or more individuals to assess their opinions, observations, and beliefs
2. Questionnaire	A standardized set of questions intended to assess opinions, observations, and beliefs
3. Direct Observation	Observing a task or set of tasks as they are performed and recording what is seen
4. Tests and Simulations	Structured situation to assess an individual's knowledge or proficiency to perform some task or behavior
5. Archival Performance Data	Use of existing information, such as files or reports

FIGURE 6-2	A PARTICIPANT REACTION QUESTIONNAIRE

Title of the session: _____

The purposes of this rapid-feedback evaluation are to find out how you are doing, to find out how we are doing as facilitators of your learning experience, and to get your opinions about the content of the course and the training methods we are using together.

Please circle the number on the 1–5-point scale that best expresses your opinion for each question.

	No, waste of time		It was useful		Yes, very worthwhile
1. Do you think that this session was worthwhile?	1	2	3	4	5
	Not at all		It was useful		Very much
2. How much did you personally need this session?	1	2	3	4	5
	Not at all		To some degree		Completely
3. To what extent were you able to participate actively in the learning experience?	1	2	3	4	5
	Poorly		Well		Very Well
4. How well did the trainer(s) do the job?	1	2	3	4	5

5. What did you like most about this session?

6. What did you like least, and how could we improve?

7. Do you have any comments or suggestions?

SOURCE: From "Rapid Response with Spreadsheets" by N. L. Weatherby and M. E. Gorosh, 1989, *Training and Development Journal, 43*(9), p. 76. Reprinted by permission.

job. One problem with using supervisor observations of job behavior has been their difficulty in recalling specific behaviors an employee has engaged in. Ostroff's method involves presenting supervisors or others observing employee performance with a scripted situation and asking them to check off which of several behaviors the employee has engaged in or would be most likely to perform.

Ostroff compared this technique to more traditional behavior and performance measures in assessing the effectiveness of a training program for school principals (see Figure 6-4). Only the scripted situation method revealed significant effects of a training program. While further research is needed to assess the effectiveness and generalizability of the scripted situation method, Ostroff's findings represent the kind of research that will make data collection and evaluation studies in general more accurate and feasible in organizational settings.

FIGURE 6-3   **GUIDELINES FOR WRITING EFFECTIVE QUESTIONNAIRES**

---

1. *Write simply and clearly, and make the meaning obvious.*

   Good example: How often does your boss give you feedback on your job performance?

   Bad example: To what extent do administrative superiors provide information regarding the quality of performance of people on your level?

2. *Ask discrete questions.*

   Good example: 1. The organization's goals are clear.
   2. My role within the organization is clear.

   Bad example: 1. The organization's goals and your role within the organization are clear to you.

3. *Provide discrete response options and explain them.*

   Good example: During the past three months, how often did you receive feedback on your work?

not once	about every month	about once/ week	about every day or so	several times a day
1	2	3	4	5

   Bad example: During the past three months, how often did you receive feedback on your work?

rarely		occasionally		frequently
1	2	3	4	5

4. *Limit the number of response options.*

   Good example: What percent of the time are you generally sure of what the outcomes of your work efforts will be?

0–20%	21–40%	41–60%	61–80%	81–100%
1	2	3	4	5

   Bad example: What percent of the time are you generally sure of what the outcomes of your work efforts will be?

0–20	21–30	31–40	41–50	51–60	61–70	71–80	81–90	91–100
1	2	3	4	5	6	7	8	9

5. *Match the response mode to the question.*

   Good example: To what extent are you generally satisfied with your job?

not at all	a little	some	quite a bit	very much
1	2	3	4	5

   Bad example: To what extent are you generally satisfied with your job?
   YES   NO

6. *Get all the important information.*

SOURCE: From "Constructing Good Questionnaires" by J. H. Maher, Jr. and C. E. Kur, 1983, *Training and Development Journal*, 37(6), p. 106. Reprinted by permission.

TABLE 6-3	ADVANTAGES AND LIMITATIONS OF VARIOUS DATA COLLECTION METHODS	
Method	**Advantages**	**Limitations**
Interview	Flexible Opportunity for clarification Depth possible Personal contact	High reactive effects High cost Face-to-face threat potential Labor intensive Trained observers needed
Questionnaire	Low cost Honesty increased if anonymous Anonymity possible Respondent sets pace Variety of options	Possible inaccurate data On-job responding conditions not controlled Respondents set varying paces Return rate beyond control
Direct Observation	Non-threatening Excellent way to measure behavior change	Possibly disruptive Reactive effect possible May be unreliable Trained observers needed
Written Test	Low purchase cost Readily scored Quickly processed Easily administered Wide sampling possible	May be threatening Possible low relation to job performance Reliance on norms may distort individual performance Possible cultural bias
Simulation/Performance Test	Reliable Objective Close relation to job performance	Time consuming Simulation often difficult High development cost
Archival Performance Data	Reliable Objective Job-based Easy to review Minimal reactive effects	Lack of knowledge of criteria for keeping or discarding records Information system discrepancies Indirect Need for conversion to usable form Record prepared for other purposes May be expensive to collect

SOURCE: From *Handbook of Training Evaluation and Measurement Methods* (p. 92) by J. J. Phillips, 1983, Houston, TX: Gulf. Adapted by permission.

Choosing Data Collection Methods

Three additional issues to consider when deciding which data collection method to use are reliability, validity, and practicality. **Reliability** is the accuracy, or freedom from error and bias, of a data collection method. A method that has little

---

FIGURE 6-4	THE SCRIPTED SITUATION DATA COLLECTION METHOD: ITEM FROM A SCHOOL PRINCIPAL PERFORMANCE SURVEY

The administrator receives a letter from a parent objecting to the content of the science section. The section topic is reproduction. The parent objects to his daughter having exposure to such materials and demands that something be done. The administrator would most likely (check one):

———— Ask the teacher to provide handouts, materials, and curriculum content for review

———— Check the science curriculum for the board approved approach to reproduction and compare board guidelines to course content

———— Ask the head of science department for his/her own opinion about the teacher's lesson plan

———— Check to see if the parent has made similar complaints in the past

---

SOURCE: From "Training Effectiveness Measures and Scoring Schemes: A Comparison" by C. Ostroff, 1991, *Personnel Psychology, 44,* p. 360. Reprinted by permission.

---

or no error or bias is highly reliable. On the other hand, the results of a method that has significant error or bias cannot be trusted. Decisions based on unreliable information are likely to be poor ones.

For example, suppose employee leadership skills will be judged by having supervisors watch employees interact with each other in a role playing exercise. If one of the supervisors assigns consistently harsher scores than the others, that personal bias and error will be reflected in low leadership ability scores for certain employees who might otherwise be considered excellent leaders.

Another issue to consider in selecting a data collection method is validity. Validity is concerned with whether the data collection method actually measures what we want it to measure. For example, suppose a trainer decides to use a written test to measure whether trainees have learned the procedure for completing travel expense forms. The test is valid to the extent that the scores on the test indicate whether the employee actually knows how to complete the forms. If the items on the test focus more on performing calculations, which was not the focus of training, rather than trainees knowing which information to report on the expense form, which was the focus of training, the test scores may be measuring the wrong thing. If this is the case, the test will likely lead to poor decisions.

Reliability and validity are complex issues, and assessing them often requires a knowledge of statistics and measurement concepts, a complete discussion of which is beyond the scope of this book. HRD professionals who are unfamiliar with these concepts should read more about the topic (see Anastasi, 1982; Cook & Campbell, 1979; and Schmitt & Klimoski, 1991) or consult other members of the organization, knowledgeable professors, or consultants who are familiar with these issues.

In addition to being reliable and valid, data collection methods must also be practical, given the constraints of the organization. Practicality concerns the time, money, and resources available for the evaluation method. For example, conducting interviews with all supervisors to assess employee job behavior may take more time than the staff has available. In this case, interviewing a sample of the supervisors or using a questionnaire may be practical alternatives. As we mentioned earlier, realistic and creative trade-offs can ensure that the evaluation effort is carried out and yields useful information.

Types of Data

At least three types of data are available for evaluating HRD effectiveness: individual performance, system-wide performance, and economic (Phillips, 1983; Robinson & Robinson, 1990). Individual performance data emphasize the individual trainee's knowledge and behaviors. Examples of this kind of data include an employee's test scores, number of units produced, timeliness of performance, quality of performance, attendance, and attitudes. System-wide performance data concern the division in which the HRD program was conducted or the entire organization. Examples of system-wide data include productivity, rework, scrap, customer/client satisfaction, and timeliness. Economic data report the financial and economic performance of the organization or unit—the "bottom line"—and include profits, product liability, avoidance of penalties (such as fines for non-compliance with laws and regulations), and market share.

A complete evaluation effort is likely to include all three types of data. Different questions demand different kinds of information. For example, Robinson and Robinson (1989, p. 263) list possible data choices to determine whether a sales training program has affected an organization's operations, including:

- Ratio of new accounts to old accounts

- Call-to-close ratio

- Average sale size

- Items per order

- Add-on sales

These and other data could be tracked for individuals, organizational units, or the entire organization. Again, the key is to carefully examine the questions being asked or the decisions being made when selecting which data to use.

Limits of Self-Report Data

Self-report data, or data provided directly by individuals involved in the training program, is probably the most commonly used type of data in HR evaluation (Podsakoff & Organ, 1986). Self-reports can offer personality data, attitudes, perceptions, and provide information to measure the effectiveness of HRD or other programs. For example, the trainer may measure learning by asking trainees to judge how much they knew before training and how much they feel they know after training. Information collected this way, whether through interviews or questionnaires, can be useful and meaningful.

However, Podsakoff and Organ (1986) identify two problems that can occur when relying on self-report data:

1. **Mono-method bias.** If both reports in a before-and-after evaluation come from the same person at the same time (say, after training), conclusions may be questionable. The respondents may be more concerned about being consistent in their answers than about accurate reporting.

2. **Socially desirable responses.** Respondents may report what they think the researcher wants to hear, rather than the truth. For example, employees may be too embarrassed to admit that they learned nothing in the training program.

In addition, Sprangers and Hoogstraten (1989) warn of a possible **response shift bias,** in which respondents' perspectives of their skills before training change during the training program and affect their after-training assessment. For example, the trainee may discover during training that their pre-training judgment of skill was unrealistically high, and adjust the post-training evaluation accordingly. As a result, the data may show no improvement of skill after training, even though such an improvement may have occurred.

Self-report data can be useful in HRD evaluation, but sole reliance on self-reports can be limiting. Depending on the question being asked, direct observation by trained observers (like supervisors), tests, or simulations may yield better, more conclusive information than self-reports.

Research Design

A research design is a plan for conducting an evaluation study. Research design is a complex topic, and much has been written about it (e.g., Campbell & Stanley, 1963; Cook & Campbell, 1979; Schmitt & Klimoski, 1991). Our goal in this section is to introduce the reader to some basic issues in research design, and discuss some of the possibilities available when evaluating HRD programs.

Research design is a critical aspect of any evaluation effort. It specifies the expected results of the evaluation study, the methods of data collection, and how the data will be analyzed. Awareness of research design issues and possible research design alternatives can help a manager or HRD professional do a better job of conducting evaluations and critiquing the results of evaluation studies.

Research Design Validity

The validity of a research design is the extent to which one can be confident that the conclusions drawn from it are true (Cook & Campbell, 1976). Validity of a design is judged on a continuum from high (confidence that the design yields truthful conclusions) to low (doubtfulness about the design's conclusions).

Research design validity has at least four aspects: internal, external, construct, and statistical conclusion (Cook & Campbell, 1976). The most important of these aspects is internal validity.

Internal validity concerns a judgment as to whether conclusions about the relationship between the variables being studied could have been due to some other variable. In the case of HRD evaluation, if an increase in employee performance is observed after an HRD program, we want to assess whether the program was responsible for the change, rather than some other factor such as experience or work rules.

For example, when a sales training program is being evaluated to determine whether it improves sales, one hopes to conclude that any observed increases in sales are a result of the training program. However, there are other factors that could encourage sales, such as economic conditions, the sales territory, or an employee's years of experience in selling. If the evaluation study does not control for these factors (i.e., ensure they don't affect the results), we cannot be sure whether any increases in sales are due to the training program or not. So, if sales after the training program are 15 percent higher than before, but the HRD evaluation did not control or adjust for economic conditions or trainee experience, it will not be clear whether the training or something else caused the increase in sales. Therefore, the study's internal validity is low: we cannot be confident that any conclusions based on this study are true.

Cook and Campbell (1976, 1979) identified a number of factors that can threaten or reduce internal validity if they are not controlled for. Table 6-4 lists these threats to internal validity in regards to HRD evaluation.

Any of these factors, if present or not controlled for by the research design, can undermine the results of the study. The HRD professional should always select a research design that will ensure that a valid conclusion can be drawn from it. Many of the conditions present within an organization can make it difficult to ensure a high degree of validity. Concerns over validity and rigor in research design can inhibit people from conducting training evaluation. However, as suggested by Goldstein (1980), creatively matching the research effort to the organizational constraints can ensure that evaluation is done and meaningful conclusions are drawn. Three categories of research designs that we will now discuss are nonexperimental designs, experimental designs, and quasi-experimental designs.

Nonexperimental Designs

A nonexperimental research design leaves a great deal of doubt as to whether the HRD program has in fact worked. Such designs include the case study, relational research, and the one group pre-test/post-test design (Schmitt & Kilmoski, 1991). Each of these designs is poorly suited for making conclusive statements about training effectiveness. There are simply too many plausible alternative explanations for any observed changes when using these methods.

TABLE 6-4	FACTORS THAT CAN AFFECT INTERNAL VALIDITY

1. **History** Unrelated events occurring during the training period that can influence training measurements.

2. **Maturation** Ongoing processes within the individual, such as aging or gaining job experience, that are a function of the passage of time.

3. **Testing** The effect of a pre-test on post-test performance.

4. **Instrumentation** The degree to which criterion instruments may measure different attributes of an individual at two different points in time.

5. **Statistical Regression** Changes in criterion scores resulting from selecting extreme groups on a pre-test.

6. **Differential Selection** Using different procedures for selecting individuals for experimental and control groups.

7. **Experimental Mortality** Differential loss of respondents from various groups.

8. **Interaction of Differential Selection and Maturation** Assuming that experimental and control groups were different to begin with, the compounding of the disparity between the groups by maturational changes occurring during the experimental period.

9. **Interaction of Pre-test with the Experimental Variable** During the course of training, something reacting with the pre-test in such a way that the pre-test affects the trained group more than the untrained group.

10. **Interaction of Differential Selection with Training** When more than one group is trained, because of differential selection, the groups are not equivalent on the criterion variable to begin with; therefore, they may react differently to the training.

11. **Reactive Effects of the Research Situation** When the research design itself so changes the trainees' expectations and reactions that results cannot be centralized to future applications of the training.

12. **Multiple Treatment Interference** Differential residual effects of previous training experiences.

SOURCE: From *Applied Psychology in Personnel Management* (4th ed, p. 395) by W. F. Cascio, 1991, Englewood Cliffs, NJ: Prentice-Hall. Adapted by permission.

However, these designs can provide detailed information about the training program and can be used as a basis for ideas to investigate in future studies.

Case Study   The **case study research design** involves an intensive, descriptive study of a particular trainee, training group, or organization to determine what has occurred and reactions to it. If diagrammed, this design would look like this:

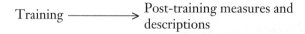

Training ⟶ Post-training measures and descriptions

The sources of data frequently used in case studies usually include archival data and reports of participants and observers. Because no pretraining information is collected, and there is no untrained comparison group, many threats to validity exist. However, a carefully conducted case study can create a record of the training program.

Relational Research   **Relational research** involves measuring two or more variables in an attempt to describe and/or explain their relationship to one another (Schmitt & Klimoski, 1991). For example, a manager may distribute a questionnaire to managers who attended an assessment center asking them to rate the value of each of the activities conducted during the program (such as a leaderless group discussion or in-basket exercise). Typically, relational research includes computing correlation coefficients (a numerical index of a relationship between two variables) between the variables measured.

While the pattern of correlations can give an idea of how the variables are related, the conclusions drawn can only be suggestive since measurements are taken at only one point in time. This makes it difficult to assess the direction of the relationships measured. For example, suppose a study shows a strong relationship between attitude toward training and attitude toward one's supervisor. Did one's feeling about the supervisor affect feelings toward training, or did one's feeling toward training affect feelings toward the supervisor?

One-Group Pre-test/Post-test Design   In this design, the trainees are assessed on the variables being observed before training and again after training.

$$\text{Pre-test} \longrightarrow \text{Training} \longrightarrow \text{Post-test}$$

This design can help to determine whether the trainees have changed as a result of the training program. For example, if a customer service program is intended to improve the trainees' attitudes toward customers, the tests would measure their attitudes toward customers before and after training. However, if a change is noticed, this design does not show whether the training program was the cause of the change. Many factors could threaten its validity, such as history, maturation, and instrumentation.

Experimental Designs

Experimental designs are constructed to show that any effects observed in the study have resulted from training and not from other factors. These designs include two significant factors:

1.   A **control group** that does not receive training.

2.   **Random assignment** of participants to the training and control groups.

Use of a control group allows the researcher to rule out the effects of factors outside of training (like maturation and history). Usually, the hopes are that the group receiving training improves and the control group does not.

However, if the training and control groups differ on some important factor, such as experience, prior training, sex, or educational level, then the comparison of the groups is compromised—these factors may be the cause of observed changes. The easiest way to do this is to randomly assign participants to the two groups. Random assignment permits the researcher to assume the groups are equivalent (Cook and Campbell, 1976).

Alternatively, a matching strategy could also create equivalent groups, by:

1. Identifying the factors, such as experience or job category, that are likely to affect the groups on the variables being measured;

2. Measuring potential participants on those factors; and then

3. Assigning subjects to balance each group on those factors.

For example, if women are known to be better listeners than men, and listening skills may have an effect on learning what is being trained, the proportion of men and women in both the experimental and the control groups should be the same.

Experimental designs include the two-group pre-test/post-test design, the two-group post-test–only design, and the Solomon four-group design.

Two-Group Pre-test/Post-test Design   This design allows control for outside influences by including a group that is not trained as a comparison group.

Group 1:   Pre-test ———→ Training ——→ Post-test
Group 2:   Pre-test ———————————→ Post-test

This design allows the researcher to make three comparisons (Schmitt & Klimoski, 1991):

1. Are the two groups in fact equivalent before training? This is assessed with the pre-test.

2. Did training improve the trainees? This is assessed by comparing Group One's pre- and post-test scores.

3. Did the untrained group remain unchanged during course of the study? This is assessed by comparing Group Two's pre- and post-test scores.

If the answer to all three questions is "yes," it is safe to conclude that training has had an effect.

Two-Group Post-test–Only Design   Sometimes, there is not enough time to gather pre-test measurements. Also, the use of some pre-test procedures may affect the outcome of training. For example, if one is measuring attitudes toward sexual harassment before a workshop about sexual harassment, simply answering questions about the topic may motivate the trainees to seek out more information or be more sensitive to the issue. Therefore, it is possible that changes in attitudes may be results of the pre-training measure rather than the training. Alternatively, if the same test (such as a test on pricing procedures) is used as both a pre- and post-test, participants may remember the items, calling the results of the post-test into question.

To resolve these situations, and still have the benefit of an untrained comparison group, a **two-group post-test–only design** could be used.

$$\text{Group 1:} \quad \text{Training} \longrightarrow \text{Post-test}$$
$$\text{Group 2:} \quad \underline{\qquad\qquad\qquad} \longrightarrow \text{Post-test}$$

The effectiveness of this design relies on the assumption that the two groups are equivalent (using a method like random or matched assignment) prior to the study.

Solomon Four-Group Design   Solomon (1949) was one of the first researchers to point out how a pre-test can affect the results of an evaluation study. His research design therefore uses one experimental group and three different groups to control for the effects of the pre-test.

$$\text{Group 1:} \quad \text{Pre-test} \longrightarrow \text{Training} \longrightarrow \text{Post-test}$$
$$\text{Group 2:} \quad \text{Pre-test} \longrightarrow \text{Post-test}$$
$$\text{Group 3:} \quad \longrightarrow \text{Training} \longrightarrow \text{Post-test}$$
$$\text{Group 4:} \quad \longrightarrow \text{Post-test}$$

This design is a combination of the two-group pre-test/post-test and two group post-test–only designs. Therefore, it allows the researcher to make strong conclusions about the effectiveness of the HRD program. The main disadvantage to this design is that the number of participants it requires prevents many organizations from being able to conduct it.

It should be noted that if the experimenter is concerned about whether the effects of training are long lasting, or if it may take a while for training to take effect, multiple post-test measures can be taken. This works best with routine data collection methods that do not affect employee performance, such as personnel (attendance, for example) or operations data.

Experimental designs also require that adequate statistical power be used (Arvey, Cole, Hazucha, & Hartanto, 1985). In a training evaluation study, **statistical power** is the probability of concluding there is a difference between the training and control groups when a difference actually exists. The higher the power, the greater the chances of finding the difference; the lower the power, the greater the chances that a true difference between the groups will go undetected.

One of the best ways to increase statistical power is to increase the number of participants in the study. However, many organizations do not have this option given their number of employees. Arvey et al. (1985) reported that the median sample size in training evaluation is 43. Studies with this number of participants have a relatively low statistical power (which can be modified somewhat according to the statistical analysis procedure used). This means that in many organizations, reliance on low power experimental designs may lead to the mistaken conclusion that training is ineffective (Cascio, 1991a).

While experimental designs are the most rigorous of the research designs and permit the greatest confidence in conclusions drawn from them, organizational constraints can make it difficult to use them. In many organizations, it is difficult to use random assignment to groups. If employees work in distant locations, or if training some employees and not training others will cause friction among employees, using a pure experimental design is not possible.

Quasi-Experimental Designs

Some people feel that if rigorous adherence to an experimental design cannot be achieved, then evaluation is not worth doing. This is a short-sighted point of view. Campbell and Stanley (1966) and Cook and Campbell (1976, 1979) have offered **quasi-experimental designs** as a way to conduct evaluation. In these designs, the researcher attempts to control as many threats to validity as possible while matching evaluation research concerns to organizational constraints. Two quasi-experimental designs include the nonequivalent control group design and the time series design.

Nonequivalent Control Group Design   In a nonequivalent control group design, one cannot assume that the two groups—the control group and the group about to receive training—are equivalent. For example, if employees in one location are the trainees and employees at another location make up the control group, any number of factors may lead to nonequivalence, such as years of experience, economic conditions, and equipment.

The threats to validity most likely to affect conclusions from a nonequivalent control group design are selection-maturation interaction, testing-training interaction, and regression effects (Cascio, 1991a). (See Table 6-4.) The burden for the evaluation researcher is to attempt to discover the factors on which the groups differ and then attempt to control for them, either statistically or in the way the experiment is conducted.

Time Series Design   In the time series design, the researcher takes multiple measures on the variables of interest (for instance, skill operating a lathe) before and after training. This can be done using a training group alone, or with a training and control group.

Simple Time Series Design

Group 1: $M_1 M_2 M_3 M_4 M_5 \longrightarrow$ Training $\longrightarrow M_6 M_7 M_8 M_9 M_{10}$

Multiple Time Series Design

Group 1: $M_1 M_2 M_3 M_4 M_5 \longrightarrow$ Training $\longrightarrow M_6 M_7 M_8 M_9 M_{10}$

Group 2: $M_1 M_2 M_3 M_4 M_5 \longrightarrow M_6 M_7 M_8 M_9 M_{10}$

In the diagrams above, the M indicates the criterion measure.

Multiple measures allow the researcher to have a better idea of the employee's standing on the criterion both before and after training. The measurements can be graphed to help determine any change in the trends before and after training. If a change is observed, the training program is likely to be the cause.

Time series designs are well suited for handling the validity threat of history, but may be susceptible to an instrumentation threat if the measurement method can affect employee performance on the criterion. As with all quasi-experimental designs, the researchers must be vigilant for possible threats to validity and attempt to control for them.

Table 6-5 shows the experimental designs we have discussed and the potential effects of the 12 threats to validity (Cascio, 1991a).

TABLE 6-5

THE EFFECT OF THREATS TO VALIDITY ON VARIOUS RESEARCH DESIGNS

Design \ Sources	History	Maturation	Testing	Instrumentation	Regression	Selection	Mortality	Interaction of Selection and Maturation	Interaction of Testing and Training	Interaction of Selection and Training	Reactive Arrangements	Multiple Treatment Interference
A. AFTER-only (one control)	+	+	+	+	+	+	+	+	+		?	?
B. BEFORE-AFTER (no control)	-	-	-	-	?	+	+	-	-	-		?
C. BEFORE-AFTER (one control)	+	+	+	+	+	+	+	+	-		?	?
D. BEFORE-AFTER (three controls) Solomon Four-Group Design	+	+	+	+	+	+	+	+	+		?	?
E. Time series design Measure (M) M (Train) MMM	-	+	+	?	+	+	+	+	-		?	?
F. Nonequivalent control group design												
I. M train M												
II. M no train M	+	+	+	+	?	+	+	-	-		?	?

Note: "M" means measure. A "+" indicates that the factor is controlled, a "-" indicates that the factor is not controlled, a "?" indicates a possible source of concern, and a blank indicates that the factor is not relevant.

SOURCE: From *Applied Psychology in Personnel Management* (4th ed, pp. 400, 403) by W. F. Cascio, 1991, Englewood Cliffs, NJ: Prentice-Hall. Adapted by permission.

Selecting a Research Design

As we have indicated, there are a number of possible research designs to use when conducting an HRD evaluation study. Therefore, what factors should an HRD professional consider when selecting a design to use for an evaluation study?

Obviously, the validity of the conclusion drawn from the study is an important concern. Without valid conclusions, the evaluation effort is compromised. But other issues besides validity also need to be considered. Schmitt and Klimoski (1991) offer four additional criteria: conceptual issues, the costs associated with making a decision error, resources, and the value system and skills of the investigator.

Conceptual issues concern the purpose of the evaluation study and previous research conducted on the training program being evaluated. The design or designs used should permit the investigator to answer the questions they are charged with asking. In addition, if previous research indicates that certain factors may affect training effectiveness (like experience or gender), the research design should address these factors.

Second, it is possible that the investigator will make an incorrect conclusion based on the study. The study may show that the training program did not improve job performance, when in fact it did. Or, the study may show a high degree of transfer of training, while employees actually apply little of what they learned to their jobs. When selecting a research design, the investigator must consider the costs associated with making an incorrect decision based on the study. If the costs are very high (that is, the company will spend a large amount of money using the program or will exclude employees from promotions if they do not successfully complete training), validity of the design becomes more important.

Third, certain designs, such as a pre-test/post-test design or the Solomon four-group design, use more resources than others. The investigator may have limited time, money, facilities, and subjects for the evaluation effort. Evaluation should be as valid as possible within resource constraints.

Finally, some organization members may be more committed and able to conduct some approaches to evaluation research (e.g., more or less rigorous) than other approaches. The expertise and attitudes of those involved in the evaluation effort should be considered (Schmitt & Klimoski, 1991).

Ethical Issues of Evaluation Research

Some of the decisions supervisors and HRD professionals make when conducting HRD evaluations have ethical dimensions. While resolving the paradoxes inherent in ethical dilemmas is no easy task, it is important that these issues be addressed. Actions such as assigning participants to training and control groups, reporting results, and the actual conduct of the evaluation study itself all raise ethical questions. Schmitt and Klimoski (1991) have identified four ethical issues relating to HRD evaluation: informed consent, withholding training, the use of deception, pressure to produce findings. To this list, we will add the issue of confidentiality.

Confidentiality

Some evaluation research projects involve asking participants questions about their own or others' job performance. The results of these inquiries may be embarrassing or lead to adverse treatment by others if they are made public. For example, if evaluation of a management development seminar involves asking participants their opinion of their supervisors, supervisors may become angry with participants who report that they don't think the supervisors are doing a good job. Similarly, employees who perform poorly or make mistakes on criterion measures (like written tests or role playing exercises), may be ridiculed by other employees.

Wherever possible, steps should be taken to ensure confidentiality of attitudes, results, and other information collected during an evaluation study. Using code numbers rather than names, collecting only necessary demographic information, reporting group rather than individual results, using encrypted computer files, and securing research materials are all ways to maintain confidentiality. And as a result, others may be more willing to participate in the evaluation project.

Informed Consent

In many research settings, such as hospitals and academic institutions, evaluation studies are monitored by a review board to ensure that participants are aware that they are participating in a study and know its purpose, what they will be expected to do, and the study's potential risks and benefits. In addition, participants are asked to sign a form stating that they have been informed of these facts and agree to participate in the study. This is called obtaining the participants' **informed consent.**

Review boards and informed consent are not common to many industrial settings; often the norm in these organizations is that management has control over and responsibility for employees, and that this is sufficient. We agree with Schmitt and Klimoski (1991) that ethical considerations and good management are compatible. Wherever possible, informed consent should be obtained from employees who will participate in the evaluation study. This not only encourages fair treatment of employees, but providing complete information may actually improve the effectiveness of the training intervention (Hicks & Klimoski, 1987).

Withholding Training

Research designs involving control groups require that some employees receive training while others do not. This can be problematic if the training is believed to improve the employee's performance, pointing towards organizational benefits like a raise or promotion, or increase the employee's well-being, as in health-related programs. If the training is expected to be effective, is it fair to train some employees and not others just for purposes of evaluation?

There are at least three possible resolutions to this dilemma (Cook & Campbell, 1976). First, an unbiased procedure, such as a lottery, can be used to assign employees to training groups. Second, employees who are assigned to a control group can be assured that if the training is found to be effective they will have the option of receiving the training. Third, the research design can be modified so that both groups are trained, but at different times. One possible design is illustrated below.

Group 1:   Measure ——→ Training ——→ Measure ————————————→ Measure
Group 2:   Measure ————————————→ Measure ——→ Training ——→ Measure

Finding ways to address the issue of withholding training is a matter of practicality, in addition to its ethical nature. Employees assigned to a control group may refuse to participate in the study or be less motivated to complete the criterion measures.

Use of Deception

In some cases, the investigator may feel that the study will yield better results if employees don't realize they are in an evaluation study or if they are given false or misleading information during the study. We believe this practice is unethical and should be used only as a last resort. Employees who are deceived will probably become angry with the management, damaging a trust that is difficult to reestablish. Any benefits of the HRD program are likely to be undermined by the effects to employees who feel they have been betrayed.

Alternatives to deception should be considered. If deception is used, it should be as minimal as possible and employees in the study should be informed of the deception and the reasons for it as soon as their participation or the study ends (Fromkin & Streufert, 1976).

Pressure to Produce Positive Results

HRD professionals and their managers may feel pressure to make certain the results of the evaluation show the program is effective, which may be one reason why rigorous evaluation of HRD programs is not done more often. The HRD people are the ones who design and develop (or purchase), deliver, and evaluate the program. If the evaluation shows the program is not effective, the HRD department may lose funding, support, and have their activities curtailed.

While the possibility of fraud—in the form of doctored results, reporting partial results, or setting up biased studies—exists, it is unclear how often this occurs in HRD evaluation. Given that reports of evaluation fraud in other areas of organizational life are fairly common, one cannot help but be pessimistic about the state of affairs in HRD evaluation.

Professional standards and ethical conduct call for those conducting HRD evaluations and report complete results. That having been said, it is no doubt difficult for many people to face the potential consequences of bad results.

Assessing the Impact of HRD Programs in Dollar Terms

Following Kirkpatrick's levels of evaluation, one of the issues to examine is the effect of the HRD program on the organization's effectiveness. This can be done using a variety of performance indexes, such as productivity and timeliness, but dollars are the most common language understood by managers in most functional areas of an organization. It is important to demonstrate effectiveness on the reaction, learning, and job behavior levels, but HR managers may be at a disadvantage when their results are compared to other divisions that express their results in monetary terms.

One of the goals of translating the effects of training and HRD programs into dollar terms is to make clear that the programs are investments, and as such will lead to payoffs for the organization in the future. While many managers and supervisors pay lip service to this idea, they often see HRD and other HR interventions as *costs*— exemplified by the fact that HR programs are often the first to be cut when financial and economic pressures force the organization to reduce its expenses.

While it has been long believed that HR programs are difficult to assess in financial terms, *evaluation of training costs* and *utility analysis* are two practical options to help the HRD professional determine the financial impact of various programs.

Evaluation of Training Costs[1]

Evaluation of training costs compares the costs incurred in conducting an HRD program to the benefits received by the organization, and can involve two categories of activities: cost benefit evaluation and cost effectiveness evaluation (Cascio, 1987). Cost benefit evaluation involves comparing the monetary costs of training to the benefits received in nonmonetary terms, like improvements in attitudes, safety, and health. Cost effectiveness evaluation focuses on the financial benefits accrued from training, such as increases in quality and profits, and reduction in waste and processing time (Cullen, Sawzin, Sisson, & Swanson, 1978).

Models, including the model of cost effectiveness offered by Cullen et al., (see Figure 6-5), can be very helpful in evaluating the costs of training. This model distinguishes between structured and unstructured training, and lists possible training costs (training development, materials, time, and production losses) and benefits (improvements in time to reach job competency, job performance, and work attitudes).

Robinson and Robinson (1989) have developed a similar model, dividing training costs into five categories: direct costs, indirect costs, development costs, overhead costs, and compensation for participants (see Table 6-6). These training costs are then compared to benefits as measured by improvements in operational indicators, such as job performance, quality, and work attitudes.

The general strategy for evaluating training costs is to measure cost and benefit indicators in dollar terms (or translate them to dollar terms) and then compare them. For example, a program's return on investment can be calculated by dividing total results by total benefits:

---

[1]A helpful source for assessing training and other HRD costs can be found in *Training Cost Analysis* by G. E. Head, 1985, Washington, DC: Marlin Press. This book also contains a number of useful worksheets.

| FIGURE 6-5 | TRAINING COST EFFECTIVENESS MODEL |

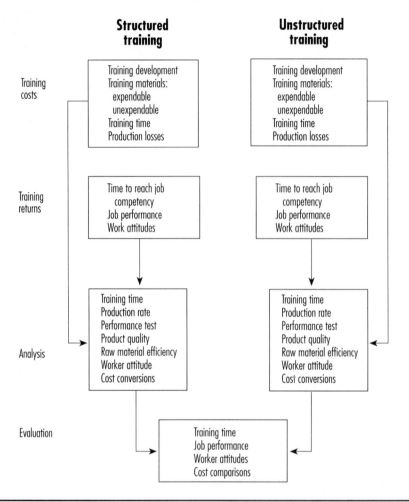

SOURCE: From "Cost-Effectiveness: A Model for Assessing the Training Investment" by J. G. Cullen, S. A. Sawzin, G. R. Sisson, and R. A. Swanson, 1978, *Training and Development Journal, 32*(1), p. 27. Reprinted by permission.

$$\text{Return on investment} = \frac{\text{Results}}{\text{Training costs}}$$

The greater the ratio of results to costs, the greater the benefit the organization receives by conducting the training program. If the ratio is less than 1, then the training program costs more than it returns to the organization.

Table 6-7 shows how Robinson and Robinson (1989) applied their model to calculate the costs for a training program they conducted at a wood panel producing plant. Table 6-8 shows how they calculated the results and return on investment for the same plant.

TABLE 6-6	TRAINING PROGRAM COSTS

To calculate the cost of a training program, an HRD professional should consider five categories of expenses.

Direct costs

These are costs directly associated with the delivery of the learning activities. They include course materials (reproduced or purchased), instructional aids, equipment rental, travel, food and other refreshments, and the instructor's salary and benefits.

Such costs are so directly tied to the delivery of a particular program that if you canceled the program the day before you planned to conduct it, you would not incur them. (While program materials may have been reproduced or purchased, they would not be consumed, and so they would be available for a future program.)

Indirect costs

These costs are incurred in support of learning activities, but cannot be identified with any particular program. Even if the program were canceled at the last minute, such costs could not be recovered.

Examples would be costs for instructor preparation, clerical and administrative support, course materials already sent to participants, and time spent by the training staff in planning the program's implementation. Expenses for marketing the program (for example, direct-mail costs) would also be considered indirect costs. Marketing may have cost $2,000. If there is insufficient registration and if the program is canceled, the $2,000 cannot be recovered.

Development costs

All costs incurred during the development of the program go in this category. Typically, they include the development of videotapes and computer-based instructional programming, design of program materials, piloting of the program, and any necessary redesign. This category also

includes the cost of the front-end assessment, or that portion of the assessment directly attributed to the program. In addition, the costs of evaluation and tracking are included.

If a program is to be conducted for a few years, the cost is often amortized over that period. For example, one-third of the development cost may be charged off in the first year of implementation, one-third in the second year, and one-third in the last year. Otherwise, there is a real "bulge" in the budget, because of development costs during the first year.

Overhead costs

These costs are not directly related to a training program, but are essential to the smooth operation of the training department.

If you have audiovisual equipment that has been purchased specifically for your department, there is a cost to maintain that equipment. Some portion of that annual cost should be charged to the various training programs. If you have classroom space available to you, there is an overhead cost for supplying heat and lighting. The cost of supporting that space for days when the classroom is used for particular courses should be charged to those programs.

Compensation for participants

These costs comprise the salaries and benefits paid to participants for the time they are in a program. If the program is two days long, salaries and benefits for your participants for those two days are costs of the program.

Typically, HRD professionals do not know what individual people earn, but can obtain that information by asking the compensation department to provide a figure for an average salary paid to the various levels of people who will be attending. The average salary is then multiplied by the number of people attending the program, to derive a compensation estimate.

SOURCE: From "Training for Impact" by D. G. Robinson and J. Robinson, 1989, *Training and Development Journal, 43*(8), p. 39. Reprinted by permission.

TABLE 6-7	EXAMPLE OF TRAINING COST ANALYSIS

Direct costs: The travel and per-diem cost is zero, because training took place adjacent to the plant. There is a cost for classroom space and audiovisual equipment, because these were rented from a local hotel. Refreshments were purchased at the same hotel. Because different supervisors attended the morning and afternoon sessions, lunch was not provided.

Direct Costs	
Outside Instructor	0
In-house instructor—12 days x $125	$ 1,500.00
Fringe benefits @ 25% of salary	$ 375.00
Travel and per-diem expenses	0
Materials—56 x $60/participant	$ 3,360.00
Classroom space and audiovisual equipment—12 days @ $50	$ 600.00
Food; refreshments— $4/day x 3 days x 56 participants	$ 672.00
Total direct costs	$ 6,507.00

Indirect costs: The clerical and administrative costs reflect the amount of clerical time spent on making arrangements for the workshop facilities, sending out notices to all participants, and preparing class rosters and other miscellaneous materials.

Indirect Costs	
Training management	0
Clerical/administrative	$ 750.00
Fringe benefits—25% of clerical/ administrative salary	$ 187.00
Postage, shipping, telephone	0
Pre- and postlearning materials—$4 x 56 participants	$ 224.00
Total indirect costs (rounded to nearest dollar)	$ 1,161.00

Development costs: These costs represent the purchase of the training program from a vendor. Included are instructional aids, an instructor manual, videotapes, and a licensing fee. The instructor-training costs pertain to the one-week workshop that the instructor attended to become prepared to facilitate the training. Front-end assessment costs were covered by the corporate training budget.

Development Costs	
Fee to purchase program	$ 3,600.00
Instructor training	
Registration fee	$ 1,400.00
Travel and lodging	$ 975.00
Salary	$ 625.00
Benefits (25% of salary)	$ 156.00
Total development costs	$ 6,756.00

Overhead costs: These represent the services that the general organization provides to the training unit. Because figures were not available, we used 10 percent of the direct, indirect, and program development costs.

Overhead Costs	
General organization support	10% of direct, indirect, and development costs
Top management's time	
Total overhead costs	$ 1,443.00

Compensation for participants: This figure represents the salaries and benefits paid to all participants while they attended the workshop.

Compensation for Participants	
Participants' salary and benefits (time away from the job)	
Total compensation	$16,696.00
Total training costs	$32,564.00
Cost per participant	$ 581.50

SOURCE: From "Training for Impact" by D. G. Robinson and J. Robinson, 1989, *Training and Development Journal, 43*(8), p. 40. Reprinted by permission.

TABLE 6-8		EXAMPLE OF CALCULATING TRAINING RETURN ON INVESTMENT			
Operational Results Area	**How Measured**	**Results Before Training**	**Results After Training**	**Differ- ences (+ or -)**	**Expressed in $**
Quality of panels	% rejected	2% rejected 1,440 panels per day	1.5% rejected 1,080 panels per day	.5% 360 panels	$720 per day $172,800 per year
Housekeeping	Visual inspection using 20-item checklist	10 defects (average)	2 defects (average)	8 defects	Not measur- able in $
Preventable accidents	Number of accidents	24 per year	16 per year	8 per year	
	Direct cost of each accident	$144,000 per year	$96,000 per year	$48,000	$48,000 per year
				Total savings:	$220,800.00

$$\text{ROI} = \frac{\text{Return}}{\text{Investment}} = \frac{\text{Operational Results}}{\text{Training Costs}}$$

$$= \frac{\$220,800}{\$32,564} = 6.8$$

SOURCE: From "Training for Impact" by D. G. Robinson and J. Robinson, 1989, *Training and Development Journal, 43*(8), p. 41. Reprinted by permission.

Utility Analysis

Usually, the results of an evaluation study express the effect of an HRD program in terms of a change in some aspect of the trainee's performance or behavior. For example, if untrained employees average 22.5 units produced and trained employees average 26 units produced, the gain due to training is 3.5 units per employee. **Utility analysis** provides a way to translate these results into dollar terms. One popular approach to utility analysis is the Brogden-Cronbach-Gleser model (Brogden, 1949; Cronbach & Gleser, 1965; Schmidt, Hunter, & Pearlman, 1982). This model computes the gain to the organization in dollar terms (ΔU) using the following variables:

N = Number of trainees

T = Length of time the benefits are expected to last

d_t = True difference of job performance between the trained and untrained groups (expressed in standard deviation units)

SD_y = Dollar value of job performance of untrained employees (expressed in standard deviation units)

C = Costs of conducting the training

Cascio (1987) combines these elements in the following formula to compute the dollar value of improved performance due to training:

$$\Delta U = (N)\ (T)\ (d_t)\ (SD_y) - C$$

Some of the terms in the equation can be directly measured, such as N, C, and d_t, but others, such as T and SD_y, must be estimated. More complicated versions of this formula have been developed to account for other factors that may affect the real monetary value of the benefits accrued, such as attrition and decay in the strength of training effects over time (Cronshaw & Alexander, 1985; Cascio, 1989; Boudreau, 1983).

Cascio (1989) also suggests a method for incorporating the results of utility analysis into cost-benefit analysis for training and HRD programs. Drawing upon techniques of capital budgeting, the three phases of Cascio's approach are as follows:

1. Compute the minimum annual benefits required to break even on the program. (How much of a payback must the program generate in order to cover its costs?)

2. Use break-even analysis to determine the minimum effect size (d_t) that will yield the minimum required annual benefit. (How much of an improvement in job performance must the trained employees show for the program to generate the payback needed to break even?)

3. Use meta-analysis results to determine expected effect size and expected payoff from the program. (What is the likely degree of improvement in job performance that the HRD program being proposed has shown in previously conducted research?)

Cascio also shows how the gains produced by a training program can be expressed in terms of reductions in the size of the work force and the savings in payroll costs associated with the reduced work force.

The goal of this analysis is to put HRD professionals on equal footing with other managers, so they can demonstrate the expected gains of their programs and compare the gains from several HRD programs or to compare other potential investments (like the purchase of a new piece of equipment). While the computational formulas for this approach are somewhat complex, Cascio argues that they can be computerized, thereby only requiring that the HRD manager or professional determine and input the values that correspond to each of the key parameters (like cost, benefits, effect size, and so on).

While utility analysis can help to translate the benefits of training programs into dollar terms, some researchers have questioned its value due to the questionable nature of the estimates used to determine some of the factors in the formula (Dreher & Sackett, 1983). Latham (1988) reports that economists have not accepted this form of analysis as offered by psychologists, who have developed and refined it. It is also unclear to what extent HR and HRD professionals use utility analysis to communicate the effectiveness of HRD programs. Even so, the development and continued refinement of utility analysis creates some exciting possibilities and represents a big step toward enabling HRD managers and professionals to address the issue of accountability, which will likely increase in importance in the future.

We agree with Latham's (1988) suggestion that HRD professionals find out from senior managers what they consider when they determine the value of HRD programs and provide management with information in those terms. For some organizations this may include the dollar value, while in others demonstrating positive improvements in non-monetary terms may be preferred.

A Closing Comment on HRD Evaluation

HRD professionals should recognize the importance of evaluating HRD programs and the variety of ways evaluation can be conducted. Given the myriad choices and the many constraints placed upon HRD efforts, Grove and Ostroff (1991) recommend following these six steps:

1. Perform a needs analysis;

2. Develop an explicit evaluation strategy;

3. Insist on specific training objectives;

4. Obtain participant reactions;

5. Develop criterion instruments; and

6. Plan and execute the evaluation study.

Not every program needs to be evaluated to the same extent. New programs and those with high visibility and expense should be evaluated more rigorously and more thoroughly than proven programs and those that are offered less frequently. The key is to have a well planned evaluation strategy that sets the stage for how and to what extent each program will be evaluated. While those with little evaluation experience may see this task as daunting and burdensome, it is essential. The challenges organizations now face, and the importance of HRD in meeting those challenges, demand it.

RETURN TO OPENING CASE

To prove the bottom line value of its EAP, McDonnell Douglas hired Alexander & Alexander Consulting Group, a Connecticut based consulting firm, to conduct a four year evaluation study focusing on the cost-effectiveness of the EAP.

The study, which began in 1985 and was completed in 1989, examined the substance abuse and mental health components of the EAP. Three groups of employees were studied:

1. EAP users (employees who sought assistance from the EAP and were referred for treatment for substance abuse or mental health problems);

2. Troubled employees who did not use the EAP (employees who were treated for substance abuse or mental illness but who elected not to use EAP services); and

3. A control group of volunteers (employees who were not treated at any time for substance abuse or mental health problems).

For employees in each group, absenteeism and medical claim data were collected over the five-year period.

The results of the study showed that employees treated for substance abuse or mental illness who chose not to use the EAP (the second group) had significantly higher rates of absenteeism and turnover as compared to the control group. There were also significant differences between employees who chose treatment by the EAP compared to troubled employees who did not. During the five-year study period, employees who were treated for substance abuse by the EAP averaged:

*   29 percent fewer days absent

*   42 percent fewer terminations

* $7,150 less in medical costs

* $14,728 less in dependent medical costs

compared to employees with substance abuse problems who were not treated. In addition, employees treated for mental health conditions during the study period averaged:

*   25 percent fewer days absent

*   28 percent fewer terminations

- $3,975 less in employee medical costs

- $8,762 less in dependent medical costs

compared to employees who did not receive treatment for mental health conditions.

The study also demonstrated the pattern of cost savings over the five-year period. The results showed that the cost savings were not achieved during the first year after treatment, but rather during subsequent years as a result of lower relapse rates and related consequences. Utilization rates for McDonnell Douglas's EAP were also impressive. For example, during 1988, the total EAP caseload was 5,800 employees, 602 of which were individuals who had conditions that could benefit from EAP services and who accepted EAP assistance.

The results of this evaluation study enabled Mardee Beckman and the decision makers at McDonnell Douglas to justify the cost-effectiveness of continued use of the EAP. The company predicted that for employees who entered the EAP for treatment in 1989, there would be an offset value during the following four years of $6 million ($2.1 million in employee medical claims, $3.0 million in dependent medical claims, and $0.9 million in a reduction in absenteeism of 7,761 days). In a time where organizations are trying to maximize the contribution from each of their employees and control rising health care costs, McDonnell Douglas appears to have an EAP program that helps them accomplish both of these goals.[2]

Summary

In this chapter we introduced the third and last phase of the training process: HRD evaluation. HRD evaluation is defined as the systematic collection of descriptive and judgmental information necessary to make effective training decisions related to the selection, adoption, value, and modification of various instructional activities. The purposes of HRD evaluation include determining whether the programs have achieved their objectives, building credibility and support for programs, and establishing the value of HRD programs.

We discussed five models of the evaluation process to emphasize the many options available when evaluating HRD programs. Kirkpatrick's model, which is the earliest and most popular, proposes four levels of evaluation: participant reaction, learning, behavior, and results (bottom line). Four other evaluation models (CIPP, CIRO, Brinkerhoff's model, and Bushnell's systems model) were also compared. Each of the models shares common elements with Kirkpatrick's model, but they expand the focus of evaluation beyond measuring post-program effectiveness.

---

[2]*SOURCE*: Adapted from "How McDonnell Douglas Cost-justified Its EAP" by P. Stuart, 1993, *Personnel Journal, 72*(2), p. 48.

Data collection is central to HRD evaluation. Among the types of information that may be collected are individual, system-wide, and economic data. Some of the data collection methods used in HRD evaluation include interview, survey, observation, archival data, and tests and simulations.

Options for designing the evaluation study were also presented. The research design provides a plan for conducting the evaluation effort. It spells out the types of information to be collected, how it will be collected, and the data analysis techniques to be used. The design should balance the need for making valid conclusions with practical and ethical concerns. Research designs can be considered nonexperimental, experimental, or quasi-experimental, and we discussed several examples of each.

HRD professionals are often asked to justify the allocation of resources. This involves a financial assessment of the impact of HRD programs. This can be done by evaluating training costs using cost benefit or cost effectiveness analysis, or translating a trained employee's productivity into dollar terms through utility analysis.

Key Terms and Concepts

control group
cost benefit analysis
cost effectiveness analysis
evaluation
experimental research design
informed consent
internal validity
job behavior criteria
learning criteria
nonexperimental research design

quasi-experimental research
   design
random assignment
reaction criteria
reliability
results criteria
self-report data
utility analysis
validity

Questions for Discussion

1. Since many agree that HRD evaluation is valuable, why isn't it practiced more frequently by organizations? Identify and describe two reasons why evaluation might not be done. How could the objections raised by these reasons be overcome?

2. Describe the four levels of evaluation that make up Kirkpatrick's model of evaluation. Identify one example of data at each level that might be collected to provide evidence for the effectiveness of a class or training program you have participated in.

3. What do CIPP and Brinkerhoff's models of evaluation add to evaluation that is not included in Kirkpatrick's model? What benefit, if any, is there to viewing evaluation in this way?

4. Suppose you have been asked to design a program intended to train airline flight attendant trainees in emergency evacuation procedures. You are now designing the evaluation study to show the flight attendants understand the procedures and use them on the job. Which data collection methods do you think would be the most useful in providing this evidence? Support your choices.

5. Identify and describe three potential problems with using self-report measures (e.g., participant questionnaires) in HRD evaluation. How can these problems be minimized?

6. Compare and contrast experimental and quasi-experimental research design. Is one type of design superior to the other? Support your answer.

7. Describe the Solomon Four Group Design. What are the advantages and disadvantages to using this design to evaluate HRD programs?

8. Identify and describe three ethical considerations in conducting evaluation research. How do these factors affect the evaluation effort?

9. What is the advantage, if any, to expressing the benefits of conducting HRD programs in dollar terms? Briefly describe the cost effectiveness approach to evaluating HRD programs. What are the limitations to using this approach? How can they be overcome?

7

Employee Orientation

Learning Objectives

1. Discuss the content, outcomes, and process of organizational socialization.
2. State the challenges faced by new employees entering an organization, and the things they need in order to be successful.
3. Describe the realistic job preview method of recruiting and explain how it can benefit organizations and new employees.
4. Define and explain the goals of employee orientation.
5. Identify the characteristics of an effective orientation program.
6. Explain how to design and implement an effective orientation program.

OPENING CASE

New employee orientation is one of the most commonly used HRD approaches, but popularity is no guarantee of program quality and effectiveness. As we will discuss in this chapter, the challenge to orientation programs is significant, and problems with these programs are all too common. Ideally, an orientation program should provide new employees with the information they need in a way that helps them adjust to the organization as soon as possible. In addition, the orientation period is an opportune time to allay concerns, reinforce the organization's values, and energize new employees about their new assignments. Yet many organizations fail to take full advantage of this opportunity. Instead, they inundate the recruit with information, including information they may not need or which may be contradictory. Further, many organizations often see orientation as a way to process new employees (completing paperwork) rather than as a way to inspire them and make them feel good about the choice they have made to join the organization.

The HRD staff at Apple Training Support (ATS), a division of Apple Computer, Inc., in Cupertino, California, recognizes the potential and pitfalls of employee orientation. While a two-day orientation session has been effective in introducing new employees to Apple Computer, ATS also wanted to provide its new hires with an understanding of the uniqueness of ATS's mission, structure, and approach. With this goal in mind, Apple set about creating an orientation program that would not only fulfill the expectations of ATS managers and employees, but also demonstrate how computer-based training can enhance learning and program effectiveness.

Introduction

Starting a new job is often a stressful experience. Newcomers find themselves in an unfamiliar work environment surrounded by people they do not know. To be successful in a new position, the new employee must establish relationships and learn new behaviors, facts, procedures, expectations, and values. New employees can also expect surprises along the way that require further adaptation, such as not anticipating the emotional impact of greater responsibility or underestimating the difficulty of adjusting to a new work schedule. In addition to learning new things, new employees must also "unlearn" things that helped them succeed in previous settings (like prior jobs or school) but would be maladaptive in their new setting (Louis, 1980).

The process of adjusting to a new organization is called **organizational socialization.** Socialization is a complex, lengthy process. It may take a new employee weeks or months to understand what is expected from them on the job and how to behave before they are accepted by other organization members. Successful socialization of new members is critical to both the individual and the organization. At stake are:

- The new employee's satisfaction, performance, and commitment to the organization

- The work group's satisfaction and performance

- Start up costs invested in the new employee (such as recruiting, selection, training, and the time until the employee is up to "full speed")

- The likelihood the employee will remain with the organization

- The costs of replacing the employee if he or she leaves

Despite its importance, some organizations do little to introduce and integrate new members, forcing them to learn on their own. Some employees may flourish under this "sink or swim" approach, but even they will likely experience anxiety and frustration during their early tenure. Fortunately, many organizations do recognize the importance of successful socialization and act to facilitate the newcomer's transition into the organization. This chapter provides a discussion of organizational socialization and the nature of this complex process. We will then identify two common approaches to facilitating employee socialization—the **realistic job preview (RJP)** and **employee orientation**—and explain how they can be used to benefit both the individual and the organization.

Socialization: The Process of Becoming an Insider

Organizational socialization is defined as "the process by which an individual acquires the social knowledge and skills necessary to assume an organizational role" (Van Maanen & Schein, 1979, p. 211). The net result of this process is that someone who was considered by organization members to be an outsider is transformed into a productive and accepted insider. While this obviously applies to new hires, they are not the only ones: transferred and promoted employees are socialized, too. Unlike new hires, transfers and promotees begin their socialization as insiders to the larger organization, with an understanding of its goals and values. Yet, like new hires, they are "outsiders" to the group they will be joining and face the challenge of gaining their new colleagues' acceptance and establishing themselves in a new role.

Before we discuss the socialization process itself, it is important that we explore its fundamental concepts: organizational roles, group norms, and expectations.

The Fundamental Concepts of Socialization

Organizational Roles   A **role** is a set of behaviors expected of individuals who hold a given position in a group (Vecchio, 1991). Roles define how a person fits into the organization and what he or she must do to perform effectively. For example, when we encounter a receptionist, we expect that person to perform certain functions of that role, such as greeting us, providing us with information, and directing us to those in the organization we wish to see. When newcomers enter a new group, they must learn what role they are expected to fulfill in order to fit in and perform effectively.

Schein (1971a) observed that organizational roles have three dimensions:

1.   **Inclusionary** A social dimension (outsider, probationary status, permanent status);

2.   **Functional** A task dimension (sales, engineering, plant operations); and

3. **Hierarchical** A rank dimension (line employee, supervisor, middle manager, officer).

A new role requires learning and performing in ways that fulfill the social, functional, and hierarchical dimensions of that role. For example, a patrol officer who is promoted to shift sergeant will not be completely effective until they know the tasks a sergeant must do, are able to do those tasks, and are accepted by others in the sergeant's role.

Van Maanen and Schein (1979) suggest that the various points on these dimensions serve as boundaries that employees cross during their careers. The socialization process becomes much more intense and presents greater challenges just before and after the employee moves across a boundary. Crossing each boundary requires learning new attitudes and behaviors, and with the risk of failed socialization and negative outcomes, such as dissatisfaction and turnover.

Role communication and **role orientation** are two issues that are relevant to organizational socialization. Ideally, an individual's role would be communicated clearly and agreed upon by all concerned parties (including management, peers, and the individual). Unfortunately, roles are not always communicated clearly. Perception plays an important part in how roles are defined and communicated, and the individual, his or her co-workers, the immediate supervisor, and upper management are all likely to view a given role differently. Although many organizations consider a job description to be the official statement of an individual's role, job descriptions are often vague and open to interpretation.

The perceptual nature of organizational roles can lead to three situations that have important consequences for job satisfaction, job performance, and turnover.

1. **Role overload** When the employee perceives the role as being more than he or she can reasonably do.

2. **Role conflict** When the employee receives mixed messages about what is expected of him or her by others, such as a boss and co-workers.

3. **Role ambiguity** When the employee feels the role is unclear— often the result of assuming a newly created position.

Research has shown that role overload, role conflict, and role ambiguity are all related to stress (Jackson & Schuler, 1985), which in turn relates to job satisfaction, job performance, and other outcomes valued by the organization, including turnover and absenteeism (Sullivan & Bhagat, 1992).

The individual's role orientation is also important to socialization. Individuals do not always conform completely to the role prescribed for them. **Role orientation** is the extent to which individuals are innovative in interpreting their organizational roles (Van Maanen & Schein, 1979). Role orientation exists on a continuum, with a **custodial orientation** (conforming to established ways of doing things) at one extreme and an **innovative orientation** (taking initiative in redefining the role) at the other (Jones, 1986). For example, a market research analyst who has an innovative orientation may include educating managers in the ethics of marketing as part of her role, even though other analysts in the organization do not perform this function. It is often beneficial for employees to creatively redefine their roles (have an innovative orientation) in ways that improve their own and the organization's effectiveness. This creativity and innovation will often challenge some of the organization's accepted beliefs and established ways of doing things.

Van Maanen and Schein (1979) suggest that an individual's role orientation will be influenced by the tactics an organization uses to socialize newcomers. Recent research (Jones, 1986; Allen & Meyer, 1990) offers initial support for this suggestion, which we will return to in our discussion of socialization (or people processing) tactics later in this chapter.

Group Norms   **Norms** are the typically unwritten rules of conduct established by group members to control behavior within the group. Group norms are an important part of the socialization process because they indicate the behaviors insiders agree are appropriate. Newcomers must learn and behave in ways that are consistent with the new group's norms if they are to be accepted as an insider.

Groups do not develop or enforce norms for all possible behaviors and situations (Shaw, 1981), but rather only for significant behaviors. Schein (1971b) suggests that organizations distinguish employee behaviors in terms of three levels of importance: *pivotal* (behaviors essential to organizational membership), *relevant* (behaviors that are desirable but not essential), and *peripheral* (unimportant behaviors). He suggested that organizations are more likely to focus on pivotal and relevant behaviors during socialization, and less likely to teach the employee or pay attention to peripheral behaviors. Similarly, Feldman (1984) observed that groups will enforce norms that facilitate group survival, express central values, make expected behaviors simpler or more predictable, or help members avoid interpersonal embarrassment.

Learning a group's norms is not always easy. Norms are not only informal and unwritten, they also vary from group to group within the same organization. Organizations can facilitate the socialization process by providing ways (such as realistic job previews and orientation programs) to help newcomers learn organization and group norms.

Expectations   Expectations are also central to organizational socialization. An **expectation** is a belief about the likelihood that something will occur, and can encompass behaviors, feelings, policies, and attitudes. Newcomers have expectations about how they will be treated, what they will be asked to do, and how they will feel in the new organization, among other things. Expectations are an important variable in a variety of organizational issues, including motivation and decision making. In terms of socialization, researchers have suggested that newcomers' expectations can affect their satisfaction, performance, commitment, and tendency to remain with the organization (Porter & Steers, 1973; Wanous, 1980; Wanous, Poland, Premack, & Davis, 1992).

Researchers have found that typical recruiting practices often result in recruits having inflated expectations of their jobs and organizational life (Wanous, 1976, 1980). **Unrealistically high expectations** are not likely to be met, leading the recruit to be dissatisfied and increase the chances they will leave the organization. Therefore, Wanous (1976) suggests that adjusting new-comer expectations to more reasonable (lower) levels will reduce turnover.

A similar line of thought focuses specifically on **met expectations** (regard-less of the realism of the expectation). Porter and Steers define met expectations as ". . . the discrepancy between what a person encounters on the job and in the way of positive and negative experiences and what [that person] expected to encounter" (1973, p. 152). Unmet expectations can lead to dissatisfaction, which can eventually result in individuals quitting their jobs. This includes not only unrealistically high expectations, but any discrepancy between what the new-comers expect and what they encounter. A newcomer may have realistic expec-tations about an organization's social policies (like allowing time off for family issues), but discover the policies are different than expected (requiring that time off be earned).

Newcomers develop and test expectations throughout the socialization process. The expectations an individual will develop depend on a number of factors and a variety of sources, including the organization and its representa-tives, co-workers, friends, family, the media, as well the newcomer's own per-sonality, attitudes, values, and prior experiences.

Organizations should be aware of the impact expectations have on the new-comer's performance and satisfaction and take steps to ensure the information they provide leads to realistic, attainable expectations. While organizations can help adjust newcomer expectations, surprise cannot be completely eliminated from the newcomer's experience, in part because newcomers may not be aware of how they feel about certain things until they experience them (Louis, 1980).

Content of Socialization

Organizational socialization can be considered a learning process in that new-comers must learn a wide variety of information and behaviors to be accepted as an organizational insider. Fisher (1986) divides the content of socialization learn-ing into five categories:

1. **Preliminary learning,** including the discovery that learning will be necessary, what to learn, and who to learn from;

2. **Learning about the organization,** including goals, values, and policies;

3. **Learning to function in the work group,** including values, norms, roles, and friendships;

4. **Learning how to perform the job,** including the necessary skills and knowledge; and

5. **Personal learning** from experience with the job and organization, including identity, expectations, self-image, and motivation.

According to Fisher, learning in each of these content areas usually results in attitude and behavioral changes within the newcomer.

A related view is offered by Feldman (1981), who claims that socialization consists of three simultaneous learning processes, with each process focusing on learning a different type of content. The processes include:

1. Acquiring a set of appropriate role behaviors;

2. Developing work skills and abilities; and

3. Adjusting to the work group's norms and values.

Feldman argued that recognizing that socialization is comprised of multiple processes provides a useful framework for socialization research and practice.

Taken together, these categorization schemes make it clear that newcomers face a difficult challenge. As we discussed in Chapter 3, learning different content areas often requires different mechanisms (recall Gagne's views). Thus it follows that organizations should use multiple approaches to facilitate the learning that must occur during successful socialization.

Outcomes of Socialization

Socialization theorists have suggested a wide variety of affective, cognitive, and behavioral outcomes of the socialization process (Fisher, 1986). Our discussion of socialization to this point has mentioned a number of possible outcomes, both positive (e.g., organizational commitment) and negative (e.g., dissatisfaction). Table 7-1 lists many possible socialization outcomes that have been discussed in relevant literature. In general, successful socialization means that the

TABLE 7-1	POSSIBLE OUTCOMES OF SOCIALIZATION

1. Role conflict
2. Role ambiguity
3. Role overload
4. General job satisfaction
5. Satisfaction with various job facets
6. Job involvement
7. Self-confidence
8. Commitment to the organization
9. Internal work motivation
10. Internalized values
11. Innovation and cooperation (role orientation)
12. Tenure
13. Job performance
14. Mutual influence
15. Over-conformity
16. Acceptance by organizational members

SOURCE: From "Organizational Socialization: An Integrative Review" by C. D. Fisher, 1986, in K. Rowland & G. Ferris (Eds.) *Research in Personnel and Human Resources Management*, Vol. 4 (pp. 101–145), Greenwich, CT: JAI Press. Adapted by permission.

newcomer develops: (1) greater knowledge of the organization and work group; (2) attitudes that make performing, fitting into, and remaining with the organization and work group possible; and (3) behaviors that lead to personal and organizational effectiveness. Unsuccessful socialization is generally argued to result in unmet expectations, dissatisfaction, lack of commitment, and turnover.

Although many outcomes have been suggested, empirical research demonstrating specifically how and when these outcomes change during the socialization process has lagged behind theory development (Feldman, 1989a; Fisher, 1986). Further research that clarifies these processes is sorely needed.

So far, we have discussed what socialization is, some foundational concepts underlying socialization, and the content and proposed outcomes of socialization. Next, we consider a model of the socialization process and the people processing tactics organizations use to socialize newcomers, before discussing HRD practices that can be used to facilitate socialization.

Stage Models of the Socialization Process

Many theorists who have written about organizational socialization (e.g., Feldman, 1976, 1981; Graen, 1976; Schein, 1978; Van Maanen, 1976) have described the process using stage models, which depict the steps or stages involved in the process. Five stage models of organizational socialization (Buchanan, 1974; Feldman, 1976, 1981; Porter, Lawler, & Hackman, 1975; Schein, 1978; Wanous, 1980) are summarized in Table 7-2. Our discussion, however, will focus on a representative three-stage model developed by Daniel Feldman (1981), which is depicted in Figure 7-1.

The first stage, **anticipatory socialization,** begins prior to the individual joining the organization. In this stage, the person forms an impression about what membership in an organization is like. Information about organizations is available from a variety of sources, such as rumors, anecdotes, advertisements, the media, and employment recruiters. For example, image advertising, such as Dow Chemical's "We Let You Do Great Things" and the U.S. Army's "Be All You Can Be" and "It's a Great Place to Start" campaigns, send messages about life within those organizations. Media also plays a role in helping organizations establish reputations. Reports and ads about Apple Computer and Microsoft, for example, communicate the message that these organizations are intellectually stimulating places to work where dedicated employees put in long hours.

These impressions influence expectations that may in turn affect an individual's behavior. For example, a person's expectations when looking for a job may attract them to one organization, reject another organization from their consideration, and affect their decision to remain at an organization where they initially choose to work. As mentioned earlier, it is important that managers provide accurate information and help correct inaccurate expectations to avoid the potential negative consequences for performance, satisfaction, and tenure.

Also during the anticipatory socialization stage, the individual may be examining the extent to which their skills, abilities, needs, and values match those they perceive the organization requires or prefers. These judgments can affect the

TABLE 7-2 FIVE STAGE MODELS OF ORGANIZATIONAL SOCIALIZATION

Feldman's (1976a, 1976b) Three-Stage Model	Buchanan's (1974) Three-Stage Early Career Model	Porter, Lawler, & Hackman's (1975) Three-Stage Entry Model	Schein's (1978) Three-Stage Socialization Model	Wanous's (1980) Integrative Approach to Stages of Socialization
Stage 1: Anticipatory socialization—"getting in" Setting of realistic expectations Determining match with the newcomer	**Stage 1: First year—basic training and initiation** Establish role clarity for newcomer Establish cohesion with peers Clarify relationship of peers with rest of organization Confirmation/disconfirmation of expectations	**Stage 1: Prearrival** Setting of newcomer expectations Reward and punishment of behaviors	**Stage 1: Entry** Search for accurate information Climate of mutual settings Creation of false expectations by both parties Inaccurate information is basis for job choice	**Stage 1: Confronting and accepting organizational reality** Confirmation/disconfirmation of expectations Conflicts between personal values and organizational climates Discovering rewarded/punished behaviors
Stage 2: Accommodation—"breaking in" Initiation into the job Establish interpersonal relationships Roles clarified Congruence between self and organizational performance appraisal	**Stage 2: Performance—years two, three and four at work** Commitment to organization according to norms Reinforcement of self-image by organization Resolution of conflicts Feelings of personal importance	**Stage 2: Encounter** Confirmation/disconfirmation of expectations Reward and punishment of behaviors	**Stage 2: Socialization** Accept organizational reality Cope with resistance to change Congruence between organizational climate and person's needs Organization's evaluation of newcomer's performance Cope with either too much ambiguity or too much structure	**Stage 2: Achieving role clarity** Initiation to the job's tasks Definition of interpersonal roles Coping with resistance to change Congruence between self- and organizational performance appraisals Coping with structure and ambiguity
Stage 3: Role management—"settling in" The degree of fit between one's life interests outside of work and the demands of the organization. Resolution of conflicts at the workplace itself.	**Stage 3: Organizational dependability—the fifth year and beyond** All succeeding years are in this stage Diversity due to individual experiences	**Stage 3: Change and acquisition** Alteration of newcomer's self-image Form new relationships Adopt new values Acquire new behaviors	**Stage 3: Mutual acceptance** Signals of organizational acceptance Signals of newcomer's acceptance Commitment to the organization Commitment to work	**Stage 3: Locating oneself in the organizational context** Learning behaviors congruent with the organization's desires Outside and work interest conflicts resolved Job challenge leads to work commitments New interpersonal relations, new values and altered self-image
				Stage 4: Detecting signposts of successful socialization Company dependability and commitment High general satisfaction Feelings of mutual acceptance Job involvement and intrinsic motivation increases

SOURCE: From "Organizational Socialization and Group Development: Toward an Integrative Perspective" by J. P. Wanous, A. E. Reichers, & S. D. Malik, 1984, *Academy of Management Review*, 9, p. 674. Reprinted by permission.

FIGURE 7-1	FELDMAN'S MODEL OF ORGANIZATIONAL SOCIALIZATION

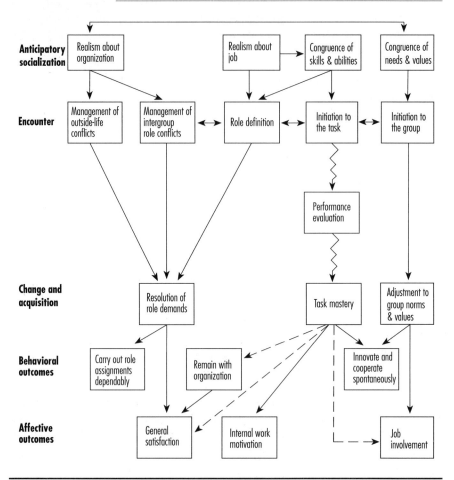

SOURCE: From "The Multiple Socialization of Organization Members" by D. C. Feldman, 1981, *Academy of Management Review*, *6*, p. 311. Reprinted by permission.

individual's behavior, both in terms of whether they will attempt to join the organization and how they may interact with organization members.

The **encounter** stage of the socialization process begins when a recruit makes a formal commitment to join the organization. A formal commitment may mean signing an employment contract or simply accepting an offer of employment or membership. At this point the individual crosses the inclusionary boundary separating the organization from the outside environment and begins to discover what the organization is really like. During this stage, pre-employment expectations may either be confirmed or disconfirmed. This can lead to some unpleasant surprises. An employee who joined an organization because of an impression that advancement into and through the management ranks will be rapid may find promotions come slowly and are fewer in number than expected. During this stage, new employees must manage conflicts between lifestyle and work, resolve any role conflicts within the work group, define and clarify their own roles, become familiar with the dynamics of the work group and job, and learn and perform the tasks required by the job.

The third and last stage in Feldman's process is called **change and acquisition.** This stage occurs when the new employees accept the norms and values of the group, master the tasks they must perform, and resolve any role conflicts and overloads. Feldman suggests that employees who successfully complete this stage will likely be satisfied, internally motivated, involved in the job, perform their jobs dependably, and remain with the organization.

It is important to recognize that socialization does not occur in a vacuum. The process is affected by group development and group dynamics, job learning, career development, and life development (Feldman, 1989a; Schein, 1978; Wanous, 1982; Wanous et al., 1984). Furthermore, it should be clear from the preceding discussion that socialization is a two-way street. Not only is the newcomer changed by events during the socialization process, but organizational insiders may be changed as well.

Two other caveats about stage models of socialization are worth mentioning. First, stage models are used to provide a framework describing what happens to a typical, or average, individual. Research testing stage models has not kept pace with model development (Fisher, 1986; Feldman, 1989a). A variety of issues, including the rate of socialization and whether individuals progress through the stages in a "lock step" order, have not been adequately addressed (Wanous, 1992). Second, stage models are not the only way to view the socialization process. For example, Louis (1980) developed a process model of events that might occur within the encounter stage. In her view, surprises are typical, and socialization occurs as newcomers find ways to explain these events and use these explanations to predict what will happen in the future. Therefore, it is important to view such models as suggestions rather than absolutes.

People Processing Tactics and Strategies

Even if the effort is not deliberate or part of a planned program, all organizations influence the adjustment of new members. Van Maanen (1978; Van Maanen & Schein, 1979) call these actions **people processing strategies,** and suggest seven pairs of tactics organizations may use when processing or socializing newcomers (see Table 7-3).

The particular tactics an organization uses are often the result of tradition rather than a conscious choice (Van Maanen, 1978). Van Maanen argues that whatever people processing strategies an organization uses, they will have a strong impact on newcomers' attitudes, behaviors, and beliefs. Further, Van Maanen and Schein (1979) and others have hypothesized that various combinations of people processing tactics will lead newcomers to develop a particular role orientation. Specifically, they suggested the following (see Table 7-4 for a summary):

TABLE 7-3	PEOPLE PROCESSING STRATEGIES

1. **Formal versus Informal** Involves the newcomer's role and whether the setting in which the activity occurs is segregated from the ongoing work content. Formal processes are segregated and make the newcomer's role explicit. Informal processes take place within the work context, do not clearly delineate the newcomer's role, and are usually unstructured. In a formal strategy, all newcomers will likely have very similar experiences (whether they are processed together or individually), whereas in an informal strategy, each newcomer's experience will likely be unique.

2. **Individual versus Collective** The degree to which newcomers are socialized individually or as a group. In a collective (or group) strategy, newcomers tend to develop a collective sense of the organization and possibly a sense of comraderie ("we're all in this together"). Here newcomers can test out their own ideas with one another and form a consensus. Individual strategies will likely be more expensive.

3. **Sequential versus Nonsequential** Sequential strategies contain a series of stages (such as probationary appointment, associate, or partner) the newcomer must progress through before gaining a recognized role and status within the organization. A nonsequential process contains one stage in which the complete transition occurs (such as a promotion to supervisor after completing a two-week training program).

4. **Fixed versus Variable** The time frame for completing the transition period. In a fixed process, the newcomer knows in advance when the transition period will end (three years in an apprenticeship program to be considered a journeyman). In a variable process, newcomers are not aware of when the process will end, and in fact the time it takes to complete the process may vary from individual to individual.

5. **Tournament versus Contest** In tournament processes, newcomers are sorted according to their potential, ambition, background, or other factors, and then assigned to separate "tracks" accordingly. For example, some systems separate new management recruits into either a fast track or a regular track. Contest processes, however, do not make such early distinctions among newcomers. Newcomers enter the process together, and they progress through various channels according to their own observed abilities and interests.

6. **Serial versus Disjunctive** Serial strategies involve having senior organization members work with newcomers to groom them to assume similar roles (as in a mentor program). In disjunctive strategies, newcomers are socialized by organization members who are not a part of their work group (as with trainers). Van Maanen hypothesizes that serial strategies are likely to perpetuate established values and norms, while disjunctive strategies are more likely to increase innovation.

7. **Investiture versus Divestiture** The degree to which the socialization process is designed to preserve or strip away the newcomer's identity. Investiture strategies reinforce the uniqueness and viability of the newcomer's individual characteristics, and are commonly used when socializing recruits for senior management positions. Divestiture strategies attempt to suppress certain characteristics of newcomers (such as their attitudes and self-confidence) and replace them with characteristics deemed of value to the organization, as is done during basic training in military organizations.

SOURCE: From "People Processing: Strategies of Organizational Socialization" by J. Van Maanen, 1978, *Organizational Dynamics*, 7, pp. 18–36. Adapted by permission.

TABLE 7-4	SOCIALIZATION STRATEGIES

Strategies	Role Orientation
Van Maanen & Schein (1979)	
Sequential, variable, serial, and divestiture	Custodial
Collective, formal, random, fixed, and disjunctive	Content Innovation
Individual, informal, random, disjunctive, and investiture	Role Innovation
Jones (1986)	
Institutionalized:	Custodial
Collective, formal, sequential, fixed, serial, and investiture	
Individualized:	Innovative
Individual, informal, random, variable, disjunctive, and divestiture	

1. A process that is sequential, variable, serial, and involves divestiture practices will lead newcomers to develop a **custodial orientation** (they will define their roles as the organization traditionally has defined them). An extreme example of this approach is the Marine Corps basic training program.

2. A process that is collective, formal, random, fixed and disjunctive will lead to a **content innovation** role orientation (newcomers will make changes and improvements in their roles but still consider their mission from the organization's traditional perspective). An example of this is General Motors Corporation's Saturn division, which was created as a way for the company to redefine how automobiles would be designed and built.

3. A process that is individual, informal, random, disjunctive, and uses investiture practices will lead to a **role innovation** orientation (creatively redefining the mission and goals of the role, going beyond merely improving the knowledge base or practices within the role). Senior managers who are hired from outside an organization are likely to be socialized in this way, taking advantage of their unique set of qualities to introduce major changes in the organization.

To date, few studies have tested these hypotheses. Jones (1986) tested Van Maanen and Schein's hypotheses in a study of a group of recent MBA recipients. As Table 7-4 illustrates, he classified socialization tactics as either institutionalized (collective, formal, sequential, fixed, serial, and investiture) or individualized (individual, informal, random variable, disjunctive, and divestiture).[1] His findings support the notion that institutionalized tactics lead to a

---

[1]Jones changed two of Van Maanen and Schein's predictions: He predicted fixed tactics and investiture tactics would decrease innovation.

custodial role orientation, and that individualized tactics lead to an innovation role orientation. Allen and Meyer (1990), also using MBA recipients, replicated Jones's (1986) findings, and further found that the serial-disjunctive dimension was the best predictor of role orientation. While these studies offer initial support for the effect socialization tactics can have on newcomer attitudes and behavior, further research using different samples and methods (beyond using self-report data) is needed before any firm conclusions can be made.

What Do Newcomers Need?

So far, we have described at some length the socialization process in terms of the key concepts involved, content, outcomes, stages, and people processing strategies. Given this knowledge, now we must ask: What do newcomers need in order to be successfully socialized? A good way to approach this question is to compare what insiders have to what newcomers lack. Insiders typically have a clear idea of their role in the organization, the group and organization's norms and values, the KSAs and experience that permit them to perform their work effectively, and they have adjusted to their roles, the work group, and the organization to the point that they have chosen to remain with the organization. In addition, insiders possess three essential elements (Louis, 1980):

1. **Accurate Expectations** Insiders normally know what to expect of the situations they find themselves in, so there are fewer surprises to confront them. Newcomers' expectations are more likely to differ from organizational reality.

2. **Knowledge Base** When surprises do occur, insiders have the knowledge base (from history and experience in the setting) to more accurately make sense of the surprising event. Newcomers lack this knowledge.

3. **Other Insiders** Insiders have other co-workers to compare their judgments and interpretations of organizational events. Newcomers have not yet developed the relationships with insiders they can trust and draw upon to help them interpret organizational events.

Not only are insiders less frequently surprised by organizational events than newcomers, they have the means available to make more accurate interpretations of such events. Newcomers are more likely to make inappropriate or dysfunctional interpretations, potentially leading to anxiety and behaviors and beliefs that differ from those of the insiders. For example, suppose the supervisor of a group of prison guards yells at several guards who arrived late for a shift, threatening them with disciplinary action. This may be typical of the way the supervisor handles rule violations, who in fact rarely carries out these threats. Therefore, insiders would simply interpret this event as their boss blowing off steam, and carry on with the shift. A newcomer to the group may view this episode differently, becoming apprehensive and worried about doing everything by the book.

Therefore, newcomers need clear information on expectations, roles, norms, values, and assistance in developing the KSAs and experience needed to perform the job effectively. Also, following Louis's (1980) view, newcomers need help interpreting events in the organization (especially surprises) and could benefit from insiders who are genuinely willing to share their knowledge and judgments. In addition, newcomers will also need help in forming accurate expectations about the organization and finding ways to cope with their new roles, both at work and in their personal lives.

As we have seen, research on organizational socialization provides managers and HRD professionals with a rich base upon which to develop programs and practices to assist newcomers in making the transition to effective, accepted insiders. We now turn our attention to two approaches used by organizations to apply these theories to increase newcomer effectiveness and satisfaction.

The Realistic Job Preview

A **realistic job preview (RJP)** involves providing recruits with complete information about the job and the organization. An RJP exists in stark contrast to the traditional approach to recruiting, sometimes referred to as the "flypaper approach" (Schneider & Schmitt, 1986), in which the organization tries to attract applicants by selectively presenting only positive aspects of the job and downplaying any negative aspects. In an RJP, the recruit is given both positive and negative information—in essence, the whole truth. Thus if a job involves long hours and extensive travel, this information would not be withheld or glossed over, but rather discussed openly.

According to Wanous (1980), the goal of an RJP is to increase the newcomer's satisfaction, commitment, and likelihood that they will remain with the organization. Wanous's (1978, 1992) model of the RJP process (see Figure 7-2) suggests four interrelated mechanisms: vaccination, self selection, coping, and personal commitment.

1. **Vaccination against Unrealistically High Expectations** Providing accurate information to outsiders is similar to vaccinating people from a disease. Recruits are given information that permits them to adjust their expectations according to the reality of the job.

2. **Self Selection** Realistic expectations enable recruits to decide whether the job and the organization match their individual needs. If they are incompatible, the recruit will probably not accept the position, thus saving the organization from hiring someone who would likely be dissatisfied and quit. The model suggests that self-selecting individuals are more likely to be satisfied employees.

3. **Coping Effect** Realistic expectations help the newcomers develop a clear idea of their roles, which in turn enables them to develop coping strategies for performing their jobs effectively.

FIGURE 7-2   **REALISTIC JOB PREVIEW EFFECTS**

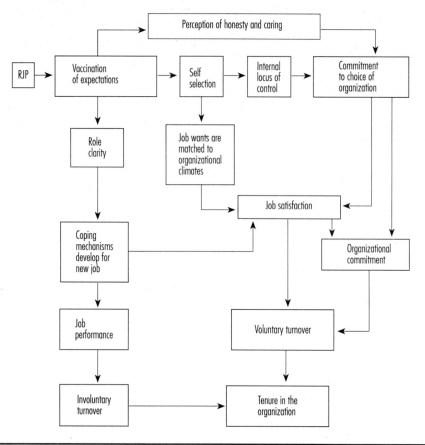

SOURCE: From "Realistic Job Previews: Can a Procedure to Reduce Turnover Also Influence the Relationship between Abilities and Performance?" by J. P. Wanous, 1978, *Personnel Psychology, 31*, p. 251. Reprinted by permission.

4. **Personal Commitment**   A recruit who makes a decision to join the organization based on a realistic perspective will likely develop a personal commitment to their choice. This encourages job satisfaction and a long-term commitment to remaining with the organization.

Although the RJP occurs during the recruitment process, it can be considered an HRD intervention in that it shares many of the same goals and techniques as other HRD approaches. The socialization process begins before an employee formally joins the organization, and the RJP addresses its initial step (anticipatory socialization) by attempting to adjust unrealistic impressions and reinforce accurate expectations.

How RJPs Are Used

The first step in developing an RJP is to assess the need for one. Wanous (1992) suggests using interviews and questionnaires to assess the satisfaction, commitment, and turnover of new employees in the organization. In addition, questions should be asked about whether recruits' expectations were realistic and the extent to which the organization met their expectations. Employees who voluntarily leave the organization should be interviewed to determine their reasons for leaving. Often, employees leave for reasons that are unrelated to their job satisfaction (including following a spouse to a new location, a change of heart about a career choice, returning to school, and receiving a better offer); in these cases, an RJP would likely do little to reduce the turnover.

Furthermore, Wanous (1992) points out that the performance of newcomers who voluntarily leave should also be considered. Some turnover is desirable, particularly that of poor performers. If this is the case and the organization would like to improve the situation (as when it is difficult to find new recruits), an alternative selection or training approach would likely be more effective than an RJP.

Advocates have suggested a number of conditions in which an RJP can be both useful and effective (Wanous, 1992; Breaugh, 1983, 1992), including:

- When job candidates can be selective about job offers, especially during times of low unemployment.

- When the selection ratio is low (the organization has many more job applicants than positions available).

- When the recruits are unlikely to have information available to develop realistic expectations (such as with entry level, complex, or "unique" jobs).

- When replacement costs are high.

A variety of media for delivering an RJP have been suggested, including printed materials (like booklets), audiovisual presentations (videos), discussions with a representative of the organization (usually a recruiter or job incumbent), oral presentations, and interviews (Wanous, 1992). Given that an RJP can be seen as a philosophy of recruiting rather than a specific program, other media are also possible, including job advertisements, recruiting literature, direct observation of the work environment (such as a tour), work simulations, and providing the recruit with actual work experience (such as a co-op or internship) (Breaugh, 1992).

Unfortunately, the research conducted to date has focused primarily on booklets and videotapes, with little research comparing the relative effectiveness of various media. An exception is a study by Colarelli (1984), which found that a two-way discussion between the recruit and a job incumbent proved more effective than an RJP booklet in reducing turnover. While it can be argued that using media that provide greater realism and immediacy (like videos) and opportunities for two-way communication may be more effective than static approaches (like booklets), the expense of using such media may outweigh the benefits. Further research that examines both the effectiveness and utility of various media is needed.

In addition to selecting what media to present the RJP, its content must be chosen, considering the following (Wanous, 1989):

- **Descriptive or Judgmental Content** Descriptive content focuses on factual information, while judgmental content communicates incumbents' feelings.

- **Extensive or Intensive Content** Extensive content contains all pertinent information, while intensive content implies selective information that is presented more briefly and forcefully.

- **Degree of Content Negativity** Should the content of the RJP be highly negative, moderately negative, or somewhere in between?

- **Message Source** If an audiovisual medium is used, should the message be presented by actors, job incumbents, or other organization members, like supervisors or trainers?

Wanous recommends using content that is judgmental, intensive, moderately negative, and presented by job incumbents. In addition, he also suggests that (a) recruits be explicitly encouraged to self select, (b) the RJP message have high credibility and match the medium used, and (c) the information presented match the organizational climate (Wanous, 1992). These recommendations seem reasonable, but the research currently available is insufficient to draw firm conclusions. Therefore, those preparing RJPs are advised to review the available literature and to examine the issues and arguments in light of their needs, budget, and available resources.

Timing is critical to the RJP. According to theory, RJPs should be given as early as possible (before an offer is made) in order to activate important mechanisms like vaccination and self selection. However, this can be an expensive proposition, depending on the number of recruits and the media used. In addition, senior management may be less likely to approve using negative information if the RJP is given early (such as in a recruiting video) rather than late in the process (after an offer is made) (Wanous, 1989).

Research conducted so far does not offer any clear guidance on the timing of RJPs because in many of the studies the RJP was presented later in the process (e.g., after an offer or after the recruit accepted an offer). Although these studies have shown RJPs are effective in lowering expectations and turnover to some extent, it may be that the timing used in these studies has led to conservative estimates of effectiveness (Breaugh, 1992). Early delivery of the RJP seems to be the best approach, using multiple forms of media—like job ads, recruiting brochures and videos—to communicate realistic information throughout the organizational entry process. Then more expensive approaches can be used later, if necessary, when there are fewer individuals to process.

Are RJPs Effective?

There are a variety of choices available to help organizations evaluate the effectiveness of their RJP, including the criteria listed in Table 7-5. We recommend organizations should evaluate their RJPs and communicate the results of their evaluations through the scientific and practitioner literature. This will serve to expand the knowledge base upon which HRD can make more informed decisions about designing and implementing RJPs.

A relatively large number of studies examining the effectiveness of RJPs have been conducted, including a number of meta-analyses (McEvoy & Cascio, 1985; Premack & Wanous, 1985; Reilly, Brown, Blood, & Malatesta, 1981; Wanous, 1977, 1980, 1992; Wanous & Colella, 1989) reviewing and combining the findings of these studies. In general, research has shown that RJPs can reduce inflated expectations and have a beneficial effect on turnover, satisfaction, and commitment. The average reduction of turnover has been between 5 and 10 percent (Premack & Wanous, 1985; Wanous, 1992). Although much research has been done, many of the studies have significant flaws. Thus, while it appears that RJPs are effective, better designed studies that examine both underlying theory and practical issues will be of great benefit.

To summarize, while the magnitude of effectiveness demonstrated thus far is not as high as advocates had hoped for, RJPs offer a practical, relatively inexpensive, ethical way to facilitate socialization for new employees. HRD

TABLE 7-5	EVALUATION CRITERIA FOR THE REALISTIC JOB PREVIEW

Stage of Entry	Evaluation Criteria
Pre-entry	1. Ability of the organization to recruit newcomers
Entry	2. Initial expectations of newcomers
	3. Choice of organization by the individual, (specific job wants being matched with climates)

Post-entry	4. Initial job attitudes
	   Satisfaction with the job
	   Commitment to the organization
	   Descriptive statements about the job (to be compared with expectations held as an outsider)
	
	   Thoughts about quitting

	5. Job performance
	6. Job survival and voluntary turnover rates

SOURCE: From *Organizational Entry: Recruitment, Selection, Orientation, and Socialization of Newcomers* (2nd ed., p. 72) by J. P. Wanous, 1992, Reading, MA: Addison-Wesley. Adapted by permission.

practitioners are encouraged to consider integrating RJPs within their organization's socialization processes.

Employee Orientation Programs

Employee orientation programs are designed to introduce new employees to the job, supervisor, co-workers, and the organization. Orientation programs typically begin after the newcomer has agreed to join the organization, usually on the individual's first day at work. Unlike realistic job previews, which affect primarily the anticipatory stage of socialization, employee orientation programs focus on the encounter stage of socialization, which is the period during which the newcomer finds out what the job and life in the organization are really like.

Commonly cited objectives of orientation programs (Feldman, 1980; Gomersall & Myers, 1966; Ivancevich & Glueck, 1986) include the following:

- Reduce the newcomer's stress and anxiety

- Reduce startup costs

- Reduce turnover

- Reduce the time it takes for the newcomer to reach proficiency (training and "break-in" time)

- Assist the newcomer in learning the organization's values and expectations

- Assist the newcomer in acquiring appropriate role behaviors

- Help the newcomer adjust to the work group and its norms

- Encourage development of positive attitudes

Orientation programs are common in organizations of all sizes. Two recent surveys of HRD professionals (Grossman & Magnus, 1989; Lee, 1991) reveal that 82 percent of responding organizations conduct some form of orientation program (including 93 percent of organizations with more than 5,000 employees, and 75 percent of those with fewer than 500 employees) (Grossman & Magnus, 1989). Orientation programs exist for a wide variety of jobs and occupations, with recent articles reporting on programs for new associates at a law firm (O'Neill, 1988), a credit union (Crumrine, 1989), and for middle and senior managers at a hospital (Compton, 1988).

Orientation Program Content

Orientation programs typically cover both general company information, which may be provided by the HRD staff, and job-specific information, which would more likely be provided by the newcomer's immediate supervisor. Company information might include an overview of the company, key policies and procedures, the mission statement, company goals and strategy, compensation, benefits, safety and accident prevention, employee and union relations, and physical facilities. Job-specific topics could include the department's function, job duties and responsibilities, policies, rules, and procedures, a tour of the department, and introduction to department employees (St. John, 1980).

Given the nature of organizational socialization, it is important that organizations clearly communicate job expectations to new employees. Such things as job responsibilities, tasks, reporting lines, accountability, and performance standards should be explained. All too often, a job description is the sole means for communicating this information, but, as mentioned earlier, important job characteristics may be missing from this description. For example, relationships with co-workers, clients, and customers; work rules; and working conditions all play roles in establishing expectations and should be discussed.

The new employee should be given an overview of the organization's mission, goals, structure, and products. These issues are critical. The organizational mission statement serves to reinforce basic values and the organization's place in the industry and society. An employee who understands the importance of the mission is more likely to behave in accordance with it. Some organizations use a "credo" to communicate the core mission and reinforce this in company policies and goals. Many organizations try to simplify these statements and refer to them in a variety of official documents (such as the employee's manual and business reports).

Compensation and benefits policies should also be explained during orientation. Some organizations devote a portion of the orientation period to completing compensation and benefit forms to make sure employees know what they are entitled to and are enrolled in the appropriate programs.

Orienting the newcomer to the department provides them with a better understanding of how different jobs fit together within the whole of that unit, as well as how the unit or department fits into the larger organization. Things such as work flow and coordination should be discussed. Finally, the physical layout of the workplace should also be explained, including the locations of supplies, facilities (like the cafeteria and rest rooms), emergency exits, and any unusual features.

A wide range of media are used in orientation programs, including lectures, videos, printed materials, and discussions. The length of orientation programs varies, from a few hours to several days to periodic sessions scheduled over several months. Table 7-6 lists a timetable of events for an orientation program developed for Corning (McGarrell, 1984).

Orientation Roles

One of the most important elements of an effective orientation experience is frequent interaction between the newcomers and their supervisors, co-workers, and other organization members. Reichers (1987) suggests that these interactions are the primary vehicle through which socialization occurs, since it is these

TABLE 7-6	**A TIMETABLE OF EVENTS FOR CORNING'S ORIENTATION PROGRAM**

Material Distribution

As soon as possible after a hiring decision is made, orientation material is distributed:

- The new person's supervisor gets a pamphlet titled *A Guide for Supervisors.*
- The new person gets an orientation plan.

The Pre-Arrival Period

During this period the supervisor maintains contact with the new person, helps with housing problems, designs the job and makes a preliminary MBO (management by objectives) list after discussing this with the new person, gets the office ready, notifies the organization that this has been done and sets the interview schedule.

The First Day

On this important day, new employees have breakfast with their supervisors, go through processing in the personnel department, attend a *Corning and You* seminar, have lunch with the seminar leader, read the workbook for new employees, are given a tour of the building and are introduced to co-workers.

The First Week

During this week, the new employee (1) has one-to-one interviews with the supervisor, co-workers, and specialists; (2) learns the how-tos, wheres and whys connected with the job; (3) answers questions in the workbook; (4) gets settled in the community; and (5) participates with the supervisor in firming up the MBO plan.

The Second Week

The new person begins regular assignments.

The Third and Fourth Weeks

The new person attends a community seminar and an employee benefits seminar (a spouse or guest may be invited).

The Second through the Fifth Month

During this period, assignments are intensified and new people have biweekly progress reviews with their supervisors, attend six two-hour seminars at intervals (on quality and productivity, technology, performance management and salaried compensation plans, financial and strategic management, employee relations and EEO and social change), answer workbook questions about each seminar, and review answers with their supervisors.

The Sixth Month

The new employee completes the workbook questions, reviews the MBO list with the supervisor, participates in a performance review with the supervisor, receives a certification of completion for Phase I orientation, and makes plans for Phase II orientation.

The Seventh through the Fifteenth Months

This period features Phase II orientation: division orientation, function orientation, education programs, MBO reviews, performance reviews, and salary reviews.

SOURCE: From "An Orientation System That Builds Productivity" by E. J. McGarrell, Jr., 1984, *Personnel Administrator, 29*(10), p. 76. Reprinted by permission.

insiders who can provide newcomers with much of the information they need to make sense of the organization. He argues that the rate of socialization during the encounter stage is dependent on the frequency of these interactions: the more interaction, the faster the newcomer becomes socialized. In one study, conducted by Louis, Posner, and Powell (1983), new employees rated interactions with peers, supervisors and senior co-workers to be the most helpful (out of ten sources) in their socialization. Furthermore, these interactions were correlated with newcomer attitudes (job satisfaction, organizational commitment, and intention to stay). By contrast, formal orientation programs (listed separately in the study) were considered to be only moderately helpful and correlated only to organizational commitment. Thus, these findings suggest that the newcomers' orientation experience should include frequent contact with their supervisors, co-workers, and the HRD staff.

The Supervisor The supervisor plays a pivotal role in the orientation process, serving as both an information source and a guide for the new employee. The supervisor can help the newcomer overcome feelings of anxiety by providing factual information, clear and realistic performance expectations, and emphasizing the employee's likelihood of succeeding in the organization. Gomersall and Myers (1966) demonstrated that an orientation program designed to reduce anxiety by communicating four key points ("Your opportunity to succeed is very good"; "Disregard 'hall talk'"; "Take the initiative in communication"; and "Get to know your supervisor") significantly reduced turnover, training time, absenteeism, waste and rejects, and costs.

In addition, the supervisor can assist new employees by encouraging their acceptance by co-workers. In some organizations, the supervisor judiciously assigns the new employee a "buddy," who is responsible for helping the new employee adjust to the job environment. Mentorship programs, which pair junior members of the organization with experienced senior members, can also be used for this purpose (see Chapter 11).

According to Feldman (1980) six other important supervisor orientation functions include:

1. Providing (or arranging for) training in job specifics

2. Buffering the newcomer from demands outside the work group for a period of time to facilitate job learning

3. Providing challenging initial assignments

4. Conducting timely, constructive performance evaluations

5. Diagnosing problems (both structural and interpersonal) that create conflicts

6. Using the newcomer's arrival as an opportunity to reallocate tasks or redesign work to improve effectiveness and employee satisfaction with the work system

It is essential that supervisors receive training to help them fulfill their orientation responsibilities effectively. At Corning, supervisors receive a written guide and a copy of the new employee workbook and attend a three-hour workshop in which they learn about the orientation system, the logic behind it, their role, and how to perform their role effectively (McGarrell, 1984). Similarly, Reinhardt (1988) recommends that supervisors be given a standardized first-day curriculum, informing them of the issues that should be discussed with new employees on their first day at work.

Co-Workers   Louis et al. (1983) show that newcomers view interactions with co-workers as particularly helpful in their socialization to the organization, by providing support, information, and training. In addition, co-workers are in a particularly good position to help the newcomer learn the norms of the work group and organization. Co-workers can also relieve newcomers' anxiety by discouraging **hazing** activities, in which new employees are targets of practical jokes or are harassed because they lack certain information. One example of hazing involves sending the new employee on an errand to get something everyone but the new employee knows doesn't exist. Although some people feel incidents of hazing are part of the socialization ritual and can lead to bonding ("welcome to the club, we've all been through it"), more often the result is increased anxiety and antagonism, which can prolong the socialization period. Using co-workers as a support system for new employees may reduce the amount of hazing that occurs.

As we mentioned, one way organizations can facilitate interaction between newcomers and their co-workers is to establish a buddy system in which newcomers are paired with experienced co-workers. Co-workers designated as buddies should be given materials that can help them fulfill their roles (such as guidebooks and information checklists) (Federico, 1991).

The HRD Staff   The primary role of the HRD staff in new employee orientation is to design and oversee the orientation program. Specifically, this may include producing or obtaining materials (such as workbooks and seminar leader guides), conducting training sessions, designing and conducting the evaluation study, and in some cases conducting some parts of the orientation program itself (focusing on such things as available services, employee rights, benefits, and workplace rules).

HRD staff members can also play an important role in encouraging all levels of management to become involved in and support the orientation program. Establishing a steering committee and finding ways for key managers to stay involved in the process (e.g., meeting with newcomers, conducting orientation sessions) are two ways this can be accomplished. Furthermore, HRD staff members should take steps (such as interviewing and surveying newcomers and supervisors) to ensure the orientation program is being carried out as planned and that the program is current.

The Newcomer   The newcomer should be encouraged to play the lead role in the orientation process by being an active learner. Research on adult learning (recall our discussion in Chapter 3) suggests that adults should be comfortable in this role in that they typically seek out information that is relevant to their situation and to the goals they are trying to achieve. In two research studies that measured the effectiveness of orientation programs at Corning and Texas Instruments, the newcomer was put in the position of guiding the learning process. At Corning, the entire orientation system was based on the principle of guided self-learning, with HRD staff members, supervisors and managers, co-workers, and resource materials playing supporting roles (McGarrell, 1984). At Texas Instruments, newcomers were encouraged to take the initiative in communication and to get to know their supervisor (Gomersall & Myers, 1966). Both of these studies demonstrated the effectiveness of this approach.

Newcomers should be explicitly encouraged to seek out both information and relationships they feel will help them in adjusting to the organization. Similarly, the organization should attempt to establish a climate in which this kind of behavior on the part of the newcomer is welcome and reinforced.

Problems with Orientation Programs

Orientation programs are no more immune from problems than any other HRD intervention. Feldman (1988) warns about the following potential problems:

- Too much emphasis on paperwork

- Information overload (giving newcomers too much information too quickly)

- Information irrelevance (general or superficial information that is not directly relevant to the newcomer's job assignment)

- Scare tactics (discussing failure rates or negative aspects of the job)

- Too much selling of the organization

- Emphasis on formal, one-way communication (using lectures and videos without giving the newcomer a chance to discuss issues of interest or ask questions)

- One-shot mentality (limiting the orientation program to only the first day at work)

- No diagnosis or evaluation of the program

- Lack of follow-up

Information overload is a particularly common problem. A person can absorb only so much information in a given period of time before learning efficiency drops and stress increases. Program designers and deliverers should be sensitive to this issue and try to prevent information overload by:

1. Including only essential information during the initial phase of orientation;

2. Providing written materials that trainees can take with them and review later, especially for complex benefits plans and important topics such as the company mission and work rules;

3. Conducting the program in phases to space out presentation of the material; and

4. Following up with the newcomers to make sure they understand major issues and to answer any additional questions they may have.

Designing an Employee Orientation Program

The orientation problems we have cited can be avoided by paying attention to the basic principles of designing any HRD program: needs assessment, design/implementation, and evaluation. McGarrell's (1984) Corning study provides a good model for developing an orientation program. Corning followed these ten steps in designing its program:

1. Set objectives:
   a. Reduce turnover in the first three years of employment by 17 percent;
   b. Reduce time to learn the job by 17 percent;
   c. Provide newcomers with a uniform understanding of the company; and
   d. Build a positive attitude toward the company and communities.

2. Form a steering committee

3. Research orientation as a concept

4. Interview recently hired people, supervisors, and corporate officers

5. Survey the orientation practices of top companies (the program at Texas Instruments proved particularly helpful)

6. Survey existing Corning orientation programs and materials

7. Select content and delivery method

8. Pilot and revise materials

9. Produce and package print and audiovisual materials

10. Train supervisors and install system

The timetable of orientation events shown in Table 7-6 is a result of the program Corning devised. Note that the Corning program begins even before the new employee's first day at work. Before then, the recruit receives material about the community, the job, and the work environment. The program is then continued for 15 months, through seminars, meetings, goal setting, and performance reviews. An evaluation study revealed that this program met or exceeded all of its objectives, including reducing voluntary turnover by 69 percent.

Orientation Program Effectiveness

Unfortunately, there is not much published research on the effectiveness of orientation programs overall, nor has the relative effectiveness of various approaches been adequately assessed. Much of the orientation literature contains suggestions for how programs can or should be conducted without the necessary data to support these suggestions.

Despite the lack of research, some guidelines can be helpful to those planning employee orientation. Feldman (1988) has found eleven design elements common to effective orientation programs, which are listed in Table 7-7 on page 232.

In closing, it should be clear that newcomers face a significant challenge when joining an organization, and it benefits both the individual and the organization to facilitate the socialization process. While we have focused our discussion on realistic job previews and employee orientation, socialization continues throughout an employee's career. HRD practitioners should not ignore other training and career development activities that facilitate this ongoing socialization. New employees need support throughout their early tenure with the organization in the form of meaningful and timely performance reviews and challenging assignments, and all employees can benefit from coaching and training, counseling to cope with stress and personal problems, and assistance in developing their careers—topics that we will explore in the following chapters.

RETURN TO OPENING CASE

Apple Training Support (ATS) took advantage of Apple's HyperCard software to design a new employee orientation program that employees could call upon both during and after the orientation period for important information about ATS and its people. Prior to designing the program, ATS identified nine principles to guide its development.

1. Assess needs as a basis for orientations. The training staff at Apple recognized that needs assessment would shape the content and approach of the program. Discussions with management and ATS employees revealed certain questions to be answered by the orientation program. (How does ATS fit into Apple? How do individual jobs fit within ATS? Who works in each group and what does each group do?) In addition, the needs assessment discussions also identified three characteristics the orientation program should have: (a) privacy, (b) ongoing access to information, resources, and people, and (c) a reflection of the tone, feeling, and spirit of ATS.

2. Establish an organizing framework. The managers encouraged program designers to organize a framework for the program that would make the information easy to find and integrate the experiences of the participants. Using a building as a metaphor, the designers classified information as individual floors in a six-story building, and each floor contained information addressing the needs identified by the needs assessment. Participants could navigate their way through the building using an elevator (press the button for a floor, and the elevator would take you there). Participants could then move around on each floor by selecting information from a menu (for example, on the ATS Technology floor, menu choices may include phones, printers, electronic mail, and fax machines).

3. Provide learner control. Program designers recognized that the learner should be able to choose the information they receive at the time they need it. Therefore, they took advantage of HyperCard's capabilities to link topics and keep track of what users have already seen (by inserting a checkmark next to the topic). Participants can also home in on a topic or issue by highlighting a word and clicking a button that takes them to the information associated with the topic.

4. Make it a process, not an event. The computer-based orientation program at ATS does not exist in a vacuum, leaving newcomers to do the best they can on their own. Instead, the orientation program is tied to regularly scheduled one-on-one meetings between the participants and ATS managers.

5. Allow people and personalities to emerge. The needs assessment at Apple showed that new hires wanted to learn more about their co-workers. To satisfy this interest, the ATS orientation program includes a floor with biographical information about ATS employees (including photographs, job duties, interests, comments, and suggestions to help new employees adjust to ATS). This information is provided by the ATS employees themselves, who are free to include whatever information they consider pertinent. Program designers found that this information is among the first selected by participants.

6. Reflect the organization and its priorities. Mission and values statements and descriptions of how they are practiced within the organization are included for both Apple and ATS.

7. Be sensitive to the politics associated with orientations. The nature of orientation has a significant political dimension. Managers who are asked to provide input for the program must answer a variety of questions that have political implications (such as, Who speaks for the organization? How do we resolve conflicts?). The program designers at Apple understood this and took steps to deal with this sensitive issue, including getting senior management support for the program and establishing policies for program development, evaluation, and revision, as well as procedures for seeking the opinions of organization members.

8. Include a system for revision and update. No organization is static. Employees come and go, responsibilities change, new technologies are introduced, and new challenges must be faced. The ATS orientation program includes a procedure for updating and revising information regularly to keep their program current and accurate.

9. Create a pleasing orientation experience. Program designers recognized that orientation is not only an information transmission process, it is also an opportunity to motivate and inspire new employees. Therefore, they made sure the ATS orientation program included attributes such as "technology, graphics, interactivity, learner control, anecdotes, opinions, and digitized images" (p. 51) to keep the participants' interest and create enthusiasm. A software program is not the only way to accomplish this goal, however. By carefully selecting components of the orientation program and ensuring that presenters are enthusiastic, knowledgeable, and sympathetic to the new employee's situation, among other things, HRD practitioners can turn a dull presentation of information into an interesting and dynamic experience.

Clearly, the ATS orientation program demonstrates how needs assessment and careful program design and implementation can lead to an orientation experience that gets new employees off to a strong start.[2]

Summary

New employees face a considerable challenge when joining an organization. They must learn the skills and behaviors necessary to perform their jobs effectively, while at the same time learning the norms and expectations of the organization and work group. Research on organizational socialization describes how outsiders to the organization are transformed into accepted and productive insiders. The success of socialization has a significant effect on outcomes that are important to both the new employee and the organization, including job satisfaction, job performance, and turnover.

Most models of the socialization process describe it in three stages: (1) anticipatory socialization, in which individuals form impressions and expectations about an organization prior to joining it; (2) encounter, the period after the individual joins the organization and discovers what life in the organization is really like; and (3) change and acquisition, which, if completed successfully, results in changes that permit the newcomer to perform effectively, be satisfied, and gain the acceptance of organization members.

---

[2]Brechlin, J. , & Rossett, A. (1991). Orienting New Employees. *Training, 28* (4), 45–51.

TABLE 7-7	**DESIGN ELEMENTS COMMON TO EFFECTIVE ORIENTATION PROGRAMS**

1. Well-run orientation programs are run on a "need to know" principle. Employees are given the information they need as they need it, and are subjected to neither cram courses nor superficial treatments of topics. The most relevant and immediate kinds of information are given first.

2. Effective orientation programs take place over a period of days and weeks. While the intensity of the orientation program is greatest on the first day, all the objectives of the orientation program cannot be met in that time frame. Good orientation programs begin even before new recruits arrive, and continue well after the first day.

3. The content of orientation programs should present a healthy balance of technical information about the job with the social aspects.

4. Orientation programs are generally more effective if they allow a lot of two-way interaction between managers and new employees. Successful socialization depends very heavily on the establishment of helpful, trusting superior-subordinate relationships.

5. The first day has a major impact on new employees: they remember those first impressions for years. Therefore, the running of that initial orientation program should be carefully planned and implemented by individuals with good social skills. Filling out paperwork should be kept to the bare minimum that day.

6. Well-run orientation programs assign the responsibility for new recruits' adjustment to their immediate supervisors. While personnel officers and other staff can serve as important resources to new recruits, one steady source of guidance and support is critical. Moreover, the immediate supervisor is in the best position to see potential problems the recruit is facing and to help him or her solve those issues.

7. Orientation programs can facilitate new recruits' adjustment by helping them get settled in the community and in new housing. When the logistics of living are up in the air, it is difficult for new hires to fully concentrate on their work assignments. For this reason, many organizations provide assistance to new recruits in house hunting and include spouses in several orientation activities.

8. New employees should be gradually introduced to the people with whom they will work rather than given a superficial introduction to all of them on the first day.

9. New employees should be allowed sufficient time to get their feet on the ground before demands on them are increased.

10. Well-run orientation programs are relaxing. They decrease anxiety, not increase it. They try to create positive attitudes toward the company by helpful and supportive behavior on the part of colleagues, not through high-toned speeches.

11. Finally, organizations should systematically diagnose the needs of new recruits and evaluate the effectiveness of their orientation programs. New topics and issues can be added to orientation programs when needed, and peripheral parts of the orientation program can be pruned.

SOURCE: From *Managing Careers in Organizations* (p. 90) by D. C. Feldman, 1988, Glenview, IL: Scott, Foresman.

Two ways to assist employees in making the transition to productive and accepted insiders are realistic job previews and employee orientation programs. RJPs involve providing recruits with a balanced view of job expectations and life within an organization, including both positive and negative attributes. This method facilitates socialization by adjusting any unrealistic expectations employees might have, thus offering them the opportunity to join the organization (or decline to join) with a clear idea of what to expect. Orientation programs are used to introduce new employees to the organization, the work group, and the job. Orientation programs facilitate socialization by providing employees with information, skills, and relationships that help them adjust their expectations, understand group norms, and learn their new jobs.

Key Terms and Concepts

anticipatory socialization
change and acquisition
employee orientation
encounter
expectations
hazing
information overload
norms *subtle / acceptable behaviors*
organizational socialization

realistic job preview (RJP) *pos + cons of their org.*
role
role ambiguity *unclear about what job is.*
role conflict
role orientation
role overload *more than you can possibly do.*
self selection *when you decide the jobs not 4 you.*
socialization (people processing)
tactics

Questions for Discussion

1. What are the differences between organizational roles and group norms? How are they similar?

2. Why are role ambiguity, role conflict, and role overload detrimental to the success of individuals and the organization?

3. Using Feldman's three stage model of organizational socialization, how would you describe the way you were socialized into an organization where you have worked? How well does the model fit your experience?

4. What three things do organizational insiders have to help them interpret organizational events that newcomers lack? How can organizations help newcomers gain these things?

5. Why might some managers resist using an RJP? What evidence could you offer to convince such managers to use one?

6. What are the benefits of using multiple forms of media (such as recruiting ads, booklets, and discussions with potential co-workers) in an RJP program?

7. Which two aspects of an orientation program do you think are the most important in socializing new employees? Support your choices.

8. Identify and describe three potential problems common to orientation programs. How can each of these problems be overcome?

9. What is the supervisor's role in employee orientation? What could be done to convince or encourage a skeptical supervisor to fulfill this role in orientation?

10. Define hazing and describe how it can be prevented. Can hazing ever play a positive role in socialization? Defend your answer.

8

Skills and Technical Training

Learning Objectives

1. *Identify and describe basic workplace competencies.*
2. *Explain the need for remedial basic skills training programs.*
3. *Explain the role of apprenticeship programs.*
4. *Describe the general technical skills training programs.*
5. *Describe the general nontechnical skills training programs.*
6. *Understand the professional development and education processes in a typical organization.*

OPENING CASE

Throughout the 1980s the auto industry in the United States was being criticized by American consumers because it could not compete with the quality, cost, and customer satisfaction achieved by the Japanese auto manufacturers. Japanese manufacturers, led by Toyota, Nissan, and Honda, captured a large share of the U.S. small-car market. The message was clear—if U.S. auto manufacturers did not change the manner in which they produced and sold their products, they would continue to lose market share.

General Motors (GM), the largest U.S. auto manufacturer, decided to challenge the Japanese where they were the strongest—the small-car market. GM managers felt that if they were going to compete successfully with the Japanese, they could not just make adjustments but would have to do things entirely differently: create a new division from the ground up using a different management philosophy. Accordingly, in 1983 GM launched Saturn Corporation. Saturn's philosophy embraced five core principles: (1) a commitment to customer satisfaction, (2) commitment to excel, (3) teamwork, (4) trust and respect for the individual, and (5) continuous improvement. Saturn management felt that the best vehicle for communicating these principles would be comprehensive training programs at all levels and functions within Saturn.

Within the retail and wholesale operations, Saturn management wanted to emphasize the commitment to "customer enthusiasm and teamwork." In order to take a fresh approach, Saturn management looked outside the organization for a training partner, a vendor with commitment to these principles. They selected Maritz Communications Company, a training and business communications subsidiary of Maritz Inc. Saturn and Maritz committed approximately 130 training professionals (e.g., designers, writers, and automotive experts) to the task of designing a retail and wholesale operations training program. The Saturn/Maritz team was given the following challenge: "to take an ideal—a belief in a better way to sell cars—and change basic attitudes enough to make it a reality."

Introduction

Organizations have become increasingly dependent on skilled technical and professional employees. Of the new jobs created between 1983 and 1990, 40 percent were skilled and technical jobs, 40 percent were classified as management and professional, and only 20 percent were lower-level unskilled positions (Carnevale et al., 1989a). The need for skilled and technical training is generally a function of changes in job requirements resulting from such things as the introduction of new technology, new organizational goals, and structural changes (Fossum & Arvey, 1990). New technology, whether it is a result of plant modernization, computerization, or other innovations, has helped to create a shift away from jobs requiring little skill to jobs demanding higher skill levels.

One factor in the success of Japanese and European manufacturers has been the manner in which they educate and train their work force. Carnevale and Johnston state that "both European and Japanese (educational systems) provide a higher quality of preparation and workplace learning for the non-college-trained workers" (1989a, p. 3). For example, Germany's current educational policy requires students to attend school full time until age 16, when they are free to enter apprenticeship programs, either directly with a company or through a technical institute (Dowling & Albrecht, 1991). This type of system ensures a steady stream of qualified young people into the work force, which has helped make Germany a formidable industrial nation.

In this chapter, we will discuss basic workplace competencies and then review some of the training programs used to improve these competencies.

There are many ways that skills training programs can be categorized. For this chapter, we organized the discussion around the categories used in the annual *Training* magazine survey: basic skills/literacy education, technical training, and nontechnical training. **Basic skills/literacy education** refers to the process of upgrading reading, writing, and computation skills needed to function on the job. **Technical training** refers to the process of upgrading a wide range of technical skills needed by virtually everyone in an organization, including professional employees. **Nontechnical training** refers to the training in which the key component is interpersonal communication. We further selected general types of training under each of the categories. These are listed in Table 8-1. In addition, we will discuss professional development activities that relate primarily to continuing education programs. Other aspects of professional development will be discussed in Chapter 11 (Career Development) and Chapter 12 (Management Development).

Basic Workplace Competencies

A major problem facing employers today is the skills gap—the difference between skill requirements of available jobs and the skills possessed by job applicants (Dole, 1991). The skills gap is the result of at least three factors: (1) the declining skills of many high school graduates and even some college graduates; (2) the growing number of racial minorities and non-English-speaking immigrants in the labor market; and (3) the increased sophistication of jobs due to increased reliance on information technology (Steck, 1992). The **declining skills of high school—and even some college—students,** particularly at a time when organizations require increasingly skilled workers, has generated much criticism of public education systems. Employers are finding that graduates with basic skill deficiencies must be given remedial training before they are job-ready.

TABLE 8-1	1992 TRAINING SURVEY PROGRAM CATEGORIES

Training Category	Subcategories
Basic skills	Remedial/basic education

Technical	Apprenticeship training
	Computer training
	Technical skills/knowledge
	New methods/procedures
	   Safety training
	   Quality training

Nontechnical	Communications/interpersonal training Customer relations/services training Sales training Team building/training

SOURCE: From B. Filipczak (1992), "What Employers Teach." *Training,* 29(10), 43–55.

This has prompted the Los Angeles School District to formulate a written warranty to accompany each of their high school diplomas, beginning in 1994, which will state that if any employer finds a graduate to be deficient in any basic skill, the school will provide remedial training at no cost to the employer (Steck, 1992). This type of commitment reflects the urgency of the problem and demonstrates how some school administrators are trying to confront the issue.

The growing number of racial minorities and non-English-speaking immigrants in the labor market was predicted in 1987 by the Hudson Report, which indicated that approximately 85 percent of new entrants into that market would be women and minorities (Johnston & Packer, 1987). A large portion of these new workers will be immigrants who not only cannot speak English, but may also have basic skill deficiencies. Thus, two kinds of training may be necessary to get them job-ready—basic skills and English-as-a-second-language (ESL). This represents a major challenge to potential employers who must rely on these workers.

The **increased sophistication of jobs,** particularly as a result of the information-technology explosion, has affected most, if not all, industries. The trend toward increasingly powerful computer hardware and user-friendly computer software systems has led to a proliferation of high-technology applications, including robotics (in the manufacturing sector), decision-support systems, electronic mail systems, and communications networks. Continuous technical training may be necessary for those occupations that rely on information technology and are directly affected by the constant changes in hardware and software.

Basic Skills/Literacy Programs

As discussed above, the basic competency skills include reading, writing, and computational skills. While the assessment of these skills is not always standardized, deficiencies in these skills are widely reported. The Business Council for Effective Literacy estimates that 27 million adults in the United States lack the basic reading, writing, and computational skills needed for the jobs of today (Gordon et al., 1989; Washburn et al., 1992). The Office of Technology Assessment estimates that 20 to 30 percent of employees lack basic writing, reading, and computational skills (Stone, 1991). These estimates reflect the depth of the problem facing employers who have the task of improving operations by introducing more efficient methods. If employees cannot read or compute, it may be virtually impossible to install new equipment that requires the operator to read instructions and make decisions.

When creating a program to address basic skill deficiencies, employers should operationally define each basic skill. An example of operationally defining literacy skills is the approach taken by Kirsch and Jungeblut (1986). In their study of literacy among young adults (ages 21 through 25), literacy skills were operationally defined according to three broad categories:

1. **Prose literacy** Skills and strategies needed to understand and use information from texts that are frequently found in the home and the community.

2. **Document literacy**   Skills and strategies required to locate and use information contained in nontextual materials that include tables, graphs, charts, indexes, forms, and schedules.

3. **Quantitative literacy**   Knowledge and skills needed to apply the arithmetic operations of addition, subtraction, multiplication, and division (either singly or sequentially) in combination with printed materials, as in balancing a checkbook or completing an order form (Kirsch & Jungeblut, 1986, p. 64).

The measurement of these skills was accomplished by devising a large number of simulated tasks that were then administered to a nationwide sample. Scores were tabulated on a scale ranging from 0 to 500, with a mean score of 305. Table 8-2 summarizes the results of the study, demonstrating that a significant number of young adults scored below the literacy average, with an even greater number of young minority adults ranking below the average.

Addressing Illiteracy in the Workplace

Many organizations have recognized the illiteracy problem among their workers. According to a 1992 *Training* magazine survey, over half the organizations with 1,000 or more employees conduct basic skills programs (Filipczak, 1992). Companies like Motorola, Ford, Xerox, Polaroid, and Eastman Kodak have already instituted comprehensive basic skills programs (Berger, 1989). The following are examples of some programs.

1. A Ford Motor Company plant spent $160,000 for a remedial reading program when it found that half of the enrollees in a process control training program could not read the training materials (Choquette, 1988).

2. Chrysler Corporation has invested $5 million in teaching basic skills to 3,000 to 4,000 workers in order to advance them to an eighth-grade level in reading, writing, and math (Filipczak, 1992).

TABLE 8-2	LITERACY RATES OF YOUNG ADULTS AGED 21–25 BY RACE			
	Literacy Scale (Mean Score = 305)			
	Below 200	201–275	276–350	351+
White	5%	17%	53%	25%
Black	18	43	35	3
Hispanic	10	33	47	10

Adapted from Kirsch & Jungeblut, 1986, p. 65–66.

3. Federal government agencies have also recognized the literacy problem. For example, the Basic Skills Education Program (BSEP) was developed by the U.S. Army in 1982 to deal with the growing problem of illiteracy among the troops. Wilson (1990) states that the BSEP "is the largest computer-based basic skills program ever developed . . . containing more than 300 lessons that cover more than 200 basic skills" (p. 38).

Some organizations have developed basic skills programs in partnership with industry associations, unions, government agencies, and outside agencies such as area adult educational programs, technical schools, and colleges to conduct the training. Some examples:

1. Eastern Michigan University provides basic skills instruction for Ford Motor Company employees as part of a partnership program with the United Auto Workers (McGee, 1989).

2. Rocco Enterprises in Harrisonburg, Virginia, in partnership with the Virginia Poultry Federation and James Madison University, initiated a two-year pilot literacy training project of 60 employees that will culminate in the administration of the General Education Development (GED) examination (May, Hugh, & Quesada, 1990).

3. Central Labor Council of the Amalgamated Clothing and Textile Workers Union (ACTWU) designed and implemented a Workplace Literacy Program funded by a New York State workplace-literacy grant. The program, directed at predominantly Spanish-speaking apparel workers throughout the five boroughs of New York, consisted of basic literacy skills, including an English-as-a-second-language component (Center for Advanced Study in Education, 1988).

Designing an In-House Basic Skills/Literacy Program

The design of basic skills/literacy programs varies widely from organization to organization. There are at least two common characteristics: (1) an aptitude test and (2) small-group and one-on-one instruction. An **aptitude** test is important for assessing the current ability level of each trainee. For example, a basic skills program developed by the Palo Verde Nuclear Generating Station begins with an assessment of each trainee's learning ability before he or she is assigned to an intense six-month study skills program (Carlisle, 1985). This data is essential for developing an individualized lesson plan that allows the trainer to pinpoint learning objectives and to select the best training methods, techniques, and materials for each trainee.

Small-group instruction and one-on-one tutoring are important for supplying feedback to the trainee, as well as for conducting remedial work in any areas of deficiency. Zaslow (1991) suggests using supervisors as writing coaches by training them to give feedback to employees on such things as writing techniques. To supplement small-group instruction, some organizations are using a self-paced, computer- interactive program that provides opportunities to practice basic concepts. Self-pacing allows the trainee to practice at his or her own rate, without the pressures of a classroom, and to repeat or skip steps or sequences in the program as necessary. This approach is best used for trainees who are motivated to learn.

The methods used for in-house basic skills training programs also vary. Table 8-3 describes some of the advantages, disadvantages, and costs of different methods. The training manual, tutorial disks, and videotapes are the least costly methods to use because they do not require a classroom or an instructor. However, these methods have significant disadvantages. When a trainer and classroom are used, the cost increases. The most costly programs are those that are customized, because they require considerable time and expertise to design. One key to a successful basic skills training program is to relate materials and examples directly to the organization (Bell, 1991). Given this single criterion, the preferred methods would be internal classroom or customized external classroom training.

Federal Support for Basic Skills Training

The federal government has long recognized its role in supporting private training initiatives that are targeted toward the unemployed, displaced, and economically disadvantaged. The 1983 **Job Training and Partnership Act (JTPA)**, which replaced the Comprehensive Employment and Training Act, is currently the largest federal skills training program. The goal of JTPA is to provide training opportunities to the unemployed, displaced, and economically disadvantaged in order to help them obtain permanent jobs.

Approximately $4 billion is funneled by the federal government through 600 individual private industry councils (PIC) to private training institutes and employers in order to fund skills training (Laabs, 1992). The PICs, which are composed of representatives from business, education, community-based agencies, and others, are appointed by local government officials. The role of a PIC is to oversee the distribution of the funds and to ensure that state JTPA standards and guidelines are followed.

Most employer-based training programs involve basic skills and job-specific training. While most of the training is conducted on-site in a classroom, JTPA will sponsor on-the-job training programs as long as the employer agrees to hire the trainees once they complete their training. The key to the success of JTPA programs is based, in part, on how well these programs are coordinated with the work of other social service agencies. For example, potential trainees can be identified and referred to a training agency by a community-based social agency that serves the economically disadvantaged target population. This was the case when the Atlanta Marquis Hotel trained 59 people; 39 were referred by Goodwill Industries, a community-based nonprofit agency, and 20 were referred by the local PIC (Laabs, 1992).

| TABLE 8-3 | SKILLS TRAINING METHODS | | |

Methods	Advantages	Disadvantages	Cost
Training manual	Reusable and self-paced.	Requires technical orientation. Examples not directly related to organization. Material presented in only one way.	Low
Tutorial disks	Same as above.	Same as above.	Low
Videotape	Presentation is more personal. Reusable, and can stop and start.	Same as above.	Moderate
Internal classroom (in-house trainer)	Customer-tailored to meet organization needs. Can adjust presentation to class abilities. Trainer understands organization.	Must have large group to justify cost. In-house trainers may not be effective instructors.	High
Internal classroom (consultant)	Customer-tailored to meet organization needs. Can adjust presentation to class abilities. Professional instructor. Consultant not tied to internal politics.	Must have large group to justify cost. Consultant does not have working knowledge of organization.	High
Customized external training	Same as above plus fewer interruptions and use of external facilities. Trainees may perceive as a reward.	Same as above.	Very high
General courses and seminars	Wide assortment of topics available. Can schedule on an individual basis.	Examples not directly related to organization.	Very high

Adapted from Callaghan, 1985, p. 29.

In addition, JTPA has been legislatively tied to the Worker Adjustment and Retraining Notification Act (WARN). WARN requires any employer with 100 or more employees to give a 60-day advance notice of plant closure to both employees and unions. When plant closings or mass layoffs are imminent, JTPA funds should be made available to set up "rapid response teams" that will work with unions and companies to administer retraining and worker-displacement programs (Holley & Jennings, 1991).

Despite successful JTPA programs, such as that of the Atlanta Marquis, several problems have been identified. First, several private institutions and employers have received funds fraudulently—some employers use JTPA funds to hire workers whom they would recruit even under normal conditions (Business Week, Reinventing America 1992). President Bush signed a bill into law on September 7, 1992, that was intended to address some aspects of the fraud. A second problem stems from the fact that while the program was intended to serve a wide target population, JTPA funds provide training programs for only 5 percent of some 33 million eligible displaced and unemployed workers. This is due in part to the fact that the JTPA budget has not increased since 1983 (Business Week, Reinventing America, 1992). The third and final problem relates to the manner in which JTPA funds are disbursed. The current system reimburses training institutes and employers for their training expenses. Typically, the employer cannot submit an invoice to the JTPA until trainees have been on the job for at least 30 days and in some cases 90 days (Laabs, 1992).

Technical Training

Due in part to the nature of the emerging global economy and fierce competition from foreign producers, U.S. organizations have been investing more dollars in a variety of technical training programs. In a 1992 survey by *Training* magazine, over one-third of respondents indicated that their 1992 training budget had increased from 1991 (Filipczak, 1992). This is a significant finding, because in tough economic times of past years, HRD programs were among those cut. The results of this survey seem to indicate that this pattern may be ending.

Technical training, as discussed earlier, is a generic term that can encompass a wide range of programs. For convenience, we will limit our discussion to five technical training programs: apprenticeship training, computer training, technical skills/knowledge training, safety training, and quality training.

Apprenticeship Training Programs

Apprenticeship training is not a new concept. As discussed in Chapter 1, apprenticeship training began during the Middle Ages as a way of passing on the knowledge of skill trades and crafts. The primary purpose of these early programs was preservation of the industrial and crafts guilds. Today the focus of apprenticeship programs is to provide trainees with the skills needed to meet continually changing job requirements. With the challenges of the global economy and the scarcity of skilled employees, it is imperative that apprenticeship programs be more responsive to these needs.

Apprenticeship programs represent a unique partnership between employers, labor unions, schools, and government agencies. In 1988 there were over 800 different apprenticeship programs enrolling 335,508 registered apprentices (Carnevale & Johnston, 1989a). Of this total, almost one-third were in carpentry, electricity, and pipe trades. A typical apprenticeship program requires a minimum of 2,000 hours of on-the-job training (OJT) experience (National Apprenticeship Program, 1987). In addition to the OJT experience, all programs require a minimum of 144 hours of classroom training. Classroom training may be given at a local vocational/technical school or community college. For example, the Community College of Rhode Island conducts training sessions for 13 different apprenticeship programs for the Electric Boat Division of General Dynamics, a large defense contractor. The average length of these programs is three years, involving 600 to 800 hours of classroom training, with the OJT component conducted at the company site by skills trainers. At the end of the program, each apprentice must be able to demonstrate all of the required skills and knowledge before being certified as a journeyman.

The U.S. apprenticeship system is regulated by the Bureau of Apprenticeship and Training (BAT) of the U.S. Department of Labor (USDOL). In 27 states, the BAT has delegated its regulatory responsibilities to state apprenticeship councils. For the remaining states, the BAT regulates standards and provides services. BAT claims that a well-planned, properly administered apprenticeship program will result in success. Table 8-4 lists some positive outcomes.

There are, however, some problems with the present apprenticeship system. A special report prepared by the National Center on Education and the Economy identified four major concerns:

1. Learning is based on time requirements rather than competency.

2. Programs are isolated from other education and training institutions.

3. Programs are concentrated in traditional blue-collar occupations.

TABLE 8-4	POSITIVE OUTCOMES OF A SUCCESSFUL APPRENTICE PROGRAM

1. Reduced absenteeism, turnover, and cost of training.
2. Increased productivity.
3. Improved community and employee relations.
4. Facilitated compliance with federal and state Equal Employment Opportunity requirements.
5. Ensured availability of related technical instruction.
6. Enhanced problem-solving ability of craftworkers.
7. Ensured versatility of craftworkers.

SOURCE: National Apprenticeship Training Program (1987)

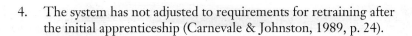

4.   The system has not adjusted to requirements for retraining after the initial apprenticeship (Carnevale & Johnston, 1989, p. 24).

Another problem with the current apprenticeship system is that it is underutilized by high school graduates. Only 2 percent of high school graduates complete such programs, even though many would benefit from apprenticeship training (Novack, 1992). This may be explained in two ways. First, there has been no linkage, until recently, between apprenticeship training and vocational high school education. Second, many high school teachers do not present apprenticeship training as a viable career alternative to prospective graduates. Until the image of apprenticeship and vocational training improves, this problem will continue. Closer relationships must be forged between workers and employers, unions, schools, and government agencies to solve these problems.

Some of these problems are being addressed by a recent initiative called Apprenticeship 2000, begun in 1987 by the U.S. Department of Labor. Based on the successes of other countries, one purpose of the program was to expand the apprenticeship concept and link it to the schools. For example, in 1991 the state of Oregon redesigned its vocational high school curriculum to allow eleventh-grade students to enter an apprentice-type training program with businesses that guaranteed the students jobs after they graduated (New York Times, July 10, 1992). This is referred to as a **school-to-work program.** The success of Oregon's program prompted other states, such as Wisconsin, Rhode Island, New York, North Carolina, and South Carolina, to seek similar reforms.

Computer Training Programs

The computer has become an integral part of many organizations and jobs. *Computerworld* magazine conducted a survey in 1992 of the Fortune 500 industrial and Fortune 500 service companies in order to assess their effective use of computers (information systems). The survey assessed, among other things, the percentage of a company's information systems (IS) budget used for training and the percentage of its employees with personal computers (PCs) or terminals. Table 8-5 summarizes the survey results, indicating industry averages for 1992. These data provide at least some sense of how great an investment companies are making in IS training.

There are two basic kinds of computer training—introductory and applications. **Introductory computer training** programs are used to introduce trainees to computer hardware and software. *Computer hardware* refers to physical equipment, such as keyboard, central processing unit, and monitor used to operate the software. Hardware is best mastered when trainees practice operating equipment. Software training is much more complex. *Computer software* refers to the computer programs used to process information. Introductory training programs focus more on mastering basic software application (i.e., word processing) through use of operating manuals and *tutorials* (software programs themselves) that provide hands-on, interactive learning. These courses are designed to help trainees overcome their fear of computers and to better understand how computers work.

TABLE 8-5	1992 AVERAGE INVESTMENT OF TOP COMPANIES IN COMPUTER TRAINING AND NUMBER OF EMPLOYEES WITH PERSONAL COMPUTERS OR TERMINALS (N = 600)

Industry	Percentage of IS[a] Budget for Training	Percentage of Employees with PCs or Terminals
Aerospace	2.0%	56%
Consumer products and services	2.7	46
Financial services	2.4	90
Industrial and automotive products	5.0	32
Manufacturing	3.4	36
Petroleum and chemicals	3.4	45
Pharmaceuticals and food	3.5	29
Retail and wholesaling	2.2	29
Transportation	2.0	36
Utilities	3.8	75

[a]Information systems.
Adapted from Computerworld Premier 100, 1992.

Applications training covers specific software applications available within the organization and instruction on applications development (Hall-Sheehy, 1985). Unlike introductory courses, which can be offered to an entire organization, applications training is provided on an "as-needed" basis.

The field of information technology, particularly its application to training, is changing rapidly. The field has begun to shift to integrated networks replacing the microcomputer with desktop workstations. Delaney (1991) predicts that workstations will be the foundation for "just-in-time" learning (immediate availability of training when needed by an employee) and that integrated networks will support text and numerical data, printing, image and communications technology, graphics, full-motion video, and two-way sound.

Technical Skills/Knowledge Training

When organizations introduce new technology (e.g., by modernizing plants, computerizing operations, etc.), they may need to update the skills of workers through job-specific technical skills/knowledge training programs. According to the 1992 survey in *Training* magazine, 82 percent of organizations conduct some type of technical skills/knowledge training (Filipczak, 1992). Examples would be training clerical workers to operate a new telephone network or providing instruction to workers after installing new equipment.

There are different levels of technical skills/knowledge training. At the lowest level, the goal is to prepare entry-level employees to assume minimum skill responsibilities. These programs are similar to basic skills programs and are combined classroom instruction with on-the-job training (OJT). As an example, Stanley-Bostitch Inc., a manufacturer of staples and fasteners, conducts a 28-

week, entry-level operator training program of six modules, encompassing basic math, basic measurement skills, blueprint reading, shop practices, basic tooling, and basic machines. The last three modules involve intensive OJT. The successful trainees are expected to operate new, advanced equipment. In a similar situation, IBM assigns entry-level clerical workers to a two-week, 68-hour training program divided into 14 modules that include automated procedures, time management, problem solving, and stress management (Henneback, 1992).

More advanced technical skills/knowledge training involves additional classroom time covering more difficult subjects. For example, Stanley-Bostitch Inc. has a 35-week technician level training program with 210 hours of classroom training.

Unions may also help provide training in addition to apprenticeship training, such as joint labor-management training programs designed to update union members' skills. For example, the Laborers' International Union and the Associated General Contractors (AGC) came together to form the Laborers-AGC Education and Training Fund. One example of the technical training provided by the Laborers-AGC group was an 80-hour certificate course in hazardous-waste removal. As of 1992, almost 9,000 of 500,000 union members had completed the training qualifying them to be hired to work on hazardous waste removal projects (Goodman, 1992).

Safety Training

According to the 1992 *Training* magazine survey, 65 percent of the responding organizations conduct some form of **safety training** (Filipczak, 1992). The need for such training has increased dramatically since the passage of the 1970 **Occupational Safety and Health Act (OSHA).** OSHA regulations cover four areas: (1) establishing safety standards; (2) conducting safety inspections; (3) granting safety variances for organizations who are unable to comply with standards; and (4) citing organizations where standards are being violated. If an organization is cited for safety violations, safety training may be required to prevent future accidents. OSHA-mandated safety training focuses on equipment safety devices, handling of toxic chemicals, safe work habits, and actions to be taken in case of an accident. For more excessive violations, OSHA has the power to levy fines, shut down an operation, or prosecute the management (or the owner).

In 1988 OSHA regulations were expanded to include hazard communications standards. These standards replaced right-to-know state laws that required organizations to (1) establish written hazard-communications policy, (2) replace old state posters with OSHA's, (3) establish procedures for obtaining material safety data sheets (MDSs) from manufacturers, (4) create notebooks containing MDSs and make them accessible to employees, (5) label hazardous materials and state effects of same, (6) provide orientation for new employees and ongoing training for other employees, and (7) prepare a safety manual (Rothwell, 1989).

Even with these regulations in place, injuries and illnesses are still common. For example, in 1989 there were approximately 6.5 million industrial accidents and illnesses on the job (Hackey, 1991). This suggests that organizations must do more to reinforce safety standards and desired work behaviors. Some desirable characteristics of an effective safety management program are as follows:

1. Top management support and reinforcement of safety standards (Thompson, 1991).

2. Employee involvement in suggesting safer work procedures and the selection of equipment (Jenkins, 1990).

3. Regular and recurring safety training programs that reinforce safety standards and behaviors (Rothwell, 1989).

4. Effective monitoring systems to ensure standards and behaviors are being practiced, and to correct any unsafe conditions (Kimmerling, 1985).

In addition to OSHA-mandated training, some companies routinely conduct safety training and retraining in order to keep liability insurance premiums to a minimum. Such training helps a company to become "certified" as a safe company. Also, being designated as a safe company can help boost employee morale and make employees feel more secure.

Safety training programs should be conducted both in the classroom and on the job site. Classroom training can focus on safety regulations, accident-reporting procedures, and other general information. On-site training can focus on actual safety standards and behaviors. Many organizations use behavior modification as a training technique to reinforce desirable behaviors.

The effectiveness of safety training can be assessed by determining if the safety standards and behaviors are being practiced. OSHA emphasizes training effectiveness in the short run by using a post-training test of safety standards and procedures and monitoring behaviors and in the long run by whether incidences of accidents, illness, and death have declined (Kimmerling, 1985).

Quality Training

Since the beginning of the 1980s, organizations have recognized the value of W. Edwards Deming's theories as a way to increase productivity and quality. Deming's 14 guiding principles have long been recognized as the foundation for many quality improvement initiatives in the United States and Japan. One outgrowth of Deming's principles is the concept of total quality management (TQM), a process of empowering all employees to seek continuous improvements in quality. TQM has become a primary vehicle for introducing quality improvement in all kinds of organizations, including those in private industry, government, and nonprofit organizations. One of the keys to successful TQM programs is quality training. According to the 1992 survey by *Training* magazine, 62 percent of the responding organizations conduct quality improvement training programs (Filipczak, 1992).

Before developing a quality training program, top management should define quality and determine how it will be measured. Quality can be defined in several ways, including product quality, service quality, and customer quality. **Product quality** is defined by the degree to which products achieve or exceed production standards. This can be measured in relation to the number of defects, recalls, and scrap. **Service quality** is defined as how well the organization responds to the customers' needs after the product or service is delivered. This can be measured by noting service response time, service backlog, and customer satisfaction ratings. **Customer quality** can be defined by whether the organization has met or surpassed each customer's expectations. This can be measured by such things as customer surveys and tracking customer complaints. Customer quality should not be ignored. Even when the product and service are technically perfect, both can fail if organizations do not meet the customer's expectations (Miller, 1992).

Once quality is defined and the organization determines how it is going to be measured, the next step is to provide training on continuous quality improvement. There are several phases of quality training. The first phase, **awareness,** involves introducing managers to the concept of quality improvement and how it will change their role. Awareness sessions should be led by a top manager who must demonstrate his or her long-term commitment to change and make sure that other managers understand their "new" role in this approach and the kind of support expected from each manager. For example, some organizations, like Rockwell Industries, ensure that middle management has a vested interest in TQM by linking the reward structure to the program (Vasilash, 1992). In turn, these managers are expected to conduct quality awareness sessions in their own units. Some organizations create a new organizational unit that is given direct responsibility for implementing the TQM program, including training programs. In addition, some organizations appoint task groups or "change committees" to oversee the process of organizational change. Organizational change processes will be discussed in more detail in Chapter 13.

The next phase of TQM generally involves more **in-depth training** in process skills and quality skills. *Process skills* refer to ways to improve work coordination, solve problems, and resolve conflicts. *Quality skills* refer to the techniques and tools that can be used for tracking quality improvements. There are at least seven quality tools (see Table 8-6) that can be used for analyzing cause and effect, problem solving, monitoring results, and recommending courses of action.

Of the quality tools described in Table 8-6, statistical process control (SPC) has been most widely applied in various organizational settings. The principle underlying SPC is that most processes demonstrate variations in output and that it is important to determine whether the causes of such a variation are normal or abnormal (Mainstone & Levi, 1989). SPC focuses on training employees to be able to discern abnormal variations so that adjustments can be made to the process in order to improve quality. Employees must learn to monitor output using control charts so that they can see variations.

There are a limited number of published evaluation studies of TQM, and only a few isolate the effects of the quality training program. One study,

TABLE 8-6	SEVEN BASIC QUALITY TOOLS

Quality Tool	How It Is Used
Process Flow Analysis	Used to chart the process or production flow that can lead to reduction of cycle time, cost savings, improvement of service to customers, and increased profitability.
Cause-and-Effect Diagram	Can help solve problems by pinpointing their root causes, differentiating between symptoms and causes of problems. Once causes are determined, information obtained can be used to develop an action plan to correct the problem.
Run Chart	Used to illustrate trends and results in terms of time and frequency of events. Information can be used for predicting future outcomes given current conditions.
Statistical Process Control (SPC)	Helps to determine if a process is stable and predictable, identify common causes of variation, and clarify when employee intervention is needed.
Scattergram	Used to determine how two variables are related (or correlated). For example, one variable (number of training days) is positively related to another variable (quality improvements) in any one department or work group. This data can be plotted and shown to management as justification for additional training days.
Histogram	Used for displaying data obtained from actual work practices, usually variations in time it takes for different employees to perform a common task. If the data represent even distribution, the majority of the employees would make up the mean (or average) with fewer performing at higher or lower levels. These data are useful for establishing work standards.
Pareto Chart	Can be used to assess different tasks or problems in terms of the time needed for performance or resolution. It is similar to a bar chart, which helps the team or manager to decide on the priority of each event.

Adapted from Carter, C. C. (1992). Seven basic quality tools. *HRMagazine*, 37(1), 81–83.

conducted by Motorola, evaluated the company's program using a multiple-group research design. Trainees were assigned to three research groups: (1) those using the entire quality training curriculum (both process skills and quality skills) followed with reinforcement from senior managers; (2) those emphasizing either process or quality skills and followed up by senior managers; and (3) those using one or both methods with no follow-up. Outcomes for the three groups were as follows: (1) the first yielded a $33 return for every dollar spent on training; (2) the second broke even; and (3) the third had a negative return (Wiggenhorn, 1990). These results suggest that quality training should be comprehensive (covering both process and quality skills) and followed up by management.

Nontechnical Training

As discussed before, a number of basic workplace competencies involve skills needed to work effectively with other people. These skills, sometimes referred to as "soft skills," include communication, interpersonal skills, customer relations, selling, and teamwork. All can be improved through training. In this section, we discuss training programs designed to help employees acquire and improve skills in each of these areas.

Communication/Interpersonal Skills Training

Training in communication and interpersonal skills training is common, being offered by 84 percent of organizations (Filipczak, 1992). Interpersonal skills training programs cover a wide range of topics, including effective speaking and listening, teamwork, problem solving, and development of negotiation skills. When the American Assembly of Colleges and Schools of Business (AACSB), a major collegiate accrediting body of business schools, studied the preparedness of business school graduates for entry-level jobs, it was found that a primary skill deficiency was a lack of interpersonal skills (Porter & McKibbin, 1988). With today's increased emphasis on interpersonal skills, some colleges are beginning to review their curricula to ensure that graduates have the necessary skills to be effective in the workplace (Grazier, 1992). Until these skills are taught on all campuses and throughout the educational system, organizations should use training to upgrade their employees' interpersonal skills.

There are two trends that have increased the need for interpersonal training. One is a movement toward team-based approaches to accomplish work, which usually involve team training with a strong interpersonal component. Another trend is the movement by some organizations toward becoming more multicultural. With changing labor market demographics and the growth of multinational organizations, more and more organizations are developing cultural diversity programs. These courses are intended to change some of the incorrect assumptions, values, and beliefs people have about other cultures, with the desired outcome being the development of more effective cross-cultural interpersonal skills. These programs will be discussed in more detail in Chapter 14.

Interpersonal skills training programs offered by organizations vary in content. For example, Duke Power Company, in Charlotte, North Carolina, includes three interpersonal training courses (Personal Development, Relationship Development, and Career Development) in their professional development core curriculum (Carnevale, et al., 1990). These courses emphasize providing trainees with a better understanding of themselves and the handling of workplace relationships.

Sales Training

Traditional sales techniques (e.g., the hard sell) are being abandoned for more consultative approaches that build trust, solve customers' problems, provide product and service options, and admit limitations (Callahan, 1992). This new approach is intended to build customer loyalty and improve long-term customer relations.

The key to adopting new sales approaches is sales training. According to the 1992 survey by *Training* magazine, 55 percent of all organizations offer some type of sales training. This figure rises dramatically for the retail and banking industries, reaching levels of 79 percent and 80 percent, respectively (Filipczak, 1992). Training varies widely, from traditional sales techniques to the new consultative approaches. Some organizations, like Saturn, are overhauling entire retail and wholesale operations through comprehensive training programs. Most, however, are not willing to make such drastic changes. Many supplement sales training with other types of training (e.g., behavior modification) that are intended to equip personnel with the interpersonal skills to be effective. Many organizations also combine sales training with customer relations/service training.

Customer Relations/Service Training

The increased emphasis on quality improvement has led more and more organizations to emphasize customer relations and customer service. According to the 1992 survey by *Training* magazine, 73 percent of the respondents conduct some form of **customer service training** (Filipczak, 1992). Customer relations/service personnel need the skills to deal effectively with customers. Any employee who interacts with a customer, even if indirectly, represents the organization. Thus, each customer's perception of the quality of that interaction may influence how the organization's products and service are perceived.

For example, Becker and Wellins (1990) surveyed over 1,300 retail customers to determine their perceptions of customer service. They concluded that (1) good service keeps customers coming back while poor service drives them away; (2) organizations should continuously monitor customers' perceptions of their service; and (3) job skills of customer-service employees most likely need to be enhanced through training.

The notion that **good service keeps customers coming back** is the crux of many customer service programs. For example, Guaranteed Eateries in Seattle instituted a customer guarantee program, referred to as "Your Enjoyment Guaranteed," which involved giving free drinks and even entire free meals, if certain service guidelines were not met. The front-line personnel were empowered to grant these guarantees. While the program is estimated to cost about $10,000 per month, sales have risen 25 percent and profits have doubled (Firnstahl, 1989).

Continuously monitoring customers' perceptions of service is also critical. Organizations must be able to get feedback from their customers in order to determine if needs were met. For example, Norand Corporation got "closer to the customer" by instituting a customer feedback system through monthly in-depth telephone surveys that were tabulated and circulated to each sales and service manager (Miller, 1992). The results can be used to make changes, including institution of training programs.

While customer service training varies considerably across both industries and companies, there are some common components. Stum and Church (1990) feel that it should include four elements:

1. **Introduce customer service training organization-wide.** Organization-wide customer service training can be a key component of a business turnaround. For example, Scandinavian Airlines Systems (SAS) in 1981 reversed several years of losses to attain a gross profit of $71 million because, among other things, "they put 27,000 employees through a company-wide (customer service) training program" (Albrecht, 1985, p. 64). Most leading service companies place the same level of importance on this training by including it in standard employee orientation programs (Desatnick, 1987).

2. **Front-line employees need to be trained in customer relations skills including interpersonal skills and operational practices.** This training is necessary for two reasons. First, customer contact employees (e.g., sales associates, customer service representatives, recruiters, secretaries, account executives, etc.) must have skills and abilities to successfully relate to customers. Important interpersonal skills include the ability to listen and speak effectively. Second, the training should reinforce the notion that the long-term health of the organization depends, in part, on front-line employees exceeding customer expectations (Cone, 1989). This is an important point. Customer-contact employees must be able to understand each customer's needs so that they can "shape" expectations. To do this, organizations must empower front-line employees to guarantee customer satisfaction, even if it means incurring additional costs.

3. **Service managers need training in how to coach employees and enforce new customer service standards.** Desatnick (1987) suggests that developing a customer-oriented work force requires the hiring of service managers to train, develop, and motivate employees. Organizations should also provide additional training to certain service managers so that they understand their roles and the need to monitor and reinforce customer service standards. The term "service manager" is used in a wider context here to include any supervisor whose employees interact with customers and other outsiders, from the sales manager to the office manager supervising secretaries who greet and interact with customers and clients.

4. **Provide incentives (and disincentives) for supporting and sustaining the new customer service philosophy, but not limited**

to recognition systems, compensation, and upgrading. Customer service training should include employee incentives (or disincentives) that serve to reinforce desired behaviors. There are a wide range of individual and group incentives that can be used for this purpose. Historically, organizations have relied on individual incentives to motivate employees. However, in recent years more and more organizations are looking more to the use of group incentives such as employee involvement and gains-sharing programs.

Team Building/Training

Another outgrowth of quality improvement movement, discussed earlier, is the emphasis on team-based approaches. W. Edwards Deming has advocated the empowerment of individuals and work groups to make them responsible for productivity and quality improvements. The application of Deming's principles has resulted in a proliferation of team-based approaches including quality circles, focus groups, cross-functional teams, problem-solving groups, and self-directed (or self-managed) teams. This trend is seen in the recent 1992 *Training* survey, which showed that 82 percent of all organizations designated employees as team members and 68 percent of these conducted some type of team building or training programs (Gordon, 1992; Filipczak, 1992).

There are at least two sets of skills involved in team building or training—task skills and process skills. **Task skills** are necessary for performing group tasks and roles. In a typical organization, qualified employees must learn how to apply those skills in a particular group setting. For example, a work team may be responsible for servicing an airplane. Each technician and mechanic may have prescribed tasks to perform. **Process skills** are essential for coordinating work between group members, providing necessary support, solving problems, and resolving conflicts. A common approach used to train team members in process skills is team building. The emphasis of this approach is on enhancing the team's ability to work together more effectively, to communicate better, to improve problem-solving capabilities, and to make better decisions.

Team building is often part of a larger change strategy. The nature of the intervention will depend upon the goals of top management and the structural components that need to be changed. Of the team-based approaches just mentioned, self-directed teams (SDTs) would involve the most dramatic structural change because the role of the immediate supervisor is minimized or eliminated. The SDT approach typically involves giving team members more responsibility for such things as assignments, work schedules, quality control, budget, performance appraisal, training, and discipline. Such an approach would normally involve a full-blown change strategy using organization development (OD) techniques (which will be discussed in Chapter 13).

Even though the use of the team approach is fairly widespread, practitioners lack the methods and tools to analyze team tasks, behaviors, and skills (Tannebaum & Yukl, 1992). This means that organizations must rely solely on organizational output measures to determine the effectiveness of team building/training, as illustrated in the following examples:

1. The team-based approach used at the Vickers AMD plant in Jackson, Mississippi, in the early 1980s produced significant improvement in the number of products passing inspection and a reduction in the cost of scrap material (Nichols, 1991).

2. At Northern Telecom in Morrisville, North Carolina, a team-based approach resulted in increased revenue and earnings (Versteeg, 1990).

3. At Johnsonville Foods in Sheboygan, Wisconsin, productivity rose over 50 percent after a team-based program was implemented (Lee, 1990).

4. The Long Island Railroad in New York introduced a team-oriented approach that has resulted in reduction of the number of lost days due to injuries (Powell, 1990).

5. Probably the most widely known SDT approach is the one used at Saturn Corporation, where work teams of 5 to 15 employees are empowered to make most of the supervisory decisions. The output measures for Saturn show that it has outsold its next immediate competitor by a 2 to 1 ratio while chalking up one of the highest customer satisfaction ratings (*Business Week*, Reinventing America 1992).

Professional Development and Education

Professionals are typically distinguished by the fact that they have qualifications, such as a college degree or certificate, and in some cases (e.g., physician, attorney, teacher) may be required to be licensed by a state regulatory agency. Certification or licensing requirements often include a review of credentials and/or an examination. In addition, some professions may also impose other requirements. To maintain a license or certificate, many professions require periodic examinations and completion of a minimum number of continuing-education courses. This section will focus on continuing education for professionals.

Continuing Education at Colleges and Universities

Many colleges and universities offer courses to meet the continuing-education needs of professionals. Some benefits of this arrangement are (1) organizations are able to use the expertise available at colleges, (2) organizations can help design the courses that are job-specific, (3) organizations can choose instructors, and (4) college credit may be granted, making it possible for employees to obtain a college degree. In some cases, the cost of these courses is refunded by the employer through a tuition-reimbursement program. Overall, the success of this arrangement depends on the demand for the courses and the flexibility of the academic institution to meet the needs of professional employees.

There are many examples of joint or partnership programs between colleges and other organizations. For instance, the Center for Financial Studies at Fairfield University, Fairfield, Connecticut, developed a cooperative venture with the National Council of Savings Institutions, which offers workshops to area banks and other financial organizations. Companies like NCR, Pacific Bell, and Control Data have developed college-credit courses approved by the American Council on Education Program on Non-collegiate Sponsored Instruction (ACE/PONSI), which uses administrators and faculty from local colleges to evaluate programs (Forsyth & Galloway, 1988). American College offers specialized training for insurance professionals, including those from John Hancock Financial Services (Crosson, 1990).

Some states have experimented with partnership programs. The state of New York began an experiment in 1983 with the Public Employees Federation, a government employees' union, in which public administration courses were designed and offered at area colleges and universities. The uniqueness of this program was that it was tied to the union contract, and thus protected somewhat from budget cuts (Faerman, Quinn, & Thompson, 1987). Similarly, the Governmental Services Center at Kentucky State University provides mandatory training and career-management workshops to a full spectrum of public-sector employees (Childress & Bugbee, 1986).

Continuing Education by Professional Associations

It is estimated that, of the over 20,000 professional associations in the United States, approximately 3 percent provide training as part of a certification program (Carnevale et al., 1990c). Professional associations provide both pre-certification and continuing-education opportunities to their members. Pre-certification programs can be offered at the association's training center or at local colleges. For instance, the National Institute of Credit provides on-site instruction for member organizations as part of their certification programs (Margotta, 1986). The insurance industry sponsors two pre-certification programs leading to the chartered life underwriter (CLU) and chartered financial consultant (ChFC) designations at the American College (Crosson, 1990). Also, the Stonier Graduate School of Banking at the University of Delaware and the School for Bank Administration at the University of Wisconsin offer certification for banking professionals (Green, 1987).

In addition to pre-certification training, many professional associations require members to attend continuing-education courses in order to qualify for recertification, including the following:

1.   Several engineering associations believe that the best way for engineers to keep up with the latest technologies is to require their recertification every three years (Howell, 1988).

2.   The American Institute of Certified Public Accountants has recommended the adoption of a national standard that requires practicing CPAs to attend mandatory continuing professional education courses (Plewa et al., 1990).

3. A number of trade associations and professional associations within the insurance industry have directed their members to meet continuing-education requirements (Ballew, 1990).

4. Over 50 percent of the states require practicing attorneys to obtain a specified number of continuing-education credits (Eckel, 1988).

5. Hospitals are requiring physicians to complete continued medical education courses approved by the American Medical Association (Wentz et al., 1989).

These examples illustrate the high priority many professional associations place on continuing education.

Continuing-Education Programs Offered On-Site

When continuing-education programs are not made available at colleges, universities, and professional associations, organizations must be able to design their own programs. Some organizations have developed college-level curricula within their own training centers. Organizations like Motorola hire faculty both from among their senior professionals (many of them at retirement age) and from outside experts. This arrangement not only makes the program organization-specific, but enables it to incorporate training in the latest technology.

Continuing education does not have to be technical or job-related. Landon (1990) states that the average professional works 52.5 hours per week and as a result may experience "energy malady." Such demands on time can lead to stress-related illnesses that could be remedied through an education program. Landon surveyed 200 Fortune 500 companies and found that over 70 percent offer some type of stress-management training. Such programs include outdoor leadership programs, time management, on-site fitness programs, and stop-smoking clinics. Stress management will be discussed in more detail in Chapter 10.

HRD Department's Role in Continuing Education

The HRD department has three distinct roles to play with respect to continuing education—as an enabler, a resource provider, and a monitor. As an **enabler,** the HRD department must establish policies and procedures that foster an effective and equitable distribution of training programs throughout the organization. Such policies should be an integral part of the mission of the organization to the extent that it brings about adjustments in attitude, perspective, and thinking (Jacobsen and Kaye, 1988).

As a **resource provider,** the HRD department should consider the program-support options discussed earlier, including tuition reimbursement, educational leave, paid professional association fees, and compensation of travel expenses to off-site professional development sites. A tuition-reimbursement program is an important part of a career-development program because it increases the chances employees will continue their education. Most programs reimburse educational expenses, including tuition and fees, provided the course is job-related and the employee receives a specified grade. Many feel that such programs will make employees more valuable to the organizations because, through it, they will become more creative, innovative, or entrepreneurial (Toomey & Connor, 1988).

Education leaves (sabbaticals) offer employees an opportunity to continue their education or conduct research while they continue to receive pay for up to 12 months. Such programs are generally made available after a certain length of employment within the organization. Some organizations also offer these leaves to senior managers so that they can pursue other interests (e.g., teaching, volunteering time in a nonprofit organization, or writing). There are usually conditions that must be met by the employee to qualify for such leave, such as not having other means of support (e.g., another job) while on leave. In addition, return to the former job or organization is mandatory, as well as the production of a detailed report, conducting seminars, or some other evidence to show that the leave was used productively.

Employers may also pay fees and expenses to allow employees to attend professional meetings and seminars. These sessions provide an opportunity to share ideas, discuss common issues, and contribute to the field of knowledge. Such meetings are invaluable to employees who want to remain current in their fields and who want to write and present professional papers. Because of limited resources for such activities, an equitable process of approving these kinds of expenditures must be established. To be equitable, the policy should specify how employees can qualify for programs, provide justification for expenditures, and be approved by management. This policy should be made known throughout the organization.

The HRD department serves as a **monitor** by ensuring that the professional development process is working as planned. For instance, General Foods has a professional development process that requires supervisors to develop skills-assessment and development plans with each subordinate. These are used to organize training and development efforts in critical skill areas and allow HRD staff to monitor changes in the skills base of the individual unit or entire department (Courtney, 1986).

RETURN TO OPENING CASE

The Saturn/Maritz design team completed the design of the retail and wholesale operations training program, the Saturn Training and Partnership (STEP), in 1989. STEP included several training programs directed at all franchise employees, from sales managers to receptionists. The training materials totaled 5,000 pages of printed material and 600 minutes of videotape, with 325 hours of training allocated per retail facility.

The sales training program emphasized a major shift from traditional hard-sell tactics to a "consultative" approach, which involved six steps:

1. Listen to customers.

2. Create an environment of mutual trust.

3. Exceed customer expectations.

4. Create a "win-win" culture.

5. Follow up with customers to make sure their expectations were met.

6. Continually improve customer perceptions of quality in products and services.

The design team studied psychological profiles of a typical salesperson, as a result producing a series of "brainstorming" sessions to look at various training designs.

The final design of the training program consisted of self-study modules and seminars conducted at Saturn's Spring Hill, Tennessee, facility, the site of its manufacturing plant. The **self-study** training method of approximately 11 hours was selected over more traditional methods because the design team felt that this approach more easily fit into employee work schedules. The self-study modules were designed around "learning maps" that detailed either reading assignments or review of video vignettes. **Seminars** covered various subjects (e.g., experimenting with concepts and practice skills) that would best be delivered in a group setting. Several modules were listed as prerequisites to attending a seminar.

Program evaluation activities included a survey assessing trainee reactions to the training design and materials, a post-training mastery examination, and a 60-day performance evaluation to assess whether the skills the trainees learned were being used back on the job. Other indicators of training effectiveness included sales volume and customer satisfaction ratings.

Since the first Saturn rolled off the assembly line, dealers have outperformed their closest competitor by 2 to 1 in terms of car sales per facility. In fact, many Saturn dealers are finding it difficult to meet demand. The level of customer satisfaction is also impressive. According to J. D. Power and Associates, which surveys new car buyers as to their rating of both car and the dealership, Saturn ranked 3rd overall among dealerships, scoring 160 points in 1992, well above the industry average of 129. Saturn management feels that, if they become the success story of the 1990s, much credit should go to the STEP program.[1]

---

[1]Cottrell, D., Davis, L., Detrick, P., & Raymond, M., 1992. "Sales training and the Saturn difference." *Training and Development Journal, 46* (12), 38–43.

Summary

The need for skilled and technical workers is on the rise. Employers are complaining that many young adults are graduating from schools lacking the skills needed to perform their current job. We reviewed six categories of workplace competencies: basic competency skills, communication skills, adaptability skills, developmental skills, group effectiveness skills, and influencing skills. The workforce deficiency in basic competency skills has caused many organizations to develop basic skills programs.

Two categories of technical training were examined—technical and nontechnical. Technical training programs included apprenticeships, and those in computers, technical skills/knowledge, safety, and quality. Apprenticeship training, the most formalized employer-based program, involves both on-the-job (OJT) and classroom training. Computer training typically involves either introductory or applications training. Technical skills/knowledge programs are generally job-specific and are offered organization-wide. Quality and team training programs are typically part of a larger quality improvement agenda.

Nontechnical programs included those in communications/interpersonal, sales, and customer relations. Each of these emphasize interpersonal skills. The last category of training is that of professional development and continuing education. Continuing-education programs can be offered by colleges and universities and professional associations, as well as the employer.

Key Terms and Concepts

apprenticeship training	professional associations
basic skills/literacy education	quality training
customer service training	safety training
Job Training and Partnership Act (JTPA)	team training
	technical training
Occupational Safety and Health Act (OSHA)	

Questions for Discussion

1. Explain why skills training programs are important for the long-term vitality of organizations.

2. Describe how skills training programs differ from other types of such programs.

3. If you were responsible for designing a basic skills/literacy training program, what approach would you take? How would you determine the effectiveness of this program?

4. Colleges and universities are primarily service enterprises. What key components would you include in customer service training for college personnel, such as security or records office staff, who interact with students?

5. Is it likely that by the year 2000 most workers will need to be skilled in using computers? What can organizations do to prepare for this?

6. Why is quality training so popular today? Provide an example where, in your experience, this type of training has been successful.

7. Explain why continuing education for professionals is important to both organizational and individual success. What kinds of program options would you provide for professionals—such as accountants and dieticians—who need professional certification?

9

Coaching

Learning Objectives

1. Define coaching and explain the need for it.

2. Explain how to analyze employee performance to set the stage for the coaching discussion.

3. Describe the steps involved in coaching to improve poor performance.

4. Explain how coaching can be used to maintain effective performance and encourage superior performance.

5. Identify the skills necessary for effective coaching.

6. Describe the evidence supporting the effectiveness of coaching.

OPENING CASE

Selling is one of the most challenging and critical jobs within any organization. While many organizations provide training to ensure sales personnel are ready and able to perform, much of the benefit of this training goes untapped. This happens because many sales managers lack the skills or motivation to reinforce what is learned in training, reducing the chances that what sales people learn in training will be used back on the job. Furthermore, sales managers often overlook opportunities to help employees continue learning from their everyday performance.

The sales executives at Xerox Corporation understand this and provide their sales managers with the skills and understanding to **coach** sales employees toward effective performance. Coaching involves helping employees recognize performance problems and opportunities for improvement while making them partners in increasing their own (and the organization's) effectiveness.

But coaching is not easy. According to Derwin Fox, a vice-president of development and consulting services at Xerox Learning Systems in Stamford, Connecticut, sales managers often have a difficult time coaching. To address this problem, researchers there have studied the coaching process and developed training guidelines for their sales managers.

The Need for Coaching

Many managers and supervisors have a narrow, reactive, and negative view of their role in managing employee performance. Their approach to managing performance can actually create or compound performance problems rather than solve them. This negative view includes beliefs such as:

1. All employees know what they should do and how to do it.

2. Performance management is a simple matter of expecting tasks to be done correctly and on time.

3. If a problem occurs, the appropriate action is to give the employee a stern lecture or to threaten punishment. The problem will then go away—after all, the employee already knows what should be done and how to do it.

4. If the problem does not go away, the employee must be stupid, lazy, or have a "bad attitude." Therefore, punishment is called for.

5. If punishment fails, the only reasonable course of action is to terminate or transfer the employee.

Managers and supervisors who attempt to manage employees this way are frequently frustrated because their intervention is often ineffective or creates opportunities for conflict. Performance management becomes aversive. Therefore, many managers and supervisors choose to ignore poor performance and poor performers altogether. Instead, they may choose to assign the work to effective employees or even to do it themselves. This approach can lead to further problems, such as feelings of inequity and low morale among the employees assigned the extra work, while the initial problem remains unresolved.

Furthermore, this negative approach may lead to frustration when changes in the organization's goals demand higher levels of employee performance. Managers who believe all they need to do to improve employee performance is to relay the orders issued from above and give employees a pep talk are stymied when these actions fail to achieve the goal. These actions may seem sensible to the manager who thinks employees already know what they are doing and how to do it. Unfortunately, if improvement does not occur, yelling, threats, or punishment may be the next, seemingly logical, course of action.

The reality is that sometimes employees know what to do and how to do it, but sometimes they do not. The recruiting and selection process may be flawed; orientation and training may have been done poorly (if at all). In addition, changes in the task, organization, or environment may prompt the need for new knowledge or skills. Even the manager or supervisor's own behavior may undermine employee motivation. For example, if superior performance is neither noticed nor rewarded, a climate may exist in which effective performance is actually discouraged. Conflicting, confusing, or incomplete requests will also cause employees to wonder what the manager really expects.

Further, taking a negative approach to managing performance may mean the only time the supervisor discusses performance with employees is when there is a problem or request for improvement. Effective performance is ignored because it is expected. Employees may resent this treatment, and the employees' supervisor misses opportunities to encourage effective performance and prevent problems.

Coaching: A Positive Approach to Managing Performance

Effective managers and supervisors realize that they must take an active and positive role in employee performance to ensure that goals are met. These managers and supervisors realize that they are paid not for what they do, but for what their subordinates do. Therefore, they define their role in managing employee performance as one of empowering employees. Their role is to ensure that employees know specifically what to do and can actually do it. When changes in the environment, goals, or task do occur, employees are informed and given the opportunity for training so they can adapt to the changes.

Effective managers and supervisors also make sure employees know how they are performing and reward effective performance when it occurs. They don't intervene only to correct problems or increase production. Therefore, performance discussions are less likely to be seen as opportunities for conflict.

In short, managing employee performance effectively requires that managers and supervisors become coaches rather than controllers. We believe coaching is one of the most important functions a manager or supervisor can perform. A manager can be a superb planner, organizer, and decision maker, but without the effective management of employee performance that coaching provides, objectives will be difficult to achieve. Coaching creates a partnership between supervisor and employees that is dedicated to helping employees get the job done. The current popularity of *participative management* approaches (e.g., employee empowerment and self-directed teams) requires managers and supervisors to function primarily as coaches for those who report to them (e.g., Geber, 1992; Kiechel, 1991). In this chapter, we discuss what is involved in coaching and describe how it can be used to improve poor performance and ensure continued effective performance. We also describe the skills and training necessary to be an effective coach.

Definition of Coaching

There is no single agreed upon definition of coaching. Some authors define it narrowly as a performance-improvement technique. For example, Fournies (1978) defines coaching as a face-to-face discussion between a manager and a subordinate to get the subordinate to stop performing an undesirable behavior and begin performing desirable behaviors. Similarly, Kinlaw (1989) defines coaching as a "mutual conversation between a manager and an employee that follows a predictable process and leads to superior performance, commitment to sustained improvement, and positive relationships" (p. 31). In Kinlaw's view, effective coaching becomes a matter of learning how to conduct the coaching discussion.

Other authors see coaching in broader terms and draw upon similarities between organizational managers and athletic coaches. For example, Kirkpatrick (1982) argues that sports coaches and managers have similar responsibilities (e.g., recruiting, motivating, ensuring results, working with individuals and the team) and work under similar conditions (e.g., limited resources, time constraints). Therefore, many of the characteristics of an effective athletic coach should also be present in the effective manager-coach. These characteristics include optimism, a strong sense of moral values, honesty, humility, warmth, and self-confidence.

Evered and Selman (1990) take the model of "manager as athletic coach" one step further. They argue that it is the "context of committed partnership" in which athletic coaching occurs that is the key to defining management coaching. The communication and relationship between coach and performer that spring from this partnership are the essence of coaching. They contend that to coach effectively, there must be a shift from seeing management as controlling employees to management as empowering or enabling employees. Similarly, Peters and Austin (1985) describe the manager-coach as one who brings individuals together and "encourages them to step up to responsibility and continued achievement, treating them as full-scale partners and contributors (p. 325)."

To complicate matters further, some authors use the term *coaching* to describe both a broad approach to performance management and a specific technique to facilitate it. Peters and Austin (1985) define coaching broadly (as described earlier) as an overall approach to performance management, while at the same time naming five distinct though related roles that together make up coaching. One of these five roles is given the name *coaching;* the other roles are called educating, sponsoring, counseling, and confronting. The coaching role is likened to leadership, whereas the other roles involve teaching (educating), mentoring (sponsoring), dealing with personal problems (counseling), or getting employees to face up to performance problems (confronting). Similarly, Kinlaw (1989) sees coaching as both problem solving and performance improvement, and argues that it is made up of four functions: counseling, mentoring, tutoring, and confronting.

So what is coaching? It would be easy to narrow the use of the term to refer to a specific performance-management technique. The disadvantage of this would be to risk creating the assumption that a manager can be controlling and manipulative and still effectively use the coaching technique to improve performance. This is not likely to be the case. We agree with Fournies (1978) and Everett and Selman (1989) that effective coaching requires an optimistic, humanistic belief in the desire of employees to be committed to the task and the organization without coercion (similar to McGregor's [1960] Theory Y philosophy). Coaching encompasses more than mere technique; it is a day-to-day approach to managing performance. Acting as a coach makes the manager or supervisor a partner with employees and a facilitator of their performance. The coach/manager thus sees himself as serving employees and as getting paid for what they achieve (Fournies, 1978). Traditional managers, on the other hand, tend to assume a monitor/controller role, in which they "use" and control employees as they would any other resource. At its heart, coaching requires the manager to take interest in and interact with subordinates to encourage effective performance.

We define **coaching** as a process used to encourage employees to accept responsibility for their performance, enable them to achieve and sustain superior performance, and treat them as partners in working toward organizational goals. This is done by performing two distinct activities: (1) **coaching analysis,** which involves analyzing performance and the conditions under which it occurs, and (2) **coaching discussions,** or face-to-face communication between employee and supervisor both to solve problems and to enable the employee to maintain and improve effective performance (Fournies, 1978; Kinlaw, 1989).

Role of Supervisor and Manager in Coaching

It should now be clear that an employee's direct supervisor or manager bears the responsibility for coaching. While other managers in the organization can serve as mentors, teach a new skill, or help overcome a specific problem, coaching occurs within the context of an ongoing relationship between employee and supervisor. It is the supervisor's responsibility to ensure his or her unit meets its goals, and that means ensuring employees perform their tasks effectively. The supervisor delegates assignments, establishes standards, and monitors performance, and is therefore uniquely equipped with sufficient information, opportunity, and authority to carry out coaching effectively. Someone outside the work unit who does not perform these tasks lacks sufficient information, opportunity, and authority to coach effectively.

The HRD Professional's Role in Coaching

HRD professionals can help managers and supervisors become effective coaches by providing training in the coaching process and ensuring the coaches have the interpersonal skills needed to be effective. In addition, problems uncovered by a coaching analysis may be solved by using other HRD programs, such as training. HRD professionals can also help management create a climate that encourages coaching through the use of organizational development (OD) techniques.

As we will see, resolving performance problems may require the use of HRM or other management activities beyond development. For example, a performance problem may be caused by an inadequate reward system, and resolved by revising the compensation system. Similarly, if a manager discovers the same skill deficiency in all employees, the recruiting or selection system may need to be changed, rather than relying on training to ensure that new employees can perform the job. And, if the information or production system contributes to or causes the problems, such as poorly maintained or outdated equipment or erroneous reports, correcting these systems can ultimately lead to improved performance.

We believe it is important that HRD professionals understand the coaching process and the skills necessary to conduct it well. While they may not have to conduct coaching themselves, they can help managers and supervisors prepare for this challenging and rewarding responsibility.

Coaching to Improve Poor Performance

Poor performance is a fact of life in many organizations. While most employees perform as expected, there will always be those employees who fail to meet expectations. According to Viega (1988), "If there is one universal truth about managers, it is that all of them have problem subordinates" (p. 145).

There are many reasons for poor performance. It is a manager's job to confront and deal with poor performance, and to create conditions that minimize the chances that it will occur again. Coaching is one way to do this. In this section we will address three issues: (1) the definition of poor performance, (2) how coaching analysis can be conducted to determine the cause of poor performance, and (3) how the coaching discussion can be used to improve poor performance.

Defining Poor Performance

Defining what sorts of behavior comprise poor performance is not as simple as it may first appear. A given behavior, such as the time one arrives at work or the number of apartments a sales agent rents in a given month, is itself neither good nor bad. A behavior must be evaluated with respect to some standard or expected level of performance before it may be labeled "good" or "poor." If the behavior meets or exceeds the standard, then it is typically considered good. If the behavior fails to meet the standard, it may be considered poor.

But how much must a behavior deviate from what is expected before it is considered poor performance? The answer depends both on who is making the evaluation and that person's perception of the situation. Supervisors may differ as to how large a deviation from the standard can be tolerated. Furthermore, the same supervisor may tolerate different deviations at different times for different employees. For example, it may be more acceptable for a sales person to fail to reach a sales goal during traditionally slow seasons than during other times of the year. Similarly, the supervisor may ignore deviations from performance standards if she believes the employee is having personal problems, while at the same time holding other employees rigidly accountable for their behavior.

Furthermore, employees and supervisors may interpret performance differently, either because they apply different standards to the same behavior or because they selectively attend to different aspects of the same behavior. For example, suppose a chef uses more expensive ingredients to prepare dishes than authorized by the restaurant manager. The chef may define this as effective behavior because it satisfies customers and may induce them to return. The manager, meanwhile, may interpret this as poor performance because it reduces the profit margin on the meals the chef prepares; the manager may consider the chef's behavior an instance of not following the rules.

In short, what is poor performance is not as clear-cut as it first appears; it depends on the standards established for performance and how those standards are applied. The following definition of **poor performance** takes these issues into account: "Specific, agreed-upon deviations from expected behavior" (Mitchell & O'Reilly, 1983, p. 205). This definition makes two important points. First, the extent of the deviation from a performance standard to be considered poor must be specifically defined. If absolutely no deviation will be tolerated, then this must be stated. If some deviation will be tolerated (e.g., two absences per quarter), then this amount must be made clear. Second, the amount of deviation that constitutes poor performance should be agreed to by both the evaluator and the performer. This is not to say every performance standard must be negotiated; rather, the performer must be made aware of what the standard is and understand that it will be used to evaluate performance. The employee must agree the standard is legitimate.

This definition of poor performance does not restrict the type of standard that may be used. For example, a supervisor can use an *absolute* standard, which would be applied to all subordinates, or a *relative* standard, which considers the employee's progress or performance in light of the performance of others. Requiring all employees to achieve an error rate of no more than 1 percent is an absolute standard; requiring an employee to be in the top 50 percent of his or her training class to be eligible for permanent position is a relative standard. The choice of the standard should be guided by the organization's (and unit's) goals and methods used to achieve those goals (e.g., policies, practices, and the task itself).

Responding to Poor Performance

Once a supervisor has determined that poor performance has occurred, he or she must diagnose the cause of the deviation and select an appropriate response (Mitchell & O'Reilly, 1983). One way to do this is to conduct a coaching (or performance) analysis. Before we describe one approach to coaching analysis, two issues need to be discussed that affect how it is conducted:

- Poor performance may have **multiple** causes.

- The process of **causal attribution** may affect what the supervisor considers an appropriate response.

Poor performance does not always result from a single cause, and the same type of performance problem may be caused by different factors at different times. As discussed in Chapter 2, employee behavior has many causes. These causes may exist within the individual, such as motivation or attitudes, or the organization, such as co-workers or reward systems, or the outside environment, such as social or family events. Solving a performance problem depends on identifying and dealing with the cause of the problem. For example, if a radiology technician is abrupt with patients because of anxiety over the prospect of being laid off or because of a family crisis, sending the technician to courtesy training will probably not eliminate the problem. Coaching analysis can help the supervisor identify the cause or causes of poor performance and thus help determine the appropriate response.

Causal attribution theory describes the process by which people assign causes to their own and others' behavior. Attribution theory suggests that supervisors may use both rational information and biases in determining the cause of employee performance (Mitchell & O'Reilly, 1983). Weiner (Weiner et al., 1972) suggests that there are four categories of causes of performance, two within the employee (effort and ability) and two in the situation (task difficulty and luck). The supervisor's response to poor performance will vary depending on whether he or she concludes the cause is within the employee or the situation.

One of the biases that may occur when attempting to find the cause for the employee's behavior is the **fundamental attribution error.** This error is the tendency to overattribute a behavior to a cause within a person (e.g., effort or ability), rather than considering the cause is in the situation (e.g., task difficulty or luck). A supervisor who commits this error is likely to overlook real environmental causes of poor performance and thus blame the employee for poor performance that was not under the employee's control. For example, suppose a manager notices a serious error in a contract drawn up by a subordinate. It could be that a tight time deadline or inadequate information provided by another employee led to the error. A manager affected by the fundamental attribution error will tend to overlook these possibilities and instead try to find a cause within the subordinate, such as laziness or carelessness. This may lead the manager to choose punishment as a response to the problem rather than more correctly focusing on making a change in the environment so the error is unlikely to occur in the future.

In addition, an employee's response to a performance problem may affect the way a supervisor evaluates and responds to it. Employees are likely to attribute their failures to factors beyond their control (e.g., task difficulty, obstacles in the environment) rather than to a lack of ability or effort (Mitchell, Green, & Wood, 1981), thereby helping to maintain their self-esteem (Larson, 1977). Furthermore, employees may select feedback-seeking strategies that minimize the amount of negative feedback they receive (Larson, 1989). When discussing performance problems with supervisors, employees may volunteer information that they hope will deflect the responsibility for poor performance from themselves to the environment (Gioia & Sims, 1986), hoping that the supervisor will view the poor performance less negatively. There is some evidence that these attempts at deflecting blame are successful. Gioia and Sims (1986) found that supervisors who heard employee explanations for their poor performance saw the employee as less responsible for the performance than before the discussion. In addition, research suggests that supervisors who viewed employees in this way evaluated the employee less negatively and provided less negative performance feedback (Knowlton & Mitchell, 1980; Ilgen & Knowlton, 1980).

A complete discussion of the attribution process is beyond the scope of this chapter. The main point to be made is that the judgments supervisors make when diagnosing the causes of poor performance can be affected by biases. This means that the coaching analysis can be adversely affected by such biases. Supervisors should be trained to guard against bias to ensure they correctly identify the cause for poor performance. Training that may be useful in this regard will be discussed in the rater training section of Chapter 12.

Conducting the Coaching Analysis

Coaching analysis is the process of analyzing the factors that contribute to unsatisfactory performance and deciding on the appropriate response to improve performance. Fournies (1978), building on Mager & Pipe's (1970) model of performance analysis, describes a nine-step process designed to identify the causes of poor performance and suggest possible solutions. In each step, the supervisor answers a question about the performance incident and determines how to proceed.

The coaching analysis process is based on the assumption that poor performance can have multiple causes, some of which are within the employee's control and some of which are not. The process leads the supervisor to examine common causes for performance problems. If the answer to a question in the analysis reveals the cause, the supervisor should take the appropriate action and then monitor performance to determine whether it improves. If it does not, the supervisor should continue the analysis until the employee's performance does improve. Some of the actions recommended in the coaching analysis process involve HRM and HRD actions such as providing **feedback,** removing obstacles to performance, or providing training. A description of the steps in the process follows:

Step 1: Identify the unsatisfactory performance. Coaching cannot begin until the supervisor defines in specific behavioral terms what the employee is doing wrong or failing to do. While this may seem the obvious first step, Fournies and others (e.g., Mager & Pipe, 1970; Viega, 1988) observe that managers and subordinates are notoriously poor at identifying the specific behavior or performance result that makes up the poor performance. Descriptions such as "She just won't listen" or "He's surly when dealing with customers" do little to provide insight to solve the real problem. A clear, specific description of the problem permits examination of exactly what is occurring and may yield ideas about what is causing it. Furthermore, a supervisor who knows specifically what is happening now can better determine whether any action he or she takes improves the situation or worsens it. Without this information, it is impossible to accurately monitor change.

Describing the unsatisfactory performance requires careful observation and recording of a specific behavior or behavior pattern. For example, if the supervisor is concerned with an employee's tardiness, details of late arrival should be observed and recorded, such as date and time of arrival in each instance. With this information, the supervisor can judge the extent of the problem, whether and by how much the employee has violated company policy, and gain insight as to the cause of the problem.

Step 2: Is it worth your time and effort? After the problem has been clearly defined, the supervisor can estimate its severity. At this point, the supervisor must determine whether the performance problem is worth fixing. The problem may not be as bad as was initially thought. For example, after charting an employee's tardiness, the supervisor may realize the employee is only occasionally rather than consistently late. Furthermore, some employee behaviors may be annoying to the supervisor or may not be in keeping with the supervisor's preferences but do not detract from individual or work-group performance. For example, a supervisor may prefer that female employees not wear perfume or may be upset with an employee's political views as related to the company's business (e.g., clean-air policies in a manufacturing plant). The supervisor should identify specifically why he or she considers a problem important (Mager & Pipe, 1970). If the so-called problem does not hinder individual, unit, or organizational effectiveness, then the supervisor should ignore it. Spending time and effort on matters that neither affect results, nor violate important rules or policies, nor interfere with co-workers, will do nothing more tangible perhaps, than please the supervisor. If the supervisor indulges in preferences, however, he or she may alienate the employee or waste time that can be better spent managing the things that do make a real difference.

Step 3: Do subordinates know that their performance is not satisfactory? One reason employees may perform poorly is that they do not realize what they are doing constitutes a problem. For example, a shipping clerk may not realize 10 percent of the orders he ships lack a packing list, especially if he is not provided with performance feedback or evaluation standards. In addition, without feedback, the employee may assume everything is going well and see no reason to change. Therefore, the employee should be asked if he realizes what he is doing is wrong. Simply pointing out faulty behavior and requesting correct performance may be enough to solve the problem.

Step 4: Do subordinates know what is supposed to be done? Not knowing what to do and when to do it may be another reason employees fail to perform correctly. For example, an employee who has never prepared a quarterly quality report or has never seen what a finished quality report looks like is not likely to produce a satisfactory report. In this step of coaching analysis, the supervisor should ask the employee if she knows what she is supposed to be doing. If the answer indicates that she does not, the supervisor should tell the employee what is required. This may be enough to eliminate the problem performance.

Step 5: Are there obstacles beyond the employee's control? Sometimes poor performance is due to factors beyond the employee's control. For example, a loan officer may make a bad loan based on incorrect information provided by the bank itself or because a credit-reporting agency provided the bank with erroneous information. Many times the obstacles that cause poor performance can be removed by the supervisor. For example, if a supplier is delivering parts late, the supervisor should take steps to correct this. Such action may result in satisfactory performance.

Step 6: Does the subordinate know how to do what must be done? Many supervisors assume an employee who attends a training or orientation session will have learned the content of the session. As we discussed in Chapter

3, learning is a complex process. Not all training results in learning. It is also possible that if a task is performed infrequently, the employee's skills may become "rusty." For example, the first presentation an employee performs after a break of several months is always the toughest. Therefore, employees who have received training may not know, or may have forgotten, how to execute performance correctly. If this is the case, the supervisor should ensure the employee receives training (and/or opportunities to practice) and that the employee has learned what is needed to perform the task.

Step 7: Does a negative consequence follow performance? It is possible an employee knows what to do and how to do it, but has learned not to do the behavior because it is always followed by an unpleasant consequence. Recalling the discussion of motivation in Chapter 2, the law of effect states that behavior followed by an aversive consequence will be less likely to occur. Therefore, if effective performance is followed by an aversive consequence, the employee will learn not to perform effectively.

For example, suppose a computer programmer who writes clear documentation is frequently asked by her supervisor to write documentation for other programmers. If the programmer prefers doing other tasks (e.g., writing programs), being asked to write more than her share of documentation would be an aversive consequence to doing this task well. This is especially true if other programmers in the unit get to write less documentation as a result. Therefore, the programmer may change her behavior to avoid this consequence by writing documentation of poorer quality in hopes of being assigned less of it.

Supervisors should attempt to determine whether an unpleasant consequence follows effective behavior. If it does, the supervisor has two alternatives. First, if possible, the aversive consequence should be removed. Returning to our example, if the programmer understands that she will no longer be given other employees' documentation to write if she does her own well, she will likely go back to writing clear documentation. Second, if the aversive consequence cannot be removed (e.g., if it is a part of the task itself), then the supervisor should provide a positive consequence that outweighs the aversive consequence. For example, cleaning restrooms is an unpleasant but necessary part of a custodian's job. If the supervisor provides custodians who do this part of the job well with a reward, such as being able to leave work early or being given first choice of vacation periods, the custodians will have good reason to perform this part of the job well.

Step 8: Does a positive consequence follow nonperformance? Sometimes employees engage in poor performance because a positive consequence follows it. In effect, they are rewarded for poor performance. Sometimes supervisors unwittingly reward poor performance. For example, suppose an employee who doesn't like to work weekends becomes disruptive during weekend shifts. If the supervisor remedies the problem by not assigning the employee to weekend shifts, the supervisor has shown the employee that the way to get what he wants is to be disruptive.

Supervisors should examine poor performance to see what consequence is reinforcing it. The supervisor should then remove the positive consequence and arrange for a positive consequence to follow effective performance. This course of action removes the reason the employee was performing poorly and gives the employee a reason to engage in effective performance.

Step 9: Could the subordinate do it if he or she wanted to? Sometimes employees perform poorly because they lack the skills, knowledge, or ability to perform effectively. Some employees will not be effective even after extensive training. If this is the case, the employee should be transferred to perform work that that employee is capable of doing well or be terminated from the organization. This is not necessarily bad for the employee. Some employees are relieved when given a way out of a situation they cannot handle. For example, if a salesperson is uncomfortable using the tactics necessary to close a sale or doesn't understand the technical nature of the products to be sold, that employee may be better suited to other kinds of work. A better match serves both the organization and the individual.

Another Question: Can the Task or Job Be Modified?   In addition to the issues Fournies describes, Mager and Pipe (1970) suggest the supervisor determine whether the task or job can be modified or simplified to increase the chances it will be performed correctly. For example, some tasks, such as maintenance checks, require multiple steps. While it may be reasonable to require the maintenance workers to remember all of these steps, an easier way would be to provide them with a job aid, such as a checklist that would be completed each time the worker services a piece of equipment.

What If the Problem Persists?   If the employee is capable of performing effectively, and if the coaching analysis has failed to improve performance, then Fournies states that the coaching discussion is called for. During this discussion, the employee and supervisor talk over the problem and its causes, and agree on a course of action to improve performance. The mechanics of this discussion are discussed next.

The Coaching Discussion

As stated earlier, the coaching discussion is designed to help the employee perform effectively. There are at least two approaches to this discussion, Fournies' (1978) five-step process, and Kinlaw's (1989) three-stage process. Because both approaches have merit, we will briefly discuss each.

Fournies's Approach   Fournies (1978) suggests a five-step coaching-discussion process that assumes the supervisor has conducted a thorough coaching analysis and has determined that the employee could perform the task if he or she wanted to. **The goal of the discussion is to get the employee to agree a problem exists and commit to a course of action to resolve it.**

Step 1: Get the employee's agreement that a problem exists. Fournies points out that unless the employee believes there is a performance problem, he or she will have no reason to change. Getting agreement involves describing the problem behavior and its consequences for the supervisor, co-workers, and the employee. Fournies recommends that the supervisor ask the employee questions designed to extract a statement of the problem behavior and its consequences (e.g., "And who has to take your calls when you come back late from lunch?"; "What happens if these calls aren't taken?"). This ensures the employee understands the situation.

This first step ends when the employee explicitly agrees a problem exists. This step may consume as much as 50 percent of time given for the coaching discussion, but Fournies is adamant that the discussion should not go forward without explicit agreement from the employee that a problem does indeed exist. At this point, Fournies asserts most employees will commit themselves to changing the behavior. But, in dealing with those who will not, the supervisor must decide whether to (1) drop the problem as one not really worth resolving, or (2) take disciplinary action. A supervisor who has already done the coaching analysis may have determined the problem is important. If not, the supervisor is paying the price for not doing the necessary homework and will be faced with having to back out of a messy situation. In our view, employees who do not agree at this point that a problem exists should be disciplined according to organizational policies (e.g., with warnings, letters to file, suspension, etc.). It is hoped that the disciplined employee will realize the consequences of their actions and agree to help resolve the performance problem. If not, the supervisor can feel a good-faith effort to resolve the problem has been made and can view the prospect of dismissing the employee—by transfer or termination—as the positive action it is.

Step 2: Mutually discuss alternative solutions to the problem. During this part of the discussion, the supervisor asks the employee for alternatives to solving the problem. If necessary, the supervisor should prompt the employee for ideas. Fournies believes that employees will more likely be committed to alternatives they have suggested. The supervisor's role during this part of the discussion is to help the employee come up with and clarify alternatives.

Step 3: Mutually agree on action to be taken to solve the problem. After sufficient alternatives have been discussed, the supervisor and employee can agree on which alternatives to pursue to solve the problem. At this point, both the employee and the supervisor clearly understand what will be done and when it will happen. They should also agree on a specific time to follow up on the discussion to determine whether the agreed-upon action has been taken. Fournies also suggests the supervisor thank the employee for his effort in trying to solve the problem and express confidence that it will be solved.

Step 4: Follow up to measure results. It is imperative that the supervisor follow up at the arranged time to determine whether the agreed-upon actions have been taken and the problem resolved. Without follow-up, the supervisor will not know what has happened, and the employee may conclude that the supervisor really doesn't care about the problem.

Step 5: Recognize any achievement when it occurs. Many performance problems will not disappear overnight. Even if a problem is not completely eliminated, the employee should be recognized for any effort and improvement made. The idea is to motivate him or her to further improvement. When necessary, further discussions should be held to determine additional steps needed to resolve the problem. Follow-up, recognition of improvement, and updated improvement planning should continue until the employee is performing effectively.

If the employee is unwilling to improve performance and fails to take action as agreed, the supervisor must decide whether to live with the problem, transfer the employee, or terminate the employee. Not all performance problems can be successfully resolved through coaching.

Kinlaw's Approach   Kinlaw (1989) suggests a three-stage approach to the coaching discussion, as follows:

- Confronting/presenting;

- Using reactions to develop information; and

- Resolution.

The goals of the **confronting/presenting stage** are to limit any negative emotion the employee might feel toward the problem situation, to specify the performance to be improved, and to establish that the goal is to help the employee change and improve. Kinlaw argues this can be done by specifically describing the performance that needs to be changed, limiting the discussion to a specific problem behavior, and avoiding assignment of blame by focusing on the future.

After the employee has confronted the problem performance, the supervisor must help the employee examine the causes for poor performance. This is done during the second stage of the discussion, **using reaction to develop information.** Kinlaw notes that employees may resist dealing with the problem after being confronted with it and argues that supervisors can reduce this resistance by focusing on the employee's concerns rather than their own. The supervisor may then develop information by attending to the employee's explanations, acknowledging important points, probing for information, and summarizing what has been discussed. At the end of this second stage of the coaching discussion, the employee and supervisor should be in a position to agree on the nature of the problem and its causes.

The third and final stage of Kinlaw's coaching discussion is called **resolving.** In this stage, the employee takes ownership of the problem and agrees upon the steps needed to solve it. Both parties at this point express commitment to improving performance and to establishing a positive relationship. This is done by examining alternative courses of action, reviewing key points of the session, and affirming that performance can be successfully improved.

An Analysis of the Two Approaches   Kinlaw and Fournies have much in common in their approach to the coaching discussion. Both emphasize the need to get the employee to verbally accept responsibility for improving performance and to involve the employee in developing the courses of action needed to solve the problem. They differ most in terms of the assumptions made about employee willingness to address performance problems. Kinlaw's approach highlights the emotional aspect of discussing performance problems with employees, and offers more guidance to supervisors in how to deal with the employee's emotions and resistance. Fournies's approach is more rational in the sense that he strongly maintains that an employee faced with evidence of a performance problem and its consequences will almost always be willing to deal with it. He states that employee unwillingness must either be based in the supervisor doing an insufficient job of analyzing the performance (e.g., not dealing with a specific behavior, dealing with an unimportant behavior, the employee not believing the supervisor will actually do anything about poor performance), or that the subordinate is engaging in self-destructive behavior and "is too mentally ill to be managed" (1978, p. 149).

We believe that both approaches offer a constructive way to discuss performance problems and that a supervisor can benefit from adopting either approach or a combination of both. One point neither approach makes clear is the importance of **setting specific goals** for performance improvement. While this is implicit in each approach (e.g., agreeing on what will be done and when), we believe that the supervisor and subordinate must agree upon a clearly stated performance goal before generating alternative solutions to the problem. As mentioned in Chapter 2, research has definitively shown specific performance goals lead to performance improvement (see also Locke & Latham, 1990). Establishing a performance goal can also provide a focus for the later steps of the discussion, where discussion alternatives, action plan, and follow-up are covered.

What If the Coaching Discussion Fails? There is no guarantee that the coaching process will resolve all performance problems. Some employees are unable or unwilling to improve performance even after being given an opportunity to do so. If the employee is unable to improve, the supervisor should either transfer the employee to work he or she can perform effectively or terminate the employee. If the employee is unwilling to improve performance, the supervisor should discipline (and if that fails, terminate) the employee according to the organization's policies. One potential advantage of the coaching process is that it provides the employee with a fair opportunity to recognize performance that is poor and take steps to improve it. If termination is the only choice left to the supervisor after coaching fails, then the supervisor should have adequate documentation to justify the termination and withstand challenges by the employee of unfair treatment.

Maintaining Effective Performance and Encouraging Superior Performance

Supervisors and managers should be interested not only in eliminating poor performance, but also in ensuring that good performers remain effective or become even better. This means they should reward effective performance and provide employees who want to become superior performers with the necessary support and opportunity. Motivational approaches, including goal setting, job redesign, employee participation programs, and the like, are ways of increasing the employees' sense of ownership of their performance, thereby encouraging them to remain successful.

Coaching can also be an effective way to encourage and enhance effective performance. Evered and Selman (1990) suggest that managers must create an environment that acknowledges employee contributions to the organization and empowers them to move forward. Managerial supportiveness, availability, and willingness to work with employees will create an environment where employees will demand coaching from their managers because they will be energized to improve. This is important, because if the employee does not have the desire to improve, the coaching discussion will likely be perceived negatively, and the employee will resist the manager's efforts.

The manager-coach can provide employees with a unique perspective on employee performance (Evered & Selman, 1990). Because it is difficult to observe oneself while performing a task, it is often difficult for employees to know exactly what they are doing during performance. The manager-coach can observe the employee, describe specifically what the employee is doing and how he or she is doing it, and then make suggestions for improvement. For example, a sales manager can accompany an employee on several sales calls to develop a complete description of the employee's approach to selling. Then the employee and sales manager can review the description and discuss ways the employee can overcome problems, build on strengths, and try new approaches. This approach to coaching effective employees is similar to Peters and Austin's (1985) idea of "skill stretching."

Evered and Selman (1990) stress that communication and partnership are vital to effective coaching. If the employee does not invite coaching, he or she may resent the manager's efforts and feel threatened or insulted. Instead of seeing the manager's actions as helpful, the employee will feel the manager is trying to monitor and control him or her.

Another way to encourage continued effective performance through coaching is to communicate and reinforce the organization's values. Peters and Austin (1985) call this aspect of coaching **value shaping.** Value shaping begins with recruiting and orientation of new employees, and is continued through training and in the manner that the manager relates to employees every day. In Peters and Austin's view, a manager must reinforce organizational values through recognition, storytelling, and work relationships, and never compromise in adherence to those values. They argue that values can serve as guides for behavior that help employees know what is expected and how to behave even in novel situations. Obviously, value shaping can only occur if the organization has a clear set of values to begin with.

Skills Necessary for Effective Coaching

According to the coaching literature, the skills needed to be an effective coach can be grouped into two categories: communication and interpersonal skills. The authors we have cited in this chapter all agree that **communication** is an essential skill in coaching. A common theme has been that unless a manager has the ability both to listen to employees and to get them to understand what effective performance is and how to achieve it, coaching will not succeed.

Fournies (1978), who takes a more behavioral tack than some other advocates of coaching, argues that the only way a manager knows whether an employee understands what has been said is if the employee restates it himself or herself. The process of getting employees to state what the problem performance is, why it is a problem, and what they are going to do to remedy the problem, as the manager expressed agreement with what the employee has said, is what Fournies calls "thought transmission."

In addition to active listening, Kinlaw (1989) and Fournies (1978) emphasize the need for managers to **be specific and descriptive** in communicating with employees. This can increase the chance that the employee will understand what is expected and will offer less resistance to coaching. These authors argue that if a coach is descriptive rather than evaluative, the employee will realize that the coach is trying to help him or her rather than place blame.

Kikoski and Litterer (1983) describe an approach called "microtraining" that can be used to train managers and supervisors in the communication skills necessary for effective coaching. This approach, which has proven effective in developing face-to-face communication skills (Ivey & Authier, 1978; Ivey & Litterer, 1979), isolates the specific verbal and nonverbal skills that make up effective communication and then trains participants in each skill. The skills developed in the microtraining approach that are relevant to coaching include basic attending skills (e.g., maintaining eye contact), feedback, paraphrasing, reflection of feeling, open and closed questions, and focusing. A list of these skills and the components that are taught in the program is provided in Table 9-1.

The **interpersonal skills** that are important to effective coaching (Kinlaw, 1990; Peters & Austin, 1985) include:

1. Indicating respect.

2. Immediacy (i.e., focusing on the present; dealing with problems as they occur).

3. Objectivity.

4. Planning.

5. Affirming (i.e., commenting on the employee's successes and positive prospects for improvement).

6. Consistency of behavior.

7. Building trust.

8. Demonstrating integrity.

Finally, Evered and Selman (1990) stress the importance of **demonstrating commitment to and respect for the employee.** If an employee believes the manager is genuinely interested in and cares about him or her, the employee will seek out coaching and make an honest effort to improve.

HRD staff members can design and conduct programs to help managers and supervisors develop and practice these skills. Training programs that use role

TABLE 9-1	THE SIX SKILLS OF MICROTRAINING IN FACE-TO-FACE COMMUNICATION

1. **Basic attending skills** to help involve the employee in the discussion. These include
   a. a slight, but comfortable, forward lean of the upper body and trunk;
   b. maintaining eye contact;
   c. speaking in a warm, but natural voice;
   d. using minimal encouragers (e.g., head nods, saying "yes," and "uh-huh"); and
   e. staying on the topic.

2. **Feedback**
   a. providing clear and concrete data;
   b. using a nonjudgmental attitude;
   c. using timely/present-tense statements (e.g., "Max, I just made some suggestions for how you can present your ideas more clearly. But you don't seem interested. How can I help you improve your presentations?" as opposed to, "Your last four presentations were disasters. I won't tolerate another one."); and
   d. providing feedback that deals with correctable items over which the employee has some control.

3. **Paraphrasing** a concise restatement, in your own words, of what the employee has just said. Paraphrasing helps clarify the issue, lets the employee know you understand what has been said, and encourages him or her to continue. Paraphrases should be nojudgmental and matter-of-fact.

4. **Reflection of feeling** reinforces the employee for expressing feelings and encourages open communication. Identifying and recognizing an employee's feelings can help the supervisor establish a closer rapport. Reflections of feeling have a structure:
   a. employee's name or pronoun;
   b. stem (e.g., "It sounds as if you feel . . . ");
   c. label for the emotion; and
   d. final stem to check whether you understood employee correctly (e.g., "Am I right?").
   An example: "Maria, you seem very nervous about working in front of others. Would you like to talk about that?".

5. **Open and closed questions** to support your purpose.
   a. Open questions (e.g., those beginning with "How," "Would," "Could," or "Why") encourage employees to talk and share their ideas (e.g., "Why do you think that is?").
   b. Closed questions (e.g., those beginning with "Did," "Is," "Are," or "How many") invite a response of a few words which can be used to clarify, identify specific points, and speed the discussion (e.g., "Did you close the sale?").

6. **Focusing** helps identify five potential areas of organizational difficulty (person, problem, context, other, and self) and ways to deal with each.

SOURCE: From "Effective Communication in the Performance Appraisal Interview" by J. F. Kikoski and J. A. Litterer, 1983, *Public Personnel Management Journal, 12,* pp. 33–42. Copyright 1983. Adapted by permission.

playing and behavior modeling can be effective in building the skills needed for effective coaching. For example, Weyerhauser Company's coaching training program uses a combination of modeling films, role-playing activities, and workbook exercises to teach coaching skills (Wexley & Latham, 1991). Silverman (1990) describes a two-day performance-appraisal training program called

ADEPT (Appraising and Developing Employee Performance Training) that includes a module on diagnosing and coaching employee performance. The module teaches participants how to identify performance problems, diagnose causes, and reach agreement on steps to be taken to solve the problems using two video scenes and a role-play exercise. It also teaches participants to give positive reinforcement to effective employees (Silverman, 1990). ADEPT has been used by firms such as Allstate Insurance, Goodyear Tire & Rubber, and Ohio Edison (Wexley & Latham, 1991).

The Effectiveness of Coaching

There is very little empirical literature that directly addresses the effectiveness of coaching as a way to improve poor performance and encourage and enhance effective performance. Could it be that managers and professionals see the effectiveness of coaching as self-evident ("Of course it works. Why test it?")? However, research on the **performance-appraisal interview,** which shares much in common with coaching, clearly demonstrates the effectiveness of many aspects of the coaching discussion.

The performance-appraisal interview is a meeting between a supervisor and subordinate in which the supervisor reviews the evaluation of an employee's performance and seeks to help the employee maintain and improve performance. While some aspects of the performance appraisal discussion are not relevant to coaching (e.g., timing of the discussion, discussion of salary or promotions), many of the same techniques used in coaching are used in the performance-improvement portion of the discussion. In this section, we provide a sampling of the findings from empirical research on the performance-appraisal interview that are relevant to the effectiveness of coaching.

Employee Participation in Discussion

A number of studies have addressed the extent to which providing employees an opportunity to contribute during the discussion affects discussion outcomes. Research shows that the more an employee participates, the greater is the employee's satisfaction with the discussion and the manager, and the more likely it is that performance goals will be met (Latham & Wexley, 1975; Nemeroff & Wexley, 1979; Wexley, Singh, & Yukl, 1973). Positive outcomes (e.g., feeling the supervisor is more helpful and constructive) have also been demonstrated when supervisors explicitly welcome employee participation during the discussion (Burke & Wilcox, 1969; Burke et al., 1978; Greller, 1975). Employees are more likely to participate when they perceive that the threat from the supervisor is low (Basset & Meyer, 1968; French et al., 1966). Finally, subordinates see the performance discussion as more fair when they are given a chance for two-way communication, especially when they are given the opportunity to challenge or rebut their evaluation (Greenberg, 1986).

Being Supportive

Supportiveness is one of the recurring themes of coaching. The extent to which the supervisor is helpful and supportive has been shown to affect employee acceptance of the performance evaluation and satisfaction with the manager (Burke & Wilcox, 1969; Burke et al., 1978; Kay et al., 1965; Nemeroff & Wexley, 1979). Managerial supportiveness has also been shown to be associated with higher levels of employee motivation (Dorfman et al., 1986). Furthermore, when employees perceive that the supervisor has constructive reasons for providing performance feedback, they are less likely to show anxiety and more likely to see the feedback as having greater utility (Fedor et al., 1989).

Using Constructive Criticism

Advocates of coaching urge managers to adopt a descriptive, nonjudgmental approach and offer feedback that is specific and factual. Criticism during the performance-appraisal interview has been shown to lead to high levels of anxiety (Kay, Meyer, & French, 1965). Furthermore, a series of studies investigating the effects of destructive criticism (i.e., feedback that is delivered inconsiderately, that is vague, or that attributes poor performance to internal causes) demonstrated that destructive criticism:

- Increases anger and tension;

- Leads to intent to handle further disagreements with resistance and avoidance;

- Leads employees to set lower goals and report lower self efficacy; and

- Is cited by employees as an important cause of conflict (Baron, 1988).

Employees will accept some criticism, but it must be specific and behavioral (Cascio, 1982).

Setting Performance Goals During Discussion

Setting goals during the performance discussion leads to positive outcomes, such as satisfaction with the discussion (Burke & Wilcox, 1969; Burke et al., 1978; Greller, 1975, 1978), perceived fairness and accuracy of feedback (Burke et al., 1978; Landy et al., 1978), and perceived utility of feedback (Greller, 1978). As was cited earlier, setting specific goals has been clearly shown to lead to behavior change (Locke & Latham, 1990).

Training and the Supervisor's Credibility

Training supervisors to discuss performance with employees has been shown to be important to the performance discussion (e.g., DeCotiis & Petit, 1978; Landy & Farr, 1980). Further, when employees perceive the supervisor as credible (e.g., knowledgeable about the employee's job and performance), they are more likely to accept the supervisor's evaluation (Stone et al., 1984), perceive the feedback as accurate, perceive the supervisor as more helpful, and report that they intend to use the feedback (Bannister, 1986).

Closing Comment

Taken together, research on the performance-appraisal interview supports the effectiveness of many of the components used in coaching as we have described it in this chapter. Thus it appears that coaching can indeed be an effective way to manage employee performance. Having the employee participate in the discussion, setting goals for improvement, offering specific, behavioral feedback, being supportive and helpful, training supervisors, and ensuring the supervisor is knowledgeable about the employee's job and performance are all related to positive outcomes. Table 9-2 lists suggestions for effective coaching. Finally, while these findings from research on the performance-appraisal interview give us some confidence in the effectiveness of coaching, further research devoted specifically to coaching can help to establish this conclusion more firmly.

TABLE 9-2	SUGGESTIONS FOR EFFECTIVE COACHING

1. Provide managers and supervisors with training in coaching skills and techniques.
2. Perform a thorough coaching analysis.
3. Prepare in advance for the coaching discussion.
4. Be constructive, helpful, and supportive.
5. Involve the employee in the discussion.
6. Provide constructive, specific, behavioral feedback.
7. Set specific goals during the discussion.
8. Jointly establish an action plan with the employee.
9. Follow-up to ensure the employee is following the action plan and to recognize performance improvements when they occur.

RETURN TO OPENING CASE

Behavioral research done at Xerox Learning Systems to investigate how coaching might improve sales performance revealed the following reasons why coaching was often either neglected or not done well:

1. **Day-to-day pressures** (e.g., revenue goals, profits) can make time spent on coaching a low priority for many sales managers.

2. Sales managers could readily identify their best and worst performers, but they often **could not explain why these individuals performed as they did** (e.g., which skills or tactics they used).

3. **Misconceptions** sales managers held about coaching (e.g., coaching equals criticism) made them reluctant to engage in it.

4. Effective coaching was hindered by the **manager's own experiences and style.** For example, a recently promoted manager may be more likely to take over a sales call from a struggling employee, rather than use the occasion as an opportunity for coaching and reinforcement.

5. Some sales managers were **unsure about what the coaching process involved.**

Having recognized these problems, Xerox Learning Systems developed a description of coaching and designed a course that ensures coaching is an integral part of sales training. The Xerox approach to coaching recognizes that coaching helps both effective and ineffective salespeople analyze their job performance to identify problems and opportunities to improve and provides partnership to address these problems and opportunities.

The coaching course is based on the following guidelines:

1. Managers must **see a benefit** for investing their time in coaching.

2. Managers must select sales calls in which they **observe everyday selling situations.**

3. Managers must **know what skills to look for** on a call.

4. Managers must be **taught how to observe, give feedback, and troubleshoot.**

5. Managers must be **given the tools to implement** the coaching process (including knowledge of how to begin coaching, select calls to observe, introduce coaching to staff members and gain staff acceptance and enthusiasm).

The coaching course developed by Xerox Learning Systems is a good example of preparing sales managers (and others) to coach in a way that ensures performance improvement while enlisting employees as partners in the process.[1]

Summary

One of a manager's primary responsibilities is to ensure employees perform their tasks effectively. Many managers choose to notice only poor performance and

---

[1]From "Coaching: The Way to Protect Your Sales Training Investment" by D. Fox, 1983, *Training and Development Journal, 37* (11), pp. 37–39. Copyright 1983 by The American Society for Training and Development. Adapted by permission.

attempt to remedy it using threats and punishment. Coaching is a positive problem-solving approach to performance management that requires managers to enter into a partnership with employees. Managers who are effective coaches are more knowledgeable about employee performance and can help employees adjust to changes in goals, tasks, and expectations.

Coaching is defined as the process a manager or supervisor uses to encourage employees to accept responsibility for performance, enable them to achieve, and sustain, superior performance, and treat them as partners in working toward organizational goals. It involves both analyzing performance and conducting a discussion with employees to solve performance problems and determine ways to enhance performance.

Performance analysis involves clearly defining a performance problem, examining the factors that affect poor performance, and determining the action required to ensure effective performance. Some of the factors that are examined in a performance analysis include the importance of the behavior in question, whether employees know their performance is unsatisfactory and know what should be done about it, the presence of environmental obstacles to effective performance, the consequences of both effective and ineffective performance, and the employee's ability.

The chapter presents two views of the coaching discussion. Fournies's approach involves getting the employee to agree that a problem exists, discussing alternative solutions, agreeing on actions to be taken, following up to measure results, and recognizing achievements. In Kinlaw's three-stage approach, the supervisor confronts the employee and presents the performance problem, uses the employee's reactions to develop information about possible causes and solutions, and agrees with the employee on what will be done to solve the problem. Coaching to maintain effective performance and encourage superior performance should focus, in part, on increasing the employee's sense of ownership of performance.

Coaching draws upon a supervisor's skills in analyzing employee performance and in using effective communication and interpersonal skills, including objectivity, immediacy, indicating respect, affirming, building trust, and demonstrating integrity. Training programs that use role playing and behavioral modeling can help supervisors and managers acquire these skills.

Key Terms and Concepts

coaching	goal setting
coaching analysis	performance-appraisal interview
coaching discussion	poor performance
feedback	

Questions for Discussion

1. Explain why it is important to coach both employees with performance problems and employees who are performing well.

2. Imagine that you are an HRD professional who has just finished conducting a training program for a group of supervisors at an air conditioner manufacturing plant. When you ask if there are any questions, one of the supervisors says, "You seem so good at this coaching business. Why can't you coach my people for me?" How would you respond to that supervisor? Support your reasoning.

3. Describe the things necessary for defining poor performance. What do you feel is difficult about defining performance as poor? Make one practical recommendation that you believe could make this task easier for managers. Support your choice.

4. Think about the last time you had a problem with your own performance, either on the job or in one of your classes. Using Fournies's performance-analysis model, try to identify the cause(s) of this problem, and state what you think could be done to correct it.

5. Many managers and supervisors find coaching difficult to do or are reluctant to do it. What do you believe are two important reasons for this? How do you think the obstacles you identify can be overcome?

6. Explain why it is necessary, during the coaching discussion, for the supervisor to get the employee to verbally agree that a performance problem exists.

7. Suppose you are a police sergeant who is conducting a coaching discussion with one of your patrol officers about her failure to complete arrest reports on time. You have conducted a coaching analysis and have determined that the officer is able to complete the reports on time, that all obstacles to doing so have been removed, and that this is an important part of a patrol officer's job. Describe how you would get the patrol officer to agree that a problem exists, and what you would do if the officer refuses to acknowledge a problem exists. Describe the options available to you in dealing with this situation. Which option would you select? Support your choice.

10

Employee Counseling Services

Learning Objectives

1. Explain the need for counseling in organizations and why counseling is an HRD activity.
2. Describe the typical activities included in employee counseling programs.
3. Describe the focus and effectiveness of three types of employee counseling programs: employee assistance programs, stress management interventions, and health promotion programs.
4. Describe the role of supervisors in employee counseling programs.
5. Explain the legal and ethical issues raised by employee counseling programs.

OPENING CASE

Central States Health & Life Company of Omaha, a medium-sized life and health insurance firm founded during the Depression, may seem an unlikely place for the beginning of a revolution. But for almost three decades the company has been in the vanguard of the employee wellness movement that has swept U.S. organizations. They have demonstrated that helping employees stay well can yield benefits for employer and employee alike.

This revolution did not happen overnight. The wellness program at Central States began more than 25 years ago, not as a result of a direct interest in employee health and well-being, but out of concern for the company's claims and loss ratio. Current chairman and CEO William M. Kizer, at that time an executive in the firm, became interested in the reasons why many policyholders were hospitalized or died prematurely. The answer was that in many cases hospitalization and early death were due to policyholders' lifestyles. Factors within an individual's control, such as smoking and obesity, appeared to be the main culprits. Kizer hypothesized that if these factors were addressed, many self-induced illnesses could be prevented—a hypothesis that has since been supported by scientific evidence.

While he couldn't do much to alter the health of policyholders, Kizer realized that he could help his firm's employees avoid such problems. Beginning with a few small steps, such as providing executives with an opportunity to exercise during the lunch period, Central States has created a wellness program that has become a model for other organizations to follow. Kizer has hit upon a way that even businesses of small and medium size, such as his own, can create relatively inexpensive and effective wellness programs for their employees.

He calls his model the SANE approach. At the end of the chapter, we will examine exactly how Kizer's SANE approach can help an organization meet its wellness goals.

The Need for Employee Counseling Programs

Personal problems are a part of life. Stress, alcohol and drug abuse, cardiovascular disease, obesity, and emotional problems abound in modern society. Whether these problems are chronic, as in the case of alcoholism, or situational, as in the case of financial problems, they can affect behavior at work as well as one's personal life. Such problems contribute to accidents, absenteeism and turnover, poor decisions, decreases in productivity, and increased costs. Estimates of losses incurred due to the problems experienced by troubled workers are staggering, ranging in the tens to hundreds of billions of dollars annually (e.g., Everly, Feldman, & Associates, 1985; Harwood, Napolitano, Kristiansen, & Collins, 1985; Maiden, 1988; Symonds, Ellis, Siler, Zellner, & Garland, 1991).

Rising health care costs are one reason organizations are so interested in helping employees with their personal problems. Health care costs rose sharply during the 1970s and 1980s to reach approximately $400 billion in 1987 (Renner, 1987). It is estimated that organizations pay approximately 80 percent of that cost (Clement & Gibbs, 1983). A dramatic example of the impact of such high costs is the experience of Chrysler Corporation, which pays $700 in health care costs for every car it produces in the United States (Gordon, 1991).

Besides reducing health care costs, employer efforts to improve employee well-being are also purported to reduce worker's compensation costs, tardiness, absenteeism, turnover, lost time from work because of illness and injury, and accidents, while enhancing morale, loyalty, creativity, productivity, decision-making effectiveness, labor relations, recruiting, and company image (Terborg, 1986). Given the potential gains, it is not surprising that organizations are looking for ways to enhance employee well-being.

Another factor promoting organizational interest in employee well-being is a shortage of skilled workers. Given the reduced birth rate following the baby boom, labor is less plentiful than it was when the baby boom generation was entering the work force. Shortcomings in the educational system have only exacerbated the problem. As a result, many organizations have adopted the HR strategy that it is better to retain and help workers with problems than to discard them and be faced with recruiting new ones (Walker, 1988, 1989), even as many companies are considering a probable need for downsizing.

How are organizations addressing the issue of employee well-being? In addition to traditional HR programs like training and motivation, organizations are also making a major investment in providing **employee counseling services** as a way to promote employee well-being. In the literature describing employee counseling services, the term "counseling" has been used to refer to a variety of activities, from informal discussions with a supervisor to intensive one-on-one discussions with a trained professional (Cairo, 1983). Masi's (1984) four-part definition of mental health counseling provides a good general description of what is typically involved in this activity at the workplace:

(1) a relationship established between a trained counselor and the employee; (2) thoughtful and candid discussion of personal problems experienced by the employee; (3) an appropriate referral that secures the necessary assistance; and (4) the provision of short-term counseling, when a referral is not necessary (p. 117).

Employee counseling services have existed since the turn of the century. In 1917 Macy's Department Store established an employee assistance program to help workers deal with personal problems, and by 1920 over 100 of the largest companies in the United States employed a welfare secretary whose responsibilities in part included employee counseling (Popple, 1981). Growth in wellness-related activities has been explosive. Recent estimates suggest there are over 13,000 employee assistance programs (Masi, 1992), which deal with substance abuse and mental health problems, and over 50,000 health promotion programs (Glasgow & Terborg, 1988), which typically focus on physical well-being. It is obvious from these numbers that organizations strongly believe employee counseling is an effective way to ensure employee well-being.

Employee Counseling as an HRD Activity

Employee counseling serves the same goal as any other HRD activity: to ensure the employee is now and will continue to be an effective contributor to the organization's effectiveness. Employee assistance and health promotion programs use the same techniques as other HRD interventions. These techniques include workshops, role playing, behavior modeling, discussions, lectures, coaching, and audiovisual presentations. In addition, the process of delivering counseling services is the same as that of any other HRD program, and includes needs assessment, planning and implementation, and evaluation. Designing, delivering, and evaluating employee counseling programs offer ample opportunity for HRD professionals to use their expertise.

An Overview of Employee Counseling Programs

Organizations use a wide variety of activities and programs to help ensure employee emotional and physical health. These activities range from health-risk appraisals to on-site counseling centers and stress reduction workshops. They may take the form of a one-session discussion, a series of sessions, or an ongoing organizational activity. In this section, we discuss the components of a typical program, who provides the services, and characteristics of an effective counseling program.

Components of the Typical Program

While employee counseling programs vary in terms of problems addressed and specific techniques used, it is possible to identify six main events fairly typical of such programs:

1. Problem identification

2. Education

3. Counseling

4. Referral

5. Treatment

6. Follow-up

Problem Identification Problem identification usually involves use of a screening device (e.g., a questionnaire or diagnostic test) and/or the training of employees and supervisors in identification of a problem. For example, employees may volunteer to have their cholesterol level assessed as part of a wellness program. Or supervisors may be trained to identify the behavioral patterns that indicate possible substance abuse.

Education Education typically includes providing information about the nature, prevalence, likely causes and consequences of the problem, and perhaps ways the problem can be avoided. For example, a program focusing on hypertension (high blood pressure) might use pamphlets, videos, or a lecture to raise employee awareness of the problem and how it can be treated or avoided.

Counseling At a minimum, counseling involves a person with whom employees can discuss difficulties and/or seek further help. The type of counseling can vary from a frank discussion with a supervisor about work-related stress or performance problem to meeting with a mental health professional skilled in diagnosing and treating problems such as depression or substance abuse.

Referral Referral involves directing the employee to the appropriate resources for assistance. For example, if an employee shows signs of cocaine addiction, he or she may be referred to a drug treatment facility that specializes in treating that addiction.

Treatment Treatment includes actual intervention to solve the problem. For example, a nutrition program may include cooking classes or offer healthy foods in the cafeteria and nutritious snacks in vending machines.

Follow-up As with any organizational activity, some form of monitoring is needed to ensure the employee is carrying out the treatment and to obtain information on progress. For example, if the employee agrees to seek alcohol abuse treatment as part of an agreement to try to improve performance, it is necessary to determine whether the employee actually attends and completes treatment.

Not all employee counseling programs include all six types of activities listed. Use of activities depends upon the type of problem addressed, the appropriate response to the problem, and the resources the organization chooses to commit to the program. Take the example of a program to address employee physical fitness. The organization may choose to renovate part of its facility or build a new structure to house a fitness center, complete with a trained staff, locker room, showers, athletic courts, and exercise equipment. Alternatively, the organization may offer employees free or reduced-fee membership in a local health club. Another, less expensive, option would be to make fitness information available and encourage employees to exercise on their own time.

Who Provides the Service?

An organization may offer a counseling program in-house or contract it out. In-house programs involve using current employees or hiring specialists, such as psychologists or social workers, to operate the program. For example, the post office in northern England established a mental health improvement program staffed internally by full-time specialists in counseling whose responsibilities covered confidential counseling to employees and advising management on mental health-related issues (Sadu, Cooper, & Allison, 1989). Contracting the service out to a third party involves hiring a local specialist or organization to provide the service. For example, an organization may decide to use a free-standing employee assistance program to help addicted employees or work with several local psychologists in private practice to help employees deal with emotional problems.

Phillips and Older (1981) list a number of advantages and disadvantages for each approach. Advantages attributed to in house programs include (1) internal control of the program, (2) familiarity with the organization (e.g., its policies, procedures, and work force characteristics), (3) better coordination of treatment and follow-up, (4) communication within the organization, (5) a sense of ownership of the program, and (6) greater credibility with some supervisors. Disadvantages of in-house programs may include (1) real or perceived problems with confidentiality, (2) lack of resources needed, (3) reluctance of some employees to use the service (e.g., a vice-president of finance may be reluctant to go to a lower-level employee to admit a drinking or marital problem), and (4) possible limitations in staff skills and expertise.

An advantage of contracting the service out is that the organization can rely on the services of trained professionals whose business it is to treat the problem in question. In addition, confidentiality may be easier to maintain, cost may be lower, and there may be better identification and utilization of community resources. Disadvantages include the lack of on-site counseling, possible communication problems, and lack of knowledge of the organization and its employees.

Characteristics of Effective Employee Counseling Programs

Communicating the service to managers, supervisors, and employees, and following up with them, is critical in getting organizational members to use it. Harris & Fennell (1988) found that employee willingness to use an employee assistance program was related to their familiarity with and trust in the program, and personal attention provided by it. Similarly, in a comparative study of four wellness programs, Erfurt, Foote, and Heirich (1992) found programs using systematic outreach and follow-up counseling were more effective than those that did not.

It is also important that managers and supervisors receive training in identifying problems and in how to counsel employees to seek treatment when needed (Masi, 1992; Swanson & Murphy, 1991). In many counseling programs, especially those in addiction and mental health, the supervisor's role in helping the employee seek treatment and supporting the treatment effort is critical to success (e.g., Trice & Beyer, 1984). (We will discuss the supervisor's role in counseling in greater detail later in the chapter.) Other ingredients believed to be necessary for an effective counseling program (Swanson & Murphy, 1991) include:

1. Top management commitment and support.

2. A clearly written set of policies and procedures outlining the program's purpose and its function within the organization.

3. Cooperation with local union(s) if any.

4. A "continuum of care" (p. 272) (e.g., referral to community resources, follow-up).

5. A clear employee information-confidentiality policy.

6. Maintaining records for program evaluation.

7. Health insurance benefit coverage for services.

Employee Assistance Programs

Employee assistance programs (EAPs) are defined as "job-based programs operating within a work organization for the purposes of identifying troubled employees, motivating them to resolve their troubles, and providing access to counseling or treatment for those employees who need these services" (Sonnenstuhl & Trice, 1986, p. 1). Although they have their origins in the occupational alcoholism programs begun in the 1940s, modern EAPs also help employees with drug and mental health problems that may be affecting their work (Masi, 1992; Sonnenstuhl, 1988). Possible outcomes that may be affected by EAPs include productivity, turnover, unemployment costs, treatment for substance abuse, absenteeism, use of supervisors' time, accidents, training and replacement costs, and insurance benefits (Cascio, 1991b). As mentioned earlier, the number of EAPs in the United States has grown dramatically since the 1970s, with the current number estimated at over 13,000 (Masi, 1992). In this section of the chapter, we will (1) discuss the extent of the problem organizations face with respect to substance abuse and mental problems, (2) describe the approach taken by EAPs, and (3) discuss the effectiveness of EAPs in dealing with these problems.

Substance Abuse

Reports of the prevalence of alcohol and drug abuse and the problems they create are commonplace. Federal, state, and local governments spend billions of dollars dealing with the problems brought on by substance abuse, from crime to sickness. It is clear that substance abuse has a powerful impact on modern society and on business and industry.

It is estimated that 18 million Americans have a serious drinking problem and that alcohol is involved in 47 percent of industrial accidents (Symonds et al., 1991). While it is commonly assumed that between 5 percent and 10 percent of all workers are alcoholics (Weiss, 1987), accurate figures are difficult to come by (Hollinger, 1988; Weiss, 1987). Reported rates of on-the-job alcohol use vary by industry and culture, and even within a given industry (Hollinger, 1988). Recent surveys do indicate that a significant percentage of employees use alcohol and drugs on the job. Some examples:

1. Two recent studies of preemployment urine testing programs in the U.S. Postal Service reported that 10 percent (Normand, Salyards, & Mahoney, 1990) and 12 percent (Zwerling, Ryan, & Orav, 1990) of applicants during the study periods tested positive for illicit drugs.

2. Hollinger (1988) reported that 6.5 percent of respondents in a survey of over 9,000 retail, manufacturing, and hospital organization employees admitted to having come to work while under the influence of drugs or alcohol in the previous year. Just over 1 percent reported they came to work under the influence weekly or daily.

3. Mensch and Kandel (1988) found that 8 percent of survey respondents reported being under the influence of marijuana, and 5 percent reported being inebriated at work at least once during the last year.

4.   In terms of specific companies, General Motors' EAP treats more than 6,000 employees annually for alcohol problems, and AT&T treats about 1,000 employees per year for alcohol abuse (Symonds et al., 1991).

Exactly how much substance abuse costs business in terms of lost productivity is difficult to determine, but recent estimates place the amount at $60 billion for alcohol abuse and $30 billion for drug abuse (Faley, Kleiman, & Wall, 1988). Recent studies have shown that marijuana and cocaine users are at greater risk for accidents, injuries, disciplinary problems, and involuntary turnover, although the level of risk is less than previously thought (Normand, Saylards, & Mahoney, 1990; Zwerling, Ryan, & Orav, 1990).

Mental Health

According to the President's Commission on Mental Health (1978), about 10 to 15 percent of the American population needs some kind of mental health services. It has been estimated that up to 25 percent of medical claims filed can be tied to mental and emotional illnesses (Lee & Schwartz, 1984). Among the mental and emotional health problems commonly seen by counselors in industry are:

- Individual adjustment problems (neurosis to psychosis);

- External factors such as battering, incest, rape, or crime;

- Sexual problems, including impotence;

- Divorce and marital problems;

- Depression and suicide attempts;

- Difficulties with family or children;

- Sexual harassment in the workplace; and

- Legal and financial problems (Masi, 1984, p. 118).

Mental health problems are not only brought into the workplace from employees' personal lives, but the work itself can lead to a decline in mental health. Two studies of factory workers in the United Kingdom showed that employees in simplified jobs who felt their skills were underused and who spent a great deal of time daydreaming had poorer mental health than other employees in the study (Clegg, Wall, & Kemp, 1987; Clegg & Wall, 1990).

Organizations are affected by employee mental health problems in the form of absenteeism, poor work habits, low job satisfaction, interpersonal conflicts, and indecisiveness (President's Commission on Mental Health, 1978). For example, Engleken (1987) estimates that businesses lose $3 to $5 billion per year as a result of absenteeism due to spouse abuse.

The EAP Approach

EAPs are based on the notion that work is very important to people and that work performance should be used to identify employee personal problems and motivate them to seek help (Masi, 1992). Originally developed to deal with alcohol abuse, the EAP approach assumes—as does the Alcoholics Anonymous (AA) movement—that substance abusers will deny their problem until they are faced with a crisis. From the EAP point of view, that crisis is created by confronting the employee with evidence of substandard work performance, meanwhile making counseling available and attempting to motivate the employee to seek help (Sonnenstuhl, 1988). In addition, Masi (1982) argues that the workplace is an "ideal place" for employees to receive treatment for mental health problems because many of the obstacles to seeking help, such as transportation and time off, are removed. A conceptual framework of the EAP approach is shown in Table 10-1, and a model for delivering mental health services in organizations is shown in Table 10-2.

TABLE 10-1	EAP CONCEPTUAL FRAMEWORK

1. EAPs are based on the premise that work is very important to people (it is ego reinforcing); the work itself is not the cause of the employee's problem. Consequently, the workplace can be a means to get people help.
2. The supervisor plays a key role in getting help for the employee. Often, however, the supervisor denies the problem and even enables the troubled employee to continue the problem behavior. The supervisor is critical in the confrontational process with the troubled employee. Therefore, education is necessary to eliminate the supervisor's tendency to enable the employee by denying the problem.
3. Information about the employee's job performance is extremely important in diagnosis and treatment. It can be used to measure and track whether treatment is successful.
4. Workplace peers and union stewards are very important; however, they too can deny the problem and enable the employee to continue the behavior. Teaching them to confront and consequently break the denial barrier is an important element.
5. Job leverage is the key ingredient. The counselor must be able to use this with the supervisor.
6. EAPs concentrate on personnel issues and job performance. They are not a medical program.
7. Cost-effectiveness is an important consideration and must be addressed with upper management.
8. The EAP practitioner's knowledge about addiction is paramount. Every EAP should be staffed by clinically licensed professionals from the mental health field who are familiar with addictions.

SOURCE: From "Employee Assistance Programs" by D. A. Masi, *The AMA Handbook for Developing Employee Assistance and Counseling Programs* (p. 5) by D. A. Masi (Ed.), 1992, New York: AMACOM.

TABLE 10-2	**MASI'S MODEL FOR DELIVERING MENTAL HEALTH SERVICES IN INDUSTRY (1984)**

1. Counseling in the workplace is short term. Long-term therapy is appropriate in the community.

2. There are logistical as well as legal problems when families are included. Although EAP programs often offer services to families, they are based on self-referral.

3. The manager or supervisor is the key person in the client's work life. The work associates are similar to family members. The counselor should learn their configuration and how it operates on the employee.

4. The counselor assumes the role of a "broker" or go-between for the employee between the supervisor and the therapist in the community.

5. The counselor should have skills in management consultation, that is, meeting with supervisors to determine whether they have a problem employee, advising them on a course of action, and supporting them through the referral and after-care process.

6. The need for crisis counseling (to deal with emergency episodes such as suicide attempts) is present in the workplace.

7. The counselor must have special skills in confrontation to break the denial of the employee appropriately, especially the addicted person.

8. Confidentiality is more of an issue in the workplace than in a community mental health clinic or social agency because of the uniqueness of the host setting. Competition for jobs, as well as an environment that does not necessarily understand employees' personal problems, mandate a clearly defined and enforced confidentiality policy.

9. Record-keeping procedures need to be carefully developed and delineated so that employees are assured of their privacy. This is not as necessary to explain to clients in a hospital or social agency; it is accepted in such situations. Employees worry about who will read their records (especially personnel officials). The Privacy Act and the Alcohol and Drug Regulations are guideposts that I recommend all EAPs follow, to be sure of protecting their employees.

10. Executive stress does not carry a stigma in the workplace and is a good subject for workshops that will reach managers in the workplace.

11. The counselor must also design and implement educational programs in the workplace.

12. There is little group counseling and interaction.

13. The counselor is a part of the same system as the client and must adapt to seeing him or her in other situations.

14. One goal of counseling is adjusting to the work situation.

15. The unique work system (personnel, company physicians) can be used to help the employee. The counselor needs to understand how these systems work.

16. Some clients may have more authority in the workplace and earn much higher salaries than the counselor.

17. Unions are extremely important in the workplace, and the counselor needs to work with them as appropriate.

SOURCE: From *Designing Employee Assistance Programs* (pp. 119–120) by D. A. Masi, 1984, New York: AMACOM.

An important aspect of the modern treatment of substance abuse in the workplace is that abuse is operationally defined in terms of job performance rather than clinically defined in terms of addiction. The pattern of behaviors that indicate a substance abuse problem typically include absenteeism, erratic performance, poor quality work, poor judgment, and complaints by clients or customers. Table 10-3 suggests behaviors supervisors should monitor to help them identify changes in employee appearance or behavior that may indicate impairment due to substance abuse.

In most EAPs, supervisors are trained to use the **constructive confrontation** approach in dealing with troubled employees. The constructive confrontation process is described as follows:

> This strategy calls for supervisors to monitor their employees' job performance, confront them with evidence of their unsatisfactory performance, coach them on improving it, urge them to use the EAP's counseling service if they have personal problems, and emphasize the consequences of continued poor performance. Constructive confrontation proceeds in progressive stages; at each stage, employees must choose whether to seek help from the EAP, manage their problems themselves, or suffer the consequences of their actions (Sonnenstuhl, Staudenmeier, & Trice, 1988, p. 385).

According to this approach, the supervisor need not, and perhaps should not, say that the employee has a drug or alcohol problem. Rather, the supervisor should treat the problem like any other performance problem, and leave it for the employee to seek help from the appropriate source. Recommending the employee contact the EAP or other agency "if they need to" should be the extent of the supervisor's intervention.

Referral by a supervisor is not the only method by which employees may contact an EAP. Employees with personal problems may contact the EAP directly and receive counseling without the supervisor's knowledge. This is seen by some as the preferred referral strategy because the employee receives help before job performance is affected (Santa-Barbara, 1984). It is also possible for a fellow employee to encourage a peer with a problem to seek help from an EAP.

The components of the typical EAP can vary in terms of organizational policy, referral method, departmental involvement (e.g., HRM or medical), use of in-house and external resources, types of problems treated, and staffing (Walsh & Hingson, 1985). The typical EAP consists of the following:

- A policy and procedures statement that makes clear the responsibilities of both company and employee concerning health and personal problems impacting the job;

- Employee education campaign, which may include letters, poster campaigns, or extensive training programs;

- A supervisory training program that teaches problem recognition and performance documentation;

TABLE 10-3	BEHAVIOR PATTERNS THAT MAY INDICATE A SUBSTANCE ABUSE PROBLEM

Absenteeism

- Frequent unauthorized absences.
- Excessive sick days.
- Frequent absences of short duration, with or without medical corroboration.
- Frequent Monday, Friday, day before and day after holiday absences.
- Frequent use of vacation days to cover absences.
- High absentee rate for vague ailments: colds, flu, headache.

On the Job Absences

- Frequently away from workstation.
- Excessive tardiness after lunch, breaks.
- Frequent trips to the water fountain, parking lot, locker room, restroom.

High Accident Rate

- Accidents off the job that affect job performance.
- Accidents on the job due to carelessness.
- Failure to wear safety gear (helmets, gloves, etc.).

Poor Job Performance

- A pattern of diminished morning or afternoon performance.
- Complaints from co-workers, clients, etc.
- Missed deadlines.
- Taking longer to do less.
- Wasting materials, damaging/losing equipment.
- Improbable excuses.
- Alternating periods of high and low performance, which becomes increasingly unsatisfactory.
- Difficulty with instructions, procedures.
- Difficulty recalling mistakes.
- Difficulty understanding new information.
- Difficulty with complex assignments.
- Uneven work habits.

Changes in Personal Habits

- Reporting to work in abnormal condition (drunk, dazed, vague, etc.).
- Different behavior after lunch than before.
- Increasing lack of attention to personal hygiene.
- Increasing lack of interest in personal appearance.

Poor Relationships with Co-workers

- Overreaction to real or implied criticism.
- Unrealistic resentments.
- Excessive talking with co-workers.
- Wide mood swings.
- Borrowing money.
- Avoiding co-workers and friends.
- Complaints from co-workers and friends.
- Increasing irritability.
- Increasingly argumentative.
- Inappropriate outbursts of anger, tears, laughter.

SOURCE: From Campell, D., & Graham, M. *Drugs and Alcohol in the Workplace: A Guide for Managers.* NY: Facts on File, pp. 100–101.

- Clinical services that may be provided by a professional in-house staff or community agencies; and

- Follow-up monitoring to ensure real problem resolution has occurred (Luthans and Waldersee, 1989, pp. 386–387).

Examples of EAPs have appeared frequently in the literature. Some of these include EAPs at Detroit Edison (Nadolski & Sandonato, 1987), professional sports (Dickman & Hayes, 1988), the Association of Flight Attendants (Feuer, 1987), and school teachers and school personnel (Emener, 1988).

Another way organizations can assist employees with mental health problems and their families is to provide mental health benefits in the employee benefit package (Rosen & Lee, 1987). Many employers now provide employees with coverage for a given number of visits (e.g., 25) to a therapist per year. The limitation of visits is one way the companies attempt to control the cost of providing mental health benefits. In addition, it should be noted that many organizations are turning to preemployment drug screening as a way to avoid hiring substance abusers while deterring substance abuse in the workplace (e.g., Axel, 1990) with some success (see Harris & Heft, 1992, for a review). However, such programs are beyond the focus of this text. We encourage the interested reader to consult other sources (e.g., Axel, 1990; Faley, Kleiman, & Wall, 1988; Harris & Heft, 1992).

Effectiveness of EAPs

The effectiveness of EAPs is widely accepted (Blum & Bennett, 1990). Evaluation studies have used a wide range of outcomes to measure success, including percentage of employees entering treatment, percentage returning to work following treatment, changes in the nature of the problem following treatment, improvements in work performance, and cost savings (Swanson & Murphy, 1991). Tersine and Hazeldine (1982) reviewed the literature on effectiveness of such programs and reported most studies claim a 50 to 85 percent success rate. Pelletier (1984) states the success rates reported in the literature range from 65 to 80 percent for long-term treatment of excessive drinking. Reported estimates of cost savings have ranged from $2 to $20 per dollar invested in the program (Cascio, 1991b). Reports of EAP effectiveness include results such as:

- Absenteeism reduced by 52 percent in EAP users and cuts in worker's compensation and health care costs of 74 percent and 55 percent, respectively (Skidmore, Balsam, & Jones, 1974);

- Reduction of sick leave usage among users by 74–80 percent (Wrich, 1984); and

- 75 percent of problem drinkers improved work performance as a result of constructive confrontation and counseling (Trice and Beyer, 1984).

Critics (e.g., Kurtz, Googins, & Howard, 1984; Luthans & Waldersee, 1989; Weiss, 1987) charge that this evidence is tainted by the fact that EAP evaluation studies suffer from serious methodological and design flaws, such as lack of comparison groups and random assignment to treatments (Kurtz, Googins, & Howard, 1984). Luthans and Waldersee (1989) argue that much of the available evidence is anecdotal and based on testimonials. Flaws such as these make it difficult to determine whether results reported are in fact due to the EAP.

Furthermore, success rates reported in EAP literature have been noted as exceeding those reported for governmental and social service agencies that treat problem drinkers (Tersine & Hazeldine, 1982; Wagner, 1982). Studies that have examined the effectiveness of other alcoholism treatment programs report far lower rates of success than EAPs. For example, Madsen (1976) reported that AA programs help only 1 out of 18 alcoholics, and Polich, Armor, and Braker (1981) found that four years after treatment only 28 percent of alcoholics who completed a formal treatment program had abstained from drinking in the past six months. These discrepancies may be due to the lack of well-operationalized definitions of success, insufficiently long follow-up periods, and the mislabeling of those entering treatment in the EAP studies; the masking of symptoms for long periods by employees hoping to avoid dismissal may also skew results (Luthans & Waldersee, 1989).

Two other criticisms of the EAP approach deserve note. Weiss (1987) states that job behaviors commonly used to identify alcoholic employees have not been supported by the literature. He also claims that by using job performance to identify employees with substance abuse problems, "it is possible a poor-performing person could be labeled an alcoholic, treated for alcoholism, and be pronounced rehabilitated with no necessary reference at any point in the process to consumption of alcohol (but merely to working harder)" (Weiss, 1982, reported in Weiss, 1987, p. 348). The research on constructive confrontation is not plentiful, but the evidence so far does offer some support for its efficacy in dealing with both substance abuse and other problems (e.g., Trice & Beyer, 1984).

What are we to conclude, then, about the effectiveness of EAPs? Given the number of EAPs currently in operation, it is obvious that organizations agree that they are effective in dealing with troubled employees. However, we agree that flaws in much of the EAP evaluation literature make it difficult to unequivocally claim that they are effective. While the rigorous evaluation studies called for by critics would help resolve the issue, the obstacles to conducting such studies (e.g., limited access to EAPs by researchers, confidentiality of records, reluctance to use random assignment to study groups) are formidable (Swanson & Murphy, 1984). Given these constraints, we agree with Harris and Heft (1992) that research on various aspects of EAPs, such as constructive confrontation, are possible and would offer some useful evidence.

Industry's commitment to EAPs and other programs (e.g., preemployment drug screening) makes it clear that the motivation and resources to deal with substance abuse and troubled employees are available; we owe it to all concerned to use them in the most effective way possible. We agree with Luthans and Waldersee (1989) that HRD professionals considering adopting an EAP for their organization should determine whether it is likely to be a cost-effective solution for their organization, and if so, determine the types of programs needed. This can be done by (1) calculating the per-person cost of treating problems to obtain the desired outcomes, and (2) comparing those costs to the cost of replacing the person rather than offering treating (Luthans & Waldersee, 1989). Information needed to determine the per-person cost of EAP programs includes:

- The frequency and types of problems present in the organization (best performed by a qualified external agent); and

- The types of outcomes that can be expected from treating these problems and the length of treatment to obtain these outcomes using various treatment options (determined by reviewing relevant clinical literature and consulting EAP providers and peer organizations who use EAPs).

Stress Management Interventions

Stress and its effects are among the most popular topics in both research and practical literature in recent years. The authors of a recent review of the work stress literature identified over 300 scholarly articles published on that subject during the last decade, with hundreds more articles in the popular press and in trade journals (Ganster & Schaubroeck, 1991). A commonly cited estimate is that stress costs the U.S. economy between $50 and $90 billion a year (Ivancevich & Matteson, 1980).

While methodological limitations of much stress research (e.g., reliance on self-reports of stress and its effects rather than objective measurements) have made firm cause-effect statements about the relationship of work stress to other factors, such as mental and physical health, job performance, and job satisfaction, the research done to date is strongly suggestive of such a relationship (Ganster & Schaubroeck, 1991; Sullivan & Bhagat, 1992). For example, Sullivan and Bhagat's (1992) review of the literature reported that, in general, work stress has been shown to have a *negative* relationship with:

- Psychological well-being (Tetrick & LaRocco, 1987);

- Psychosomatic symptoms (Gavin & Axelrod, 1977);

- Mental health (Gavin, 1975);

- Commitment (Erickson, Pugh, & Gunderson, 1972);

- Job threat and anxiety (Tosi, 1971);

- Non-work satisfaction (Lance & Richardson, 1988); and

- Job involvement (Hollon & Chesser, 1976).

Sullivan and Bhagat also reported that stress has been shown to have a *positive* relationship with turnover, turnover intentions, and absenteeism (e.g., Jamal, 1984; Kemery et al., 1985) and tension (e.g., Erickson et al., 1972; Kemery et al., 1985).

Stress management programs or interventions (SMIs) are defined as "any activity, program, or opportunity initiated by an organization, which focuses on reducing the presence of work-related stressors or on assisting individuals to minimize the negative outcomes of exposure to these stressors" (Ivancevich, Matteson, Freedman, & Phillips, 1990, p. 252). SMIs are among the most widely offered employee counseling programs and are a significant part of the over 50,000 health promotion programs that exist in organizations (Howe, 1983). The techniques used to treat excessive stress vary widely, including such activities as education, time management, physical exercise, assertiveness training, biofeedback, meditation, and communications training (Everly, 1984; Ivancevich et al., 1990). While stress management interventions are popular, two important issues have yet to be completely addressed: the definition of stress, and the effectiveness of SMIs.

Defining Stress

Stress has been a difficult concept to define. According to Matteson & Ivancevich (1987), hundreds of definitions of stress can be found in the literature. This lack of a clear, agreed-upon definition limits a researcher's ability to compare results across studies, since what is called stress in one study may differ from what is called stress in another. Although there is yet to be complete agreement on a definition, there is some agreement that **stress** includes three components:

- Some environmental force affecting the individual, which is called a **stressor;**

- The individual's psychological or physical response to the stressor; and

- Sometimes the interaction of the stressor and the individual's response (Ivancevich et al., 1990).

Stressors can include a wide variety of stimuli both within and outside the organization. Organizational stressors can be such factors as poorly defined rules, lack of control, inconsistent policies, work overload, and inadequate rewards (Matteson & Ivancevich, 1987). A more inclusive list of organizational stressors is shown in Table 10-4.

Research has also examined a wide range of variables that may moderate the effect of stress on organizationally valued outcomes. Possible moderators include the individual's sense of competence, perceived control, locus of control, job characteristics, social support, and organizational level (Sullivan & Bhagat, 1992).

| TABLE 10-4 | ORGANIZATIONAL STRESSORS |

1. Factors Intrinsic to the Job
   Role Conflict
   Role Ambiguity
   Workload
   Insufficient Control

2. Organizational Structure and Control
   Red Tape
   Politics
   Rigid Policies

3. Reward Systems
   Faulty and Infrequent Feedback
   Inequitable Rewards

4. Human Resource Systems
   Inadequate Career Opportunities
   Lack of Training

5. Leadership
   Poor Relationships
   Lack of Respect

SOURCE: From *Controlling Work Stress* (p. 27) by M. T Matteson and J. M. Ivancevich, 1987. San Francisco: Josey-Bass.

The way a person cognitively evaluates stress can play an important role in how stress is experienced. A force that feels like overwhelming stress to one person may be experienced as stimulating to another. For example, some employees may prefer loosely defined roles because they then have the freedom to determine the activities that can be legitimately performed in the job. Other employees may experience a poorly defined role as stressful because they are confused about what they should and should not be doing. Some SMIs take advantage of this by providing employees with new ways of evaluating the stressors in their lives. For example, employees can be taught to view assignments that require them to use new skills as opportunities for growth rather than opportunities for failure.

The way individuals cope with stress can also have an effect on whether the stressor has a negative effect on performance. Learning relaxation exercises that help employees dissipate anxiety experienced when they are under stress can reduce the physical effects of the stressor (e.g., headaches, rapid breathing) and help the employee view the stressor in a more realistic way, rather than inflating its significance.

A Model of SMIs

SMIs can be categorized as either educational or skill-acquisition oriented (Matteson & Ivancevich, 1987). **Educational interventions** are designed to inform the employee about the sources of stress, what stress feels like, how stressors can be avoided, and how the individual can better cope with stress. **Skill-acquisition interventions,** such as time management or assertiveness training, are designed to provide employees with new ways to cope with stressors affecting their lives and performance and help keep the effects of stress in check.

Ivancevich et al. (1990) developed a model of SMIs that depicts the targets of the intervention, the type of intervention, and likely outcomes. Their model, shown in Figure 10-1, categorizes SMIs as focusing on the individual (e.g., goal setting), the organization (e.g., job redesign), or the individual-organizational interface (e.g., co-worker relationships). Currently, most workplace SMIs focus on helping the individual cope with stress (Ivancevich et al., 1990) through activities such as meditation, exercise, and time management. However, researchers are increasingly recommending that SMIs should focus on the characteristics of the work environment that cause stress (Ganster & Schaubroeck, 1991; Murphy, 1984). We agree with this point of view. Focusing on work environment fac-

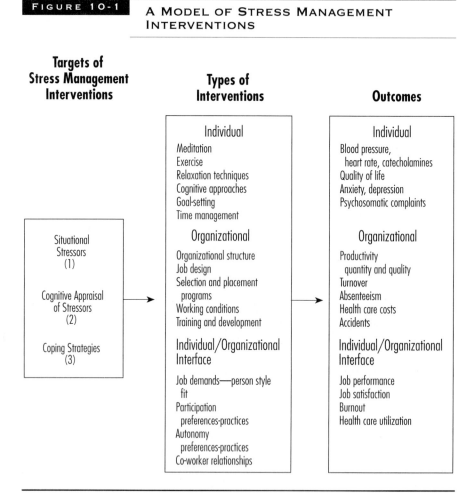

FIGURE 10-1   A MODEL OF STRESS MANAGEMENT INTERVENTIONS

Targets of Stress Management Interventions

Situational Stressors (1)

Cognitive Appraisal of Stressors (2)

Coping Strategies (3)

Types of Interventions

Individual
Meditation
Exercise
Relaxation techniques
Cognitive approaches
Goal-setting
Time management

Organizational
Organizational structure
Job design
Selection and placement programs
Working conditions
Training and development

Individual/Organizational Interface
Job demands—person style fit
Participation preferences-practices
Autonomy preferences-practices
Co-worker relationships

Outcomes

Individual
Blood pressure, heart rate, catecholamines
Quality of life
Anxiety, depression
Psychosomatic complaints

Organizational
Productivity quantity and quality
Turnover
Absenteeism
Health care costs
Accidents

Individual/Organizational Interface
Job performance
Job satisfaction
Burnout
Health care utilization

SOURCE: From "Worksite Stress Management Interventions" by J. M. Ivancevich, *American Psychologist, 45,* p. 254. Copyright 1990 by American Psychological Association. Reprinted by permission.

tors may not only yield significant benefits to both the individual and the organization, but may also be a way for organizations to assume their responsibility in creating and managing stress.

The Effectiveness of SMIs

The picture for SMIs is similar to that for EAPs—not enough rigorously conducted studies exist to allow firm conclusions. A number of reviews of SMI research have been conducted (e.g., DeFrank & Cooper, 1987; Ivancevich & Matteson, 1986; Ivancevich et al., 1990; Matteson & Ivancevich, 1987; Murphy, 1984, 1986; Newman & Beehr, 1979). While there are many anecdotal reports suggesting that SMIs are effective in helping employees manage stress and saving organizations money, the reviewers cited earlier note that much SMI research is poorly conducted, having been based on anecdotes or testimonials and lacking in scientific rigor. The well-conducted studies that do exist, however, provide some evidence to support the effectiveness of commonly used SMI tactics, such as meditation, biofeedback, and increased participation (Ivancevich et al., 1990). Table 10-5 summarizes some of these studies. These results give rise to optimism that SMIs are in fact effective. Further studies of the type listed in Table 10-5 will provide the information organizations and HRD professionals need to make informed choices about which SMIs are most effective for dealing with work stress.

Health Promotion Programs

Wellness or health promotion programs (HPPs) are comprised of activities that promote behavior and company practices that ensure employee health and fitness (e.g., Gebhardt & Crump, 1990; Terborg, 1986). Unlike disease prevention and health protection programs, HPPs and wellness programs are based on the premise that wellness is more than mere absence of disease. These programs attempt to encourage individuals to adopt lifestyles that maximize overall well-being (Terborg, 1986). While stress management may be a component of HPPs, they also deal with non-stress issues, such as obesity and smoking cessation (Fielding & Piserchia, 1989). Interest in health promotion and fitness is very strong. As mentioned earlier, it is estimated that there are over 50,000 programs that promote physical fitness among employees (Driver & Ratliff, 1982; Howe, 1983; Jacobs, 1983). Table 10-6 lists the frequency of worksite health promotion activities in private-sector places of employment.

O'Donnell (1986) describes three levels at which fitness and wellness programs can be implemented. **Level I** programs primarily cover educational activities and may not attempt to directly change employee behavior. Techniques used in Level I programs include newsletters, posters, classes, and health screening. **Level II** programs are those that attempt to bring about direct behavior change. The activities in such programs may include supervised exercise classes, memberships in fitness centers, and classes on how to properly perform physical work tasks, like lifting. **Level III** programs try to create an organizational environment that helps employees maintain healthy lifestyles. These programs

TABLE 10-5 RECENT SMI EVALUATION STUDIES

Researchers	Subjects	Intervention Target	Intervention Type	Outcome Measures	Results/ Comments
Carrington et al. (1980)	Telephone company workers	CS	Meditation, muscle relaxation	Depression, anxiety, hostility	Corporate program. Meditation was superior to relaxation. Control group used.
Manuso (1980)	Clerical and managerial workers	CS	Relaxation (via biofeed-back)	Anxiety, headaches, health care utilization	Corporate program. Significant symptom reduction, cost savings reported. No controls used.
Peters (1981)	Office workers	CS	Relaxation	Blood pressure, performance, satisfaction	Good controls. Identified conditions important in relapse prevention.
Wall & Clegg (1981)	Departmental work teams	SS	Work redesign, autonomy increase	Job satisfaction, emotional distress	Significant changes in outcome measures, with 6- and 18-month follow-ups. No controls used.
Ganster, Mayes, Sime, & Tharp (1982)	Public agency workers	CA CS	Cognitive modification, relaxation	Epinephrine, depression, anxiety, somatic complaints	Epinephrine and depression levels were better for trained subjects than for controls. True experimental design used.
Jackson (1983)	Hospital employees	SS	Increasing participation practices	Emotional strain, absenteeism, role conflict and ambiguity	Some effects (less distress, lower turnover intention) significant at three months, others (reduced role ambiguity and conflict) at six months. Solomon four-group design used.

Study	Type	Intervention	Outcome measures	Comments
Murphy (1984b)	CS	Muscle relaxation	Muscle tension, anxiety, sleep disturbances	Controls showed changes on most measures. Trained groups showed less baseline regression on follow-up. Blue-collar sample used.
Bruning & Frew (1987)	CA CS	Cognitive modification, meditation, exercise	Blood pressure, heart rate, skin response	Each intervention led to improvement in outcome measures. Combination of interventions led to greater improvement. Good design, with controls, was used.
Murphy & Hurrell (1987)	CA CS	Cognitive modification, relaxation	Job satisfaction, work environment scale	Moderate changes reported. No controls used. Described formation of Stress Reduction Committee to make recommendations regarding strategies for reducing stress, but no data yet collected on this interesting intervention.
Jones et al. (1988)	SS CS	Increased participation, work redesign, relaxation exercise instruction	Job satisfaction, objective job performance error rate	Series of four related studies. Excellent example of combining good design with practical questions. Significant improvement was shown in intervention compared with matched controls.

Note: CS = Coping Strategies; SS = Situational Stressors; CA = Cognitive Appraisal

SOURCE: From "Worksite Stress Interventions" by J. M. Ivancevich, 1990, *American Psychologist, 45*, p. 256–257. Copyright 1990 by American Psychological Association. Reprinted by permission.

| TABLE 10-6 | FREQUENCY OF HPP ACTIVITIES |

Activity	Percent of Respondents Reporting Activity
Any activity	65.5
Health risk assessment	29.5
Smoking cessation	35.6
Blood pressure control	16.5
Exercise fitness	22.1
Weight control	14.7
Nutrition education	16.8
Stress management	26.6
Back-problem prevention and care	28.5
Off-the-job accident prevention	19.8

SOURCE: From "Frequency of Worksite Health Promotion Activities" by J. E. Fielding and P. V. Piserchia, 1989, *American Journal of Public Health, 79*, pp. 16–20.

may include corporate fitness centers and making healthy foods available to employees in cafeterias and vending machines. Two examples of Level III programs are Johnson & Johnson's "Live for Life" program (Wilber, 1983) and Control Data's "Staywell" program (Fielding, 1984), which the company is also selling to other organizations.

HPPs can be divided into three areas (Terborg, 1986):

1. **Screening programs** that identify individuals who may be at risk for various problems.

2. **Educational programs** that relate information on health-related topics.

3. **Behavior change programs** that encourage employees to participate in health-related activities.

Table 10-7 lists activities that might take place in each of these areas. The sequence of events common to many HPPs can be described as follows:

> [T]he program begins with employee health screening, results of the health screen are fed back to the employee in some type of counseling session, employees are advised to participate in one or more health promotion activities consistent with their current health status, and follow-up counseling and health assessment reinforces and maintains employee involvement (Terborg, 1986, p. 231).

Four common components of HPPs are exercise and fitness, smoking cessation, nutrition and weight control, and hypertension (high blood pressure) control. We will examine each of these components and their effectiveness below.

TABLE 10-7	ACTIVITIES THAT MAY BE INCLUDED IN AN HPP

Screening Programs	Educational Programs	Behavioral Change Programs
Annual medical exam	Alcohol and drug use	Exercise and fitness
Blood analysis	Breast self-exam	Aerobics
Cervical cancer	Cancer prevention	Calisthenics
Colon and rectal cancer	Coronary disease risk	Recreational sports
Diabetes	factors	Competitive sports
Fitness assessment	Cardiopulmonary resusci-	Weight training
Health fairs	tation	Exercise instruction
Health-risk appraisal	Weight control	EAPs
Height and weight	Exercise and fitness	Healthy back
High blood pressure	First aid	Self-defense
Preemployment medical	Cancer detection	Smoking cessation
exams	Low back pain	Stress management
Pulmonary function tests	Nutrition	Weight loss
Screening for job-specific	Seat-belt use	Cooking classes
health	Smoking cessation	
	Stress	

SOURCE: From "Worksite Health Promotion in Colorado" by M. F. Davis, K. Rosenberg, D. C. Iverson, T. M. Vernon, & J. Bauer, 1984, *Public Health Reports, 99*, pp. 2.

Exercise and Fitness Interventions

Corporate exercise and fitness programs are among the most popular employee well-being interventions. These programs can supply a range of services for employees, from jogging trails and on-site fitness centers to exercise breaks and company-sponsored sports leagues. Companies such as Xerox, Kimberly-Clark, Goodyear Tire and Rubber, and Tenneco have sponsored such programs.

One of the driving forces behind the strong interest in exercise and fitness programs is evidence that the risk of developing coronary heart disease, cancer, and other leading causes of death can be reduced by adopting a healthy lifestyle (Harris, 1981; Mattzarro, 1984; Miller, 1983). Organizations supporting fitness and health programs expect to generate benefits such as a greater ability to attract and retain employees, more positive employee attitudes, and increased productivity through reduced absenteeism, turnover and a heightened physical capacity to perform work (Howard & Mikalanchki, 1979). Organizations also use fitness programs as a way to cut rising health care costs (Herzlinger & Schwartz, 1985).

The physical and psychological benefits of exercise and fitness have been demonstrated. For example, a study performed at Xerox showed that employees who participated in an exercise program showed improvements in heart rate, blood pressure, cholesterol, and triglycerides after 14 weeks (Pauly, Palmer, Wright, & Pfeiffer, 1982). Other studies have yielded similar positive results (e.g., Blair, Jacobs, & Powell, 1985; Cady, Thomas, & Karwasky, 1985). Fitness and exercise programs can also affect job performance. A study at Tenneco

(Bernacki & Baun, 1984) found that employees who stuck with fitness programs tended to earn above-average to outstanding job-performance ratings from their supervisors. Studies have also shown a positive effect on employee attitudes, such as greater self-confidence, reduced stress, more energy, and greater job satisfaction (e.g., Rhodes & Dunwoody, 1980; Cox, Shepard, & Corey, 1981). Other studies have also shown long-term participation in fitness programs has a positive effect on employee mental health (e.g., Lichtman & Poser, 1983).

Still, many studies evaluating workplace fitness and exercise programs are limited by methodological problems (Falkenberg, 1987), like the other employee well-being programs cited in this chapter. Even so, it appears that these fitness and exercise programs are effective in improving employee health, attitudes, and job behavior and reducing turnover and absenteeism (Gebhardt & Crump, 1990).

The major obstacle to the effectiveness of fitness and exercise programs may be persuading employees who would most benefit from them to participate. Participation rates in fitness and exercise programs tend to be low, around 30 percent or less (Fielding, 1984; Shepard, 1983), with rates for blue collar workers tending to be much lower than that for white collar workers, at about 3 to 5 percent (Gebhardt & Crump, 1990). This problem is exacerbated by the fact that many participants in such programs tend to be those who are already physically active (Fielding, 1982).

Organizations that use fitness programs should identify the needs of all employees and provide incentives to ensure that those at greatest risk also participate (Conrad, 1987). Systematic outreach and follow-up counseling have also been found to increase effectiveness and cost-effectiveness of fitness programs (Erfurt, Foote, & Heirich, 1992). Other aspects of an effective fitness and exercise program include establishing program goals and objectives, obtaining management commitment, hiring quality staff for the program, developing an evaluation strategy, and recruiting participants (Gebhardt & Crump, 1990).

Smoking Cessation

Smoking is one of the best-publicized health risks in society and the workplace. It has been amply demonstrated for some time that smoking is linked to greater incidence of coronary heart disease, stroke, cancer, and emphysema (Fielding, 1984). Even so, it is estimated that 25 percent of Americans still smoke (Cascio, 1991b). Not only does the smoker suffer increased health risks, but there is mounting evidence that nonsmokers exposed to cigarette smoke (i.e., second-hand smoke) also incur greater health risks. The additional annual cost of employing smokers and allowing smoking in the workplace has been estimated to be $2,853 per smoker (Cascio, 1991b).

Organizations have been increasingly willing to sponsor smoking cessation programs as a way to help employees, reduce costs, and provide a safer workplace. In many cases, state and local laws banning smoking in public areas have also prodded organizations to help employees quit smoking. The New York Times reported that 70 to 80 percent of U.S. organizations have already adopted or plan to adopt policies that restrict smoking (McFadden, 1989). Fielding and

Piserchia (1989) surveyed a random sample of private work sites and found that 35 percent of respondents had a smoking cessation program. Organizations can either sponsor smoking cessation programs in-house, as part of an EAP, stress management, or wellness program, or refer interested employees to an outside organization, such as the American Cancer Society or a local hospital.

Two related indexes of the success of smoking cessation programs are the quit rate and the percent of smokers who participate in the program. An impressive quit rate is less significant to the organization if only a small proportion of smoking employees enter the program. Quit rates reported in the literature are typically in the area of 25 to 60 percent (Matteson & Ivancevich, 1987). Participation rates are not reported as frequently as quit rates (Matteson & Ivancevich, 1988), but are typically lower than quit rates. For example, Brennan (1986) reported a participation rate of only 7.5 percent in four smoking cessation programs offered at the Metropolitan Life Insurance Company. If incentive programs such as competitions are used, participation rates can be much higher. For example, Klesges and Glasgow (1986) reported an 88 percent participation rate in a program that pitted employees of four banks in a smoking cessation competition.

Nutrition and Weight-Control Interventions

Approximately 14 percent of men and 21 percent of women can be considered obese, which is defined as being 20 percent or more over ideal body weight (Fielding, 1982). Obesity has been associated with musculoskeletal problem, hypertension, and high levels of blood sugar and cholesterol (Fielding, 1984). Because of health and cost consequences of obesity, and because of employee concerns about appearance (Terborg, 1986), workplace weight-control and nutrition interventions are becoming more common.

The content of such programs varies widely, and can include educational activities, such as newsletters, leaflets, cooking demonstrations, weigh-ins, and advice on developing weight-loss programs (Ford & Ford, 1986). Organizations may also stock cafeterias and vending machines with healthy, low-fat foods, and post nutritional information on food sold in the cafeteria (Pelletier, 1984; Salcedo, 1986).

The effectiveness of nutritional and weight-control programs has not been conclusively demonstrated, since many reports in the literature are based on testimonials rather than controlled studies (Terborg, 1986). One commonly cited study reported an average weight loss of 7.6 pounds (Brennan, 1986). As is the case with other health improvement programs, participation is an important aspect of program effectiveness. Competition seems to improve both participation and the success rate (e.g., Feuer, 1985; Brownell, et al., 1984).

Control of Hypertension

Approximately 15 to 25 percent of the U.S. work force suffers from **hypertension,** which is a blood pressure greater than 140/90 millimeters of mercury (mm Hg) over repeated measurements (Terborg, 1986). Health problems linked to hypertension include a significantly greater incidence of heart disease and stroke (Fielding, 1984). Cohen (1985) estimated organizations lose 52 million workdays per year because of heart and vascular disease.

The high incidence of hypertension and the relative ease with which it can be detected and controlled have made hypertension screening and control programs popular in the workplace. Despite the potentially devastating effects of hypertension, it can often be controlled through exercise, weight reduction, medication, stress reduction, and a low-salt diet (Fielding, 1984). Organizations need not have a full-blown fitness or health promotion program to help employees reduce hypertension. According to Terborg (1986), a typical screening and control program may include:

- Providing educational materials;

- Conducting blood pressure screenings to identify hypertensive employees;

- Referral of such employees for treatment;

- Installing blood pressure screening equipment for employees to use to monitor their blood pressure;

- Providing low-salt foods in both cafeteria and vending machines; and

- Periodic monitoring of employee progress.

Success rates of hypertension control programs in the workplace, as measured by percentages of employees who manage to control blood pressure over a period of time, range from 50 to 75 percent, which is often superior to programs offered in other settings (Matteson & Ivancevich, 1988). Such programs also appear to be cost-effective. Foote & Erfurt (1991) reported a benefit of $1.89 to $2.72 in reduced health care claims per dollar spent on running a hypertension control program.

Issues in Employee Counseling

Each of the employee counseling approaches discussed previously is affected by a common set of issues, including effectiveness, ethical and legal issues, responsibility, and unintended negative consequences. We will discuss each of these issues.

Effectiveness of Employee Counseling Interventions

A common theme among the interventions cited previously is a lack of scientifically sound studies demonstrating effectiveness. While much of the evidence to support these interventions is based on anecdotes and testimonials, the trend is toward more rigorous studies. However, until a greater number of such studies is conducted and reported, the evidence cited earlier is more suggestive than conclusive. Several factors make it difficult for better research to be conducted.

First, the personal nature of many problems addressed by counseling, such as substance abuse and mental illness, may make organizations reluctant to allow researchers access to the settings and data needed. Second, defining success and effectiveness for many of these problems is a difficult task. In the case of alcohol abuse, for example, many programs define alcoholism indirectly, in terms of changes in job behavior, rather than directly, in terms of alcohol consumption volume or pattern. Is an alcohol abuse program effective if treated employees return to normal working patterns, even if the employees still drink? Similarly, what period of time is suitable to establish that a problem has been resolved? Does a reduction of stress for six months signify success? The prevention of relapse is a significant factor, whether in the case of weight control, hypertension, or fitness interventions. We agree with Matteson and Ivancevich (1988) and Luthans and Waldersee (1989) that effectiveness needs to be defined by multiple criteria, including cost effectiveness, short- and long-term behavior and attitude changes, participation rates, and direct impact on the cause of the problem.

Third, and finally, the reasons an organization has begun intervention in the first place may affect whether research is done and how effectiveness is defined. Some organizations launch employee counseling programs because they believe it is the right thing to do or because the program is consistent with the organization's philosophy (as is the case with Xerox and its emphasis on employee fitness). Other organizations implement such programs to enhance the organization's image, both internally and externally. Effectiveness data in these cases may not affect whether the organization continues to offer the program; the fact that the program is being offered is the key concern.

One way to encourage organizations to evaluate their programs is to provide a model that identifies the data needed for sound evaluation. Gebhardt and Crump (1990) describe a strategy for evaluating wellness programs that we believe could be used as a guideline for evaluating EAPs and SMIs as well. The strategy includes these steps:

1. Determine the demographics of the organization (e.g., age, sex, etc.).

2. Determine expected participation rates.

3. Estimate program start-up and maintenance costs needed to meet objectives.

4. Implement a testing and tracking system to quantify program outcomes.

5. Measure pre- and post-program changes for relevant outcomes.

6. Analyze program variables separately by relevant demographic groups and by measuring participation versus nonparticipation in the program.

7. Perform cost-benefit analyses of present and future benefits, expressed in current-dollar value.

Following this model is not necessarily easy, as it is often difficult to identify all the costs and benefits of a program and to express them in economic terms (Cascio, 1991b). However, conducting an evaluation study based on this strategy can provide the data needed to make informed decisions about the program.

Legal Issues in Employee Counseling Programs

Federal and state legislation has had a significant impact on the growth of employee counseling programs, especially in the area of alcohol and drug abuse. Federal laws such as the Federal Rehabilitation Act of 1973, the Drug-Free Workplace Act of 1988, and Executive Order 12564 (called the Drug-Free Federal Workplace and signed by President Reagan in 1986) have been seen by some (e.g., Masi, 1992) as encouraging the adoption of EAPs. For example, the Drug-Free Workplace Act requires federal contract and grant recipients of more than $25,000 to have a written policy regarding drug use in the workplace and to notify employees of the availability of related counseling, rehabilitation, and employee assistance programs. State laws, such as that of Rhode Island, and federal agency rules, such as those of the Department of Transportation, require drug testing programs to be accompanied by EAPs or some other form of rehabilitation counseling (Axel, 1990).

Some proponents of employee counseling programs cite a legal advantage to such programs, pointing out that they help the organization comply with existing laws such as the Rehabilitation Act (1973) and the Americans with Disabilities Act of 1990 (ADA). These laws prohibit employers from discriminating against individuals with disabilities and require that employers make "reasonable accommodations" to help such employees perform their job functions. Both of these laws cover employees with alcohol and drug problems (e.g., ADA includes in its definition of disability such individuals who have successfully completed or are currently using a supervised drug rehabilitation program and who are no longer using illegal drugs).

The Rehabilitation Act, which applies to federal contractors and government-supported organizations, specifies that employees with handicaps may be discharged only for job-performance reasons. An alcoholic employee may not be fired because of alcoholism, but only for the negative effects the alcoholism has had on performance. In addition, it is unlawful to simply permit the employee's performance to deteriorate to a level that would justify termination. According to the law, the employer must make reasonable accommodations that help the employee resolve the problem and improve performance. In the case of substance abuse, "reasonable accommodation" has been interpreted to mean the employee must be offered the opportunity for treatment and permitted the time necessary for the treatment to take effect before firing for poor performance is justified (Luthans & Waldersee, 1989). Some authors (e.g., Good, 1986) see EAPs as a way to prevent lawsuits relating to wrongful discharge or reasonable accommodation.

ADA, which was passed in 1990 and became effective in July of 1992, broadly defines reasonable accommodation to include modification of facilities, materials, procedures, and jobs, and states employers must take such action provided these modifications do not create "undue hardship" (e.g., significant difficulty or expense). The impact of ADA is likely to be greater than that of the Rehabilitation Act because it applies to all employers of fifteen or more employees. ADA has created considerable concern among employers (primarily with regard to its impact on employee selection practices) who fear the cost of complying with the act and feel that its definitions of disability, reasonable accommodation, and undue hardship are too vague to provide clear guidance as to ways to comply with it. While ADA does not explicitly mention counseling services, it is likely some employers will see EAPs, SMIs and/or HPPs as a way to help them comply with the law. Because ADA only recently took effect and little case law exists to aid in interpreting it, the real impact (beyond the considerable concern created prior to its becoming effective) remains to be seen.

The potential legal advantage of using counseling programs to comply with existing laws may be offset to the extent that the counseling program exposes employers to lawsuits charging erroneous assessment, failure to refer to appropriate treatment, or for not being referred to treatment (Loomis, 1986). Further, in the case of fitness and wellness programs, litigation may also be encountered if the employee becomes injured while participating in company-sponsored events or while working out in its fitness facility.

Clearly, there are both legal pros and cons to engaging in employee well-being programs. The rapid growth of these programs may indicate that such problems are either not prevalent or are not considered significant by many organizations (although the recent enactment of ADA remains a wild card). Nevertheless, legal issues should be examined when an organization is planning and implementing counseling programs.

Whose Responsibility Is Employee Counseling?

Employees, the organization, supervisors, and unions all have a role to play in employee well-being. As stated earlier, organizations stand to gain significant benefits from taking steps to improve employee mental and physical health, and many have seen fit to implement programs to do this. It should be noted that labor unions can and have played a role in employee well-being also. Several unions, such as the Association of Flight Attendants (Feuer, 1987), have sponsored EAPs to assist members with alcohol and drug abuse problems.

Proponents of union involvement in employee counseling (e.g., Akabus, 1977; Feuer, 1987; Perlis, 1980) contend that union-sponsored programs can help reduce members' negative perceptions of counseling. In addition, union-based programs can take advantage of peer pressure and referrals to encourage troubled employees to seek assistance (Trice, Hunt, & Beyer, 1977).

Furthermore, employees may be more likely to seek help from a union than an employer, perceiving the union's interest in offering help as a genuine "brotherly" concern, while the employer's interest may be seen as self-serving (Steele, 1988).

Observers have noted that management has typically involved unions in counseling programs such as EAPs almost as an afterthought (Trice, Hunt, & Beyer, 1977). We believe opportunities exist for joint counseling programs that can motivate increased employee use, and therefore effectiveness, of these programs. However, critics note that union cooperation will not necessarily facilitate the effectiveness of EAPs (Weiss, 1987), and adoption of an EAP has been hindered by union involvement (Fennell, 1984).

Obviously, the individual bears primary responsibility for his or her own well-being. Given the impact of lifestyle choices on health and longevity, individuals are ultimately responsible for the course of their lives. Still, many of the factors leading to stress and poor coping result from the interaction of the organization and the individual (Ivancevich et al., 1990). Individuals should be trained to recognize these sources so that they can determine when help is needed.

Finally, supervisors and managers play a key role in the effectiveness of any employee counseling effort. Because supervisors are in regular contact with employees, responsible for their development and evaluation, and ultimately held responsible for their performance, they occupy a unique position in the counseling process. The supervisor's primary responsibility is to ensure the effective functioning of the work unit. Supervisory counseling should focus on being aware of employee performance problems that might be the result of personal problems, supporting troubled employees by helping them to obtain the care they need to improve performance, motivating the employee to improve, and monitoring performance to ensure that it does.

Confronting problem employees and dealing with them sensitively and effectively is a challenging task. Care must be taken to train supervisors and managers to fulfil the counseling role. A supervisor who is too zealous in undertaking counseling can be as counterproductive as one who avoids the role completely (Ramsey, 1985). Training programs should help the supervisor acquire both the skills and attitudes needed to fulfill this important role. Suggestions for the content of a supervisory counseling training program that addresses these issues is shown in Table 10-8.

Ethical Issues in Employee Counseling

Matteson & Ivancevich (1988) identify two ethical issues relating to employee counseling services that we believe merit discussion: confidentiality and nature of participation (i.e., whether mandatory or voluntary). Each is discussed here.

Confidentiality is a key concern in all types of employee counseling interventions. We emphatically agree with the position taken by Matteson and Ivancevich (1988):

Simply put, all records of program utilization should be held in the strictest confidence, should be maintained separate and apart from an

TABLE 10-8	POSSIBLE CONTENT OF A SUPERVISORY COUNSELING TRAINING PROGRAM

1. Identification of supervisor's initial reactions to prospect of counseling (e.g., using comfort reaction questionnaire).
2. Lecture and discussion of various counseling topics, which may include
   a. emotional needs of individuals (e.g., using Maslow's Need Hierarchy);
   b. potential signs of employee problems;
   c. signs of overinvolvement in counseling (e.g., loss of objectivity, focusing beyond job performance, guidelines for giving advice;
   d. structure of a counseling session, including decisions to be made therein;
   e. counseling terminology to facilitate discussion of feelings, reactions, and behaviors; and
   f. nonverbal communication.
3. Training in counseling skills, perhaps using case studies and behavior modeling.
4. Role play of counseling sessions.
5. Discussion of counseling's relationship to coaching and performance management.
6. Evaluation of counseling options and resources available.

SOURCE: From "Counseling Employees" by K. B. Ramsey, 1985, *Handbook of Human Resource Management and Development*, pp. 829, 832.

employee's personnel file, and should be released only with the express permission of the employee (p. 293).

While data generated by participation in, for example, a nutrition program may be less sensitive than that gained from a drug treatment program, it is nevertheless important to guarantee confidentiality of all employee counseling records. Program policy statements should include an explicit description of the confidentiality policy and the steps involved in implementing it.

A second ethical consideration concerns whether participation in a counseling program should be voluntary or mandatory. While organizations stand to gain greater benefits if all members of a target group participate in a program (e.g., all smokers, all obese employees), we believe participation should be voluntary. Employees should have the right to determine their lifestyle, and should not be forced to engage in behavior change other than that of performance on the job. Even an employee with a substance abuse problem should be free to choose whether and how to deal with that problem. The organization can offer assistance in treating the problem, but it should not attempt to force acceptance of treatment. If the employee's substandard performance does not improve after he or she has had ample opportunity to improve, then the organization may legally terminate the employee.

Unintended Negative Outcomes of Employee Counseling Programs

It is possible that participating in a counseling or fitness program can have unintended negative consequences. This is particularly true of health promotion programs. Some potential unintended negative consequences include:

- Worker's compensation costs may increase;

- Employees who participate in fitness programs may experience scheduling problems, increased fatigue and accidents, and lower performance;

- Health care unit costs may rise as employees use health care benefits less;

- Reduced turnover could reduce promotional opportunities and increase payroll costs;

- Smoking bans may lead to conflicts between smokers and nonsmokers (Terborg, 1986).

There is little research on this topic to guide organizations in making decisions. Decision-makers concerned about such consequences may find some help by investigating the experiences of other organizations.

Closing Comment

Both organizations and employees have much to gain from workplace counseling interventions. While the numbers of active programs indicate that employers already see and are acting upon this opportunity, we need to know more about what works, how well it works, and under what conditions it works. Economic conditions and changing business strategies often lead to cost-cutting initiatives, and counseling programs (like all others) will be closely examined. HRD professionals have the skills and expertise (in needs assessment, program design and implementation, and evaluation) to provide this information and to help see that their organization's resources are used wisely.

RETURN TO OPENING CASE

The SANE approach to wellness programs advocated by CEO William Kizer of Central States Life & Health Company of Omaha is a good way for organizations to adopt a wellness program gradually and with little initial investment. SANE stands for the four components of the wellness program: Smoking, Alcohol, Nutrition, and Exercise.

Central States began its smoking cessation program by establishing a company smoking policy, which created smoking and nonsmoking areas and smoking-cessation classes. These activities set the stage for a smoking ban, which was introduced some years later. The alcohol portion of the program can also start inexpensively by writing a policy on the use of alcohol at company-sponsored events. This can be followed by a program to help employees who have alcohol or substance abuse problems to get help. Central States uses an outside provider that is skilled in treating such problems and can maintain confidentiality for those who seek help. They followed that action in 1990 by instituting a drug and alcohol testing program to catch problems early, and introduced an alcohol and drug abuse education program in 1991.

The nutrition portion of Central States' SANE approach focuses on food at the work site, offering employees healthy snack alternatives in vending machines and making refrigerators and microwave ovens available that encourage them to bring healthy food for lunch. And, while Central States provides a relatively expensive, fully equipped fitness center for employees, Kizer points out there are less expensive ways to furnish opportunities for and encouragement to exercise. Subsidizing memberships in a YMCA or health club are one approach, and sponsoring competitions, such as the company's Walk 100 Miles in 100 Days for $100 incentive campaign, is another option. Central States has found such competitions effective in increasing employee participation. The walking campaign resulted in a participation rate of more than one-third of its employees.

Central States also ensures their program will enjoy both management support and employee ownership through its More Life Committee, which is made up of a cross section of Central States employees and managers.

Has the company's wellness program paid off? It has resulted in controlled health insurance premium costs at a time when other organizations are struggling with rising premiums. Another benefit to the company was its nomination as one of the "60 Best Companies for Working Mothers" in the United States by *Working Woman* magazine.[1]

Summary

Employee well-being affects the ability, availability, and readiness of employees to perform their jobs. The effects of problems with alcohol and drug abuse, mental health, smoking, and stress are widespread and are estimated to cost organizations billions of dollars in lost productivity. Both the organization and the individual stand to gain from employer attempts to provide information and programs that help employees deal with these problems.

Employee counseling programs, which can include employee assistance programs, health promotion programs, and stress management programs, include activities such as problem identification and diagnosis, education, counseling or

---

[1]From "Wellness with a Track Record," by F. W. Schott and S. Wendel, 1992, *Personnel Journal, 71*(4), pp. 98–104.

advising, referral to appropriate treatment, actual treatment, and follow-up. Employee counseling can be considered an HRD activity because it shares the same purpose as HRD: to ensure employees are now and will continue to be effective contributors to organizational goals.

While each of these programs is believed to be effective in helping at least some participants, the data available is based largely on studies that lack scientific rigor and appropriate conceptualization of the main variables. While the data so far suggest these programs can yield benefits both to individual and organization, further, more rigorous research is needed to determine the true effectiveness of these interventions. Solving the problem of how to get employees who would benefit from using these programs to participate is also an important issue.

Supervisors can play a key role in an effective counseling program, and must be aware of what programs are available to their employees and what employees need to do to participate. In addition, for many programs, such as alcohol abuse counseling, the supervisor often serves as the person who first identifies an employee may be in trouble and refers the employee for treatment. In addition, the supervisor is also in a position to participate in the follow-up effort to determine whether the employee is carrying out the treatment and whether the problem is in control or has been solved. Training supervisors to perform the counseling role is an important aspect of program effectiveness.

Employee counseling programs also face legal and ethical issues. Laws and regulations have both fueled the growth of counseling programs and raised questions about the role counseling programs may play in providing disabled employees with "reasonable accommodation" to perform job duties. Ensuring the confidentiality of an employee's participation in counseling and the nature of participation (e.g., whether voluntary or mandatory) are two ethical issues to be dealt with, as is the possible presence of negative consequences from participation.

Key Terms and Concepts

counseling	reasonable accommodation
constructive confrontation	stress
employee assistance program (EAP)	stress management intervention (SMI)
health promotion program (HPP)	stressor
hypertension	wellness

Questions for Discussion

1. Explain why employee counseling services can be considered HRD programs. Describe two elements counseling programs have in common with other HRD programs.

2. Suppose you were asked by your employer to develop a proposal for an EAP. Which approach would you recommend: An in-house program run by company employees, or a service provided by an

outside contractor? Support your choice. Suppose financial constraints limited the company to offering only two areas of service (e.g., mental health, substance abuse, gambling, financial problems, etc.). Which services do you think are most important? Support your choices. Describe how you would make sure the services you select are the ones the company and the employees would benefit the most from.

3. There is some disagreement as to the effectiveness of EAPs and the constructive confrontation approach in treating alcohol abuse. Present the positions supporting both sides of the argument. Given what you have learned about this issue, where do you think the truth lies? Support your choice.

4. Stress management interventions commonly focus on helping employees find ways to deal with the stressors in their lives. Yet some experts believe organizations should modify jobs or other organizational attributes (e.g., management style) to remove or reduce the impact of such stressors themselves, rather than teaching coping skills alone. What is your opinion on this matter? Support your position.

5. Some believe that programs like wellness programs infringe on an individual's right to choice of lifestyle, maintaining that an individual has the right to smoke cigarettes, eat junk food, and avoid exercise. What argument can you make to support the use of workplace wellness and health promotion programs? What argument would support the critics of workplace wellness programs? If you were a director of a workplace wellness program at a large banking firm, how would you balance needs of the company with the rights of individuals? Support your position.

6. Employee counseling programs of all types are popular in the United States, despite the lack of scientific evidence that conclusively supports the efficacy of these programs. If managers are such "bottom-line" decision makers, why do they continue to offer these programs when an iron-clad case for effectiveness has not yet been made? Describe two reasons why it is difficult to conduct conclusive scientific studies as to the effectiveness of employee counseling services.

11

Career Development

Learning Objectives

1. *Define the term* career, *and explain the role that both the individual and the organization play in career development.*
2. *Describe how models of life and career development enhance our understanding of careers.*
3. *Explain what is involved in career management.*
4. *Describe five career management activities and practices.*
5. *Understand what is involved in designing a career management program.*

OPENING CASE

Like many organizations, the Exploration Division of British Petroleum (BPX), the third-largest oil company in the world, is flattening its structure and shifting from bureaucracy to teamwork as a way to maximize organizational performance. At the same time, BPX wants to become a more attractive place to work (e.g., providing more interesting and challenging work roles) and establish a global identity. An integral part of BPX's strategy is redesigning the company's career path structure.

The career paths at BPX prior to the redesign were similar to those at many organizations. Employees who wanted to move up in the organization had only one way to go: become a manager. While managing may be attractive to some employees, many lack the interest and/or aptitude to become successful managers. Furthermore, this single-track approach has at least two drawbacks. First, the organization may be making reluctant managers of persons who could better serve the organization as individual contributors in the areas of their experience and expertise (e.g., engineering, product development). Second, and even worse, the organization may be encouraging key employees—who want to advance, but not to management—to leave for better opportunities in other organizations or to remain in positions that do not make full use of their talents.

Some organizations have addressed the career track problem by creating **dual career paths.** Each of these separate but parallel paths—that of management and individual contributor—offers comparable increases in responsibilities, influence, and rewards at each level. Still, in many organizations, dual career paths have met with mixed success because the paths failed to be comparable, did not mesh with organizational and individual needs, were blocked by managers, or became stigmatized as a refuge for failed managers.

Mindful of these potential pitfalls, BPX believed dual career paths could meet its needs, and set about designing and implementing dual career paths that would succeed.

Introduction

The study of careers and how they develop is one of the most active areas of inquiry in the social sciences. Psychologists, educators, sociologists, economists, and management scientists are all trying to understand how a person selects, works within, and makes decisions to change the focus of his or her working life. It is not surprising that careers should be the focus of such intensive study. We spend most of our lives working. The choices we make about what our work will involve determine to a large degree the success, happiness, and financial well-being of ourselves and our children.

Understanding and finding ways to influence the careers of employees in an organization is also an integral part of HRD. Career development provides a future orientation to HRD activities. It is a fact of life that people and organizations change. Organizational objectives, and the blend of knowledge, skill, and abilities (KSAs) it will take to reach those objectives change in response to challenges from the environment. As employees grow and change, the types of work they may want to do may change as well. If organizations can assist employees in making decisions about future work, they can better prepare employees to be effective when they take on new positions. Similarly, if the organization understands how employees make decisions about future work, it can do a better job of planning for its human resource needs.

Career development is such a broad field that it is beyond the scope of this book to survey it in its entirety. Instead, we will focus on discussing career development concepts and practices that managers and HR professionals can use to fulfill their role as developers of human resources.

Defining Career Concepts
What Is a Career?

The word *career* means many things to many people. It also has different meanings among researchers. Greenhaus (1987) and Schein (1987a) described several themes underlying different definitions of the term, including:

1. *The property of an occupation or organization* (Dalton, Thompson, & Price, 1977; Van Maanen & Schein, 1977). When used in this way, *career* describes the occupation itself (e.g., sales or accounting) or an employee's tenure within an organization (e.g., my college career).

2. *Advancement* (Hall, 1976; Van Maanen & Schein, 1977). In this sense, *career* denotes one's progression and increasing success within the occupation or organization.

3. *Status of a profession* (Hall, 1976). Some use the term *career* to separate the "professions," such as law or engineering, from other occupations, such as plumbing, carpentry, or being a clerk. The lawyer is said to have a career, while the carpenter does not.

4. *Involvement in one's work* (Schein, 1987a). Sometimes *career* is used in a negative sense to describe being extremely involved in the task or job one is doing, as in "Don't make a career out of it."

5. *Stability of a person's work pattern* (Van Maanen & Schein, 1977). A sequence of related jobs is said to describe a *career*, while a sequence of unrelated jobs does not.

Each of these definitions is limiting in that it defines career too narrowly. Several authors, including Feldman (1989b) and Greenhaus (1987) have offered definitions that are more expansive and therefore more useful. We agree with Greenhaus that a **career** is best described as "the pattern of work-related experiences that span the course of one's life" (1987, p. 6).

This definition includes both *objective* events, such as jobs, and *subjective* views of work, such as the person's attitudes, values, and expectations (Greenhaus, 1987). Therefore, both a person's work-related activities and his or her reactions to those activities are part of the career. Further, this definition is consistent with the notion that careers develop over time, and that all persons have careers, regardless of profession, level of advancement, or stability of work pattern.

This definition of career also underscores the influence and importance of both the individual and the organization on the individual's work life. While the job and occupational choices an individual makes during a career are determined in large part by forces within the individual, the organization and other external forces (e.g., society, family, the educational system) also play a role.

The individual is driven by his or her skills, knowledge, abilities, attitudes, values, and life situation. Organizations provide the jobs and information about jobs, as well as the opportunities and constraints within which one may pursue other jobs in the future (especially if one chooses to remain employed within the same organization). Both the individual and organization have needs and priorities. While some perspectives within the study of careers emphasize one set of influences over the other, it is important to remember that both are critical to the development of one's career.

Relationship of Career to Nonwork Activities

While the definition of career that we have chosen focuses on work-related events and the individual's reactions to those events, some career theorists recognize the importance of nonwork events on one's career. Super (1986) argues that to truly understand and manage careers, one must take into account all of an individual's skills, abilities, and interests. Placing the notion of career within the larger context of one's life, Super views offering employees opportunities to use all their talents—and thus attain real life satisfaction—as a way for organizations to best use the people within the organization. He further suggests that if organizations don't attempt to understand the whole person, they may be less able to compete in the future as the mix of skills needed to reach organizational objectives changes.

Even if one does not take as expansive view of career management as Super does, it is difficult to ignore the impact of nonwork influences on an individual's career. People come to organizations for specific reasons, and those reasons change as the person ages. The effect of family and society on a person's interests and aspirations play a significant part in determining the role work and career play in the person's life. Ignoring these influences will limit the organization's ability to understand and manage employee careers.

Career Development

Over the past 20 years, much attention has been given to addressing the question of how careers, and adult lives, develop or change over time. Recent research provides strong evidence to support the notion that careers do develop in a predictable, common sequence of stages (Hall, 1976; Levinson, 1986; Levinson, Darrow, Klein, Levinson, and McKee, 1978; Schein, 1978, 1987a). These researchers have found that at various ages people face common issues and pressures that they attempt to resolve in their lives. The stages affect, and are affected by, the career activities and choices the individual has made.

The overall process of **career development** can be defined as "an ongoing process by which individuals progress through a series of stages, each of which is characterized by a relatively unique set of issues, themes, and tasks" (Greenhaus, 1987, p. 9). We will present a model of career development in the next section of this chapter. However, it is useful to distinguish between two sets of activities that can be subsumed within career development: career planning and career management.

Career Planning and Career Management

As stated earlier, both the individual and the organization have interests in an individual's career, and both parties may take actions to influence that career. These sets of related activities are referred to as *career planning* and *career management*. These two sets of activities can be viewed as existing along a continuum (Storey, 1976).

Career planning is defined as "a deliberate process of (1) becoming aware of self, opportunities, constraints, choices, and consequences, (2) identifying career-related goals, and (3) programming work, education, and related developmental experiences to provide the direction, timing, and sequence of steps to attain a specific career goal" (Storey, 1976, in Hall, 1986, p. 3). Viewed in this way, career planning is an activity performed by the individual to understand and attempt to control his or her work life. The individual need not perform these activities alone. Assistance from counselors, supervisors, and others within and outside the organization can be helpful, but the focus of career planning is on the individual. For example, completing a career awareness workbook that helps the employee understand his or her skills, abilities, and preferences would be considered a career planning activity. If career planning is done successfully, the individual will know what he or she wants and have a set of action steps that, if followed, should allow achievement of these goals.

On the other end of the continuum of career development activity is **career management,** defined as "an ongoing process of preparing, implementing, and monitoring career plans undertaken by the individual alone or in concert with the organization's career systems" (Storey, 1976, in Hall, 1986, p. 3). Career management may include activities that help the individual develop and carry out career plans, but the focus is on taking actions that increase the chances the organization's anticipated HR needs will be met. At its most extreme, career management is largely an activity carried out by the organization. An example of such an activity is **succession planning,** which is typically carried out by senior management in secret to determine which employees can and should be prepared to replace people in positions of greater responsibility.

Figure 11-1 describes where various career development activities fit along the career planning/career management spectrum (Hall, 1986). These activities vary along this spectrum according to (1) the amount of influence by the individual, (2) the amount of information provided to the individual, (3) the amount of influence by the organization, and (4) the amount of information provided to the organization. Career management and career planning activities can be complementary and can reinforce each other. For example, it is difficult to monitor career plans of an individual who has not made specific plans to be monitored. A balance between the two (management and planning) can make for effective career development (Gutteridge, 1986). The organization can act at any point on the spectrum, assisting the employee with career planning as well as conducting career management activities, and thus play a role in effective career intervention.

Greenhaus (1987) uses the term *career management* to refer to all phases of career development activities, from gaining self-awareness, to developing

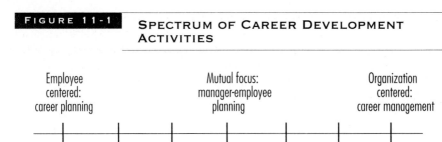

SOURCE: From "An Overview of Current Career Development Theory, Research, and Practice" by D. T. Hall, 1986, in D. T. Hall and associates (Eds.), *Career Development in Organizations* (p. 4), Copyright 1986 by Jossey-Bass, Inc., Publishers. San Francisco: Jossey-Bass. Reprinted by permission.

career goals and plans, to enacting those plans. Because planning is a significant activity within management, we will adopt Greenhaus's more inclusive use of the term *career management* and will use his model to form the framework of our discussion of how individuals and organizations can influence career development. Before discussing how one can influence the course of one's career, however, it is important to examine the career development process.

Stages of Career Development

One way to characterize a person's life or career is by identifying common experiences, challenges, or tasks most people seem to go through as their life or career progresses. For example, psychologists and others such as Freud (1959) have long argued that aspects of human nature such as personality, intelligence, and morality all develop in a predictable, common sequence closely tied to a person's age. Research by Levinson (1986; Levinson et al., 1978) and Erikson (1963) suggests that adult life follows a series of common stages. Work done by Schein (1987a, 1978), Super (1980), and others suggests that careers also develop in stages.

Visualizing career development as unfolding in stages permits us to understand why some experiences—such as difficulties in adjusting to one's first position, or mid-career problems—occur, and why they are so common. From a practical perspective, a stage view helps both the individual and the organization to predict likely crises and challenges and therefore plan ways to resolve or minimize them. For example, if initial job challenge is an issue for most young, new employees, then these individuals can be made to understand the nature of the problem and organizations can ensure that initial assignments have sufficient challenge to overcome this problem.

It is also true that stage views of development have their limitations. First, they describe what happens to the normal, or typical, individual. As we know, all individuals are unique and will not have the same experience. For example, many people do experience a period of self-questioning and reevaluation at mid-career, but not all people do. Levinson et al. (1978) found that 80 percent of the men they interviewed experienced such a crisis, but a sizable minority (20 percent) did not. So when using a stage approach, one gets only an average view, not one that applies to all people.

In addition, many stage views use age and/or life experiences to define when a stage is likely to begin and end. Some criticize using age as a criterion, arguing that major life events such as marriage and one's first job occur at different ages for different individuals. However, Levinson (1986) argues that the age ranges he uses, while flexible, are based on empirical research evidence. He states that it is hard to ignore the data, though more research needs to be done to confirm the validity of age anchors.

We believe that the usefulness of stage views outweighs the limitations. While age ranges may have to be interpreted liberally, and any given individual may not fit the stage model, there is enough evidence to support the usefulness of stage models as a way to understand and respond to career development.

Stage Views of Adult Development

A person's career is but one part of life, influenced by (and influencing) major events. Therefore, it is useful to briefly examine two stage models of adult development before we discuss a model of career development. At least two theorists, Erik Erikson (1963) and Daniel Levinson (1986, Levinson et al., 1978) have offered stage models of adult development that provide a meaningful basis for understanding career development.

Erikson's Model of Adult Development Erikson (1963) proposed that people progress through eight stages during the course of their life. These stages focus on both psychological and social issues, as are depicted in Table 11-1. In each stage of development, the person is faced with a challenge that he or she must resolve in order to develop.

TABLE 11-1	ERIKSON'S STAGES OF HUMAN DEVELOPMENT
Stage of Development (Issue)	**Age Range (Years)**
1. Basic trust versus mistrust	Infancy
2. Autonomy versus shame and doubt	1–3
3. Initiative versus guilt	4–5
4. Industry versus inferiority	6–11
5. Identity versus role confusion	Puberty and adolescence
6. Intimacy versus isolation	Young adulthood
7. Generativity versus stagnation	Middle adulthood
8. Ego integrity versus despair	Maturity

For example, the fifth stage, which occurs during adolescence, is defined by a conflict between **identity** and role confusion. If individuals successfully resolve this issue, they will enter adulthood with a clear sense of who they are in relation to others in the world. If they do not successfully resolve this issue, they will enter adulthood with confusion over who they are and what their role in the world is to be. It is the positive and negative experiences in each stage that determine its outcome.

The last three stages of Erikson's model focus on the issues facing adult development. As a young adult, one is faced with the challenge of developing meaningful relationships with others, which Erikson calls **intimacy.** If the individual successfully resolves this stage, he or she will be able to make a commitment to other individuals and groups; otherwise, the individual is likely to experience feelings of isolation.

In middle adulthood, the challenge is to develop the capacity to focus on the generations that will follow, which Erikson calls **generativity.** This can take the form of becoming more involved in one's children's lives, social issues affecting future generations, or in serving as a mentor for younger colleagues. Erikson argues failure to resolve this stage will lead to feelings of stagnation, in that one has made no contribution to the world that will last after he or she is gone.

Finally, in maturity the individual is faced with developing **ego integrity,** which involves developing an understanding and acceptance of the choices one has made in life. Successful development of ego integrity permits one to be at peace with one's life as one faces death. Failure at this stage leads to despair over the meaninglessness of one's existence.

Erikson's view of adult development identifies some of the issues (ego integrity, generativity, and intimacy) that can affect the career choices employees make. Organizations can serve as places for the individual to successfully resolve these challenges. For example, participating in mentoring programs serves the needs of young adults to develop meaningful relationships as well as the needs of middle adults to find a way to "give something back" to members of future generations.

Knowledge of these challenges also helps the organization understand some of the changes employees go through. Employees nearing retirement are facing many sources of stress (e.g., the loss of work and part of the social support system). **Preretirement counseling** and motivational programs geared toward older workers can yield benefits for both the individual and organization. Finally, Erikson's model also provides evidence that there is a predictable order to the issues individuals face as they develop.

Levinson's "Eras" Approach to Adult Development Levinson and his colleagues (1986; Levinson et al., 1978) have developed a widely cited view of how adults develop based on the notion that adult lives progress through *seasons,* not unlike the seasons of the year. He discovered these stages by collecting intensive biographical information from individuals in different walks of life over a period of years.

Levinson, like Erikson, argues that there is an underlying order to adult life called the *life cycle.* He uses the metaphor of seasons to indicate that major phases of a person's life (called **eras**) are like seasons of the year in the following ways:

1. They are qualitatively different;

2. Change occurs within each season;

3. There is a transitional period between each season that is part of both seasons;

4. No season is superior or inferior to another season;

5. Each season contributes something unique to life; and

6. There are four seasons or eras in a person's life (Levinson, 1986).

The four eras proposed by Levinson are preadulthood, early adulthood, middle adulthood, and late adulthood. Each era contains a series of stable and transitional periods. The stable periods last about six years, and the within-era transitional periods last about four or five years. The transitional periods between eras, called *cross-era transitions*, last about five years and signal the end of one era and the beginning of a new one. Figure 11-2 depicts the eras model.

The general pattern of progress through life is not from an inferior mode of being to a superior one. Rather, the transitional periods raise issues that cannot be dealt with by the life structure that exists at the current stage of a person's life. During these transitions, the individual questions and reexamines that structure and searches for new, different ways of dealing with these issues. New life structures supplant the old until the next transition period.

Levinson also discovered that the stages of a person's life are closely related to age. For example, preadulthood, which ranges from infancy to age 22, is a period in which we struggle to develop a sense of self. Levinson's research showed some variation in the age ranges among individuals, but also showed amazing constancy. Because careers occur primarily during Levinson's eras of young adulthood and middle adulthood, it is useful to examine each of these eras in more detail.

Early Adulthood (Ages 17–45)   Early adulthood includes four periods: the early adult transition (ages 17–22), entry life structure for early adulthood (ages 22–28), age 30 transition (ages 28–33), and the culminating life structure for early adulthood (ages 33–40). In general, early adulthood is a period of great energy and great stress. During this era, the person is at a biological peak and is striving to attain the goals and desires of youth. Finding a place in society, obtaining meaningful work, realizing a lifestyle, establishing meaningful relationships (including marriage), and raising a family are all a part of this period. Many people experience occupational advancement during this period as well. However, the stresses present are also great. Family and society place demands on the individual at the same time he or she is dealing with individual ambitions and passions.

FIGURE 11-2   LEVINSON'S ERAS MODEL OF ADULT
DEVELOPMENT

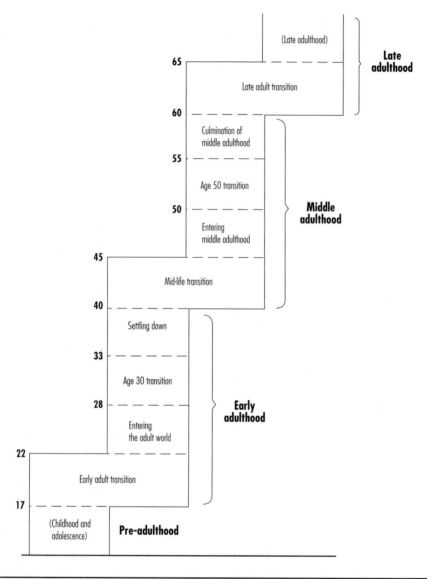

SOURCE: From *Seasons of a Man's Life* (p. 57) by D. J. Levinson, C. N. Darrow, E. B. Klein, M. H. Levinson, and B. McKee, 1978, New York: Knopf. Copyright 1978 by Daniel J. Levinson. Reprinted by permission of Alfred A. Knopf, Inc.

Of particular note in early adulthood is the "age 30 transition." For those in Levinson's studies, this is a time of questioning and reappraisal about the path one has initially chosen and whether it is adequate for helping the individual realize major life goals. Levinson refers to major life goals as the "Dream." If the age 30 transition is successfully resolved, the individual experiences a period of stability in which the Dream is vigorously pursued and work is done towards becoming "one's own man."

Middle Adulthood (Ages 40–65) The midlife transition (ages 40–45) leads from early adulthood to the beginning of middle adulthood. Research by Levinson and others shows that a person's life changes significantly between early and middle adulthood (Levinson, 1986). During this period there is a major questioning of the life structure (goals, ambitions, etc.) and Dream that was so vigorously pursued at the end of early adulthood. Questions often asked during this transition include, "What have I done with my life? What is it I want to accomplish before I die? What do I want to leave behind for my family and others?" It is not surprising this transition is so universal and so powerful. At this time in life, the individual is experiencing declines in physical functioning as his or her children are becoming adults. The individual's parents may be in significant physical decline or may die, and the individual may also witness the deaths of friends and peers.

The midlife transition can lead to an even stronger sense of self, allowing one to become more accepting of one's self and others, more judicious, and more compassionate. On the other hand, unsuccessful resolution of this transition can lead to bitterness and stagnation (notice the similarity to Erikson's idea of generativity). The midlife transition is followed by a period of stability (ages 45–50), the age 50 transition (ages 50–55), and another stable period (ages 55–60) that leads to the end of middle adulthood. During one's late forties and fifties, one typically becomes a senior member of the groups and organizations he or she is involved with. This can be a period of great satisfaction or great frustration.

Late Adulthood (Age 60–Death) Late adulthood begins with the late adulthood transition (ages 60–65). During this period, the individual faces additional major life events, including retirement, further physical decline, and the loss of family and loved ones. The major challenge in this era (similar to that described by Erikson) is to come to terms with one's life and accept things as they have been, rather than dwelling on what might have been. Less research has been done on this era than on the earlier ones.

Contributions of Levinson's Model to Career Development Levinson's ideas are significant. His model is based on empirical evidence and is consistent with, but expands upon, earlier ideas (e.g., Erikson's) about adult life development. While Levinson himself acknowledges that the model must undergo additional testing and refinement, research does support the sequence of events the model suggests and the age boundaries he has set. In addition, there is some evidence that the model, which was developed initially with white men, also applies to black men, women, and those in other cultures (Levinson, 1986).

There are similarities between Levinson's and Erikson's models. For example, they both rely on age ranges as markers for development, and identify similar issues that all adults must deal with as they develop (e.g., identity and intimacy). Levinson's model differs, however, in that it makes finer distinctions and describes adult development as progressing through alternating periods of stability and transition.

More important for our purposes, the notion that early adulthood, middle adulthood, and late adulthood represent a predictable, more or less universal sequence of life events provides a useful way to examine career development. A career is a part of a person's total life, and will be affected by these life issues. HRD professionals can use these ideas to help identify the particular issues employees in their organizations may face and plan career development programs accordingly. In addition, Levinson's model also suggests that there are periods of stability in a person's life that can be both productive and satisfying. This notion challenges the traditional assumption regarding **career plateaus** (periods lacking significant increases in responsibility) as consistently problematic (Feldman & Weitz, 1988).

A Model of Career Development

Numerous models of career development (e.g., Hall & Nougaim, 1968; Schein, 1978; Super, 1980, 1992) have been offered to explain the sequence of stages adults progress through during their work lives. Each of these models emphasizes the notion of an orderly series of career stages linked to age ranges, places the career into the context of a person's life, and contains overlapping concepts (Greenhaus, 1987). Given the similarities among these models, Greenhaus (1987) combined these approaches into a five stage model, which is shown in Table 11-2. Each stage is described here.

Stage 1: Preparation for Work (Age 0–25)   The major tasks during this period involve forming and defining an idea of the occupations one would like to engage in, and making necessary preparations for entry into those occupations. These activities include assessing possible occupations, selecting an occupation, and obtaining the necessary education. A great deal of research has been done to identify the factors that influence occupational choice, with at least nine theories offered (Brown, Brooks, et al., 1990). The choices one makes during this stage represent initial decisions rather than final ones, and establish the first direction of the individual's career (Greenhaus, 1987).

Stage 2: Organizational Entry (Ages 18–25)   At this stage, the individual selects a job and an organization in which to begin employment in the chosen career field. The amount and quality of information obtained can affect whether the initial job choice will be a fulfilling introduction to one's career or a disappointing false start. Among the obstacles the individual faces in this stage are initial job challenge (is it sufficient?), initial job satisfaction (typically lower than at later career stages, due to the disparity between initial expectations and organizational realities), and organizational socialization (becoming an insider).

The last three career stages in the model are organized around Levinson's life eras (e.g., early adulthood, middle adulthood, and late adulthood). Greenhaus believes these eras each present significant issues that affect a career.

TABLE 11-2	GREENHAUS'S FIVE-STAGE MODEL OF CAREER DEVELOPMENT

Stage 1. Preparation for Work

Typical Age Range: 0–25
Major Tasks: Develop occupational self-image, assess alternative occupations; develop initial occupational choice; pursue necessary education.

Stage 2. Organizational Entry

Typical Age Range: 18–25
Major Tasks: Obtain job offer(s) from desired organization(s); select appropriate job based on accurate information.

Stage 3. Early Career: Establishment and Achievement

Typical Age Range: 25–40
Major Tasks: Learn job; learn organizational rules and norms; fit into chosen occupation and organization; increase competence; pursue Dream.

Stage 4. Mid-Career

Typical Age Range: 40–55
Major Tasks: Reappraise early career and early adulthood; reaffirm or modify Dream; make choices appropriate to middle adult years; remain productive in work.

Stage 5. Late Career

Typical Age Range: 55–retirement
Major Tasks: Remain productive in work; maintain self-esteem; prepare for effective retirement.

SOURCE: From *Career Management* (p. 87) by J. H. Greenhaus, 1987, Hinsdale, IL: The Dryden Press.

Stage 3: The Early Career (Age 25–40)   During this stage, the individual is dealing with finding a place in the world and pursuing his or her life dream; this also involves becoming established in a career and in an organization. The specific challenges that must be met to do this include becoming technically proficient and becoming assimilated into an organization's culture (that is, learning its norms, values, and expectations). Successful resolution of these challenges can result in job satisfaction, advancement in terms of position and responsibility, and increased financial and social rewards. In short, the early career stage is about becoming established and "making it."

Stage 4: The Mid-Career (Age 40–55)   Following Levinson's model, the mid-career stage begins at the same time as the midlife transition. Therefore, one of the tasks the individual faces at mid-career is a reexamination of the life structure and choices that were adopted during the early career. The individual may reaffirm or modify the Dream, make choices appropriate to middle adulthood, and remain productive at work. These challenges are congruent with the popular notion of a "mid-career crisis." The crisis may be severe for some and not even seen as a crisis by others. Two events that often occur during the mid-career are *plateauing* (a lack of significant increases in responsibility and/or job advancement) and *obsolescence* (finding one's skills are not sufficient to perform tasks required by technological change). As stated earlier, the individual who successfully resolves these challenges will remain productive, while one who does not will experience frustration and stagnation.

Stage 5: The Late Career (Age 55–Retirement)   The individual faces two challenges during the late career. First, he or she must strive to remain productive and maintain a sense of self-esteem. This can sometimes be hampered by the negative (and incorrect) beliefs society has regarding the performance and capabilities of older workers. Second, this individual faces the challenge of disengaging from work and retiring. Retirement brings many emotional, financial, and social changes, and should be planned for well in advance of the actual retirement date. Given current trends in social security, the abolition of the mandatory retirement age, instability in the banking system, and questions about the management of pension funds, many people in the future will be facing a career without a planned retirement. Rather than retirement, the individual may have to deal with occupational change at the age their parents were dealing with a shift from work to non-work. On the other hand, pressures toward early retirement by organizations trying to reduce personnel costs may at the same time force some workers into retirement sooner than planned, creating an additional set of problems.

Greenhaus's model is useful for identifying the normal, or typical, sequence of events that occur within one's working life. Some individuals, such as those who begin new occupations late in life, will deviate from the age ranges suggested in the model. However, even though the ages will vary, the challenges are likely to stay the same. For example, is establishment as an actor at age 22 that much different from establishment as a politician at age 45? It is important to note that this model does not attempt to describe what an ideal career should be like, only what is likely to happen as it proceeds. It should be clear that the notion of the ideal in a career will vary from individual to individual.

Life Stage and Career Stage Models as Conceptual Base for Career Development

Taken together, the models of life stages and career stages provide a rich foundation for the practice of career development. By understanding the issues raised in these models, individuals can anticipate and manage the transitions they will experience during their lives. Similarly, this knowledge can help organizations develop strategies and tactics to manage the career transitions their employees will experience in a way that will both meet the organization's HR needs and satisfy the needs of employees.

The Process of Career Management

So far, we have discussed issues that provide a context within which career management occurs. We turn our attention now to the specific activities individuals and organizations can use to actively manage careers. As discussed earlier, career management involves both planning for career activities and putting those plans into action. Figure 11-3 presents a model that depicts the decisions and activities involved in this process (Greenhaus, 1987), one that we feel provides an excellent guide for career management in organizations.

FIGURE 11-3   **A MODEL OF CAREER MANAGEMENT**

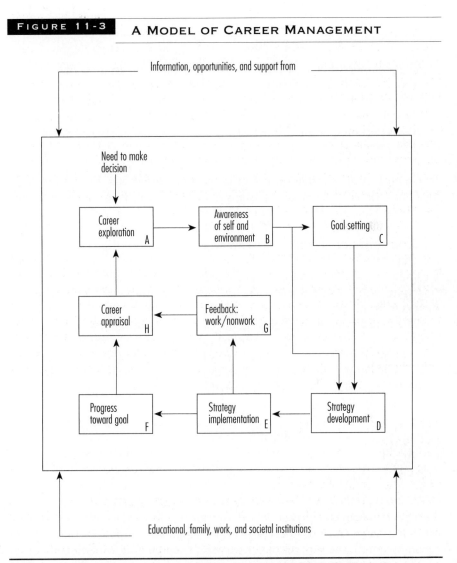

SOURCE: From *Career Management* (p. 18) by J. H. Greenhaus, 1987, Hinsdale, IL: The Dryden Press.

Greenhaus (1987) states that this model represents the ideal career management process—the way he believes people should conduct career management, not a description of what the typical person actually does. The model states that effective career management begins as the individual responds to the need to make a career decision. That response includes eight activities: career exploration, awareness of self and environment, goal setting, strategy development, strategy implementation, progress toward the goal, feedback from work and non-work sources, and career appraisal. These activities are described in greater detail in Table 11-3. To perform them, the individual uses information, opportunities, and support both from family and from educational, work and societal institutions. The model suggests career management occurs in a series of steps, though the order of progression through these steps may vary. The process may be summed up this way:

> [T]he career management cycle is a problem-solving, decision-making process. Information is gathered so individuals can become more aware of themselves, and the world around them. Goals are established, plans or strategies are developed and implemented, and feedback is obtained to provide more information for ongoing career management (Greenhaus, 1987, p. 20).

It is important to note that the career management process is cyclical and ongoing. The need to make career decisions can result from changes within the individual (e.g., questioning done at mid-career), and changes in the environment (e.g., organizational decisions such as firing and downsizing).

As discussed earlier, individual advancement and satisfaction may not be reliable indicators of success. Effective application of the career management model, including knowledge of both self and the environment, realism of goals, career strategies, and continual feedback, are more meaningful indicators of career success (Greenhaus, 1987).

We believe following such a model can assist both the individual and the organization in understanding what should be done to effectively manage careers. Obviously, it is to the individual's benefit to establish and work toward career goals. But it is also beneficial for organizations to manage careers in this way. The organization's needs are likely to change over time, given loss of key personnel through turnover and retirement and responding to competitive and other environmental challenges. Assisting employees in career management can help the organization ensure that human resources available will be adequate to perform important tasks and accomplish organizational objectives.

The Supervisor's Role in Career Management

The career management process just described presents a number of opportunities for managers and supervisors to become involved. For example, during career appraisal, the supervisor can serve as a source of information about the employee's capabilities and limitations through performance evaluations. Also,

TABLE 11-3	CAREER MANAGEMENT ACTIVITIES

1. **Career exploration.** Career exploration involves gathering information about one's self and the environment. For example, a young woman engaged in career exploration would collect information about her skills, values, and preferences as well as information about the possible jobs and organizations available to her in the environment.

2. **Awareness of self and environment.** Successful career exploration will lead the individual to a deeper self-awareness and an understanding of both opportunities and constraints present in the environment. This awareness of self and environment can lead the individual to set or revise career goals, or, if such goals are already set, it would lead to strategy development.

3. **Goal setting.** A career goal is an outcome the individual decides to try to obtain. Such goals may be specific (e.g., I want to become a partner in my accounting firm by age 35) or general (e.g., I want to be a successful and respected chef). To the extent career goals are based on an awareness of the self and environment, they are likely to be realistic.

4. **Strategy development.** A career strategy is an action plan for accomplishing the career goal. An effective strategy should include the actions that should be carried out and a timetable for performing them. Many of the HRD practices and programs presented in this book can serve as part of an individual's career strategy. For example, a police officer whose career goal is to become a police sergeant may develop a strategy that includes attending college and other training courses and successfully completing the sergeant's examination. The strategy will be more effective if it is based on realistic self-awareness and environmental awareness. Greenhaus (1987) lists seven career strategies: competency in the current job, increased involvement in work, developing skills, developing opportunities, cultivating mentor relationships, image building, and engaging in organizational politics.

5. **Strategy implementation.** Strategy implementation involves carrying out the strategy the individual has developed. Following a realistic strategy as opposed to acting without a clearly defined plan increases the likelihood of attaining the career goal. It is easier to get where you want to go if you have a plan to follow. However, some people may develop elaborate plans, but then fail to implement them. Strategy implementation can lead to progress toward the goal and feedback from work and nonwork sources.

6. **Progress toward the goal.** This is the extent to which the individual is nearing the career goal.

7. **Feedback from work and nonwork sources.** Valuable information about the progress toward the career goal can be obtained from both work sources—such as co-workers, supervisors, and specialists—and nonwork sources—such as friends, family, and teachers.

8. **Career appraisal.** Feedback and information on progress toward the career goal permit the individual to appraise his or her career. This appraisal leads to reengagement in career exploration, and the career management process continues with another cycle of activities.

SOURCE: From *Career Management* (p. 19–20) by J. H. Greenhaus, 1987, Hinsdale, IL: The Dryden Press.

the supervisor can provide accurate information about career paths and opportunities within the organization, support the employee's career plans (e.g., nominate the employee for training, adjust the employee's schedule to permit attendance in a training program), and serve as a key source of feedback to the employee on career progress.

Based on analysis of critical incidents gathered from employees, Leibowitz and Schlossberg (1981) identified four roles managers and supervisors should be trained to perform to fulfill their responsibility as career developers. These roles include:

1. **Coach**—one who listens, clarifies, probes, and defines employee career concerns

2. **Appraiser**—one who gives feedback, clarifies performance standards and job responsibilities

3. **Adviser**—one who generates options, helps set goals, makes recommendations, gives advice

4. **Referral Agent**—one who consults with employee on action plan and links the employee to available organizational people and resources.

Supervisor involvement has been cited as a key component of successful career development programs (e.g., Leibowitz, Feldman, & Mosley, 1992; Russell, 1984). An outline of a training design that can be used to prepare managers and supervisors for this important role (Leibowitz et al., 1986) is presented in Table 11-4.

In the next section of this chapter, we will present some common career development practices and activities currently used in organizations. These practices can serve multiple purposes in the career management process.

Career Development Practices and Activities

Organizations have a wide range of possible career development tools and activities to choose from. Some of these, such as self-awareness workshops, are intended primarily for career development, while others, such as recruitment, are a part of normal HR management activities. A working model that depicts the subprocesses underlying career development activities (Gutteridge & Otte, 1983) is shown in Figure 11-4. The subprocesses that concern the individual include occupational choice, organizational choice, choice of job assignment, and career self-development. The subprocesses that concern the organization include recruitment and selection, human resource allocation, performance appraisal, and training and development activities.

Gutteridge (1986) placed organizational career development tools and activities into five categories: self-assessment tools, individual counseling, internal labor market information/placement exchanges, potential assessment processes,

TABLE 11-4	DESIGN FOR TRAINING MANAGERS AND SUPERVISORS FOR THEIR ROLE IN CAREER DEVELOPMENT

Day 1

Overview of program
Goals and objectives
The career development model
Assessing manager strengths in career coaching
The role of the coach
Practicing coaching skills and behaviors
The role of appraiser
Practicing appraising skills

Day 2

The role of the adviser: understanding the organization
Multiple goal setting
The role of the referral agent: force field analysis
The development plan
The four Cs of career discussions: climate building, clarifying, collaborating, and closing
Closure/evaluation

SOURCE: From *Designing Career Development Systems* (p. 130) by Z. B. Leibowitz, C. Farren, and B. L. Kaye, 1986, San Francisco: Jossey-Bass.

and developmental programs. Table 11-5 lists the categories and the career development practices included within each category.

For clarity of presentation, we will use this typology as a framework for describing these activities and will discuss various types of career development practices separately. However, it is important to keep in mind that many organizations use these tools and activities as a part of an overall career development program or strategy. For example, organizations such as Mattel, NASA, Gulf Oil, and AT&T all have integrated career development programs that use a variety of activities.

Self-Assessment Tools and Activities

Self-assessment activities are among the most commonly used career development interventions (Gutteridge & Otte, 1983). These activities, which can include self-study workbooks or career planning workshops, focus on providing the individual with a systematic way to identify capabilities and career preferences. Self-assessment is best used as a first step in the career management process (at the stage of self-exploration) rather than as the only activity in a career management program (Gutteridge, 1986; Leibowitz, Farren, & Kaye, 1986). Self-assessment activities can be done by the individual alone, in groups, or in some arrangement combining the two. Effective self-assessment should (1) set the stage for the self-assessment experience, and (2) help the individual explore

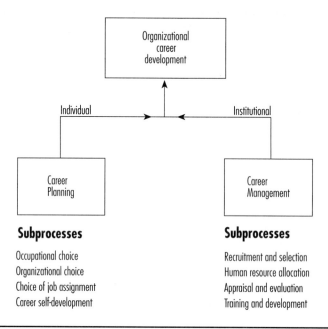

SOURCE: From *Organizational Career Development: State of the Practice* (p. 7) by T. G. Gutteridge and F. L. Otte, 1983, Washington, DC: ASTD Press.

his or her values, interests, skills, feelings, personal resources, goals for timing, and decision-making styles (Smith, 1988). This information can help answer questions such as, "Who am I?" "What do I want out of my life and my career?" and "How can I achieve my career goals?"

Self-assessment workbooks provide information and a series of exercises to help an individual discover his or her values, abilities, and preferences. These workbooks can be purchased from a third party or designed specifically for the organization. For example, the best-selling book, *What Color Is Your Parachute?* (Bolles, 1991), includes a series of self-discovery exercises along with information about various occupations and job search skills. Similarly, *The Self Directed Search* (Holland, 1977) helps the individual identify his or her interests and can suggest possible occupations that match these interests.

Self-assessment exercises developed by third-party sources have the advantages of being readily available and of being designed by career development experts. However, they are not specifically designed to fit within the organization's HRD and career development strategy. The HRD staff may need to develop supplementary material to fill these gaps.

Workbooks designed to complement the organization's overall HRD strategy may better make employees aware of resources and opportunities within the organization. Such workbooks can include:

TABLE 11-5	ORGANIZATIONAL CAREER DEVELOPMENT TOOLS

A. Self-Assessment Tools
   1. Career planning workshops
   2. Career workbooks
   3. Preretirement workshops

B. Individual Counseling
   1. Personnel staff
   2. Professional counselor (internal and external)
   3. Outplacement
   4. Supervisor or manager

C. Internal Labor Market Information/Job Placement Exchanges
   1. Job posting
   2. Skills inventories
   3. Career ladders/career-path planning
   4. Career resource center
   5. Other career communications formats

D. Organizational Potential Assessment Processes
   1. Assessment centers
   2. Promotability forecasts
   3. Replacement/succession planning
   4. Psychological testing

E. Developmental Programs
   1. Job rotation
   2. In-house human resource development programs
   3. External seminars/workshops
   4. Tuition reimbursement/educational assistance
   5. Supervisor training in career counseling
   6. Dual-career programs
   7. Mentoring programs

SOURCE: From *Organizational Career Development Systems: State of the Practice*, (p. 61) by T. G. Gutteridge and F. L. Otte, 1983, Washington, DC: ASTD.

1. A statement of the organization's career development policy and associated procedures;

2. Information on the organization's structure, career paths, and job specifications;

3. Information about related training, education, and development programs; and

4. Instructions on how employees can obtain further information within the organization, such as names, addresses and phone numbers of resource persons within the organization (Burack & Mathys, 1980).

The activities included within a workbook can also be delivered via computer. For example, the U.S. Army uses a microcomputer-based self-assessment system for officers called Officer Career Information and Planning System (OCIPS), and the American College Testing Program publishes a microcomputer-based system called DISCOVER. Each of these programs provides career information and self-discovery exercises similar to those found in workbooks.

One of the advantages of using self-assessment workbooks and computer programs is that they can be completed at the employee's convenience. However, it can also be beneficial to provide self-assessment information in an interactive group session where employees can share and discuss their insights. Career planning and preretirement workshops are well suited for this purpose. Table 11-6 provides a more extensive list of the advantages and disadvantages of using career awareness workbooks.

TABLE 11-6   ADVANTAGES AND DISADVANTAGES OF CAREER AWARENESS WORKBOOKS

A. Advantages

1. Provides a structured approach to career planning which is self-scheduled and self-paced.
2. Can be used alone or as a supplement to other career development approaches. Can extend the efficiency and effectiveness of career workshops and career counseling.
3. Amenable to low cost, mass use with individuals at various organizational layers and in various life/career stages.
4. Completely private; no breach of confidentiality possible.
5. Responds to need to conduct career planning over a span of time rather than in one or two concentrated settings.
6. Can be customized to incorporate organizational data.
7. Emphasizes learning through self-initiated exploration and discovery.
8. Scheduling and convening of individuals in groups is unnecessary.

B. Disadvantages

1. Some individuals will be too impatient to work through all the materials.
2. Can be a lonely experience. Many individuals need support groups for critique, feedback, and reinforcement.
3. Frequently, workbooks overemphasize career planning at expense of plan execution.
4. It can be difficult to tie career workbook into other segments of career development process, e.g., supervisory career discussions.
5. Usually, a career workbook assumes all career problems are alike. Thus, it fails to respond to unique needs of specific target groups, e.g., women, minorities, mid-career employees.
6. Individuals who fear initiating contacts with others may fail to extend their learning beyond the boundaries of their own self-knowledge.
7. Considerable start-up investment.

SOURCE: From *Organizational Career Development: State of the Practice* (p. 56) by T. G. Gutteridge and F. L. Otte, 1983, Washington, DC: ASTD Press. Copyright 1983, the American Society for Training and Development. Reprinted with permission.

Like other self-assessment approaches, career planning workshops provide a structured experience in which participants develop, share, and discuss personal information about their strengths and weaknesses, goals, and values (Gutteridge, 1986). Workshops can be comprised of one or more sessions that focus on what career planning and management is all about, self-discovery, reality testing of insights gained during self-discovery through discussions with the facilitator and other participants, identification of possible career directions and opportunities, and career goal setting (Leibowitz et al., 1986).

A list of the advantages and disadvantages of group career awareness workshops is provided in Table 11-7. The advantages of workshops include the ability to reach many people at once, opportunities to gain support from peers and develop networks, and obtaining the ideas and reactions of others. In addition, feedback from the facilitator and other group members may help the individual recognize any self-deception or self-ignorance that might go undetected if a self-assessment workbook were used alone. Potential disadvantages include

| **TABLE 11-7** | **ADVANTAGES AND DISADVANTAGES OF GROUP CAREER AWARENESS WORKSHOPS** |

A. Advantages

1. Provides a definitive structure for career planning, thereby enhancing likelihood participant will complete planning task.
2. By virtue of a pre-scheduled time and place, the workshop helps participants decide when they will take the time to do career planning.
3. Useful vehicle for communicating organization's career philosophy.
4. Demonstrates a visible commitment to career development on part of organization.
5. Provides participants an opportunity to learn from each other.
6. Provides non-threatening setting within which participant can do some reality testing.
7. The interaction itself can be fun in a group setting.

B. Disadvantages

1. Logistics and costs of convening a critical mass of participants may be impractical or prohibitive.
2. Unless well-designed and conducted, workshop can be fun, yet unproductive.
3. Usually, the most important career thinking cannot be done during one or two concentrated sessions; the career choice process requires a span of time to complete.
4. Some of the most important career planning competencies cannot be adequately learned in a classroom setting, e.g., self-initiated exploration and reality testing must be practiced on the job or at home.
5. Participants may not be ready or willing to do many of the same things at the same time due to age group differences, differing career stages, learning styles, etc.
6. Getting people together from the same firm to do career planning can lead to some embarrassing questions.

SOURCE: From *Organizational Career Development: State of the Practice* (p. 56) by T. G. Gutteridge and F. L. Otte, 1983, Washington, DC: ASTD Press. Copyright 1983, the American Society for Training and Development. Reprinted with permission.

scheduling problems, difficulty in designing an experience that suits all the participants' needs (especially if they come from different organizational levels), and the possibility that some may be intimidated by the group setting (Leibowitz et al., 1986).

If performed effectively, self-assessment activities can provide the individual with a sound basis on which to develop realistic career goals and strategies. As suggested by the career management model presented earlier in the chapter, self-assessment and evaluation of the environment are important first steps in establishing effective career goals and strategies. Career counseling and information about the internal labor market can also provide useful information for this task. These career management activities will be discussed next.

Individual Career Counseling

Individual career counseling involves one-on-one discussions between the employee and an organizational representative. A survey by Gutteridge and Otte (1983) revealed that organizations used a variety of people as counselors, including supervisors, managers, specially trained HRD professionals, and outside professional counselors. They also reported that counseling sessions ranged from brief, informal talks, to the annual performance evaluation discussion to a series of discussions with a manager or counseling professional.

Individualized counseling can be used to answer a wide range of questions and can either stand alone or supplement other career development activities. Burack and Mathys (1980) suggest the counseling process is made up of three stages:

1. **Opening and probing.** This stage establishes rapport and determines the employee's goals for the counseling session(s).

2. **Understanding and focusing.** This includes providing assistance in self-assessment and establishing career goals and strategies.

3. **Programming.** This stage provides support for implementing the career strategy.

During this process, the counselor can suggest actions to the employee and provide support and feedback about the ideas and results of actions taken by the employee.

Counseling can be used for continuing employees as well as employees who are approaching retirement, are laid off, or are terminated. **Outplacement** counseling focuses on assisting terminated employees in making the transition to a new organization (Gutteridge, 1986). The use of outplacement counseling has become widespread during the 1980s and 1990s, especially in the wake of the downsizing, mergers, and acquisitions that organizations experienced during this period. These sessions can focus on job-search skills, stress management, and career planning. Of all the forms of individualized counseling, outplacement counseling is the most likely to be performed by a counselor who is not an organization member. Many consulting firms offer outplacement services for hire.

Preretirement counseling involves activities that help employees prepare for the transition from work to nonwork. As stated earlier, retirement is filled with great uncertainty on both the personal and financial levels. Preretirement counseling programs typically involve discussions about financial planning, social adjustment, family issues, and preparing for leisure activities.

An important issue in individualized counseling centers on the individual selected to be the counselor. In some ways, managers and supervisors are well suited to serve as counselors. They are knowledgeable about the organization and should be familiar with the employee's performance and some of his or her capabilities. In addition, they are in an ideal position to offer support and follow up on actions taken by the employee. However, there are disadvantages to using supervisors and managers as career counselors. First, unless they receive training in career development issues and counseling skills such as listening, questioning, and clarification, they may lack the skills to perform effective counseling. Second, even with training, some supervisors and managers lack the abilities and/or desire to perform the task well. They may view it as an added burden and may not be rewarded by the organization for performing it. Finally, employees may be reluctant to discuss their career plans with current bosses or take advice from a nonprofessional (Leibowitz et al., 1986).

Gutteridge (1986) suggests that if managers and supervisors are to be used as counselors, the following steps should be taken:

1. Their role in the career development process must be clarified;

2. They must be trained to perform this role;

3. They must have the opportunity to discuss their own career development concerns; and

4. The role of counselor/developer should be incorporated into the organizational reward system (e.g., included in managers' performance evaluations).

One element of this approach is used at Metropolitan Life, where the performance evaluation process for managers and supervisors includes an evaluation of how well they perform employee development.

Internal Labor Market Information/Job Placement Exchanges

Employees engaged in career planning need accurate environmental information in addition to an accurate self-assessment. To this end, the organization should provide employees with information about job opportunities within the organization. Two commonly used methods of doing this are job-posting systems and establishing career paths.

Job posting involves making open positions in the organization known to current employees before advertising them to outsiders. In a typical job posting program, the organization publishes the job description, job requirements, pay range, an application procedure for vacancies, and provides a form for employees to submit. The vacancies can either be posted in a common area, such as near the cafeteria, or on a bulletin board reserved for that purpose. Interested employees can then apply and be considered for the vacant positions. Job posting systems are widely used in both government and private organizations.

Job posting is a source of career information as well as a recruiting and selection tool. Employees can learn which skills and abilities are needed for various positions and can use that information as a springboard for career development discussions and to establish career goals and strategies. If they are administered openly and fairly, job postings can help employees realize they have a future in the organization and can improve morale. However, job posting systems can also create problems if employees suspect only low-level or undesirable positions are being posted, or if the job requirements listed are rigged to ensure an "inside" candidate is the only one qualified for a position.

A **career path** is a sequence of jobs, usually involving related tasks and experiences, that employees move through over time (Walker, 1976). For example, a career path in a city police department may include the positions of patrol officer, desk sergeant, lieutenant, captain, and chief of police. Career paths communicate to employees the possibilities for job movement. Together with job descriptions and job specifications, these paths can aid the employee in developing a career strategy.

Career paths can be developed using either a political/traditional or a job/behavioral approach (Shippeck & Taylor, 1985). In the political/traditional approach, the career path represents what has typically happened in the organization and usually represents a consensus among managers about logical job movements within a particular department. For example, if computer operators typically become technical advisors before becoming supervisors, the career path will reflect this. In the job/behavioral approach, the path is created by analyzing the similarities and differences among jobs in the organization. For example, if the positions of market research analyst and personnel research analyst require similar skills, these jobs may be listed on the same career path even though they exist in different departments. The job/behavior approach can include jobs from throughout the organization and, as a result, open up more possibilities for movement than the traditional approach (Shippeck & Taylor, 1985).

Some organizations use a dual career path or dual-track system in which the path to greater responsibility includes both management and nonmanagement tracks. The presence of nonmanagement paths, with relatively equivalent esteem and pay, can serve the needs of employees who either lack the skills or the desire to become managers, and open up more possibilities than the traditional pyramid structure provides (Tucker, Moravec, & Ideus, 1992).

While career paths can help provide information to employees as to career progression possibilities, they may rely too much on what the organization has typically done rather than what it is likely to need in the future (Gutteridge, 1986). And, given the trend toward reducing the layers of management in organizations, vertical progressions will be shorter and therefore unavailable to many employees. To guard against this, career paths should be developed within the context of human resource planning and strategic planning activities. In addition, care should be taken to identify possible lateral career movement. This is included in the career grid approach (Walker, 1992), in which career grids, based on job content, specify possible vertical and horizontal sequences of positions employees may hold. The grids can communicate not only the potential paths, but the competencies required for each position in the paths and developmental ideas for moving through these positions as well (Tucker, Moravec, & Ideus, 1992). From the organization's point of view, this approach is beneficial in that it provides skilled and valued employees (e.g., the organization's top engineers or accountants) a career option that promises progression while allowing them to remain in their specialty. It also provides a learning and developmental incentive for employees who lack the skills or desire to become managers.

Beyond using career paths and job posting, internal information can also be supplemented by publishing booklets and flyers that inform employees of career enhancement possibilities. Knowledge of available resources such as upcoming training programs and tuition assistance programs can help employees develop and implement their career strategy.

Another source of internal labor market information useful to organizations is a **skills inventory** (Kaumeyer, 1979). A skills inventory is a database that contains information about employee skills, education, performance evaluation, and career preferences. The HRD department can use this information during the organizational needs assessment phase to identify the capabilities of the work force and pinpoint any skill shortages that should be addressed. Skills inventory information is usually collected from voluntary reports from employees. Potential shortcomings of voluntary self-reports include the possibility of incomplete, inaccurate, or outdated information.

Organization Potential Assessments

Organizations have a vested interest in ensuring that they have available individuals who are ready to fill key positions when these positions become vacant. To this end, many organizations evaluate the *potential*, or *promotability*, of managerial, professional, and technical employees. Those judged as high-potential employees can then be "groomed" for these positions. Three ways **potential assessment** can be done are through potential ratings, assessment centers, and succession planning.

Potential ratings are similar to employee performance evaluations. They are typically performed by the employee's manager or supervisor, measure multiple dimensions, and include a summary or overall rating of the employee's potential for advancement. The main difference between potential ratings and performance ratings is that potential ratings focus on the future rather than the past or present. This requires the rater to judge whether the employee is likely to be successful in jobs requiring skills he or she may not currently use. Also, the results of potential evaluations are unlikely to be made known to the employee. Ratings of potential are subject to the same problems as performance evaluations (i.e., rating errors) and raters should be trained in the proper way to conduct the evaluation.

Assessment centers, which can be used as employee selection tools, can also be used to assess potential for advancement (Boehm, 1988). In an assessment center, small groups of employees perform a variety of exercises while being evaluated by a group of trained assessors. The exercises can include simulations, group discussions, tests, and interviews. The exercises used are chosen to ensure that relevant skills and aptitudes can be measured. The assessors are typically managers who are one or two organizational levels above the assessees and are specifically trained for this task. The assessors write a detailed report on each assessee and usually make an overall judgment about the assessee's promotability. When used for developmental purposes, the intensive assessment feedback is provided to the employee to increase self-awareness. The feedback from a developmental assessment center can be used by the employee to develop career goals and strategy. While career development assessment centers can be expensive to use, they provide a rich source of data. Care should be taken in designing these centers to include assessment of skills that can be developed in a reasonable amount of time and to include exercises that permit multiple opportunities to observe participants in each dimension (Thornton, 1992). Examples of this approach include developmental assessment centers at AT&T (Cairo & Lyness, 1988) and Kimberly Brothers Manufacturing Company (Thornton, 1992).

Succession plans are a third way of conducting potential evaluations. Succession planning, which is usually done for senior management positions, requires senior managers to identify employees who should be developed to replace them. Information generated during succession planning may not be communicated to the employee. If potential evaluations are made known to the employee and his or her superiors, this information can be used to create a self-fulfilling prophecy. That is, if managers believe the employee has high potential for advancement, they may be more likely to evaluate this person favorably and promote them more quickly than actual performance warrants (Schein, 1987a). On the other hand, if succession plans are not communicated to the employee, the organization runs the risk of a mismatch between the employee's career plans and its plans for the employee. Making this information available to the employee can ensure that the employee develops realistic career plans (Leibowitz et al., 1986) and reduces the chances an employee will refuse a position the organization was planning that he or she fill.

Developmental Programs

The final group of career management activities we will examine concerns developmental programs. These include job rotation, in-house HRD programs, external workshops and seminars, tuition assistance and reimbursement plans, and mentoring programs. These programs provide the employee with opportunities to learn new ideas and skills, thus preparing them for future positions as well as introducing new challenges.

Job rotation involves assigning an employee to a series of jobs in different functional areas of the organization. These assignments are typically lateral rather than vertical moves, and can involve service on task forces and movement from line to staff positions. Job rotation is a good way to introduce variety into an employee's career, particularly if the employee has become bored with the current work assignment, as may be the case at mid-career. In addition, it provides the employee with a chance to learn and use new skills and to better understand different organizational functions. It can also serve to help the employee build networks within the organization. Care should be taken to ensure that the job assignments used in job rotation offer developmental opportunities rather than just the chance to do something different (White, 1992).

Mentoring refers to a relationship between a junior and senior member of the organization that contributes to the career development of both members. Mentoring relationships can be important from both a life development and career development perspective. From a life development perspective, recall from Levinson's Era approach to adult development that young adults seek to establish meaningful relationships, while middle-aged adults want to make an impact on the generation to follow them. From a career development perspective, the younger employee wishes to become established in the organization, while the middle-aged employee wants to remain productive at work and make choices appropriate to his or her stage in life. From either perspective, the mentor relationship serves the needs of both members.

The mentoring relationship serves both career and psychosocial (e.g., social support) functions (Kram, 1986; Noe, 1988; Scandura, 1992). The mentor provides the protege with career support, opening doors, teaching the ropes of the organization, creating potential opportunities to demonstrate competence, enhancing visibility, and ensuring the protege has challenging work. The protege provides the mentor with a meaningful, mutually reinforcing relationship that demonstrates both parties' commitment and value to the organization. The mentor has a chance to serve as a role model and share what he or she knows with someone who can benefit from such knowledge. In return, the mentor receives respect, support, and in many cases, friendship.

In many organizations, mentoring relationships are formed as a result of mutual attraction between the two parties. Some organizations, such as the Internal Revenue Service (Klauss, 1979) and Federal Express (Lean, 1983), have created formal mentoring programs in which mentors and proteges are paired by the organization and provided with support for the relationship. An example of a formal mentoring program is shown in Table 11-8.

Research has shown mentoring can yield these organizational benefits:

1. Facilitate socialization of new members in the organization;

2. Reduce turnover;

3. Minimize mid-career adjustments;

4. Enhance transfer of beneficial knowledge and values; and

5. Facilitate adjustment to retirement (Kram, 1986).

Mentoring relationships are complex. While they serve a variety of needs for both mentor and protege, they are subject to potential limitations and problems. Limitations of formal mentoring programs include the small number of

TABLE 11-8	EXAMPLE OF A FORMAL MENTORING PROGRAM

Sample Implementation

1. Define a population for whom relationships should be established. Invite potential mentors and proteges to help define the criteria for matching pairs and the process for doing so.

2. Collect data on potential participants that are needed to maximize an effective matching process (such as career goals, performance records, developmental needs).

3. Assign juniors and seniors to each other *or* foster a voluntary selection process. Provide guidelines on goals of the program, role expectations, and staff support services, and encourage participation in relevant educational offerings.

4. Set up monitoring procedures for providing feedback to the organization concerning how the program affects employee development over time.

Advantages	Disadvantages
• Ensures that juniors and seniors find each other.	• Individuals may feel coerced and confused about responsibilities.
• Increases the likelihood that matches will be good ones.	• Those who are not matched feel deprived and pessimistic about their futures.
• Provides ongoing support to the pairs.	
• Makes mentoring relationships legitimate and more accessible.	• Assumes that volunteers can learn the requisite skills; some may be ill suited.
	• Destructive dynamics may evolve within formal pairs or with immediate supervisors.

SOURCE: From "Mentoring in the Workplace" by K. E. Kram, 1986, in D. T. Hall and associates (Eds.), *Career Development in Organizations* (p. 183). San Francisco: Jossey-Bass.

mentor pairs that they can accommodate, the depth and scope of mentor-protege relationships, and unintended negative consequences (e.g., dissatisfaction with the relationship, negative feelings of those not involved in the program) (Kram & Bragar, 1992). There may also be problems in cross-gender mentoring relationships (Ragins, 1989). Research on cross-gender mentoring suggests that:

1. Concern exists between the parties about intimacy and sexual attraction (Kram, 1985; Bowen, 1985).

2. There is an inclination for men and women to rely on sex-role stereotypes (Kanter, 1977).

3. Dissatisfaction with the role-modeling aspect of the relationship may be felt (Kanter, 1977).

4. The relationship is subject to public scrutiny (e.g., jealous spouses, office gossip) (Bowen, 1985).

5. Peer resentment may occur (Kram, 1985; Bowen, 1985).

However, two recent studies (Dreher & Ash, 1990; Whitely, Dougherty, & Dreher, 1992) have found no gender differences in the amount of career mentoring that proteges receive.

Research on cross-racial mentoring also suggests problems. Thomas (1990) found that black proteges with white mentors reported less satisfaction with the mentoring relationship and less support than did members of same-race mentoring relationships. Even within same-race and same-sex mentoring relationships, lack of support from the organization and incompatibility of the parties can undermine the relationship.

Given these problems, some authors have questioned the value of mentoring. Clawson (1985) argues that mentoring is not essential, and that employees can gain some of the same benefits by learning from their current supervisors while seeking sponsorship at the appropriate time from someone else. Kram (1986) recognizes that it may not be necessary to look for everything mentoring can provide in a single relationship. In addition, relationships with peers can also provide some of the same functions that relationships with mentors do (e.g., information, career strategies, emotional support, personal feedback) and may be more suitable for individuals without mentors or those who don't want mentors (Kram & Isabella, 1985).

Given the potential benefits for both the individual and the organization, we believe mentoring is a viable and appropriate career development strategy. If an organization choose to develop a formal mentoring program, three conditions seem to increase the chances of success (Kram & Bragar, 1992):

1. The program should be clearly linked to the business strategy and existing HR policies and practices so as to increase the chances potential participants and senior management will accept and actively support the program.

2. Core components of the program (objectives, guidelines, training and education, communication strategy, monitoring and evaluation, and coordination) should be designed for effectiveness rather than expediency.

3. Voluntary participation and flexible guidelines are critical to success.

In addition, Kram and Bragar (1992) suggest that formal mentoring programs be used as one part of an overall development strategy that is tied to strategic business needs and takes advantage of natural learning opportunities and HR systems that encourage mentoring.

Issues in Career Development

Several issues should be considered when formulating or modifying an organization's career development program. These include generating career motivation, career plateauing, career development for nonexempt workers, career development without advancement, and the effect of baby boomers' changing attitudes toward work and careers. We will discuss each of these issues briefly.

Developing Career Motivation

Developing career motivation is a significant goal of effective career management (London, 1983, 1985). According to London (1985, London & Mone, 1987) **career motivation** affects how people choose their careers, how they view their careers, how hard they work in them, and how long they stay in them. London (1985) sees career motivation as a set of characteristics grouped into three facets: career resilience, career insight, and career identity. Each of these facets is defined in Table 11-9. A person can have a high, moderate, or low level of career motivation depending on his or her position in each of these categories. For example, a person with high career motivation will continue to pursue career goals in the face of obstacles and setbacks (career resilience), formulate and pursue realistic career goals (career insight), and be highly involved in work and aggressively pursue career goals (career identity).

While career motivation is partly determined by the individual's life experiences, career activities and practices can help develop a person's career motivation. For example, self-awareness workbooks and personal journals can be used to build career insight. Because career motivation can affect both decision making and commitment to the career, it would be beneficial for organizations to offer career development activities to enhance such motivation. Table 11-10 provides some suggestions as to ways this can be accomplished.

The Career Plateau

The pyramidal structure of many organizations together with a shrinking number of management positions typically means that a time will come in an individual's career when he or she will no longer be able to "move up" in the organization. In addition, career progress is not likely to be a continuous upward journey, but rather one that includes periods of movement and periods of stability. These factors contribute to what has been termed a career plateau. Ferrence, Stoner, and Warren (1977) define a **career plateau** as "the point in a

---

TABLE 11-9   **DEFINITIONS OF THE THREE FACETS OF CAREER MOTIVATION**

1. **Career resilience**—the extent to which people resist career barriers or disruptions affecting their work. This consists of self-confidence, need for achievement, the willingness to take risks, and the ability to act independently and cooperatively as appropriate.

2. **Career insight**—the extent to which people are realistic about themselves and their careers and how these perceptions are related to career goals. This includes developing goals and gaining knowledge of the self and the environment.

3. **Career identity**—the extent to which people define themselves by their work. This includes involvement in job, organization, and profession and the direction of career goals (e.g., toward advancement in an organization).

SOURCE: From *Career Management and Survival in the Workplace* (p. 54) by M. London and E. M. Mone, 1987, San Francisco: Jossey-Bass.

TABLE 11-10	METHODS FOR INCREASING CAREER MOTIVATION

1. To support career resilience
  a. Build employees' self-confidence through feedback and positive reinforcement.
  b. Generate opportunities for achievement.
  c. Create an environment conducive to risk-taking by rewarding innovation and reducing fear of failure.
  d. Show interpersonal concern and encourage group cohesiveness and collaborative working relationships.

2. To enhance career insight
  a. Encourage employees to set their own goals.
  b. Supply employees with information relevant to attaining their career goals.
  c. Provide regular performance feedback.

3. To build career identity
  a. Encourage work involvement through job challenge and professional growth.
  b. Provide career development opportunities, such as leadership positions and advancement potential.
  c. Reward solid performance through professional recognition and/or financial bonus.

SOURCE: From "Career Development" by M. London, 1991, in K. N. Wexley and J. Hinrichs (Eds.), *Developing Human Resources* (pp. 5–159). Washington, DC: BNA Books.

career where the likelihood of additional hierarchical promotion is very low" (p. 602). Early writing on career plateaus suggested that this is a traumatic experience for many employees (especially those who desire career growth), accompanied by feelings of stress, frustration, failure, and guilt (e.g., Latack, 1984; Schein, 1978).

The empirical research on the consequences of career plateaus has been mixed, with some verification of negative consequences of plateauing coupled with some data to suggest employees at such a plateau can be happy and productive (see Feldman & Weitz, 1988, and Elsass & Ralston, 1989, for reviews). At least two explanations for these mixed findings have been offered. First, Feldman and Weitz (1988) argue that the factors that lead to a plateau affect the consequences of the plateau. For example, if employees become plateaued because they lack the skills and ability to advance, they will likely exhibit poor performance and job attitudes. Alternatively, if the plateau occurs because of self-imposed constraints or a low need for growth, the employee will likely continue to perform well and have positive job attitudes. Feldman and Weitz suggest a model (presented in Table 11-11) that specifies six causes of career plateaus together with their impact on performance and attitudes and possible managerial interventions to address them. While this model awaits empirical testing, it presents an encouraging and intuitively realistic explanation for and approach to career plateaus.

A second explanation for the mixed findings regarding the consequences of career plateaus, offered by Chao (1990), centers on the way the concept has

TABLE 11-11	CAUSES OF CAREER PLATEAUS AND SUGGESTED MANAGERIAL INTERVENTIONS

Source of Career Plateaus	Impact on Performance and Attitudes	Managerial Interventions
I. Individual Skills and Abilities		
Selection system deficiencies.	Poor performance.	Redesign of selection system.
Lack of training.	Poor job attitudes.	Improved training.
Inaccurate perceptions of feedback.		Improved performance appraisal and feedback systems.
II. Individual Needs and Values		
Low growth need strength.	Solid performance.	Continue to reward, contingent on no downturn in performance.
Career anchors of security and autonomy.	Good job attitudes.	Career information systems.
Self-imposed constraints.		
III. Lack of Intrinsic Motivation		
Lack of skill variety.	Minimally acceptable job performance.	Combining tasks.
Low task identity.	Declining job attitudes.	Forming natural work units.
Low task significance.		Establishing client relationships.
		Vertical loading.
		Opening feedback channels.

been measured. Studies have tended to operationally define a career plateau as a dichotomy (as in plateaued versus not plateaued) and have used job tenure (e.g., number of years since last promotion) to indicate whether the individual is plateaued. Chao (1990) observed that viewing plateaus as a dichotomy ignores the fact that individuals gradually become aware that careers are in plateau, and that different levels of awareness may lead to different consequences. Second, and more important, Chao argued that what is critical to defining career plateaus is the individual's perception of being plateaued, because the individual's perception of career progress will likely determine how he or she feels about it and reacts to it. Consequently, she hypothesized that a continuous perceptual measure of career plateaus will better explain the consequences of being plateaued than the traditional job tenure approach. Chao (1990) tested this hypothesis by developing a perceptual measure of plateauing and found that perception accounted for more variance in four outcomes (including satisfaction and career planning) than did job tenure. In addition, she also found that the negative effects of a plateau were worse during the early years of an employee's career.

Source of Career Plateaus	Impact on Performance and Attitudes	Managerial Interventions
IV. Lack of Extrinsic Rewards		
Small raises, few promotions.	Poor performance. Poor job attitudes.	Redesign of compensation system.
Inequities in reward systems.		Redesign of promotion policies.
Uncontingent rewards.		Encourage highly dissatisfied to leave.
V. Stress and Burnout		
Interpersonal relationships on job.	Poor performance. Poor job attitudes.	
Organizational climate.		Job rotation. Preventive stress management.
Role conflict.		
VI. Slow Organizational Growth		Sabbaticals; off-site training.
External business conditions.	Continued good performance in short-run.	Provide "stars" with increased resources.
"Defender" corporate strategy.	Declining job attitudes.	Provide poorer performers with incentives to leave or retire.
Inaccurate personnel forecasts.		

SOURCE: From "Career Plateaus Reconsidered" by D. C. Feldman and B. A. Weitz, 1988, *Journal of Management, 14,* p. 71.

Taken together, Feldman and Weitz's (1988) and Chao's (1990) findings suggest that career plateauing is more complex than previously thought. These findings suggest two implications for career development practice. HRD professionals should (1) assess whether employees are plateaued by determining employees' perceptions of the extent to which their careers are stalled and attempt to identify the reasons for the plateau, and (2) tailor the action used to resolve the employee's problem according to the cause of the plateau.

Career Development for Nonexempt Employees

While a great deal of the literature on career development focuses on the needs of and programs for developing managers and professionals, the career development needs of blue-collar and nonexempt employees (e.g., clerical and support staff and technicians, who are paid hourly or weekly rates and are entitled to overtime) have been almost completely ignored. One reason for this situation is the assumption by managers and HR professionals that these employees do not have long-term ambitions that need to be addressed (Leibowitz, Feldman, & Mosley, 1992). Given the great number of such employees and the critical role they play in organizational effectiveness, it would be wise for HRD professionals to consider career development activities that allow the organization to better use the potential of these employees and serve their long-term needs.

Some HRD professionals are beginning to examine this issue. A recent survey of career development professionals about the development needs of nonexempt employees revealed the following:

1. Job satisfaction often comes from the work itself, which can often be repetitive and unchallenging.

2. Changing current status (e.g., union to nonunion, blue-collar to white-collar) requires both a significant personal investment and a significant cultural adjustment. For example, white-collar positions may require higher education levels than blue-collar positions, and employees who cross the "collar line" may not receive the support they may need from co-workers.

3. Nonexempt employees may become more frustrated during their careers than exempt employees because opportunities to make a vertical transition are more limited and more difficult for them (Leibowitz, Feldman, & Mosley, 1992).

Some organizations, such as Corning and Lockheed Marine, have implemented career development programs for nonexempt employees to better serve them and at the same time ensure future manpower needs of the organization will be met. Both programs recognize that nonexempt employees need to be encouraged to take the initiative in their career development and be supported by management for doing so. Lockheed Marine's program includes career/life planning workshops (open to all employees), a career development resource center, and support for lifelong learning activities (e.g., tuition reimbursement for relevant courses, in-house seminars) (Russell, 1984). Corning's program includes four components: career exploration and planning software, videos, information books describing career possibilities at Corning, and supervisory training in career counseling (Leibowitz, Feldman, & Mosley, 1992). Both programs have been successful in terms of high levels of employee participation and greater levels of career development actions on the part of nonexempt employees.

Both of these programs serve as good examples of how organizations can address both their own needs and the career development needs of this large pool of employees. It is our hope that these initiatives stimulate more research and practice in this area.

Enrichment: Career Development without Advancement

Many organizations find themselves faced with the prospect of downsizing their workforces and reducing the numbers of management positions in response to competition and changing business conditions. Even with fewer employees, organizations will still have to engage in career development activities, because HR needs will change as business strategy and technology change. These forces increase the likelihood that organizations will have to develop career development programs without being able to offer upward movement or the promise of job security as benefits to employees. Instead, career development programs will have to focus on enriching employees in their current jobs and/or areas of expertise to increase employee satisfaction, maintain the skill base the organization needs, and to offer employees a sense of career security by providing the best chance of gaining meaningful employment if they are laid off (London, 1991).

Career development options within an enrichment strategy include (London, 1991):

1. Certification programs and mastery paths that specify selection criteria, and identify performance expectations, and training requirements to move through various levels of expertise within a job;

2. Retraining programs; and

3. Job transfers or rotation.

Enrichment programs not only raise the level of skills and professionalism of the workforce, but also can increase the employee's sense of self-esteem and sense of self-determination in guiding his or her own career.

Career Development and the Baby Boom Generation

One demographic change with which organizations must currently deal is the arrival of the baby boom generation (i.e., people born between 1946 and 1964) as the largest age cohort in the workforce (almost 55 percent; Kiechel, 1989). There is some evidence that members of this generation hold views toward work and careers that differ from previous generations (Hall & Richter, 1990). Baby boomers have been described as having:

1. A strong concern for basic values, especially in terms of questioning why they seek success and what it means to them personally;

2. A sense of freedom to act on their values;

3. A focus on self (e.g., a strong sense of self-awareness);

4. The need for autonomy and to question authority;

5. Less concern with advancement;

6. A need for high quality in the current job (called *crafting*);

7. Entrepreneurship; and

8. Concern with the work-family balance (taking a whole life perspective) (Hall & Richter, 1990).

To the extent these characteristics typify members of this generation, organizational career development practices and policies may need to be adapted to more effectively use the potential of this group. Hall and Richter (1990) proposed a list of guidelines for this purpose (shown in Table 11-12). For example, to take advantage of individuals with a strong focus on the self, organizations could stress ongoing career development activities that encourage self-development and lifelong learning. It seems reasonable for HRD professionals, by way of needs assessment, to determine the extent to which these characteristics typify employees in their organization and adjust career development policies accordingly.

Delivering Effective Career Development Systems

It should be clear by now that any HRD program has the best chance of succeeding if care and attention are paid to performing needs analysis, design and implementation, and evaluation of the program. The same is true for career development programs. The earlier discussion highlights some of the relevant issues in the design and implementation of an effective system. Tables 11-13 and 11-14 provide two views of the steps involved in putting together and delivering an effective career-development system. Both views share the need to obtain senior management support and to conduct and evaluate pilot programs before implementing a full-blown program.

We have noted several times in this chapter (and in the text) that rapid changes in the environment (e.g., demographics, technology, competition) have meant changes in organizational operations and their effects on employees (e.g., the advent of downsizing). Managing career development efforts well in the current turbulent environment makes it even more important that such activities be tied to the organization's strategic plan. As we noted in Chapter 4, this means that needs assessment data should include organization level data on goals, strengths, weaknesses, resource availability, organizational climate, and on the current human resource plan. Career development, like all HRD activities, should fit into the overall HR strategy. Recruiting, selection, compensation, benefits, and HRD activities have an impact on career development, and all can be used to facilitate the process. A model depicting the relationship between career development and HRM functions is shown in Figure 11-5.

Another issue in developing and delivering career development activities is the attitude held by many people that career development is seen as an individual's responsibility rather than a beneficial organizational activity. This attitude must be overcome if a career development system is to gain wide acceptance. One way to overcome this attitude, and benefit both the organization and the individual, is to make clear from the start what purpose the career development programs will serve. Are they to enhance employee growth and decision making? Address EEO and affirmative action pressures? Improve the organization's

TABLE 11-12	SUMMARY OF BABY BOOMER CHARACTERISTICS AND RECOMMENDED ORGANIZATIONAL ACTIONS

Profile of Baby Boom Characteristics	Recommended Organizational Action
1. Concern for basic values	1. a. Replace promotion culture with psychological success culture. b. Examine, change corporate career criteria. c. Focus on corporate ethics.
2. Freedom to act on values	2. a. Support protean career paths. b. More lateral mobility. c. De-couple rewards and the linear career path.
3. Focus on self	3. Build ongoing development into the job through • Self-development. • Lifelong learning.
4. Need for autonomy	4. More flexible careers.
5. Less concern with advancement	5. More diversity in career paths. More change • within present job. • within present function. • within present location. • across function and locations.
6. Crafting	6. Reward quality performance, not potential.
7. Entrepreneurship	7. a. Create internal enterpreneurial assignments. b. Encourage employee career exploration (internally and externally).
8. Concern for work-home balance	8. a. More organizational sensitivity to home life. b. Training for managing the work-home interface. c. Inclusion of spouse in career discussions. d. Career assistance for employed spouse. e. Flexible benefits to help meet family needs (e.g., child care, elder care, care for sick children). f. More flexible work arrangements.

SOURCE: From "Career Gridlock: Baby Boomers Hit the Wall" by D. T. Hall and J. Richter, 1990, *The Executive, 4,* p. 19.

image? Ensure the organization has the necessary talent to remain effective? Whatever the purposes, they should be clearly stated. Achievement of these goals should then be evaluated once the program is in operation. The use of a steering committee, together with input from a variety of employees as to the

TABLE 11-13	PRINCIPLES OF EFFECTIVE CAREER DEVELOPMENT SYSTEMS

Analyze Needs

1. Address specific needs and target groups.
2. Tie the program to HRD practices and policies.
3. Tailor the program to fit the culture.

Build a Vision and a Model

1. Build from a conceptual base.
2. Create long-term approaches with short-term payoffs.
3. Formalize some aspects of the program.
4. Design multiple approaches/methods.

Develop and Implement a Strategy

1. Codesign and manage project with advisory group.
2. Ensure visible top-management support.
3. Involve managers.
4. Publicize accomplishments.
5. Start small—pilot, evaluate, redesign.

SOURCE: From "The 12-Fold Path to CD Enlightenment" by Z. B. Leibowitz, C. Farren, and B. L. Kaye, 1985, *Training and Development Journal, 39*(4), p. 50.

TABLE 11-14	CAREER DEVELOPMENT PLANNING PROGRAM MODELS

1. Identify problems, pressures, needs, opportunities.
2. Identify success indicators
   - Employees (career plan prepared, career discussion held).
   - Managers (better employee performance ratings, less time required to fill job openings).
   - Top management (improved employee morale, lower turnover).
   - Human resource development staff (greater employee use of existing development programs, positive internal evaluation of career systems).
3. Evaluate existing processes, tools, and techniques.
4. Design program.
5. Develop implementation strategy
   - Resource requirements (human and budgetary).
   - Support elements and barriers.
   - Approaches for enhancing organizational commitment.
   - Time priorities and sequencing.
   - Communication of program effectiveness to organization.
   - Evaluation strategy.
6. Introduce and evaluate pilot.
7. Begin full-scale implementation/ongoing evaluation.

SOURCE: From "Organizational Career Development Systems: The State of the Practice" by T. G. Gutteridge, 1986, in D. T. Hall and associates (Eds.), *Career Development in Organizations* (p. 78), San Francisco: Jossey-Bass.

FIGURE 11-5
SCHEIN'S MODEL OF THE RELATIONSHIP BETWEEN HUMAN RESOURCE PLANNING AND CAREER DEVELOPMENT

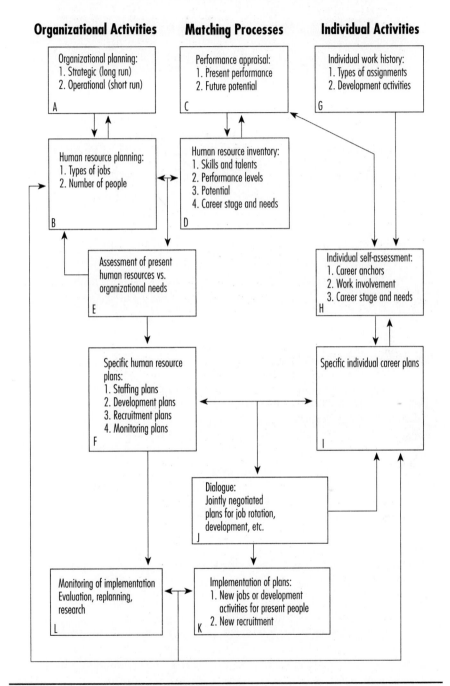

Organizational Activities   **Matching Processes**   **Individual Activities**

Organizational planning:
1. Strategic (long run)
2. Operational (short run)
A

Performance appraisal:
1. Present performance
2. Future potential
C

Individual work history:
1. Types of assignments
2. Development activities
G

Human resource planning:
1. Types of jobs
2. Number of people
B

Human resource inventory:
1. Skills and talents
2. Performance levels
3. Potential
4. Career stage and needs
D

Assessment of present human resources vs. organizational needs
E

Individual self-assessment:
1. Career anchors
2. Work involvement
3. Career stage and needs
H

Specific human resource plans:
1. Staffing plans
2. Development plans
3. Recruitment plans
4. Monitoring plans
F

Specific individual career plans
I

Dialogue:
Jointly negotiated plans for job rotation, development, etc.
J

Monitoring of implementation Evaluation, replanning, research
L

Implementation of plans:
1. New jobs or development activities for present people
2. New recruitment
K

SOURCE: From *Career Dynamics: Matching Individual and Organizational Needs* (p. 191) by E. H. Schein, 1978, Reading, MA: Addison-Wesley. Reprinted by permission.

planning, design, and testing of these programs can further build support, understanding, and commitment.

RETURN TO OPENING CASE

BPX established four parameters for its dual career path structure:

1. Both the management and individual contributor tracks must be **consistent with the company's mission and values.**

2. The tracks must be **based on how things ought to be done,** not how they were currently being done.

3. The tracks must be **flexible** (i.e., permitting employees to move between management and individual contributor tracks).

4. There must be **a common set of dual tracks within each functional area,** with each set of tracks **applying to worldwide operations** within each functional area (thus reinforcing a global identity).

The process BPX used to design these career tracks mirrored certain company goals: to use networking, open thinking, and empowerment. After external consultants collected job analysis data and identified the nontechnical skills used in each area, teams of BPX employees met to design the paths. The employee teams identified the factors that should be the basis for the paths, delineated the number of levels in each path, and described each level. The teams ensured that each level was clearly distinguished from the next and that responsibility was pushed down to the lowest level possible within each path.

Employee design teams also developed a matrix that spelled out the competencies required for each factor at each level of the path. The purpose of the matrix was to clearly identify the competencies employees would need to progress from level to level along a career path. Finally, the teams created developmental guidelines that employees could use to guide their thinking about how they could develop the competencies needed to achieve their career goals. Taken together, the career matrices, competencies, and developmental guidelines would allow employees to take control of their own career progress as well as facilitate career discussions between employees and their supervisors.

A team approach was also used to implement the new dual career paths. Teams of BPX line managers and HR employees trained and coached their colleagues on how to adopt the career-planning process and use the dual paths.

BPX's future career management plans include integrating the dual-track system with the company's performance appraisal and reward programs. While the dual career paths have only recently been implemented, BPX expects the system to meet its goals and help the organization be both successful and a rewarding place to work.[1]

Summary

A career is the pattern of work-related experiences that span the course of a person's life. While the individual is ultimately responsible for his or her own career, which includes developing a clear understanding of self and the environment in order to establish career goals and plans, the organization can assist the individual by providing information, opportunities, and assistance. It is in the organization's interest to assist the employee in order to enhance its internal labor market and ensure that employees will be available and motivated to perform the activities that will be needed in the future for the organization to compete.

Erikson described our lives as progressing through a series of stages, with each stage presenting the individual with a challenge he or she must meet in order to develop further and achieve happiness and a clear sense of self. Levinson similarly describes adult life as progressing through a series of stages, with each stage or era representing a season in a person's life. In each season, the demands on the individual change, and the individual works to make changes in his or her life to meet those demands. Both models teach us that change is a normal and inevitable part of adult life, and that the challenges faced in life will affect career plans and decisions.

Greenhaus (1987) describes the process of career management as one in which the individual (1) explores the environment, (2) develops a clear sense of environment and self-awareness, (3) sets career goals, (4) develops a strategy to reach the goal, (5) implements the strategy, (6) makes progress toward the goal, (7) obtains feedback on progress from work and nonwork sources, and (8) appraises his or her career. Using this process can enable the individual to achieve career satisfaction and greater life happiness.

Organizations use a variety of tools and techniques to manage employee careers. These include self-assessment tools and activities, such as workbooks, workshops, and computer programs, individual career counseling, job placement exchanges, organizational potential assessment, and developmental programs such as job rotation and mentoring. These activities and practices help employees gather information to develop career awareness and career plans and offer opportunities to implement these plans.

Designing a career management program involves steps similar to those for developing any HRD intervention: conducting a needs analysis, identifying the

---

[1]From "Designing a Dual Career-Track System" by R. Tucker, M. Moravec, and K. Ideus, 1992, *Training & Development, 6*, p. 55–58. Copyright 1992 by The American Society for Training and Development. All rights reserved. Adapted by permission.

goals and components of the program, establishing criteria to measure effectiveness, implementing the program, and evaluating its effectiveness. Because career management programs affect the human resource function in an organization, developers and deliverers of such programs must be aware of issues involved in HR planning, equal employment opportunity and affirmative action, and labor relations. In addition, organizations should consider the issues of career motivation, career plateaus, and career development for nonexempt workers when designing career development programs.

Key Terms and Concepts

assessment center	generativity
career	job posting
career development	job rotation
career management	mentoring
career motivation	potential assessment
career path	preretirement counseling
career planning	self-assessment activities
career plateau	succession planning
ego integrity	

Questions for Discussion

1. Explain the significance of defining the term "career" broadly as the pattern of work-related experiences that span the course of one's life.

2. Using your knowledge of the stages of life and career development, explain how the career issues of a 27-year-old individual differ from those faced by a 45-year-old. What are the organizational implications of the issues you identified?

3. Describe how career management is a problem-solving and decision-making process.

4. Explain how both organizations and individuals can benefit from a well-designed career management system.

5. Discuss the value of self-assessment tools and activities to effective career development.

6. Given the potential benefits of and problems linked to mentoring as a career development tool, describe how you feel about the prospect of becoming involved in a mentoring relationship as part of your own career development. What would your concerns be, and what would you like to see an organization do to ensure the mentoring experience is a positive one?

7. Recent research suggests that career plateaus are more complex than previously thought. Briefly explain why the individual's perception of being plateaued is important and how organizations may want to develop multiple ways for dealing with plateaued employees.

8. The flattening of many organizations is forcing many individuals and organizations to change their perception of what career advancement is all about. What are some alternatives to upward movement as a career option? How do you feel about the prospect of these alternatives as opposed to the traditional upward progress within your own career?

12

Management Development

Learning Objectives

1. *Define management development and describe the extent to which it is used in U.S. organizations.*
2. *Identify the roles and competencies that make up a manager's job.*
3. *Describe the various approaches to management education.*
4. *Describe "in-house" approaches to management training and development.*
5. *Describe the components of three programs frequently used in management development programs: leadership training, rater training, and behavior modeling training.*
6. *Discuss the issues involved in designing management development programs.*

OPENING CASE

The overall success of an organization is directly related to the effectiveness of its management. Managing in a turbulent environment requires a broad range of skills and abilities, many of which need to be developed to ensure a manager's effectiveness. Most organizations recognize this and offer management development programs to ensure managers will be effective in carrying out their responsibilities.

One such organization is the Children's World Learning Centers (CWLC), a nationwide organization that includes a network of 500 individual child-care centers throughout the United States. Each of these centers is a $1 million physical plant led by a manager who is responsible for its day-to-day operation.

In 1989 CWLC hired a new CEO, Duane Larson, a former HRD professional who came to CWLC from Manpower Inc. When Larson came on board he traveled around the country visiting individual centers to get a sense of the company's operation. What he found was an organization that provided good service, but that the service was inconsistent from center to center. Furthermore, the organization was experiencing a high turnover among center directors (32 percent), as well as high turnover among clients.

One reason for these problems was inconsistency in management training and development. According to Karen Maggio, director of organization development, CWLC training was plagued by several problems: (1) the timing of the training was haphazard, (2) there were inconsistencies in topics, and (3) district managers, responsible for training the center directors in their districts, tended to conduct training when they had time regardless of the need for it.

Upon receipt of this information from Maggio, Larson directed that Maggio and Kim Moore, director of educational training and development, create a centralized management development program to ensure consistency of training for all center directors. Larson made the management development program CWLC's number one priority—he felt that until the firm was "able to guarantee consistent delivery in the business," it would not be able to grow.

Introduction

For at least the past 40 years, managers have been viewed as a dynamic and important element of business organizations. Given the turbulence in today's environment (e.g., a global economy, the emergence of regional trading blocs, increased competition, technological change), organizations need a high-quality, high-performance management team that can help them meet these challenges. This is true even for organizations that are using downsizing and employee empowerment techniques (e.g., self-directed teams, which will be discussed in Chapter 13). One way for an organization to increase the chances its managers will be up to the task of managing is through management development. While it may have once been believed that ability to manage (like the ability to lead) was primarily an inborn capability, the current view holds that the KSAs required to perform effectively as a manager can be learned and/or enhanced (Campbell, Dunnette, Lawler, & Weick, 1970).

Management development is one of the most common HRD activities. A recent survey of HRD professionals revealed that 86 percent of organizations provide some form of management development activities (Filipczak, 1992). There are almost as many definitions of management development as there are individuals who have written about the topic, with the focus ranging from subjects covered (e.g., planning, interpersonal skills) to a broad list of activities (e.g., succession planning, career development, job rotation, performance appraisal). We feel the following definition captures the essence of management development as it can and should be practiced in organizations:

> [A]n organization's conscious effort to provide its managers (and potential managers) with opportunities to learn, grow, and change, in hopes of producing over the long term a cadre of managers with the skills necessary to function effectively in that organization (McCall, Lombardo, & Morrison, 1988, p. 147).

This definition makes several key points. First, it suggests that management development should be seen as specific to a particular organization. While there may be roles and competencies that apply to managing in a variety of settings (Schoenfeldt & Steger, 1990), each organization is unique, and its goal should be to develop individuals to be more effective managers within its own context. Second, management development consists of providing employees with opportunities for improving various skills. While there is no guarantee that particular individuals will take advantage of, or profit from, these opportunities, management development cannot occur unless they are at least provided (McCall, Lombardo, & Morrison, 1988). Third, management development must be a conscious effort on the part of the organization. Leaving development to chance (which can lead to changes) reduces the likelihood that the organization will achieve the kinds of changes it needs and desires. Fourth, and finally, management development (like all HRD activities) should be part of the organization's long-term business plan if it is to be a sound investment and ultimately successful. While many current management development programs do not conform to this definition, it can serve as a benchmark to which such programs can and should aspire.

Management development has been described as having three main components: management education, management training, and on-the-job experiences (Keys & Wolfe, 1988; Wexley & Baldwin, 1986). **Management education** can be defined as "the acquisition of a broad range of conceptual knowledge and skills in formal classroom situations in degree-granting institutions" (Keys & Wolfe, 1988, p. 205). **Management training** focuses more on providing specific skills or knowledge that could be immediately applied within an organization and/or to a specific position or set of positions within an organization (e.g., middle managers) (Keys & Wolfe, 1988; Wexley & Baldwin, 1986). **On-the-job experiences** are planned or unplanned opportunities for a manager to gain self-knowledge, enhance existing skills and abilities, or obtain new skills or information within the context of day-to-day activities (e.g., mentorship, coaching, assignment to a task force).

We will group management training and on-the-job experiences together and refer to them as **management training and experiences (MTE)** for two reasons. First, the focus of these activities is essentially the same—providing KSAs that can be applied immediately within the organization. Second, both differ from management education in terms of setting (classroom), specificity to the organization involved, and time frame for application (immediate relevance for the job rather than just educational benefits over the long haul).[1]

Extent of Management Development Activities

As mentioned earlier, management development is one of the most commonly offered approaches to HRD. The percentage of organizations offering management development programs varies depending on the level of management the program is intended to develop. For example, Filipczak (1992) reported that 74 percent of respondents stated their organizations offered programs to first-line supervisors, as compared to 73 percent for middle managers, 70 percent for executives, and 65 percent for senior managers. The amount of training, as measured by the average number of hours delivered per year, did not differ among levels, however, with an average of 32 hours of training per individual at the higher management levels and 33 hours per individual for first-line supervisors (Filipczak, 1992). In addition, most organizations (57 percent or more) use a combination of in-house and external providers for their management development programs, with senior management and executive development most likely offered exclusively by external providers (Filipczak, 1992).

The most frequently cited reasons for developing managers include broadening the individual and providing knowledge or skills (Saari et al., 1988). Few organizations (5 percent in Saari's survey) cited an intent to reward managers as a reason for providing them with developmental opportunities. The types of activities used in management development vary widely across organizations. Table 12-1 lists the percentages using various approaches (Saari et al., 1988).

Organization of the Chapter

Management development comprises such a broad range of issues and approaches that it is not realistic to try to cover them all in a single chapter. Rather, we will focus our discussion on the following issues:

1. Efforts to describe the roles managers must perform and the competencies necessary for performing them effectively;

2. Options available for management education;

3. Options available for management training and experiences;

4. A description of three approaches used to develop managers (leadership training, rater training, behavior modeling training for interpersonal skills), and;

5. The design of management development programs.

---

[1]*Note:* The distinctions we make here do not apply to all activities performed under each category, but are rather intended as useful generalizations.

TABLE 12-1	PERCENTAGE OF ORGANIZATIONS REPORTING THE USE OF VARIOUS APPROACHES TO MANAGEMENT DEVELOPMENT

Approach	Percent of Respondents Indicating Use
On-the-job training	93%
Formal training/education programs	89
Special programs and task forces	80
Mentoring	57
Job rotation	40
Career planning	30
Types of Formal Programs	
External short courses	90
Company specific programs	75
University residential programs	31
Executive MBA programs	25

SOURCE: From "A Survey of Management Training and Education Practices in U.S. Companies" by L. M. Saari, T. R. Johnson, S. D. McLaughlin, and D. M. Zimmerle, 1988, *Personnel Psychology, 41*, pp. 731–743.

Describing the Manager's Job: Management Roles and Competencies

Given that almost all organizations employ managers, the scrutiny under which they operate, and the vast literature on management and its subfields, one would expect that we would have a clear idea of what managers do, the KSAs necessary to do those things effectively, and how to identify and develop those KSAs. Unfortunately, surprisingly little is known about what managers do, how they learn to do it, and how they should be developed (e.g., Beatty, Schneier, & McEvoy, 1987; Schoenfeldt & Steger, 1990). While it is true that popular conceptions of the manager's role and development are available, scientific research has yet to provide a clearly supported and accepted model that can be used to guide management development. Even among the best empirical studies in this area, such as the Management Progress Study conducted over a 30-year period at AT&T (Bray, Campbell & Grant, 1974; Howard & Bray, 1988), there are significant limitations (e.g., small sample sizes, analysis of only one organization) that make it difficult to confidently conclude what most or all managers do and how they develop.

This is not to say we know nothing about managers and the ways available to develop them. Rather, we raise this point to make the reader aware of the limitations of our present knowledge and give a sense of how far we have to go.[2] In

---

[2]*Note:* Given the differences that exist across organizations, levels of management, and the changes in approaches to management over time (e.g., a current trend is the empowerment of employees), it may not ever be possible to develop a meaningful, generalizable model of managers and their development.

this section of the chapter, we briefly describe several approaches to conceptualizing the management role to suggest a starting point in designing a reasonable management development program. As indicated in the definition of management development we presented at the beginning of the chapter, meaningful management development is likely to differ given the context and challenges facing a particular organization. We encourage designers of such programs to begin their efforts by obtaining a clear understanding of the organization (including its goals, strategic plan, culture, strengths and weaknesses, etc.) and the characteristics of the target population (managers and managers-to-be). The research available on what managers do, how they do it, and how they develop the capabilities to do it can provide a useful conceptual model to begin the needs assessment process and serve as a source of possible development topics and issues. It is unrealistic, however, to expect such research, no matter how advanced, to provide the blueprint for any particular organization's management development strategy.

Approaches to Understanding the Job of Managing

Researchers who have examined the job of managing have done so from at least three perspectives: describing the characteristics of the job as it is typically performed, describing the **roles** managers serve, and developing process models that show how the various components of managing relate to each other (Schoenfeldt & Steger, 1990). The *characteristics approach* involves observing the tasks managers perform and grouping them into meaningful categories. McCall, Morrison, and Hannan (1978) reviewed the results of a group of observational studies and concluded ten elements of managing were consistently present. These elements indicate the management job involves long hours of work, high activity levels, fragmented work (e.g., many interruptions), varied activities, primarily oral communication, many contacts, information gathering, and spending most working time within the organization. In addition, managers tend not to be reflective planners (given the variety of tasks and fragmented nature of the work) and do poorly in accurately estimating how they spend their time.

While these observations may be interesting, they are of little value in describing specifically what managers do, how they do it, and how they should be developed. A common conclusion from such studies is that important questions about the job remain unanswered (e.g., the relationship of the activities to each other) and that "knowing that the managerial job is varied and complex is not particularly helpful in the identification and/or development process" (Schoenfeldt & Steger, 1990, p. 196).

A second approach to describing the managerial job is to identify the roles that managers are typically assigned. This can be accomplished by using either an observational approach or an empirical approach. The *observational approach* is typified by Fayol's (1949) five management functions (planning, organizing, commanding, coordinating, and controlling) and Mintzberg's (1973, 1975) ten managerial roles: interpersonal (figurehead, leader, liaison), informational (monitor, disseminator, spokesperson), and decisional (entrepreneur, disturbance handler, resource allocator, and negotiator). While these categorizations are extremely popular, they do not appear to accurately describe what managers do. They also lack specificity and do not adequately describe the interrelations among the various roles (Carrol & Gillen, 1987).

The *empirical approach* relies on a descriptive questionnaire (e.g., Management Position Description Questionnaire) as completed by managers themselves and/or by others who work with them (Tornow & Pinto, 1976). This approach has failed to provide practical, meaningful descriptions of the job (Schoenfeldt & Steger, 1990). Taken together, the observational and empirical approaches to categorizing the managerial role have not proven useful in defining the managerial job or as guides to developing managers.

One way researchers have tried to overcome the limitations of the previous approaches is to develop process models that take into account the particularly relevant competencies and constraints involved in performing the management job. Two process models of particular note to the discussion of management development are the **integrated competency model** (Boyatzis, 1982) and the **four-dimensional model** (e.g., Manners & Steger, 1976, 1979; Schoenfeldt, 1979). The integrated competency model was based on interviews of over 2,000 managers in 12 organizations that were conducted by the consulting firm of McBer and Company. The model focuses on *managerial competencies,* skills and/or personal characteristics that contribute to effective performance (Albanese, 1988), rather than the roles managers perform. The model identifies 21 competencies that are grouped into six categories: human resource management, leadership, goal and action management, directing subordinates, focus on others, and specialized knowledge (Boyatzis, 1982). Table 12-2 shows the specific competencies included in each cluster. The human resources, leadership, and goal and action clusters are seen as most central to managing. The model also depicts the relationships among the first four clusters, shown in Figure 12-1. "Focus on others" is not shown in the model at the skill level because its key competencies do not exist at that level. "Specialized knowledge" is not shown because Boyatzis sees its impact on the other competencies as "pervasive."

While the model makes other important distinctions (e.g., competencies versus threshold competencies, competencies relevant for various management levels and for public and private sector organizations), the main contribution of the model is its attempt to describe the managerial job in terms of the competencies that contribute to performance and the relationships among these competencies. This approach can be useful in guiding management development programs, and in fact it has been used as the basis for those programs as offered by the American Management Association. The primary weakness of the model is that it is based on a narrow range of measuring devices (McClelland's need theory and Kolb's learning style theory), which likely do not represent all of the traits, skills, and knowledge needed for managerial performance (Schoenfeldt & Steger, 1990).

The second process model of the managerial role that can contribute to designing management development efforts is the four-dimensional model (Schoenfeldt & Steger, 1990). Based on various information sources (e.g., managerial diaries, interviews, performance evaluation documents, observation), this model depicts the managerial role as having the following dimensions:

TABLE 12-2	CLUSTERS AND COMPETENCIES ASSOCIATED WITH THE INTEGRATED COMPETENCY MODEL

Cluster	Competencies
Human Resource Management	Use of socialized power Positive regard[a] Managing group processes Accurate self-assessment[a]
Leadership	Self-confidence Use oral presentations Conceptualization Logical thought[a]
Goal and Action Management	Efficiency orientation Proactivity Concern with impact Diagnostic use of concepts
Directing Subordinates	Use of unilateral power[a] Spontaneity[a] Developing others[a]
Focus on Others	Perceptual objectivity Self-control Stamina and adaptability Concern with close relationships
Specialized Knowledge	Memory Specialized job knowledge[a]

Note: [a]Identified as threshold competencies, that is, characteristics essential to performing a job, but not causally related to superior job performance.

SOURCE: From "Identification and Development of Managerial Talent" by Schoenfeldt, L. F. and Steger, J. A., 1990, in G. R. Ferris and K. M. Rowland (Eds.), *Organizational Entry* (p. 210). Greenwich, CT: JAI Press.

1. Six **functions**—forecasting and planning, training and development, persuasive communication, influence and control, expertise/functional area, and administration;

2. Four **roles**—innovator, evaluator, motivator, director;

3. Five (relational) **targets**—peers, subordinates, superiors, external, and self;

4. An unspecified number of managerial **styles** (attributes that describe the image and approach of the manager)—examples include objectivity, personal impact, leadership, energy level, and risk-taking.

The four-dimensional model states managers interact with various targets (e.g., subordinates), carrying out an assortment of functions by performing specific roles (i.e., the roles that exist within each of the functions). The way they perform these functions and roles is consistent with their managerial style. For example,

FIGURE 12-1	AN INTEGRATED MODEL OF MANAGEMENT COMPETENCIES AT THE SKILL LEVEL

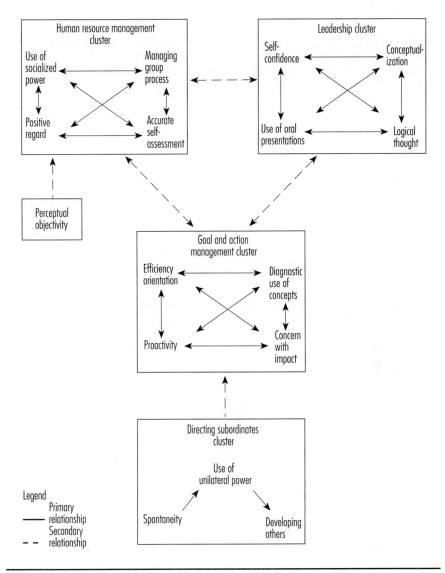

SOURCE: From *The Competent Manager: A Model for Effective Performance* (p. 194) by R. E. Boyatzis, 1982, New York: Wiley. Copyright 1982 by John Wiley & Sons, Inc. Reprinted by permission.

in performing the training and development function with a subordinate (the target), the manager may have to direct the subordinate, motivate him or her during training, and evaluate progress (all roles contained within the training and development function). The manager may do this using a particular style (e.g., objectivity, which involves evaluating and responding to the subordinate in an unbiased manner). Table 12-3 describes each of the elements within

TABLE 12-3	**DEFINITIONS OF COMPONENTS OF THE FOUR DIMENSIONAL MODEL**

Dimension	Definition
Functions	
Persuasive Communication	The manager, as spokesperson for the group, must persuade various targets. This function involves articulation of a position and, through logic, persuasion, and argumentation, convincing others to accept those positions.
Administration	The degree to which the position requires the manager to sort and react to the rules of the organization, and to work within organizational policies. Included would be such things as budget activities, paper work, scheduling of activities, coordinating, and so forth.
Functional Expertise	The level of required proficiency, specialized knowledge, or technical expertise required by the managerial assignment. Although the manager may not be the most competent in the organization in some specific area of specialized knowledge, the manager must have a level of expertise to ask critical questions and provide substantive direction.
Influence and Control	The degree to which the position requires the manager to impose his/her wishes on others from the managerial base of recognized organizational authority.
Training and Development	The degree to which the position requires the manager to train and develop his/her own talents as well as those of others. This training could be through formal programs or informal opportunities tailored to the individuals involved.
Forecasting and Planning	The degree to which the position requires the manager to predict trends and understand the requirements and resources necessary to meet future needs.
Roles	
Motivator	The necessity of the manager through action, inspiration, and encouragement, to arouse, excite, and energize others. The degree to which the manager is required to provide others with an incentive or stimulus to act.
Evaluator	The degree to which the position requires the manager to examine and judge situations or options. The manager as evaluator is assessing and appraising options for some action.
Director	The requirement that the manager lead the way. The director role is one of selecting and defining end points or directions. Taken together, the evaluator and director roles constitute decision making; that is, the process of evaluating alternatives and selecting the most appropriate one for achieving a particular goal.

Dimension	Definition
Innovator	This role is the degree to which the managerial functions require the manager to be creative and innovative to gain better outcomes, either in terms of efficiency or quality of interactions.
Targets	
Peers	Managers of equivalent level within the same organization.
Subordinates	Individuals who report directly to the manager. The traditional managerial target in the literature on the conceptualization of the role.
Superiors	Those at higher organizational levels.
External	Individuals outside the organization, such as customers, suppliers, elected or appointed officials, and members of other external constituencies.
Self	Literature on the management role suggests that self-discipline is required to be effective. A manager must supervise his or her own activity.
Style[a]	
Objectivity	The degree to which the manager is required to evaluate and respond to inputs in an unbiased manner.
Personal Impact	The requirement that the manager act, speak, and dress in a particular manner. The required sensitivity to social demands for credibility.
Leadership	The leadership demands of the managerial role. This could be further subdivided to include such things as power mode (autocratic versus participative), consideration, and openness.
Energy Level	The degree to which personal energy is required to successfully operate in the managerial role. This could be subdivided into such components as work pace and endurance.
Risk-Taking	The degree to which the manager is required to take a chance or to take action in the face of uncertainty.

Note: [a]The style dimensions given are a few examples of the many elements possible.

SOURCE: From "Identification and Development of Managerial Talent" by Schoenfeldt, L. F. and Steger, J. A., 1990, in G. R. Ferris and K. M. Rowland (Eds.), *Organization Entry* (pp. 214, 215). Greenwich, CT: JAI Press.

the four dimensions, while Figure 12-2 depicts the relationships among the dimensions.

The four dimensional and integrated competency models include similar skills, roles, and activities and provide a better basis for describing the managerial job and designing management development programs (see Schoenfeldt & Steger, 1990, for a discussion of the relationships among the models). Either of these models provide a useful conceptual basis to begin viewing the role of managers within a specific organization and the competencies they need to perform effectively. It should be emphasized that these models have not been validated by research and are not substitutes for a thorough needs assessment.

Importance of Needs Assessment in Determining Managerial Competencies

As we have stated in Chapter 4 and in subsequent chapters, needs assessment provides critical information in determining the conditions for training, where training is needed, what kind of training is needed, and who needs training. Given the fact that research on the managerial job has left many unanswered questions, the importance of conducting a thorough needs assessment prior to designing a management development program is amplified. Despite this, many organizations fail to do needs assessment. According to a survey of 1,000 organizations by Saari et al. (1988), only 27 percent of respondents reported conducting any needs assessment prior to designing management development programs. This means that many organizations are leaving much to chance and are likely wasting critical resources.

Some organizations are doing a good job of needs assessment for management development and as a result have a clearer idea of the competencies and issues their development programs should address. Two examples illustrate this approach: New York Telephone and the U.S. Office of Personnel Management. According to Sutton and McQuigg-Martinez (1990), New York Telephone (a NYNEX company) found itself, after the court-ordered breakup of AT&T, facing competition for the first time in its more than 100 years of existence. As a part of a reexamination of the way it conducted business, company officials realized they needed to identify the skills managers required to respond to a competitive environment.

The human resource department of New York Telephone developed a series of program and policy changes called the Development Partnership designed to help managers improve their abilities (particularly in managing people), perform their nonsupervisory functions better, and to aspire to greater responsibility. The Partnership focuses on the relationship between a manager and his or her superior, with the individual manager playing the initiating role. The new program includes three key components: an annual development cycle (in which the manager and superior create a development plan), on-the-job development opportunities (such as task forces and transfers), and managerial accountability for the development of subordinates.

Of particular interest to our discussion is the study New York Telephone conducted to establish its management skills curriculum, a series of courses man-

---

FIGURE 12-2   FUNCTIONS, ROLES, AND TARGETS FROM
THE FOUR DIMENSIONAL MODEL OF THE
MANAGER'S JOB

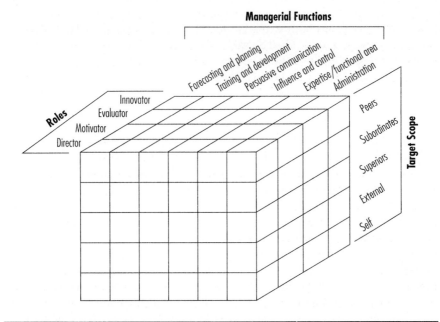

SOURCE: From "Identification and Development of Managerial Talent" by Schoenfeldt, L. F. and Steger, J. A., 1990, in G. R. Ferris and K. M. Rowland (Eds.), *Organization Entry* (pp. 212). Greenwich, CT: JAI Press.

---

agers may take as part of achieving their development goals. The study began by having a task force of managers from three levels identify essential, generic management skills. The 30 skills identified by this task force were then included in a questionnaire that asked respondents to rate the importance of each skill in managing effectively in the present and future. After pilot testing, the questionnaire was mailed to a random sample of over 3,000 managers from various levels. The results of the survey indicated consensus on what were the most important and least important managerial skills. The 20 most important skills were then combined into six groups (personal, communications, organizing and planning, people and performance management, business, and independent thinking) and used as the basis for identifying the courses to include in the company's management skills curriculum. The final curriculum included some already existing company courses, as well as some new ones developed in-house or purchased from vendors. The organization considered the skills study a success in identifying the mix of skills needed for its development program to ensure New York Telephone would have the quality of management necessary to face future challenges. New York Telephone's experience illustrates the value of determining necessary skills as well as conducting regular assessment of individual employees and planning (as part of the annual development cycle).

The second example focuses on the U.S. government's efforts to train its managers. The federal government is huge by any measure, whether in terms of numbers of employees (over 2 million civilian employees, including over 280,000 managers and supervisors and 9,000 executives), the range of services provided (both in number and variety), or the number of locations in which it operates (hundreds of locations both in the United States and abroad) (Eurich, 1990). In 1978 Congress passed the Civil Service Reform Act, which, among other things, dictated that systematic training be offered to prepare employees for the managerial role. The act created the Office of Personnel Management (OPM) and the Senior Executive Service (SES) and charged them with the responsibility to establish educational programs for the government's managers (in addition to other human resource management functions). Currently, OPM provides guidance to various government agencies (e.g., the Department of Agriculture, the Department of Defense) and either operates educational programs itself or in conjunction with individual agencies (most of the larger agencies have their own programs) (Eurich, 1990).

Of particular interest to our present discussion is OPM's study to describe the managerial job in government. The study resulted in a model called the Management Excellence Framework, which is used as the basis for its competency-based education program for managers (OPM, 1985). The model describes the managerial job in three dimensions: effectiveness characteristics (e.g., strategic view, flexibility, communication); management functions (e.g., coordination, work unit planning, personnel management) and management level (supervisor, manager, executive). (See Figures 12-3 and 12-4.) The study identified the importance of each function and each skill for each level of management. According to Eurich (1990) the model is used as an "organizing principle for management education throughout the government and form[s] a way of evaluating managers' development needs (p. 143)." In part, this model ensures that the management training and development the government offers will be responsive to both participants' and the agencies' needs.

The efforts by New York Telephone and OPM illustrate the value of conducting a thorough investigation of the managerial job and the competencies needed to perform effectively prior to designing a management development program.

The Globally Competent Manager

The advent of the global economy has led some writers to suggest organizations should create management development programs to produce globally competent managers (e.g., Adler & Bartholomew, 1992; Bartlett & Ghoshal, 1992; Bogorya, 1985; Murray & Murray, 1986). Organizations such as Corning Glass, ITT and General Electric have incorporated this perspective into their management development programs. We will present two of many possible points of view to serve as examples of how the competencies needed to be an effective global manager have been conceptualized.

Bartlett and Ghoshal (1992) take the position that in order to succeed in today's global environment, organizations need a network of managers who are

FIGURE 12-3

OFFICE OF PERSONNEL MANAGEMENT'S MANAGEMENT EXCELLENCE FRAMEWORK

Effectiveness Characteristics

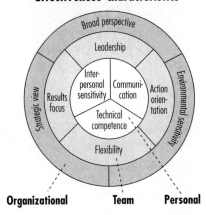

Organizational   Team   Personal

Management Functions

External awareness	Representation	Work unit planning
Interpretation	Coordination	Work unit guidance
Budgeting	Personnel management	Work unit monitoring
Material resources administration	Supervision	Program evaluation

Management Levels

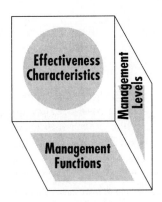

SOURCE: From *The Managerial Excellence Framework: A Competency-based Model of Effective Performance for Federal Managers* (p. 2) by U.S. Office of Personnel Management, 1985.

FIGURE 12-4

OFFICE OF PERSONNEL MANAGEMENT'S MANAGEMENT EXCELLENCE FRAMEWORK: RELATIVE DUTIES BY MANAGERIAL LEVEL

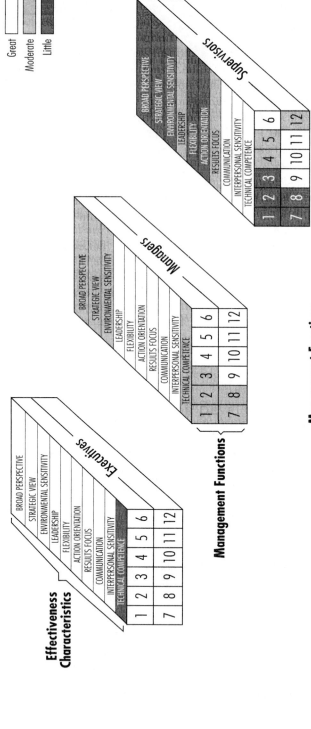

SOURCE: From *The Managerial Excellence Framework: A Competency-based Model of Effective Performance for Federal Managers* (p. 8) by U.S. Office of Personnel Management, 1985.

specialists as opposed to globalizing all managers. They suggest four categories of managers are needed:

1. **Business Managers** This type of manager plays three roles, serving as "the **strategist** for the organization, the **architect** of its worldwide asset configuration, and the **coordinator** of transactions across national borders" (p. 125).

2. **Country Managers** This type of manager, who works in the organization's national subsidiaries, also plays three roles, serving as "the **sensor** and interpreter of local opportunities and threats, the **builder** of local resources and capabilities, and the **contributor** to active participation in global strategy" (p. 128).

3. **Functional Managers** These managers are functional specialists (e.g. in engineering, marketing, human resources) who "**scan** for specialized information worldwide, '**cross-pollinate**' leading-edge knowledge and best practice, and **champion** innovations that may offer transnational opportunities and applications" (p. 130).

4. **Corporate Managers** These managers serve in corporate headquarters and orchestrate the organization's activities, playing the roles of **leader, talent scout** (i.e., by identifying potential business, country and functional managers), and **developing** promising executives.

Bartlett and Ghoshal (1992) illustrate these roles by using case studies of managers at Procter & Gamble, Electrolux, and NEC. They suggest organizations need to develop management teams capable of performing these functions in concert to achieve the organization's goals. While this categorization of the global manager's role is interesting and provides some sense of how these roles and managers interrelate, further research is needed to determine whether it can be a useful basis for developing global managers.

A second point of view is offered by Adler and Bartholomew (1992). These authors identify seven transnational skills they believe are necessary to managing effectively in a global environment: global perspective, local responsiveness, synergistic learning, transition and adaptation, cross-cultural interaction, collaboration, and foreign experience. They argue that transnationally competent managers need a broader set of skills than traditional international managers, who were developed with a narrower perspective of their role in the global environment. Table 12-4 displays the contrast of skills in the transnational and international approach. Adler and Bartholomew (1992) state that an organization's human resource management strategies must be modified in order to manage and develop such managers, and conclude from a survey of 50 North American firms that their present HRM strategies are less global than their business strategies. These authors also provide recommendations for how HRM systems can be modified to become more global—for example, they say that developmental

TABLE 12-4	TRANSNATIONALLY COMPETENT MANAGERS	
Transnational Skills	**Transnationally Competent Managers**	**Traditional International Managers**
Global perspective	Understand worldwide business environment from a global perspective.	Focus on a single foreign country and on managing relationships between headquarters and that country.
Local responsiveness	Learn about many cultures.	Become an expert on one culture.
Synergistic learning	Work with and learn from people from many cultures simultaneously.	Work with and coach people in each foreign culture separately or sequentially.
	Create a culturally synergistic organizational environment.	Integrate foreigners into the headquarters' national organizational culture.
Transition and adaptation	Adapt to living in many foreign cultures.	Adapt to living in a foreign culture.
Cross-cultural interaction	Use cross-cultural interaction skills on a daily basis throughout one's career.	Use cross-cultural interaction skills primarily on foreign assignments.
Collaboration	Interact with foreign colleagues as equals.	Interact within clearly defined hierarchies of structural and cultural dominance.
Foreign experience	Transpatriation for career and organization development.	Expatriation or inpatriation primarily to get the job done.

SOURCE: From "Managing Globally Competent People" by N. J. Adler and S. Bartholomew, 1992, *The Executive*, 6(3), p. 54.

activities should prepare managers to work "anywhere in the world with people from all parts of the world" (p. 59).

Adler and Bartholomew's (1992) view of the globally competent manager differs from Bartlett and Ghoshal's (1992) approach in at least two significant ways. First, Bartlett and Ghoshal adopt a role-oriented view, while Adler and Bartholomew focus on the competencies managers need. Second, Adler and Bartholomew suggest that all managers become "globalized," while Bartlett and Ghoshal argue that global management requires a team of managers who perform different functions and roles (and who would require significantly different sets of competencies).

Our purpose in raising these two points of view is not to suggest which is "correct" or would make the better foundation for describing the managerial job and the development of managers. Both models (as well as other ideas about achieving global competency) require further research, testing, and modification. Rather, these two approaches illustrate the impact that consideration of the global environment can have on the approach to developing an organization's managers. In addition, they underscore the need to consider an organization's business strategy and the environment in which it operates as a foundation for determining how to develop its managers.

Having explored the nature of the management job and competencies that managing requires, we turn our attention to some of the options organizations use to develop their managers.

Management Education

As defined earlier, management education involves activities designed to help participants gain a broad range of conceptual knowledge and skills in formal classroom situations, typically in degree-granting institutions. Management education continues to be an extremely popular choice among college students. Enrollments in Bachelor's and Master's degree programs in the U.S. grew rapidly during the 1980s, with over 200,000 of bachelor's degrees and over 50,000 master's degrees awarded each year (e.g., Porter & McKibbin, 1988). Management education activities can be grouped into three categories:

1. Bachelor's or master's programs in business administration (B.B.A. or M.B.A.) offered at colleges and universities;

2. Executive M.B.A. programs, similar in content to other M.B.A. programs but usually conducted at an accelerated pace; and

3. Short courses ranging from one day to 14 weeks in length offered by colleges, universities, or industry associations.

Each category is discussed below.

Bachelor's or Master's Degree Programs in Business Administration

Traditional management education offered at four year colleges and universities, leading to a bachelor's or master's degree, generally focuses on management knowledge and general concepts. While there has been some debate as to whether to focus such management education programs on providing primarily conceptual knowledge (e.g., market research techniques, planning and decision models) or developing the skills (e.g., communication, interpersonal) managers need to be successful, most business school programs focus on providing both. The curriculum of most B.B.A. and M.B.A. programs, particularly those accredited by the American Assembly of Collegiate Schools of Business (AACSB), is built around providing a common body of knowledge (the core) made up of seven content areas representing the functional areas of business: accounting, business environment and strategy, finance, human resources and organization theory, marketing, management information systems, quantitative analysis, and operations management. The skill areas these programs attempt to develop include leadership, oral communications, planning and organizing, decision making, and problem analysis, among others (e.g., Porter & McKibbin, 1988). This curriculum at the undergraduate level may take up between 40 percent to 80 percent or more of the student's total program, although the AACSB recommends that the range be between 40 percent and 60 percent. The remainder of the student's curriculum is made up of general education and/or unrestricted electives.

A recent comprehensive review of business school training conducted by the AASCB (summarized in Porter & McKibbin, 1988) addressed concerns that business schools were not satisfying the needs of organizations in terms of providing students with the education needed to become effective managers. Concerns focused on the lack of cross-functional integration in coursework (e.g., finance, human resource management), perceptions of graduates' levels of "soft" skills (e.g., communication, interpersonal), lack of an international perspective, and a lack of breadth in the students' preparation (i.e., too much focus on business issues at the expense of providing a broad education). Among Porter and McKibbin's (1988) recommendations were that business schools should modify their curricula to address these shortcomings and thus become more responsive to making students and organizations more competitive in the current and future environment. These changes would have far-reaching consequences both in terms of knowledge of subject matter needed by the faculty to develop the content of these programs and the educational techniques needed to deliver them.

Schools are responding to these needs. For example, the Wharton School at the University of Pennsylvania offers one of the first M.B.A. programs to completely overhaul its curriculum to meet what are perceived to be the realities of doing business in the next century. Rather than offering semester-long courses in separate disciplines, the new Wharton program offers courses in four six-week modules that integrate the disciplines to solve problems. The new program also places a heavy emphasis on the development of "people skills," practical problem solving, and acquiring a global perspective. The new curriculum, which was developed with the input of students, faculty, alumni, futurists, CEOs, and corporate recruiters, was to be phased in over a two-year period, with the first class beginning in the Fall of 1991 (Byrne, 1991).

It should be noted that degree programs at both the graduate and undergraduate levels should be seen as only one component of a manager's development. It is unreasonable to expect that education at these levels will result in a "whole manager" who has all of the KSAs needed to manage effectively. We agree that business programs at their best can provide a valuable foundation for a manager's development. Graduates of such programs should be seen as "works in progress" with the potential to become effective managers with further development and experience (e.g., Linder & Smith, 1992).

Executive M.B.A. Programs

Because of the length of time it can take to complete an M.B.A. program and the crowded lives of many full-time managers, many institutions have repackaged the traditional M.B.A. program into executive M.B.A. (EMBA) programs. A recent survey (Saari et al., 1988) revealed that 25 percent of respondents use such programs for management development. It is estimated that over 9,500 executives attend such programs at 102 business schools in North America (Byrne, 1991). EMBA programs can be very expensive, with the cost per student for the total program ranging from about $20,000 (e.g., at Georgia State University) to over $58,000 (e.g., at Wharton) (Byrne, 1991). Most of these programs condense or accelerate the coursework, with courses meeting once per week (typically on weekends). These programs are typically designed to be completed in two years. Students tend to be older, full-time managers from a variety of organizations who have a significant amount of experience as managers. Such programs have become big moneymakers for the institutions that offer them.

Commonly perceived advantages of EMBA programs include the opportunity to interact with managers from other organizations, maximum input of new ideas, high quality of instruction, and the prestige afforded by having a university affiliation. Commonly perceived disadvantages include inadequate exposure to information specific to the organization's needs, the high price, and insufficient numbers of instructors within a given program who are effective at teaching adults (Porter & McKibbin, 1988). In addition, critics charge that some programs are merely watered-down versions of M.B.A. programs, with poor quality of instruction and lax admission standards, and with the primary goal of generating income for the school (Byrne, 1991).

Are EMBA programs an effective approach to developing managers? Unfortunately, there is little existing research to answer the question. Evaluations are generally based on anecdotal information. Typical results of the few evaluation studies of EMBA programs indicate that participants are generally satisfied with their experience, feeling that they have been broadened by the resultant exposure to new ideas and people and have gained increased levels of self-confidence (e.g., Andrews, 1966; Hollenbeck, 1991). Despite the lack of hard evidence, organizations continue to support such programs.

Most organizations use EMBA programs as one component of their executive development efforts in addition to other in-house and external activities (e.g., succession planning, short courses) (Fresina, 1988). We recommend that organizations interested in using EMBA programs carefully examine their development needs and investigate the programs they consider using. Discussions with administrators, faculty members, and alumni can yield useful information.

Short Courses in Management

Short courses in management are offered by a wide range of providers, including colleges, universities, industry associations, and consultants. These courses are generally focused on a particular topic, issue, or skill, and are freestanding (i.e., do not exist within a degree-oriented curriculum). Prior to 1980, the dominant external provider of such programs was the American Management Association (AMA), which continues to offer hundreds of courses on a wide range of topics. While other providers did offer courses and programs (e.g., the National Training Laboratories), the AMA nearly held a monopoly on providing such training (Eurich, 1990; Porter & McKibbin, 1988). The current picture is different in that no single provider dominates the field. In addition to colleges and universities, organizations such as the Center for Creative Leadership, Wilson Learning, industry associations, and a host of consultants offer short courses that can be used as part of a total management development program.

The intent of many short courses is to mix some theory with a great deal of practical relevance. The intent is to provide trainees with information and tools that have immediate application to their current jobs. Advantages to using such courses offered by external providers include controlling the costs of in-house courses, the specialized expertise of the provider, the design and packaging of such courses, and a practitioner-oriented approach (particularly among non-university courses) (Porter & McKibbin, 1988). One of the significant disadvantages of such courses is a lack of quality control. Operating in a highly competitive environment, many of these providers are under pressure to stay in business and may reduce their standards to ensure they generate sufficient business in the short-term. While market forces will eventually (and ideally) weed out the poor quality programs, this may take time and many clients may purchase poor quality courses during the process (Porter & McKibbin, 1988).

One potential disadvantage to short courses offered by colleges and universities is a real or perceived lack of relevance and practical orientation. One way some organizations are addressing these concerns is by working with colleges and universities to customize courses that will meet their specific needs. For example, Hoffman-LaRoche Inc., a New Jersey–based health care and pharmaceutical company, convinced the Massachusetts Institute of Technology (MIT) to customize a course that would provide managers with training in strategic management of technology, leadership, and quality (Hequet, 1992). Other similar partnerships exist between Ford Motor Company and the University of Michigan and IBM and Wharton. While this approach may resolve the issues of quality and relevance, it is not inexpensive, with costs per program (e.g., a three- or four-day course) ranging from $50,000 to $80,000 (Hequet, 1992). In addition, some schools may be reluctant to customize their offerings. Hequet (1992) recommends that organizations interested in such an approach should "shop around" by discussing their needs with a variety of schools, explaining specifically what they want and finding out what the school can offer (i.e., in terms of times, locations, instructors) and then negotiate for a reasonable price.

Customized or not, short courses offered by external providers are likely to remain a significant part of the management development scene in the future, especially in light of the convenience and variety of the options that are available. One of the best ways an organization can ensure it purchases courses that will meet its needs is to conduct a thorough needs analysis and evaluate the programs both before and after they are used.

Management Training and Experiences

As cited earlier, recent surveys indicate that almost 90 percent of organizations provide training and on-the-job experiences as part of their efforts to develop managers (Lee, 1991; Saari et al., 1988). The majority of organizations use a combination of externally provided and internally developed courses and programs to achieve this goal. In this section of the chapter, we focus briefly on company-specific management training approaches. A wide variety of possibilities exist. To illustrate the options in use, we will discuss three approaches: company-designed courses, company academies or "colleges," and on-the-job experiences.

Company-designed Courses

Organizations frequently design their own courses and seminars as one way to develop their managers. Such courses have the advantage of being tailored to the specific issues, skills, and individual attributes of the organization and its managers. These efforts can range from a specific course focusing on one skill or issue (e.g., evaluating employee performance, budgeting) to a series of interconnected courses (e.g., a two-week-long series of workshops to expose key nonmanagers to all company divisions and products and acquaint them with the challenges the company faces). For example, General Electric (GE) developed a series of courses to prepare managers to compete successfully in a global environment. The program, offered at the company's Crotonville, New York, management development center, is comprised of a core curriculum that includes courses offered in a five-stage developmental sequence—Corporate Entry Leadership Conferences, New Manager Development Courses, Advanced Functional Courses, Executive Programs, and Officers' Workshops. This program services employees ranging from new college hires to corporate officers (Tichy, 1989). The courses are tailored to the challenges faced by GE's managers, including the use of GE-specific issues to provide an opportunity for participants to solve problems.

The issues in designing and implementing such courses are the same as for any HRD program. Of particular note for such courses is to ensure they fit within an overall framework for developing managers. The idea is to avoid redundancy and help participants see the relevance of the courses to their overall developmental plan. It also helps managers, who are responsible for developing their subordinates, to understand the relationships of the courses the organization offers to the overall development effort. For example, GE makes clear its assumption that 80 percent of development occurs through on-the-job experience, with only 20 percent taking place through formal development (e.g., such as the Crotonville courses; Tichy, 1989). This perspective makes clear to managers that the bulk of their developmental efforts should be focused on providing subordinates with meaningful developmental experiences.

Company Academies or "Colleges"

A number of organizations have concluded that a significant component of their management development strategy should include a company academy or college in which all managers at certain levels are required to complete a specific curriculum. Organizations who have taken this approach include GE, IBM, McDonald's, Dunkin' Donuts, Holiday Inn, and Xerox. The facilities used for these academies can be quite elaborate (e.g., hundred-acre, landscaped campuses with multiple buildings and residential facilities located away from other company facilities). They have a specific educational mission geared toward the organization's specific needs and preferred ways of doing things. For example, McDonald's, the worldwide fast-food chain, teaches managers its approach to ensuring quality, service, and cleanliness at Hamburger University in Oak Brook, IL. The courses at Hamburger University include operational procedures that reinforce the organization's philosophy. Hamburger University uses a wide range of training methods, including lecture and discussion, audiovisuals, and hands-on experiences with equipment (Eurich, 1990; Odiorne & Rummler, 1988).

Xerox Corporation devotes a portion of its over 2,000-acre corporate living, learning, and fitness center in Leesburg, Virginia, to its corporate education center. The center is capable of handling 1,000 students at a time, and offers curricula in sales training, service training, and management training. The management training curriculum focuses on teaching participants about the business, their jobs as managers, and about themselves. Faculty for the center are drawn from the company's employees and course design is performed by a group of professionals (Educational Services) specifically trained in course design that has access to production facilities capable of creating courses using a wide range of technologies (e.g., video, computer-assisted instruction). Members of this group identify needs and develop courses in collaboration with clients, subject matter experts, and instructors (Odiorne & Rummler, 1988).

While not all company academies are as elaborate as those run by McDonald's and Xerox, they are an expensive component of management development. Some organizations permit members of outside organizations to use their facilities and attend their courses for a fee when space permits. Critics charge that the standardized curricula at corporate academies can lead to problems (e.g., unresponsiveness to the organization's needs, detachment from the realities of the operating divisions). Eurich (1990) suggests, however, that such curricula can be useful if they transmit knowledge and skills that all participants at a particular level should know, and that some of the problems that accompany this approach can be mitigated by a "vigilant management and training staff to ensure that a curriculum admits new ideas and responds to change" (p. 167).

On-the-Job Experiences

It is generally believed that most managers develop their expertise as a result of on-the-job experiences (e.g., Digman, 1978; McCall, Lombardo, & Morrison, 1988; Zemke, 1985). Organizations also recognize what experience contributes to development (e.g., GE assumes that 80 percent of management development occurs on-the-job [Tichy, 1989]). Despite the importance of on-the-job experience to management development, many organizations leave such development to chance, hoping managers discover the lessons to be learned on their own. In addition, not much is known about how these events influence development and how we can make the most of such experiences (e.g., Wexley & Baldwin, 1986). Some observers have noted that many on-the-job experiences tend to reinforce old attitudes and behaviors rather than encourage managers to adopt new ones that can make them more effective (Keys & Wolfe, 1988).

Clearly, research on the types of events that have developmental potential, the lessons they can teach, and how such lessons can be learned is needed if we are to harness the power of experience. An important step in that direction is a series of studies of the role of experience in executive development conducted at the Center for Creative Leadership (CCL) (this research is summarized in McCall, Lombardo, & Morrison, 1988). Researchers from CCL studied 191 successful executives from six major organizations by asking them to describe the key events in their careers and explain what they learned from them. These inquiries yielded over 1,500 lessons executives learned from 616 events. Content analysis of these statements resulted in 32 types of lessons that can be grouped into five themes: setting and implementing agendas, handling relationships, basic values, executive temperament, and personal awareness. The developmental events were summarized into five categories: setting the stage, leading by persuasion, leading on the line, when other people matter, and hardships. Table 12-5 lists the themes and the lessons that make up each theme, and Table 12-6 lists the categories of events and types of events that make up each category.

McCall, Lombardo, and Morrison (1988) observe that the lessons learned from on-the-job events are hard-won, involving emotion, reflection, and assistance from others to extract the meaning. They conclude that it is management's responsibility (shared with the individual) to be vigilant for opportunities to develop subordinates (e.g., task-force assignments, challenging assignments), and to provide the necessary support, resources, feedback, and time necessary for subordinates to learn from these events. While recognizing that firm conclusions are hard to come by, McCall, Lombardo, and Morrison suggest that an effective management development system is one that is characterized by the following:

1. **Opportunism**—taking advantage of opportunities for growth and learning;

2. **Individualism**—taking into account the unique attributes of the individuals being developed;

3. **Long-term perspective**—taking the view that developing managers is a multi-year process (e.g., 10–20 years);

4. **Encouragement of self-motivation** by the individuals being developed; and

5. **On-line approach**—centered around learning on the job.

The events approach described by the CCL research is intriguing and presents a variety of useful suggestions for using experiences deliberately to develop managers. However, this work is only an initial step toward understanding what can be done and how to do it. Generalizations to be taken from this research thus

TABLE 12-5	POTENTIAL LESSONS OF EXPERIENCE

Setting and Implementing Agendas
- Technical/professional skills.
- All about the business one is in.
- Strategic thinking.
- Shouldering full responsibility.
- Building and using structure and control systems.
- Innovative problem-solving methods.

Handling Relationships
- Handling political situations.
- Getting people to implement solutions.
- What executives are like.
- How to work with executives.
- Strategies of negotiation.
- Dealing with people over whom you have no authority.
- Understanding other people's perspectives.
- Dealing with conflict.
- Directing and motivating subordinates.
- Developing other people.
- Confronting subordinate performance problems.
- Managing former bosses and peers.

Basic Values
- You can't manage everything all alone.
- Sensitivity to the human side of management.
- Basic management values.

Executive Temperament
- Being tough when necessary.
- Self-confidence.
- Coping with situations beyond your control.
- Persevering through adversity.
- Coping with ambiguous situations.
- Use (and abuse) of power.

Personal Awareness
- The balance between work and personal life.
- Knowing what really excites you about work.
- Personal limits and blind spots.
- Taking charge of your career.
- Recognizing and seizing opportunities.

SOURCE: From *The Lessons of Experience: How Successful Executives Develop on the Job* (p. 6) by M. W. McCall, Jr., M. M. Lombardo, and A. M. Morrison, 1988, Lexington, MA: Lexington Books.

far are limited (e.g., the sample studied was composed almost entirely of male, white, middle-aged managers from six large organizations). Nevertheless, we believe this research is a significant step forward in an important area.

In addition to the "events" view, there are at least two other approaches to using on-the-job experiences systematically in management development: mentoring and action learning. Mentoring was discussed at some length in Chapter

TABLE 12-6	THE DEVELOPMENTAL EVENTS

Setting the Stage
- Early work experience.
- First supervisory job.

Leading by Persuasion
- Project/task-force assignments.
- Line to staff switches.

Leading on Line
- Starting from scratch.
- Turning a business around.
- Managing a larger scope.

When Other People Matter
- Bosses.

Hardships
- Personal trauma.
- Career setback.
- Changing jobs.
- Business mistakes.
- Subordinate performance problems.

SOURCE: From *The Lessons of Experience: How Successful Executives Develop on the Job* (p. 10) by M. W. McCall, Jr., M. M. Lombardo, and A. M. Morrison, 1988, Lexington, MA: Lexington Books.

11, so we will not revisit that topic here. **Action learning** is a European concept that has recently been applied in the United States (Keys & Wolfe, 1988). Originally developed as a way to encourage line managers to provide input to modify operating systems (e.g., Morgan & Ramirez, 1983; Revans, 1982), action learning as it is currently practiced involves having participants select an organizational problem, write a case study describing the problem, and meet with a group of other managers who face similar problems to discuss ways the problem can be dealt with (Keys & Wolfe, 1988). This idea is sort of a "living case" approach, where instead of analyzing situations that have been resolved in the past, participants deal with ongoing problems and issues. Among the potential advantages of an action learning approach is the discovery of a structured way to examine and analyze on-the-job events. Action learning also provides the opportunity to motivate participants to seek additional development (e.g., negotiation skills) that will help them resolve the type of problem discussed. In addition, because participants focus on existing issues, their motivation to learn and seek further development may be stronger. While there has been some descriptive writing about the action learning approach (e.g., Mumford, 1987), empirical research is lacking.

In summary, there are a variety of ways organizations can systematically use on-the-job experiences to develop managers. While there is much research to be done, on-the-job experience should be a significant component of an organization's management development strategy. We recommend organizations examine the opportunities available to them in this area to determine how they can make the most of experiences in their managers' development.

Examples of Approaches Used to Develop Managers

There are many options for conducting management training and development. Not only are there many training techniques available (see Chapter 5), but the topics are also diverse, including leadership, motivation, interpersonal skills, decision making, cultural training, and technical knowledge. We will describe three types commonly used in management development programs: leadership training, rater training, and the use of behavior modeling to develop interpersonal skills.

Leadership Training

Leadership has been one of the most heavily researched and popularly discussed topics in management. There is a widespread belief that leadership skills are essential to effective management. At any point in time, dozens of books and popular press articles are available to managers to help them learn how they can become more effective leaders. One of the problems with advice in the popular press on leadership is that it is usually anecdotal, lacks a sound theoretical basis, and is often contradictory.

Two widely used approaches to leadership training, Leader Match and Managerial Grid training, and one more recent approach, Leader-Member Exchange (LMX) training, overcome many of these problems. Each of these programs is based on a theory about what leadership is and how it can be acquired. Each has also been the subject of empirical research, and is backed by at least some evidence that it can improve one's leadership effectiveness. While these programs are not without problems or critics, they do represent a clearheaded, systematic approach to training and development.

Fiedler's Leader Match Program   Leader Match training (Fiedler & Chemers, 1984) is based on the notion that effective leadership occurs when there is a match between the leader's style and the situation he or she faces. The theoretical foundation for the program is Fiedler's contingency theory of leadership (e.g., Fiedler, 1964, 1967; Fiedler & Chemers, 1974). Fiedler believes that each person has a particular leadership style, based on his or her needs, that dictates how he or she will act. Because this style is based on the leader's needs, it is very difficult for the leader to change it. According to Fiedler, that style will not be effective in all situations. It is therefore the leader's task to diagnose the situation, and either place himself in a situation favorable to his style or modify the situation so that it becomes favorable to his style.

The **Leader Match** program (Fiedler & Chemers, 1984; Fiedler, Chemers, & Mahar, 1976) is a self-administered programmed instruction technique (it is sold as a workbook) designed to help the leader:

1. Diagnose his or her leadership style;

2. Diagnose the situation and categorize it as favorable or unfavorable; and

3. Change the critical elements of the situation so that it will match the leader's style.

The program takes about 5 to 12 hours to complete and can be supplemented by lectures, discussions, and other training media (Wexley & Latham, 1991).

Trainees use measuring scales provided in the programmed instruction book to assess their leadership style and situational favorableness. The leader's style is measured by the **Least Preferred Co-Worker (LPC) scale** shown in Figure 12-5. This instrument requires the leader to describe the person he or she would least like to work with using a series of bipolar adjectives (e.g., friendly-unfriendly, supportive-hostile). The leader's responses indicate whether the leader has a stronger need for relationships (a high-LPC leader) or for task accomplishment (a low-LPC leader). Fiedler argues that all leaders have both needs, but that one need will be dominant and must be satisfied first. Therefore, relationship-motivated leaders will behave in ways to establish relationships first, and will then focus primarily on task accomplishment. The opposite is true of task-motivated leaders.

Whether the situation is favorable or unfavorable depends on the leader's control over the situation, which is measured by three factors: leader-member relations, task structure, and the leader's position power. The Leader Match book contains measuring scales for each of these dimensions. Contingency theory states that task-motivated leaders are effective in highly favorable and highly unfavorable situations. A highly favorable situation is one that permits a high degree of control (e.g., good relationships with followers, a highly structured task, and adequate power to reward and punish subordinates). An unfavorable situation is one with a low degree of control (e.g., poor relationships with followers, an ambiguous or unstructured task, and inadequate power to reward and punish). The theory further states that relationship-motivated leaders are effective in situations that are moderately favorable (i.e., provide the leader with moderate control).

After the trainee has diagnosed his or her leadership style and the favorableness of the situation he or she manages in, the training program focuses on ways in which the leader can modify the situation to match his or her style. Suggestions are made as to how one can modify leader-member relations, task structure, and position power. For example, to increase position power, the leader can "show [her] subordinates 'who's boss' by exercising fully the powers that the organization provides" or "make sure that information to [her] group gets channeled through [her]" (Fiedler & Chemers, 1984, p. 183).

Both Fiedler's contingency theory and the Leader Match program have been extensively researched (see Strube & Garcia, 1981, and Burke & Day, 1986, for reviews). The program has been tested in a variety of settings using working

FIGURE 12-5	LEAST PREFERRED CO-WORKER (LPC) SCALE

Pleasant	__ __ __ __ __ __ __ __	Unpleasant
	8 7 6 5 4 3 2 1	

Friendly	__ __ __ __ __ __ __ __	Unfriendly
	8 7 6 5 4 3 2 1	

Rejecting	__ __ __ __ __ __ __ __	Accepting
	1 2 3 4 5 6 7 8	

Tense	__ __ __ __ __ __ __ __	Relaxed
	1 2 3 4 5 6 7 8	

Distant	__ __ __ __ __ __ __ __	Close
	1 2 3 4 5 6 7 8	

Cold	__ __ __ __ __ __ __ __	Warm
	1 2 3 4 5 6 7 8	

Supportive	__ __ __ __ __ __ __ __	Hostile
	8 7 6 5 4 3 2 1	

Boring	__ __ __ __ __ __ __ __	Interesting
	1 2 3 4 5 6 7 8	

Quarrelsome	__ __ __ __ __ __ __ __	Harmonious
	1 2 3 4 5 6 7 8	

Gloomy	__ __ __ __ __ __ __ __	Cheerful
	1 2 3 4 5 6 7 8	

Open	__ __ __ __ __ __ __ __	Guarded
	8 7 6 5 4 3 2 1	

Backbiting	__ __ __ __ __ __ __ __	Loyal
	1 2 3 4 5 6 7 8	

Untrustworthy	__ __ __ __ __ __ __ __	Trustworthy
	1 2 3 4 5 6 7 8	

Considerate	__ __ __ __ __ __ __ __	Inconsiderate
	8 7 6 5 4 3 2 1	

Nasty	__ __ __ __ __ __ __ __	Nice
	1 2 3 4 5 6 7 8	

Agreeable	__ __ __ __ __ __ __ __	Disagreeable
	8 7 6 5 4 3 2 1	

Insincere	__ __ __ __ __ __ __ __	Sincere
	1 2 3 4 5 6 7 8	

Kind	__ __ __ __ __ __ __ __	Unkind
	8 7 6 5 4 3 2 1	

SOURCE: From *Improving Leadership Effectiveness: The Leader Match Concept (2nd Ed)* (p. 19) by F. E. Fiedler and M. M. Chemers, 1984, New York: Wiley. Copyright 1984 by John Wiley & Sons, Inc. Reprinted by permission.

adult leaders, including public health volunteer workers (Fiedler & Mahar, 1979a), ROTC military leaders (Fiedler & Mahar, 1979b), police and county government middle managers (Fiedler, Mahar, & Schmidt, 1976). Overall, there is evidence that Leader Match can improve a leader's effectiveness. Burke and Day (1986), in a meta-analysis of 70 published and unpublished studies of management development programs, concluded that Leader Match is effective when using subjective behavioral criteria (i.e., ratings of changes in on-the-job behavior) and generalized across situations. They recommend the use of Leader Match training based on both the research evidence and cost-effectiveness of the program.

Leader Match and the contingency theory have not been without controversy. Researchers have questioned the soundness of the LPC scale and the linkage between Leader Match and the contingency theory (e.g., Schriesheim, Bannister, & Money, 1979; Jago & Ragan, 1986a, 1986b; Kabanoff, 1981), with rejoinders from Fiedler and his associates (Rice, 1978, 1979; Chemers & Fiedler, 1986). Despite the lack of closure on the controversial aspects of the theory and program, Leader Match and Fiedler's efforts to develop and substantiate a training program based on theory and empirical research are impressive given the tendency in the past for the training and development and the HRD fields to rely on fads and testimonials. This approach should be a model for others in these fields to emulate.

Grid Training Grid® training is another approach to leadership training that has been systematically developed and refined. Developed by Blake and Mouton (1964, 1985; Blake & McCanse, 1991), Grid training is based on the idea that it is a leader's behavior (and the attitudes and motivations that create that behavior) that makes him or her effective. Blake and Mouton believe that there are two dimensions to a leader's behavior:

1. **Concern for people**—the extent to which the leader demonstrates respect, warmth, sympathy, trust and respect for others through his or her actions; and

2. **Concern for production**—the extent to which the leader's behavior focuses on results, whether it be in the form of profits, mission, performance, costs, and the like.

A leader's consistent pattern of behavior, or style, can be represented as a combination of these two factors. Blake and Mouton developed a chart, called the **Managerial Grid** (and renamed and trademarked as the Leadership Grid® in 1991), to graphically depict a leader's style (see Figure 12-6). The *y*-axis of the Grid shows concern for people and the *x*-axis shows concern for production. Both factors are rated on a scale of 1 (low) to 9 (high).

A leader's style can be represented by two numbers that show the rating the leader receives on each dimension. For example, if a leader is rated 3 on concern for production, and 5 on concern for people, the leader would be referred to as a 3,5 leader. Five styles are prominent and are described on the Grid:

FIGURE 12-6 **THE LEADERSHIP GRID®**

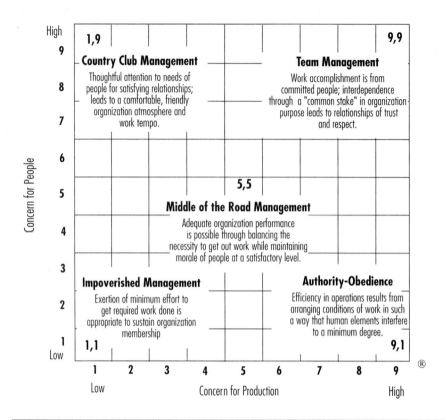

SOURCE: From *Leadership Dilemmas—Grid® Solutions* (p. 29), by R. R. Blake and A. A. McCanse, 1991, Houston, TX: Gulf Publishing. Copyright 1991 by Scientific Methods, Inc. Reprinted by permission.

(1) Impoverished Management, (2) Authority-Obedience, (3) Middle of the Road Management, (4) Country Club Management, and (5) Team Management. In addition, Blake and McCanse (1991) describe two additional prominent leadership styles, Opportunism and Paternalism, and describe all seven leadership styles in terms of key issues and behaviors (e.g., motivation, conflict solving, initiative, inquiry, advocacy, subordinate interactions).

According to the Grid approach, the extent to which a leader engages in each type of behavior is based on his or her assumptions about leadership. Grid training is designed to help trainees examine their assumptions about leadership and adopt a more effective and humane leadership style.

The goal of Grid training is to help the manager become a 9,9 leader (i.e., high concern for production and high concern for people). Blake and Mouton argue that this style will make one an effective leader in all situations. They argue that this style is a "goal-centered, team approach that seeks to gain optimum results through participation, involvement, commitment, and conflict solving from everyone who can contribute" (Blake & Mouton, 1985, p. 13).

The full Grid training program involves six phases that may take up to five years for an organization to complete. In total, the six phase program is an organizational development approach. The six phases, as described by Blake and Mouton (1985) and Blake and McCanse (1991) include:

1. **Phase 1: Grid® Seminars** Training programs for managers and executives designed to teach the Leadership Grid and therefore increase self-understanding, experience team problem-solving, learn about managing conflict, and understand the implications to the organization of managing according to the Grid approach. This is followed by Phase 1a projects, the purpose of which is to get those who can solve a problem to take responsibility for it, applying what has been learned in the Grid Seminar to solving real-world problems.

2. **Phase 2: Team building** A five-day, on-the-job program designed to bring together managers to make decisions and solve problems. The goals include creating a team culture, increasing objective views of one's behavior, setting standards for excellence, and establishing team objectives.

3. **Phase 3: Interface development** Focuses on the activities between departments or units experiencing resistance and barriers to effectively working together. This is implemented only between departments that have problems with cooperation and coordination.

4. **Phase 4: Designing an ideal strategic organization model** The goal is for the organization to establish the way it will conduct business activity in the future, based on the concepts of 9,9 managing.

5. **Phase 5: Implementing development** Involves identifying and implementing actions needed to put into practice the ideal model developed in Phase 4.

6. **Phase 6: Consolidation** This phase includes activities to ensure the model is working as planned, evaluating activities, and scanning the environment to ensure any changes needed for the organization to remain competitive are identified and implemented.

Grid training, at least at the Phase 1 level, has been widely implemented in industry and government. Wexley and Latham (1991) report that over 400,000 managers have attended Grid Seminars since 1964. Is Grid training effective? It is difficult to tell at this point. According to Wexley and Latham (1991), there are no published evaluative studies of Phase 1 training, and research that has been offered to examine the overall effectiveness of the Grid approach, while supportive, was anecdotal, subjective, and lacked an experimental control group. We agree that more research is needed before any firm statements can be made about the program's effectiveness.

Leader-Member Exchange (LMX) Training   The third type of leadership training discussed here, **Leader-Member Exchange (LMX),** is designed to improve the relationships between supervisors and their subordinates. According to Vertical Dyad Linkage (VDL) theory (Graen, 1976; Liden & Graen, 1980), subordinates and supervisors have a relationship based on exchange, with each party having something the other wants. Supervisors have control over organizational resources and rewards (e.g., opportunity for decision-making, access to information, access to work assignments) and subordinates have control over their commitment to the organization and the effort they put forth. Subordinates exchange involvement for organizational outcomes controlled by the supervisor, and vice versa.

Research on this relationship has shown that supervisors behave consistently toward subordinates over time, treating some more favorably than others, resulting in the formation of favored in-groups and less favored out-groups (Dansereau, Graen, & Haga, 1975). In high LMX relationships, the relationship is characterized by high productivity and satisfaction. In low LMX relationships, the opposite is true. To the extent an out-group exists, the supervisor (leader) is not making the best use of resources and the unit is less effective than it should be, with a negative impact on turnover (Graen, Liden, & Hoel, 1982) and productivity (Graen, Novak, & Sommerkamp, 1982).

The goal of LMX training is to get supervisors to examine the relationships they have with subordinates and improve low LMX relationships. The program involves a series of two-hour sessions, covering topics such as LMX theory, listening skills, resource exchange, and one-on-one relationships. Leader-member relationships are measured using the seven-item LMX scale (Liden & Graen, 1980). Like Fiedler's LPC scale, the psychometric properties of the LMX scale have been criticized (see Dienesch & Liden, 1986).

There is evidence to suggest LMX training is effective in improving leader-member relations. For example, Scandura and Graen (1984) tested the effectiveness of LMX training using a pre-test/post-test design with a placebo control group (in which managers received six hours of training in other issues). They found an improvement in out-group relationships and an increase in job satisfaction and productivity. Research on both VDL theory and LMX training has also examined factors that may effect the application of LMX training. For example, Graen, Scandura, and Graen (1986) showed that employees with high growth-need strength responded positively to offers of vertical collaboration, which is one aspect of LMX, while employees with low growth-need strength did not.

Comment on Leadership Training   Leadership training programs such as Leader Match and LMX training represent a positive approach to management development (and to HRD in general). These programs are based on theory and have been examined using research designs that can actually answer questions about program effectiveness. The willingness of the developers of these programs to go the extra mile is exactly what is needed if HRD is to advance and serve the needs of organizations.

Performance Rater Training

Rating employee performance is commonly described as one of the least liked aspects of managing. Over the last 20 years, a great deal of attention has been paid to how managers and supervisors can be trained to make fewer errors and rate employee performance more accurately. Accurate performance ratings are essential if the decisions they are used to make (e.g., as to promotion, pay, access to training) are to be correct.

The primary concern of many **rater training** approaches is to reduce rating errors. **Rating errors** are tendencies or biases managers may have when evaluating performance that interfere with accuracy. Among the errors commonly highlighted in training programs are halo error, leniency error, central tendency error, and contrast error. These errors are defined in Table 12-7.

Smith (1986) reviewed the results of 24 empirical studies that tested the effectiveness of rater training. He grouped rater training programs into three categories:

1. **Rater error training (RET)** The purpose of this training is to directly reduce the incidence of errors, usually by explaining and demonstrating errors to trainees and encouraging them to avoid them.

2. **Performance dimension training (PDT)** This approach familiarizes trainees with the aspects of performance to be rated by having

---

TABLE 12-7   **FOUR COMMON RATING ERRORS**

1. **Halo error**—Allowing evaluation of one dimension of an employee's performance to affect evaluation of other dimensions. For example, if an employee works well with others, a supervisor's evaluation of this aspect of performance may lead him or her to overlook poor quality work, tardiness, or other undesirable aspects of performance. Consequently, the supervisor's ratings on all dimensions will be similar, even though actual performance on these dimensions is not.

2. **Leniency error**—The tendency to use only the favorable end of the rating scale, thus rating all employees positively regardless of true performance. For example, a professor who refuses to give students D and F grades would be committing leniency error. The opposite of this is *stringency error*, which involves using only the unfavorable end of the rating scale, as when a professor refuses to give any student an A.

3. **Central tendency error**—The tendency to use only the middle portion of the rating scale, regardless of employee performance. As a result, no employees are rated at the extreme positive or negative end of the scale.

4. **Contrast error**—This can occur if a supervisor rates several employees in succession and allows the evaluation of the previous employee to affect the rating of the subsequent one.

them read job descriptions and qualifications, review the rating scales they will use, or actually assist in developing those scales.

3. **Performance standard training (PST)** Trainees are given common perceptions of the performance standards, usually by showing them samples of performance and the ratings "expert" raters would give each sample.

Smith (1986) also categorized the training programs according to the method used to present material. The categories include lecture, group discussion, and practice and feedback. He reports several conclusions.

First, training becomes more effective as trainees become more involved in the process: practice and feedback is superior to discussion, which is superior to lecture.

Second, rater error training (RET) is effective in reducing errors, including those in the halo and leniency categories. However, RET cannot guarantee ratings will be more accurate—absence of rating errors is not the same as accurate ratings. As Bernardin and Buckley (1984) point out, rater error training may merely encourage trainees to substitute one response set (e.g., halo error with similar ratings across dimensions) for another (e.g., giving different ratings on different dimensions whether performance on those dimensions is different or not).

A third conclusion was that performance standard training (PST) and performance dimension training (PDT) can improve rater accuracy. Smith (1986) argues the best approach to improving accuracy is to combine PDT and PST by first having trainees discuss the performance dimensions they will use, then providing them with examples of performance in each dimension, then allowing them to practice using the rating scales, and finally having them compare their ratings with those of experts.

Despite these conclusions, the message sent by this research is not as clear. Several problems with these studies limit the generalizability of their results to real-world settings. First, researchers cannot agree on the criteria that should be used to evaluate the effectiveness of rater training programs. Many studies use how close the subjects' ratings are to "true score" ratings, which are usually determined by having a panel of observers who evaluate the stimulus material before the study. However, these so-called true scores may be in fact wrong and unclear, especially if they are developed by observers who have never performed the job being rated (Zedeck & Cascio, 1984). In addition, focusing on true-score criteria and eliminating rating errors may fail to serve the real goal of rater training, which is to improve the rater's ability to observe performance accurately (Bernardin & Villanova, 1986).

Furthermore, most rater training studies have been conducted using college students as raters in laboratories rather than managers in a real-world setting (Bernardin & Villanova, 1986; Goldstein & Musicante, 1986; Smith, 1986). It is unclear whether the behavior of student raters in laboratories is similar to that of managers in the real world. Similarly, in many of these studies subjects rated either written descriptions of performance or videotapes of performance by actors. There is some research (Murphy et al., 1986) that shows ratings of "paper people" are different than ratings of actual behavior. It appears, therefore, "that we have failed to understand the dynamics of organizations and thus our research does not seem to be focusing on the issues that makes (sic) a difference" (Goldstein & Gessner, 1988, p. 57). We agree with Goldstein and Gessner (1988) and Latham (1988) that future research on rater training should focus on improving rater accuracy and be conducted within the organizational context.

Behavior Modeling Training

Behavior modeling training is a popular training technique that has been used primarily to train people to perform both manual, interpersonal, and cognitive skills. The technique is based on Bandura's Social Learning Theory, which was applied to supervisory training by Goldstein and Sorcher (1974). The underlying rationale for this form of training is that people can learn by observing other people (models) perform a task provided they are shown clearly what the components of the behavior are, remember what the behavior is, actually perform the behavior, and are motivated to use what they have learned (Decker & Nathan, 1985).

Behavior modeling typically involves five steps: modeling, retention, rehearsal, feedback, and transfer of training. During the *modeling phase*, trainees are usually shown a film or videotape in which a model performs the behavior to be learned. The desired behavior is broken into a series of discrete *learning points*, or key behaviors that make up the overall behavior. For example, if supervisors are being trained to handle employee complaints, the film would show a supervisor handle complaints in the desired manner. The learning points for this behavior might include:

1. Listen openly.

2. Do not speak until the employee has had his or her say.

3. Avoid reacting emotionally. (Don't get defensive.)

4. Ask for the employee's expectations about a solution to the problem.

5. Agree on specific steps to be taken and specific deadlines (Decker & Nathan, 1985, p. 145).

In the *retention phase*, trainees perform activities to enhance the memory of what they have observed. These activities include reviewing the learning points, discussing the rationale underlying each point, and talking over the behaviors the model performed to illustrate those points. In the *rehearsal phase*, each trainee role plays the desired behavior with another trainee. For example, each trainee learning how to handle employee complaints would have an opportunity to role play resolving a complaint from a fellow trainee representing the complaining employee. During the *feedback phase*, each trainee receives feedback on his or her performance based on what was done well and what should be improved. Finally, in the *transfer of training phase*, trainees are encouraged to practice the newly learned behavior on the job. In some behavior modeling programs, trainees regroup later to discuss problems and successes in using their newly learned skills.

An example of behavior modeling training applied to the mastery of a computer software program is reported by Gist, Schwoerer, and Rosen (1989). Trainees observed a videotape in which the model illustrated the steps involved in performing each task to be learned. The video also reviewed key learning points and showed trainees the responses to expect from the program on the computer monitor. Following a demonstration of each step, the trainer stopped the videotape to allow trainees to perform it, with the responses from the program on the computer monitor providing feedback as to the correctness of the trainee's performance.

There is research evidence to support the effectiveness of behavior modeling training. Although studies conducted during the mid-1970s (e.g., Burnaska, 1976; Byham, Adams, & Kiggins, 1976; Moses & Ritchie, 1976; Smith, 1976) supporting behavior modeling were criticized as having flaws that compromised the findings, subsequent research (e.g., Gist et al., 1989; Latham & Saari, 1979; McGehee and Tullar, 1978; Meyer & Raich, 1983) correcting these problems has supported the technique's effectiveness. Although behavior modeling is not always effective (see Russell, Wexley & Hunter, 1984), Burke and Day's (1986) meta-analysis of management training also shows behavior modeling is among the most effective management training techniques.

One of the reasons that behavior modeling seems to be effective is that it increases a trainee's feelings of self-efficacy (Bandura, 1986), which is one's belief in his or her capacity to perform a particular task (see Chapter 2). Individuals with high self-efficacy tend to perform better than individuals with low self-efficacy (e.g., Taylor, Locke, Lee, & Gist, 1984).

Research has suggested how behavior modeling works and how it can be improved (e.g., Decker, 1983, 1984; Latham & Saari, 1979). For example, a series of studies has demonstrated the importance of learning points in the process. *Learning points* keyed to important behaviors and demonstrated by the model result in greater recall and performance of those behaviors (Latham & Saari, 1979; Mann & Decker, 1984). In addition, research suggests that learning points generated by trainees led to better performance than learning points generated by "experts" (Hogan, Hakel, & Decker, 1986).

A recent study (Baldwin, 1992) examined two ways such training may be improved: by providing multiple scenarios during training and by exposing trainees to both positive and negative models. Baldwin suggested providing multiple scenarios may increase the chances trainees would generalize the skills they learn to apply them to other situations. Baldwin also theorized that providing negative models as well as positive models would help trainees not only learn new behaviors but also help them unlearn prior, ineffective behaviors. Baldwin reported two significant findings: (1) that providing positive and negative models did lead to greater generalization than using positive models only, but (2) that viewing positive models led only to greater reproduction of the behavior learned than viewing both positive and negative models.[3] While further research into this issue is needed, these results suggest that different approaches to using models in behavior modeling training may be needed, depending on the goals of the training (e.g., reproducing a behavior in a particular type of situation or being able to use the behavior in a variety of situations).

Behavior modeling is not without its critics. Parry and Reich (1984) argue that the technique can have several weaknesses that trainers should take care to avoid:

1. The use of simplistic behavior models.

2. Not explaining the theory underlying why the behaviors being taught are needed. For example, suppose the training session focuses on handling abusive customers. If trainees are told they should let the customer vent his feelings, they should be told why.

3. The classes are boring because they follow a similar format and have all trainees in a session perform the same role playing.

4. Examples of incorrect behavior are seldom used, even though they provide opportunities for learning.

5. If verbal behavior is what is being taught, then the use of film or video might interfere by adding extraneous stimuli. Written models may be better for these cases.

6. Many trainees engage in improvisational acting rather than true role playing.

7. While focusing on behaviors rather than underlying attitudes may be effective in the short run, it is important to change attitudes as well; otherwise, employees will not stick with the newly learned behaviors over the long haul.

Parry and Reich (1984) do believe the technique can be effective if these limitations are overcome. Rosenbaum (1984) replied to Parry and Reich's (1984) criticisms, suggesting, among other things, that the design and delivery of behavior modeling training requires rigorous technique, that models serve as points of reference rather than purporting to show the only way to handle a situation, and

---

[3]*Note:* Baldwin's (1992) study also illustrates the importance of evaluating training at different levels, as suggested in Chapter 6.

that modeling conforms to the tenets of adult learning. This sort of debate is healthy, and, combined with research on ways to improve modeling training, can lead to better ways of using behavior modeling to help managers (and others) improve their interpersonal skills. Those who wish to use the technique should consult Goldstein and Sorcher (1974) and especially the excellent book written by Decker and Nathan (1985) for specifics on how to develop a program.

Designing Management Development Programs

Management development programs should be constructed the way any sound HRD program is: through needs assessment, design and implementation, and evaluation. More specifically, the issues discussed in this chapter lead to several recommendations and reminders:

1. Management development must be **tied to the organization's strategic plan** to be responsive to the needs of the organization and those of the individuals being developed.

2. A **thorough needs analysis,** including investigating what managers in the organization do and the skills they need to perform effectively, is essential.

3. **Specific objectives,** both for the overall program and each of its components, (e.g., on-the-job experiences, classroom training) should be established.

4. **Involvement in and commitment of senior management in all phases** of the process, from needs assessment to evaluation, is critical. Simply stated, it is management's responsibility to ensure the organization has a high-quality management team.

5. A **variety of developmental opportunities,** both formal and on-the-job, should be used.

6. The program should be designed to ensure that the individuals to be developed are **motivated to participate** in such activities. The day-to-day demands placed on managers at all levels make it easy to put development on the back burner.

7. Action should be taken to **evaluate** the program regularly, and **modify and update** same as needs change.

While this list contains nothing new or startling (especially coming as it does in the twelfth chapter of this text), many management development programs do not conform to these basic expectations.

RETURN TO OPENING CASE

After a thorough needs analysis and examining management development programs at similar organizations, such as Manpower Inc., Children's World Learning Center (CWLC) created a centralized management development program that had two key components: MDS1 and MDS2. The program was developed through subject-matter and training experts. The design process took about one year and cost the company $300,000.

MDS1 included a self-study package of materials and focused on candidates with on-the-job field experience. Employees who wanted to become center directors were given the self-study package to complete at their own pace. The participant's district director was responsible for monitoring progress and could customize parts of the program if needed.

After completing MDS1, participants hired as center directors began the second phase, MDS2. MDS2 training was conducted at the company's management development center in Golden, Colorado. By the time each new center director was on the job six months, he or she would have received over 50 hours in training.

Karen Maggio estimates that the cost of operating the program is about $1,500 per trainee. She believes that this cost is justified by indications that training helps reduce turnover. Data collected to date show that there has been a 5 percent drop in CWLC's turnover rate for those serving as center directors. According to Maggio, "The only drawback that we've encountered so far is that the demand for the training is greater than we expected."[4]

Summary

Management development is one of the most widely offered and important forms of HRD. It should be deliberate, long-term, specific to the organization, and tied to the organization's business plan.

While one would expect that existing research on the managerial job would provide a clear picture of what managers do, the competencies they need, and how they develop, there is much we do not yet know. We have presented several ways this issue has been addressed and suggested that two process models, the integrated competency model and the four-dimensional model, may be the most advanced and useful approaches available to date. However, this discussion also emphasized the importance of careful study by HRD practitioners to better answer these questions when designing management development programs for their own organizations.

---

[4]From "When the CEO is on Your Side" by P. A. Galagan, 1992, *Training and Development Journal, 43*(9). Copyright 1992 by The American Society for Training Development. All rights reserved. Adapted by permission.

Options for management education, such as college and university degree programs, executive M.B.A. programs, and short courses offered by external providers, were discussed. In addition, we also explored organizationally based training and experience methods, including courses and programs, corporate academies, and on-the-job experiences.

To illustrate the content of some of the approaches used in management development, we described three common training programs: leadership training, rater training, and behavior modeling training for interpersonal skill development. Three approaches to leadership development that are grounded in leadership theory are Leader Match, Grid Training, and Leader-Member Exchange (LMX) training. Leader Match is based on the idea that a manager should diagnose his or her leadership style and then match the situation to that style. Grid training involves measuring a manager's leadership style and then training the manager to adopt a style that shows both high concern for production and high concern for people. LMX training is aimed at helping managers improve their relationships with subordinates. Rater training focuses on helping managers learn to evaluate employee performance accurately. Several approaches, including rater error training, performance dimension training, and performance standard training, are available. Finally, behavior modeling training involves learning through observing a model perform the behavior in question. Trainees are usually shown a videotape or film of a model performing the behavior, discuss the components of the behavior, practice the behavior by role playing, and receive constructive feedback on their performance. This form of training has been shown to be effective for training both in motor and interpersonal skills.

The chapter closed with a list of recommendations for designing an effective management development program.

Key Terms and Concepts

assessment center
behavior modeling
competencies
executive M.B.A. programs
four dimensional model
integrated competency model
interpersonal skills
Leader Match
Least Preferred Co-worker (LPC) scale

Leader-Member Exchange
  (LMX) training
management development
management education
Managerial Grid
on-the-job experiences
rater training

Questions for Discussion

1. Explain why management development is one of the most common HRD activities found in organizations today. Provide evidence.

2. Give the current trends toward empowerment and employing fewer levels of management, how important do you believe management development will be in the near future? Support your answer.

3. Why is it important for a HRD practitioner to understand managerial roles and competencies? How are these assessed? How is this information used as a needs assessment in designing a management development program?

4. Efforts to accurately and completely describe the job of managing have met with considerable frustration. Why do you think the job of managing has proven so difficult to pin down? Which of the ideas and models offered so far do you believe to be the most useful in guiding management development? Support your choice.

5. Compare and contrast management education, management training, and on-the-job experiences. Which of these would you emphasize for a new manager? Explain?

6. Briefly describe the key advantages and disadvantages of the three approaches to management education. Under what conditions would you recommend that an organization send its managers to an executive MBA program?

7. Explain how management education prepares a manager for his or her role. What are the different forms of management education? Can they be substituted by training or on-the-job experiences? Why or why not?

8. Explain the role on-the-job experience plays in a manager's development. Identify two ways an organization can increase the chances that the on-the-job experiences its managers encounter will be developmental experiences.

9. Describe how managing in a global environment can differ from the traditional approach to managing. Describe one way that we can develop managers to be more successful in a global environment.

10. Briefly describe the components of the behavior modeling approach to training and development. Describe how you would use these components to design a behavior modeling session that trains supervisors to effectively obtain an employee's agreement for improved performance.

13

Organization Development and Change

Learning Objectives:

1. *Define organization development (OD).*
2. *Understand the basic theories and concepts of OD.*
3. *Describe the planned-change model.*
4. *Explain the roles of the change agent, manager, and the system in developing an intervention strategy.*
5. *Understand the basic steps involved in designing an implementation strategy.*
6. *Explain the different types of human processual intervention strategies.*
7. *Explain the different types of technostructural intervention strategies.*
8. *Explain the different types of sociotechnical intervention strategies.*
9. *Explain the different types of large-systems change intervention strategies.*
10. *Describe the role of HRD practitioners in OD interventions.*

OPENING CASE

Throughout the 1970s, Xerox Corporation was the dominant player in the domestic copier market. However, Xerox's market share was eroded, when in 1979, Canon, a Japanese competitor, introduced a midsize copier priced under $10,000. Xerox responded by claiming that Canon was using unfair trade practices, specifically, underpricing its products in order to capture a larger share of the U.S. copier market. However, Xerox engineers soon learned that the price differential was due to Canon's operating efficiency, which resulted in production of copiers at a lower cost than Xerox. Xerox management realized it needed to become more efficient to compete in a changing market place.

At the same time, Xerox was facing another problem: poor relations with the unions that represented its employees. According to Joseph Laymon, Xerox's director of corporate industrial relations, poor union-management relations were caused by "an inability to listen and effectively understand the other side's issues. . . . [The] union would come to the table with 150 to 200 demands, and the company would come in with 75 to 150 demands, and both sides would waste hours and months trying to understand the legitimate needs of both sides." This sort of environment would make it difficult for any organization to achieve greater levels of efficiency.

It became clear to Xerox's management that improved efficiency would require greater employee involvement, but to do so it would need to have the unions on its side.

Organization Development (OD) Defined

Organization development (OD) is defined as a process used to enhance the effectiveness of an organization and the well-being of its members through planned interventions (Alderfer, 1977; Beckhard, 1969; Beer & Walton, 1990; French & Bell, 1990; Friedlander & Brown, 1974). This definition makes three key points. First, OD **enhances the effectiveness of the organization.** *Effectiveness,* in this context, is defined as achieving organizational goals and objectives. Second, OD **enhances the well-being of organization members.** The term *well-being* refers to the perceived overall satisfaction each organization member feels toward job and work environment. Generally speaking, "having challenging and meaningful work leads to high work satisfaction and, if rewarded by the organization, to higher satisfaction with rewards as well" (Locke & Latham, 1990, p. 16). Thus, OD is used to enhance both personal and work satisfaction.

Third, OD is used to enhance the effectiveness of organizations and individual well-being **through planned interventions.** Planned interventions refer "to sets of structured activities in which selected organizational units (target groups or individuals) engage with a task or sequence of tasks where the task goals are related directly or indirectly to organizational improvement" (French & Bell, 1990, p. 102). Thus, planned interventions, or **intervention strategy,** are the primary means through which organizational improvement and changes take place.

Organization Development Theories and Concepts

OD theories have evolved primarily from three disciplines—psychology, the social sciences, and management. OD theory can be divided into two categories—change process theory and implementation theory.

Change Process Theory

Change process theory tries to explain the dynamics through which organizational improvement and changes take place (Woodman, 1989). The change process was first depicted by Kurt Lewin (1958) as occurring in three stages—unfreezing, moving, and refreezing. The *unfreezing* stage involves the process of getting people to accept the change as inevitable and to stop doing certain things (e.g., as to policy, practice, behavior, etc.). The *moving* stage involves getting people to accept the new, desired state (e.g., new policies, practices, etc.). The last stage, *refreezing*, involves making the new practices and behaviors a permanent part of the operation or role expectations. Lewin viewed change as deriving from two forces: (1) those internally driven (from a person's own needs) and (2) those imposed or induced by the environment. Environmental forces can be further distinguished between *driving* (pushing for change) and *restraining* forces (those seeking to maintain the status quo). In order for change to be environmentally imposed, driving forces must outnumber restraining forces.

Schein (1987b) further delineated each stage of Lewin's model (see Table 13-1). The emphasis of Schein's Change Model is on the dynamics of individual change and how a **change agent** must be able to manage these changes. At Stage 1 (unfreezing), the change agent motivates the person to accept change by disconfirming his or her attitudes, behaviors, or performance. For example, in order for an employee to correct poor work habits, he or she must first accept that his or her performance is not acceptable. At Stage 2 (changing through cognitive

---

TABLE 13-1	SCHEIN'S THREE-STAGE MODEL OF THE CHANGE PROCESS

Stage 1 Unfreezing: Creating motivation and readiness to change through
    a. Disconfirmation or lack of confirmation
    b. Creation of guilt or anxiety
    c. Provision of psychological safety

Stage 2 Changing through cognitive restructuring: Helping the client to see, judge, feel, and react differently based on a new point of view obtained through
    a. Identifying with a new role model, mentor, etc.
    b. Scanning the environment for new relevant information

Stage 3 Refreezing: Helping the client to integrate the new point of view into
    a. The total personality and self-concept
    b. Significant relationships

SOURCE: From *Process Consultation* (Volume II) (p. 93) by E. H. Schein, 1987, Reading, MA: Addison-Wesley.

restructuring), the emphasis is on getting the employee to see and do things differently and actually believe that by changing work habits his or her performance will improve. Finally, at Stage 3 (refreezing), the change agent helps the person to integrate these new behaviors (work habits) into his or her thinking patterns. This stage focuses on helping the employee to reconfirm his or her self-concept and reinforce desired performance standards.

Implementation Theory

Implementation theory focuses on specific intervention strategies designed to induce changes. We will discuss some of the underlying theories and concepts of four types of interventions: human processual, technostructural, sociotechnical systems (STS) designs, and large systems.

Human Processual Intervention Theory   Human processual theories focus on changing behaviors by modifying individual attitudes, values, problem-solving approaches, and interpersonal styles. The theoretical underpinnings of this approach have been derived from the behavioral sciences, particularly the need, expectancy, reinforcement, and job-satisfaction theories. The application of these theories to human processual intervention was pioneered in the 1950s by Kurt Lewin, in collaboration with Lippitt, White, Likert, McGregor, and others. Lewin was able to transfer his knowledge of the way planned interventions produce desired behavioral changes in a social setting, to an organizational setting (Bennis, Benne, & Chin, 1961). Lewin hypothesized that interventions should be directed at the group level rather than at the individual level. He felt that changing an individual's behavior without first changing group norms would be fruitless because that individual would be viewed as a deviate and pressured to return to his or her former behavior pattern. Lewin's work led to the development of several OD intervention techniques, including survey feedback and force field analysis, which will be discussed later in the chapter.

Chris Argyris (1970), another early pioneer of human processual intervention strategies, postulated that the basic requirements of an intervention activity are valid information, free choice, and internal commitment. In order to facilitate change, the person involved in the change should have useful information with which to diagnose the situation and then act on that information. Free choice implies that the person involved in the change process has the autonomy, control, and motivation to implement the intervention activity. Internal commitment implies that the person(s) involved in the change process have "ownership" of the strategy. This also implies that the person(s) "have processed valid information and made an informed free choice" (Argyris, 1970, p. 20). Argyris's early work led to the development of several **team building** techniques, including process consultation, role clarification, and confrontation meetings. Team building will be discussed later in the chapter.

Technostructural Intervention Theory   Technostructural theory focuses on improving work content, work method, work flow, performance factors, and relationships among workers (Friedlander & Brown, 1974). One of the key con-

TABLE 13-2	W.E. DEMING'S FOURTEEN GUIDING PRINCIPLES

1. Create constancy of purpose toward improvement of product and service, with the aim to become competitive and to stay in business, and to provide jobs.

2. Adopt the new philosophy. We are in a new economic age. Western management must awaken to the challenge, must learn their responsibilities, and take on leadership for change.

3. Cease dependence on inspection to achieve quality. Eliminate the need for inspection on a mass basis by building quality into the product in the first place.

4. End the practice of awarding business on the basis of price tag. Instead, minimize total cost. Move toward a single supplier for any one item, on a long-term relationship of loyalty and trust.

5. Improve constantly and forever the system of production and service, to improve quality and productivity, and thus constantly decrease costs.

6. Institute training on the job.

7. Institute leadership. The aim of supervision should be to help people and machines and gadgets to do a better job. Supervision of management is in need of overhaul, as well as supervision of production workers.

8. Drive out fear, so that everyone may work effectively for the company.

9. Break down barriers between departments. People in research, design, sales, and production must work as a team to foresee problems of production and in use that may be encountered with the product or service.

10. Eliminate slogans, exhortations, and targets for the work force asking for zero defects and new levels of productivity. Such exhortations only create adversarial relationships, as the bulk of the causes of low quality and low productivity belongs to the system and thus lies beyond the power of the work force.

11a. Eliminate work standards (quotas) on the factory floor. Substitute leadership.

  b. Eliminate management by objective. Eliminate management by the numbers, numerical goals. Substitute leadership.

12a. Remove barriers that rob the hourly worker of his right to pride of workmanship. The responsibility of supervisors must be changed from sheer numbers to quality.

  b. Remove barriers that rob people in management and in engineering of their right to pride of workmanship. This means, inter alia, abolishment of the annual or merit rating and of management by objective.

13. Institute a vigorous program of education and self-improvement.

14. Top management will accomplish the transformation.

SOURCE: Schuler, R. S. & Harris, D. L. (1992). "Deming Quality Improvement: Implications for Human Resource Management as Illustrated in a Small Company." *Human Resource Planning, 14*(3), p. 194. Reprinted with permission.

principles that can be translated into mission and goals. The mission and goals should form the basis for managing the organization, effective use of technology, and the distribution of rewards. To do this effectively, organizational leaders must understand

> the nature of culture and what it takes to change it; the significant role of values in an organization's life; the general sociopolitical nature

TABLE 13-3	CHALLENGES FACING ORGANIZATIONAL LEADERS

1. Changing the shape of the organization.
2. Changes in the mission or "reason for being."
3. Changes in ways of doing business.
4. Changes in ownership.
5. Downsizing.
6. Changes in the culture of the organization.

SOURCE: From *Organizational Transitions* (2nd edition) by R. Beckhard and R. T. Harris, 1987, Reading, MA: Addison-Wesley.

of the world; impacts of currencies and East-West/North-South issues; and, finally, the technology and concepts of managing effective change and of balancing stability and change (Beckhard and Harris, 1987, p. 8).

Limitations of Research Supporting OD Theories

As in many areas of HRD, there are limitations in the research that has been conducted to test the underlying theoretical constructs of OD and the effectiveness of interventions (Alderfer, 1977; Beer & Walton, 1987; Bullock & Svyantek, 1987; Porras & Berg, 1977). These limitations include:

1. The lack of true experimental designs in OD research;

2. The lack of resources available to OD practitioners;

3. The limitations of field research designs;

4. Bias by OD evaluators (the designer of the intervention); and

5. Simply a "lack of motivation" by the OD evaluator to do the job correctly (Bullock & Svyantek, 1987).

In particular, it is difficult to isolate causality. Applying traditional experimental strategies, which attempt to isolate causation, to OD interventions forces researchers to focus on a single intervention episode and overlook the systematic nature of organizations (Beer & Walton, 1987). In addition, most OD research results are measured by changes in attitudes and behaviors. This is a limitation because attitudinal and behavioral changes are considered intervening variables and may have very little to do with improvements in group and organization performance (Nicholas, 1982).

One significant development is the application of meta-analysis to OD research. Meta-analysis is a set of analytical techniques that can be used to statistically combine results across studies investigating the same variable or intervention, making it easier to draw conclusions from prior research. In addition to examining the effects of change interventions on dependent variables, meta-analysis also makes it possible to examine the effects of moderator variables (e.g., technology of the organization, organization types, and rigor of study) (Neuman et al., 1989). Meta-analysis also makes it possible to statistically remove possible effects of things such as reviewer bias and insensitivity (Guzzo et al., 1985). Meta-analytic studies of OD research have made it easier to determine what we can reasonably conclude from prior research.

Model of Planned Change

The lack of fundamental OD research has underscored the need for a universally accepted model of planned change (Bennis, et. al., 1961; Porras & Hoffer, 1986). Because of the lack of a generic model, change process and intervention theories are "recklessly combined and crossed levels of abstraction, levels of analysis, and narrowly defined discipline boundaries" (Woodman, 1989, p. 206). The purpose of this section is to present a model of planned change that attempts to provide a framework for integrating OD theory, research, and practice.

The Porras and Silvers (1991) model of planned change (see Figure 13-1) provides a framework for introducing change within an organizational setting.

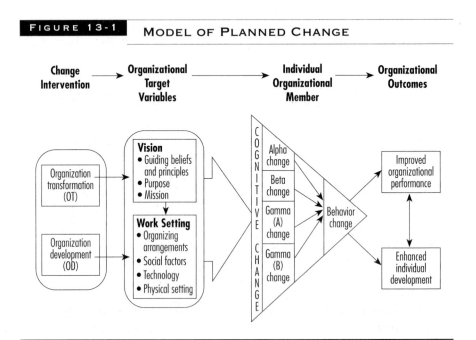

FIGURE 13-1   MODEL OF PLANNED CHANGE

SOURCE: From "Organization Development and Transformation" by J. I. Porras and R. C. Silvers, 1991, *Annual Review of Psychology, 42,* p. 53. Copyright 1991 by Annual Reviews, Inc. Reprinted by permission.

Specifically, it addresses how planned interventions targeted at specific organization variables with a desired affect on individual change will result in organizational outcomes. There are four distinct parts to this model. First, it distinguishes two types of intervention strategies—OD and *organization transformation* (OT). OT involves the application of large systems change theory discussed earlier. Porras and Silvers (1991) feel that OT should be a separate entity because the underlying theories and concepts are still not well-defined. In comparison, human processual and technostructural theories and concepts have gained widespread acceptance among OD practitioners.

The second part of the model shows the relationship between change interventions with organizational target variables. The model shows two sets of target variables. The first is *vision* variables, which are the underlying organizational values, beliefs, and principles that guide management decisions. Vision variables also provide the foundation for the purpose and mission of the organization. The second type of target variables are identified as *work setting* variables, which are directly related or influenced by OD interventions and vision variables. Work setting variables include policies, procedures, work rules, job descriptions, formal reporting lines, social factors, and communication patterns. In essence, these form the framework for organization structure.

The third part of the model focuses on predicted individual changes. Porras and Silvers (1991) conceptualize organizational change as the alteration of a person's perception of some existing organizational variable or paradigm. An *organizational paradigm* can be defined as a generally accepted view or belief that is based on unquestioned and unexamined assumptions (Golembiewski et al., 1976; Porras & Silvers, 1991). Organization change can occur at four cognitive levels:

1. *Alpha changes* are possible when individuals perceive a change in the levels of variables (e.g., a perceived improvement in skills) within a paradigm without altering their configuration (e.g. job design);

2. *Beta changes* are possible when individuals perceive a change in value of variables (e.g., change in work standards) within an existing paradigm without altering their configuration;

3. *Gamma (A) changes* are possible when individuals perceive a change in the configuration of an existing paradigm without the addition of new variables (e.g., changing the central value of a "product-driven" paradigm from "cost-containment" to "total quality focus"; this results in the reconfiguration of all variables within this paradigm); and

4. *Gamma (B) changes* are possible when individuals perceive a replacement of one paradigm with another that contains new variables (e.g., replacing a product-driven paradigm with a customer-responsive paradigm) (p. 57).

As the definitions indicate, each level of cognitive change represents change as occuring on a broader scope, from individual to organizational. For example, suppose a shipping clerk attends a training program to improve her reading skill. An alpha change can be said to have occurred if at the end of training she perceives that her reading skill has improved. Further, suppose that the shipping department manager attempts to improve productivity by reducing the standard for effective order processing time from 48 hours to 24 hours. A beta change can be said to have occurred if the shipping clerks accept this new standard as legitimate. This is so because the employees now define success as processing an order in less than 24 hours as opposed to less than 48 hours.

Gamma A and B changes refer to changes occurring at the organization level. Gamma A changes are directed at the manner in which the operation's mission or philosophy is accomplished, but where the core mission would remain intact. For example, if a product-driven organization introduced new cost-containment procedures, without changing its operation philosophy, a gamma A change would have occurred. Alternatively, gamma B changes are directed at the core mission or philosophy. Alternatively, a gamma B change has occurred if the organization redefines itself from being product-driven to being customer-driven. Unlike a gamma A change, a gamma B change "alters existing behaviors, creates new behaviors, and gives individual employees a totally new of way of viewing their work" (Porras & Silvers, 1991, p. 58).

There are several benefits of distinguishing the levels of cognitive change. First, it will help the change agent to pinpoint the scope of the desired change. Second, this approach provides a conceptual framework for doing evaluative research on OD interventions. Third, effectiveness can be reported as a change at one or more of the four cognitive levels, making communication of results clearer.

The fourth, and last, part of the model focuses on how individual behavioral changes can lead to two possible outcomes—improved organizational performance and enhanced individual development. Organizational performance, in this context, refers to improvement in efficiency, effectiveness, productivity, and profitability. Enhanced individual development refers to the alteration of behaviors and/or skills resulting in such things as improved work habits, increased commitment, and improved performance. These outcomes are consistent with the definition of OD, which referred to enhancing the effectiveness of an organization and the well-being of its members through planned interventions.

Designing an Intervention Strategy

The model of planned change is an attempt to provide a framework for integrating OD theory, research, and practice. In this section, we will discuss how organizations go about designing an intervention strategy that targets specific organizational variables. We will first discuss specific roles in the design and implementation phases. Next we will examine some steps in designing an intervention strategy. Last, we will look at the role of the HRD practitioner in this process.

Specific Roles

There are at least three distinct sets of roles with respect to designing and implementing intervention change strategy—the change manager, the system, and the change agent.

Role of Change Manager

The **change manager** oversees the design of the intervention strategy. This person would have overall responsibility for assessing the need for change, determining the appropriate intervention activities, implementing the strategy, and evaluating the results. Some organizations elect to develop a parallel structure—one person responsible for ongoing management functions and another person responsible for managing change. However, using this structure may mean that the change manager may not have sufficient power to create the conditions for change, particularly if the functional manager is perceived, by others in the organization, as not supporting the change process.

Rather than create a parallel structure, most organizations look to the functional manager to assume the additional duties of change manager. For example, if the target variable is team building involving a single department, the change manager would be the department manager. If the target variable is the mission of the organization, the appropriate change manager would be the CEO.

Managers must understand the nature of planned change as opposed to "forced" change. Forced change, which uses coercive tactics (e.g., threat of discipline), may produce immediate results, but these changes (in behavior) may not be permanent. Individuals may react immediately to forced change in order to avoid the consequences. However, when the consequences are removed, the person may revert to old habits or behaviors. Managers will continue to use forced change until they learn to balance their short-term needs with the potential for the long-term benefits of planned change. Planned change focuses on seeking permanent changes, as discussed earlier. Frequently, managers who attempt to create planned change call on others to assist them in developing and implementing a planned change strategy. Individuals who perform this function are referred to as change agents.

Role of Change Agent

The **change agent** assists the change manager in designing and implementing the change strategy. Among other things, the change agent, under the direction of the change manager, has primary responsibility for facilitating all of the activities surrounding the design and implementation of the strategy. This person should have knowledge of OD theories, concepts, practices, and research results so that he or she can advise the change manager of the efficacy of different intervention strategies.

The change agent can be an internal staff person (e.g., HRD practitioner) or an external consultant. *Internal change agents* generally are knowledgeable regarding the organization's mission, structural components, technology, internal politics, and social factors. This knowledge can be very important for establishing a trusting relationship with the change manager and members of the system. However, system members may feel the internal change agent is too close to the existing situation and cannot be objective. In addition, the internal change agent may not possess specialized knowledge needed for a particular intervention strategy. If this is the case, the organization may decide to hire an external consultant with specialized OD knowledge and skills.

External change agents are hired to fulfill a specific function or role for a specified period of time. The external change agent's role is determined by the change manager and outlined in a contract. The contract should specify the exact nature of the work to be performed, the timetable for the work, length of service, method and amount of payment, and some way of evaluating the change agent's performance. Some organizations negotiate a performance clause, which gives the organization the right to evaluate the change agent's efforts at any time and provides that the contract can be terminated if the work is not up to established standards.

Burke (1987) described eight different roles of a change agent (see Table 13-4). The differences between the roles are based upon the relationship between the change agent and the change manager or client. For example, when a change agent assumes the advocate role (i.e., becomes highly directive), he or

TABLE 13-4	**CHANGE AGENT'S ROLES**	
Role	**Definition**	**When Appropriate**
Advocate	Highly directive role in which the change agent tries to influence the client to use a certain approach.	When client is not sure of the approach to take and needs a lot of direction.
Technical Specialist	Provides specific technical knowledge on special problems.	When client seeks direction on a special problem.
Trainer or Educator	Provides information about OD or different intervention strategies.	When client needs training in some aspect of OD.
Collaborator in Problem Solving	Provides assistance in problem analysis, identifying solutions, and action steps.	When client needs assistance in decision making.
Alternative Identifier	Same as above, but does not collaborate.	When client needs assistance in developing a decision-making process.
Fact Finder	Serves as a research or data collector	When client needs are very specific.
Process Specialist	Facilitates meetings and group processes.	When client's needs are for process consultation.
Reflector	Helps client to understand situation by reacting to information.	When client is not sure of the data and seeks clarification.

SOURCE: From *Organization Development* (pp. 146–148) by W. W. Burke, 1987, Reading, MA: Addison-Wesley.

she is attempting to influence the change manager to select a certain strategy. At the other extreme, when the change agent assumes the role of a reflector (i.e., becomes nondirective), he or she is attempting to clarify information so that the change manager can make the decision. For each intervention strategy it is possible for the change agent to serve in one or more of these roles. For example, if during the initial stages of designing the intervention strategy the change manager lacks understanding of some of the key concepts of planned change, the change agent may act as a trainer and educator to ensure these concepts are understood. Having gained sufficient knowledge, the change manager will look to the change agent to assume additional roles (e.g., fact finder, process specialist, etc.).

Roles within System   The roles within the *system*, or the target of the intervention strategy, are determined by the change manager. The system can be a small work group or the entire organization. Individuals or groups within the system may be asked by the change manager to take on a specific role in the change process. For example, some organizations create a change committee whose role it is to work with both the change manager and the change agent in the design and implementation of the intervention strategy. Committees are important for helping to collect data, develop team skills, and define the emerging tasks and roles within the system (Beer & Walton, 1987). Ideally, these individuals will be energized by their involvement, allowing them to put forth the extra effort needed for committee work (Kanter, 1983).

Designing the Intervention Strategy

In order to design an intervention strategy, the change manager, with the help of the change agent and others in the system, must be able to diagnose the existing environment for change, develop a plan of action, and evaluate the results of the action plan to determine if the desired (behavioral) changes have occurred. Each of these steps is discussed below.

Diagnosing the Environment   Diagnosing the environment focuses on the readiness of the target group to accept change. The change manager and change agent need to know if the members are ready to accept change. One way to determine readiness to accept change is by conducting force field analysis. Lewin developed **force field analysis** to analyze the driving and restraining forces of change. Figure 13-2 illustrates force field analysis graphically using the example of a company that plans to introduce new production standards. The change manager, change agent, and possibly a change committee would diagnose the environment to determine possible forces both for and against change. These forces are shown as "force" lines. The length of the lines indicates the relative force—the longer the line, the greater the force. Theoretically, if change is going to take place, the accumulation of forces for change would have to exceed the accumulation of forces against change. In the example in Figure 13-2, the restraining forces would seem to prevent the introduction of new product standards unless the present situation were modified. Thus, the value of a force field

FIGURE 13-2 **FORCE FIELD ANALYSIS (INTRODUCING NEW PRODUCTION STANDARDS)**

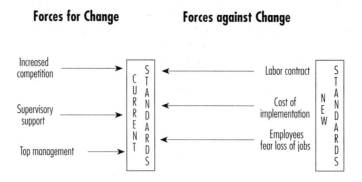

analysis is that it allows the intervention strategists to pinpoint specific support and resistance to a proposed change program. In this situation, the change manager must be able to reduce the resistance (e.g., renegotiate the contract) or increase the forces for change.

Developing an Action Plan Developing an action plan involves the identifying specific target variables and determining the techniques to bring about change. Identifying specific target variables (e.g., resistance points, existing policies, etc.) allows the intervention strategists to better understand the relative complexity of the change program. Using the earlier example of changing production standards, the change manager may view the union, supervisors, and production workers as possible resisters to change. The union will have to agree to a change in production standards; supervisors must understand the need to change those standards, and why their active support is critical to the outcome; and employees need to know that the change will not affect their job security. Determining the specific techniques to bring about change is necessary to institute change. Continuing with the example, the following techniques may be considered:

1. Scheduling a supervisory meeting and follow-up sessions to communicate the critical need for changing standards and impress key personnel with need to actively support the change.

2. Conducting meetings with union officials to determine their interpretation of the labor contract and whether they agree that management has the "right" to change production standards unilaterally. Depending upon the results of the meetings, other sessions may be necessary.

3. Conducting an awareness/training session for production workers to set forth how the changes in production standards will affect them personally and how those changes will be implemented.

The **action plan** specifies the intervention strategy. Like any other plan, the action plan should specify the objective of each change activity, who will be involved, who is responsible, and when the activity must be completed. Implementation of the action plan involves carrying out each step in the intervention strategy. This may require at least as much energy and commitment of the change manager and change agent as all of the previous steps combined. Too often, people in organizations get bogged down with the planning process and see it as an end in itself rather than as a means to an end. Thus, when the action plan is prepared, participants may be unwilling to see it through. The role of the change manager, with the assistance of the change agent, is to oversee the implementation of the plan and ensure that all of the steps are followed, that responsible individuals are completing their tasks, and that deadlines are met. If there is any delay in carrying out an activity, the change manager should intervene and find out the cause of the delay. The change manager should continually confer with the members of the system to review results, get feedback, and make adjustments to the plan.

Evaluation of Results of Action Plan The results of the action plan must be evaluated to determine whether behavior has changed and whether other problems have emerged (e.g., new standards may be in place, but the union wants the workers upgraded). It is important that members of the system be involved in these steps to determine whether the action plan was effective. Evaluation results should be provided to demonstrate the degree to which the intervention was effective. If there are other problems identified, the change manager may want to repeat the action planning process.

Role of HRD Practitioners in Design of OD Interventions

HRD practitioners have two primary roles in the design of OD interventions. First, they can serve as change agents. As discussed in Chapter 1, OD competencies are part of the overall competencies of an HRD professional. In planned change situations, particularly those that involve HRD programs and processes such as intervention techniques (e.g., training), the HRD practitioner can help the change manager understand the full range of HRD programs and processes and which ones work best under different conditions. The HRD practitioner, as the change agent, can facilitate some of the change activities (e.g., awareness sessions) that are part of the action plan.

The second role that an HRD practitioner can play in design and implementation is to serve as the evaluator of intervention strategies. Even in situations where the HRD practitioner was not directly involved in the intervention strategy, he or she could be responsible for designing the evaluative component. Again, it is expected that this person possesses the competencies to conduct the needed research and can use the appropriate methodology to evaluate the effects of the change program.

The Role of Labor Unions in OD Interventions

OD interventions and labor relations are inextricably linked. While most OD intervention strategies are considered to be a rational process, labor relations are often perceived as irrational and unpredictable, particularly if past relations have been less than satisfactory. If union members generally mistrust management, it is not likely that they will be willing partners in a planned change program. Rather, they may attempt to obstruct the process.

Some OD practitioners would argue that if an organization truly wants to bring about lasting change in a union environment, management must first attempt to make labor relations a more rational process. They must view the union leaders as partners in change, and emphasize that their commitment to long-term goals for change is as important as that of the top managers. Management and union leaders must share the reality that organizational changes must be made if the organization is to remain a viable entity and prosper. Furthermore, they must be willing to make fundamental changes in accountability and in ways employees perform their jobs. This kind of arrangement is generally known as a *cooperative agreement.*

Cooperative agreements are generally accomplished within normal contract negotiations. Generally, unions will make certain trade-offs as long as they appear to be in the best interest of the membership. Certainly, during tough economic times, or when the organization faces financial or market problems, management and union leaders may be more willing to agree on a cooperative arrangement without any significant change to wage structure, as long as the change is expected to improve business and save jobs. But during stable times, or even boom times, the union may expect something in return for buying into the change.

Types of Interventions: Human Processual

Most of the OD interventions in the 1960s and 1970s were human processual. These interventions are directed at improving interpersonal, intragroup, and intergroup relations. Two of the most common human processual intervention strategies are survey feedback and team building (Friedlander & Brown, 1974: Guzzo, Jette, & Katzell, 1985; Neuman, Edwards, & Raju, 1989; Nicholas, 1982; Nicholas & Katz, 1985).

Survey Feedback

Survey feedback is defined as "the systematic feedback of survey data to groups with the intent of stimulating discussion of problem areas, generating potential solutions, and stimulating motivation for change" (Nicholas, 1982). The data provides a "snapshot" of an existing situation, usually measuring some aspect of the group or organization, which can be used to compare its current state with some desired state. Ideally, the end result of survey feedback sessions is that changes will be attempted to bridge the gap between the current state and desired state.

There are many different refinements of survey feedback systems. Alderfer and Holbrook's (1973) peer-intergroup model (cited in Alderfer, 1977) is used to supply feedback data to superiors and subordinates when relations are strained between them. This approach, involving two or more groups, focuses on organization-wide issues only. The groups meet separately to discuss how the data reflects their concerns and then join the other groups to share their reactions. Significant concerns are then addressed through the development of action plans.

When using survey feedback as an intervention strategy, it is important for the change manager and change agent to be clear on (1) what organizational variables they are trying to measure; (2) how these measurements will be made in order to have a valid and reliable survey; and (3) how best to present the survey results to the intended audience. There are many commercially produced (*attitude* or *climate*) surveys available which provide a range of normative items, along with comparative data (Lawler, 1986).

Team Building

Team building is a process used to improve a work group's problem solving ability and effectiveness (Nicholas, 1982). Groups, like individuals, experience problems. Groups can become dysfunctional when they experience internal problems that members cannot resolve or when they are unable to adapt to external changes (e.g., changes in technology). When a group becomes dysfunctional, relationships are strained, conflicts increase among the members, group output declines, and turnover of membership increases. In this situation, a team building intervention can be used to address some of these problems.

Even when groups are able to solve problems, management and/or members of the group may feel that the group is not effective. Group effectiveness depends upon three elements:

1. The degree to which the group's productive output (its product or service) meets the standards of quantity, quality, and timeliness of the people who receive, review, and/or use the output;

2. The degree to which the process of carrying out the work enhances the capability of members to work together interdependently in the future; and

3. The degree to which the group experience contributes to the growth and personal well-being of team members (Hackman & Walton, 1986, pp. 78–79).

Before team building is attempted, several things should occur. First, there should be a preliminary diagnosis of the group's need for team building. There should be a "strongly felt need to improve some basic condition or process that is interfering with the achievement of organizational goals" (Dyer, 1987, p. 36). Without this kind of diagnosis, it is likely that some members of the group will resist any efforts to bring about change.

Second, a change agent should be selected who is able to use a wide range of OD skills and techniques to facilitate change. One technique important to team building is **process consultation** (PC), which is used by change agents to facilitate meetings and encounters with the work group. In this role, the change agent observes group activities and processes, and conducts a feedback session on those observations at the end of the meeting.

Third, the change manager and the change agent should develop a general approach to the team building sessions. Their roles should be specified clearly, in terms of who is going to facilitate different team building activities. The approach should also specify the team building cycle (e.g., action planning steps). Fourth, the change manager and change agent should establish a schedule outlining when these activities take place, including evaluation and follow-up sessions.

Effectiveness of Human Processual Interventions

There is some evidence that human processual interventions can be effective in bringing about change. Two recent meta-analyses of the OD literature (Guzzo et. al., 1985; Neuman et al., 1989) showed, among other things:

1. Team building was the most effective intervention for modifying satisfaction and other attitudes (Neuman et al., 1989).

2. Team building showed strong effects on productivity measures (Guzzo et al., 1985).

Types of Interventions: Technostructural

The purpose of technostructural interventions is to: (1) improve work content, work method, and relationships among workers (Friedlander & Brown, 1974) and (2) lower cost by replacing inefficient materials, methods, equipment, work-flow designs, and costly unnecessary labor with more efficient technology (Gerstein, 1987). Given today's competitive climate, more organizations are turning to technostructural interventions to increase worker efficiency and satisfaction. The most common technostructural intervention strategies are job design/enlargement, job enrichment, alternative work schedules, and sociotechnical interventions (Guzzo, Jette, & Katzell, 1985; Neuman, Edwards, & Raju, 1989; Nicholas, 1982; Nicholas & Katz, 1985). We will first discuss job design/enlargement, job enrichment, and alternative work schedules in this section. The sociotechnical interventions (e.g., quality circles, total quality management, and self-directed work teams) will be examined separately in the next section.

Job Design/Enlargement

Job design/enlargement interventions are "attempts to increase satisfaction and performance by consolidating work functions from a 'horizontal slice' of the work unit to provide greater variety and a sense of the whole task" (Nicholas, 1982). Job enlargement is probably carried out as a normal supervisory practice in most organizations. That is, a supervisor may observe boredom in a worker and diagnose that this person is not being challenged. The supervisor's normal coaching response, given no major obstacles (e.g., union contract), may be to reassign this person to a more challenging job. Thus, some job enlargement interventions are done informally.

The job enlargement interventions discussed in this chapter refer to large-scale interventions involving several workers. There are, unfortunately, very few published studies which isolate the effects of job enlargement. One study, conducted by Campion and McClelland (1991), focused on the effects of job enlargement on clerical positions. They concluded that job enlargement had a greater effect on employee satisfaction and on customer service, but less effect on mental overload, meaning that employees had greater chances of making errors. Results from meta-analytic studies investigating this approach will be presented at the end of this section.

Job Enrichment

Job enrichment involves varying some aspect of the job in order to increase motivational potential. Job enrichment is one area in which there has been a significant amount of research, particularly as to the efficacy of Hackman and Oldham's **job characteristics model** (JCM) as an intervention strategy (Fried & Ferris, 1987). The JCM is based on the premise that jobs have five core dimensions (i.e., skill variety, task identity, task significance, autonomy, and feedback). The core job dimensions affect work outcomes by determining employees experience of:

1. *Meaningfulness* of the work itself.

2. *Responsibility* for the work and its outcomes.

3. *Knowledge of actual results* of the work.

Hackman and Oldham developed the *job diagnostic survey* (JDS), a self-report instrument, to measure worker perception of each core job dimension. The scores on each core job dimension are combined into an overall *motivation potential score* (MPS) that is an indicator of whether the job can be "enriched" by modifying one or more of the core job dimensions.

The JCM has been the subject of considerable empirical testing and discussion. Overall, researchers (e.g., Fried & Ferris, 1987) have concluded that the model should be refined (e.g., clarifying the relationships among some variables, modifying calculation of the Motivational Potential Score). Further, research suggests that the job characteristics included in the model are related to job satisfaction (e.g., Loher et al., 1985; Neuman et al., 1989) and to a lesser degree to job performance (e.g., Fried & Ferris, 1987). These relationships are stronger for individuals who have high growth need strength. Taken together, research supports the conclusion that the job characteristics approach can be an effective technostructural intervention.

Alternative Work Schedules

Alternative work schedules allow employees to modify their work requirements to satisfy their personal needs. According to a study of 521 corporations, 93 percent of the responding organizations have some type of **alternative work schedules** (AWS) (Christensen, 1990). The two most common AWS interventions are the **compressed workweek** and **flextime** (Neuman et al., 1989).

Compressed Workweek The compressed workweek involves reducing the number of work days in a week, usually from five to four. Typically, the compressed schedule provides an option to employees to work four ten-hour days, known as the 4/40 schedule. Research of the 4/40 plan seems to show a positive effect on employee attitudes, but results as to effects on work productivity are mixed (Dunham et al., 1987; Newman, 1989; Pierce et al., 1989).

Flextime Work Schedule The flextime schedule allows employees some latitude in determining their starting and ending times in a given workday. This allows employees, particularly those with young children, the option of changing their working hours to conform to their family patterns. According to Tarrant (1992), in approximately 53 percent of all U.S. families both parents are employed, and of the remaining, 25 percent of the families are headed by a single parent. This suggests that almost three-quarters of all employees may have some restrictions due to parental responsibilities.

There are two conditions that define the extent of flexibility: (1) the employee must work some standard number of hours per day (e.g., eight hours) and (2) all employees must work a common core period of the day (usually during the middle of the day). On either side of the core time, usually four hours, each employee can make a decision as to when to begin and end the workday. A review of recent research (Pierce et al., 1989) suggests that flextime schedules are positively related to a number of factors, including organizational attachment, attendance, performance, stress, off-job satisfaction, and attitudes. The effects of flextime were strongest on job attitudes (e.g., job satisfaction, satisfaction with work, and satisfaction with supervisor).

Effectiveness of Technostructural Interventions

Recent meta-analyses of technostructural interventions (Nicholas, 1982; Guzzo et al., 1985; and Neuman et al., 1989) have shown:

1. Alternative work schedules and job redesign had a moderate effect on measures of work output, such as quality and quantity of production (Guzzo et al., 1985).

2. Work rescheduling interventions had a small but significant effect on measures of withdrawal behavior (e.g., absenteeism), whereas work redesign has a larger but not statistically significant effect on measures of withdrawal behavior (Guzzo et al., 1985).

3. Overall, technostructural interventions had less effect than human processual interventions (Neuman et al., 1989).

4. Alternative work schedules had a greater effect on attitude than did job design/enlargment or job enrichment (Neuman et al., 1989).

5. Job enlargement and job enrichment interventions brought about the same amount of overall change (42 percent change) with enrichment having a greater affect on productivity (Nicholas, 1982).

It appears then that technostructural interventions had less effect, overall, than human processual interventions. The general explanation for this difference is that human processual interventions are intended to "affect changes in organizations through the employees rather than through modifications in the work or work environment (technostructural approaches)" (Neuman et al., 1989, p. 480). Of the three types of technostructural interventions, job design had the greatest effect on productivity, while alternative work schedules had the greatest effect on attitude. All three types affected managerial/professional employees the most, an important point when considering using these techniques throughout an organization.

Types of Interventions: Sociotechnical Systems

Since the 1970s, organizations have used *sociotechnical systems* (STS) designs as a way to increase productivity and worker satisfaction. Where as human processual and technostructural interventions focus on interpersonal relationships and job design, STS designs are defined as interventions that focus on a combination of organizational structural demands (e.g., workflow, task accomplishment, and performance) and social demands (e.g., relationship among workers) (Fagenson & Burke, 1990; Guzzo et al., 1985; Neuman et al., 1989). These interventions include quality circles, total quality management, and self-directed work teams. STS interventions have been among the most widely implemented OD interventions and for good reasons. Research suggests STS interventions have had a greater effect on productivity than either human processual or technostructural interventions (Guzzo et al., 1985). We will discuss each one and provide some empirical evidence of their overall effectiveness.

Quality Circles

The **quality circle** (QC) approach is a process of involving employees in meaningful work decisions including, but not limited to, solving job-related problems. While most QC programs are designed to meet an organization's unique needs, there are some common features. First are the QC roles—the steering committee, the facilitator, and the circle leader. The *steering committee*, composed of key managers and staff persons, is responsible for implementing the QC process and making decisions about such things as resource allocation, production or operation changes, and personnel assignments. The *facilitator*, selected by the steering committee, has responsibility for training the circle leaders and overseeing the operation of all of the circles. The facilitator must have OD competencies. *Circle leaders*, usually supervisors, are responsible for such things as calling meetings, encouraging active participation among the members, and the preparation of reports for submission to the steering committee.

The second common characteristic of QCs is that participants are provided training in group process, diagnosing problems, and problem-solving skills. Group leaders will generally be given additional training. A third common characteristic is that each circle meets on a regular basis to discuss issues like improving work procedures and product quality, working conditions and facilities. Priority is usually given to problems in that QC's work area and/or under the direct control of the circle leader. While participation is strictly voluntary, the employees are usually given time off to attend meetings.

The empirical evidence of the overall effectiveness of QC is mixed. Steel and Lloyd (1988) studied the effects of participation in QC programs on several organizational variables. They found that:

1. There were significant effects on cognitive measures of sense of competence and interpersonal trust and on some measures related to properties of the task environment such as goal congruence (p. 13);

2. QC participants reported significantly greater attachment to the organization as the study progressed (p. 13); and

3. The QC process generally produced little overt enhancement in participants' work performance (p. 15).

Park (1991) analyzed evaluative data from 154 QC programs in both private and public organizations and found that, overall, QC programs have shown an increase in organizational effectiveness and the empowerment of employees. This conclusion was supported by Botch and Spangle (1990), who found the QC to be a powerful employee development tool, primarily because participants perceive their involvement as a way of getting personal recognition. Others disagree with these findings. They feel that while there are some decreases in operating costs, there is no evidence that productivity, quality, or attitudes have improved where QCs are used (Verney et al., 1989; Townsend, 1990; Adam, 1991).

Even with the mixed reviews on the QC, there seems to be a consistent feeling among researchers that, in order for QC intervention strategies to be effective, they must possess (1) comprehensive training for the facilitator, group leaders, and group members; (2) active support from top and middle management; (3) supervisors who possess good communications skills; and (4) inclusion of labor unions (Clark & McGee, 1988; Piczak, 1988; Honeycutt, 1989; Berman & Hellweg, 1989; Lansing, 1989; Tang et al., 1989, Steel et al., 1990).

Total Quality Management

Faced with increasingly stiff competition from both domestic and foreign companies, organizations have identified quality as a critical competitive factor. One way to improve quality is to design and implement a popular technostructural intervention strategy referred to as the **total quality management program** (TQM).

TQM is defined as a "set of concepts and tools for getting all employees focused on continuous improvement, in the eyes of the customer" (Schonberger, 1992, p. 17). Based on the work of Deming, TQM seeks to make every employee responsible for continuous quality improvement. It involves a significant change in the way employees do their work.

Most TQM intervention strategies involve five basic components—total commitment from senior management, standards and measures, training for employees, communication, and reward, recognition, and celebration. Senior management must guide the implementation of TQM. For example, Tenant Company, which established a quality program in 1979, found that managers are often isolated and need to be kept informed and involved (Hale, 1989). A study of the TQM program at Digital Equipment Corporation revealed that the success of the program was dependent on how well management established clear quality goals and related them to business, communicated and reinforced them, and demonstrated behavior consistent with those values (Salemme, 1991).

Standards and measures serve as benchmarks for TQM. Organizations that establish clear quality goals must be able to quantify these in terms of standards. TQM emphasizes the role of each manager in terms of reducing cost, particularly nonconformance cost (which accounts for about 20 percent of revenues in most organizations) caused by deviations from performance standards (McCormack, 1992). Supervisors must be able to:

1. Specify current performance standards;

2. Identify where outputs are at variance with standards;

3. Determine the causes of variances;

4. Identify and initiate actions to correct causes;

5. Specify desired performance;

6. Compare the desired standards to current standards and identify gaps;

7. Develop alternatives to close the gaps; and

8. Institutionalize new standards (McCormack, 1992).

Training of participants is critical to the overall success of TQM. Therefore, organizations that elect to implement TQM must make a major investment in training. Training should begin with sensitizing managers at all levels to the philosophy and principles of TQM. All managers need training in both TQM awareness and how to implement TQM principles (Ferketish & Hayden, 1992). In addition, employees may need training in statistical process control (SPC) techniques and, if an organization incorporates problem-solving groups (i.e., quality circles), employees may need training in group process and group decision making (Bowen & Lawler, 1992; Tollison, 1992).

Rewards, recognition, and celebration are used to keep employees energized and working toward the goals of total quality. Many organizations have linked TQM participation and success to three kinds of rewards: (1) individual monetary, (2) group monetary, and (3) nonmonetary (Schonberger, 1992). Individual monetary rewards, the more traditional form of compensation, are still important for linking TQM to a manager's participation and success. However, because individual compensation systems "place a strong emphasis on individual performance, almost always creating a competitive situation among employees," (Bowen & Lawler, 1992, p. 38) some organizations have abandoned merit increases. In its place, many organizations are emphasizing gainsharing programs.

Overall, recognition and celebration begins with national awards to organizations who have successful TQM programs. The most prestigious award is the Malcolm Baldrige National Quality Award, which has been instrumental in promoting the concept of TQM. Organizations that want to be recognized must adhere to a nationally accepted set of criteria for evaluating their TQM program. In the public sector, NASA's Quality and Excellence Award is given annually to contractors, subcontractors, and suppliers who consistently improve the quality of their products and services (Axland, 1991). Most organizations with TQM programs also recognize groups for their successes.

Communication begins with the CEO "going public" with the commitment to TQM and how it will change the direction of the company (Johnson, 1991). A communication network needs to be devised whose sole purpose is to inform employees of TQM and their role in the process. In addition, communication networks should be used to provide performance feedback and reviews. Another component should be a continuous flow of information on product and service quality improvements so that employees can track their group progress. Many organizations display results on wall charts for this purpose.

Before considering TQM as an intervention strategy, the change manager should solve preexisting problems. If employees are dissatisfied with some aspect of the organization, it will be very difficult for them to focus on quality issues. For example, Wallace Company in Houston, Texas, a recipient of the Baldrige Award in 1990, took the advice of an external change agent and addressed a problem that irritated employees before launching their now successful TQM program (Altany, 1992). Another preexisting condition that could delay implementing TQM is organizational **downsizing,** particularly at the management levels. Employees who are in fear of losing their jobs may not be able to focus on TQM principles, unless they see this as a means of saving their jobs.

The practitioner literature suggests that there is a high rate of success with TQM, particularly from the organization's perspective. For many companies, TQM has led to significant improvements in product quality and service leading to increased market share, profits, and company image. For example, in 1987 Rockwell Tactical Systems was cited by the U.S. Army for having 1,744 quality problems in its Hellfire anti-armor missile production. But by applying TQM principles they were able to save the existing program and, in 1990, won a new contract for 100 percent production of the missile (Velocci, 1991).

In addition to extensive applications to industry, many sectors of public service, including government, hospitals, and universities, have introduced innovations with TQM. The federal government has established The Federal Quality Institute, which offers quality seminars and in-house consulting to approximately 30 federal agencies (Reynolds, 1992). State and local governments have also launched innovations with TQM. For example, the city of Madison, Wisconsin, has realized significant budgetary savings through TQM (Sensenbrenner, 1991). Hospitals across the United States have been adopting TQM as a means of improving patient care, performance, and market share (McCarthy, 1991). In the face of declining budgets and enrollments, universities and colleges are using TQM techniques to help focus on the needs of the market and ways to improve delivery systems. However, to be successful, colleges and universities need the cooperation of their faculty (or their labor unions) to change the tradition of life-long tenure and peer review of their teaching (McWilliams, 1991).

While there are many anecdotal examples in the practitioner literature of successful organizational outcomes of TQM interventions in both the private and public sectors, there is, unfortunately, little evidence from controlled studies showing effects on individual productivity and attitudes.

Self-Directed Teams

Self-directed teams (SDTs) are defined as structures empowering employees to assume more autonomy and responsibility, enabling them to make decisions that are reserved for management (Schilder, 1992). SDTs represent a fundamental change to management authority. The team takes on supervisory, and, in some cases, managerial tasks, decreasing the number of management layers until the organization becomes flatter (Lee, 1990). This kind of change must be managed from the top, using a "hands-on" approach with the CEO serving as change manager. To move the organization to embrace the philosophy of empowerment, top management must continually reinforce this philosophy at each stage of the intervention.

One key intervention technique is training, which should be continuous throughout the process. There are several levels of training suggested. First, awareness training should be used to initiate the process and explain its benefits to individuals. Second, team members should be provided with skills training in a wide range of skills and competencies, including budgeting and planning, problem solving, and communication. Skills training in TQM may have to include basic skills for employees with literacy problems. Third each team member needs to be trained in all of the team tasks. Once the initial skills training is completed, each team becomes responsible for ongoing training.

Since SDTs are a major departure from the traditional hierarchical design, not many organizations have moved in this direction. According to a recent study of Fortune 1,000 companies by the American Productivity and Quality Center in Houston, only 7 percent indicated that they have adopted SDTs, but over half said that they would consider them in the future (Schilder, 1992). The increased visibility of SDTs has organizations thinking that "this is the only way to successfully meet business pressures in the 1990s and on into the twenty-first century, especially when those pressures demand fuller involvement and utilization of human resources" (Shipper & Manz, 1992, p. 49).

Some results attributed to SDTs include the following:

- At Northern Telecom Canada Ltd.'s Morrisville, North Carolina, repair facility, revenue increased by 63 percent, sales by 26 percent, and earnings by 46 percent in the three years since implementing SDTs (Versteeg, 1990).

- At General Electric's plant in Salisbury, North Carolina, part of the work force of 24,000 was organized into SDTs, resulting in an increase of 250 percent in productivity (Schilder, 1992).

- At Johnsonville Foods in Sheboygan Falls, Wisconsin, which has had SDTs since 1986, productivity has risen over 50 percent (Lee, 1990).

- During the three-year period covering 1969 through 1971, Donnelly Mirrors, Inc., of Holland, Michigan introduced SDTs, along with other innovations (e.g., in compensation, administration, etc.), that resulted in a 48 percent increase in productivity, reduction of absenteeism from 5 percent to 2 percent, and an overall increase on the return on investment of 220 percent (Iman, 1975).

- General Mills experimented with SDTs in the early 1970s. The work teams made decisions on the speed of the line, work assignments, rest breaks, and quality inspection. The teams encountered some early problems, but soon began to achieve their objectives, including high levels of satisfaction among the participants (Walton, 1975).

Beyond productivity increases, organizations have received other benefits of successful SDT applications. These include better quality products and services, higher employee morale, reduced or flatter management hierarchy, and more responsive organizational structures (Musselwhite & Moran, 1990).

Empirical evidence regarding the effectiveness of SDTs is mixed. Beekun (1989) studied the effects of different work group designs (autonomous, semi-autonomous, and nonautonomous) on productivity and escape behavior (e.g., absenteeism, turnover, etc.). Autonomous work groups were more productive (by 38 percent), but experienced less improvement in escape behavior (by 35 percent) than nonautonomous groups (those under direct supervision). Another interesting finding was that the nonautonomous groups were more productive (by 37 percent) and engaged in less escape behavior (by 104 percent) than semi-autonomous groups. These findings suggest that nonautonomous groups are best for curbing escape behavior, but that autonomous groups can be more productive.

There is other evidence that the results of SDTs are not always positive. Wall et al. (1986) conducted a long-term field experiment involving autonomous work groups in a manufacturing setting. The intervention involved giving shop floor employees substantially more autonomy in carrying out their daily jobs. The results of the experiment showed positive results on intrinsic job satisfaction, but effects on motivation, organizational commitment, mental health, work performance, and turnover were not very positive. These kinds of results point out the problem of field research and isolating the effects of change.

Differences Between TQM and SDT

There are some significant differences between the total quality management program (TQM) and the self-directed team (SDT). TQM is a participative process and "participation per se does not always equalize power and may even increase discrepancies" (Kanter, 1983, p. 258). In an SDT approach, each team is empowered with the authority to make decisions affecting the output of that team without the concurrence of a supervisor. Under TQM, while teams are encouraged to participate in problem solving, they do not have the authority to implement changes. TQM focuses exclusively on quality, as compared with the SDT, in which quality is one of several goals.

The SDT approach requires significant changes in organizational structure, including accountability systems, policies, procedures, and job descriptions. Changing job descriptions requires collaboration with labor unions and possible changes in the labor contract. To a lesser degree, TQM may require minor structural changes which may need to be reflected in the labor contract.

Both TQM and SDT focus on customers. TQM programs focus on both internal and external customers equally, which can often create internal conflict, as opposed to SDT programs that focus on external customers, while treating internal customers as partners (Holpp, 1992).

Another difference between the two is the manner in which employees are trained. Using a TQM approach, the concept of lifelong training may be emphasized, but in reality employees may only be trained in a limited number of TQM skills (e.g., process flow analysis, problem solving, etc.). SDT training provides more lifelong learning in practice. Team members are subjected to some initial awareness and skills training. After that, training is continuous and self-directed, with the expectation that each team member will become a subject matter specialist and teach others in his or her team (Holpp, 1992).

Another difference is the manner in which the two approaches are implemented. Table 13-5 lists some common implementation phases and the differences between TQM and SDT.

HRD Programs as Sociotechnical Intervention Techniques

The role HRD professionals play in STS design changes is similar to their role with respect to human processual and technostructural interventions. There are three specific roles. First, because the major emphasis of STS designs is on training, HRD practitioners can be responsible for the design and implementation of the several levels of training programs. Second, there is probably a less evident, but equally great, need for them to help employees to adjust to new roles within the STS design. With so much emphasis on productivity and quality improvement, there is considerable pressure on employees to change. HRD practitioners must be able to assist the change manager in correctly diagnosing the system's readiness to accept change and provide help in designing the appropriate change strategy.

Third, because STS designs also emphasize participation, the HRD practitioner should also assist in determining the level of participation of employees. There are two basic types—representative and consultative. *Representative* programs allow employee participation on organizational committees including advisory committees, employee councils, grievance committees, safety committees, and even boards of directors. Membership on these committees can be determined through appointment, self-selection, or election. It is particularly important for appointed members to make sure that they reflect the needs and concerns of the employees they represent. In terms of attitudes, there are studies which demonstrate that members have been found to have more positive attitudes than nonmembers (Nurick, 1982; Cotton et al, 1988). *Consultative* programs allow employees to participate directly in job-related issues. They have an opportunity to influence the decisions affecting their daily worklife. Probably the best example of this kind of program is the self-directed work team, which allows team members to set production and quality goals, hire, train, and schedule employees, and order materials.

Types of Interventions: Large Systems Change

Large systems change is defined as a multifaceted approach to organization change that can affect human processual, technostructural, and sociotechnical dimensions of the organization. Typically, large systems change focuses on organization-wide interventions (e.g., re-organization, cultural change). Even through large systems intervention strategies are still ill-defined and highly experimental, they are very common (Fagenson & Burke, 1990; Mirvis, 1988;

TABLE 13-5	COMPARING TQM AND SDT IMPLEMENTATION PHASES	

Phases	Self-Directed Teams	Total Quality Management
Start-up	Identify work units that are candidates for SDTs.	Create a vision statement accompanied by clear values.
Awareness and training	Charter a steering or design committee and begin education process.	Share the vision and solicit feedback. Provide examples of quality.
Initial planning	Identify all stakeholders and clarify barriers and sources of resistance.	Identify critical corporate performance targets and sponsor task teams.
Communication	Create a working plan for an SDT organization, including boundaries, roles, expectations, and related goals.	Hold "TQM Awareness" sessions to provide a common language for improvement.
Training and education	Provide regular facilitation and support for teams on a nearly full-time basis. Train managers and supervisors in new roles.	Begin extensive top-down process for all staff in leadership, teamwork, tools, and techniques.
Measuring and monitoring	Facilitate teams in setting their own benchmarks and goals.	Set up apparatus to track completion of projects and provide feedback. Establish recognition-and-rewards teams.
Managing ongoing performance	Assist teams in setting goals and managing performance. Provide resources to help teams with discipline, selection and compensation.	Provide additional training and education to reinforce the use of new tools and processes. Set up performance indicators and guidelines to ensure compliance and equitable administration.

SOURCE: From "Making Choices: Self-Directed Teams or Total Quality Management?" by L. Holpp, 1992, *Training, 29*(5), pp. 69–74.

Porras & Silvers, 1991; Tichy & DeVanna, 1986). In order to be effective, large system intervention strategies must be managed from the top of the organization (Beckhard and Harris, 1987). The CEO must be the driving force that leads the organization from its present state to some desired future state. The manager must develop a vision for the future and create the environment in which this vision can be realized. The person in charge of the change program should:

1. Define the transition state as a set of conditions separate from both the present and future state;

2. Determine what type of governance or management would be most effective;

3. Set up the management structure and system; and

4. Communicate the existence of this structure or system to all relevant parties (Beckhard & Harris, 1987, p. 78).

Defining the transition state helps the organization members adjust to the change. They will understand that, while it may be unsettling now, the ultimate change will improve the present situation. For example, if the organization makes a decision to move from a product-driven to a customer-driven operation, the transition state would normally be somewhat chaotic while employees learn their new roles and responsibilities. In addition, management must determine the most appropriate governance or management structure to oversee the transition. We will discuss two types of large systems interventions—cultural interventions and strategic interventions.

Cultural Interventions

Organization culture is defined as a system of learned, shared values, beliefs, and norms that are used to interpret elements in the environment and as a guide for all kinds of behavior (Geertz, 1973: Ott, 1989). Organizational culture is not something that is found in a mission statement or corporate policy manual. Rather, organizational culture is communicated and reinforced through organizational mechanisms (see Table 13-6).

Organizational cultural interventions involve more than simply restating values, beliefs, or norms, and communicating them to individuals. **Cultural changes** involve a complex process of replacing an existing paradigm with another. For example, if an organization wants to become *multicultural* (integrating aspects of other cultures into the fabric of the organization), it must be able to make some fundamental changes to existing organizational paradigms (e.g., valuing cultural differences). This will be discussed in more detail in Chapter 14.

Strategic Changes

Strategic change is defined as any fundamental change in organizational purpose or mission requiring system-wide changes (e.g., downsizing). System-wide

---

TABLE 13-6   **MECHANISMS THAT SUSTAIN ORGANIZATIONAL CULTURE**

1. What managers pay attention to.
2. The ways managers react to critical incidents.
3. Role modeling, coaching, and organizational training programs.
4. Criteria for allocating rewards and status.
5. Criteria for recruitment, selection, promotion, and removal from the organization.

SOURCE: From "Organization Change and Development: New Areas for Inquiry and Action" by R. W. Woodman, 1989, *Journal of Management, 15*(2), p. 217.

changes can be perceived as having three dimensions—size, depth, and pervasiveness (Ledford et al., 1989). *Size* refers to the number of employees in an organization. Generally speaking, the larger the organization, the greater the complexity involved in the change. *Depth* of the change refers to the extent to which the change involves limited structural changes or goes to core values of the organization. *Pervasiveness* of the change refers to how many functions and hierarchical levels of the organization will be directly impacted by the change.

Strategic interventions may be necessary when an organization is faced with external pressures to change and adapt. External pressures come from many sources, including the economic, social, legal, and political arenas. Table 13-7 lists some of the more common economic pressures. Organizations unable to create a "dynamic fit" between their own variables and the demands imposed by their environments will face decline and possible elimination (Lawrence, 1989). For example, with the cutback in defense spending, many defense-oriented manufacturers have been faced with a reduction in the size and number of defense contracts. In order to adapt to this change, these organizations may consider changing their purpose or mission so that they can convert their manufacturing focus to nonmilitary purposes.

When large systems change involves reorganizing parts of the organization, the effects are felt by the employees. For example, since 1980 over 500 of the largest organizations have reorganized their operations, many as a result of mergers and acquisitions, resulting in layoffs and job changes (Leana & Feldman, 1990). One such company, General Electric, acquired 338 businesses and sold off 232—in addition closing 73 plants—between 1980 and 1986, resulting in the loss of tens of thousands of jobs (Leana & Feldman, 1990). Beyond the elimination of employees, **mergers** may require realignment of reporting lines, policies, procedures, allocation processes, and control systems. Depending upon the size of the merging organizations, the effects can be very disruptive, particularly to the managers.

Acquisitions may be less disruptive than mergers. It is possible that many of the operational components of the acquired organization will remain intact. Some acquisitions involve merging executive offices to establish command and

TABLE 13-7	ECONOMIC PRESSURES ON ORGANIZATIONS
External Pressures	**How Organizations Perceive Pressures**
Increasing competition.	Market imperatives.
Changing stakeholder expectations.	New opportunities.
Changing work force.	Cultural pressures.
Technological developments.	Technological imperatives.
New laws and regulations.	Legal constraints.
Change in financial markets.	Economic pressures.

SOURCE: From Mohrman, S. A. & Mohrman, A. M. (1989). "The Environment as an Agent of Change." In A. M. Mohrman, S. A. Mohrman, G. E. Ledford, T. G. Cummings, and E. E. Lawler (Eds.), *Large Scale Organizational Change* (pp. 35–47). San Francisco: Jossey-Bass Publishers.

control functions. In most acquisitions, the employees face many job-related losses that may affect their ability to perform their jobs (Galosy, 1990). These are listed and explained in Table 13-8; the feelings they generate must be addressed as part of the change strategy.

One possible large systems change intervention technique is downsizing of the organization—reducing the number of departments, management levels, and/or overall number of employees. As stated earlier, most of the larger organizations have announced cutbacks in recent years. Even the few U.S. organizations (e.g., IBM, Digital Equipment Corp.) that have historically avoided layoffs in favor of retraining, have joined the ranks by making major cutbacks. An anticipated cutback can paralyze some organizations and employees, particularly if they have a history of continued employment. The effects of a cutback also linger well beyond its implementation among employees who survive the purge. These employees may experience low morale, a decline in productivity, greater distrust of management, and become excessively cautious (Rice & Dreilinger, 1991).

Effectiveness of Large Systems Change Strategies

There are many reports of successful strategic change strategies. Organizations that have successfully undergone large systems change strategies include Honeywell, Polaroid, and General Electric (Kanter, 1983) and Chrysler, the American Can Company (now called Primerica), AT&T, TRW, Westinghouse, and General Motors (Galbraith, 1989). Successes are not limited to the private sector. Weisbord (1987) described the successful strategic change of a government-owned utility (Atomic Energy of Canada Limited) that in 20 weeks:

- Evolved a new mission;

- Developed a new strategic plan;

- Reorganized its work force;

- Involved everybody who wished to be involved, in the change;

- Created a new level of labor-management cooperation;

- Turned around its sales and costs;

- Implemented a participative, no-layoff downsizing; and

- Established a firm future base (p. 364).

While the evidence that large systems change strategies can lead to an organizational improvement is mostly anecdotal, there is limited empirical evidence to support their effect on micro level organizational variables such as communication and support. One such study of the effectiveness of large systems change

TABLE 13-8	HOW EMPLOYEES FEEL ABOUT MERGERS

Feeling	Why?
1. Loss of hierarchical status.	Often the acquiring company becomes the "boss."
2. Loss of knowledge of firm.	Procedures and people change.
3. Loss of trusted subordinates.	People tend to be shifted around.
4. Loss of network.	New connections are formed.
5. Loss of control.	Acquiring company usually makes the decisions.
6. Loss of future.	No one knows what will happen.
7. Loss of job definition.	Most things are in flux for a while.
8. Loss of physical location.	Moving is typical in mergers.
9. Loss of friends or peers.	Often people leave, are fired, or transfer.

SOURCE: From "The Human Factors in Mergers and Acquisitions" by J. R. Galosy, 1990, *Training & Development Journal, 44,* p. 90. Copyright 1990, the American Society for Training and Development. All rights reserved. Reprinted with permission.

strategies on organizational variables examined the coping mechanisms used by employees involved in large systems change at AT&T (Ashford, 1988). This study showed that:

1. Transition-related stressors occurred both while workers anticipated the change and six months after it occurred;

2. Personal control and tolerance of ambiguity appeared to be the most useful buffers against transition-related stressors; and

3. Sharing worries and concerns appeared to be the most effective buffering response.

These findings suggest that during strategic change managers should target these organizational variables as part of their overall intervention strategy.

Role of HRD Practitioners in Design of Large Systems Change

To say that large systems change will have an impact on employees is an understatement. With that in mind, there are several roles that can be assumed by HRD practitioners. First, they can serve on strategic change committees—not only to give advice on training and development, but also to help strategic planners look at various alternatives and their potential impact on people (Gall, 1986). This role is key in both cultural and strategic changes. Second, given the impact of mergers, acquisitions, and downsizing on workers HRD practitioners must be involved in addressing these issues during the planning stages of such changes. Among other things, management must pay special attention to communicating with employees as to the reasons for cutbacks and why they had to be made. HRD practitioners can help facilitate awareness sessions. In this role, they can help employees deal with the realities of change.

There are many different HRD programs and processes discussed in this book that can be used as part of an overall intervention strategy. OD and HRD are closely related. Since the intent of most planned interventions is to ultimately bring about changes in individual behavior, it is difficult to introduce change without using HRD programs and processes. While the relationship between OD and HRD is more apparent at the human processual and technostructural levels, the need for HRD programs and processes is just as critical in large systems change interventions. Table 13-9 describes some examples of how HRD programs and processes contained in this text can be used as part of OD interventions.

TABLE 13-9	**HRD APPLICATIONS TO OD INTERVENTIONS**

OD Intervention		
Level	**Emphasis**	**HRD Application**
Human processual	Human needs; job satisfaction.	Career development; stress management; coaching.
	Individual differences.	
	Norms and values.	Cross-cultural training.
	Team effectiveness.	Orientation; socialization.
Technostructural	Job competencies.	Team training.
		Skills and technical training.
Sociotechnical	Self-directed teams.	Team training.
	Total quality management.	Quality training.
Large systems	Reorganization (downsizing).	Employee assistance programs; management development.

RETURN TO OPENING CASE

In 1980, Xerox embarked on a ten-step, system-wide change effort known as the Total Quality Management program. The program emphasized many of Deming's 14 principles. One aspect of the program focused on a process referred to as "benchmarking," which involves emulating competitors' best practices. This was the first time that a U.S. company used this approach to improve efficiency. At the time, Paul Allaire, President of Xerox, simply explained the program as "involving all of our people—union and nonunion alike—in problem-solving and quality improvement."

Xerox's program was based on all four aspects of a successful TQM process: senior management guidance, standards and measures, training, and rewards and recognition. But success was also made possible by convincing the leaders of the Amalgamated Clothing & Textile Workers Union (ACTWU), who today represent 4,000 Xerox employees, to accept the change program and to try alternative bargaining approaches. As a result, more cooperative programs were developed between company management and the union, including training courses for both union and management members and benchmarking best practices.

The results of the change program have been dramatic. In the five-year period from 1980 through 1985, Xerox was able to cut unit production costs by 50 percent and make a sixty-seven percent cut in inventory. The firm also received national recognition in 1989 when it received the prestigious Malcolm Baldrige National Quality Award for its effective TQM approach. Many companies have now adopted Xerox's approach, including Ford, AT&T, Hewlett-Packard, and IBM (in the 1980s). Most recently, President Clinton, upon taking office, cited Xerox's TQM successes as a worthy model for emulation by the federal government.[1]

Summary

Organization development (OD) is defined as a process used to enhance the effectiveness of an organization and the well-being of its members through planned interventions. OD theory is divided into change process theory and implementation theory. Change process theory tries to explain the dynamics by which individuals, groups, and organizations change. Lewin views change as a three-stage process of unfreezing, transitional action, and refreezing. Implementation theory focuses on specific intervention strategies designed to induce changes. We discussed some of the underlying theories and concepts of four different types of interventions: human processual, technostructural, sociotechnical systems (STS) designs, and large systems.

We also introduced a model of planned change that consisted of four interrelated parts: (1) change interventions that alter (2) key targeted organizational variables that then affect (3) individual organizational members and their on-the-job behaviors, resulting in changes in (4) organizational outcomes. The focus of this model is on changing individual behaviors, which ultimately leads to improved organizational outcomes (e.g. performance) as well as individual development.

[1]From Anonymous (Nov. 30, 1992). "Beg, Borrow—and Benchmark." *Business Week*, p. 74; Anonymous (Feb. 15, 1993). "Bargaining in Laymon's Terms." *Industry Week*, p. 18; Caudron, S. (Feb. 1993). "Keys to Starting a TQM Program." *Personnel Journal*, pp. 28–35; Cocheu, T. (1992). "Training with Quality." *Training & Development Journal 47*(5), pp. 23–32; and Hillkirk, J. (Feb 25, 1993). "Clinton Copies Xerox Way of Management." *USA Today* p. B-1.

There are three ways to introduce organizational change—through the manager (client), the system, and the change agent. The manager's role is to oversee the process. The influences generated within the system to promote change can vary, but the most important is that of members who participate directly in the process. The change agent's role is to consult, advise, and assist the manager in developing appropriate strategies for introducing change. In addition, some organizations hire external change agents (consultants).

We discussed some basic steps involved in designing a change strategy. In order to design an intervention strategy, the change manager, with the help of the change agent and others in the system, must be able to diagnose the existing environment for change, develop a plan of action, and evaluate the results of the action plan to determine if the desired (behavioral) changes have occurred. HRD practitioners have a definite role in this process. Among other things, an HRD practitioner can help the change manager understand the full range of HRD programs and processes and determine which works best under different conditions.

We introduced four types of planned interventions—human processual, technostructural, sociotechnical, and large systems change. Human processual interventions are directed at improving interpersonal, intragroup, and intergroup relations. The most common human processual intervention studies are laboratory training, survey feedback, and team building. Technostructural interventions focus on improving the work content, work method, and relationships among workers, and lowering cost by replacing inefficient materials, methods, equipment, workflow designs, and costly unnecessary labor with more efficient technology. One type of technostructural intervention is the sociotechnical. This focuses more on seeking innovative ways of increasing productivity and worker satisfaction through redesigning workflow structures, work methods, and work content. Large-systems interventions are used for large-scale reorganizations or cultural changes. Both of these approaches are very complex and need to be managed from the top of the organization.

Key Terms and Concepts

action planning	intervention strategy
alpha changes	job characteristics model
alternative work schedules	job design/enlargement
beta changes	job enrichment
change agent	organization development
change manager	process consultation
client	quality circles
cultural change	self-directed teams
downsizing	sociotechnical systems interventions
gamma changes	survey feedback
flextime	team building
force field analysis	technostructural interventions
human processual interventions	total quality management

Questions for Discussion

1. Describe how an organization introduces change and how such changes can produce desired effects. Can an organization replicate another organization's procedure and get the same results each time? Why or why not?

2. Why is the role of the manager critical to the success of the intervention? Is it possible to have a successful intervention without the manager's direct involvement? If yes, under what conditions?

3. When are internal change agents more likely to be successful as compared to external change agents? If both are involved in the same intervention, what kinds of problems could arise? How are these problems resolved?

4. What change agent skills are necessary for helping a dysfunctional group become more effective? What if the problems are between the respective managers? What happens if they refuse the help of the change agent?

5. Describe how the skills needed for designing and implementing human processual interventions as opposed to technostructural interventions differ.

6. If you were a manager in a shoe manufacturing plant and you were asked to design and implement self-directed work teams, what kind of intervention strategy would you use? How would you involve first-line supervision in this process? What kinds of problems would you anticipate?

7. Is large systems change a necessity for maintaining an efficient organization? Why or why not? Even though there is limited empirical evidence to support large systems change intervention strategies, why do organizations still use this approach? Identify and describe a situation where this approach would not be effective. Support your answer.

14

HRD in a Multicultural Environment

Learning Objectives:

1. *Understand how new entrants into the labor market may change the cultural fabric of organizations.*

2. *Describe the effects a greater percentage of women in the workforce has on organizational culture and the challenges to HRD posed by these effects.*

3. *Describe the effects that a greater percentage of racial minorities in the workforce will have, and resultant challenges to HRD.*

4. *Become familiar with the challenges to HRD professionals in a multicultural environment.*

5. *Understand how programs for "valuing differences" and "managing diversity" can achieve multiculturalism.*

6. *Describe HRD programs and processes that can support multiculturalism.*

OPENING CASE

Armco Steel, a major U.S. steel producer, has a heritage common to most U.S. steel companies: macho and conservative. The composition of the company's management team has reflected this tradition—it was almost exclusively white and male and saw little reason to change. In 1988 Bob Boni, then chief executive, assembled Armco's top executives for a meeting in Princeton, New Jersey, to discuss the issue of diversity. The meeting was designed to confront and discuss discriminatory attitudes, particulary among executives. Mike Wilson, a human resource manager at Armco, stated that "participants at the meeting denied they discriminated . . . tended to view the exercise as a waste of time and money and paid lip service to equal employment afterwards."

The Princeton meeting led to several important decisions about the company's approach to diversity. First, Armco changed its recruitment policy, particularly for professional employees. Rather than recruit at the local level, the company decided to recruit from universities throughout the country and even overseas. Second, Armco decided to foster an awareness and understanding of discriminatory attitudes among employees and how to avoid them. This would involve a long-term effort to change stereotypical attitudes (e.g., sexist, racist, etc.) and the behavior they led to. As a first step toward implementing these initiatives, Armco management decided to concentrate its efforts on the research laboratory located in Middletown, Ohio. This was an appropriate choice—the laboratory had very few employees who were not white males.[1]

Introduction

In order for organizations to compete successfully in a global economy, they must be willing to attract and retain the best possible employees. For some organizations, this may mean recruiting and hiring more women and minorities for roles that are nontraditional for them—such as management. As discussed in Chapter 1, the Hudson Institute published a major report, based on the study of demographic changes, which, among other things, predicted that women and minorities would represent approximately 85 percent of all *new workers* entering the work force between 1988 and 2000 (Johnston & Packer, 1987). This report, although controversial, forced many organizations to rethink their organizational policies and programs and to begin to make necessary adjustments.

The focus of this chapter will be on the changing labor market and how it is influencing organizations like Armco Steel to make changes. We will discuss the effects of hiring more women and minorities on an organization's culture. Then, we will discuss several approaches used by organizations to become multicultural and what the implications of those actions are for HRD practitioners.

Organizational Culture

Every person exists within a sociopolitical culture. **Culture** can be defined as a set of shared values, beliefs, norms, and artifacts that are used to interpret the environment and as a guide for all kinds of behavior. Each culture is distinguished by a unique set of attributes, described in Table 14-1. These attributes help people to differentiate one culture from another. For example, when these attributes are used to describe a nationality (e.g., American), the primary descriptors would be geographic origin, language, and political institutions. These attributes can also describe groupings or subcultures within a larger culture.

TABLE 14-1	**COMMON CULTURAL CHARACTERISTICS**

1. Common geographic origin.
2. Migratory status.
3. Race.
4. Language or dialect.
5. Religious faith.
6. Ties that transcend kinship, neighborhood, and community boundaries.
7. Shared traditions, values, and symbols.
8. Literature, folklore, music.
9. Food preferences.
10. Settlement and employment patterns.
11. Special interests in regard to politics.
12. Institutions that specifically serve and maintain the group.
13. An internal perception of distinctness.
14. An external perception of distinctness.

SOURCE: From Thernstrom, S., Orlov, A., & Handlin, O. (Eds.). (1980). *Harvard Encyclopedia of American Ethnic Groups*. Cambridge, MA.

When describing a subset of the American culture, the descriptors might include race, food preference, religion, employment practices, migratory status, and internal/external distinctness. A visitor to the United States, for example, would notice stark cultural differences between residents of New Orleans, Louisiana and residents of Provo, Utah.

Organizational Culture Defined

Organizational culture was defined in Chapter 13 as a set of shared values, beliefs, norms, artifacts, and patterns of behavior that is used as a frame of reference for the way one looks at, attempts to understand, and works within any organization (Ott, 1989). Organizations are subsets of larger sociopolitical cultures. Relationships between the larger sociopolitical culture and organizational cultures are referred to "as cultural 'paradigms'" which tie together the basic assumptions about humankind, nature, and activities" (Schein, 1987b, p. 264); these assumptions are reflected in the way that key members of an organization view relationships as domineering, submissive, or harmonizing. These assumptions are the building blocks or the roots of an organizational culture. They are often unseen and can be inferred only through artifacts and patterns of behavior.

Artifacts are "material and nonmaterial objects and patterns that intentionally or unintentionally communicate information about the organization's technology, beliefs, values, assumptions, and ways of doing things" (Ott, 1989, p. 24). Material artifacts include documents, physical layout or arrangements, furnishings, patterns of dress, and so on. Nonmaterial artifacts include organizational stories, ceremonies, and leadership styles. In organizations, leadership style can be influenced by assumptions about gender and racial roles. For example, if a male manager assumes that it is women's nature or role to give family issues priority over work issues, then he would not likely promote women to higher levels of responsibility. This kind of attitude is prevalent in our society and will be discussed later in this chapter.

Patterns of behavior help to reinforce an organization's assumptions, beliefs, and ways of doing things through such things as staff meetings, training programs, filing forms, and other normal organizational practices (Ott, 1989). For example, if an organization initiates a sexual harassment policy by scheduling a mandatory training program for all employees, it is communicating a high level of importance and value to this responsibility. Conversely, even if an organization talks up the importance of curbing incidences of sexual harassment, but fails to provide adequate training to reach that goal, it will be communicating that it places the issue at a much lower level of importance. Thus, patterns of behavior help to reinforce important assumptions, beliefs, and values.

Both artifacts and patterns of behavior play an important role in the socialization process. As discussed in Chapter 7, socialization is the process whereby new members learn how to function (e.g., learn norms) in a group or organization. In the absence of a prescribed code of conduct, new members typically learn how to behave by observing artifacts and patterns of behavior in an organization.

The match between people in an organization with the organizational culture is very important. If an organization employs people who make similar assumptions about people and have similar values and beliefs, then there is greater likelihood that they will demonstrate loyalty and commitment to organizational goals. This kind of organization is often referred to as a *monoculture*. Conversely, organizations who employ people from diverse cultures or subcultures, where there may be divergent assumptions, values, and beliefs, may have different experiences. These experiences, however, are not necessarily bad. In fact, there is growing feeling among many authors that cultural diversity can have many positive outcomes. This diversity, among other things, can bring a richness of perspective to an organization.

Effects of Labor-Market Changes on Organizational Culture

As we discussed earlier, the 1987 *Work Force 2000* report has increased the awareness of the effects of demographic changes on organizations. Nowhere is that effect stronger than on an organization's culture. The prediction that women and racial minorities will represent 85 percent of all new entrants into the labor market by the turn of the century was based, in part, on Department of Labor statistical projections (see Table 14-2). Basically, the projections are that:

1. The participation rate among white, black, and Hispanic women in the workforce will increase by 4.3, 4.9, and 6.8 percent, respec-

TABLE 14-2	CHANGES IN PARTICIPATION RATES OF WORKERS BY SEX, RACE, AND HISPANIC ORIGIN, AGED 16 AND OLDER, FROM 1986 AND PROJECTED TO 2000

	Participation Rate		Number (in thousands)		Percent Change
	1986	2000	1986	2000	
Whites–Total	65.5%	68.2%	101,801	116,701	14.6%
Men	76.9	75.3	57,216	62,252	8.8
Women	57.2	61.5	44,585	54,449	22.1
Blacks–Total	63.5%	66.0%	12,684	16,334	28.8%
Men	71.2	70.7	6,373	7,926	24.4
Women	57.2	62.1	6,311	8,408	33.2
Hispanics–Total	65.4%	68.7%	8,076	14,086	74.4%
Men	81.0	80.4	4,948	8,303	67.8
Women	50. 1	56.9	3,128	5,783	84.9

SOURCE: Bureau of Labor Statistics, 1987.

tively, while the participation rate among men in all categories will decrease slightly.

2. The total number of minority workers in the labor market, particularly Hispanics, will increase at a faster rate than whites.

The **participation rate** refers to the estimated number of people over the age of 16 in any demographic category who are currently *available to work* (excluding students, retirees, people who are institutionalized, or those receiving total disability) compared to the number of people who are *currently employed.* Thus, a participation rate of 80 percent means that if 10 people are available to work, only 8 are actually working. The higher the participation rate is, the larger the number of people in any single category who are (or are predicted to be) employed. The impact of the changing employment patterns of women and minorities on organizations, and specifically on an organization's culture, will be discussed next.

Women and Organizational Culture

The continued increase in participation rates among women will mean that more and more women, both white and nonwhite, will be seeking job opportunities. Some women will continue to seek job opportunities in traditionally female-dominated occupations (e.g., nursing, secretarial, etc.). However, a substantial number of women will be seeking employment opportunities in nontraditional, male-dominated jobs. This trend is shown in Table 14-3.

TABLE 14-3	**THE PRESENCE OF WOMEN IN THE WORKPLACE**

- Since 1950, college undergraduate female students have doubled from 20 to 54 percent.
- Since 1960, female lawyers increased from 7,500 to 180,000.
- Since 1960, female engineers increased from 7,404 to 174,000.
- Since 1960, working mothers, with children under the age of 18, have increased from 28 to 68 percent.
- Since 1970, the number of women in management has quadrupled.

SOURCE: From "Careers under Glass" by C. Solomon, 1990, *Personnel Journal, 69*(4), pp. 96–105.

The "Glass Ceiling"

Even though the number of women in professional occupations has increased significantly, very few have been promoted to policy-making and executive-level positions. In a recent review of literature on women and minorities in management, Morrison and Von Glinow (1990) reported the following:

1. Women comprise nearly a third of all holders of managerial positions (up from 19 percent in 1972), but most have little authority and low pay;

2. A survey report concluded that women consisted of 2 percent of 1,362 senior executives;

3. A study of *Fortune Service 500* and the 190 largest health care organizations found that only 3.6 percent of positions on boards of directors and 1.7 percent of positions as corporate officers were held by women;

4. U.S. government report showed women hold 8.6 percent of senior executive-level positions;

5. A survey in 1987 found that women at the vice-presidential level earn 42 percent less than their male counterparts; and

6. Between 1979 and 1984, women were six times more likely than men to leave corporate management to start their own businesses. (p. 200)

These trends not only reveal a pattern of exclusion, but they also indicate that some women have become frustrated with the lack of mobility and pay differentials and are leaving corporate life to pursue their own career goals. This also suggests that organizations must make some changes if they want to retain qualified women.

Even though research has shown that women can be successful managers, negative attitudes toward their ability to manage persist. The rise of women to management positions, particularly upper-level executive and policy-making positions, has been slow. It appears that there is an invisible but impenetrable boundary preventing women from advancing to senior management levels. This barrier has been described as the **"glass ceiling."** The glass ceiling is defined as subtle attitudes and prejudices that block women and minorities from upward mobility, particularly into management jobs (Garland, 1991; Mize, 1992; Morrison & Von Glinow, 1990; Solomon, 1990). More specifically, the glass ceiling symbolizes prevailing attitudes about different cultural groups and their general abilities, or the lack thereof, to perform some role or occupation. Thus, when a qualified woman enters an occupation, there may be a prevailing attitude among male managers that this person will not be groomed for one of the top jobs. Even when women are promoted into management positions, they tend to be in staff functions (e.g., human resources, public relations, etc.) that have limited authority and not considered developmental assignments for promotion into executive and policy-making positions (Morrison & Von Glinow, 1990). Morrison et al. (1987) researched the experiences of successful and unsuccessful women and found that, overall, women were not given the difficult on-the-job assignments (e.g., start-up or turnaround) that were considered essential leadership assignments for upward mobility. This is substantiated by the fact that there are very few women in executive and policy-level positions.

Lack of Role Models and Mentors

One of the insidious aspects of the glass ceiling is that many women in entry-level and mid-level positions are excluded from the informal mentoring system. **Mentoring** is defined as a process by which an older and more experienced person provides career guidance and psychological support to a protege (Noe, 1988). (Recall our discussion of mentoring in Chapter 11.) While some organizations have used formal mentoring systems (e.g., Digital Equipment Corporation), informal systems are still prevalent. Noe (1988) found several barriers (that can serve as a glass ceiling) to building mentor relationships between men and women:

1. Women lack the knowledge of how to develop informal networks, which are dominated by white males (p. 67);

2. When women are given preferential treatment for certain jobs, particularly those that are male-dominated, other employees may feel resentful; thus, the new employees are considered tokens (p. 68);

3. Women are sometimes socialized by their managers and peers to accept certain roles and role expectations that do not include

performing and mastering behavior that is required for managerial performance (p. 69);

4. There are no norms for establishing cross-gender mentor relationships; thus, men tend to avoid developing mentor relationships with women (p. 70); and

5. Women rely on more indirect and acquiescent strategies for influence, while men tend to exert direct power, and these differences may be perceived by men as being ineffective (p. 71).

As a result of not having a mentor, women in management may experience isolation and choose to leave the organization (Haller, 1989).

Department of Labor Study

The glass ceiling has been recognized by the U.S. Department of Labor (DOL). Under the direction of former Secretary of Labor Elizabeth Dole, the DOL initiated a study of the effects of the "glass ceiling" on upward mobility. The goals of the initiative were:

1. To promote a quality, inclusive, and diverse work force capable of meeting the challenge of global competition;

2. To promote good corporate conduct through an emphasis on corrective and cooperative problem solving;

3. To promote equal opportunity, not mandated results; and

4. To establish a blueprint of procedures to guide the department in conducting future reviews of all management levels of the corporate work force (U.S. Department of Labor, p. 3).

The study investigated several companies to determine the extent to which an organization's promotion patterns showed a glass ceiling pattern. Some of the findings were:

1. Neither women nor minorities tended to advance as far as their white male counterparts, but women advanced further than minorities;

2. While most organizations made a concerted effort to identify and develop key (white male) employees, few organizations had taken any ownership for equal employment opportunity and access;

3. The few women and minorities who held executive jobs were in staff positions (e.g., human resources, research, and administration) which were considered outside the corporate mainstream; and

4. While most organizations held federal government contracts, most of them had inadequate equal-employment and affirmative-action record keeping.

The report also identified some potential barriers to upward mobility. In addition to recruitment practices, the report cited the "lack of opportunity to contribute and participate in corporate developmental experiences" (U.S. Department of Labor, p. 21). This suggests that organizations must be able to formalize the career development process in order to eliminate the effects of the glass ceiling. The sole reliance on informal mentoring is insufficient to ensure that every qualified person is given an opportunity for advancement.

The effect of the lack of an informal mentor is further complicated when women represent a small minority within an organization or group. Kanter (1977) suggests that when there are 15 to 35 percent or less of any single group in an organization or unit, **tokenism** will likely occur. One impact of tokenism is on performance evaluation ratings. For example, Sackett et al. (1991) compared male and female performance ratings and found that when women make up less than 20 percent of the work force, they tend to be rated about one-half a standard deviation below men, as compared with results when women make up over 50 percent of workers. Surprisingly, when women represent over half of the work force, they tend to be rated higher than men.

Challenges to Human Resource Development

The increase in the number of women entering the work force represents a challenge to organizations specifically to HRD staff. The challenge will be the greatest for those organizations that are male-dominated and/or those that have not created access to all occupational areas for women. Leaving equal employment laws aside, if these organizations want to attract and retain highly qualified women, they must address some of the underlying assumptions, beliefs, and values that men have about women. These attitudes may be the result of sex-characteristic stereotyping, beliefs regarding women's preferences, attributions regarding performance outcomes, and sex-role stereotyping (Noe, 1988).

HRD professionals must be willing to confront some of the underlying assumptions, beliefs, and attitudes within themselves and be willing to challenge different aspects of the prevailing organizational culture that support stereotyping. We will discuss several educational and training options to accomplish this goal later in this chapter.

Minorities and Organizational Culture

The continued increase in the total population of racial minorities will mean that more and more blacks, Hispanics, Asians, and other minority groups will be seeking better job opportunities. Minorities, like women, are faced with two kinds of job discrimination—access and treatment. **Access discrimination** occurs when an organization places limits on job availability through such means as limiting advertisement and recruitment, rejecting applicants, or offering a lower starting salary (Ilgen & Youtz, 1986). **Treatment discrimination** occurs after the minority person is hired and on the job, and takes the form of limited opportunities for training, promotion, and pay raises. Each form of discrimination is discussed below.

Access Discrimination

The effect of access discrimination is illustrated by the fact that racial and ethnic minorities have had the highest unemployment rates of all groups and have held a disproportionately high number of low-skill jobs. This is reflected in the economic status of racial minorities. Mantsios (1992) stated that, using the 1990 poverty level of $12,675 for an urban family of four and $9,736 for a family of three, the following estimates can be made:

1. More than one out of every five children in the United States (all races) lives below the poverty line;

2. Thirty-nine percent of Hispanic children and 45 percent of black children in the United States live below the poverty line;

3. One out of every four rural children is poor;

4. One out of every three black persons over 65 years of age lives below the poverty line;

5. Approximately 60 percent of people below the poverty line do part-time or seasonal work; and

6. Two million people below the poverty line work full time (p. 98).

These estimates make two things clear. First, the data illustrate the dismal economic status of a large percentage of minority families in the United States. Second, the data suggest that while many of the people in a poverty situation may be eligible to work, many, if not most, may not have the education and training to compete for jobs in the future. With the growing numbers of low-skill jobs being transferred to foreign subsidiaries by companies seeking cheaper wage rates, this problem becomes magnified.

Treatment Discrimination

While there has been some significant progress made by educated and trained minority workers, they are still subjected to **treatment discrimination.** This is illustrated in a study of formal training programs in the United States that revealed a significant discrepancy in the rate of participation in training programs between white and nonwhite employees (Carnevale and Gainer, 1989). Table 14-4 shows the discrepancy between numbers of whites attending training programs as opposed to those of blacks and Hispanics. Such information does indicate, in part, the existence of barriers faced by blacks and Hispanics.

The projected increase in the total number of workers of racial and ethnic minorities entering the work force represents a significant challenge to organi-

TABLE 14-4	BREAKDOWN OF FORMAL TRAINING BY RACE		
	Whites	**Blacks**	**Hispanics**
Percent of work force	86.0%	9.5%	5.5%
Percent of work force in formal training	92.2%	5.1%	2.7%

SOURCE: From *The Learning Enterprise* (p. 13) by A. P. Carnevale and L. J. Gainer, 1989, Alexandria, VA: The American Society for Training and Development.

zations. Like women, minorities have begun to enter many of the nontraditional occupations (e.g., management) and also have had difficulty in moving into key executive and policy-making positions. Morrison and Von Glinow's (1990) review of the literature regarding participation of women and minorities in management found that minorities have made less progress than women. Specifically:

1.   Only one *Fortune 1000* company has a black CEO;

2.   Of the 1,708 senior executives surveyed in 1979 and 1985, the number of those who were minorities showed modest increases: for blacks, from 3 to 4; Asians, from 2 to 4; and Hispanics, from 2 to 3.

3.   In a survey of 400 *Fortune 1000* companies, fewer than 9 percent of all managers were minorities, including those who were black, Asian, and Hispanic.

These findings can be explained, in part, by differences in performance evaluation and developmental opportunities made available to racial minorities. For example, Greenhaus et al. (1990) examined the relationship between race (black versus white employees) and career options, and concluded that there were significant differences in each of the career outcomes when controlled by race. Specifically, black employees "received less favorable assessments of promotability from their supervisors, were likely to have plateaued in their careers, and were more dissatisfied with their careers than whites" (Greenhaus et al., 1990). Ilgen and Youtz (1986) examined the factors affecting the evaluation and development of minorities in organizations, including bias effects, lost opportunities, and self-limiting behaviors. In terms of development, they found that the development of minorities in organizations is affected by such things "as absence of mentors, less interesting or challenging work as a result of being in the outgroup, and being left out of the informal social network" (Ilgen & Youtz, 1986, p. 326). This suggests that if organizations are going to attract and retain qualified minorities, they must address the developmental needs of those groups.

Impact of Recent Immigration Patterns

One reason for the tremendous growth in the number of minority workers is the continuing influx of immigrants during the 1980s and 1990s. Table 14-5

TABLE 14-5	SURGE OF IMMIGRANTS IN THE 1980S

- Today's immigrants represent a wide range racial and ethnic groups.
- Almost 9 million immigrants arrived in the 1980s, which represents 43.8 percent of the nation's 19.8 million foreign-born.
- Foreign-born U.S. residents represent 1 of 7 people in the country.
- The Hispanic population grew by 60 percent; the total Mexican population alone is 13.5 million.
- The Asian population doubled between 1970 and 1980, from 1.4 million to 3.5 million.
- The Chinese population, the largest Asian group, doubled to 1.6 million.

SOURCE: From "Immigrant Tide Surges in the 80s" by M. L. Usdansky, May 29–31, 1992, *USA Today,* p. 1.

describes some of the immigration patterns in the 1980s. Hispanics, the largest foreign-born group, are quite diverse, separated by socioeconomic class, national origin, citizenship status, length of residence in the United States, and the degree of assimilation into the American culture (Heskin & Heffner, 1987). The fastest growing group is Mexicans, who currently represent approximately 70 percent of the foreign-born U.S. population. Because many Mexican immigrants have limited education, language skills, and work skills, they are generally relegated to low-skilled jobs. Preparing these workers for higher-skilled jobs will mean making a considerable investment in education and training.

The number of Asians, who are the second-largest immigrant group, doubled in size between 1970 and 1980, from 1.4 million to 3.5 million. This number is predicted to triple again between 1980 to 2000 (Patel, 1988). Asians have made considerable advancements in education. For example, while Asian Americans represented 2 percent of the population in 1986, they represented 12 percent of the freshman class at Harvard that year (Ramirez, 1986). Asians, like Hispanics, come from different cultures and religious backgrounds, and speak different languages.

The Chinese, who are the largest Asian group, have been successful in gaining professional status. A large number of Chinese immigrants entered this country after restrictive immigration laws were lifted in the 1960s, most of whom were very poor and looking for low-skilled work. In the intervening years, however, they have made great strides in assimilating into the American culture. Today, a large proportion of foreign-born and native Chinese hold jobs as small business owners, managers, professionals, and executives (Hess et al., 1992).

The Japanese followed the Chinese in terms of immigration patterns, but not in the same numbers. Today, the growth of Japanese manufacturing industries and Japanese foreign investment in the United States has made them a significant force in U.S. financial markets. As the number of Japanese-owned businesses in the United States has increased, the number of Japanese executives working here has also increased. Asian groups from the southeast region, referred to as the Indochinese, have also grown in size since the end of the Vietnam War. These groups include Laotians, Vietnamese, Cambodians, Thais, and Indonesians.

As we noted earlier, Asians hold very few corporate executive positions, and also face the discrimination and cultural indifference experienced by other racial minorities and women (Ramirez, 1986). While Asians have experienced discrimination, sociological studies of discrimination have generally excluded scrutinizing these groups. However, with the tremendous growth in Asian immigration over the past ten years, it is expected that more data will be generated about the impact of these groups on society.

Challenges to Human Resource Development

In organizations that want to attract and retain racial minorities, HRD professionals have several challenges. First, they must be willing to confront some of the underlying assumptions, values, and beliefs that support stereotyping behavior. Second, HRD professionals must be willing to modify existing policies, or create new ones, that are sensitive to problems like the glass ceiling. These include changing orientation programs, developing a formal career development and mentoring process, and offering training programs that address some of the underlying assumptions, beliefs, and values that become manifested as sexist and racist attitudes. These approaches will be discussed later in this chapter.

Adapting to Demographic Changes

Many organizations have recognized the demographic changes that have occurred in the work force over the past 30 years. In response to the civil rights and feminist movements in the 1960s, some organizations established programs to facilitate the recruitment and retention of qualified women and minorities. This inclusion of women and minorities has made organizations more culturally diverse.

Cultural diversity is defined as the existence of two or more persons from different cultural groups in any single group or organization. Most organizations are culturally diverse because their employees are from different cultural subgroups (e.g., with regard to gender, race, ethnic origin, etc.). But even if an organization is culturally diverse, it may not be multicultural. This distinction is significant. **Multicultural** organizations are those designed for the express purpose of serving a combination of needs. Thus, multicultural organizations acknowledge differences of members and make the necesssary adjustments to ensure that everyone is treated fairly, without excluding any group. Multicultural organizations deliberately capitalize on the diversity of their employees by ensuring that all organizational policies and practices are responsive to all employees (Morrison & Von Glinow, 1990).

Becoming a multicultural organization may not only be desirable, it may become necessary if organizations are to survive in the global economy and rapidly changing labor market. Multiculturalism can be an important strength for succeeding in foreign markets and in attracting qualified women and minority candidates from the labor market of the future.

In this section we will discuss three common approaches to achieving multiculturalism—affirmative action, valuing differences, and managing diversity.

Affirmative Action Programs

Since the 1960s, the U.S. government has established laws intended to protect the civil rights of U.S. citizens. One important group of civil rights laws is those mandating **equal employment opportunity** (EEO). EEO is defined as the right to obtain jobs and be rewarded in them regardless of non-job-related factors. EEO laws (the most recent being the Civil Rights Act of 1991) make it unlawful for employers to make employment decisions on the basis of race, sex, national origin, age, religious beliefs, mental or physical disability, Vietnam-era or disabled veteran status, or pregnancy, unless these factors can be shown to be job-related. These laws are directed primarily at employment practices and decisions, including access to HRD programs, that have an unfair exclusionary impact on any of the groups specified in the legislation. Essentially, EEO provides a basis for ensuring that illegal discrimination no longer occurs in the workplace.

Affirmative action goes well beyond the obligations specified in EEO legislation. The purpose of affirmative action programs (AAPs) is "to bring members of underrepresented groups, usually groups that have suffered discrimination, into a higher degree of participation in some beneficial program" (Rosenfeld, 1991, p. 42). The concept of affirmative action was written into law in 1965 as part of Executive Order 11246 (as amended by Order 11375), which was issued by President Johnson. This order requires certain government agencies and employers (and their subcontractors) who hold federal contracts in excess of $10,000 to undertake affirmative action processes to ensure equal employment opportunity. It also established the Office of Federal Contract Compliance Programs (OFCCP), which was given the responsibility of overseeing the affirmative action process (AAP). According to OFCCP guidelines, organizations should take the following steps to meet affirmative action requirements:

1. Prepare a written policy statement on equal employment opportunity/affirmative action (EEO/AA).

2. Designate an affirmative action officer.

3. Publicize an EEO/AA policy statement.

4. Conduct an analysis of the surrounding labor market to determine if the current labor force is representative.

5. If a protected group is underrepresented in any area within the organization (e.g., by department, occupation, etc.), develop goals and timetables in order to achieve parity with the external labor market.

6. Develop specific programs and activities to achieve these goals and timetables.

7. Establish an internal auditing and reporting system of its programs and activities.

8. Develop support for affirmative action, both inside and outside the company.

In essence, AAPs require actions such as preferential recruiting and hiring or placement of certain groups when those groups are underrepresented in any occupation within an organization. These actions may involve HRD programs.

Affirmative action is a volatile topic. Historically, there has been some justification offered for giving some groups preferential treatment. First, supporters of affirmative action believe that AAPs are necessary for correcting patterns of discrimination, particularly when an AAP has been ordered by the courts in cases where an organization is found guilty of longstanding discrimination. For example, this line of reasoning was supported by the U.S. Court of Appeals (Second Circuit) in the case of the *United States v. the National Association for the Advancement of Colored People, Inc.*, (779 f.2d 881, 1985). This decision allowed an affirmative action decree to stand because the court found the City of Buffalo, New York, was guilty of longstanding discrimination against blacks, women, and Hispanics.

The second justification offered for AAPs is the belief that, because of institutional racism, minorities have been subjected to inferior conditions (e.g., lack of good education) and that they have thus been inhibited in their ability to compete against better-prepared whites. Therefore, preferential treatment can be one way to equalize their chances. This was the reasoning supported in the case of *Weber v. Kaiser Aluminum and Chemicals* (415 F. Sup. 761, 1976). This decision allowed a temporary preference for admitting qualified members of underrepresented groups to jobs and training opportunities when a company could show imbalances in its work force. In this case, Kaiser had negotiated exclusionary terms with a union that barred blacks from accessing in-house training programs required for promotion (Milkovich & Boudreau, 1991).

While affirmative action has resulted in some employment gains for women and minorities, particularly in the professional ranks, it has vocal opponents and has created several problems. Critics argue that AAPs go beyond providing equal employment opportunity by allowing employers to give preference to members of protected groups at the expense of majority-group members who themselves are not guilty of illegal discrimination. They claim that this preference leads to so-called "reverse discrimination" against such individuals. Furthermore, AAPs have created feelings of animosity toward individuals and groups who have been perceived to have benefited from them. A second problem with AAPs is that they can **stigmatize** qualified minorities and women who have been hired or promoted based on their achievements. When an AAP is present, some employees claim that the successes of all minority and women candidates are the result of affirmative action alone. This tends to undermine the self-esteem of people who have worked hard to educate themselves and develop the necessary skills to be successful.

While affirmative action contributes to the goal of achieving cultural diversity, it does not make an organization multicultural. There are a number of reasons for this. First, because AAPs (particularly court-ordered ones) are seen as a reaction to external forces and not accepted as part of the organizational culture, organizational members see them as an imposition. These feelings can lead to the sexist and racist attitudes described earlier (e.g., those that comprise the glass ceiling). Second, as long as organizational members perceive AAPs as unfair preferential treatment, women and minorities, even if not directly helped by an AAP, will likely be stigmatized. Thus, co-workers will undervalue the education, experience, and contributions of minority and women colleagues. R. Roosevelt Thomas, executive director of the American Institute of Managing Diversity, feels that "affirmative action gets blamed for failing to do things it could never do . . . so long as racial and gender equality is something we grant to minorities and women there will be no racial and gender equality" (Thomas, 1990, p. 109). Something beyond affirmative action must be done to achieve the goal of multiculturalism.

Valuing Differences

According to Barbara Walker, former manager of the International Diversity Program at Digital Equipment Corporation, **valuing differences** is defined as "building an environment in which all people—each one a person of difference—could feel that their interests mattered and would at least be taken into account." In essence, this approach tries to create an environment in which each person's cultural differences are respected.

The valuing differences approach emphasizes education as a means of confronting some of the underlying causes of cultural bias—primarily racism and sexism. The intent of this approach is to expose employees to an analysis of some of the faulty assumptions people make about members of other groups. This will help them to increase their awareness of themselves and others. For example, US WEST, a Denver-based telecommunications company, developed a diversity program that includes two kinds of training: (1) a three-day program called "Managing a Diverse Workforce" for managers and union stewards and (2) a one-day version called "The Value of Human Diversity" for the remaining 65,000 employees (Caudron, 1992). Pacific Gas & Electric (PG&E), a major public utility in California, takes a different approach to valuing differences. PG&E's program is built on the assumption that a cadre of internal trainers is needed to cultivate the underpinnings of a multicultural organization. Employees are selected to attend a six-day certification ("train-the-trainer") diversity awareness program and, upon graduation, are expected to champion diversity in their day-to-day interactions with others (Johnson & O'Mara, 1992). Corning Inc. requires its employees to attend two cultural awareness programs— "Women and Men as Colleagues" and "Valuing Racial Diversity" (Solomon, 1990).

Digital Equipment Corporation's (DEC's) valuing differences program also emphasizes education and training, but places more emphasis on follow-up programs. DEC begins its program with a two-day cultural awareness session followed by assignment to core groups. The core groups are composed of eight to ten employees from diverse backgrounds who explore their underlying assumptions, beliefs, values, and perceptions about people. The intent is to strip away some of the cultural stereotypes that can create barriers to communication and ongoing relationships. In addition to the awareness training and core groups, DEC provides many different support activities including leadership groups, networking, celebrating awareness events, resource libraries on valuing differences, a formal mentor process, and a strong commitment to affirmative action.

While the valuing differences approach has the potential benefit of generating greater respect among members of diverse cultural groups, encouraging upward mobility for women and minorities and greater receptivity for affirmative action, it does not empower members of a diverse group to reach their full potential (Thomas, 1991). One criticism of the valuing differences approach is that its primary emphasis is on improving interpersonal relations and not on providing the skills needed for working with diverse cultural groups (Galagan, 1991). In order to learn these skills, a managing diversity approach may be needed.

Managing Diversity

Thomas (1991) defines **managing diversity** as "a comprehensive managerial process for developing an environment (organizational culture) that works for all employees" (p. 10). This definition gets at the core of multiculturalism—creating an environment designed for a combination of several distinct cultures. This approach goes beyond both affirmative action and valuing diversity because it focuses on building an environment for everyone and on full utilization of the total work force. It does not exclude women or minorities, nor does it exclude whites or males. It is an attempt to create a level playing field for all employees without regard to cultural distinction. To do this, the managing diversity approach requires: (1) a long-term commitment to change; (2) substantive change in organizational culture; (3) a modified definition of leadership and management roles; (4) both individual and organizational adaptation; and (5) structural changes (Thomas, 1991).

The **long-term commitment to change,** particularly from top management, is necessary to allow sufficient time and resources to bring about a change in organizational culture. For example, Pillsbury has created the following managing diversity three-year objectives for its division heads:

1. To develop and implement strategic plans for creating more culturally diverse organizations;

2. To increase leaders' and managers' knowledge and skills in managing a culturally diverse workplace; and

3. To attract, motivate and retain people of color and women (Greenslade, 1991).

In order to achieve these objectives, managers must be totally committed to the program. Commitment from key organizational members (e.g., top managers, union leaders, etc.) is an important part of managing diversity. How to gain their commitment will be discussed later in this chapter.

The **substantive change in culture** is necessary if an organization expects to change the underlying assumptions, values, and beliefs that have fostered sexist and racist attitudes. Employees must learn to be more understanding of language and cultural differences and be able to identify and reject cultural stereotypes. Most organizations that have developed managing diversity programs rely on education and training programs, much as the valuing differences approach does. For example, organizations like Avon, Apple Computer, DEC, and Xerox have made diversity education the cornerstone of their managing diversity programs.

Modified definition of leadership and management roles is needed in order to accommodate the changes in organizational culture. Not only is it important that management roles be redefined during the change process, they may also be redefined as part of the managing diversity program. For example, managers may be required to serve as formal mentors to one or more of the women and minorities in their organization. Other organizations may require managers to lead a diversity core group. In order to ensure that these roles are institutionalized, some organizations have created a new corporate office for managing diversity. This office not only gives the program high visibility, but ensures that all activities are coordinated.

Managing diversity requires **both individual and organizational adaptation** because as the organizational culture undergoes a redefinition and begins to take on new characteristics, employees must be able to adapt to these changes. How well the organization and its employees adapt is highly dependent upon the management and leadership of the change process. Sufficient support systems must be available for people who are not sure about what is expected of them and how to adapt to these new expectations. For example, some employees may feel this program is affirmative action under a new name. Managers must be able to reinforce the point that a managing diversity program favors no subgroup.

Structural changes are necessary to accommodate the changes in management and leadership roles and changes in individual expectations. For example, several structural changes within the HRD function may need to be made. These include (1) developing new policies that support management diversity initiative; (2) changing formal orientation programs to place more emphasis on diversity issues; (3) developing formal career development programs; (4) adding a diversity component to some of the ongoing training programs, particularly management and supervisory training; and (5) developing a diversity resource library for all types of ongoing diversity programs.

Potential Roadblocks to Multiculturalism

While there is growing awareness of the need to address diversity issues, there is some reluctance to move in this direction. A Towers/Perrin survey of 645 national companies revealed that there was a widespread acknowledgement (75 percent) of labor-market changes, but that only 29 percent of those firms have initiated a diversity program (cited in Galagan, 1991). Even though there is considerable acceptance for managing diversity as a means for achieving multiculturalism, there is very little evidence of its effectiveness. Beyond the fact that a number of organizations (e.g., Armco Steel Company, Avon, DEC, PG&E, Pillsbury, etc.) have achieved some successes, there is very little empirical evidence of the overall effectiveness of their managing diversity programs. PG&E, for example, claims that managing diversity "improves its competitive advantage in recruiting and retaining employees and that it increases productivity, quality, creativity, and morale" (Johnson & O'Mara, 1992). Further, a survey of 400 Society for Human Resource Management (SHRM) members found that while there was some criticism (as to communication problems and training costs), almost half of the respondents indicated that managing diversity has created a more tolerant organizational culture (Rosen & Lovelace, 1991). Most of the respondents also indicated that the successful programs were the direct result of corporate efforts to open up communication channels and increase sensitivity to cultural and gender differences (Rosen & Lovelace, 1991).

Another roadblock to multiculturalism is the resistance of long-held attitudes to change. Even when organizations bolster multicultural programs with education and training programs, there is no guarantee that everyone will place the same value on learning about their own attitudes and about other cultures, particularly if they feel they have nothing in common with members of those cultures. The fact remains that people tend to feel most comfortable among those with whom they share things in common (e.g., cultural attributes).

Furthermore, there is evidence of a "backlash" among whites, particularly white males. Mobley and Payne (1992) cited reports of a backlash to diversity education and training programs, including:

1. Deep-seated biases and prejudices that are emerging as a reaction to fast-paced social change;

2. Lack of jobs and increased competition for resources, creating what some people see as a threatening environment;

3. Race and gender issues used increasingly as a political football;

4. Sensationalistic journalism, creating scapegoats and highlighting stereotypes;

5. The tendency of some people to see the "political correctness" movement as a direct threat to the First Amendment—which has created a legal and social mine field;

6. The tendency of some to feel that a focus on multiculturalism will dissolve the unity of the United States; and

7. A confusion about such terms as *political correctness, diversity, multiculturalism, pluralism, equal opportunity,* and *affirmative action* (Mobley & Payne, 1992, p. 46).

This perceived backlash should not be ignored in the process of forced change. As discussed in Chapter 13, resistance to change is rooted in personal values, beliefs, and attitudes. To overcome this resistance, we feel that organizations should consider introducing multiculturalism through a planned change strategy.

Introducing Multiculturalism through Change Strategy

One way to introduce multiculturalism, particularly if the approach is one of managing diversity, is by developing a large systems change strategy. As discussed in Chapter 13, large systems change is a very complex process. It will involve, among other things, defining the role(s) of a change manager, a change agent, and a change committee. In most large systems change strategies, it is important that a top manager, preferably the CEO, serve as the change manager. Because of the complexity of large systems change programs, it is also recommended that the CEO appoint a change committee that will oversee day-to-day implementation. For example, Avon appointed a Multicultural Participation Council that has responsibility for overseeing their diversity program (Thomas, 1990). Some organizations designate a manager (e.g., corporate director for diversity) who, along with the change manager and change agent, has ongoing responsibility for implementing the change strategy. The leadership of large systems change should:

1. Determine the readiness of the organization to accept change;

2. Develop a commitment plan (gaining commitment);

3. Develop an action plan (change strategy); and

4. Evaluate results.

Each of these will be described.

Determining Readiness of the Organization to Accept Change

The first step of determining the readiness usually involves assessing key individuals' perceptions of the existing situation. This may involve collecting data through such means as focus group sessions and/or a questionnaire administered to a larger group. The purpose of data collection is to better understand prevailing organizational assumptions, values, and beliefs and how they have manifested as different attitudes. Focus groups are useful in generating discussion as to how people perceive different aspects of the organization and how prevailing attitudes may result. Questionnaires or attitude surveys are useful for assessing perceptions of a group of people.

Developing a Commitment Plan

Developing a commitment plan is an essential step in large, complex change strategies. Beckhard and Harris (1987) state that, in order to make complex, large system changes, the commitment of a critical mass of people (key organizational members) is necessary to provide the impetus for change. Thus, before initiating a large systems change strategy, it is important to determine who people are and what level of commitment is needed from them. This process, referred to as **commitment planning,** involves analyzing each organization member's role and desired commitment to the proposed change program. Beckhard and Harris (1987) identified four commitment categories: (1) no commitment; (2) let it happen; (3) help it happen; and (4) make it happen. Each person's role is analyzed in two ways—as to whether the person supports change currently and what commitment is needed from him or her in the future. For those individuals who are categorized lower than desired, the commitment strategy should include the activities needed to gain the necessary support and commitment. One way that people can be influenced is by helping them understand the need to change and by using the top manager as a role model for accepting change.

Developing Change Strategy

Developing a change strategy involves determining the kinds and levels of intervention that will be needed. Assuming that the critical mass of people is in place to generate change, it is safe to conclude that some, if not all, of these people may have a stake in the outcome of the proposed change program. Key people should be directly involved in formulating the intervention strategy. Strategy sessions should be headed by the top manager and facilitated by the change agent (e.g., HRD practitioner). The goals of the program should be clearly defined. This will help the key individuals to better understand and develop objectives for each component.

Table 14-6 describes Pillsbury's managing diversity strategy, which involves six stages (Greenslade, 1991). Stages 1 and 2 are used for developing the context in which the change will take place. The activities include awareness sessions with senior management who need to understand their role in the change process and how to manage diversity. The briefing sessions are followed by team sessions that focus on educating employees as to some of the issues that underlie cultural diversity. If necessary, the change agent(s) may review cultural data to illustrate important aspects of the organization's culture (e.g., minorities feel isolated). The desired outcome of these first two stages is that everyone will feel a shared need to change.

Stages 3 through 5 involve more in-depth education as to how diversity can bring added value to the organization. These three-day sessions explore the underlying assumptions that lead to racist and sexist attitudes. The goal is to expand each participant's understanding and valuing of cultural differences, and ways that inclusion of women and minorities will enhance the organization. The last stage, Stage 6, involves integrating the cultural strategy into the organization's business plan. Since the philosophy of managing diversity is predicated on how well managers and other members of an organization view the utilization of people from all cultures, it is essential that the long-term strategy of the organization reflect this philosophy. This strategy also includes any changes in human resource management policies that will be necessary for achieving the

TABLE 14-6	SAMPLE PROGRAM FOR MANAGING DIVERSITY

Stage	Objectives
I. Briefing session, half day–2 days	a. Review organization's cultural assessment data. b. Learn basic concepts regarding high-performing, culturally diverse organization. c. Review organization's diversity plan.
II. Team session, 2 days	a. Build team skills necessary for addressing cultural diversity. b. Clarify business rationale for cultural diversity. c. Understand differences in business style. d. Understand differences in interpersonal style.
III. Added value (race), 3 days	a. Enhance racial interactions and communications. b. Identify stereotyping (racist) behaviors. c. Identify and address organizational barriers to contributions of racial minorities. d. Develop strategies for greater inclusion of racial minorities.
IV. Added value (gender), 3 days	a. Enhance gender interactions and communications. b. Identify stereotyping (sexist) behaviors. c. Identify and address organizational barriers to women's successful contributions. d. Develop strategies for greater inclusion of women.
V. Added value (style), 3 days	a. Identify the value that differences in style, ethnic/race, gender, and culture bring to the workplace. b. Practice teamwork that enhances the contribution of each member.
VI. Strategic planning, 1–2 days	a. Integrate cultural diversity into the business plan. b. Develop plans to (1) Expand educational process to the total organization, (2) Enhance the human resource system, and (3) Strengthen recruitment and retention.

SOURCE: From "Managing Diversity: Lessons from the United States" by M. Greenslade, 1991, *Personnel Management* (United Kingdom), p. 30.

long-term strategy, including strengthening recruitment, hiring, and retention of women and minorities.

Evaluating Results

Evaluating the results of the change strategy means focusing on whether there has been a fundamental change to the organization's culture. Given the complex nature of large systems change, designing an evaluation strategy may involve three sources of information: (1) pilot projects; (2) an examination of every area of the organization, to determine if there are any barriers to subsequent implementation; and (3) an analysis of the impact of the entire program on the organization (Kilmann, 1989). One of the difficulties in determining the effectiveness of cultural change is the lack of standardized measurement scales. Organizational culture researchers are using a "triangulation approach" involving survey data on several organizational dimensions combined with qualitative (through observations) and archival data (records) (Ott, 1989). This method increases the availability of data that can be cross-referenced.

Multicultural Education and Training Programs

Achieving multiculturalism, whether it involves valuing differences or managing diversity, relies heavily on education and training programs. These programs are typically referred to as **cultural awareness training** and should be designed just like any other training program. Most cultural awareness training programs deal with at least four elements:

1. Raising the awareness of cultural differences;

2. Focusing on ways attitudes are shaped;

3. Providing factual information about each culture; and

4. Building skills in the areas of language, nonverbal communication, cultural stress management and adjustment adaptation skills (Callahan, 1989).

In **raising the awareness of cultural differences,** there are some questions that need to be asked in order to generate discussion in this area. Table 14-7 summarizes some of these questions. The discussion should focus on understanding some of the assumptions, beliefs, and values people have about other cultures. Without first developing insight as to these elements, it will be difficult for people to value cultural differences. For example, some Asian cultures (e.g., Japanese) have difficulty assimilating with the aggressiveness and self-promotion that is common within many U.S. workplaces (Cox, 1991). Without understanding these differences, Americans may misinterpret the motive of a Japanese manager who is unwilling to confront an American worker who has been overly aggressive toward him.

Focusing on how attitudes are shaped helps people to understand how cultural stereotypes are formed and the destructiveness of cultural bias. Even though people may understand cultural differences, they may not truly understand how assumptions, values, and beliefs underlie sexist and racist attitudes. For example, a male manager may take extra effort to understand gender differences and learn to value women's contributions at the workplace. However, because there is a limited number of female managers, he may assume that most women lack the desire (or ability) to become managers. This assumption may result in his

TABLE 14-7	**QUESTIONS FOR CULTURAL AWARENESS TRAINING**	

Question	Potential Areas of Discussion	Examples
What are some key dissimilarities between people from different cultures?	1. Physical traits. 2. System of values. 3. Language or dialect. 4. Religion. 5. Institutions.	1. Sex, age, race. 2. Work ethic. 3. Hispanic. 4. Judaism. 5. Economic.
How do these differences come about?	1. Custom. 2. Lifestyle. 3. Shared norms. 4. Shared experiences. 5. Communication patterns.	1. Clothing. 2. Food. 3. Conforming. 4. War veteran. 5. Nonverbal symbols.
What are the implications when different cultures interact?	1. Conflict. 2. Stereotyping or ethnocentrism. 3. Sexism or racism.	1. When there is a misunderstanding. 2. When a group refuses to accept a person from another group. 3. Discrimination.

SOURCE: From *Management: An International Perspective* by H. Mason and R. S. Spich, 1987, Homewood, IL: Irwin.

not actively encouraging female subordinates to develop the skills needed to qualify for a management position. This may help create a glass ceiling. Without focusing on how these attitudes are developed, it will be difficult to change them.

Providing factual information about each culture is necessary to reinforce new assumptions, values, beliefs, and attitudes about different cultures. Since some people tend to be ethnocentric—that is, feeling that their culture is superior—they need constant reinforcement that every culture brings its own unique and valuable experience, perspective, and style of approaching problems to the organization. There is empirical evidence suggesting that cultural diversity brings together different experiences, perspectives, and different styles that can be used for approaching problems and situations resulting in more productivity (Gordon, 1992). People need to know what these strengths are and how they can help individual workers and the organization to do a better job.

Building skills in the areas of language, nonverbal communication, cultural stress management, and adjustment adaptation addresses critical interpersonal relations of employees both inside and outside the organization. In order for people to establish effective relations, they must learn how to communicate. Nonverbal communication, including body language (e.g., gestures, handshakes, etc.), is particularly important. Table 14-8 describes how some common forms of body language used by Americans can be misinterpreted by other cultures. Part of the communication training effort should focus on learning to

TABLE 14-8	BODY LANGUAGE IN CULTURES WORLDWIDE

- Acceptable interpersonal distance in various countries is

0 to 18 inches	Middle Eastern males, eastern and southern Mediterraneans, and some Hispanic cultures.
18 inches to 3 feet	U.S. and Western Europe.
3 feet or more	Asians (Japanese the farthest) and many African cultures.

- It is inappropriate behavior to touch Asians on the head.

- Acceptable length of eye contact in various countries is

0 to 1 second	Native Americans, East Indians, and Asian cultures (least is the Cambodian culture, which believes that direct eye contact is flirtatious).
1 second	U.S. (to continue direct eye contact beyond 1 second can be considered threatening, particularly between Anglo- and African-American persons).
1 second or more	Middle Eastern, Hispanic, southern European, and French cultures generally advocate very direct eye contact.

- Variations of handshakes in various countries are

Firm	Americans, Germans.
Moderate grasp	Hispanics.
Light	French (not offered to superiors).
Soft	British.
Gentle	Middle Easterners.
Gentle	Asians (for some cultures, though not Koreans, shaking hands is unfamiliar and uncomfortable).
Pointing	Generally poor etiquette in most countries, except in Asian countries where it is considered rude and in poor taste. If pointing is necessary, in Hong Kong you use your middle finger, in Malaysia it is the thumb, and the rest of Asia it is the entire hand.
Beckoning	The American gesture of using upturned fingers, palm facing the body, is deeply offensive to the Mexicans, Filipinos, and Vietnamese. For example, this gesture in the Philippines is used to beckon prostitutes.
Signs of approval	The use of the "okay" sign, the "thumbs-up" signal, and the "V" for "victory" are among the most offensive to other cultures.
Signaling "no"	This can be confusing. In Mexico and the Middle East, a "no" is indicated by a back-to-forth movement of the index finger.
The left hand	Gesturing or handling something with the left hand among Muslims is considered offensive because they consider this the "toilet" hand.

- Crossing legs is in poor taste among most Asians and Middle Easterners. The Russians find it distasteful to place the ankle on the knee.

SOURCE: From *Bridging Cultural Barriers for Corporate Success* (p. 133–141) by S. Thiederman, 1990, Lexington, MA: Lexington Books.

understand cultural differences in body language when dealing with different cultural groups.

Many organizations schedule cultural events that coincide with national events or celebrations (e.g., Black History Month) as part of their cultural awareness programs. These events provide an opportunity for others to learn more about a certain culture. Some organizations also provide resource libraries that contain literature, films, and other reference materials. Cultural awareness classes may include assignments that require participants to conduct small research projects using these materials.

Potential Problems with Diversity Education and Training

Just as there are roadblocks to achieving multiculturalism, there are also potential problems that can hamper diversity education and training programs. In particular, the design of the training program and the selection of the trainer should be given close scrutiny. There are many potential pitfalls that should be avoided—see the listing provided in Table 14-9. It is very important that HRD professionals consider all of these issues when designing a program.

TABLE 14-9	POTENTIAL PROBLEMS WITH MANAGING DIVERSITY TRAINING
When trainers . . .	**When the training program . . .**
• Use their own psychological issues (e.g., trust or group affiliation) as template for training.	• Is not integrated into the organization's overall approach to diversity.
• Have their political agenda.	• Is too brief, too late, or reactive.
• Do not model the philosophy or skills associated with valuing diversity.	• Is presented as remedial and trainees as people with problems.
• Are chosen because they represent or advocate for a minority group.	• Does not distinguish the meanings of valuing diversity, pluralism, EEO, AA, and managing across cultures.
• Are not competent at facilitation and presenting, have poor credibility with trainees, or are known to be insensitive.	• Does not make a link between stereotyping behavior and personal and organizational effectiveness.
• Force people to reveal their feelings about people.	• Is based on philosophy of political correctness.
• Do not respect individual styles of trainees.	• Is too shallow or too deep.
• Pressure only one group to change.	• Resource materials are outdated.
• Cover too few issues and do not engage participants individually.	• Curriculum is not adapted to trainees' needs or not matched with the skills and experience of the trainer.
	• Discussion of certain issues (e.g., reverse discrimination) is not allowed.

SOURCE: From "Backlash: The Challenge to Diversity Training" by M. Mobley and T. Payne, 1992, *Training & Development Journal, 43*(12), p. 47. Copyright 1992, the American Society for Training and Development. All rights reserved. Reprinted with permission.

Human Resource Development Programs for Multiculturalism

In order to achieve multiculturalism, organizations should look beyond education and training and review existing HRD policies and practices to ensure that they meet the needs of all employees. As discussed earlier, existing sexist and racist attitudes have been manifested in such practices as the glass ceiling. In order to eliminate these practices, fundamental changes in the way employees are socialized and developed are needed. In particular, organizations should examine their practices in the areas of socialization/orientation and career development. These two areas, along with other human resource programs and practices that can be used to further multiculturalism, are discussed here.

Socialization, Orientation, and Career Development

In Chapter 7 we defined socialization as the process by which an individual becomes an insider through assimilation of the roles, norms, and expectations of the organization. A new employee's initial experiences in an organization are particularly significant in influencing later decisions about career choices and whether to remain in an organization. For example, organizations must understand that when they design learning experiences for new employees, they should consider the following issues:

1. The sexist and racist attitudes held by the majority of employees (Ilgen & Youtz, 1986; Kanter, 1977; Morrison & Von Glinow, 1990).

2. Feelings of isolation experienced by new employees (women and minorities) when their cultural differences prevent them from obtaining the interesting and challenging work assignments needed to learn important job-related skills and to qualify for promotions (Kanter, 1977).

3. Additional stresses experienced by women and minorities who must become bicultural in order to be accepted by co-workers in the majority group (Cox et al., 1991).

4. The holding of women and minorities to higher standards than co-workers as they enter nontraditional occupations (Fernandez, 1988; Solomon, 1990).

Failure to consider these issues may result in the loss of talented female and minority employees.

Some organizations have recognized the influences of cultural differences on the socialization process and have taken steps to incorporate them into their orientation and socialization practices. For example, Armco, discussed in the opening case, not only recognized potential negative effects of subtle attitudes and prejudices that black women and minorities from upward mobility, but also how these are manifested during the socialization process. Specifically, they began to look for ways in which existing employees can serve as role models during the socialization process. Having same gender and racial role models makes it easy for new employees to confront issues like sexism and racism without fearing reprisal from co-workers.

There is some disagreement about the value of holding training and orientation programs that are targeted to a segregated audience (women or minority only). Some organizations believe that if the goal of managing diversity is to get employees to work together, it is important not to segregate women or minorities at any point in their development. Other organizations see such sessions as important in meeting the special needs of these groups. Organizations like DuPont and GTE do provide additional classroom training for newly hired women, but the trend is to avoid the impression of preferential treatment (Morrison & Von Glinow, 1990). Morrison and Von Glinow argue that "because women and minorities face special situations as tokens, they may need to perfect certain competencies such as conflict resolution" (1990, p. 204). While we agree it may be beneficial for incoming women and minorities to be given special awareness and training programs to help them to make the adjustment and deal with difficult cultural issues, these programs should exist within an overall plan targeted toward all employees to achieve the goal of multiculturalism.

Career Development

Most career development models and programs (recall our discussion in Chapter 11) do not explicitly deal with the special concerns of a culturally diverse work force. Given the continued existence of the glass ceiling and the failure of affirmative action to completely address inequities in the career advancement of women and minorities, more direct action should be taken in modifying career development systems.

Programs that promote valuing differences and managing diversity can be useful in creating a positive climate for career advancement. Although both of these approaches rely on education and training to change some of the underlying assumptions, values, and beliefs that support and sustain barriers like the glass ceiling, only managing the diversity approach attempts to integrate these efforts into the organizational strategy. Jim Preston, CEO of Avon Products, who sees managing diversity as a significant part of business strategy, states that "if you are going to attract the best . . . people into your organization, you'd better have a culture; you'd better have an environment in which those people feel they can prosper and flourish" (Thomas, 1991, p. 164).

Organizations can modify or create career development policies and programs without using a managing diversity approach. However, we believe that if sexist and racist attitudes are prevalent, an organization would have limited success using career development techniques for achieving multiculturalism. Therefore, we feel that career development policies and programs should be explicitly included in a strategy of managing-diversity intervention. The "new" career development program should include specific roles for managers (e.g., serving as mentors or advocates) and a formal role for HRD departments to monitor the process.

Other Human Resource Management Programs and Processes

Some organizations have extended managing diversity programs beyond HRD programs and processes by changing human resource management (HRM) policies and programs to meet the special needs of the new work force. Through the development of affirmative action programs, many organizations have been able to develop effective recruitment methods that are more effective in attracting qualified women and minority candidates. This influx of women and minorities into the work force has led organizations to modify some of their HRM practices to meet the needs of a culturally diverse work force. For example, some organizations have devised **flexible work schedules** and child care programs directed at the growing number of working mothers who are reentering the work force. IBM, after realizing that 30 percent of its employees had child care needs and an equal number had elder care responsibilities, revised its child care program and established a program for elder care (Sourentian, 1989).

Some organizations have responded to the problems of communicating with non-English-speaking employees. A small survey of companies within the southeastern New England region discovered that those organizations that acknowledged problems with non-English-speaking employees identified communication as the major problem. The survey respondents said that using the services of language interpreters and multilingual supervisors was the most effective means of resolving this problem. The language interpreters can help to establish expectations, convey organizational messages, and intervene when there are problems (Heskin & Heffner, 1987). All of these roles help to support an effective managing diversity policy and program. Hiring multilingual supervisors is probably one of the most effective means of communicating with non-English-speaking employees because they can communicate directly without an interpreter.

Closing Comment

We hope the reader has gained an appreciation for the importance of multiculturalism and how HRD programs can be used to achieve this goal. Obviously, no one can provide concrete evidence that organizations that are moving toward multiculturalism will be more successful in the future than those that resist change. However, we are convinced that working toward the goal of multiculturalism is not only fair and ethical, it will ultimately lead to a climate in which all employees can thrive within and contribute to the organization's success.

RETURN TO OPENING CASE

Prior to 1968, the Middletown, Ohio, research laboratory of Armco Steel Company was staffed predominantly by white males. Realizing the need to increase the representation there of women and minorities, Armco focused an effort for change on two activities: (1) altering the recruitment policy to establish a more diverse employment pool and (2) creating an awareness and understanding of discriminatory attitudes among employees and providing ways for these attitudes to be changed.

This awareness training effort was spearheaded by Mike Wilson, the human resource manager at the research laboratory. Wilson hired two Cincinnati consultants, Merline and Pat Pope, to help him create and deliver the program. Wilson chose the Popes because of their experience in developing a long-term program to change discriminatory behavior at Procter & Gamble.

The awareness training strategy Armco used included two interventions: seminars and the creation of "consultant pairs." The seminar intervention included a series of one-day seminars for the laboratory's top management and two-day seminars for the remaining 435 employees. The seminars, held off-site, involved presentation and discussion about different forms of discrimination and sexist and racist attitudes. The second intervention strategy included the selection and training of 17 "consulting pairs" who would serve as facilitators/mentors for socializing new employees. All of the pairs included people with fairly long service in the company.

The consulting pairs process is initiated with a meeting between the hiring manager and the new recruit. The pairs were chosen based on their ability to reflect the viewpoint of the hiring manager and the new recruit. For example, a white male manager and black male recruit would be accompanied by a white male pair and black male pair.

The results of these two initiatives have been successful so far. In 1991, 12 percent of the professional work force at the laboratory were ethnic minorities and 24 percent were women. While these numbers are not reflected in management positions—of the 120 managers, there is only one black and one woman—it is expected that, in time, the pairs program will bring greater equity to that area, as well. The consultant pairs program, even though initiated in early 1991, has met with a uniformly positive response from participants. Mike Wilson feels that this program will bring about genuine, deep-rooted change in the company power structure. He feels that it will take five to ten years to make the change.[1]

Summary

The demographic changes in today's work force may dictate needed changes to organizational culture. The prediction is that approximately 85 percent of new workers will be women and minorities. If this prediction is true, organizations must make some fundamental changes in the way they manage. First, they must address the underlying causes of sexism and racism, and reinforce new attitudes that respect and value each person's culture.

---

[1]From "Steel Partners" by J. Pickard, 1991, *Personnel Management* (United Kingdom), p. 32. Adapted by permission of Personnel Publicatons, Ltd.

There are at least three ways this can be accomplished: affirmative action, valuing differences, and managing diversity. Affirmative action has made a definite impact on organizations, but it is not a panacea for fostering multiculturalism. The valuing differences approach is a major adjustment in how women and minorities are valued within the organization, but does not address the problem of integrating multiculturalism into the mainstream of an organization. The managing diversity approach combines the goals of both affirmative action and valuing differences. It looks at multiculturalism as a long-term program for change in which ultimately every person in an organization will have not only value, but also will be a contributing member throughout the organization.

Since both valuing differences and managing diversity require significant changes in organizational culture, the implementation should be looked at as a large systems change strategy. The strategy should be led by a top manager, preferably the CEO. There are at least four steps in the process: (1) determining the readiness of the organization to change; (2) commitment planning; (3) developing the change strategy; and (4) evaluating the results. Since the major goal of the strategy is to change some of the underlying assumptions, beliefs, and values people have about others, one of the change activities usually involves cultural awareness training.

The change strategy may include changes in other HRD and HRM programs and processes. HRD practitioners must be able to adapt current socialization/orientation and career development processes to the needs of the new work force. HRM professionals should consider adapting other policies (e.g., benefits) in order to meet the special needs of new groups, including day-care services, flextime, interpreters, and multilingual supervisors.

Key Terms and Concepts

access discrimination	multiculturalism
affirmative action	participation rate
cross-awareness training	tokenism
cultural diversity	treatment discrimination
glass ceiling	valuing differences
managing diversity	

Questions for Discussion

1. Compare and contrast affirmative action and managing diversity programs. Can they occur simultaneously? Why or why not?

2. How has cultural bias affected women and minorities in terms of employment opportunities? Do you feel this can change? Provide an example of this type of change in your own life experiences.

3. Why is it important to acknowledge, understand, and value differences in your organization? How are you and your friends from culturally different backgrounds different? How are you the same?

4. How common is multiculturalism in our society? Provide at least two examples. How does multiculturalism affect individuals?

5. Describe the role of HRD practitioners with respect to managing diversity. What kinds of programs support this approach?

6. In some organizations, cultural diversity efforts meet with resistance from key managers and employees. Identify one reason for this resistance and make a recommendation as to ways it can be overcome. Support your recommendation.

REFERENCES

Abbott, J. (1988). The multicultural workforce: New challenges for trainers. *Training and Development Journal, 42*(8), 12–13.

Abramms-Mezoff, B., & Johns, D. (1988/89). Dealing with diversity: Playing with a mixed deck. *Management Quarterly, 29*(4), 17–19.

Adam, E. E. (1991). Quality circle performance. *Journal of Management, 17*(1), 25–39.

Adams, J. S. (1963). Toward an understanding of inequity. *Journal of Abnormal and Social Psychology, 67,* 422–436.

Addams, H. L. (1985). Up to speed in 90 days: An orientation plan. *Personnel Journal, 64*(12), 35–38.

Adler, N. J., & Bartholomew, S. (1992). Managing globally competent people. *The Executive, 6*(3), 52–65.

Ajzen, I., & Fishbein, M. (1977). Attitude-behavior relations: A theoretical analysis and review of empirical research. *Psychological Bulletin, 84,* 888–918.

Ajzen, I., & Fishbein, M. (1980). *Understanding attitudes and predicting social behavior.* Englewood Cliffs, NJ: Prentice-Hall.

Akabus, S. (1977). Labor: Social policy and human services. *Encyclopedia of Social Work,* 727–744.

Al-Gattan, A. A. (1985). Test of the path-goal theory of leadership in the multinational domain. *Group and Organizational Studies, 10,* 425–429.

Albanese, R. (1988). Competency-based management education. *Journal of Management Development, 8*(2), 66–76.

Albrecht, C. (1985). Achieving excellence in service. *Training and Development Journal, 39*(12), 64–67.

Alderfer, C. P. (1969). An empirical test of a new theory of human needs. *Organizational Behavior and Human Performance, 4,* 143–175.

Alderfer, C. P. (1972). *Existence, relatedness, and growth.* New York: The Free Press.

Alderfer, C. P. (1977). Organization development. *Annual Review of Psychology,* *28,* 197–223.

Alderfer, C. P., & Brown, L. D. (1975). *Learning from changing: Organizational diagnosis and development.* Beverly Hills: Sage Publications.

Alderfer, C.P. & Holbrook, J. (1973). A new design for survey feedback. *Education Urban Society, 5,* 437–464.

Allen, N. J., & Meyer, J. P. (1990). Organizational socialization tactics: A longitudinal analysis of links to newcomers' commitment and role orientation. *Academy of Management Journal, 33,* 847–858.

Alliger, G. M., & Janak, E. A. (1989). Kirkpatrick's levels of training criteria: Thirty years later. *Personnel Psychology, 42,* 331–342.

Altany, D. (1992). Cinderella with a drawl. *Industry Week, 241*(1), 49–51.

Anastasi, A. (1982). *Psychological testing.* New York: Macmillan.

Anderson, J. R. (1983). *The architecture of cognition.* Cambridge, MA: Harvard University Press.

Anderson, J. R. (1993). Problem solving and learning. *American Psychologist, 48,* 35–44.

Anderson, J. R., & Bower, G. H. (1973). *Human associative memory.* Washington, DC: Winston.

Anderson, J. R., Farrell, R., & Sauers, R. (1984). Learning to program in LISP. *Cognitive Science, 8,* 87–129.

Andrews, E. S., & Noel, J. L. (1986). Adding life to the case study method. *Training and Development Journal, 40*(2), 28–29.

Andrews, K. R. (1966). *The effectiveness of university management development programs.* Boston: Harvard University.

Anonymous (1992, November 30). Beg, borrow . . . and benchmark. *Business Week,* 74.

Anonymous (1993, February 15). Bargaining in Layman's terms. *Industry Week,* 18.

Argyris, C. (1957). *Personality and organization.* New York: Harper.

Argyris, C. (1970). *Intervention theory and method: A behavioral science view.* Reading, MA: Addison-Wesley.

Argyris, C. (1980). Some limitations to the case method: Experiences in a management development program. *Academy of Management Review, 5,* 291–298.

Argyris, C. (1985). *Strategy, change, and defensive routines.* Boston: Pitman.

Argyris, C. (1986). Skilled incompetence. *Harvard Business Review, 64*(5), 74–79.

Arvey, R. D., Cole, D. A., Hazucha, J. F., & Hartanto, F. M. (1985). Statistical power of training evaluation designs. *Personnel Psychology, 38,* 493–507.

Ashford, S. J. (1988). Individual strategies for coping with stress during organizational transitions. *Journal of Applied Behavioral Science, 24,* 19–36.

Atwater, S. K. (1953). Proactive inhibition and associative facilitation as affected by degree of prior learning. *Journal of Experimental Psychology, 46,* 400–404.

Axel, H. (1990). *Corporate experiences with drug testing programs.* New York: The Conference Board.

Axland, S. (1991). Two awarded NASA's prize trophy. *Quality Progress, 24*(12), 51–52.

Baldwin, T. T. (1987, August). *The effect of negative models on learning and transfer from behavior modeling: A test of stimulus variability.* Presented at the 47th annual meeting of the Academy of Management, New Orleans, LA.

Baldwin, T. T. (1992). Effects of alternative modeling strategies on outcomes of interpersonal skills training. *Journal of Applied Psychology, 77,* 147–154.

Baldwin, T. T., & Ford, J. K. (1988). Transfer of training: A review and directions for future research. *Personnel Psychology, 41,* 63–103.

Ballew, J. A. (1990). Follow a program of continuing education. *Insurance Sales, 133*(7), 2–22.

Bandura, A. (1977). Self-efficacy: Toward a unifying theory of behavior change. *Psychological Bulletin, 84,* 122–147.

Bandura, A. (1977). *Social learning theory.* Englewood Cliffs, NJ: Prentice-Hall.

Bandura, A. (1986). *Social foundations of thought and action.* Englewood Cliffs, NJ: Prentice-Hall.

Bandura, A., & Cervone, D. (1983). Self-evaluation and self-efficacy mechanisms governing the motivational effects of goal systems. *Journal of Personality and Social Psychology, 45,* 1017–1028.

Bandura, A., & Cervone, D. (1987). Differential engagement of self-reactive influences in cognitive motivation. *Organizational Behavior and Human Decision Processes, 38,* 92–113.

Bannister, B. D. (1986). Performance outcome feedback and attributional feedback: Interactive effects on recipient responses. *Journal of Applied Psychology, 71,* 203–210.

Baran, S., Zandan, P., & Vanston, J. H. (1986). How effectively are we managing innovation? *Research Management, 29*(1), 23–25.

Barkley, W. J., Jr., & Green, T. B. (1992). Safe landings for outplaced employees at AT&T. *Personnel Journal, 71*(6), 144–147.

Barnard, C. (1938). *The functions of the executive.* Cambridge, MA: Harvard University.

Baron, R. A. (1988). Negative effects of destructive criticism: Impact on conflict, self-efficacy, and task performance. *Journal of Applied Psychology, 73,* 199–207.

Barrick, M. R., & Mount, M. K. (1991). The big-five personality dimensions and job performance: A meta-analysis. *Personnel Psychology, 44,* 1–26.

Bartlett, C. A., & Ghoshal, S. (1992). What is a global manager? *Harvard Business Review, 70*(5), 124–132.

Bass, B. M., & Vaughn, J. A. (1966). *Training in industry.* Belmont, WA: Wadsworth.

Basset, G. A., & Meyer, H. H. (1968). Performance appraisal based on self-review. *Personnel Psychology, 21,* 421–430.

Baumgartel, H., Reynolds, M., & Pathan, R. (1984). How personality and organizational-climate variables moderate the effectiveness of management development programmes: A review and some recent research findings. *Management and Labour Studies, 9,* 1–16.

Baxter, P. (1984). Bring your computer training manuals down to earth. *Training and Development Journal, 38*(8), 55–59.

Beatty, R. W., Schneier, C. E., & McEvoy, G. M. (1987). Executive development and management succession. *Personnel and Human Resources Management, 5,* 289–322.

Becker, W. S., & Wellins, R. S. (1990). Customer-service perceptions and reality. *Training and Development Journal, 44*(3), 49–51.

Beckhard, R. (1969). *Organization development: Strategies and models.* Reading, MA: Addison Wesley.

Beckhard, R., & Harris, R. T. (1987). *Organizational transitions* (2nd ed.). Reading, MA: Addison Wesley.

Beckhard, R., & Pritchard, W. (1992). *Changing the essence: The art of creating and leading fundamental change in organizations.* San Francisco: Jossey-Bass Publishers.

Beehr, T. A., & Bhagat, R. S. (Eds.) (1985). *Human stress and cognition in organizations.* New York: Wiley.

Beekun, R. I. (1989). Assessing the effectiveness of sociotechnical interventions: Antidote or fad? *Human Relations, 42,* 877–897.

Beer, M. (1980). *Organization change and development: A systems view.* Glencove, IL: Goodyear/Scott Foresman.

Beer, M., & Walton, E. (1987). Organization change and development. *Annual Review of Psychology, 38,* 339–367.

Beer, M., & Walton, E. (1990). Developing the competitive organization: Interventions and strategies. *American Psychologist, 45,* 154–161.

Behling, O., & Starke, F. A. (1973). The postulates of expectancy theory. *Academy of Management Journal, 16,* 373–388.

Bell, B. L. (1991). Illiteracy: It's cheaper to train them. *Supervisory Management, 36*(9), 4–5.

Bennis, W. G., Benne, K. D., & Chin, R. (1961). *The planning of change.* New York: Holt, Rinehart and Winston.

Berdiansky, H. (1985). The invisible trainer. *Training and Development Journal, 39*(3), 60–63.

Berger, M. A. (1983). In defense of the case method: A reply to Argyris. *Academy of Management Review, 8,* 329–333.

Berkowitz, D., & Donnerstein, E. (1982). External validity is more than skin deep: Some answers to criticisms of laboratory experiments. *American Psychologist, 37,* 245–257.

Berman, S. J., & Hellweg, S. A. (1989). Perceived supervisor communication competence and supervisor satisfaction as a function of quality circle participation. *Journal of Business Communication, 26*(2), 103–122.

Bernacki, E. J., & Baun, W. B. (1984). The relationship between job performance to exercise adherence in a corporate fitness program. *Journal of Occupational Medicine, 26,* 529–531.

Bernardin, H. J., & Beatty, R. W. (1984). *Performance appraisal: Assessing human behavior at work.* Boston, MA: Kent.

Bernardin, H. J., & Villanova, P. (1986). Performance appraisal. In E. A. Locke (ed.), *Generalizing from laboratory to field settings.* Lexington, MA: Lexington Books.

Bernstein, A. (1991, August 10). The global economy: Who gets hurt. *Business Week,* pp. 48–53.

Blair, S. N., Jacobs, D. R., & Powell, K. E. (1985). Relationships between exercise or physical activity and other health behaviors. *Public Health Reports, 100,* 172–180.

Blake, R. R., & McCanse, A. A. (1991). *Leadershp Dilemmas—Grid® Solutions.* Houston, TX: Gulf Publishing.

Blake, R. R., & Mouton, J. S. (1964). *The managerial grid.* Houston, TX: Gulf Publishing.

Blake, R. R., & Mouton, J. S. (1985). *The managerial grid III: The key to leadership excellence.* Houston, TX: Gulf Publishing.

Blum, M. L., & Naylor, J. C. (1968). *Industrial psychology.* New York: Harper & Row.

Blum, T., & Bennett, N. (1990). Employee assistance programs: Utilization and referral data, performance management, and prevention concepts. In P.M. Roman ed., *Alcohol Problem Intervention in the Workplace* (pp. 144–162). New York: Quorum Books.

Boal, K. B., & Cummings, L. L. (1981). Cognitive evaluation theory: An experimental test of processes and outcomes. *Organizational Behavior and Human Performance, 28,* 289–310.

Boehm, V. R. (1988). Designing developmental assessment centers. In M. London and E. M. Mone (Eds.), *Career growth and human resource strategies: The role of the human resource professional in employee development.* New York: Quorum Books, 173–182.

Bogorya, Y. (1985). Intercultural development for managers involved in international business. *Journal of Management Development, 4*(2), 17–25.

Bolles, R. N. (1991). *What color is your parachute?* San Francisco: Ten Speed Press.

Bolt, J. F. (1989). Executive development as a competitive weapon. *Training and Development Journal, 43*(7), 71–76.

Botch, K., & Spangle, R. (1990). The effects of quality circles on performance and promotions. *Human Relations, 43,* 573–582.

Boudreau, J. W. (1983). Economic considerations in estimating the utility of human resource productivity improvement programs. *Personnel Psychology, 36,* 551–576.

Bourne, L. E., & Ekstrand, B. R. (1973). *Psychology: Its principles and meanings.* Hinsdale, IL: The Dryden Press.

Bove, R. (1984). Reach out and train someone. *Training and Development Journal, 38*(7), 26.

Bove, R. (1985). HRD takes its place in the executive suite. *Training and Development Journal, 39*(9), 81.

Bowen, D. W. (1985). Were men meant to mentor women? *Training and Development Journal, 39*(2), 31–34.

Bowen, D. E., & Lawler III, E. E. (1992). Total quality-oriented human resources management. *Organizational Dynamics, 20*(4), 29–41.

Boyatzis, R. E. (1982). *The competent manager: A model for effective performance.* New York: Wiley.

Bray, D. W., Campbell, R. J., & Grant, D. L. (1974). *Formative years in business: A long-term AT&T study of managerial lives.* New York: Wiley.

Breaugh, J. A. (1983). Realistic job previews: A critical appraisal and future research directions. *Academy of Management Review, 8,* 612–619.

Breaugh, J. A. (1992). *Recruitment: Science and practice.* Boston: PWS Kent.

Brechlin, J., & Rosett, A. (1991). Orienting new employees. *Training, 28*(4), 45–51.

Brennan, A. J. J. (1982). Health promotion, health education, and prevention at Metropolitan Life Insurance Companies. *Health Education Quarterly, 9,* 49–54.

Brief, A. P., & Hollenbeck, J. R. (1985). An exploratory study of self-regulating activities and their effects on job performance. *Journal of Occupational Behavior, 6,* 197–208.

Briggs, G. E., & Naylor, J. C. (1962). The relative efficiency of several training methods as a function of transfer task complexity. *Journal of Experimental Psychology, 64,* 505–512.

Brinkerhoff, R. O. (1986). Expanding needs analysis. *Training and Development Journal, 40*(2), 64–65.

Brinkerhoff, R. O. (1987). *Achieving results from training.* San Francisco: Jossey-Bass.

Brogan, J. E, (1991). Driven to improve safety performance. *Occupational Health & Safety, 60*(8), 40–42, 44.

Brogden, H. E. (1949). When testing pays off. *Personnel Psychology, 2,* 171–185.

Brown, A. (1986). Career development 1986: A look at trends and issues. *Personnel Administrator, 31*(3), 45–48, 109.

Brown, A. L. (1978). Knowing when, where, and how to remember: A problem of metacognition. In R. Glaser (Ed.), *Advances in instructional psychology* (Vol. 1). Hillsdale, NJ: Lawrence Erlbaum Associates.

Brown, A. L., & Palinscar, A. S. (1984). Reciprocal teaching of comprehension-fostering and monitoring activities. *Cognitive Instruction, 1*(2), 175–177.

Brown, A. L., & Palinscar, A. S. (1988). Guided, cooperative learning and individual knowledge acquisition. In L. B. Resnick (Ed.), *Knowing, learning and instruction: Essays in honor of Robert Glaser.* Hillsdale, NJ: Lawrence Erlbaum Associates.

Brown, D., Brooks, L., & Associates (Eds.) (1990). *Career choice and development* (2nd ed.). San Francisco: Jossey-Bass.

Brown, L. D. (1983). *Managing conflict at organizational interfaces.* Reading, MA: Addison-Wesley.

Brownell, K. D., Cohen, R. Y., Stunkard, A. J., Felix, M. R., & Cooley, N. B. (1984). Weight loss competitions at the worksite: Impact on weight, morale, and cost-effectiveness. *American Journal of Public Health, 74,* 1283–1285.

Bruner, J. S. (1966). *Toward a theory of instruction.* New York: Norton.

Buchanan, B. (1974). Building organizational commitment: The socialization of managers in work organizations. *Administrative Science Quarterly, 19,* 533–546.

Bullock, R. J., & Svyantek, D. J. (1987). The impossibility of using random strategies to study the organization development process. *Journal of Applied Behavorial Science, 23,* 255–262.

Burack, N. L., & Mathys, N. J. (1980). *Career management in organizations: A practical human resource planning approach*. Lake Forest, IL: Brace-Park Press.

Burke, M. J., & Day, R. R. (1986). A cumulative study of the effectiveness of managerial training. *Journal of Applied Psychology, 71*, 232–245.

Burke, R. J., Weitzel, W., & Weir, T. (1978). Characteristics of effective employee performance review and development interviews: Replication and extension. *Personnel Psychology, 31*, 903–919.

Burke, R. J., & Wilcox, D. S. (1969). Characteristics of effective employee performance review and development interviews. *Personnel Psychology, 22*, 291–305.

Burke, W. W. (1987). *Organization development*. Reading: Addison Wesley.

Burnaska, R. F. (1976). The effect of behavior-modeling training upon managers' behaviors and employee's perceptions. *Personnel Psychology, 29*, 329–335.

Bushnell, D. S. (1990). Input, process, output: A model for evaluating training. *Training and Development Journal, 44*(3), 41–43.

Business Week/Reinventing America (1992).

Butler, J. L., & Keys, J. B. (1973). A comparative study of simulation and rational methods of supervisory training in human resource development. In T. B. Green & D. F. Ray (Eds.), *Academy of Management Proceedings* (pp. 302–305). Boston, MA: Academy of Management.

Byham, W. C., Adams, D., & Kiggins, A. (1976). Transfer of modeling training to the job. *Personnel Psychology, 29*, 345–349.

Byrne, J. A. (1991, May 13). Wharton rewrites the book on B-schools. *Business Week*, p. 43.

Byrne, J. A. (1991, October 28). Back to school. *Business Week*, pp. 102–107.

Cady, L. D., Thomas, P. C., & Karweisky, R. J. (1985). Program for increasing health and physical fitness of fire fighters. *Journal of Occupational Medicine, 7*, 110–114.

Cairo, P. C. (1983). Counseling in industry: A selected review of the literature. *Personnel Psychology, 36*, 1–18.

Cairo, P., & Lyness, K. S. (1988). Stimulating high-potential career development through an assessment center process. In M. London and E. M. Mone (Eds.), *Career growth and human resource strategies: The role of the human resource professional in employee development*. New York: Quorum Books, 183–194.

Callaghan, D. R. (1985). Realistic computer training. *Training and Development Journal, 39*(7), 27–29.

Callahan, M. R. (1989). Preparing the new global manager. *Training and Development Journal, 43*(3), 28–32.

Callahan, M. R. (1992). Tending the sales relationship. *Training and Development Journal, 43*(12), 31–55.

Campbell, D. T., & Stanley, J. C. (1966). *Experimental and quasi-experimental designs for research*. Chicago: Rand McNally.

Campbell, D., & Graham, M. (1988). *Drugs and alcohol in the workplace: A guide for managers*. New York: Facts on File.

Campbell, J. P. (1971). Personnel training and development. *Annual Review of Psychology, 22*, 565–602.

Campbell, J. P. (1988). Training design for performance improvement. In J. P. Campbell and R. J. Campbell (Eds.), *Productivity in organizations*. San Francisco: Jossey-Bass.

Campbell, J. P., Dunnette, M. D., Lawler, E. E., & Weick, K. E. Jr. (1970). *Managerial behavior, performance, and effectiveness*. New York: McGraw-Hill.

Campbell, J. P., & Pritchard, R. D. (1976). Motivation theory in industrial and organizational psychology. In M. D. Dunnette (Ed.), *Handbook of Industrial and Organizational Psychology*. Chicago: Rand McNally.

Campion, M.A., & McClelland, C. L. (1991). Interdisciplinary examination of the costs and benefits of enlarged jobs: A job design quasi-experiment. *Journal of Applied Psychology, 76*, 186–198.

Carlisle, K. E. (1985). Learning how to learn. *Training and Development Journal, 39*(3), 75–80.

Carnevale, A. P., & Gainer, L. J. (1989). *The learning enterprise*. Alexandria, VA: The American Society for Training and Development and Washington DC: Government Printing Office.

Carnevale, A. P., Gainer, L. J., & Meltzer, A. S. (1991). *Workplace basics: The essential skills employers want*. San Francisco: Jossey-Bass.

Carnevale, A. P., Gainer, L. J., & Villet, J. (1991). *Training in America: The organization and strategic role of training*. San Francisco: Jossey-Bass.

Carnevale, A. P., Gainer, L. J., Villet, J. & Holland, S. L. (1990). *Training partnerships: Linking employers and providers*. Alexandria, VA: American Society for Training and Development.

Carnevale, A. P., & Johnston, J. W. (1989). *Training America: Strategies for the nation*. Alexandria, VA: American Society for Training and Development.

Carrell, M. R., & Dittrich, J. E. (1978). Equity theory: The recent literature, methodological considerations, and new directions. *Academy of Management Review, 3*, 202–210.

Carroll, S. J., & Gillen, D. J. (1987). Are the classical management functions useful in describing managerial work? *Academy of Management Review, 12*, 38–51.

Carroll, S. J., Paine, F. T., & Ivancevich, J. J. (1972). The relative effectiveness of training methods—Expert opinion and research. *Personnel Psychology, 25*, 495–510.

Carter, C. C. (1992). Seven basic quality tools. *HRMagazine, 37*(1), 81–83.

Carter, S. (1991). *Reflections of an affirmative action baby*. New York: Basic Books.

Cascio, W. F. (1982). *Applied psychology in personnel management*. Reston, VA: Reston Publishing Co.

Cascio, W. F. (1987). *Costing human resources: The financial impact of behavior in organizations* (2nd ed.). Boston, MA: PWS-Kent.

Cascio, W. F. (1989). Using utility analysis to assess training outcomes. In I. L. Goldstein and Associates, *Training and development in organizations*. San Francisco: Jossey-Bass.

Cascio, W. F. (1991a). *Applied psychology in personnel management* (4th ed.). Englewood Cliffs, NJ: Prentice-Hall.

Cascio, W. F. (1991b). *Costing human resources: The financial impact of behavior in organizations* (3rd ed.). Boston: PWS-Kent.

Cattan, P. (1988). The growing presence of Hispanics in the U.S. work force. *Monthly Labor Review, 111*(8), 9–14.

Caudron, S. (1991). Training ensures success overseas. *Personnel Journal, 70*(12), 27–30.

Caudron, S. (1992). U S WEST finds strength in diversity. *Personnel Journal, 71*(3), 40–44.

Caudron, S. (1993). Keys to starting a TQM program. *Personnel Journal, 72*(2), 28–35.

Center for Advanced Study in Education (August, 1988). *Evaluation report of the Workplace Literacy Program.* City University of New York Graduate School, Technical Report #2.

Chacko, T. I., & McElroy, J. C. (1983). The cognitive component in Locke's theory of goal setting: Suggestive evidence for a causal attribution interpretation. *Academy of Management Journal, 26,* 104–118.

Chao, G. T. (1990). Exploration of the conceptualization and measurement of career plateau: A comparative analysis. *Journal of Management, 16,* 181–193.

Chemers, M. M., & Fiedler, F. E. (1986). The trouble with assumptions: A reply to Jago and Ragan. *Journal of Applied Psychology, 71,* 560–563.

Cherns, A. (1987). Principles of sociotechnical design revisited. *Human Relations, 40,* 153–162.

Chi, M. T. H., Glaser, R., & Rees, E. (1982). Expertise in problem solving. In R. J. Sternberg (Ed.), *Advances in the psychology of human intelligence* (Vol. 1). Hillsdale, NJ: Lawrence Erlbaum Associates.

Childress, G. W., & Bugbee, J. A. (1986). Kentucky's across-the-board effort at making HRD work. *Public Personnel Management, 15*(4), 369–376.

Chisman, F. P. (1989). *Jump start: The federal role in adult literacy.* Southport, CT: The Southport Institute for Policy Analysis.

Choquette, Jr., P. J. (1988). Literacy, training and competitiveness: The strategic link. *Connection: New England's Journal of Higher Education and Economic Development, 2*(4), 14–16.

Christensen, K. (1990). Here we go into the "high flex" era. *Across the Board, 27*(7), 22–23.

Chu, G. C., & Schramm, W. (1967). *Learning from television: What the research says.* Washington, DC: National Association of Educational Broadcasters.

Clancey, W. J. (1984). Teaching classification problem solving. *Proceedings of the Cognitive Science Society Conference,* Boulder, 44–46.

Clark, S. G., & McGee, W. (1988). Evaluation: A method of transition—Our program is great . . . isn't it? *Journal for Quality & Participation, 11*(4), 50–54.

Clawson, J. G. (1985). Is mentoring necessary? *Training and Development Journal, 39*(4), 36–39.

Clegg, C., & Wall, T. (1990). The relationship between simplified jobs and mental health: A replication study. *Journal of Occupational Psychology, 63,* 289–296.

Clegg, C., Wall, T., & Kemp, N. J. (1987). Women on the assembly line: A comparison of main and interactive explanations of job satisfaction, absence, and mental health. *Journal of Occupational Psychology, 60,* 273–287.

Clement, J., & Gibbs, D. A. (1983). Employer consideration of health promotion programs: Financial variables. *Journal of Public Health, 4,* 45–55.

Cocheu, I. (1992). Training with quality. *Training and Development Journal, 47*(5), 23–32.

Cohen, D. J. (1990). What motivates trainees? *Training and Development Journal, 44*(11), 91–93.

Cohen, S. L. (1991). The challenge of training in the nineties. *Training and Development Journal, 45*(7), 30–36.

Cohen, W. S. (1985). Health promotion in the workplace. *American Psychologist, 40,* 213–216.

Colarelli, S. M. (1984). Methods of communication and mediating processes in realistic job previews. *Journal of Applied Psychology, 69,* 633–642.

Comeau, B. J. (1986). Does your CBT course teach performance? *Training and Development Journal, 40*(7), 42–44.

Compton, D. O. (1988). Orienting new managers with a transition workshop. *Healthcare Financial Management, 42*(8), 84–87.

Cone, J. (1989). The empowered employee. *Training and Development Journal, 43*(6), 96–98.

Connor, K. T. (1984). How to put your sale in someone else's hand and still succeed. *Training and Development Journal, 38*(11), 40–43.

Conrad, P. (1987). Who comes to work-site wellness programs? *Journal of Occupational Medicine, 29,* 317–320.

Cook, T. D., & Campbell, D. T. (1976). The design and conduct of quasi-experiments and true experiments in field settings. In M. D. Dunnette (Ed.), *Handbook of Industrial and Organizational Psychology.* New York: Rand McNally.

Cook, T. D., & Campbell, D. T. (1979). *Quasi-experimentation: Design and analysis issues for field settings.* Chicago: Rand-McNally.

Copeland, L. (1988a). Valuing diversity, part 1: Making the most of cultural differences at the workplace. *Personnel, 65*(6), 52–60.

Copeland, L. (1988b). Valuing workplace diversity. *Personnel Administrator, 33*(11), 38, 40.

Cose, E. (1991, December 24). Are quotas really the problem? *Time,* p. 70.

Cotton, J. L., Vollrath, D. A., Froggatt, K. L., Lengnick-Hall, M. L., & Jennings, K. R. (1988). Employee participation: Diverse forms and different outcomes. *Academy of Management Review, 13,* 8–22.

Cottrell, D., Davis, L., Detrick, P. & Raymond, M. (1992). Sales training and the Saturn difference. *Training and Development Journal, 46*(12), 38–43.

Courtney, R. S. (1986). A human resources program that helps management and employees prepare for the future. *Personnel, 63*(5), 32–40.

Cox, M. H. (1984). Fitness and lifestyle programs for business and industry: Problems in recruitment and retention. *Journal of Cardiac Rehabilitation, 4,* 135–142.

Cox, M., Shepard, R. J., & Corey, P. (1981). Influence of an employee fitness programme upon fitness, productivity, and absenteeism. *Ergonomics, 24,* 795–806.

Cox, T. H., Lobel, S. A., & McLeod, P. L. (1991). Effects of ethnic group cultural differences on cooperative and competitive behavior on a group task. *Academy of Management Journal, 34,* 827–847.

Cox, T. Jr., (1991). The multicultural organization. *The Executive, 5*(2), 34–47.

Crocker, O. L., Charney, C., & Chui, S. L. (1984). *Quality circles.* New York: Methuen Publications.

Cronbach, L. J. (1965). Comments on "A dollar criterion in fixed-treatment employee selection programs" in L. J. Cronbach & G. C. Gleser (Eds.), *Psychological tests and personnel decisions* (2nd ed.). Ubana, IL: University of Illinois Press.

Cronbach, L. J. (1967). How can instruction be adapted to individual differences. In R. M. Gagne (Ed.), *Learning and individual differences.* Columbus, OH: Charles E. Merrill.

Cronbach, L. J., & Snow, R. E. (1977). *Aptitudes and instructional methods.* New York: Irvington.

Cronshaw, S. F., & Alexander, R. A. (1985). One answer to the demand for accountability: Selection utility as an investment decision. *Organizational Behavior and Human Decision Processes, 35*, 102–118.

Crosson, C. (1990). Hancock enlists American College for courses. *National Underwriter, 94*(12), 7, 36.

Crumrine, L. (1989). Training programs: Here's what credit unions are doing. *Credit Union Executive, 29*(1), 20–21.

Cullen, J. G., Swazin, S. A., Sisson, G. R., & Swanson, R. A. (1978). Cost effectiveness: A model for assessing the training investment. *Training and Development Journal, 32*(1), 24–29.

Cureton, J. H., Newton, A. F., & Tesolowski, D. G. (1986). Finding out what managers need. *Training and Development Journal, 40*(5), 106–107.

Daft, R. L. (1991). *Management* (2nd ed). Fort Worth, TX: The Dryden Press.

Dailey, N. (1984). Adult learning and organizations. *Training and Development Journal, 38*(12), 64, 66, 68.

Daloisio, T., & Firestone, M. (1983). A case study in applying adult learning theory in developing managers. *Training and Development Journal, 37*(2), 73–78.

Dalton, G. W., Thompson, P. H., & Price, R. L. (1977). The four stages of professional careers: A new look at performance by professionals. *Organizational Dynamics, 6*(1), 19–42.

Danaher, B. G. (1980). Smoking cessation programs in occupational settings. *Public Health Reports, 95*, 149–156.

Dansereau, F., Graen, G., & Haga, B. (1975). A vertical dyad linkage approach to leadership within formal organizations: A longitudinal investigation of the role making process. *Organizational Behavior and Human Performance, 13*, 46–78.

Darraugh, B. (1991). Course construction. *Training and Development Journal, 45*(5), 66–71.

Davenport, J., & Davenport, J. A. (1985). A chronology and analysis of the andragogy debate. *Adult Education, 35*, 152–159.

Davis, G., & Watson, G. (1978). *Black life in corporate America.* Garden City, NY: Anchor Press.

Davis, M. F. (1984). Worksite health promotion. *Personnel Administrator, 29*(12), 45–50.

Davis, M. F., Rosenberg, K., Iverson, D. C., Vernon, T. M., & Bauer, J. (1984). Worksite health promotion in Colorado. *Public Health Reports, 99,* 538–543.

Deal, T. D., & Kennedy, A. A. (1982). *Corporate cultures.* Reading, MA: Addison-Wesley.

Deci, E. L. (1975). *Intrinsic motivation.* New York: Plenum Press.

Deci, E. L., & Porac, J. (1978). Cognitive evaluation theory and the study of human motivation. In M. R. Lepper and D. Greene (Eds.), *The hidden costs of rewards.* Hillsdale, NJ: Lawrence Erlbaum Associates.

Decker, P. J. (1980). Effects of symbolic coding and rehearsal in behavior modeling training. *Journal of Applied Psychology, 65,* 627–634.

Decker, P. J. (1982). The enhancement of behavior modeling training of supervisory skills by the inclusion of retention processes. *Personnel Psychology, 32,* 323–332.

Decker, P. J. (1983). The effects of rehearsal group size and video feedback in behavior modeling training. *Personnel Psychology, 36,* 763–773.

Decker, P. J. (1984). Effects of different symbolic coding stimuli in behavior modeling training. *Personnel Psychology, 37,* 711–720.

Decker, P. J., & Nathan, B. R. (1985). *Behavior modeling training: Principles and applications.* New York: Praeger.

Decotiis, T., & Petit, A. (1978). The performance appraisal process: A model and some testable propositions. *Academy of Management Review, 3,* 635–646.

DeFrank, R. S., & Cooper, C. L. (1987). Worksite stress management interventions: Their effectiveness and conceptualization. *Journal of Managerial Psychology, 2,* 4–10.

Delaney, C. (1991). The revolution (yawwnnnn!) keeps rolling along. *Training and Development Journal, 45*(3), 45–49.

Desatnick, R. L. (1987). Building the customer-oriented work force. *Training and Development Journal, 41*(3), 72–74.

Deterline, W. A., (1968). *Instructional technology workshop.* Palo Alto, CA: Programmed Teaching.

Dickman, F., & Hayes, B. (1988). Professional sports and employee assistance programs. In F. Dickman, B. R. Challenger, W. G. Emener, and W. S. Hutchinson, Jr. (Eds.), *Employee assistance programs: A basic text* (pp. 425–430). Springfield, IL: Charles C. Thomas.

Diener, E., & Dweck, C. S. (1978). An analysis of learned helplessness: Continuous changes in performance, strategy, and achievement cognitions following failure. *Journal of Personality and Social Psychology, 31,* 451–462.

Dienesch, R. M., & Liden, R. C. (1986). Leader member exchange model of leadership: A critique and further development. *Academy of Management Review, 11,* 618–634.

Digman, L. A. (1978). How well-managed organizations develop their executives. *Organizational Dynamics, 7*(2), 63–80.

Dole, E. (1990). "Ready, set, work," says labor secretary. *Training and Development Journal, 44*(5), 17–22.

Donaldson, L., & Scannell, E. E. (1986). *Human resource development: The new trainer's guide* (2nd ed.). Reading, MA: Addison-Wesley.

Dorfman, P. W., Stephan, W. G., & Loveland, J. (1986). Performance appraisal behaviors: Supervisor perceptions and subordinate reactions. *Personnel Psychology, 39,* 579–597.

Dowling, M. J., & Albrecht, K. (1991). Technical workers and competitive advantage: What we can learn from the Germans. *Business Horizons, 34*(6), 68–75.

Downey, R. G., & Lahey, M. A. (1988). Women in management. In London, M. & Mone, E. M. (Eds.) *Career growth and human resource strategies: The role of the human resource professional in employee development.* (pp. 241–255) New York: Quorum Books.

Downs, S. (1970). Predicting training potential. *Personnel Management, 2,* 26–28.

Dreher, G. F., & Ash, R. A. (1990). A comparative study of mentoring among men and women in managers, professional, and technical positions. *Journal of Applied Psychology, 75,* 539–546.

Dreher, G. F., & Sackett, P. R. (Eds.) (1983). *Perspectives on employee staffing and selection.* Homewood, IL: Richard D. Irwin.

Driver, R. W., & Ratliff, R. A. (1982). Employers' perceptions of benefits accrued from physical fitness programs. *Personnel Administrator, 27*(8), 21–26.

Drucker, P. F. (1974). *Management: Tasks, responsibilities, practices.* New York: Harper & Row.

Dumas, M. A., & Wile, D. E. (1992). The accidental trainer: Helping design instruction. *Personnel Journal, 71*(6), 106–110.

Dunbar, E., & Katcher, A. (1990). Preparing managers for foreign assignments. *Training and Development Journal, 44*(9), 45–47.

Dunham, R. B., Pierce, J. L., & Casteneda, M. B. (1987). Alternate work schedules: Two field quasi-experiments. *Personnel Psychology, 40,* 215–242.

Dunnette, M. D. (1976a). Mismash, mush, and milestones in organizational psychology. In H. Meltzer and F. R. Wiskert (Eds.), *Humanizing organizational behavior* (pp. 86–102). Springfield, IL: Charles C. Thomas.

Dunnette, M. D. (1976b). Aptitudes, abilities, and skills. In M. D. Dunnette (Ed.), *The handbook of industrial and organizational psychology.* Chicago: Rand McNally.

Dyer, W. G. (1987). *Team building.* Reading, MA: Addison-Wesley.

Early, P. C. (1987). Intercultural training for managers: A comparison of documentary and interpersonal methods. *Academy of Management Journal, 30,* 685–698.

Eckel, K. (1988). Staying abreast of the law. *Satellite Communications, 12*(12), 21–22.

Eden, D. (1984). Self-fulling prophecy as a management tool: Harnessing Pygmalion. *Academy of Management Review, 9,* 64–73.

Eden, D., & Ravid, G. (1982). Pygmalion versus self-expectancy: Effects of instructor and self-expectancy on trainee performance. *Organizational Behavior and Human Performance, 30,* 351–364.

Eden, D., & Shani, A. B. (1982). Pygmalion goes to boot camp: Expectancy, leadership, and trainee performance. *Journal of Applied Psychology, 67,* 194–199.

Ellis, H. C. (1965). *The transfer of learning.* New York: Macmillan.

Elsass, P. M., & Ralston, D. A. (1989). Individual responses to the stress of career plateauing. *Journal of Management, 15,* 35–47.

Emener, W. S. (1988). School teachers and school personnel. In F. Dickman, B. R. Challenger, W. G. Emener, & W. S. Hutchinson, Jr. (Eds)., *Employee assistance programs: A basic text* (pp. 443–453). Springfield, IL: Charles C. Thomas.

Engleken, C. (1987). Fighting the costs of spouse abuse. *Personnel Journal, 66*(3), 31–34.

Erfurt, J. C., Foote, A., & Heirich, M. A. (1992). The cost-effectiveness of work-site wellness programs for hypertension control, weight loss, smoking cessation, and exercise. *Personnel Psychology, 45,* 5–27.

Ericksen, S. C. (1974). *Motivaton for learning.* Ann Arbor: The University of Michigan Press.

Erickson, J. M., Pugh, W. M., & Gunderson, E. E. (1972). Status as a predictor of job satisfaction and life stress. *Journal of Applied Psychology, 56,* 523–525.

Erikson, E. H. (1963). *Childhood and society* (2nd ed.). New York: W.W. Norton & Company.

Eurich, N. P. (1990). *The learning industry: Education for adult workers.* Lawrenceville, NJ: Princeton University Press.

Evans, M. G. (1986) Organizational behavior: The central role of motivation. *Journal of Management, 12,* 203–222.

Evered, R. D., & Selman, J. C. (1990). Coaching and the art of management. *Organizational Dynamics, 18*(2), 16–32.

Everly, G. S. (1984). The development of occupational stress management programs. In G. S. Everly and R. H. L. Feldman (Eds.), *Occupational health promotion* (pp. 49–73). New York: Wiley.

Everly, G. S., Feldman, R. H. L., & Associates (1985). *Occupational health promotion: Health behavior in the workplace.* New York: Wiley.

Faerman, S. R., Quinn, R. E. & Thompson, M. P. (1987). Bridging management practice and theory: New York's public service training program. *Public Administration Review, 47*(4), 310–319.

Fagenson, E. A., & Burke, W. W. (1990). Organization development practitioners' activities and interventions in organizations during the 1980s. *Journal of Applied Behavioral Science, 26,* 285–297.

Faley, R., Kleiman, L., & Wall, P. (1988). Drug testing in public and private-sector workplaces: Technical and legal issues. *Journal of Business and Psychology, 3,* 154–186.

Falkenberg, L. (1987). Employee fitness programs: Their impact on the employee and the organization. *Academy of Management Review, 12,* 511–522.

Fayol, H. (1949). *General and industrial management.* (C. Storrs, Translator). London: Pitman.

Federico, R. F. (1991). Six ways to solve the orientation blues. *HRMagazine, 36*(6), 69–70.

Fedor, D. B., Eder, R. W., & Buckley, M. R. (1989). The contributory effects of supervisor intentions on subordinate feedback responses. *Organizational Behavior and Human Decision Processes, 44,* 396–414.

Feldman, D. C. (1976a). A contingency theory of socialization. *Administrative Science Quarterly, 21*, 433–452.

Feldman, D. C. (1976b). A practical program for employee socialization. *Organizational Dynamics, 5*(2), 64–80.

Feldman, D. C. (1980). A socializaiton process that helps new recruits succeed. *Personnel, 57*(2), 11–23.

Feldman, D. C. (1981). The multiple socialization of organization members. *Academy of Management Review, 6*, 309–318.

Feldman, D. C. (1984). The development and enforcement of norms. *Academy of Management Review, 9*, 47–53.

Feldman, D. C. (1988). *Managing careers in organizations.* Glenview, IL: Scott, Foresman.

Feldman, D. C. (1989a). Socialization, resocialization, and training: Reframing the research agenda. In I. L. Goldstein and Associates (Eds.), *Training and development in organizations* (pp. 376–416). San Francisco: Jossey-Bass.

Feldman, D. C. (1989b). Careers in organizations: Recent trends and future directions. *Journal of Management, 15*, 135–156.

Feldman, D. C., & Weitz, B. A. (1988). Career plateaus reconsidered. *Journal of Management, 14*, 69–80.

Fennell, M. (1984). Synergy, influence, and information in the adoption of administrative innovations. *Academy of Management Journal, 27*, 113–129.

Ferketish, B. J., & Hayden, J. W. (1992). HRD & quality: The chicken or the egg? *Training and Development Journal, 46*(1), 38–42.

Fernandez, J. P. (1988). Human resources and the extraordinary problems minorities face. In London, M. and Mone, E. M. (Eds.), *Career growth and human resource strategies: The role of the human resource professional in employee development* (pp. 227–239). New York: Quorum Books.

Ferrence, T. P., Stoner, J. A. F., & Warren, E. K. (1977). Managing the career plateau. *Academy of Management Review, 2*, 602–612.

Ferris, G. R. (1985). Role of leadership in the employee withdrawal process: A constructive replication. *Journal of Applied Psychology, 70*, 777–781.

Fetteroll, E. C. (1985). 16 tips to increase your effectiveness. *Training and Development Journal, 39*(6), 68–70.

Feuer, B. (1987). Innovations in employee assistance programs: A case study at the association of flight attendants. In A. W. Reilly and S. J. Zaccaro (Eds.), *Occupational stress and organizational effectiveness* (pp. 217–227). New York: Praeger.

Feuer, D. (1985). Wellness programs: How do they shape up? *Training, 22*(4), 25–34.

Feuer, D. (1986). A training department of independent means. *Training, 23*(9), 75–78.

Feuer, D. (1988). Tales of small-time training. *Training, 25*(2), 29–36.

Fiedler, F. E. (1964). A contingency model of leadership effectiveness. In L. Berkowitz (Ed.), *Advances in experimental social psychology* (pp. 149–190). New York: Academic Press.

Fiedler, F. E. (1967). *A theory of leadership effectiveness.* New York: McGraw-Hill.

Fiedler, F. E., & Chemers, M. M. (1974). *Leadership and effective management.* New York: Scott, Foresman.

Fiedler, F. E., & Chemers, M. M. (1984). *Improving leadership effectiveness: The leader match concept* (2nd ed.). New York: Wiley.

Fiedler, F. E., Chemers, M. M., & Mahar, L. (1976). *Improving leadership effectiveness: The leader match concept.* New York: Wiley.

Fiedler, F. E., & Mahar, L. (1979a). The effectiveness of contingency model training: A review of the validation of Leader Match. *Personnel Psychology, 32,* 45–62.

Fiedler, F. E., & Mahar, L. (1979b). A field experiment validating contingency model leadership training. *Journal of Applied Psychology, 64,* 247–254.

Fielding, J. E. (1982). Effectiveness of employee health improvement programs. *Journal of Occupational Medicine, 24,* 907–916.

Fielding, J. E. (1984). Health promotion and disease prevention at the worksite. *Annual Review of Public Health, 5,* 237–265.

Fielding, J. E., & Piserchia, P. V. (1989). Frequency of worksite health promotion activities. *American Journal of Public Health, 79,* 16–20.

Figueroa, J. R., & Silvanik, R. A. (1990). *State welfare-to-work programs: Four case studies.* Training and Employment Program, Center for Policy Research, Washington: National Governors' Association, 1990.

Filipczak, B. (1992). What employers teach. *Training, 29*(10), 43–55.

Finkel, C. (1986). Pick a place, but not any place. *Training and Development Journal, 40*(2), 51–53.

Firnstahl, T. W. (1989). My employees are my guarantee. *Harvard Business Review, 67*(4), 28–31.

Fishbein, M., & Ajzen, I. (1975). *Belief, attitude, intention, and behavior.* Reading, MA: Addison-Wesley.

Fisher, C. D. (1986). Organizational socialization: An integrative review. In K. Rowland and G. Ferris (Eds.), *Research in personnel and human resources management* (Vol. 4, pp. 101–145). Greenwich, CT: JAI Press.

Fitts, P. M. (1965). Factors in complex skill training. In R. Glaser (ed.), *Training research in education.* New York: Wiley.

Flanagan, J. C. (1954). The critical incident method. *Psychological Bulletin, 51,* 327–358.

Fleishman, E. A. (1967). Development of a behavior taxonomy for describing human tasks: A correlational-experimental approach. *Journal of Applied Psychology, 51,* 1–10.

Fleishman, E. A. (1972). On the relation between abilities, learning, and human performance. *American Psychologist, 27,* 1017–1032.

Fleishman, E. A. (1975). Toward a taxonomy of human performance. *American Psychologist, 30,* 1127–1149.

Fleishman, E. A., & Mumford, M. D. (1988). The ability requirement scales. In S. Gael (Ed.), *The job analysis handbook for business, government, and industry.* New York: Wiley.

Fleishman, E. A., & Quaintance, M. K. (1984). *Taxonomies of human performance: The description of human tasks.* Orlando, FL: Academic Press.

Foegen, J. H. (1987). Too much negative training. *Business Horizons, 30*(5), 51–53.

Foote, A., & Erfurt, J. C. (1991). The benefit to cost ratio of work-site blood pressure control programs. *Journal of the American Medical Association, 265*(10), 1283–1286.

Ford, J. D., & Ford, J. G. (1986). Health promotion: Competitor or resource? *EAP Digest, 6,* 23–28.

Ford, J. K., & Noe, R. A. (1987). Self-assessed training needs: The effects of attitude toward training, managerial level, and function. *Personnel Psychology, 40,* 39–53.

Ford, J. K., and Wroten, S. P. (1984). Introducing new methods for conducting training evaluation and for linking training evaluation to program redesign. *Personnel Psychology, 37,* 651–665.

Forsyth, S., & Galloway, S. (1988). Linking college credit with in-house training. *Personnel Administrator, 33*(11), 78–79.

Fossum, J. A., & Arvey, R. D. (1990). Marketplace and organizational factors that contribute to obsolescence. In S. L. Willis and S. S. Dubin (Eds.), *Maintaining professional competence: Approaches to career enhancement, vitality, and success throughout a work life* (pp. 44–63). San Francisco: Jossey-Bass.

Foster, B., Jackson, G., Cross, W. E., Jackson, B., & Hardiman, R. (1988). Workforce diversity and business. *Training and Development Journal, 42*(4), 38–42.

Fournies, F. F. (1978). *Coaching for improved work performance.* New York: Van Nostrand Reinhold.

Fox, D. (1983). Coaching: The way to protect your sales training investment. *Training and Development Journal, 37*(11), 37–39.

Fraker, S. (1984, April 16). Why women aren't getting to the top. *Fortune,* pp. 40–45.

Framholtz, E. G. (1990). Toward a holistic model of organizational effectiveness and organization development at different states of growth. *Human Resource Development Quarterly, 1*(2), 109–127.

Frayne, C. A., & Latham, G. P. (1987). The application of social learning theory to employee self-management of attendance. *Journal of Applied Psychology, 72,* 387–392.

Freedman, S. M., & Phillips, J. S. (1988). The changing nature of research on women at work. *Journal of Management, 14,* 231–251.

French, J. R. P., Kay, E., & Meyer, H. (1966). Participation and the appraisal system. *Human Relations, 19,* 3–20.

French, W. L., & Bell C. H. Jr. (1990). *Organization development.* Reading, MA: Addison-Wesley.

Fresina, A. J., & Associates. (1988). *Executive education in corporate America.* Palatine, IL: Anthony J. Fresina and Associates.

Freud, S. (1959). *Collected papers.* New York: Basic Books.

Fried, Y., & Ferris, G. R. (1987). The validity of the job characteristics model: A review and meta-analysis. *Personnel Psychology, 40,* 287–318.

Friedlander, F., & Brown, L. D. (1974). Organization development. *Annual Review of Psychology, 25,* 313–341.

Fromkin, H. L., & Streufert, S. (1976). Laboratory experimentation. In M. D. Dunnette (Ed.), *Handbook of industrial and organizational psychology.* New York: Rand McNally.

Fulmer, R. M. (1986). Mergers and acquisitions, 2: The role of management development. *Personnel, 63*(9), 38–40.

Gael, S. (Ed.) (1988). *The job analysis handbook for business, industry, and government* (Vol. I & II). New York: Wiley.

Gage, N. L., & Berliner, D. C. (1988). *Educational psychology* (4th ed.). Boston: Houghton Mifflin Co.

Gagné, R. M. (1962). Military training and principles of learning. *American Psychologist, 17*, 83–91.

Gagné, R. M. (1972). Domains of learning. *Interchange, 3*, 1–8.

Gagné, R. M. (1984). Learning outcomes and their effects: Useful categories of human performance. *American Psychologist, 39*, 377–385.

Gagné, R. M. (1985). *The conditions of learning and theory of instruction* (4th ed.). New York: Holt, Rinehart and Winston.

Gagné, R. M., & Briggs, L. J. (1979). *Principles of instructional design* (2nd ed.). New York: Holt, Rinehart and Winston.

Gagné, R. M., & Dick, W. (1983). Instructional psychology. *Annual Review of Psychology, 34*, 261–295.

Gagné, R. M., & Glaser, R. (1987). Foundations in learning research. In R. M. Gagné (Ed.), *Instructional technology: Foundations.* Hillsdale, NJ: Lawrence Erlbaum Associates.

Gagné, R. M., Briggs, L. J., & Wagner, W. W. (1988). *Principles of instructional design* (4th ed.). New York: Holt, Rinehart and Winston.

Galagan, P. (1986). Focus on results at Motorola. *Training and Development Journal, 40*(5) 43–47.

Galagan, P. (1987). Computers and training: Allies or enemies? *Training and Development Journal, 41*(4), 73–76.

Galagan, P. (1989). *Training America: Learning to work for the 21st century.* Alexandria, VA: American Society for Training and Development.

Galagan, P. A. (1991). Tapping the power of a diverse workforce. *Training and Development Journal, 45*(3), 38–44.

Galagan, P. A. (1992). When the CEO is on your side. *Training and Development Journal, 46,*(9), 47–51.

Galagan, P. (1993). Training keeps the cutting edge sharp for the Anderson Companies. *Training and Development, 47*(1), 30–35.

Galbraith, J. R. (1989). From recovery to development through large-scale changes. In A. M. Mohrman, S. A. Mohrman G. E. Ledford, T. G. Cummings, and E. E. Lawler (Eds.), *Large scale organizational change* (pp. 62–88). San Francisco: Jossey-Bass Publishers.

Gall, A. L. (1986). What is the role of HRD in a merger? *Training and Development Journal, 40*(4), 18–23.

Galosy, J. R. (1983). Curriculum design for management training. *Training and Development Journal, 37*(1), 48–51.

Galosy, J. R. (1990). The human factor in mergers and acquisitions. *Training and Development Journal, 44*(4), 90–95.

Galvin, J. C. (1983). What trainers can learn from educators about evaluating management training. *Training and Development Journal, 37*(8), 52–57.

Ganger, R. E. (1990). Computer-based training works. *Personnel Journal, 69*(9), 85–91.

Ganster, D. C., & Schaubroeck, J. (1991). Work stress and employee health. *Journal of Management, 17*, 235–271.

Garland, S. B. (1991, April 29). Can the Feds bust through the "glass ceiling?" *Business Week*, p. 33.

Gatewood, R. D., & Field, H. J. (1990). *Human resource selection* (2nd ed). Hinsdale, IL: The Dryden Press.

Gavin, J. F. (1975). Employee perceptions of the work environment and mental health: A suggestive study. *Journal of Vocational Behavior, 6*, 217–234.

Gavin, J. F., & Axelrod, J. F. (1977). Managerial stress and strain in a mining organization. *Journal of Vocational Behavior, 11*, 66–74.

Geber, B. (1989). Industry report 1989: Who, how & what. *Training, 26*(10), 49–63.

Geber, B. (1990). Simulating reality. *Training, 27*(4), 41–46.

Geber, B. (1992). From manager into coach. *Training, 29*(2), 25–31.

Gebhardt, D. L., & Crump, C. E. (1990). Employee fitness and wellness programs in the workplace. *American Psychologist, 45*, 262–272.

Geering, A. (1985). The development and qualifications of trainers. *Work and People, 1*, 15–19.

Geertz, C. (1973). *The interpretation of culture.* New York: Basic Books.

Geidt, T. E. (1985). Drug and alcohol abuse in the work place: Balancing employer and employee rights. *Employee Relations Law Journal, 11*, 181–205.

Gerber, B. (1987). HRD degrees. *Training, 24*(7), 49.

Gerstein, M. S. (1987). *The technology connection.* Reading, MA: Addison-Wesley.

Gilley, J. W., & Eggland, S. A. (1989). *Principles of human resource development.* Reading, MA: Addison-Wesley.

Gilley, J. W., & Galbraith, M. W. (1986). Examining professional certification. *Training and Development Journal, 40*(6), 60–61.

Gioia, D. A., & Sims, H. P. (1986). Cognition-behavior connections: Attribution and verbal behavior in leader-subordinate interactions. *Organizational Behavior and Human Decision Processes, 37*, 197–229.

Gist, M. E. (1987). Self-efficacy: Implications for organizational behavior and human resource management. *Academy of Management Review, 12*, 472–485.

Gist, M. E., Schwoerer, C., & Rosen, B. (1989). Effects of alternative training methods on self-efficacy and performance in computer software training. *Journal of Applied Psychology, 74*, 884–891.

Giusti, J. P., Baker, D. R., & Graybash, P. J. (1991). Satellites dish out global training. *Personnel Journal, 70*(6), 80–84.

Glaser, R. (1982). Instructional psychology: Past, present, and future. *American Psychologist, 37*, 292–305.

Glaser, R. (1984). Education and thinking: The role of knowledge. *American Psychologist, 39*, 93–104.

Glaser, R., & Bassok, M. (1989). Learning theory and the study of instruction. *Annual Review of Psychology, 40*, 631–666.

Glaser, S. R., Zamanou, S., & Hacker, K. (1987). Measuring and interpreting organization culture. *Management Communication Quarterly, 1*(2), 173–198.

Glasgow, R. E., & Terborg, J. R. (1988). Occupational health promotion programs to rescue cardiovascular risk. *Journal of Consulting and Clinical Psychology, 56,* 365–373.

Goldstein, A. P., & Sorcher, M. (1974). *Changing supervisor behavior.* Elmsford, NY: Pergamon Press.

Goldstein, I. L. (1980). Training in work organizations. *Annual Review of Psychology, 31,* 229–272.

Goldstein, I. L. (1986). *Training in organizations: Needs assessment, development, and evaluation* (2nd ed.). Pacific Grove, CA: Brooks-Cole.

Goldstein, I. L. (1991). Training in work organizations. In M. D. Dunnette and L. M. Hough (Eds.), *The handbook of industrial and organizational psychology* (2nd ed., Vol. 2, pp. 507–619). Palo Alto, CA: Consulting Psychologists Press.

Goldstein, I. L., & Gessner, M. J. (1988). Training and development in work organizations. In C. L. Cooper and I. Robertson (Eds.), *International review of industrial and organizational psychology 1988* (pp. 43–73). London: John Wiley & Sons.

Goldstein, I. L., & Gilliam, P. (1990). Training system issues in the year 2000. *American Psychologist, 45,* 134–143.

Goldstein, I. L., Macey, W. H., & Prien, E. P. (1981). Needs assessment approaching for training development. In H. Meltzer and W. R. Nord (Eds.), *Making organizations more humane and productive: A handbook for practitioners.* New York: Wiley-Interscience.

Goldstein, I. L., & Musicante, G. R. (1986). The applicability of a training transfer model to issues concerning rater training. In E. A. Locke (Ed.), *Generalizing from laboratory to field settings.* Lexington, MA: Lexington Books.

Golembiewski, R. T., Billingsley, K., & Yeager, S. (1976). Measuring change and persistence in human affairs: Types of change generated by OD designs. *Journal of Applied Behavioral Science, 12,* 133–157.

Gollnick, D. M., & Chinn, P. C. (1986). *Multicultural education in a pluralistic society* (2nd ed.). Columbus: Charles E. Merrill.

Gomersall, E. R., & Myers, M. S. (1966). Breakthrough in on-the-job training. *Harvard Business Review, 44*(4), 62–72.

Good, R. K. (1986). Employee assistance. *Personnel Journal, 65*(2), 96–101.

Goodman, F. F. (1992). A union trains for the future. *Training and Development Journal, 46*(10), 23–29.

Goodman, P. S. (1986). Impact of task and technology on group performance. In P. S. Goodman and Associates (Eds.), *Designing effective work groups* (pp. 120–167). San Francisco: Jossey-Bass.

Gordon, C. (1991). Health care the corporate way. *The Nation, 252*(11), 276, 378–380.

Gordon, E. E., Ponticell, J. & Morgan, R. R. (1989). Back to basics. *Training and Development Journal, 43*(8), 73–76.

Gordon, J. (1986). Organization development: Next time, just smile and nod. *Training, 23*(9), 93–98.

Gordon, J. (1988). The case for corporate colleges. *Training, 25*(3), 25–31.

Gordon, J. (1992). Rethinking diversity. *Training, 29*(1), 23–30.

Gordon, J. (1992). Work teams: How far have they come? *Training, 29*(10), 59–65.

Gordon, L. V. (1955). Time in training as a criterion of success in radio code. *Journal of Applied Psychology, 39,* 311–313.

Gordon, M. E., & Klieman, L. S. (1976). The predication of trainability using a work sample test and an aptitude test: A direct comparison. *Personnel Psychology, 29,* 243–253.

Graen, G. (1976). Role-making processes within complex organizations. In M. D. Dunnette (Ed.), *Handbook of industrial and organizational psychology* (pp. 1201–1245). Chicago: Rand McNally.

Graen, G., Liden, R., & Hoel, W. (1982). Role of leadership in the employee withdrawal process. *Journal of Applied Psychology, 67,* 868–872.

Graen, G., Novak, M., & Sommerkamp, P. (1982). The effects of leader-member exchange and job design on productivity and satisfaction: Testing manual attachment mode. *Organizational Behavior and Human Performance, 30,* 109–131.

Graen, G., Scandura, T. A., & Graen, M. R. (1986). A field experimental test of the moderating effects of growth need strength on productivity. *Journal of Applied Psychology, 71,* 484–491.

Graham, J. K., & Mihal, W. L. (1986). Can your management development needs surveys be trusted? *Training and Development Journal, 40*(3), 39–42.

Grazier, P. B. (1992). Leadership for high performance. *Journal for Quality & Participation, 15*(2), 66–69.

Green, A. (1987). Business schools that breed the best bankers. *Bankers Monthly, 104*(10), 51–56.

Greenberg, J. (1986). Determinants of perceived fairness of performance evaluations. *Journal of Applied Psychology, 71,* 340–342.

Greenhaus, J. H. (1987). *Career management.* Hinsdale, IL: The Dryden Press.

Greenhaus, J. H. Parasuraman, S. & Warmley, W. M. (1990). Effects of race on organizational experiences, job performance evaluations, and career outcomes. *Academy of Management Journal, 33,* 64–86.

Greenslade, M. (1991). Managing diversity: Lessons from the United States. *Personnel Management, 23*(12), 28–33.

Greiner, L. E., & Schein, V. E. (1988). *Power and organizational development.* Reading: Addison-Wesley.

Greller, M. M. (1975). Subordinate participation and reaction in the appraisal interview. *Journal of Applied Psychology, 60,* 544–549.

Greller, M. M. (1978). The nature of subordinate participation in the appraisal interview. *Academy of Management Journal, 21,* 646–658.

Gridley, J. D. (1986). Mergers and acquisitions, 1: Premerger human resources planning. *Personnel, 63*(9), 28–36.

Grossman, M. E., & Magnus, M. (1989). The $5.3 billion tab for training. *Personnel Journal, 68*(7), 54–56.

Grove, D. A., & Ostroff, C. (1991). Program evaluation. In K. N. Wexley (Ed.), *Developing human resources.* Washington, DC: BNA Books.

Guilford, J. P. (1967). *The nature of human intelligence.* New York: McGraw-Hill.

Guion, R. M. (1977). Content validity: The source of my discontent. *Applied Psychological Measurement, 1,* 1–10.

Gutteridge, T. G. (1986). Organizational career development systems: The state of the practice. In D. T. Hall and Associates (Eds.), *Career development in organizations* (pp. 50–94). San Francisco: Jossey-Bass.

Gutteridge, T. G., & Otte, F. L. (1983). *Organizational career development: State of the practice.* Washington, DC: ASTD Press.

Guzzo, R. A. (1979). Types of rewards, cognitions, and work motivation. *Academy of Management Review, 4,* 75–86.

Guzzo, R. A., Jette, R. D., & Katzell, R. A. (1985). The effects of psychologically based intervention programs on worker productivity: A meta-analysis. *Personnel Psychology, 38,* 275–291.

Hackey, M. K. (1991). Injuries and illness in the workplace, 1989. *Monthly Labor Review, 114*(5), 34–36.

Hackman, J. R. (1977). Work design. In J. R. Hackman & J. L. Suttle, (Eds.), *Improving life at work.* Santa Monica, CA: Goodyear.

Hackman, J. R. & Oldham, G. R. (1975). Development of the Job Diagnostic Survey. *Journal of Applied Psychology, 60,* 159–170.

Hackman, J. R., & Oldham, G. R. (1976). Motivation through the design of work: Test of a theory. *Organizational Behavior and Human Performance, 16,* 250–279.

Hackman, J. R., & Oldham, G. R. (1980). *Work redesign.* Reading, MA: Addison-Wesley.

Hackman, J. R., & Walton, R. E. (1986). Leading groups in organizations. In P. S. Goodman and Associates (Eds), *Designing effective work groups* (pp. 72–119). San Francisco: Jossey-Bass.

Hagman, J. D., & Rose, A. M. (1983). Retention of military tasks: A review. *Human Factors, 25,* 199–213.

Halcrow, A. (1988). A day in the life of Levi Strauss. *Personnel, 67*(11), 14–15.

Hale, R. L. (1989). Tennant Company: Instilling quality from top to bottom. *Management Review, 78*(2), 65.

Hall, D. T. (1976). *Careers in organizations.* Pacific Pallisades, CA: Goodyear.

Hall, D. T. (1986). An overview of current career development theory, research, and practice. In D. T. Hall and Associates (Eds.), *Career development in organizations* (pp. 1–20). San Francisco: Jossey-Bass.

Hall, D. T., & Nougaim, K. (1968). An examination of Maslow's need hierarchy in an organizational setting. *Organizational Behavior and Human Performance, 3,* 11–35.

Hall, D. T., & Richter, J. (1990). Career gridlock: Baby boomers hit the wall. *The Executive, 4,* 7–22.

Hall-Sheey, J. (1985). Course design for PC training. *Training and Development Journal, 39*(3), 66–67.

Haller, E. (1989). Four by four. *Training and Development Journal, 43*(11), 24–27.

Hamburg, S. K. (1988). Manpower Temporary Services: Keeping ahead of the competition. In J. Casner-Lotto & Associates (Eds.), *Successful training strategies.* San Francisco: Jossey-Bass.

Hamilton, R. A. (1986). HRD value in mergers and acquisition. *Training and Development Journal, 40*(6), 31–33.

Harris, M. M., & Fennell, M. L. (1988). Perceptions of an employee assistance program and employees' willingness to participate. *Journal of Applied Behavioral Science, 24,* 423–438.

Harris, M. M., & Heft, L. L. (1992). Alcohol and drug use in the workplace: Issues, controversies, and directions for future research. *Journal of Management, 18,* 239–266.

Harris, P. R. (1981). *Health United States 1980: With prevention profile.* Washington, DC: U.S. Government Printing Office.

Harris, P. R., & Moran, R. T. (1987). *Managing cultural differences.* Houston: Gulf Publishing.

Harris, P. R., & Moran, R. T. (1991). *Managing cultural differences* (3rd ed.). Houston: Gulf Publishing.

Harwood, H. J., Napolitano, D. M., Kristiansen, P. L., & Collins, J. J. (1985). *Economic costs to society of alcohol and drug abuse and mental illness: 1980.* (Publication No. RTI/2734/00-01FR). Research Triangle Park, NC: Research Triangle Institute.

Head, G. E. (1985). *Training cost analysis: A practical guide.* Washington, DC: Marlin Press.

Hellriegel, D., Slocum, J. W., & Woodman, R. W. (1989). *Organization behavior.* St. Paul: West Publishing.

Hendrikson, G., & Schroeder, W. (1941). Transfer of training to hit a submerged target. *Journal of Educational Psychology, 32,* 206–213.

Henne, D., Levine, M., Usery, W. J., & Fishgold, H., (1986). A case study in cross-cultural mediation: The General Motors-Toyota joint venture. *Arbitration Journal, 41,* 5–15.

Henneback, C. (1992). Instant secretaries: Just add training. *Training and Development Journal, 46*(11), 63–65.

Hequet, M. (1992). Executive education: The custom alternative. *Training, 29*(4), 38–41.

Herbert, G. R., & Doverspike, D. (1990). Performance appraisal in the training needs analysis process: A review and critique. *Public Personnel Management, 19*(3), 253–270.

Herzberg, F. H. (1966). *Work and the nature of man.* Cleveland: World Publishing Co.

Herzberg, F. H., Mausner, B., & Snyderman, B. B. (1959). *The motivation to work.* New York: Wiley.

Herzlinger, R. E., & Schwartz, J. (1985). How companies tackle health care costs: Part I. *Harvard Business Review, 63*(4) 68–81.

Heskin, A. D., & Heffner, R. A., (1987). Learning about bilingual, multicultural organizing. *Journal of Applied Behavioral Science, 23,* 525–541.

Hess, B. B., Markson, E. W., & Stein, P. J. (1992). Racial and ethnic minorities: An overview. In P. S. Rothenberg (Ed.), *Race, class, and gender in the United States* (pp. 96–110). New York: St. Martin's Press.

Hicks, W. D., & Klimoski, R. J. (1987). Entry into training programs and its effects on training outcomes: A field experiment. *Academy of Management Journal, 30,* 542–552.

Hillelsohn, M. J. (1984). How to think about CBT. *Training and Development Journal, 38*(1), 42–44.

Hillery, J. M., & Wexley, K. N. (1974). Participation effects in appraisal interviews conducted in a training situation. *Journal of Applied Psychology, 59,* 168–171.

Hillkirk, J. (1993, February 25). Clinton copies Xerox way of management. *USA Today,* B-1.

Hodges, H. G., & Ziegler, R. J. (1963). *Managing the industrial concern.* Boston: Houghton Mifflin.

Hogan, P. M., Hakel, M. D., & Decker, P. J. (1986). Effects of trainee-generated versus trainer-provided rule codes on generalization in behavior-modeling training. *Journal of Applied Psychology, 71,* 469, 473.

Holden, S. J. (1984). The science of developing technical training. *Training and Development Journal, 38*(8), 35–41.

Holding, D. H. (1965). *Principles of training.* London: Pergamon Press.

Holland, J. L. (1977). *The self-directed search.* Palo Alto, CA: Consulting Psychologists Press.

Hollenbeck, G. P. (1991). What did you learn in school? Studies of a university executive program. *Human Resource Planning, 14*(4), 247–260.

Holley, W. H., & Jennings, K. M. (1991). *The labor relations process* (4th ed). Hinsdale, IL: The Dryden Press.

Hollinger, R. C. (1988). Working under the influence (WUI): Correlates of employees' use of alcohol and other drugs. *Journal of Applied Behavioral Science, 24,* 430–454.

Hollon, C. J., & Chesser, R. J. (1976). The relationship of personal influence dissonance to job tension, satisfaction, and involvement. *Academy of Management Journal, 19,* 308–314.

Holpp, L. (1992). Making choices: Self-directed teams or total quality management? *Training, 29*(5), 69–74.

Homans, G. C. (1989). The Western Electric researchers. In M. T. Matteson & J. M. Ivancevich (Eds.), *Management and organizational behavior classics* (pp. 193–202). Homewood, IL: Richard D. Irwin.

Honeycutt, A. (1989). The key to effective quality circles. *Training and Development Journal, 43*(5), 81–84.

House, R. J. (1971). A path-goal theory of leader effectiveness. *Administrative Science Quarterly, 16,* 321–338.

Howard, A., & Bray, D. W. (1988). *Managerial lives in transition: Advancing age and changing times.* New York: Guilford Press.

Howard, J., & Mikalachki, A. (1979). Fitness and employee productivity. *Canadian Journal of Applied Sport Sciences, 4,* 191–198.

Howe, C. (1983). Establishing employee recreation programs. *Journal of Physical Education, Recreation, and Dance, 54,* 34–52.

Howell, V. W. (1988). What it takes to be a certified professional. *Automation, 35*(2), 10–12.

Howell, W. C., & Cooke, N. J. (1989). Training the human information processor: A review of cognitive models. In I. L. Goldstein and associates, *Training and development in organizations.* San Francisco: Jossey-Bass.

Huczynski, A. A., & Lewis, J. W. (1980). An empirical study into the learning transfer process in management training. *Journal of Management Studies, 17,* 227–240.

Huse, E. F., & Cummings, T. G. (1985). *Organization development and change* (3rd ed.). St. Paul: West Publishing.

Huseman, R. C., Hatfield, J. D., & Miles, E. W. (1987). A new perspective on equity theory: The equity sensitivity construct. *Academy of Management Review, 12,* 222–234.

Ilgen, D. R., Fisher, C. D., & Taylor, M. S. (1979). Consequences of individual feedback on behavior in organizations. *Journal of Applied Psychology, 64,* 349–371.

Ilgen, D. R., & Youtz, M. A. (1986). Factors affecting the evaluation and development of minorities in organizations. *Research in Personnel and Human Resource Management, 4,* 307–337.

Ilgen, D. R., & Klein, H. J. (1988). Individual motivation and performance: Cognitive influences on effort and choice. In J. P. Campbell and R. J. Campbell (Eds.) *Productivity in organizations.* San Francisco: Jossey-Bass.

Ilgen, D. R., & Knowlton, W. A. Jr. (1980). Performance attributional effects on feedback from supervisors. *Organizational Behavior and Human Decision Processes, 25,* 441–456.

Iman, S. C. (1975). The development of participation by semiautonomous work team: The case of Donnelly Mirrors. In L. E. Davis & A. B. Cherns (Eds.), *The quality of working life.* New York: The Free Press.

Irons, E. D., & Moore, G. W. (1985). *Black managers: The case of the banking industry.* New York: Praeger.

Ivancevich, J. M., & Glueck, W. (1986). *Personnel/human resource management* (4th ed.). Plano, TX: Business Publications, Inc.

Ivancevich, J. M, & Matteson, M. T. (1980). *Stress and work.* Glenview, IL: Scott, Foresman.

Ivancevich, J. M, & Matteson, M. T. (1986). Organizational level stress management interventions: Review and recommendations. *Journal of Occupational Behavior Management, 8,* 229–248.

Ivancevich, J. M., Matteson, M. T., Freedman, S. M., & Phillips, J. S. (1990). Worksite stress management interventions. *American Psychologist, 45,* 252–261.

Ivey, A., & Authier, J. (1978). *Microcounseling.* Springfield, IL: Charles C. Thomas.

Ivey, A., & Litterer, J. (1979). *Face to face.* Amherst, MA: Amherst Consulting Group.

Jackson, C. N. (1985). Training's role in the process of change. *Training and Development Journal, 39*(2), 70–74.

Jackson, S. E., & Schuler, R. S. (1985). A meta-analysis and conceptual critique of research on role ambiguity and role conflict in work settings. *Organizational Behavior and Human Decision Processes, 36,* 16–78.

Jacobs, B. A. (1983). Sound minds, bodies . . . and savings. *Industry Week, 216,* 67–78.

Jacobson, B. & Kay, B. (1988). How do you view your work? *Training and Development Journal, 42*(4), 43–47.

Jago, A. G. (1982). Leadership: Perspectives in theory and research. *Management Science, 22,* 315–336.

Jago, A. G., & Ragan, J. W. (1986a). Some assumptions are more troubling than others: Rejoinder to Chemers and Fiedler. *Journal of Applied Psychology, 71,* 564–565.

Jago, A. G., & Ragan, J. W. (1986b). The trouble with LEADER MATCH is that it doesn't match Fiedler's contingency model. *Journal of Applied Psychology, 71,* 555–559.

Jamal, M. (1984). Job stress and job performance controversy: An empirical assessment. *Organizational Behavior and Human Performance, 33,* 1–21.

James, W. (1890). *Principles of psychology.* New York: Holt, Rinehart and Winston.

James, W., & Galbraith, M. W. (1985, January). Perceptual learning styles: Implications and techniques for the practitioner. *Lifelong Learning,* 20–23.

Janis, I. (1982). *Groupthink* (2nd ed.). Boston: Houghton Mifflin.

Jelinek, M., & Litterer, J. A. (1988). Why OD must become strategic. In W. A. Pasmore and R. W. Woodman (Eds.), *Research in organizational change and development* (Vol. 2, pp. 135–162). Greenwich, CT: JAI Press.

Jenkins, J. A. (1990). Self-directed work force promotes safety. *HRMagazine, 35*(2), 54–56.

Johnson, J. G. (1991). The culture clock: TQM and doing the right thing right at the right time. *Journal for Quality & Participation, 14*(6), 1–14.

Johnson, R. B., & O'Mara, J. (1992). Shedding new light on diversity training. *Training and Development Journal, 43*(5), 45–52.

Johnston, W. B., & Packer, A. (1987). *Work Force 2000: Work and workers for the 21st century.* Indianapolis: Hudson Institute.

Jones, G. R. (1986). Socialization tactics, self-efficacy, and newcomers' adjustments to organizations. *Academy of Management Journal, 29,* 262–279.

Kabanoff, B. (1981). The critique of LEADER MATCH and its implications for leadership research. *Personnel Psychology, 34,* 749–764.

Kanter, R. (1983). *The change masters.* New York: Simon & Schuster.

Kanter, R. M. (1977). *Men and women of the corporation.* New York: Basic Books.

Kaplan, R. E., Lombardo, M. M., & Mazique, M. S. (1985). A mirror for managers: Using simulation to develop management teams. *Journal of Applied Behavioral Science, 21,* 241–253.

Katzell, R. A., & Thompson, D. E. (1990). Work motivation: Theory and practice. *American Psychologist, 45,* 144–153.

Kaumeyer, R. A. (1979). *Planning and using skills inventory systems.* New York: Van Nostrand Reinhold.

Kay, E., Meyer, H. H., & French, J. P. R., Jr. (1965). Effects of threat in a performance appraisal interview. *Journal of Applied Psychology, 49,* 311–317.

Kazdin, A. E. (1975). *Behavior modification in applied settings.* Homewood, IL: Dorsey Press.

Kearsley, G. (1984). *Training and technology.* Reading, MA: Addison-Wesley.

Kearsley, G. (1986). 33 ways to better software design. *Training and Development Journal, 40*(7), 47–48.

Kelley, H. H. (1973). The process of causal attribution. *American Psychologist, 28,* 107–128.

Kemery, E. R., Bedeian, A. G., Mossholder, K. W. & Touliatos, J. (1985). Outcomes of role stress: A multi-sample constructive replication. *Academy of Management Journal, 28,* 363–375.

Keys, B., & Wolfe, J. (1988). Management education and development: Current issues and emerging trends. *Journal of Management, 14*, 205–229.

Kiechel, W. III (1989, April 10). The workaholic generation. *Fortune*, pp. 50–62.

Kiechel, W. III (1991, November 4). The boss as coach. *Fortune*, pp. 201, 204.

Kikoski, J. F., & Litterer, J. A. (1983). Effective communication in the performance appraisal interview. *Public Personnel Management Journal, 12*, 33–42.

Kilmann, R. H. (1989). A completely integrated program for organizational change. In A. M. Mohrman, Jr., S. A. Morhman, G. E. Ledford, Jr., T. G. Cummings, and E. E. Lawler (Eds.), *Large scale change* (pp. 200–228). San Francisco: Jossey-Bass.

Kimmerling, G. F. (1985). Warning: Workers at risk, train effectively. *Training and Development Journal, 39*(4), 50–55.

Kinlaw, D. (1989). *Coaching for commitment: Managerial strategies for obtaining superior performance.* San Diego, CA: University Associates, Inc.

Kirkpatrick, D. L. (1967). Evaluation. In R. L. Craig and L. R. Bittel (Eds.), *Training and development handbook* (pp. 87–112). New York: McGraw-Hill.

Kirkpatrick, D. L. (1982). *How to improve performance through appraisal and coaching.* New York: AMACOM.

Kirkpatrick, D. L. (1987). Evaluation. In R. L. Craig (Ed.) *Training and development handbook* (3rd ed.) (pp. 301–319). New York: McGraw-Hill.

Kirsch, I. S., & Jungeblut, A. (1986). *Literacy: Profiles of America's young adults.* National Assessment of Educational Progress. Princeton, NJ: Educational Testing Service.

Klauss, R. (1981). Formalized mentor relationships for management and development programs in the federal government. *Public Administration Review, 4*(4), 489–496.

Klesges, R. C., & Glasgow, R. E. (1986). Smoking modification in the worksite. In M. F. Cataldo and T. J. Coates (eds.), *Health and Industry.* New York: Wiley.

Knowles, M. S. (1970). *The modern practice of adult education: Andragogy versus pedagogy.* New York: Association Press.

Knowles, M. S., & Associates, (1984). *Andragogy in action: Applying modern principles of adult learning.* San Francisco: Jossey-Bass.

Knowlton, W. A. Jr., & Mitchell, T. R. (1980). Effects of causal attributions on supervisor's evaluations of subordinate performance. *Journal of Applied Psychology, 65*, 459–466.

Kohler, W. (1927). *The mentality of apes.* New York: Harcourt Brace Jovanovich.

Kolb, D. A. (1984). *Experiential learning.* Englewood Cliffs, NJ: Prentice-Hall.

Komaki, J., Heinzemann, A. T., & Lawson, L. (1980). Effects of training and feedback: Component analysis of a behavioral safety program. *Journal of Applied Psychology, 65*, 261–270.

Korman, A. K. (1971). *Industrial and organizational psychology.* Englewood Cliffs, NJ: Prentice-Hall.

Kram, K. E. (1985). *Mentoring at work.* Glenview, IL: Scott, Foresman.

Kram, K. E. (1986). Mentoring in the workplace. In D. T. Hall and associates (Eds.), *Career development in organizations.* San Francisco: Jossey-Bass, 160–201.

Kram, K. E., & Bragar, M. C. (1992). Development through mentoring: A strategic approach. In D. H. Montross and C. J. Shinkman (Eds.), *Career development: Theory and practice* (pp. 221–254). Springfield, IL: Charles C. Thomas.

Kram, K. E., & Isabella, L. A. (1985). Mentoring alternatives: The role of peer relationships in career development. *Academy of Management Journal, 28,* 110–132.

Kreitner, R., & Kinicki, A. (1989). *Organizational behavior.* Homewood, IL: Richard D. Irwin.

Krepchin, I. P. (1990). Report from Sweden: The human touch in automobile assembly. *Modern Materials Handling, 240*(4), 39–46.

Kruck, R. S. & Mueire, P. (1987). Reading continuous text on video screens. *Human Factors, 26*(1), 339–345.

Kuhn, N. J. (1987). Merging high touch with high tech. *Training and Development Journal, 41*(6), 64–65.

Kung, E. Y., & Rado, R. N. (1984). Teletraining applied. *Training and Development Journal, 38*(7), 27–28.

Kurtz, N. R., Googins, B., & Howard, W. C. (1984). Measuring the success of occupational alcoholism programs. *Journal of Studies on Alcohol, 45,* 33–45.

Laabs, J. J. (1992). How federally funded training helps business. *Personnel Journal, 71*(3), 35–39.

Lambert, L. I. (1985). Nine reasons that most training programs fail. *Personnel, 64*(1), 62–67.

Lance, C. E., & Richardson, D. R. (1988). Correlates of work and nonwork stress and satisfaction among American insulated sojourners. *Human Relations, 41,* 725–738.

Landon, L. (1990). Pump up your employees. *HR Magazine, 35*(5), 34–37.

Landy, F. J., Barnes, J. L., & Murphy, K. R. (1978). Correlates of perceived fairness and accuracy of performance evaluation. *Journal of Applied Psychology, 63,* 751–754.

Landy, F. J., & Becker, L. J. (1987). Motivational theory reconsidered. In L. Cummings & B. Staw (Eds.), *Research in Organizational Behavior* (Vol. 9). Greenwich, CT: JAI Press.

Landy, F. J., & Farr, J. L. (1980). Performance ratings. *Psychological Bulletin, 87,* 72–107.

Lansing, R. L. (1989). The power of teams. *Supervisory Management, 34*(2), 39–43.

Larkin, J. H., McDermott, J., Simon, D. P., & Simon, H. A. (1980). Models of competence in solving physics problems. *Cognitive Science, 4,* 317–345.

Larson, J. R. Jr. (1977). Evidence for a self-serving bias in the attribution of causality. *Journal of Personality, 45,* 430–441.

Larson, J. R. Jr. (1989). The dynamic interplay between employees' feedback-seeking strategies and supervisors' delivery of performance feedback. *Academy of Management Review, 14,* 408–422.

Latack, J. C. (1984). Career transitions within organizations: An exploratory study of work, non-work, and coping strategies. *Organizational Behavior and Human Performance, 34,* 296–322.

Latane, B., Williams, K., & Harkins, S. (1979). Many hands make light the work:

The causes and consequences of social loafing. *Journal of Personality and Social Psychology, 37,* 822–832.

Latham, G. P. (1988). Human resource training and development. *Annual Review of Psychology, 39,* 545–582.

Latham, G. P. (1989). Behavioral approaches to the training and learning process. In I. L. Goldstein and Associates (Eds.), *Training and development in organizations.* San Francisco: Jossey-Bass.

Latham, G. P., & Saari, L. E. (1979). The application of social learning theory to training supervisors through behavior modeling. *Journal of Applied Psychology, 64,* 239–246.

Lawler III, E. E. (1986). *High-involvement management.* San Francisco: Jossey-Bass.

Lawrence, P. R. (1989). Why organizations change. In A. M. Mohrman, S. A. Mohrman, G. E. Ledford, T. G. Cummings, and E. E. Lawler (Eds.), *Large scale organizational change* (pp. 48–61). San Francisco: Jossey-Bass.

Lawrence, P. R., & Lorsch, J. W. (1967). *Organizations and environment: Managing differentiation and integration.* Homewood, IL: Richard D. Irwin.

Lean, E. (1983). Cross-gender mentoring—Downright upright and good for productivity. *Training and Development Journal, 37*(5), 60–65.

Leana, C. R., & Feldman, D. C. (1990). When mergers force layoffs: Some lessons about managing the human resource problems. *Human Resource Planning, 12*(2), 123–140.

Ledford, G. E., Mohrman, S. A., Mohrman, A. M., & Lawler, E. E. (1989). The phenomenon of large scale organizational change. In A. M. Mohrman, S. A. Mohrman, G. E. Ledford, T. G. Cummings, and E. E. Lawler (Eds), *Large scale organizational change* (pp. 1–32). San Francisco: Jossey-Bass.

Ledvinka, J. (1982). *Federal regulation of personnel and human resource management.* Boston: PWS-Kent Publishing.

Lee, C. (1986). Certification for trainers: Thumbs up. *Training, 23*(11), 56–64.

Lee, C. (1990). Beyond teamwork. *Training, 27*(6), 25–32.

Lee, C. (1991). Who gets trained in what—1991. *Training, 28*(10), 47–59.

Lee, F. C., & Schwartz, G. (1984). Paying for mental health care in the private sector. *Business and Health, 1*(19), 12–16.

Lefton, R. E., & Hyatt, M. T. (1984). The professional sales training system. *Training and Development Journal, 38*(11), 35–37.

Leibowitz, Z. B., Farren, C., & Kaye, B. L. (1985). The 11-fold path to CD enlightenment. *Training and Development Journal, 39*(4), 29–32.

Leibowitz, Z. B., Farren, C., & Kaye, B. L. (1986). *Designing career development systems.* San Francisco: Jossey-Bass.

Leibowitz, Z. B., Feldman, B. H., & Mosley, S. H. (1992). Career development for nonexempt employees: Issues and possibilities. In D. H. Montross and C. J. Shinkman (Eds.), *Career development: Theory and practice* (pp. 324–335). Springfield, IL: Charles C. Thomas.

Leibowitz, Z., & Schlossberg, N. (1981). Training managers for their role in a career development system. *Training and Development Journal, 35*(7), 72–79.

Leifer, M. S., & Newstrom, J. W. (1980). Solving the transfer of training problem. *Training and Development Journal, 34*(8), 42–46.

Levinson, D. J. (1986). A conception of adult development. *American Psychologist*, *41*, 3–13.

Levinson, D. J., Darrow, C. N., Klein, E. B., Levinson, M. H., & Mckee, B. (1978). *Seasons of a man's life*. New York: Knopf.

Lewin, K. (1947). Group decision and social change. In T. M. Newcomb and E. L. Hartley (Eds.), *Readings in Social Psychology* (pp. 330–344). New York: Holt, Rinehart and Winston.

Lewin, K., (1958). Group decision and social change. In E. E. Maccoby, T. M. Newcomb, and E. L. Hartley (Eds.), *Readings in Social Psychology* (pp. 197–211). New York: Holt, Rinehart and Winston.

Lewis, M. W., Milson, R., & Anderson, J. R. (1988). Designing and intelligent authoring system for high school mathematics ICAI: The teacher apprentice project. In G. Kearsley (Ed.), *Artificial intelligence and instruction: Applications and methods*. New York: Addison-Wesley.

Lichtman, S., & Poser, E. G. (1983). The effects of exercises on mood and cognitive functioning. *Journal of Psychosomatic Research*, *27*, 43–52.

Liden, R., & Graen, G. (1980). Generalizability of the vertical dyad linkage model of leadership. *Academy of Management Journal*, *23*, 451–465.

Linder, J. C., & Smith, H. J. (1992). The complex case of management education. *Harvard Business Review*, *70*(5), 16–33.

Lindsey, E. H., Homes, V., & McCall, M. W. (1987). *Key events in executives' lives* (Technical Report No. 32). Greensboro, NC: Center for Creative Leadership.

Lippitt, R., & Lippitt, G. (1975). Consulting process in action. *Training and Development Journal*, *29*(5), 48–54.

Locke, E. A. (1968). Toward a theory of task motivation and incentives. *Organizational Behavior and Human Performance*, *3*, 157–189.

Locke, E. A. (1976). The nature and causes of job satisfaction. In M. D. Dunnette (Ed.), *The handbook of industrial and organizational psychology*. Chicago: Rand McNally.

Locke, E. A., Frederick, E., Lee, C., & Bobko, P. (1984). Effects of self-efficacy, goals, and task strategies on task performance. *Journal of Applied Psychology*, *69*, 241–251.

Locke, E. A., & Latham, G. P. (1990). *A theory of goal setting and task performance*. Englewood Cliffs, NJ: Prentice-Hall.

Locke, E. A., Shaw, K. N., Saari, L. M., & Latham, G. P. (1981). Goal setting and task performance: 1969–1980. *Psychological Bulletin*, *90*, 125–152.

Loher, B. T., Noe, R. A., Moeller, N. L., & Fitzgerald, M. P. (1985). A meta-analysis of the relation of job characteristics to job satisfaction. *Journal of Applied Psychology*, *70*, 280–289.

London, M. (1983). Toward a theory of career motivation. *Academy of Management Review*, *8*, 620–630.

London, M. (1985). *Developing managers: A guide to motivating people for successful managerial careers*. San Francisco: Jossey-Bass.

London, M. (1991). Career development. In K. N. Wexley and J. Hinrichs (Eds.), *Developing human resources* (pp. 152–184). Washington, DC: BNA Books.

London, M., & Bassman, E. (1989). Retraining midcareer workers for the future workplace. In I. L. Goldstein and Associates (Eds.), *Training and development in organizations.* San Francisco: Jossey-Bass.

London, M., & Mone, E. M. (1987). *Career management and survival in the workplace.* San Francisco: Jossey-Bass.

Loomis, L. (1986). Employee assistance programs: Their impact on arbitration and litigation of termination cases. *Employee Relating Law Journal, 12,* 275–288.

Louis, M. R. (1980). Surprise and sensemaking: What newcomers experience in entering unfamiliar organizational settings. *Administrative Science Quarterly, 25,* 226–251.

Louis, M. R., Posner, B. Z., & Powell, G. N. (1983). The availability and helpfulness of socialization practices. *Personnel Psychology, 36,* 857–866.

Lowenthal, J., & Jankowski, P. (1983). A checklist for selecting the right teleconferencing mode. *Training and Development Journal, 37*(12), 47–50.

Lubliner, M. (1978). Employee orientation. *Personnel Journal, 57*(4), 207–208.

Luthans, F., & Waldersee, R. (1989). What do we really know about EAPs? *Human Resource Management, 28,* 385–401.

Mabe, P. A., & West, S. G. (1982). Validity of self-evaluation of ability: A review and meta-analysis. *Journal of Applied Psychology, 67,* 280–296.

Madkins, J. (1989). Affirmative action is ethical. *Personnel Administrator, 68*(8), 29–30.

Madsen, W. (1976). Alcoholics Anonymous as a crisis cult. *Journal of Studies on Alcohol, 37,* 482.

Mager, R. F. (1984). *Preparing instructional objectives* (2nd ed.). Belmont, CA: Pitman Learning.

Mager, R. F., & Pipe, P. (1970). *Analyzing performance problems.* Belmont, CA: Fearon Publishers.

Maher, J. H. Jr., & Kur, C. E. (1983). Constructing good questionnaires. *Training and Development Journal, 37*(6), 100–110.

Mahoney, F. X., & Lyday, N. L. (1984). Design is what counts in computer-based training. *Training and Development Journal, 38*(7), 40–41.

Maiden, R. P. (1988). Employee assistance program evaluation in a federal government agency. In M. J. Holosko and M. D. Feit (Eds.), *Evaluation of employee assistance plans* (pp. 191–203). New York: Haworth Press.

Maier, N. R. F. (1973). *Psychology in industrial organizations* (4th ed.). Boston: Houghton Mifflin.

Mainstone, L. E., & Levi, A. S. (1989). Fundamentals of statistical process control. *Organization Behavior Management, 9*(1), 5–21.

Mandler, G. (1954). Transfer of training as a function of response overlearning. *Journal of Experimental Psychology, 47,* 411–417.

Mann, R. B., & Decker, P. J. (1984). The effect of key behavior distinctiveness on generalization and recall in behavior-modeling training. *Academy of Management Journal, 27,* 900–909.

Manners, G., & Steger, J. A. (1976). Behavioral specifications of the R&D management role. *IEEE Transactions in Engineering Management, 23,* 139–141.

Manners, G., & Steger, J. A. (1979). Implications of research in the R&D management role for the selection and training of R&D managers. *R & D Management, 9,* 85–92.

Mantsios, G. (1992). Rewards and opportunities: The politics and economics of class in the U.S. In P. S. Rothenberg (Ed.). *Race, class, and gender in the United States* (pp. 96–110). New York: St. Martin's Press.

Margotta, M. H. (1986). Positioning for promotion. *Credit and Financial Management, 88*(4), 13–18.

Marx, R. D. (1982). Relapse prevention for managerial training: A model for maintenance of behavioral change. *Academy of Management Review, 7,* 433–441.

Masi, D. A. (1984). *Designing employee assistance programs.* New York: AMACOM.

Masi, D. A. (1992). Employee assistance programs. In D. A. Masi (Ed.), *The AMA handbook for developing employee assistance and counseling programs* (pp. 1–35). New York: AMACOM.

Maslow, A. H. (1943). A theory of human behavior. *Psychological Review, 50,* 370–396.

Maslow, A. H. (1954). *Motivation and personality.* New York: Harper & Row.

Maslow, A. H. (1968). *Toward a psychology of being* (2nd ed.). New York: Van Nostrand Reinhold.

Mason, H., & Spich, R. S. (1987). *Management: An international perspective.* Homewood, IL: Richard D. Irwin.

Masterson, B., & Murphy, B. (1986). Internal cross-cultural management. *Training and Development Journal, 40*(4), 56–60.

Matteson, M. T., & Ivancevich, J. M. (1987). *Controlling work stress.* San Francisco: Jossey-Bass.

Matteson, M. T., & Ivancevich, J. M. (1988). Health promotion at work. In C. L. Cooper and I. Robertson (Eds.), *International review of industrial and organizational psychology* (pp. 279–306). London: Wiley.

Mattzarro, J. D. (1984). Behavioral health: A 1990 challenge for the health science professions. In J. D. Mattzarro, S. M. Weiss, J. A. Herd, N. E. Miller, and S. M. Weiss (Eds.), *Behavioral health: A handbook of health enhancement and disease prevention* (pp. 3–40). New York: Wiley.

May, P. L., Hugh, S. E., & Quesada, E. A. (1990). Back to basics. *Personnel Journal, 69*(10), 62–71.

McCall, M. W., & Lombardo, M. M. (1982). Using simulation for leadership and management research: Through the looking glass. *Management Science, 28,* 533–549.

McCall, M. W., & Lombardo, M. M. (1983, February). What makes a top executive? *Psychology Today,* pp. 26–31.

McCall, M. W. Jr., Lombardo, M. M., & Morrison, A. M. (1988). *The lessons of experience: How successful executives develop on the job.* Lexington, MA: Lexington Books.

McCall, M. W., Jr., Morrison, A. M., & Hannan, R. L. (1978). *Studies of managerial work: Results and methods.* (Tech Report No. 14). Greensboro, NC: Center for Creative Leadership.

McCalla, G. I., & Greer, J. E. (1987). *The practical use of artificial intelligence in automated tutoring systems: Current status and impediments to progress.* Saskatoon, Canada: University of Saskatchewan, Department of Computational Science. Cited in N. P. Eurich (1990), *The learning industry: Education for adult workers.* Lawrenceville, NJ: Princeton University Press.

McCarthy, G. J. (1991). TQM is key to improving services but it's not for every hospital. *Health Care Strategic Management, 9*(11), 18–20.

McCauley, C. D., Lombardo, M. M., & Usher, C. J. (1989). Diagnosing management development needs: An instrument based on how managers develop. *Journal of Management, 15,* 389–403.

McClenahan, J. S. (1987, November 16). Why U.S. managers fail overseas. *Industry Week,* pp. 71–74.

McCormack, S. P. (1992). TQM: Getting it right the first time. *Training and Development Journal, 46*(6), 43–46.

McCullough, R. C. (1987). To make or buy. *Training and Development Journal, 41*(1), 25–26.

McDermott, L. C. (1984). The many faces of the OD professional. *Training and Development Journal, 38*(2), 15–19.

McEnery, J., & McEnery, J. M. (1987). Self-rating in management training needs assessment: A neglected opportunity? *Journal of Occupational Psychology, 60,* 49–60.

McEvoy, G. M., & Cascio, W. F. (1985). Strategies for reducing employee turnover: A meta-analysis. *Journal of Applied Psychology, 70,* 342–353.

McFadden, R. D. (1989, September 15). Smoking restrictions increased dramatically in recent years. *The New York Times,* p. A20.

McGarrell, E. J. Jr. (1984). An orientation system that builds productivity. *Personnel Administrator, 29*(10), 75–85.

McGee, L. F. (1989). Teaching basic skills to workers. *Personnel Administrator, 34*(8), 42–47.

McGee, L., (1989). Innovative labor shortage solutions. *Personnel Administrator, 34*(8), 56–60.

McGehee, W. (1948). Cutting training waste. *Personnel Psychology, 1,* 331–340.

McGehee, W., & Thayer, P. W. (1961). *Training in business and industry.* New York: Wiley.

McGehee, W., & Tullar, W. L. (1978). A note on evaluating behavior modification and behavior modeling as industrial training techniques. *Personnel Psychology, 31,* 477–484.

McGregor, D. (1960). *The human side of the enterprise.* New York: McGraw-Hill.

McKenna, J. F. (1992). Apprenticeships: Something old, something new, something needed. *Industry Week, 241*(2), 14–21.

McLagan, P. A. (1989). Models for HRD practice. *Training and Development Journal, 41*(9), 49–59.

McLagan, P. A., & Bedrick, D. (1983). Models for excellence: The results of the ASTD Training and Development Competency Study. *Training and Development Journal, 37*(6), 49–59.

McMahan, I. D. (1973). Relationships between causal attributions and expectancy of success. *Journal of Personality and Social Psychology, 28,* 108–114.

McWilliams, G. (1991, October 25). The public sector: A new lesson plan for college. *Business Week,* pp. 144–145.

Meglino, B. M., DeNisi, A. S., Youngblood, S. A., & Williams, K. J. (1988). Effects of realistic job previews: A comparison using an "enhancement" and a "reduction" preview. *Journal of Applied Psychology, 73,* 259–266.

Mensch, B. S., & Kandel, D. B. (1988). Do job conditions influence the use of drugs? *Journal of Health and Social Behavior, 29*, 169–184.

Mento, A. J., Steele, R. P., & Karren, R. J. (1987). A meta-analytic study of the effects of goal setting on task performance: 1966–1984. *Organizational Behavior and Human Performance, 39*, 52–83.

Meyer, H. H., & Raich, M. S. (1983). An objective evaluation of a behavior modeling training program. *Personnel Psychology, 36*, 755–761.

Michalak, D. F. (1981). The neglected half of training. *Training and Development Journal, 35*(5), 22–28.

Milkovich, G. T., & Boudreau, J. W. (1991). *Human resource management* (6th Ed.). Howmewood, Il: Richard D. Irwin.

Miller, N. E. (1983). Behavioral medicine: Symbiosis between laboratory and clinic. *Annual Review of Psychology, 34*, 1–31.

Miller, R. B. (1962). Task description and analysis. In R. M. Gagné (Ed.), *Psychological principles in systems development.* New York: Holt, Rinehart and Winston.

Miller, T. O. (1992). A customer's definition of quality. *Journal of Business Strategy, 13*(1), 4–7.

Miller, V. A. (1987). The history of training. In R. L. Craig (Ed.), *Training and Development Handbook* (pp. 3–18). New York: McGraw-Hill.

Mills, G. E., Pace, R. W., & Peterson, B. D. (1988). *Analysis in human resource training and organizational development.* Reading, MA: Addison-Wesley.

Miner, J. B. (1984). The validity and usefulness of theories in an emerging organizational science. *Academy of Management Review, 9*, 296–306.

Mintzberg, H. (1973). *The nature of managerial work.* New York: Harper & Row.

Mintzberg, H. (1975). The manager's job: Folklore and fact. *Harvard Business Review, 53*(4), 49–61.

Mirvis, P. H. (1988). Organization development: Part I—Evolutionary perspective. In W. A. Pasmore and R. W. Woodman (Eds.), *Research in organizational change and development* (Vol. 2, pp. 1–57). Greenwich, CT: JAI Press.

Mirvis, P. H., Sales, A. L., & Hackett, E. J. (1991). The implementation and adoption of new technology in organizations: The impact on work, people, and culture. *Human Resource Management, 30*, 113–139.

Mitchell, T. R. (1974). Expectancy models of satisfaction, occupational preference, and effort: A theoretical, methodological, and empirical appraisal. *Psychological Bulletin, 81*, 1053–1077.

Mitchell, T. R. (1982). Motivation: New directions for theory, research, and practice. *Academy of Management Review, 7*, 80–88.

Mitchell, T. R., Green, S. G., & Wood, R. E. (1981). An attributional model of leadership and the poor performing subordinate: Development and validation. In L. L. Cummings and B. M. Staw (Eds.), *Research in organizational behavior* (Vol. 3, pp. 197–234.). Greenwich, CT: JAI Press.

Mitchell, T. R., & O'Reilly, C. A. (1983). Managing poor performance and productivity in organizations. *Research in Personnel and Human Resources Management, 1*, 201–234.

Mitchell, V. F., & Moudgill, P. (1976). Measurement of Maslow's need hierarchy. *Organizational Behavior and Human Performance, 16*, 334–349.

Mitchell, W. S. Jr. (1984). Wanted: Professional management training needs analysis. *Training and Development Journal, 38*(10), 68–70.

Miyake, N., & Norman, D. A. (1979). To ask a question one must know enough to know what is known. *Journal of Verbal Learning and Verbal Behavior, 18,* 357–364.

Mize, S. (1992). Shattering the glass ceiling. *Training and Development Journal, 46*(1), 60–62.

Mobley, M., & Payne, T. (1992). Backlash: The challenge to diversity training. *Training and Development Journal, 43*(12), 45–52.

Mohrman, S. A., & Mohrman, A. M. (1989). The environment as an agent of change. In A. M. Mohrman, S. A. Mohrman, G. E. Ledford, T. G. Cummings, and E. E. Lawler (Eds.), *Large scale organizational change* (pp. 35–47). San Francisco: Jossey-Bass.

Moore, L. L. (1986). *Not as far as you think.* Lexington, MA: Lexington Books.

Moore, M. L. & Dutton, P. (1978). Training needs analysis: Review and critique. *Academy of Management Review, 3,* 532–545.

Morgan, G., & Ramirez, R. (1983). Action learning: A holographic metaphor for guiding social change. *Human Relations, 37,* 1–28.

Morris, L. (1992). Research capsules. *Training and Development Journal, 46*(4), 74–76.

Morrison, A. M., & Von Glinow, M. A. (1990). Women and minorities in management. *American Psychologist, 45,* 200–208.

Morrison, A. M., White, R. P., Van Velsor, E., & the Center for Creative Leadership (1987). *Breaking the glass ceiling: Can women reach the top of America's largest corporations?* Reading, MA: Addison-Wesley.

Moses, J. L., & Ritchie, R. J. (1976). Supervisory relationships training: A behavioral evaluation of a behavior modeling program. *Personnel Psychology, 29,* 337–343.

Mowday, R. T. (1979). Equity theory predictions of behavior in organizations. In R. D. Steers and L. W. Porter (Eds.), *Motivation and Work Behavior* (2nd ed.). New York: McGraw-Hill.

Mumford, A. (1987). Action learning (Special Issue). *Journal of Management Development, 6*(2), 1–70.

Murphy, K. R., Herr, B. M., Lockhart, M. C., & Maguire, E. (1986). Evaluating the performance of paper people. *Journal of Applied Psychology, 71,* 654–661.

Murphy, L. R. (1984). Occupational stress management: A review and appraisal. *Journal of Occupational Psychology, 57,* 1–17.

Murphy, L. R. (1986). A review of occupational stress management research: Methodological considerations. *Journal of Occupational Behavior Management, 8,* 215–228.

Murray, F. T., & Murray, A. H. (1986). SMR forum: Global managers for global business. *Sloan Management Review, 27*(2), 75–80.

Murray, H. (1938). *Explorations in personality.* New York: Oxford University Press.

Musselwhite, E., & Moran, L. (1990). On the road to self-direction. *Journal of Quality & Participation,* 58–63.

Nadler, L., & Nadler, Z. (1989). *Developing human resources.* San Francisco: Jossey-Bass.

Nadolski, J. N., & Sandonato, C. E. (1987). Evaluation of an employee assistance program. *Journal of Occupational Medicine, 29,* 32–37.

Nash, A. N., Muczyck, J. P., & Vettori, F. L. (1971). The relative practical effects of programmed instruction. *Personnel Psychology, 29,* 337–343.

National Apprenticeship Program (1987). Washington: Employment and Training Administration: U.S. Department of Labor.

Naylor, J. C., & Briggs, G. E. (1963). The effect of task complexity and task organization on the relative efficiency of part and whole training methods. *Journal of Experimental Psychology, 65,* 217–224.

Neel, R. G., & Dunn, R. E. (1960). Predicting success in supervisory training programs by the use of psychological tests. *Journal of Applied Psychology, 44,* 358–360.

Nemeroff, W. F., & Wexley, K. N. (1979). An exploration of the relationships between the performance feedback interview characteristics and interview outcomes as perceived by managers and subordinates. *Journal of Occupational Psychology, 52,* 25–34.

Neuman, G. A., Edwards, J. E., & Raju, N. S. (1989). Organization development interventions: A meta-analysis of their effects on satisfaction and other attitudes. *Personnel Psychology, 42,* 461–489.

Newman, J. D., & Beehr, T. (1979). Personal and organizational strategies for handling job stress: A review of research and opinion. *Personnel Psychology, 32,* 1–43.

Newstrom, J. W., & Lengnick-Hall, M. L. (1991). One size does not fit all. *Training and Development Journal, 45*(6), 43–48.

Nicholas, J. M. (1982). The comparative impact of organization development interventions on hard criteria measures. *Academy of Management Review, 7,* 531–542.

Nicholas, J. M., & Katz, M. (1985). Research methods and reporting practices in organization development: A review and some guidelines. *Academy of Management Review, 10,* 737–749.

Nichols, D. (1991). Teaching workers to team up. *Incentive, 165*(3), 44, 174.

Nickerson, R. S., Perkins, D. N., & Smith, E. E. (1985). *The teaching of thinking.* Hillsdale, NJ: Lawrence Erlbaum Associates.

Noe, R. A. (1986). Trainee's attributes and attitudes: Neglected influences on training effectiveness. *Academy of Management Review, 11,* 736–749.

Noe, R. A. (1988). An investigation of the determinants of successful assigned mentoring relationships. *Personnel Psychology, 41,* 457–479.

Noe, R. A. (1988). Women and mentoring: A review and research agenda. *Academy of Management Review, 13,* 65–78.

Noe, R. A., & Schmitt, N. (1986). The influence of trainee attitudes on training effectiveness: Test of a model. *Personnel Psychology, 39,* 497–523.

Noel, J. L., Ulrich, D., & Mercer, S. R. (1990). Customer education: A new frontier for human resource development. *Human Resource Management, 29*(4), 411–434.

Normand, J., Salyards, S., & Mahoney, J. (1990). An evaluation of pre-employment drug testing. *Journal of Applied Psychology, 75*, 629–639.

Norris, D. R., & Niebuhr, R. E. (1984). Attributional influences on the job performance-job satisfaction relationship. *Academy of Management Journal, 27*, 424–430.

Novack, J. (1992). Earning and learning. *Forbes, 149*(10), 150, 154.

Nurick, A. J. (1982). Participation in organizational change: A longitudinal field study. *Human Relations, 35*, 413–430.

O'Connor, R. (1992). New training approaches for Europe '93. *Personnel Journal, 71*(5), 96–103.

O'Donnell, M. P. (1986). *Design of workplace health promotion programs.* Royal Oak, MI: American Journal of Health Promotion.

O'Neill, S. B. (1988). Associate orientation: Fostering an effective work style. *Legal Economics, 14*(7), 46–49.

Odiorne, G. S., & Rummler, G. A. (1988). *Training and development: A guide for professionals.* Chicago: Commerce Clearing House.

Oppenheimer, R. J. (1982). An alternative approach to assessing management development needs. *Training and Development Journal, 36*(3), 72–76.

Osigweh, C. A. B. (1986–1987). The case approach in management training. *Organizational Behavior Teaching Review, 11*(4), 120–133.

Ostroff, C. (1991). Training effectiveness measures and scoring schemes: A comparison. *Personnel Psychology, 44*, 353–374.

Ott, J. S. (1989). *The organizational culture perspective.* Chicago: Dorsey Press.

Pace, R. W., Smith, P. C., & Mills, G. E. (1991). *Human resource development.* Englewood Cliffs, NJ: Prentice-Hall.

Park, S. (1991). Estimating success rates of quality circle programs: Public and private experiences. *Public Administration Quarterly, 15*(1), 133–146.

Parry, S. B., & Reich, L. R. (1984). An uneasy look at behavior modeling. *Training and Development Journal, 30*(3) 57–62.

Pasmore, W. A., & Fagans, M. R. (1992). Participation, individual development, and organizational change: A review and synthesis. *Journal of Management, 18*, 375–397.

Patel, D. I. (1988). Asian Americans: A growing force. *Journal of State Government, 61*(2), 71–76.

Pauly, J. T., Palmer, J. A., Wright, C. C., & Pfeiffer, G. J. (1982). The effects of a 14-week employee fitness program on selected physiological and psychological parameters. *Journal of Occupational Medicine, 24*, 457–463.

Pearce, J. L., & Peters, R. H. (1985). A contradictory norms view of employer-employee exchange. *Journal of Management, 11*, 19–30.

Pelletier, K. R. (1984). *Healthy people in unhealthy places.* New York: Delacorte Press.

Perlis, G. (1980). Labor and employee assistance programs. In R. H. Egdahl and D. C. Walsh (Eds.), *Mental wellness programs for employees.* New York: Springer-Verlag.

Peters, T., & Austin, N. (1985). *A passion for excellence: The leadership difference.* New York: Random House.

Petrini, C. M. (1991). Literacy programs make the news. *Training and Development Journal, 45*(2), 30–33.

Phillips, D. A., & Older, H. J. (1981). Models of service delivery. *EAP Digest, 1*(May–June), 12–15.

Phillips, J. J. (1983). *Handbook of training evaluation and measurement methods.* Houston, TX: Gulf.

Pickard, J. (1991). Steel partners. *Personnel Management, 23*(12), 32.

Piczak, M. W. (1988). Quality circles come home. *Quality Progress, 21*(12), 37–39.

Pierce, J. L., Newstron, J. W., Dunham, R. B., & Barber, A. E. (1989). *Alternative work schedules.* Boston: Allyn & Bacon.

Pinder, C. C. (1984). *Work motivation: Theory, issues, and applications.* Glenview, IL: Scott, Foresman.

Pintrich, P. R., Cross, D. R., Kozma, R. B., & McKeachie, W. J. (1986). Instructional psychology. *Annual Review of Psychology, 37*, 611–651.

Pittman, T. S., & Heller, J. F. (1987). Social motivation. *Annual Review of Psychology, 38*, 461–489.

Plewa, F. J., Ransom, G. M., & Boes, R. F. (1990). The new CPE requirements: Views of non-practicing CPAs. *Ohio CPA Journal, 49*(2), 53–55.

Podsakoff, P. M., & Organ, D. W. (1986). Self-reports in organization research: Problems and prospects. *Journal of Management, 12*, 531–544.

Polich, J. M., Armor, D. J., & Braker, H. B. (1981). *The course of alcoholism: Four years after treatment.* New York: Wiley.

Popple, P. R. (1981). Social work practice in business and industry. *Social Service Review, 6*, 257–269.

Porras, J. I. (1987). *Stream analysis.* Reading, MA: Addison-Wesley.

Porras, J. I., & Berg, P. O. (1977). The impact of organization development. *Academy of Management Review, 3*, 249–266.

Porras, J. I., & Hoffer, S. J. (1986). Common behavior changes in successful organization development efforts. *Journal of Applied Behavioral Science, 22*, 477–494.

Porras, J. I., & Silvers, R. C. (1991). Organization development and transformation. *Annual Review of Psychology, 42*, 51–78.

Porter, L. W., & McKibbin, L. E. (1988). *Management education and development: Drift of thrust into the 21st century?* New York: McGraw-Hill.

Porter, L. W., Lawler, E. E. III, & Hackman, J. R. (1975). *Behavior in organizations.* New York: McGraw-Hill.

Porter, L. W., & Steers, R. M. (1973). Organizational, work, and personal factors in employee turnover and absenteeism. *Psychological Bulletin, 80*, 151–176.

Powell, M. (1990). Long-term commitment to teamwork. *The Journal of Quality and Participation, 13*(4), 86–89.

Premack, S. L., & Wanous, J. P., (1985). A meta-analysis of realistic job preview experiments. *Journal of Applied Psychology, 70*, 706–719.

President's Commission on Mental Health (1978). *Report to the President* (Vol. 1). Washington, DC: U.S. Government Printing Office.

Rado, R. (1989). Connecting with the customer. *Training and Development Journal, 43*(7), 66–68.

Ragins, B. R. (1989). Barriers to mentoring: The female manager's dilemma. *Human Relations, 42*, 1–22.

Ramirez, A. (1986, November 4). America's super minority. *Fortune*, pp. 148–164.

Ramsey, K. B. (1985). Counseling employees. In Tracey (Ed.), *Handbook of human resource management and development* (pp. 821–836).

Reber, R. A., & Wallin, J. A. (1984). The effects of training, goal setting, and knowledge of results on safe behavior: A component analysis. *Academy of Management Journal, 27*, 544–560.

Redwood, A. (1990). Human resources management in the 1990s. *Business Horizons, 33*(1), 74–80.

Reichers, A. E. (1987). An interactionist perspective on newcomer socialization rates. *Academy of Management Review, 12*, 278–287.

Reilly, R. R., Brown, B., Blood, M. R., & Malatesta, C. Z. (1981). The effect of realistic previews: A study and discussion of the literature. *Personnel Psychology, 34*, 823–834.

Reinhardt, C. (1988). Training supervisors in first-day orientation techniques. *Personnel, 65*(6), 24–28.

Reinhart, C. (1989). Developing CBT—The quality way. *Training and Development Journal, 43*(11), 85–89.

Reinventing America [Special Issue]. (1992). *Business Week*, pp. 78–79, 82–88.

Renner, J. F. (1987). Wellness programs: An investment in cost containment. *EAP Digest, 7*, 49–53.

Resnick, L. B. (1981). Instructional psychology. *Annual Review of Psychology, 32*, 659–704.

Revans, R. (1982). What is action learning? *Journal of Management Development, 1*(3), 64–75.

Reynolds, L. (1992). The Feds join the quality movement. *Management Review, 81*(4), 39–42.

Rhodes, E. C., & Dunwoody, D. (1980). Physiological and attitudinal changes in those involved in an employee fitness program. *Canadian Journal of Public Health, 71*, 331–336.

Rice, D., & Dreilinger, C. (1991). After the downsizing. *Training and Development Journal, 45*(5), 41–44.

Rice, R. W. (1978). Construct validity of the Least Preferred Co-worker (LPC) Score. *Psychological Bulletin, 85*, 1199–1237.

Rice, R. W. (1979). Reliability and validity of the LPC scale: A reply. *Academy of Management Review, 4*, 291–294.

Roach, J. B. (1990). Education and training at Welch Allyn. *ILR Report, 28*(1), 14–17.

Robertson, I., & Downs, S. (1979). Learning and prediction of performance: Development of trainability testing in the United Kingdom. *Journal of Applied Psychology, 64*, 42–50.

Robertson, I., & Downs, S. (1989). Work sample tests of trainability: A meta-analysis. *Journal of Applied Psychology, 74,* 402–410.

Robinson, D. G., & Robinson, J. (1989). Training for impact. *Training and Development Journal, 43*(8), 34–42.

Romiszowski, A. J. (1988). *The selection and use of instructional media* (2nd ed.). New York: Nichols Publishing.

Rosen, B., & Lovelace, K. (1991). Piecing together the diversity puzzle. *HRMagazine, 36*(6), 78–84.

Rosen, R. H., & Lee, F. C. (1987). Occupational mental health: A continuum of care. In A. W. Reilly and S. J. Zaccaro (Eds.), *Occupational stress and organizational effectiveness* (pp. 245–267). New York: Praeger.

Rosenbaum, B. L. (1984). Back to behavior modeling. *Training and Development Journal, 30*(11), 88–89.

Rosenberg, M. J. (1987). Evaluating training programs for decision making. In L. S. May, C. A. Moore, and S. J. Zammit (Eds.), *Evaluating business and industry training.* Boston, MA: Kluwer Academic Publishers.

Rosenfeld, M. (1991). *Affirmative action and justice.* New Haven: Yale University Press.

Rosow, J. M., & Zager, R. (1988). *Training: The competitive edge.* San Francisco: Jossey-Bass.

Ross, I. (1986, September 29). Corporations take aim at literacy. *Fortune,* pp. 48–54.

Rossett, A. (1989). Assess for success. *Training and Development Journal, 43*(5), 55–59.

Rossett, A. (1990). Overcoming obstacles to needs assessment. *Training, 36*(3), 36, 38–40.

Rothenberg, P. S. (1992). *Race, class, & gender: An integrated study.* New York: St. Martin's Press.

Rothwell, W. J. (1989). Complying with OSHA. *Training and Development Journal, 43*(5), 52–54.

Rothwell, W. J. (1991). HRD and the Americans with Disabilities Act. *Training and Development Journal, 45*(8), 45–48.

Rubin, I., & Inguaguiato, R. (1991). Changing the work culture. *Training and Development Journal, 45*(7), 57–60.

Rumbaut, R. G. (1985). How well are Southeast Asians adapting? *Business Forum, 10*(Fall), 26–31.

Rush, H. M. F. (1989). What is behavioral science? In M. T. Matteson & J. M. Ivancevich (Eds.), *Management and Organizational Behavior Classics* (pp. 37–48). Homewood, IL: Richard D. Irwin.

Russell, J. S., Wexley, K. N., & Hunter, J. E. (1984). Questioning the effectiveness of behavior modeling training in an industrial setting. *Personnel Psychology, 37,* 465–481.

Russell, M. (1984). Career planning in a blue-collar company. *Training and Development Journal, 38*(1), 87–88.

Ryman, D. H., & Biesner, R. J. (1975). Attitudes predictive of driving training success. *Personnel Psychology, 28,* 181–188.

Saari, L. M., Johnson, T. R., McLaughlin, S. D., & Zimmerle, D. M. (1988). A survey of management training and education practices in U.S. companies. *Personnel Psychology, 41,* 731–743.

Sackett, P. R. (1987). Assessment centers and content validity: Some neglected issues. *Personnel Psychology, 40,* 13–25.

Sackett, P. R., DuBois, C. L., & Noe, A. W. (1991). Tokenism in performance evaluation: The effects of work group representation on male-female and white-black differences in performance ratings. *Journal of Applied Psychology, 76,* 263–267.

Sadu, G., Cooper, C., & Allison, T. (1989). A post office initiative to stamp out stress. *Personnel Management, 21*(8), 40–45.

Sahl, R. J. (1992). Succession planning drives plant turnaround. *Personnel Journal, 71*(9), 67–70.

Salcedo, M. (1986). The 25 healthiest companies to work for. *EAP Digest, 6,* 45–50.

Salemme, T. (1991). Lessons learned from employees about quality improvement efforts. *Tapping the Network Journal, 2*(2), 2–6.

Santa-Barbara, J. (1984). Employee assistance programs: An alternative resource for mental health service delivery. *Canada's Mental Health, 32,* 35–38.

Sayao, F. (1991, October 29). Black executives: Racism No. 1 barrier. *USA Today,* p. 6B.

Scandura, T. A. (1992). Mentorship and career mobility: An empirical investigation. *Journal of Organizational Behavior, 13,* 169–174.

Scandura, T. A., & Graen, G. B. (1984). Moderating effects of initial leader-member exchange status on the effects of a leadership intervention. *Journal of Applied Psychology, 69,* 428–436.

Schein, E. H. (1971a). The individual, the organization, and the career: A conceptual scheme. *Journal of Applied Behavioral Science, 7,* 401–426.

Schein, E. H. (1971b). Occupational socialization in the professions: The case of the role innovator. *Journal of Psychiatric Research, 8,* 521–530.

Schein, E. H. (1978). *Career dynamics: Matching individual and organizational needs.* Reading, MA: Addison-Wesley.

Schein, E. H. (1980). *Organizational Psychology* (3rd ed.). Englewood Cliffs, NJ: Prentice-Hall.

Schein, E. H. (1986). What you need to know about organizational culture. *Training and Development Journal, 40*(1), 32.

Schein, E. H. (1987a). Individuals and careers. In J. Lorsch (Ed.), *Handbook of organizational behavior* (pp. 155–171). Englewood Cliffs, NJ: Prentice-Hall.

Schein, E. H. (1987b). *Process consultation* (Vol. II). Reading, MA: Addison-Wesley.

Schein, E. H. (1987c). Coming to a new awareness of organizational culture. In E. H. Schein (Ed.), *The art of managing human resources* (pp. 261–278). New York: Oxford University Press.

Schein, V. E. (1985). Organizational realities: The politics of change. *Training and Development Journal, 39*(2), 37–41.

Schendel, J. D., & Hagman, J. D. (1982). On sustaining procedural skills over a prolonged retention interval. *Journal of Applied Psychology, 67,* 605–610.

Schilder, J. (1992). Work teams boost productivity. *Personnel Journal, 71*(2), 67–71.

Schmidt, F. L., Hunter, J. E., & Pearlman, K. (1982). Assessing the impact of personnel programs on workforce productivity. *Personnel Psychology, 35,* 333–347.

Schmitt, N. W., & Klimoski, R. J. (1991). *Research methods in human resources management.* Cincinnati, OH: South-Western.

Schneider, B., & Schmitt, N. W. (1986). *Staffing organizations* (2nd ed.). Glenview, IL: Scott, Foresman.

Schoenfeldt, L. F., & Steger, J. A. (1990). Identification and development of management talent. In G. R. Ferris and K. M. Rowland (Eds.), *Organizational entry* (pp. 191–251). Greenwich, CT: JAI Press.

Schonberger, R. J. (1992). Total quality management cuts a broad swath through manufacturing and beyond. *Organizational Dynamics, 20*(4), 16–28.

Schott, F. W., & Wendel, S. (1992). Wellness with a track record. *Personnel Journal, 71*(4), 98–104.

Schramm, W. (1962). Learning from instructional television, *Review of Educational Research, 32,* 156–167.

Schriesheim, C. A., Bannister, B. D., & Money, W. H. (1979). Psychometric properties of the LPC scale: An extension of Rice's review. *Academy of Management Review, 4,* 287–290.

Schriesheim, C., & DeNisi, A. (1981). Task dimensions as moderators of the effects of instrumental leadership: A two-sample replicated test of path-goal leadership theory. *Journal of Applied Psychology, 66,* 587–589.

Schuler, R. S., & Harris, D. C. (1992). Deming quality improvement: Implications for human resource management as illustrated in a small company. *Human Resource Planning, 14*(3), 191–207.

Schwade, S. (1985). Is it time to consider computer-based training? *Personnel Administrator, 30*(2), 25–35.

Sculnick, M. W., (1986). Sex segregation in the work place. *Employment Relations Today, 13*(Spring), 3–10.

Sensenbrenner, J. (1991). Quality for cities. *Nation's Business, 79*(10), 60, 62.

Shahandeh, B. (1985). Drug and alcohol abuse in the workplace: Consequences and countermeasures. *International Labour Review, 124,* 207–223.

Shain, M., & Groeneveld, J. (1980). *Employee-assistance programs.* Lexington, MA: Lexington Books.

Shames, G., (1986). Training for the multicultural workplace. *Cornell Hotel & Restaurant Administration Quarterly, 26,* 25–31.

Shaw, M. (1981). *Group dynamics* (3rd ed.). New York: McGraw-Hill.

Shepard, R. J. (1983). Employee health and fitness: The state of the art. *Preventive Medicine, 12,* 644–653.

Shippeck, M. A., & Taylor, C. (1985). Up the career path. *Training and Development Journal, 39*(8), 46–48.

Shipper, F., & Manz, L. L. (1992). An alternative road to empowerment. *Organizational Dynamics, 20*(3), 48–61.

Shore, B., & Sechrest, L. (1975). Concept attainment as a function of positive instances presented. *Journal of Educational Psychology, 52,* 303–307.

Siegel, A. I. (1983). The miniature job training and evaluation approach: Additional findings. *Personnel Psychology, 36*, 41–56.

Silverman, S. B. (1990). Individual development through performance appraisal. In K. N. Wexley & J. R. Hinrichs (Eds.), *Developing human resources* (pp. 120–151). Washington, DC: Bureau of National Affairs, Inc.

Simon, D. P., & Simon, H. A. (1978). Individual differences in solving physics problems. In R. S. Siegler (Ed.), *Children's thinking: What develops?* Hillsdale, NJ: Lawrence Erlbaum Associates.

Sims, H., & Manz, C. C. (1982). Modeling influences on employee behavior. *Personnel Journal, 61*(1), 45–51.

Skidmore, R. A., Balsam, D. D., & Jones, O. (1974). Social work practice in industry. *Social Work, 19*, 280–286.

Skinner, B. F. (1953). *Science and human behavior.* New York: Macmillan.

Skinner, B. F. (1974). *About behaviorism.* New York: Knopf.

Smallwood, N., & Folkman, J. (1987). Why employee surveys don't work. *Personnel, 64*(8), 20–28.

Smith, C. B. (1988). Designing and facilitating a self-assessment experience. In M. London and E. M. Mone (Eds.), *Career growth and human resource strategies: The role of the human resource professional in employee development* (pp. 157–172). New York: Quorum Books.

Smith, D. E. (1986). Training programs for performance appraisal: A review. *Academy of Management Review, 11*, 22–40.

Smith, H. W. (1985). Implementing a management development program. *Personnel Administrator, 30*(7), 75–86.

Smith, M. E. (1992). The search for executive skills. *Training and Development, 37*(9), 88–95.

Smith, P. (1976). Management modeling training to improve morale and customer satisfaction. *Personnel Psychology, 29*, 353–359.

Smith, R. E. (1984). Employee orientation: 10 steps to success. *Personnel Journal, 63*(12), 44–48.

Solomon, C. (1989). The corporate response to workforce diversity. *Personnel Journal, 68*(8), 42–53.

Solomon, C. (1990). Careers under glass. *Personnel Journal, 69*(4), 96–105.

Solomon, R. L. (1949). An extension of the control group design. *Psychological Bulletin, 46*, 137–150.

Sommer, R. F. (1989). *Teaching writing to adults: Strategies and concepts for improving learner performance.* San Francisco: Jossey-Bass.

Sonnenstuhl, W. J. (1988). Contrasting employee assistance, health promotion, and quality of work life programs and their effects on alcohol abuse and dependence. *The Journal of Applied Behavioral Science, 24*, 347–363.

Sonnenstuhl, W. J., Staudenmeier, W. J. Jr., & Trice, H. M. (1988). Ideology and referral categories in employee assistance program research. *The Journal of Applied Behavioral Science, 24*, 383–396.

Sonnenstuhl, W. J., & Trice, H. M. (1986). *Strategies for employee assistance programs: The crucial balance.* Ithaca, NY: ILR Press.

Sourentian, J. (1989). Four by four. *Training and Development Journal, 43*(11), 21–30.

Spayd, E. (1989). Gender prejudice is subtle, study says. *Washington Post*. (Published in the *Providence Journal*, October 30, 1989, pp. B16–17.)

Speroff, B. J. (1954). Rotational role playing used to develop managers. *Personnel Journal, 33*(2), 49–50.

Sprangers, M., & Hoogstraten, J. (1989). Pretesting effects in retrospective pretest-posttest designs. *Journal of Applied Psychology, 74*, 265–272.

St. John, W. D. (1980). The complete employee orientation program. *Personnel Journal, 59*(5), 373–378.

Stacey, J. (1980). Business taking a new look at health care costs. *American Medical News, 23*, 20.

Stackel, L. (1988). National Technological University: Learning by satellite. In J. Casner-Lotto and Associates (Eds.), *Successful training strategies*. San Francisco: Jossey-Bass.

Staw, B. M., & Ross, J. (1985). Stability in the midst of change: A dispositional approach to job attitudes. *Journal of Applied Psychology, 70*, 469–480.

Steck, R. N. (1992). The skills gap and how to deal with it. *D & B Reports, 40*(1), 47–48.

Steel, R. P., Jennings, K. R., & Lindsey, J. T. (1990). Quality circle problem solving and common cents: Evaluation study findings from a United States federal mint. *Journal of Applied Behavioral Science, 26*, 365–381.

Steel, R. P., & Lloyd, R. F. (1988). Cognitive, affective, and behavioral outcomes of participation in quality circles: Conceptual and empirical findings. *Journal of Applied Behavioral Sciences, 24*, 1–17.

Steele, P. D. (1988). Substance abuse in the work place, with special attention to employee assistance programs: An overview. *Journal of Applied Behavioral Science, 24*, 315–325.

Steiner, D. D., Dobbins, G. H., & Trahan, W. A. (1991). The trainer-trainee interaction: An attributional model of training. *Journal of Organizational Behavior, 12*, 271–286.

Steinmetz, C. S. (1976). The history of training. In R. L. Craig (Ed.), *Training and development handbook* (pp. 1–14). New York: McGraw-Hill.

Sternberg, R. J. (1986). *Intelligence applied*. San Diego, CA: Harcourt Brace Jovanovich.

Sterns, H. L. (1986). Training and retraining adult and older adult workers. In J. E. Birren, P. K. Robinson, and J. E. Livingston (Eds.), *Age, health, and employment*. Englewood Cliffs, NJ: Prentice-Hall.

Sterns, H. L., & Doverspike, D. (1988). Training and developing the older worker: Implications for human resource management. In H. Dennis (Ed.), *Fourteen steps to managing an aging workforce*. New York: Lexington.

Sterns, H. L., & Doverspike, D. (1989). Aging and the training and learning process. In I. L. Goldstein and Associates, *Training and development in organizations*. San Francisco: Jossey-Bass.

Stone, D. L., Gueutal, H. G., & McIntosh, B. (1984). The effects of feedback sequence and expertise of the rater on perceived feedback accuracy. *Personnel Psychology, 37*, 487–506.

Stone, N. (1991). Does business have any business in education? *Harvard Business Review, 69*(2), 46–62.

Storey, W. D. (Ed.) (1976). *A guide for career development inquiry: State-of-the-art report on career development.* ASTD Research Series Paper No. 2. Madison, WI: American Society for Training and Development.

Strube, M. J., & Garcia, J. E. (1981). A meta-analytic investigation of Fiedler's contingency theory of leadership effectiveness. *Psychological Bulletin, 93,* 600–603.

Stuart, P. (1993). How McDonnell Douglas cost-justified its EAP. *Personnel Journal, 72*(2), 48.

Stum, D. L., & Church, R. P. (1990). Hitting the long ball for the customer. *Training and Development Journal, 44*(3), 45–48.

Sullivan, S. E., & Bhagat, R. S. (1992). Organizational stress, job satisfaction, and job performance: Where do we go from here? *Journal of Management, 18,* 353–374.

Super, D. E. (1980). A life-span, life-space approach to career development. *Journal of Vocational Behavior, 16,* 282–298.

Super, D. E. (1986). Life career roles: Self-realization in work and leisure. In D. T. Hall and Associates (Eds.), *Career development in organizations* (pp. 50–94). San Francisco: Jossey-Bass.

Super, D. E. (1992). Toward a comprehensive theory of career development. In D. H. Montross and C. J. Shinkman (Eds.), *Career development: Theory and practice* (pp. 35–64). Springfield, IL: Charles C. Thomas.

Sussman, L., & Kuzmits, F. (1986). The HRD professional as entrepreneur. *Training and Development Journal, 40*(8), 43.

Sutton, E. E., & McQuigg-Martinetz, B. (1990). The development partnership: Managing skills for the future. *Training and Development Journal, 44*(4), 63–70.

Swanson, N. G., & Murphy, L. R. (1991). Mental health counseling in industry. In C. L. Cooper and I. T. Robertson (Eds.), *International review of industrial and organizational psychology* (Vol. 6, pp. 265–282). Chichester: Wiley.

Swasy, A., & Hymowitz, C. (1989, February 9). The workplace revolution. *The Wall Street Journal,* pp. 26–28.

Symonds, W. C., Ellis, J. E., Siler, S. F., Zellner, W., & Garland, S. B. (1991, March 25). Is business bungling its battle with booze? *Business Week,* pp. 76–78.

Tang, T. L., Tollison, P. S., & Whiteside, H. D. (1989). Quality circle productivity as related to upper-management, attendance, circle initiation, and collar color. *Journal of Management, 15,* 101–113.

Tannenbaum, S. I., & Yukl, G. (1992). Training and development in work organizations. *Annual Review of Psychology, 43,* 399–441.

Tarrant, S. M. (1992). How companies can become more family friendly. *Journal of Compensation & Benefits, 7*(4), 18–21.

Taylor, C. W. (1952). Pretesting saves training costs. *Personnel Psychology, 5,* 213–239.

Taylor, F. W. (1947). *Scientific Management.* New York: Harper & Row.

Taylor, J. (1984). Assessment centers: Not just for managers anymore. *Training, 21*(11), 54–59.

Taylor, M. S., Fisher, C. D., & Ilgen, D. R. (1984). Individuals' reactions to performance feedback in organizations: A control theory perspective. In K. M. Rowland and G. R. Ferris (Eds.), *Research in personnel and human resource management* (Vol. 2). Greenwich, CT: JAI Press.

Taylor, M. S., Locke, E. A., Lee, C., & Gist, M. E. (1984). Type A behavior and faculty research productivity: What are the mechanisms? *Organizational Behavior and Human Performance, 34,* 402–418.

Taylor, R. K., & Tajen, C. (1948). Selection for training: Tabulating equipment operators. *Personnel Psychology, 1,* 341–348.

Terborg, J. (1986). Health promotion at the worksite: A research challenge for personnel and human resources management. In K. H. Rowland and G. R. Ferris (Eds.), *Research in personnel and Human Resources Management, 4,* 225–267.

Tersine, R. J., & Hazeldine, J. (1982). Alcoholism: A productivity hangover. *Business Horizons, 25*(11), 68–72.

Tetrick, L. E., & LaRocco, J. M. (1987). Understanding prediction and control as moderators of the relationships between perceived stress, satisfaction, and psychological well-being. *Journal of Applied Psychology, 72,* 538–543.

Thermstrom, S., Orlou, A., & Hanolin, O. (Eds.), (1980). *Harvard Encyclopedia of American Ethnic Groups.* Cambridge, M.A.

Thiederman, S. (1988). Overcoming cultural and language barriers. *Personnel Journal, 67*(12), 42–45.

Thiederman, S. (1990). *Bridging cultural barriers for corporate success.* Lexington, MA: Lexington Books.

Thomas Jr., R. R. (1990). From affirmative action to affirming diversity. *Harvard Business Review, 68*(2), 107–117.

Thomas Jr., R. R. (1991). *Beyond race and gender.* New York: AMACOM.

Thomas, D. A. (1990). The impact of race on manager's experience of developmental relationships (mentoring and sponsorship); An intraorganizational study. Journal of *Organization Behavior, 11*(6), 479–491.

Thomas, W. G. (1988). Training and development do make better managers. *Personnel, 65*(1), 52–53.

Thompson, B. L. (1991). OSHA bounces back. *Training, 28*(1), 45–53.

Thorndike, E. L. (1913). *The psychology of learning: Educational psychology.* (Vol. 2). New York: Teachers College Press.

Thorndike, E. L. (1927). The law of effect. *American Journal of Psychology, 39,* 212–222.

Thorndike, E. L., & Woodworth, R. S. (1901). (I) The influence of improvement in one mental function on the efficiency of other functions. (II) The estimation of magnitudes. (III) Functions involving attention, observation, and discrimination. *Psychological Review, 8,* 247–261, 384–395, 553–564.

Thornton, G. C., & Cleveland, J. N. (1990). Developing managerial talent through simulation. *American Psychologist, 45,* 190–199.

Thornton, G. C. (1992). *Assessment centers in human resource management.* Reading, MA: Addison-Wesley.

Thornton, G. C. III (1980). Psychometric properties of self-appraisals of job performance. *Personnel Psychology, 33,* 263–271.

Thornton, G. C., & Byham, W. C. (1982). *Assessment centers and managerial performance.* New York: Academic Press.

Tichy, N. M., & DeVanna, M. A. (1986). *The transformational leader.* New York: Wiley.

Tichy, N. M. (1989). GE's Crotonville: A staging ground for corporate revolution. *Academy of Management Executive, 3,* 99–107.

Tollison, P. (1992). Assessing TQM training needs. *Journal for Quality & Participation, 15*(1), 50–54.

Toomey, E. L., & Connor, J. M. (1988). Employee sabbaticals: Who benefits and why. *Personnel, 65*(4), 81–84.

Topf, M. D., & Preston, R. T. (1991). Behavior modification can heighten safety awareness, curtail accidents. *Occupational Health & Safety, 60*(2), 43–49.

Tornow, W. W., & Pinto, P. R. (1976). The development of a managerial job taxonomy: A system for describing, classifying, and evaluating executive positions. *Journal of Applied Psychology, G1,* 410–418.

Tosi, H. (1971). Organizational stress as a moderator of the relationship between influence and role-response. *Academy of Management Journal, 14,* 7–20.

Townsend, T. M. (1990). Let employees carry the ball. *Personnel Journal, 69*(10), 30–36.

Training (1991). Computers in training. *Training, 28*(10), 51.

Trice, H. M., & Beyer, J. M. (1984). Work-related outcomes of the constructive-confrontation strategy in a job-based alcoholism program. *Journal of Studies on Alcohol, 45,* 393–404.

Trice, H. M., Hunt, R. & Beyer, J. M. (1977). Alcoholism programs in unionized work settings: Problems and prospects in union-management cooperation. *Journal of Drug Issues, 7,* 103–115.

Trice, H. M., & Schonbrunn, M. (1981). A history of job-based alcoholism programs: 1900–1955. *Journal of Drug Issues, 11,* 171–198.

Tubiana, J. H., & Ben-Shakhar, G. (1982). An objective group questionnaire as a substitute for a personal interview in the prediction of success in military training in Israel. *Personnel Psychology, 35,* 349–357.

Tucker, R., Moravec, M., & Ideus, K. (1992). Designing a dual career-track system. *Training & Development, 46*(6), 55–58.

U. S. Office of Personnel Management (1985). *The managerial excellence framework: A competency-based model of effective performance for federal managers.* Washington, DC: U. S. Government Printing Office.

U.S. Department of Labor. (1991). *A report of the glass ceiling initiative* (Publication Number 1992 312-411/64761). Washington, DC: U.S. Government Printing Office.

Usdansky, M. L. (1992, May 29–31). Immigrant tide surges in 80s. *USA Today,* p. 1.

Van Eynde, D. F., Church, A., Hurley, R. F. & Burke, W. W. (1992). What OD practitioners believe. *Training and Development Journal, 46*(4), 41–46.

Van Maanen, J. (1978). People processing: Strategies of organizational socialization. *Organizational Dynamics, 7*(1), 18–36.

Van Maanen, J., & Schein, E. H. (1977). Career development. In J. R.

Hackman and J. L. Suttle (Eds.), *Improving behavior at work: Behavioral science approaches to organizational change.* Santa Monica, CA: Goodyear.

Van Maanen, J., & Schein, E. H. (1979). Toward a theory of organizational socialization. In B. Staw (Ed.), *Research in organizational behavior* (pp. 209–264). Greenwich, CT: JAI Press.

Van Zwieten, J. B., & Britton, M. (1989). Training you can bank on. *Training and Development Journal, 43*(6), 59–63.

Vasilash, G. S. (1992). Driving beyond satisfaction at Rockwell Automotive. *Production, 104*(4), 40–43.

Vecchio, R. P. (1991). *Organizational behavior* (2nd ed.). Hinsdale, IL: The Dryden Press.

Vecchio, R. P., & Godbell, B. C. (1984). The vertical dyad linkage model of leadership: Problems and prospects. *Organizational Behavior and Human Performance, 34*, 5–20.

Velocci, A. L., Jr. (1991). TQM makes Rockwell tougher competitor. *Aviation Week & Space Technology, 135*(23), 68–69.

Verespej, M. A. (1990). When you put the team in charge. *Industry Week, 239*(23), 30–32.

Verespej, M. A. (1992). When workers get new roles. *Industry Week, 241*(3), 11.

Verney, T., Ackelsberg, R., & Holoviak, S. J. (1989). Participation and worker satisfaction. *Journal for Quality & Participation, 12*(3), 74–77.

Versteeg, A. (1990). Self-directed work teams yield long-term benefits. *Journal of Business Strategy, 11*(6), 9–12.

Viega, J. F. (1988). Face your problem subordinates now! *Academy of Management Executive, 2*, 145–152.

Von Glinow, M. A. (1985). Reward strategies for attracting, evaluating, and retaining professionals. *Human Resource Management, 24*(2), 191–206.

Vroom, V. H. (1964). *Work and motivation.* New York: Wiley.

Wabha, M. A., & Bridwell, L. G. (1976). Maslow reconsidered: A review of research on the need hierarchy theory. *Organizational Behavior and Human Performance, 15*, 212–240.

Wade, R. (1982). *Highlights of management education and development for the XXI century in the management for the XXI century.* The American Assembly of Collegiate Schools of Business and The European Foundation of American Development, Boston: Kluwer and Nijhoff Publishing.

Wagner, W. G. (1982). Assisting employees with personal problems. *Personnel Administrator, 61*(11), 59–64.

Wakabayashi, M., & Graen, G. B. (1984). The Japanese career progress study: A 7-year follow-up. *Journal of Applied Psychology, 69*, 603–614.

Walker, J. W. (1976). Let's get serious about career paths. *Human Resource Management, 15*(3), 2–7.

Walker, J. W. (1988). Managing human resource in flat, lean and flexible organizations: Trends for the 1990s. *Human Resource Planning, 11*(2), 124–132.

Walker, J. W. (1989). Human resource roles for the 90's. *Human Resource Planning, 12*(1), 55–60.

Walker, J. W. (1992). Career paths in flexible organizations. In D. H. Montross and C. J. Shinkman (Eds.), *Career development: Theory and practice* (pp. 385–402). Springfield, IL: Charles C. Thomas.

Wall, T. D., Kemp, N. J., Jackson, P. R., & Clegg, C. W. (1986). Outcomes of autonomous workgroups: A long-term field experiment. *Academy of Management Journal, 29,* 280–304.

Walsh, D. C., & Hingson, R. W. (1985). Where to refer employees for treatment of drinking problems. *Journal of Occupational Medicine, 27,* 745–752.

Walton, R. E. (1975). From Hawthorne to Topeka to Kalmir. In E. L. Cass and F. G. Zimmer (Eds.), *Man and the work in society.* New York: Van Nostrand Reihold.

Walton, R. E. (1985). From control to commitment in the workplace. *Harvard Business Review, 63*(2), 76–84.

Walton, R. E. (1987). *Managing conflict* (2nd ed.). Reading, MA: Addison-Wesley.

Wanous, J. P. (1976). Organizational entry: From naive expectations to realistic beliefs. *Journal of Applied Psychology, 61,* 22–29.

Wanous, J. P. (1977). Organizational entry: Newcomers moving from outside to inside. *Psychological Bulletin, 84,* 601–618.

Wanous, J. P. (1978). Realistic job previews: Can a procedure to reduce turnover also influence the relationship between abilities and performance? *Personnel Psychology, 31,* 249–258.

Wanous, J. P. (1980). *Organizational entry.* Reading, MA: Addison-Wesley.

Wanous, J. P. (1989). Installing a realistic job preview: Ten tough choices. *Personnel Psychology, 42,* 117–134.

Wanous, J. P. (1992). *Organizational entry: Recruitment, selection, orientation, and socialization of newcomers* (2nd ed.). Reading, MA: Addison-Wesley.

Wanous, J. P., & Colella, A. (1989). Organizational entry research: Current status and future directions. In K. Rowland & G. Ferris (Eds.), *Research in Personnel and Human Resources Management* (Vol. 7, pp. 59–120). Greenwich, CT: JAI Press.

Wanous, J. P., Keon, T. L., & Latack, J. C. (1983). Expectancy theory and occupational/organizational choice: A review and test. *Organizational Behavior and Human Performance, 32,* 66–86.

Wanous, J. P., Poland, T. D., Premack, S. L., & Davis, K. S. (1992). The effects of met expectations on newcomer attitudes and behaviors: A review and meta-analysis. *Journal of Applied Psychology, 77,* 288–297.

Wanous, J. P., Reichers, A. E., & Malik, S. D. (1984). Organizational socialization and group development: Toward an integrative perspective. *Academy of Management Review, 9,* 670–683.

Warr, P., Bird, M., & Rackham, N. (1970). *Evaluation of management training.* London: Gower Press.

Washburn, S. Z., & McClure, F. G. (1992). A modern workplace in the face of an age-old problem: Illiteracy. *Industrial Management, 34*(1), 2–4.

Watkins, B. T. (1991). 18 Universities join effort to offer bachelor degrees in management, entirely through cable television. *The Chronicle of Higher Education, 38*(5), A18–A19.

Watson, J. B. (1913). Psychology as the behaviorist views it. *Psychology Review, 20,* 158–177.

Watts, P., (1987). Bias busting: Diversity training in the workplace. *Management Review, 76,* 51–54.

Weatherby, N. L., & Gorosh, M. E. (1989). Rapid response with spreadsheets. *Training and Development Journal, 43*(9), 75–79.

Weiner, B. (1980). *Human motivation.* New York: Holt, Rinehart and Winston.

Weiner, B., Frieze, I., Kukla, A., Reed, L., Nest, S., & Rosenbaum, R. (1971). Perceiving the causes of success and failure. In E. Jones, D. Kanouse, H. Kelley, R. Nisbett, S. Balins, & B. Weiner (Eds.), *Attribution: Perceiving the causes of behavior.* Morristown, NJ: General Learning Press.

Weiner, B., Frieze, I., Kukla, A., Reed, L., Nest, S., & Rosenbaum, R. (1972). Perceiving the causes of success and failure. In E. Jones, D. Kanouse, H. Kelley, R. Nisbett, S. Balins, and B. Weiner (Eds.), *Attribution: Perceiving the causes of behavior.* Morristown, NJ: General Learning Press.

Weiner, B., Heckhausen, H., Meyer, W., & Cook, R. E. (1972). Causal ascriptions and achievement behavior: A conceptual analysis of effort and reanalysis of locus of control. *Journal of Personality and Social Psychology, 21,* 239–248.

Weinstein, C., & Mayer, R. (1986). The teaching of learning strategies. In M. Wittrock (Ed.), *Handbook of research on teaching* (3rd ed.). New York: Macmillan, 1986.

Weisbord, M. R. (1987). Toward a third-wave managing and consulting. *Organizational Dynamics, 15*(3), 4–24.

Weiss, R. M. (1980). *Dealing with alcholism in the workplace.* New York: The Conference Board.

Weiss, R. M. (1987). Writing under the influence: Science versus fiction in the analysis of corporate alcoholism programs. *Personnel Psychology, 40,* 341–355.

Wentz, D. K., Gannon, M. I., Osteen, A. M., Baldwin, D. C. Jr. (1989). Continuing medical education. *Journal of American Medical Association, 282,* 1043–1045.

Wertheimer, M. (1959). *Productive thinking.* New York: Harper & Row.

Wexley, K. N. (1984). Personnel training. *Annual Review of Psychology, 35,* 519–551.

Wexley, K. N. (1985). Appraisal interview. In R. A. Berk (Ed.), *Performance assessment: Methods & applications* (pp. 167–185). Baltimore, MD: Johns Hopkins University Press.

Wexley, K. N., & Baldwin, T. T. (1986). Management development. *Journal of Management, 12,* 277–294.

Wexley, K. N., & Baldwin, T. T. (1986). Post-training strategies for facilitating positive transfer: An empirical exploration. *Academy of Management Journal, 29,* 503–520.

Wexley, K. N., & Latham, G. P. (1981). *Developing and training human resource in organizations.* Glenview, IL: Scott, Foresman.

Wexley, K. N., & Latham, G. P. (1991). *Developing and training human resources in organizations* (2nd ed.). New York: HarperCollins.

Wexley, K. N., Singh, J. P., & Yukl, G. A. (1973). Subordinate personality as a moderator of the effects of participation in three types of appraisal interviews. *Journal of Applied Psychology, 58,* 54–59.

Wexley, K. N., & Thornton, C. L. (1972). Effect of verbal feedback of test results upon learning. *Journal of Educational Research, 66,* 119–121.

White, R. P. (1992). Jobs as classrooms: Using assignments to leverage development. In D. H. Montross and C. J. Shinkman (Eds.), *Career development: Theory and practice* (pp. 190–206). Springfield, IL: Charles C. Thomas.

Whitely, W., Dougherty, T. W., & Dreher, G. F. (1992). Correlates of career-oriented mentoring for early career managers and professionals. *Journal of Organizational Behavior, 13*, 141–154.

Wiggenhorn, W. (1990 July-August). Motorola U: When training becomes an education. *Harvard Business Review*, 71–83.

Wilber, C. S. (1983). The Johnson & Johnson program. *Preventive Medicine, 12*, 672–681.

Williams, E.D., Hayflich, P.F., & Gaston, J. (1986). Training: The challenges of a multi-cultural work force. *Personnel Journal, 65*(8), 148–151.

Wilson, L.S. (1990). An on-line prescription for basic skills. *Training and Development Journal, 44*(4), 36–41.

Wircenski, J.L., Sullivan, R. L., and Moore, P. (April, 1989). Assessing training needs at Texas Instruments. *Training and Development Journal, 43*(4), 61–63.

Wittock, M. (1986). *The handbook of research on teaching*. New York: Macmillian.

Woodman, R. W. (1989). Organization change and development: New areas for inquiry and action. *Journal of Management, 15*, 205–228.

Work Force 2000—Work and Workers for the 21st Century. Gary, IN: The Hudson Institute, 1987.

Wrich, J. T. (1984). *The employee assistance program*. Center City, MN: Hazelden Educational Foundation

Zaslow, R. (1991). Managers as writing coaches. *Training and Development Journal, 45*(7), 61–64.

Zedeck, S., & Cascio, W. F. (1984). Psychological issues in personnel decisions. *Annual Review of Psychology, 35*, 461–518.

Zemke, R. (1985). The Honeywell studies: How managers learn to manage. *Training, 22*(8), 46–51.

Zenger, J. H., & Hargis, K. (1982). Assessment of training results: It's time to take the plunge! *Training and Development Journal, 36*(1), 11–16.

Zwerling, C., Ryan, J, & Orav, E. J. (1990). The efficacy of preemployment drug screening for marijuana and cocaine in predicting employment outcome. *Journal of the American Medical Association, 264*(20), 2639–2643.

Adam, E. E., 434
Adams, D., 406
Adams, J. S., 32
Adler, N. J., 382–386
Ajzen, I., 40
Akabus, S., 315
Albanese, R., 375
Albrecht, K., 236
Alderfer, C. P., 10, 27, 29, 414, 419, 429
Alexander, R. A., 196
Al-Gattan, A. A., 46
Allaire, Paul, 447
Allen, Charles, 5
Allen, N. J., 207, 216
Alliger, G. M., 171
Allison, T., 291
Altany, D., 437
Anastasia, A., 178
Andersen, Arthur, 1
Anderson, J. R., 55
Anderson, John, 78
Andrews, E. S., 149, 150
Andrews, K. R., 389
Argyris, Chris, 149, 150, 416
Armor, D. M., 300
Arvey, R. D., 185, 236
Ashe, R. A., 353
Ashford, S. J., 445
Atwater, S. K., 62
Austin, N., 266, 278, 279
Authier, J., 279
Axel, H., 299, 314
Axelrod, J. F., 301
Axland, S., 436

Baldwin, T. T., 59, 64, 66, 151, 371, 392, 406
Ballew, J. A., 257
Balsam, D. D., 299
Bandura, A., 36, 405, 406
Bannister, B. D., 283, 399
Barnard, Chester, 5
Baron, R. A., 282
Barrick, M. R., 59
Bartholomew, S., 382–386
Bartlett, C. A., 382–386
Bass, B. M., 141
Basser, G. A., 281
Bassok, M., 57, 79
Baumgartel, H., 59, 66
Beatty, R. W., 373
Becker, L. J., 31
Becker, W. S., 252
Beckhard, R., 10, 414, 417, 419, 441, 442, 470, 471
Beckman, Mardee, 165, 199
Beehr, T., 305
Beekun, R. I., 439

Beer, M., 10, 414, 419, 425, 414
Behling, O., 31
Bell, B. L., 241
Bell, C. H., Jr., 414
Ben-Shakhar, G., 59
Bennett, T., 299
Bennie, K. D., 416
Bennis, W. G., 416, 420
Berdiansky, H., 145
Berger, M. A., 149, 239
Berkowitz, D., 65
Berman, S. J., 435
Bernacki, E. J., 310
Bernardin, H. J., 404
Beyer, J. M., 292, 299, 300, 315, 316
Bhagat, R. S., 206, 301, 302
Biersner, R. J., 59
Bird, M., 170
Blair, S. N., 309
Blake, R. R., 399–401
Blood, M. R., 221
Blum, M. L., 61, 62
Boal, K. B., 35
Bobko, P., 36
Boehm, V. R., 349
Bogorya, Y., 382
Bolles, R. N., 342
Boni, Bob, 451
Botch, K., 434
Boudreau, J. W., 196, 465
Bourne, L. E., 63
Bowen, D. E., 352, 436
Bower, G. H., 55
Boyatzis, R. E., 375
Bragar, M. C., 352, 353
Braker, H. B., 300
Braun, W. B., 310
Bray, D. W., 373
Breaugh, J. A., 219, 220
Brennan, 311
Bridwell, L. G., 29
Brief, A. P., 36
Briggs, G. E., 61, 62
Briggs, L. J., 79, 80
Brinkerhoff, R. O., 94, 170, 172
Brogden, H. E., 195
Brooks, L., 334
Brown, A. L., 79
Brown, B., 221
Brown, D., 334
Brown, L. D., 414, 416, 428, 430
Brownell, K. D., 311
Bruner, J. S., 56
Buchanan, B., 210, 211
Bugbee, J. A., 256
Bullock, R. J., 419
Burack, N. L., 343, 346
Burke, M. J., 141, 152, 397–399, 406

Burke, R. J., 281, 282
Burke, W. W., 417, 424, 433, 440
Burnaska, R. F., 406
Bushnell, D. S., 170, 173
Butler, J. L., 151
Byham, W. C., 151, 406
Byrne, J. A., 388, 389

Cady, L. D., 309
Cairo, P. C., 289, 350
Callahan, M. R., 252, 473
Campbell, D. T., 178–181, 184, 186,
    180, 181, 184, 186, 189
Campbell, J. P., 32, 33, 39, 99, 103,
    105, 173, 370
Campbell, R. J., 373
Campion, M. A., 431
Carlisle, K. E., 240
Carnevale, A. P., 2, 76, 77, 97, 128,
    129, 236, 244, 245, 251, 256, 460
Carrell, M. R., 32
Carrol, S. J., 375
Carroll, S. J., 141
Cascio, W. F., 181, 185–187, 191, 196,
    221, 282, 293, 299, 310, 314, 404
Caudron, S., 466
Cervone, D., 36
Chacko, T. I., 37
Chao, G. T., 355–357
Chemers, M. M., 396–399
Chesser, R. J., 301
Chi, M. T. H., 79
Childress, G. W., 256
Chin, R., 416
Choquette, P. J., Jr., 239
Christensen, K., 432
Chu, G. C., 145
Church, R. P., 253
Clancey, W. J., 62
Clark, S. G., 435
Clawson, J. G., 353
Cleese, John, 130
Clegg, C., 294
Clement, J., 288
Cleveland, J. N., 150, 151
Clinton, Bill, 447
Clinton, DeWitt, 3
Cohen, D. J., 141
Colarelli, S. M., 219
Cole, D. A., 185
Colella, A., 221
Collins, J. J., 288
Compton, D. O., 222
Cone, J., 253
Connor, J. M., 258
Conrad, P., 310
Cook, R. E., 37
Cook, T. D., 178–181, 184, 186
Cooke, N. J., 57
Cooper, C., 291
Cooper, C. L., 305
Corey, P., 310

Cotton, J. L., 440
Courtney, R. S., 258
Cox, Allan, 13
Cox, M., 310
Cox, T. H., 473, 477
Cronbach, L. J., 68, 195
Cronshaw, S. F., 196
Cross, D. R., 57
Crosson, C., 256
Crump, C. E., 305, 310, 313
Crumrine, L., 222
Cullen, J. G., 191
Cummings, L. L., 35
Cureton, J. H., 105

Daloisio, T., 70
Dalton, G. W., 325
Dandonato, C. E., 299
Dansereau, F., 46, 402
Darrow, C. N., 326
Davenport, J., 70
Davenport, J. A., 70
Davis, K. S., 207
Day, R. R., 141, 152, 397–399, 406
Deci, E. L., 34
Decker, P. J., 37, 62, 405, 406, 408
DeCotiis, T., 282
DeFrank, R. S., 305
Delaney, C., 246
Deming, W. Edwards, 130, 248, 254,
    417, 418, 435
DeNisi, A., 46, 46
Desatnick, R. L., 253
Desch, Herbert W., 20
Deterline, 104
DeVanna, M. A., 441
Dewey, John, 75
Dick, W., 57
Dickman, F., 299
Diener, E., 37
Dienesch, R. M., 402
Digman, L. A., 392
Dittrich, J. E., 32
Dobbins, G. H., 38
Dole, E., 237
Dole, Elizabeth, 458
Donaldson, Les, 161
Donnerstein, E., 65
Dorfman, P. W., 282
Dougherty, T. W., 353
Doverspike, D., 72, 73, 111
Dowling, M. K., 236
Downs, S., 32, 59, 59
Dreher, G. F., 197, 353
Dreilinger, C., 444
Driver, R. W., 305
Dunham, R. B., 432
Dunn, R. E., 59
Dunnette, M. D., 39, 42, 370
Dunwoody, D., 310
Dutton, P., 97, 99, 110
Dweck, C. S., 37

Dyer, W. G., 430

Early, P. C., 141
Eckel, K., 257
Eden, D., 45, 59
Edwards, J. E., 428, 430
Eggland, S. A., 132
Ekstrand, B. R., 63
Ellis, H. C., 65
Ellis, J. E., 288
Elsass, P. M., 355
Emener, W. S., 299
Engleken, C., 295
Erfurt, J. C., 292, 310, 312
Erickson, J. M., 301, 302
Erikson, Erik, 328–330, 333
Eurich, N. P., 78, 144, 145, 154, 382, 390, 392
Evans, M. G., 26, 26
Evered, R. D., 266, 267, 278, 279
Everly, G. S., 288, 302

Faerman, S. R., 256
Fagenson, E. A., 433, 440
Faley, R., 294, 299
Falkenberg, L., 310
Farr, J. L., 282
Farrel, R., 78
Farren, C., 341
Fayol, Henri, 374
Federico, R. F., 226
Fedor, D. B., 282
Feldman, B. H., 340, 358
Feldman, D. C., 207, 209–213, 222, 225, 227, 325, 334, 355, 357, 441
Feldman, R.H.L., 288
Fennell, M. L., 292, 316
Ferketish, B. J., 436
Fernandez, J. P., 477
Ferrence, T. P., 354
Ferris, G. R., 46, 431, 432
Fetteroll, E. C., 161
Feuer, D., 299, 311, 315
Fiedler, F. E., 396–399
Field, H. J., 101
Fielding, J. E., 305, 308, 310
Filipczak, B., 141, 143, 149, 150, 239, 243, 246–248, 251–254, 370, 372
Finkel, C., 160
Firestone, M., 70
Firnstahl, T. W., 252
Fishbein, M., 40
Fisher, C. D., 62, 208–213
Fitts, P. M., 61
Fitzgerald, M. P., 47
Flanagan, J. C., 104
Fleishman, Edwin, 41, 42, 43
Foegen, J. H., 154
Follett, Mary Parker, 5
Foote, A., 292, 310, 312
Ford, J. D., 311
Ford, J. G., 311

Ford, J. K., 64, 66, 115
Forsyth, S., 256
Fossum, J. A., 236
Fournies, F. F., 266, 267, 271, 274–279
Fox, Derwin, 264
Frayne, C. A., 36
Frederick, E., 36
Freedman, S. M., 302
French, J.R.P., 281, 282
French, W. L., 414
Fresina, A. J., 389
Freud, Sigmund, 328
Fried, Y., 431, 432
Friedlander, F., 414, 416, 428, 430
Fromkin, H. L., 190

Gael, S., 101
Gagné, Robert M., 54, 55, 56, 60, 62, 79, 80, 209
Gainer, L. J., 2, 76, 97, 460
Galagan, P., 467, 469
Galbraith, M. W., 77
Gall, A. L., 445
Galloway, S., 256
Galosy, J. R., 444
Galvin, J. C., 170, 172
Ganger, R. E., 153, 154
Ganster, D. C., 301, 304
Garcia, J. E., 397
Garland, S. B., 288, 457
Gatewood, R. D., 101
Gavin, J. F., 301
Geber, B., 265
Gebhardt, D. L., 305, 310, 313
Geertz, C., 442
Gerber, B., 18
Gessner, M. J., 405
Ghoshal, S., 382–386
Gibbs, D. A., 288
Gilbreth, Lillian, 5
Gillen, D. J., 375
Gilley, J. W., 132
Gioia, D. A., 270
Gist, M. E., 36, 406
Glaser, R., 54, 55, 56, 57, 60, 79
Glasgow, R. E., 289, 311
Glueck, W., 222
Godbel, B. C., 46
Goldstein, A. P., 37
Goldstein, I. L., 42, 61, 65, 95, 97, 99, 103, 106, 167–169, 181, 404, 405, 408
Golembiewski, 421
Gomersall, E. R., 222, 225, 227
Goodman, P. S., 247
Googins, B., 300
Gordon, C., 288
Gordon, E. E., 238, 254
Gordon, L. V., 59
Graen, G. B., 46, 210, 402
Graen, M. R., 402
Grant, D. L., 373

Grazier, P. B., 251
Green, A., 259
Green, S. G., 270
Greenberg, J., 281
Greenhaus, J. H., 11, 34, 325–328, 334–338, 461
Greenslade, M., 467, 471
Greer, J. E., 154
Greller, M. M., 281, 282
Grossman, M. E., 222
Grove, D. A., 197
Guilford, J. P., 42
Gunderson, E. E., 301
Gutteridge, T. G., 327, 340, 341, 346–348
Guzzo, R. A., 35, 420, 430–433, 420

Hackey, M. K., 247
Hackman, J. R., 47, 210, 211, 417, 429, 130
Haga, B., 46, 402
Hagman, J. D., 62
Hakel, M. D., 406
Hale, R. L., 435
Hall, D. T., 325–327, 334, 359, 360
Haller, E., 458
Hall-Sheehy, J., 246
Hamburg, S. K., 153
Hannan, R. L., 374
Hargis, K., 168
Harkins, S., 48
Harris, M. M., 292, 299, 300
Harris, P. R., 309
Harris, R. T., 419, 441, 442, 470, 471
Hartanto, F. M., 185
Harwood, H. J., 288
Hatfield, J. D., 33
Hayden, J. W., 436
Hayes, B., 299
Hazeldine, J., 299, 300
Hazucha, J. F., 185
Heckhausen, H., 37
Heffner, R. A., 462, 479
Heft, L. L., 299, 300
Heinzemann, A. T., 59, 62
Heirich, M. A., 292, 310
Heller, J. F., 35
Hellweg, S. A., 435
Hendrikson, G., 65
Henneback, C., 247
Hequet, M., 390
Herbert, G. R., 111
Herzberg, F. H., 29
Herzlinger, R. E., 309
Heskin, A. D., 462, 479
Hess, B. B., 462
Hicks, W. D., 59, 189
Hill, Anita, 96
Hillelsohn, M. J., 153
Hingson, R. W., 297
Hodges, H. G., 3
Hoel, W., 402
Hoffer, S. F., 420

Hogan, P. M., 406
Holbrook, 429
Holding, D. H., 61
Holland, J. L., 342
Hollenbeck, G. P., 389
Hollenbeck, J. R., 36
Holley, W. H., 243
Hollinger, R. C., 293
Hollon, C. J., 301
Holpp, L., 439, 440
Holt, 333
Honeycutt, A., 435
Hoogstraten, J., 180
House, R. J., 46
Howard, A., 373
Howard, J., 309
Howard, W. C., 300
Howe, C., 305
Howell, V. W., 256
Howell, W. C., 57
Huczynski, A. A., 66
Hunt, R., 315, 316
Hunter, J. E., 195, 406
Huseman, R. 33

Ideus, K., 348, 349
Ilgen, D. R., 26, 62, 270, 459, 461, 477
Iman, S. C., 438
Isabella, L. A., 353
Ivancevich, J. J., 141
Ivancevich, J. M., 222, 301–305, 311–316
Ivey, A., 279

Jackson, S. E., 206
Jacobs, B. A., 305
Jacobs, D. R., 309
Jacobsen, 257
Jago, A. G., 45
Jago, A. J., 399
Jamal, M., 302
James, W., 55, 77
Janek, E. A., 171
Janis, I., 48
Jankowski, P., 145
Jenkins, J. A., 248
Jennings, K. M., 243
Jette, R. D., 430
Johnson, Lyndon, 464
Johnson, R. B., 436, 466, 469
Johnson, T. R., 168
Johnston, J. W., 236, 244, 245
Johnston, W. B., 238, 452
Jones, G. R., 207, 215, 216
Jones, O., 299
Jungeblut, A., 238, 239
Juran, Joseph, 130

Kabanoff, B., 399
Kandel, D. B., 293
Kanter, R. M., 352, 425, 439, 444, 459, 477
Kaplan, R. E., 150

Karren, R. J., 34
Karwasky, R. J., 309
Katz, M., 428, 430
Katzell, R. A., 26, 26, 34, 430
Kaumeyer, R. A., 349
Kay, E., 282
Kaye, B. L., 341, 257
Kazdin, A. E., 65
Kearsley, G., 143, 144, 145, 148, 153
Kelley, H. H., 37
Kemery, E. R., 302
Kemp, N. J., 294
Keon, T. L., 31
Keys, B., 148, 149, 150, 151, 371, 393, 395
Keys, J. B., 151
Kiechel, W. III, 265, 359
Kiggins, A., 406
Kikoski, J. F., 279
Kilmann, R. H., 473
Kimmerling, G. F., 248
Kinicki, A., 31
Kinlaw, D., 266, 267, 276, 279
Kirkpatrick, D. L., 170–173, 190, 266
Kirsch, I. S., 238, 239
Kizer, William M., 288, 318
Klaus, R., 351
Kleiman, L., 294, 299
Klein, E. B., 326
Klein, H. J., 26, 26
Klesges, R. C., 311
Klieman, L. S., 59
Klimoski, R. J., 59, 178, 180–184, 188, 189
Knowles, M. S., 68, 70, 72
Knowlton, W. A., Jr., 270
Kohler, W., 55
Kolb, David, A., 73, 74, 75, 148, 375
Komaki, J., 59, 62
Korman, A. K., 141
Kozma, R. B., 57
Kram, K. E., 351–353
Kreitner, R., 31
Kristiansen, P. L., 288
Kruck, 154
Kurtz, N. R., 300

Laabs, J. J., 241, 243
Lance, C. E., 301
Landon, 257
Landy, F. J., 31, 282
Lansing, R. L., 435
Larkin, J. H., 79
LaRocco, J. M., 301
Larson, Duane, 370
Larson, J. R., Jr., 270
Latack, J. C., 31
Latack, L. C., 355
Latane, B., 48
Latham, G. P., 34, 36, 39, 62, 63, 99, 103, 104, 169, 197, 277, 280–282, 401, 405, 406, 414
Lawler, E. E. III, 210, 211, 370, 429, 436

Lawrence, P. R., 441
Lawson, L., 59, 62
Laymon, Joseph, 414
Lean, E., 351
Leana, C. R., 441
Ledford, G. E., 441
Lee, C., 36, 255, 390, 406, 437, 438
Lee, F. C., 294, 299
Leibowitz, Z. B., 340, 341, 345–347, 350, 358
Leifer, M. S., 66
Lengnick-Hall, M. L., 70, 72
Levinson, Daniel J., 326, 328–334, 351
Levinson, M. H., 326
Lewin, Kurt, 75, 415, 416, 425
Lewis, J. W., 66
Lewis, M. W., 78
Lichtman, S., 310
Liden, R. C., 402
Linder, J. C., 388
Lindsey, E. H., 116
Lippitt, R., 416
Litterer, J. A., 279
Lloyd, R. F., 434
Locke, E. A., 34, 36, 277, 282, 406, 414, 406
Loher, B. T., 47, 432
Lombardo, M. M., 116, 150, 371, 392, 393
London, M., 354, 359
Loomis, L., 315
Louis, M. R., 204, 208, 213, 216, 217, 225, 226
Lovelace, K., 469
Lowenthal, J., 145
Luthans, F., 299, 300, 301, 313, 315
Lyness, K. S., 350

Macey, W. H., 97, 103
Madsen, W., 300
Mager, R. F., 126, 127, 128, 271, 272, 274
Maggio, Karen, 370, 409
Magnus, M., 222
Mahar, L., 399
Mahoney, J., 293, 294
Maiden, R. P., 288
Maier, N. R. F., 58
Malatesta, C. Z., 221
Mandler, G., 62
Mann, R. B., 406
Manners, G., 375
Mantsios, G., 460
Manz, C. C., 66
Manz, L. L., 438
Margotta, M. H., 256
Marx, R. D., 66
Masi, D. A., 289, 292–296, 314
Maslow, A. H., 27
Maslow, Abraham, 5
Mathys, N. J., 343, 346
Matteson, M. T., 301–305, 311–316
Mattzarro, J. D., 309

Mausner, B., 29
May, P. L., 240
Mayer, R., 76
Mazique, M. S., 150
McCall, M. W., Jr., 116, 150, 371, 374, 392, 393
McCalla, G. I., 154
McCanse, 399–401
McCarthy, G. J., 437
McCauley, C. D., 116, 119
McClelland, C. L., 431
McClelland, D. C., 375
McCormack, S. P., 435, 436
McCullough, R. C., 157
McDermott, J., 79
McElroy, J. C., 37
McEnery, J., 115
McEnery, J. M., 115
McEvoy, G. M., 221, 373
McFadden, R. D., 310
McGarrell, E. J., Jr., 223, 226–228
McGee, L. F., 240
McGee, W., 435
McGehee, W., 59, 61, 63, 94, 99, 103, 110, 406
McGregor, D., 267, 416
McKeachie, W. J., 57
McKee, B., 326
McKibbin, L. E., 251, 387–390
McLagen, P. A., 11, 14, 15, 17
McLaughlin, S. D., 168
McMahan, I. D., 37
McQuigg-Martinez, B., 380
McWilliams, G., 437
Meltzer, A. S., 76
Mensch, B. S., 293
Mento, A. J., 34
Meyer, H. H., 281, 282, 406
Meyer, J. P., 207, 216
Meyer, W., 37
Michalak, D. F., 66
Mikalanchki, A., 309
Miles, E. W., 33
Milkovich, G. T., 465
Miller, N. E., 309
Miller, R. B., 104
Miller, T. O., 249, 253
Miller, V. A., 3, 5
Mills, G. E., 4, 104
Milson, R., 78
Miner, J. B., 34
Mintzberg, H., 374
Mitchell, T. R., 26, 31, 269, 270
Mitchell, V. F., 29
Miyake, N., 79
Mize, S., 457
Mobley, M., 469
Moeller, N. L., 47
Mone, E. M., 354
Money, W. H., 399
Moore, Kim, 370
Moore, M. L., 97, 99, 110

Moran, L., 439
Moravec, M., 348, 349
Morgan, G., 395
Morrison, A. M., 116, 371, 374, 392, 393, 456, 457, 461, 463, 477, 478
Moses, J. L., 406
Mosley, S. H., 340, 358
Moudgill, P., 29
Mount, M. K., 59
Mouton, J. S., 399–401
Mowday, R. T., 33
Mueire, 154
Mumford, A., 42, 43, 395
Murphy, L. R., 292, 299, 300, 304, 305, 405
Murray, A. H., 382
Murray, F. T., 382
Murray, H., 26, 26
Musicante, G. R., 404
Musselwhite, E., 439
Myers, M. S., 222, 225, 227

Nadler, L., 3, 6
Nadler, Z., 3, 6
Nadolski, J. N., 299
Napolitano, D. M., 288
Nathan, B. R., 37, 405, 408
Naylor, J. C., 61, 62
Neel, R. G., 59
Nemeroff, W. F., 281, 282
Neuman, G. A., 420, 430–433
Newman, J. D., 305
Newstrom, J. W., 66, 70, 72
Newton, A. F., 105
Nicholas, J. M., 417, 419, 428–432
Nichols, D., 255
Nickerson, R. S., 79
Niebuhr, R. E., 37
Noe, R. A., 40, 41, 47, 58, 115, 351, 457, 459
Noel, J. L., 149, 150
Norman, D. A., 79
Normand, J., 293, 294
Norris, D. R., 37
Nougaim, K., 334
Novack, J., 245
Nurick, A. J., 440

Obradovic, 440
Odiorne, G. S., 392
O'Donnell, M. P., 305
Older, H. J., 291
Oldham, G. R., 47, 417, 431
O'Mara, J., 466, 469
O'Neill, S. B., 222
Orav, E. V., 293, 294
O'Reilly, C. A., 269, 270
Organ, D. W., 179, 180
Osigweh, C. A. B., 149, 150
Ostroff, C., 174, 175, 197
Ott, J. S., 442, 453, 454, 473
Otte, F. L., 340, 341, 346

Pace, R. W., 4, 104
Packer, A., 238, 452
Paine, F. T., 141
Palinscar, A. S., 79
Palmer, J. A., 309
Park, S., 434
Parry, S. B., 407
Patel, D. I., 462
Pathan, R., 59
Pauly, J. T., 309
Payne, T., 469
Pearce, J. L., 46
Pearlman, K., 195
Pelletier, K. R., 311
Perkins, D. N., 79
Perlis, G., 315
Peters, R. H., 46
Peters, T., 266, 278, 279
Peterson, B. D., 104
Petit, A., 282
Pfeiffer, G. J., 309
Phillips, D. A., 291
Phillips, J. J., 167, 179
Phillips, J. S., 302
Piaget, Jean, 75
Piczak, M. W., 435
Pierce, J. L., 432
Pinder, C. C., 26, 26, 34, 33
Pinto, P. R., 375
Pintrich, P. R., 57
Pipe, P., 271, 272, 274
Piserchia, P. V., 305, 311, 312
Pittman T. S., 35
Plewa, F. J., 256
Podsakoff, P. M., 179, 180
Poland, T. D., 207
Polich, J. M., 300
Pope, Merline, 480
Pope, Pat, 480
Popple, P. R., 289
Porac, J., 34
Porras, J. I., 419–422, 441
Porter, L. W., 207, 208, 210, 211, 251,
    387–390
Poser, E. G., 310
Posner, B. Z., 225
Powell, G. N., 225
Powell, K. E., 309
Powell, M., 255
Premack, S. L., 207, 221
Preston, Jim, 478
Price, R. L., 325
Prien, E. P., 97, 103
Pritchard, R. D., 32, 33
Pugh, W. M., 301

Quinn, R. E., 256

Rackham, N., 170
Ragan, J. W., 399
Raich, M. S., 406
Raju, N. S., 428, 430

Ralston, D. A., 355
Ramirez, A., 462
Ramirez, R., 395
Ramsey, K. B., 316
Ratliff, R. A., 305
Ravid, G., 45, 59
Reagan, Ronald, 314
Reber, R. A., 59
Rees, E., 79
Reich, L. R., 407
Reichers, A. E., 223
Reilly, R. R., 221
Reinhardt, C., 226
Reinhart, C., 153
Resnick, L. B., 57
Revans, R., 395
Reynolds, L., 437
Reynolds, M., 59
Rhodes, E. C., 310
Rice, D., 444
Rice, R. W., 399
Richardson, D. R., 301
Richter, J., 359, 360
Ritchie, R. J., 406
Robbins, Sharon, 88
Robertson, I., 59
Robinson, D. G., 173, 179, 191, 192
Robinson, J., 173, 179, 191, 192
Romiszowski, A. J., 148
Rose, A. M., 62
Rosen, B., 406, 469
Rosen, R. H., 299
Rosenbaum, B. L., 407
Rosenfeld, J. M., 464
Ross, J., 40
Rothwell, W. J., 247, 248
Rummler, G. A., 392
Russell, J. S., 406
Russell, M., 340, 358
Ryan, J., 293, 294
Ryman, D. H., 59

Saari, L. M., 34, 168, 372, 380, 389,
    390, 406
Sackett, P. R., 197, 459
Sadu, G., 291
St. John, W. D., 223
Salcedo, M., 311
Salemme, T., 435
Salyards, S., 293, 294
Santa-Barbara, J., 297
Sauers, R., 78
Sawzin, S. A., 191
Sbyantek, D. J., 419
Scandura, T. A., 351, 402
Scannell, Edward, 161
Schaubroeck, J., 301, 304
Schein, E. H., 205–207, 210–215, 325,
    326, 334, 350, 355, 363, 415, 430,
    453
Schendel, J. D., 62
Schilder, 437, 438

Schlossberg, N., 340
Schmidt, F. L., 195, 399
Schmitt, N., 41, 59, 178, 180–184, 188, 189
Schmitt, N. W., 217
Schneider, B., 217
Schneier, C. E., 373
Schoenfeldt, L. F., 371, 373–380
Schonberger, R. J., 435, 436
Schramm, W., 145
Schriesheim, C. A., 46, 399
Schroeder, W., 65
Schuler, R. S., 206
Schwade, S., 153
Schwartz, G., 294
Schwartz, J., 309
Schwoerer, C., 406
Sechrest, L., 65
Selman, J. C., 266, 267, 278, 279
Sensenbrenner, J., 437
Shani, W. B., 59
Shaw, K. N., 34
Shaw, M., 207
Shepard, R. J., 310
Shippeck, M. A., 348
Shipper, F., 438
Shore, B., 65
Siler, S. F., 288
Silverman, S. B., 280, 281
Silvers, R. C., 419–422, 441
Simon, D. P., 79
Simon, H. A., 79
Sims, H., 66
Sims, H. P., 270
Singh, J. P., 281
Sisson, G. R., 191
Skidmore, R. A., 299
Skinner, B. F., 38
Smith, C. B., 342
Smith, D. E., 403, 404
Smith, E. E., 79
Smith, H. J., 388,
Smith, M. E., 408
Smith, P., 406
Smith, P. C., 4
Snow, R. E., 68
Snyderman, B. B., 29
Solomon, C., 457, 467, 477
Solomon, R. L., 185
Sommer, R. F., 70
Sonnenstuhl, W. J., 293, 297
Sorcher, M., 37, 405, 408
Sourentian, J., 479
Spangle, R., 434
Sprangers, M., 180
Stackel, L., 145
Stark, F. A., 31
Staw, B. M., 40
Steck, R. N., 237
Steel, R. P., 34, 434, 435
Steele, P. D., 316
Steers, R. M., 207, 208

Steger, J. A., 371, 373–380
Steiner, D. D., 38
Steinmetz, C. S., 3, 4
Sternberg, R. J., 79
Sterns, H. L., 72, 73
Stone, D. L., 282
Stone, J.A.F., 354
Stone, N., 19
Storey, W. D., 327
Straudenmeier, W. J., Jr., 297
Streufert, S., 190
Strube, M. J., 397
Stum, D. L., 253
Sullivan, S. E., 206, 301, 302
Super, D. E., 326, 334
Sutton, E. E., 380
Swanson, N. G., 292, 299, 300
Swanson, R. A., 191
Symonds, W. C., 288

Tajen, C., 59
Tang, T. L., 435
Tannebaum, S. I., 254
Tarrant, S. M., 432
Taylor, C., 348
Taylor, C. W., 59
Taylor, M. S., 62, 406
Terborg, J. R., 289, 305, 308, 311, 312
Tersine, R. J., 299, 300
Tesolowski, D. G., 105
Tetrick, L. E., 301
Thayer, P. W., 61, 63, 94, 99, 103, 110
Thomas, Clarence, 96
Thomas, D. A., 353
Thomas, P. C., 309
Thomas, R. Roosevelt, Jr., 466, 467, 470, 478
Thompson, B. L., 248
Thompson, D. E., 26, 26, 34
Thompson, M. P., 256
Thompson, P. H., 325
Thorndike, E. L., 38, 55, 62, 65
Thornton, C. L., 62
Thornton, G. C., 150, 151, 350
Tichy, N. M., 391, 392, 441
Tollison, P., 436
Toomey, E. L., 258
Tornow, W. W., 375
Tosi, H., 301
Townsend, T. M., 434
Trahan, W. A., 38
Trice, H. M., 292, 293, 297–300, 315, 316
Tubiana, J. H., 59
Tucker, R., 348, 349
Tullar, W. L., 406

Usher, C. J., 116

Van Maanen, J., 205–207, 210–215, 325
Vasilash, G. S., 249

Vaughn, J. A., 141
Vecchio, R. P., 39, 46, 205
Velocci, A. L., Jr., 437
Verney, T., 434
Versteeg, A., 255, 438
Viega, J. F., 268, 271
Villanova, P., 404
Villet, J., 97
Von Glinow, M. A., 46, 456, 457, 461,
    463, 477, 478
Vroom, V. H., 29

Wagner, W. G., 300
Wagner, W. W., 62
Wahba, M. A., 29
Wakabayashi, M., 46
Waldersee, R., 299, 300, 301, 313,
    315
Walker, Barbara, 466
Walker, J. W., 289, 348, 349
Wall, P., 294, 299
Wall, T. D., 439
Wallin, J. A., 59
Walsh, D. C., 297
Walton, E., 10, 414, 419, 425
Walton, R. E., 428, 429
Wanous, J. P., 31, 108, 210, 211, 213,
    217–221
Warr, P., 170
Warren, E. K., 354
Washburn, S. Z., 238
Watkins, B. T., 144
Watson, J. B., 38
Weick, K. E., Jr., 370
Weiner, B., 37, 270
Weinstein, C., 76
Weisbord, 444

Weiss, R. M., 293, 300, 316, 355
Weitz, B. A., 334, 357
Wellins, R. S., 252
Wentz, D. K., 257
Wertheimer, M., 55
Wexley, K. N., 59, 62, 63, 64, 66, 99,
    103, 104, 151, 154, 169, 280–282,
    371, 392, 401, 402, 406
White, R. P., 351, 416
Whitely, W., 353
Wigginhorn, 251
Wilber, C. S., 308
Wilcox, D. S., 281, 282
Williams, K., 48
Wilson, L. S., 240
Wilson, Mike, 452, 480
Wircenski, J. L., 109
Wittock, M., 145
Wolfe, J., 148, 149, 150, 151, 371, 393,
    395
Wood, R. E., 270
Woodman, R. W., 415, 417, 420
Woodworth, R. S., 65
Wrich, J. T., 299
Wright, C. C., 309

Yourtz, M. A., 459, 461, 477
Yukl, G., 254, 281

Zaslow, R., 241
Zedeck, S., 404
Zellner, W., 288
Zemke, R., 392
Zenger, J. H., 168
Ziegler, R. J., 3
Zimmerle, D. M., 168
Zwerling, C., 293, 294

SUBJECT INDEX

AACSB. See American Assembly of
    Colleges and Schools of Business
    (AACSB)
AAPs. See Affirmative action programs
    (AAPs)
Abilities, 41–43
    defined, 41
    training and, 57–59
    See also KSAs
Absenteeism
    employee counseling/EAPs and, 198,
        288, 293–295
    health promotion and, 309, 310

orientation and, 225
self-directed teams (SDTs) and, 439
stress and, 302
substance abuse and, 298
Abstract conceptualization (AC), 74, 75
AC. See Abstract conceptualization
    (AC)
Acceptance, as reward, 47
Access discrimination, 459, 460
Accidents, 293, 298
Accommodative learning, 75
Accountability, 8, 169, 197
    self-directed teams (SDTs) and, 439

ACE/PONSI. *See* American Council on Education Program on Non-collegiate Sponsored Instruction (ACE/PONSI)

ACG. *See* Alexander Consulting Group (ACG); Associated General Contractors (ACG)

Achievement motivation training, 29

Acquisitions, 346, 443–444
  See also Large systems change

ACT* theory, 78–79

Action learning, 395

Action plan, 426–427, 429

Active experimentation (AE), 74, 75

Active listening, coaching and, 279

Active practice, 60

ACTWU. *See* Amalgamated Clothing and Textile Workers Union (ACTWU)

ADEPT, 281

Adjustment adaptation, 474, 475

Adult development, 329–334
  mentoring and, 351

Advancement, 325
  baby boom generation and, 359
  glass ceiling and, 459
  potential for, 349–350

Adviser (in career development), 340

Advocate, 424, 425

AE. *See* Active experimentation (AE)

Aetna, 21

Affective learning strategies, 76

Affirmative action programs (AAPs), 18, 464–466, 469, 479
  career development and, 360, 478
  at Digital Equipment Corporation (DEC), 467
  glass ceiling and, 459

African Americans, 475. *See also* Blacks

Africans, 475

Age
  career development and, 329–334
  motivation and, 73
  training/learning and, 68–70, 72–73
  transitions, 332–333

Alcohol abuse
  employee counseling/EAPs for, 291, 293–294, 300, 313
  Rehabilitation Act and, 314
  See also Substance abuse

Alcoholics Anonymous (AA), 295, 300

Alderfer's ERG theory. *See* Existence, relatedness, and growth (ERG) theory

ALDO, 154

Alertness, learning and, 76

Alexander & Alexander Consulting Group, 198

Alexander Consulting Group (ACG), 123–124, 161–162

Allstate Insurance, 281

Alpha changes, 421, 422

Alternative identifier, 424

Alternative work schedules (AWS), 417, 432, 433
  cultural diversity and, 479

AMA. *See* American Management Association (AMA)

Amalgamated Clothing and Textile Workers Union (ACTWU), 240, 447

American Assembly of Colleges and Schools of Business (AACSB), 251, 387, 388

American Can Company, 444

American Council on Education Program on Non-collegiate Sponsored Instruction (ACE/PONSI), 256

American Institute of Managing Diversity, 466

American Management Association (AMA), 70, 375, 389–390

American Productivity and Quality Center, 438

American Society for Training and Development (ASTD), 6, 8, 17–18
  Award for Excellence, 20
  HRD evaluation models and, 172
  Models for Excellence study of, 109

Americans with Disabilities Act (ADA), 314–315

Analytic needs, 94

Andragogy, 68–70, 72

Announcements (for HRD program), 156

Anticipatory socialization, 210–211, 218

Anxiety
  criticism and, 282
  hazing by co-workers and, 226
  orientation and, 222, 225
  relaxation exercises for, 303
  stress and, 301, 303
  See also Test anxiety

Apple Computer, Inc., 204, 468

Apple Training Support (ATS), 204, 229–231

Applications training, 246

Appraiser (in career development), 340

Apprenticeship, 3, 19, 243–245
  in Germany, 19, 236

Apprenticeship 2000, 245

Aptitude tests, 240

Architect, manager as, 385

Archival performance data, 177

Armco Steel, 451–452, 469, 479–480
  "consulting pairs" at, 477, 480

Arousal, motivation and, 26

Arthur Andersen & Company (AA), 1–2, 20

Artifacts, 453–454

Artificial intelligence, 154

Asians, 459, 461, 473, 475
  population growth of, 462–463

Assembly line, 4

Assertiveness training, 302, 303
Assessment centers, 113, 341, 349–350
Assimilation, 75
Associated General Contractors (ACG), 247
Association, 55
Association of Flight Attendants, 299, 315
Assumptions, 76–77, 78
ASTD. See American Society for Training and Development (ASTD)
AT&T, 23–24, 48–49
    assessment center at, 350
    breakup of, 380
    career development at, 341
    EAPs at, 294
    large systems change at, 444, 445
    Management Progress Study at, 373
    total quality management (TQM) at, 447
    training at, 145
ATI. See Attribute-treatment interaction (ATI)
Atlanta Marquis Hotel, 241
Atomic Energy of Canada Limited, 444
Attending skills, coaching and, 279, 280
Attention, learning and, 57, 72
Attitude surveys, 112, 429
    cultural diversity and, 470
Attitudes
    career development and, 326
    career plateaus and, 356, 357
    career/job, 40
    change theory and, 416
    cultural diversity and, 469, 470, 473
    employee behavior model and, 25, 39–41
    leadership and, 46
    learning and, 54, 57, 59–60, 80–82
    modeling and, 407
    organization development (OD) and, 419
    orientation and, 222, 225
    quality circles and, 434
    skills assessment feedback and, 40
    sociotechnical interventions and, 440
Attribute-treatment interaction (ATI), 68, 72
Attribution theory, 27, 37–38
    See also Causal attribution theory; Fundamental attribution error
Audiovisual aids, 142–148
    employee counseling/EAPs and, 289
Authority
    baby boom generation and, 359, 361
    line vs. staff, 8
    self-directed teams (SDTs) and, 437, 439
Authority-Obedience, 400
Autocratic style, 88
Autonomy, 356, 359, 361
    change theory and, 416

job enrichment and, 431
self-directed teams (SDTs) and, 437, 439
    See also Semiautonomous groups
Avon, 468, 469, 470, 478
Awareness, 249
    cultural diversity and, 471, 473, 474
    of discrimination, 452, 466–467, 480
    large systems change and, 446, 471
    self-. See Self-awareness
    self-directed teams and, 438
AWS. See Alternative work schedules (AWS)

Baby boom, 289, 359–360, 361
Bachelor's degree programs, 387–388
Baldwin Locomotive, 4
Basic Skills Education Program (BSEP), 240
Basic skills/literacy education, 155, 237, 238–243
BAT. See Bureau of Apprenticeship and Training (BAT)
Behavior
    attitudes and, 40
    attribution theory and, 37–38
    change theory and, 416
    consistency of, 279
    environment and, 37, 43–48
    individual. See Individual behavior
    job design and, 47
    in learning, vs. cognition, 54
    learning to change, 54
    organization development (OD) and, 419
    patterns of, 454
    social learning theory and, 36–37
    See also Employee/job behavior
Behavior modeling. See Modeling
Behavior modification, 38–39
    videotape used in, 144
Behavioral intentions model, 40, 41
Behavioral science, 5
Behaviorism, 38–39
    learning and, 54
Benchmarking, 435, 446–447
Benchmarks (instrument for person analysis), 116–119
Benefits, 7, 223
Beta changes, 421, 422
Bias
    coaching and, 270–271
    cultural diversity and, 466, 469, 473
    in data for HRD evaluation, 179–181
    fundamental attribution error as, 270
    minorities and, 461. See also Discrimination organization development (OD) and, 419, 420
Biofeedback, 302
Black History Month, 476
Blacks, 18, 459, 461
    affirmative action and, 465

Blacks (continued)
    as percentage of new workers, 455
    training and, 460–461
    See also African Americans
Blue-collar employees, career development for, 357–358
Body language, 474, 475
Bonding, 226
Bonuses, 44, 47
BPX. See British Petroleum (BPX)
British culture, 475
British Petroleum (BPX), 324–325, 364–365
Brogden-Cronbach-Gleser model, 195–196
Buchanan's socialization model, 211
"Buddy system," 225, 226
Budgeting, 168, 438
Buffering response, 445
Builder, manager as, 385
Bureau of Apprenticeship and Training (BAT), 244
Burnout, career plateaus and, 357
Business Council for Effective Literacy, 238
Business HRD competencies, 15–16
Business managers, 385
Business strategy. See Strategic goals

CAI. See Computer-aided instruction (CAI)
Cambodians, 463, 475
Campbell Soup Company, 78, 154
Canon, 413, 414
Career, defined, 326
Career anchors, 356
Career development, 11, 14, 324–366
    affirmative action and, 478
    career identity, resilience, and insight in, 354, 355
    college/university courses in, 18
    counselor for, 14
    cultural diversity and, 468, 478–479
    defined, 326
    effective, 360–364
    enrichment in, 358–359
    glass ceiling and, 459
    human processual intervention and, 446
    minorities and, 461
    models for, 362–363
    for nonexempt employees, 357–358
    plateaus in, 334, 336, 354–357
    practices and activities in, 340–353
    stages of, 328–336
    subprocesses in, 340–342
    See also Management development
Career grid approach, 349
Career management, 11, 327–328, 337–340
    career motivation and, 354
Career obsolescence, 336

Career outcomes, leadership and, 46
Career path, 341, 347, 348–349
    at BPX, 364
    dual, 324, 341, 364–365
    political/traditional vs. job/behavioral approach to, 348
Career planning, 11, 327, 328, 344–345
    counseling for, 346
    management development and, 373
Career plateaus, 334, 336, 354–357
Career/job attitudes, 40
Case study, 65, 113, 148–150
    for HRD evaluation, 181, 182
Causal attribution theory, 37, 269, 270
Causality, 419
Cause-and-effect diagram, 250
CBT. See Computer-based training
CE. See Concrete experience (CE)
Celebration, 436
Center for Creative Leadership (CCL), 390, 393
Center for Professional Education (CPE), 2, 20
Central States Health & Life Company of Omaha, 287–288
Central tendency error, 403
Certification programs, 359
Chalkboards, 143
Champion, manager as, 385
Change, 413–448
    action plan for, 426–427
    attitudes and, 80
    career development and, 325, 338, 360
    cognitive levels of, 421–422
    cultural diversity and, 468, 469, 470–473
    enrichment and, 359
    evaluating strategy for, 472–473
    forced, 421, 470
    learning and, 54
    macro vs. micro, 10
    planned. See Planned change
    predictions for year 2000 regarding, 19
    resistance to, 426
    size, depth, pervasiveness of, 443
    See also Employee/job behavior, changing; Organizational change; Organization development (OD)
Change agent, 14, 415–416, 423–425
    action plan and, 427
    cultural diversity and, 471
    OD intervention and, 11, 14
    survey feedback and, 429
    team building and, 430
    total quality management (TQM) and, 437
Change and acquisition (in socialization), 213
Change committee, 425
Change manager, 421, 423, 425

action plan and, 427
cultural diversity and, 470
large systems change and, 445
self-directed teams and, 437
survey feedback and, 429
team building and, 430
total quality management (TQM) and, 436
Change process theory, 415–416
Charts, 12, 141, 250
Child-care programs, 18, 479
Children's World Learning Centers (CWLC), 370–371, 409
Chinese, population growth of, 462
Chrysler Corporation, 239, 444
CIPP model, 170, 172
Circle leader, 434
CIRO model, 170, 172–173
CIT. See Critical incident technique (CIT)
Civil rights movement, 463, 464–466
Civil Service Reform Act, 382
Classroom training, 109, 140–155, 159
on-the-job training (OJT) combined with, 246–247
for skills training, 242
CLC. See Center for Creative Leadership (CCL)
Climate, organizational, 95, 96, 97, 100
for training, 160
career development and, 360
career plateaus and, 357
realistic job preview and, 220
Climate survey, 429
Closed questions, 279, 280
Coaching, 140, 264–285
analysis, 269–274
in career development, 340, 364
closed questions and, 279, 280
constructive criticism in, 282
defined, 10, 266–267
discussion and, 274–277
effective or superior performance and, 273–274, 277–278
effectiveness of, 281–284
employee counseling/EAPs and, 289
expectations and, 45
human processual intervention and, 446
person analysis and, 113
poor performance and, 264, 268–277
supervisors and, 11
Cocaine addiction, 290–291, 294
Cognition/cognitive strategies, in learning, 54, 57, 80–82
Cognitive evaluation theory, 27
rewards and, 47
Cognitive levels of OD, 421–422
Cognitive restructuring, 415–416
Cognitive theories of motivation, 26, 27, 29–39
Collaboration, 385, 386

by change agent, 424
Collaborative learning, 82
"Collar line," 358
Colleges/universities, 10, 18, 145
basic skills/literacy programs at, 240
continuing education of professionals at, 255–256
executive M.B.A. programs at, 387–390
interpersonal skills training at, 251
total quality management (TQM) and, 437
See also Company "colleges"
Commitment
coaching and, 279
employee counseling/EAPs and, 293
expectations and, 207
internal, 416
leader-member exchange (LMX) and, 402
management development and, 408
managing diversity and, 468, 470–471
organization development (OD) and, 422
organizational culture and, 454
orientation and, 225
realistic job preview and, 218
self-directed teams (SDTs) and, 439
stress and, 301
Commitment planning, 471
Communication
career development and, 362
coaching and, 278–279
cultural diversity and, 469
discussion method as two-way, 142
employee counseling/EAPs and, 293
large systems change and, 444
lecture as one-way, 141
management development and, 378, 388
networks, 238
non-English-speaking employees and, 479
nonverbal, 474, 475
oral, 388
persuasive, 378
quality circles and, 435
self-directed teams and, 438
skills, training in, 251
stress and, 302
total quality management (TQM) and, 436
Company "colleges," 391–392
Compensation, 7
career plateaus and, 357
orientation and, 223
See also Pay; Salary
Competence
career paths and, 364
core, 120

Competence *(continued)*
 instructional psychology and, 56, 57
 technostructural intervention and,
  446
 See also HRD professionals, competencies of; Management, roles and
  competencies; Workplace competencies
Competition, global, 18–19
Component task achievement, 56
Comprehension monitoring learning
 strategies, 76
Compressed workweek, 432
Computer-aided instruction (CAI),
 153–154, 155
Computer-based training (CBT), 39, 75,
 78–79, 152–155
 conferencing in, 145, 147
 selecting, 131, 152–155
 slides used in, 143
Computers
 Basic Skills Education Program
  (BSEP) and, 240
 in career development, 342, 344,
  358
 database, 349
 integrated networks and, 246
 training programs, 240, 245–246
 See also Information systems
  (IS)/technology
"Computers in Training," 152
Concrete experience (CE), 74, 75
Conditions, objectives and, 126–127
Conferences, 113, 145
 See also Teleconferencing
Confidence, attribution theory and, 38
Confidentiality
 in employee counseling/EAPs, 293,
  296, 316–317
 in HRD evaluation research, 189
Confrontation
 change theory and, 416
 constructive, 297, 300
 presenting and, 276
Consistency of behavior, 279
Consolidation, 401
Constructive confrontation, 297, 300
Constructive criticism, 282
"Consulting pairs," 477–478, 480
Consultive STS programs, 440
Content innovation role orientation, 215
Contiguity, 55, 80
Contingency approach, to learning, 72
Contingency theory (Fiedler's), 396–397
Continuing education, 20, 255–258
"Continuum of care," 292
Contrast error, 403
Contributor, manager as, 385
Control
 change theory and, 416
 locus of, 72
 management and, 378

rewards perceived as mechanisms
 for, 47
 span of, 88
Control Data, 256, 308
Control group, 183, 184, 186–187
 ethical issues regarding, 188–189
 Out-groups, 402
 at McDonnell Douglas, 198–199
Convergent learning, 75
Cooker Maintenance Advisor, 78–79
Cooperative agreements, 428
Coordinator, manager as, 385
Coping effect, 217
Core competencies, 120
Core groups, 467, 468
Corning, Inc., 224, 226, 227, 228–229
 career development at, 358
 cultural diversity at, 466
Corporate managers, 385
Costs
 cultural diversity and, 469
 effectiveness evaluation, 191–195
 of employee counseling/EAPs, 293,
  301, 318
 orientation and, 225
 total quality management (TQM) and,
  447
 of training/HRD programs, 190–197
Counseling
 career development, 14
 crisis, 296
 defined, 10
 See also Employee counseling
Country Club Management, 400
Country managers, 385
Co-workers/peers
 employee behavior model and, 25
 as environmental influence, 47–48
 group dynamics and, 48
 mentoring and resentment from, 352
 mentoring replaced by relationships
  with, 353
 orientation and, 225, 225, 226, 230
 stress and, 304
 substance abuse and, 298
Crafting, 359, 361
Creating hierarchy (in learning), 76
Creativity
 employee counseling and, 288
 organizational roles and, 207
 tuition reimbursement and, 258
Credibility
 coaching and, 282–283
 HRD evaluation and, 168
 See also Integrity
Crisis counseling, 296
Critical incident technique (CIT), 104, 113
Criticism, constructive, 282
Cross-cultural interaction, 385, 386
Cross-cultural training, 18, 446
Cross-functional teams, 254
Cross-pollinating, 385

Cultural diversity, 451–481
  at Armco Steel, 451–452, 469, 477,
    479–480
  awareness of, 471, 473
  backlash to programs regarding,
    469–470
  defined, 463
  effectiveness of programs regarding,
    469
  evaluating programs regarding,
    472–473
  potential problems with programs
    regarding, 476
  sample program regarding, 472
  training and, 251
Cultural sensitivity, 18, 19
Culture. *See* Organizational culture
Custodial orientation, 206–207, 215,
  216
Customer loyalty, 252
Customer quality, 249
Customer service training, 252–254
Customers, self-directed teams (SDTs)
  and, 439
CWLC. *See* Children's World Learning
  Centers (CWLC)

Data collection
  cultural diversity and, 470
  in HRD evaluation, 168, 174–180
  for needs assessment, 94–119
  See also Information
Database, 349
Dayton-Hudson, 21
Decision making
  convergent learning and, 75
  employee counseling/EAPs and, 288,
    294
  groupthink and, 48
  in HRD evaluation, 168
  management development and, 388
  total quality management (TQM) and,
    436
Decision-support systems, 238
Declarative knowledge, 78
"Defender" corporate strategy, 357
Deming's fourteen principles, 417, 418,
  446
Democratic needs, 94
Demographic changes, 454, 463–470
  See also Labor market, changing
  nature of Descriptive information, 167
Design/implementation phase, 89–90,
  123–162
  in orientation program, 228, 230
  purchasing guidance in, 128
Developer, manager as, 385
Development cycle, 380, 381
Development Dimensions International
  (DDI), 131
Development Partnership, 380–381
Developmental activities, 10

Developmental needs, 115
Devised situations, 113
Diagnostic needs, 94
Diagnostic person analysis, 110
Diagnostic rating, 113
Diaries, 113
Digital Equipment Corporation (DEC), 444
  cultural diversity at, 466–467, 468,
    469
  mentoring at, 457
  total quality management (TQM) at,
    435
Direct observation, 177, 180
Direct questions, 142
Directing, management and, 378
Direction, motivation and, 26
Disciplinary actions, 44, 45, 275
DISCOVER, 342
Discrimination, 452, 480
  access and treatment types of,
    459–461
  Equal employment opportunity (EEO)
    and, 464
  reverse, 465
  See also Racism/racial discrimina-
    tion; Sexism/gender-based dis-
    crimination
Discussion, 142, 404
  employee counseling/EAPs and, 289
  for potential assessment, 350
Dissatisfaction, 28
Divergent learning, 75
Diversity, work force, 8, 18. *See also*
  Cultural diversity
Doing (as learning style), 74, 75
Domino's Pizza, 145
Donnelly Mirrors, Inc., 438
Downsizing, 442, 444, 446
  at AT&T, 24, 48
  career development and, 358–359
  employee counseling/EAPs and, 289,
    346
  enrichment and, 358
  outplacement and, 346
  at Scott Paper Company, 88
  total quality management (TQM) and,
    437
  See also Large systems change
"Dream," 332–333, 335
Driving forces, 415
Drug abuse
  legal issues in, 314–315
  See also Substance abuse
Drug/urine testing, 293, 314
Dual career paths, 324, 341, 364–365
Duke Power Company, 251
Dunkin' Donuts, 140, 391
DuPont, 478
Dynamic media, 143–144

East Indians, 475
Eastman Kodak, 239

Economy, 96, 443
  minorities and, 460
Education, 18–19
  career development and, 341
  continuing, 20, 255–258
  cultural diversity and, 467, 468, 471,
    473–476
  deficiencies in, 289. See also
    Illiteracy
  in employee counseling/EAPs, 290
  health promotion and, 308
  management. See Management
    education
  self-directed teams and, 438
  stress and, 302
  See also Training
Educational interventions, 303–304
Educator, 424, 425
Effectiveness
  of HRD program, 166–167, 169, 191
  large systems change and, 444
  management, 382, 383, 384
  management development and, 370
  organization development (OD) and,
    414, 422
  organizational roles and, 207
  of orientation programs, 229
  quality circles and, 434
  utility analysis and, 197
Efficiency
  benchmarking for, 447
  organization development (OD) and,
    422
Efficiency indexes, 97, 101
Effort, social learning theory and, 36
Ego integrity, 330
Elaboration learning strategies, 76
Elder care, 479
Electrolux, 385
Electronic mail, 238
EMBA. See Executive M.B.A. (EMBA)
  programs
Embarrassment, 44, 45
Employee assistance programs (EAPs),
  292–301
  conceptual framework of, 295
  effectiveness of, 299–301
  evaluating, 313–314
  large systems change and, 446
  legal issues regarding, 314–315
  Masi's model for, 295–296
  at McDonnell Douglas, 165, 198–199
  typical one, 297, 298
  See also Employee counseling
Employee counseling, 110, 14, 288–320
  in career development, 341, 346–347
  components of, 290–291
  effectiveness of, 292–293, 312–314
  ethical issues in, 316–317
  legal issues in, 314–315
  preretirement. See Preretirement
    counseling

providers of, 291–292
  responsibility for, 315–316
  voluntary vs. mandatory, 317
  See also Employee assistance pro-
    grams (EAPs)
Employee manual, 132, 157, 223, 242
Employee orientation. See Orientation
Employee participation, 281. See also
  Participative management
Employee/job behavior, 2–50
  changing, 275, 282, 308
  health promotion and, 310
  HRD evaluation of, 171
  model of, 25
  orientation and, 222
  pivotal, relevant, and peripheral,
    207
  poor performance and, 268–277
  supervisors' effect on, 46
  supervisors' observations of, 175
  See also Behavior; Group norms
Employee/job involvement, 325
  stress and, 301
  training and, 254
Employee-employer relations, 7, 9
Employees, well-being of, 414, 422
Employment, participation rate of, 455
Empowerment, 417
  quality circles and, 434
  self-directed teams and, 437
Encoding, 57
Encounter stage (of socialization),
  211–212, 222, 225
Encouragement, 393
Energizing, motivation and, 26
Energy level, 379
"Energy malady," 257
English-as-second-language (ESL),
  238
Enrichment, 358–359
Entrepreneurship
  baby boom generation and, 360, 361,
    361
  tuition reimbursement and, 258
Environment
  and behavior, 37, 43–48
  career development and, 360
  change theory and, 415
  constraints of, 95, 96
  diagnosing, 425–426
  employee behavior model and, 25
  external, 25
  internal, 25, 26–39
  learning and, 54, 56, 60, 66
  physical, 159–160
  strategic change and, 443
  support in work, 64, 66
Equal employment opportunity (EEO), 7,
  18, 96, 464–466, 469
  career development and, 360
  glass ceiling and, 458, 459
Equity theory, 27, 39, 44

Eras (Levinson's approach), 330–334, 351
ERG theory. *See* Existence, relatedness, and growth (ERG) theory
Erikson's model of adult development, 329–330
ESL. *See* English-as-second-language (ESL)
Ethics, in HRD evaluation research, 188–190
Ethnic minorities. *See* Minorities
European culture, 475
European manufacturers, 236
Evaluation
    career development and, 342, 362
    defined, 167
    of employee counseling/EAPs, 292
    of HRD and training, 90–91
    management and, 378
    management development and, 408
    organization development (OD) and, 419, 427–428
    phase, in orientation program, 228, 231
Evaluator, 14
"Events" approach, 393–394, 395
Executive M.B.A. (EMBA) programs, 373, 387, 388–390
    evaluation of, 168
Exercise, physical, 302, 304, 309–310
Existence, relatedness, and growth (ERG) theory, 27–28
Expectancy theory, 27, 29–32, 39
    change theory and, 416
    perception of outcomes in, 44
    rewards and, 47
Expectations
    attribution and 37
    career development and, 334
    change theory and, 416
    coaching and, 45
    defined, 207
    orientation and, 222, 223
    realistic job preview and, 217
    self-fulfilling prophecy and, 45
    socialization and, 207–208, 216, 217
Experience
    concrete, 74, 75
    life, 75, 354
    on-the-job, 371, 373, 390, 392–396
    openness to, 59
    potential lessons of, 394
    See also On-the-job experience
Experiential learning/training, 82, 148–152
Experimental designs, 183–186, 419
Extinction, 39
Extraversion, 59
Eye contact, 279, 280, 475

Facilitator, 11, 14, 434, 435
    cultural diversity and, 480

discussion method of training and, 142
Fact finder, 424, 425
Factory schools, 4
Family, work vs., 360, 361
Family-leave policies, 18
Fayol's management functions, 374
Federal Express, 21, 351
Federal Quality Institute, The, 437
Feedback
    andragogy and, 72
    from assessment center, 350
    for behavior modeling, 406
    career development and, 338–340
    career plateaus and, 356
    coaching, 270, 271, 279, 280
    criticism as, 282
    informational vs. motivational, 62
    job enrichment and, 431
    learning and, 62, 68
    modeling and, 37
    outcomes in equity theory as, 44
    in rater training, 404
    skills assessment, 40
    survey. *See* Survey feedback
    total quality management (TQM) and, 436
Feeling (as learning style), 74, 75
Fiedler's contingency theory, 396–397
Feldman's socialization model, 210–213
Feminist movement, 463
Filipinos, 475
Film (in training), 143, 144, 405, 407
Final report, 109
First Amendment, cultural diversity and, 469
Fitness programs, 10, 257, 291, 305–310
    legal issues regarding, 315
    See also Health; Physical exercise; Wellness programs
Flexible work schedules, 479
Flextime, 432
"Flypaper approach," 217
Focus groups, 254, 470
Focusing, coaching and, 279, 280
Force field analysis, 416, 425–426
Forced change, 421, 470
Ford Motor Company, 4, 20, 88–89
    basic skills/literacy program at, 239, 240
    total quality management (TQM) at, 447
    University of Michigan and, 390
Foreign experience, 385, 386
Foreign subsidiaries, 460
Fortune 500 companies
    computer training programs among, 245–246
    stress management training at, 257
    women and, 456
Fortune 1000 companies, 438, 461

Four-dimensional model (management), 375–380, 381
Four-group design, 185
Free choice, 416
French, 475
Functional managers, 385
Functions of the Executive, The, 5
Fundamental attribution error, 270
Futurists, 388

Gagné-Briggs theory, 79–82
Gains-sharing programs, 254
Games, business, 65, 113, 150
Gamma changes, 421, 422
Gatekeeper, trainer as, 142
GED. *See* General Education Development (GED) examination
General Dynamics, 244
General Education Development (GED) examination, 240
General Electric (GE), 4, 145, 438
    management development at, 391
    strategic change by, 443, 444
General Foods, 258
General Mills, 438
General Motors, 444
    EAPs at, 294
    Saturn division of. *See* Saturn division of General Motors
General principles theory, 64, 65
Generalization, in modeling, 406
Generativity, 330, 333
Georgia State University, 389
German culture, 475
German manufacturers, 19, 236
Germany, 19
Gerontology, 72–73
Gestalt psychologists, 55
Glass ceiling, 456–459, 463, 474
    affirmative action and, 466
Global economy, 18–19
    management development in, 382, 385–387
    multiculturalism and, 463
Global perspective, 385, 386
Goal setting, 27, 39
    career development and, 338, 339
    coaching and, 10, 277
    stress and, 304
    See also Objectives; Organizational goals; Performance goals
Goodwill Industries, 241
Goodyear Tire & Rubber, 4, 281, 309
Government employees, 240, 314–315
Greenhaus's model of career development, 334–336
Grid.® *See* Managerial Grid
Group dynamics, 48
Group norms, 48, 207, 217
    change theory and, 416
    human processual intervention and, 446

for mentoring women, 458
    orientation and, 222
    subjective, 40
Grouping information (in learning strategy), 76
Groups
    core, 467, 468
    "in" vs. "out," 46, 402, 461
    semiautonomous, 417, 439
    size, and social loafing, 48
    survey feedback and, 429
    total quality management (TQM) and, 436
    training and, 160
    See also Quality circle (QC); Teams
Groupthink, 48
Growth need, 432
GTE, 478
Guaranteed Eateries, 252
GUIDON, 62
Gulf Oil, 341

Hackman and Oldham's model, 47, 431
Halo error, 115, 403, 404
Hamburger University, 140, 391
Handouts, 141, 143
Handshake, 475
Hazing, 226
Health, employee, 288, 289, 302
    and costs, 198, 288, 309, 318
    See also Fitness; Insurance benefits; Wellness programs
Health promotion programs (HHPs), 305–312, 318
    legal issues regarding, 315
Herzberg's two factor theory, 27, 28, 29, 47
Hewlett Packard, 145, 447
HHPs. *See* Health promotion programs (HHPs)
Hierarchy of needs, 27–28
High schools, 237–238, 245
Hispanics, 459, 461, 475
    economic status of, 460
    as percentage of new workers, 455
    population growth of, 462
    training and, 460–461
    See also Latino workers; Spanish-speaking workers
Histogram, 250
History, 187
Hoe and Company, 4
Hoffman-LaRoche Inc., 390
Holiday Inn, 391
Honeywell, 444
HRD administrator, 14
HRD advisory committee, 119
HRD evaluation, *defined,* 167. *See also* Training/HRD programs, evaluating
HRD materials developer, 14
HRD professionals, 11–21
    academia and, 17–18

career development and, 325, 334, 357–358
certification and education for, 16–17
challenges to, 18–20
as change agent, 423, 427
coaching and, 267–268
competencies of, 14–17, 160
continuing education and, 257–258
cultural diversity and, 471, 476
employee counseling/EAPs and, 289
evaluation by, 91
job-duty-task method applied to job of, 107
large systems change and, 445–446
minorities and, 463
needs assessment by, 90, 92
organization development (OD) and, 427–428
orientation and, 226
roles of, 11, 13, 14
sociotechnical systems (STS) designs and, 440
women and, 459
See also Training/HRD programs
HRIS. See Human resource information system (HRIS)
HRM (human resource management), 6–8
career development and, 360, 363
coaching analysis and, 271
cultural diversity and, 471, 479
employee counseling/EAPs and, 297
global managers and, 385–386
Hudson Institute, 18, 238, 452
See also Work Force 2000
Human processual intervention, 416, 428–430, 446
technostructural vs., 433
Human relations movement, 5
Human resource allocation, 340, 342, 360
Human resource development (HRD). See entries beginning HRD; Training/HRD programs
Human Resource Development Quarterly, 17–18
Human Resource Development: The New Trainer's Guide, 161
Human resource information system (HRIS), 115
Human resource management. See HRM (human resource management)
Human resource planning, 7, 348
Human resource wheel, 9–10
Hygiene factors, 28
HyperCard, 230
Hypertension, 311–312

IBM, 20, 145, 390, 444
child care and elder care at, 479
company academy/college at, 391
skills training at, 247

total quality management (TQM) at, 447
ICAI. See Intelligent computer-assisted instruction (ICAI)
Ice-breaker exercise, 160
Ideas, convergent learning and, 75
Identical elements, 64, 65
Identity, 330, 335, 354, 355
career plateaus and, 356
Illiteracy, 239–240
See also Basic skills/literacy programs
Image
company/organizational, 288, 361
self-(occupational), 335
Imagination, divergent learning and, 75
Immediacy, coaching and, 279
Immigration, 238, 461–463
Implementation theory, 416–419
Impoverished Management, 400
In-basket exercise, 150–151
Incentives, 253–254. See also Rewards
Individual behavior
cultural diversity and, 468
human processual intervention and, 446
motivation as part of, 26
organization development (OD) and, 421, 422
Individualism, 393
Indochinese, 462
Indonesians, 463
Industrial democratization, 417
Industrial gerontology, 72–73
Industrial psychology, 18
Influencing, management and, 378
Information
career development and, 341, 347
career plateaus and, 356
descriptive and judgmental, 167
in employee counseling/EAPs, 290
in employee orientation, 203–204, 223, 225. See also Information overload
for HRD evaluation, 167–168
job posting as source of, 348
valid, 416
See also Data
Information overload, 227–228
Information processing models, 57
Information systems (IS)/technology, 8, 237, 238
Informed consent, 189
In-groups, 46, 402
Innovation, management and, 379
Innovative orientation, 207, 215, 216
Insight, 55
Instructional psychology, 56, 78–82
Instructional television, 144–145
Instructor, 14
Instrumentality, 30, 31, 36, 44
Instrumentation, in HRD evaluation, 187

Insurance benefits, 293. *See also* Health, employee
Integrated competency model, 375, 376–377, 380
Integrity
coaching and, 279
ego, 330
See also Credibility
Intellectual skills/competencies, 15, 17, 80–82
Intelligent computer-assisted instruction (ICAI), 154–155
Intentions, 40, 41
Interaction of selection and maturation/testing and training, 187
Interface development, 401
Interference, 63
Internal commitment, 416
Internal environment, motivation as part of, 26–39
Internal labor market, 343, 347–349
Internal Revenue Service, 351
Internal validity, 181, 182
International Harvester, 4
INTERNET, 145
Interpersonal skills
career plateaus and, 357
change theory and, 416
coaching and, 279
cultural diversity and, 467
as HRD competencies, 15, 16–17, 160
modeling and, 407
training in, 152, 251, 253
Intervention strategy, 414
designing, 422–428
human processual, 416, 428–430, 433, 446
large systems change, 417–419, 421, 440–446
quality circles, 417, 434–435
self-directed teams, 417, 437–439
sociotechnical systems, 417, 433–440, 446
survey feedback, 416, 428–429
team building, 401, 429–430
technostructural, 416–417, 430–433, 446
total quality management (TQM), 417, 435–437
types/theories of, 416–419, 428–446
Interview, 177. *See also* Performance appraisal
Intimacy, 330
Inventory. *See* Job inventory questionnaire; Manpower inventory; Skills inventory
Involvement. *See* Employee/job involvement
IS. *See* Information systems (IS)/technology

Japan, 19
Japanese culture, 473, 475
Japanese immigrants, 462–463
Japanese manufacturers, 235, 236
Japanese philosophy, 417
JCM. *See* Job characteristics model (JCM)
JCPenney, 145
JDS. *See* Job diagnostic survey (JDS)
JIT. *See* Job instruction training (JIT)
Job analysis, 101, 106
Job behavior. *See* Employee/job behavior
Job characteristics model (JCM), 431, 432
Job description, 120
career path and, 348
defined, 100
orientation and, 223
self-directed teams (SDTs) and, 439
task analysis and, 99, 100–103
Job design/redesign/enlargement, 7, 47, 431, 433
change theory and, 416–417
coaching and, 277
stress and, 304
Job diagnostic survey (JDS), 431
Job enlargement. *See* Job design/enlargement
Job enrichment, 28, 29, 417, 431–432
Job instruction training (JIT), 5, 138–139
Job inventory questionnaire, 105
Job involvement. *See* Employee/job involvement
Job placement exchanges, 343, 347–349
Job posting, 341, 347–348, 349
Job rotation, 10, 139–140
career development and, 341, 350–351, 359
career plateaus and, 357
management development and, 373
Job satisfaction, 28
attribution theory and, 37
career development and, 334, 335, 38, 358
employee counseling/EAPs and, 294
enrichment and, 359
flextime and, 432
human processual intervention and, 446
job design/enlargement and, 431
job enrichment and, 432
leader-member exchange (LMX) and, 402
leadership and, 46
organization development (OD) and, 414, 416, 417
organizational roles and, 206
orientation and, 225
self-directed teams (SDTs) and, 439
team building and, 430

Job security, career development and, 356, 359
Job specifications, 106, 348
Job tenure, 356
Job Training and Partnership Act (JTPA), 241–243
Job transfer, 44, 275, 359, 380
Job-duty-task method, 105, 106, 107
Job-search skills, 346
Johnson & Johnson, 308
Johnsonville Foods, 255, 438
Joint planning, 70
JTPA. See Job Training and Partnership Act (JTPA)
Judgmental information, 167

Kaiser Aluminum and Chemicals, 465
Kimberly Brothers Manufacturing Company, 350
Kimberly-Clark, 309
Kirkpatrick's model, 170–173, 190
Knowledge
    declarative vs. procedural, 78, 80
    defined,, 42
    learning and, 54
    in management, 375, 376
    of results of work, 431
    strategic, 80–82
    See also KSAs (knowledge, skills, and abilities); Education
Knowledge work, 9
Kodak. See Eastman Kodak
Kolb's learning styles, 73–75, 82, 375
Koreans, 475
KSAs (knowledge, skills, and abilities)
    career development and, 325
    developmental needs and, 115
    employee behavior model and, 25, 39, 41–43
    maintaining, 115
    management development and, 370, 371, 373, 388
    socialization and, 216, 217
    analysis and, 99, 101, 106–108
    training and, 10
    See also Management education

Labor contract, 439
Labor market, changing nature of, 452, 454–455, 468
Labor relations, 7, 288. See also Unions
Laborers' International Union, 247
Language comprehension, 57
Laotians, 463
Large systems change, 417–419, 421, 440–446
    cultural diversity and, 470–473
    organizational culture and, 441, 442
    strategic change and, 442–444
Latino workers, 18. See also Hispanics
Law of effect, 38, 55, 273
Layoffs, 443

aftermath of, 24
at AT&T, 23–24, 48
counseling for, 346
skills training and, 243
Leader Match, 396–397
Leader-Member Exchange (LMX) training, 396, 402
Leader-member relationships, 397
Leadership
    artifacts and, 454
    coaching and, 266, 267
    cultural diversity and, 468, 470
    diagnosing style of, 397, 399–400
    organizational culture and, 468
    performance and, 45–46
    See also Center for Creative Leadership; Leadership training
Leadership Grid. See Managerial Grid
Leadership training, 376, 379, 385, 388
    approaches to, 396–403
Learning
    action, 395
    attitudes and, 41
    audiovisual aids in, 145
    coaching analysis and, 273
    as cognitive process, 29
    contingency approach to, 72
    cultural diversity and, 477
    feedback in, 62, 68
    group dynamics and, 48
    HRD and, 53–84, 171
    individual differences in, 66–73
    instruction and, 54–57
    instructional psychology and, 78–82
    interference in, 63
    "just-in-time," 246
    "to learn," 54, 76, 82
    lifelong. See Lifelong learning
    maximizing, 57–66
    motivation and, 395
    multimedia centers for, 20
    orientation and, 226–227, 230
    original, 63
    plateaus in, 68
    principles of, 54–57
    self-questioning in, 76
    strategies and styles of, 73–77, 82
    synergistic, 385, 386
    training design and principles of, 56
    whole vs. part, 61, 63
    See also Education; Training
Learning curves, 67–68
Learning Management program, 82–83
Learning outcomes, 79–80
Learning points (in modeling), 405, 406
Learning strategies, 76–77
Learning Style Inventory (LSI), 75
Learning styles, 73–75, 82, 155
Least Preferred Co-Worker (LPC) scale, 397–399, 402
Lectures, 74, 141–142
    employee counseling/EAPs and, 289

Lectures *(continued)*
in rater training, 404
Legal environment/issues, 96, 314–315
Leniency error, 403, 404
Lesson plan, 132–136
Levinson' approach to adult development, 330–334, 351
Lewin's change model, 415–416
Life cycle/stages, in career development, 330, 336
Life experience, 75, 354
Lifelong learning, 19–20, 358, 360, 361
self-directed teams (SDTs) and, 439–440
Line authority, 8
LISP (computer language), 78, 154
List of tasks, 109
Listening skills
leader-member exchange (LMX) and, 402
See also Active listening
Literacy. *See* Basic skills/literacy education
"Living case" approach, 150, 395
LMX. *See* Leader-Member Exchange (LMX) training
Local responsiveness, 385, 386
Lockheed Marine, 358
Locus of control, learning and, 72
Long Island Railroad, 255
Long-term perspective/commitment, 393, 467–468
Looking Glass, Inc., 150
Loyalty, organizational culture and, 454
LPC scale. *See* Least Preferred Co-Worker (LPC) scale
LSI. *See* Learning Style Inventory (LSI)

Macy's Department Store, 289
Malcolm Baldrige National Quality Award, 436–437, 447
Management
difficulty in describing job of, 373
functions, 374, 376
models for, 374–380
roles and competencies, 373–387
"soft skills" of, 388
Management development, 10, 370–410
attitudes and, 40
behavior modeling in, 152
benchmark for, 371
cultural diversity and, 468
defined, 371
"events" in, 393–394, 395
in global economy, 382, 385–387
large systems change and, 446
leadership and, 46
percentage of organizations using different approaches to, 373
at Scott Paper Company, 88
"The Competency Program," 70
Management education, 373, 387–390

company "colleges"/courses for, 391–392
defined, 371
lacks in, 388
See also Education; Management training
Management Excellence Framework, 382
Management training, 373, 390–396
defined, 371
Management training and experiences (MTE), 371–372, 390–396
Managerial Grid, 396, 399–402
Managers
change. *See* Change managers
coaching by. *See* Coaching
first-level, and job rotation, 140
HRD professionals and, 13
minorities as, 480
types of global, 385–387
women as, 457, 458, 480
See also Supervisors; Top/senior management
Managing diversity, 467–468, 478
sample program for, 472
See also Cultural diversity
Manpower, Inc., 153, 409
Manpower inventory, 97, 100
Manuals, 132, 157, 223, 242
Maps, 141
Marijuana, 293, 294
Maritz, Inc., 236, 258
Marketer, 14
Martin Marietta Inc., 150
Maslow's need hierarchy theory, 27–28, 29
Mass production, 4
Massachusetts Institute of Technology (MIT), 390
Massed practice, 60–61, 63
Master's degree programs, 387–388
Mastery, modeling and, 406
Mastery paths, 359
Mattel, 341
Maturation, 187
M.B.A. education. *See* Executive M.B.A. programs
MBO, person analysis and, 113
McBer and Company, 75, 375
McClelland's need theory, 375
McDonald's, 140, 391, 392
McDonnell Douglas Corporation, 165, 198–199
McGregor's Theory Y philosophy, 267
Meaningfulness, 9, 63, 142
career development and, 359
job enrichment and, 431
Media
realistic job preview and, 219–221
static vs. dynamic, 142–143
Medical costs. *See* Health, employee; Insurance

Meditation, stress and, 302, 304
Mediterranean culture, 475
Memory, 57. *See also* Retention
Mental health, 198, 439
Mental image, 76
Mental/emotional health, 198, 439
    employee counseling/EAPs and, 288,
        289, 293–295
    stress and, 301
Mentoring, 140, 225, 341, 351
    cross-gender, 352–353, 458
    cross-racial, 352
    cultural diversity and, 468, 480
    at Digital Equipment Corporation
        (DEC), 467
    in management development, 373,
        394
    minorities and, 461, 468
    modeling and, 37
    women and, 457–458, 468
Mergers, 346, 443, 445. *See also* Large
    systems change
Meta-analysis, of organization develop-
    ment (OD), 420, 430, 432
Metropolitan Life Insurance Company,
    311, 347
Mexicans, 462, 475
Microsoft Word, 153
Microtraining, 279
Mid-career crisis/adjustment, 336, 351
Middle Easterners, 475
Middle of the Road Management, 400
Midlife transition, 333, 335–336
Miller Brewing Company, 153
Mind Extension University, 144
Minorities, 18, 459, 460–461, 479
    affirmative action and, 465, 479
    basic skills/literacy and, 238, 239
    glass ceiling and, 457
    immigration and, 461–463
    organizational culture and,
        459–463
    as percentage of new workers, 452,
        454–455
    training and, 160
Mintzberg's managerial roles, 374
Mission, 108
    career development and, 364
    large systems change and, 418
    orientation and, 223, 230
Mnemonic devices, 63
Model T car, 4
Model tracing, 78
Modeling, 37, 131, 152, 404–408
    coaching and, 280
    employee counseling/EAPs and, 289
    mentoring and, 352
    phases of, 405
Models for Excellence study, 109
Monitoring, employee counseling/EAPs
    and, 297
Monoculture, 454

Mono-method bias, 180
Morale
    downsizing and, 24, 444
    employee counseling and, 288
    job posting and, 348
    at Scott Paper Company, 88
    self-directed teams (SDTs) and, 439
Mortality, 187
Motivation, 26–39
    action learning and, 395
    andragogy and, 72
    attitudes and, 41–43
    career management and, 354
    career plateaus and, 356
    change theory and, 416
    coaching and, 273, 275, 282
    cognitive theories of, 26, 27, 29–38
    defined, 26
    employee behavior model and, 25
    factors in, 28
    job enrichment and, 431
    leadership and, 46
    management and, 378
    management development and, 408
    need-based theories of, 26–29
    non-cognitive theory of, 26, 27,
        38–39
    OD research and, 419
    orientation and, 231
    preretirement counseling and, 330
    reinforcement theory and, 39
    rewards and, 47
    self-, 393
    self-directed teams (SDTs) and, 439
    supportiveness and, 282
    training and, 57–59
Motivation potential score (MPS), 431
Motivator factors, 28
Motor skills, 80–82
Motorola, 20, 140
    basic skills/literacy program at, 239
    continuing education programs at,
        257
    quality training at, 250–251
Moving (stage of change model), 415
MPS. *See* Motivation potential score
    (MPS)
MTE. *See* Management training and
    experiences (MTE)
Multicultural organization, 442, 451–481
    affirmative action in, 464–466
    defined, 463
    HRD programs needed for becoming,
        477–479
    managing diversity in, 467–468,
        478
    roadblocks to becoming, 468–470
    valuing differences in, 442, 466–467,
        473, 478
    See also Cultural diversity
Multicultural training, 251
Multimedia learning centers, 20

Multinational organizations, training at, 251
Multiple scenarios, 406
Multiple treatment interference, 187
Muslims, 475

Nabisco. *See* RJR-Nabisco Corporation
NASA, 341
NASA's Quality and Excellence Award, 436
National Association for the Advancement of Colored People, 465
National Cash Register, 4
National Center on Education and the Economy, 244
National Council of Savings Institutions, 256
National Personnel Services Organization (NPSO), 48–49
National Technological University (NTU), 144
National Training Laboratories, 389
Native Americans, 475
NCR, 256
NEC, 385
Needs, 26–29
    career plateaus and, 356
    change theory and, 416
    hierarchy of, 27–28
    human processual intervention and, 446
Needs analyst, 14
Needs assessment, 88–89, 91–95
    in career development, 360, 362
    defined, 91
    design/implementation phase and, 124
    management development and, 374, 380–382, 408
    in orientation program, 228, 229–230
    purchasing assistance in, 128
    at Scott Paper Company, 88
Negative reinforcement, 39
Negative transfer, 63
Networks, 457, 461
New England Mutual Insurance, 143
New England Telephone, 408
New Jersey Bell Telephone, 5
New York Telephone, 380, 382
Non-English-speaking employees, 479
Nonequivalent control group, 186–187
Nonexperimental research design, 181–183
Nonmanagerial employees, career development for, 357–358
Nontechnical training, 237, 251–255
Norand Corporation, 252–253
Norms. *See* Group norms
Northern Telecom, 255, 438
Note-taking, 76, 82
NPSO. *See* National Personnel Services Organization (NPSO)
Nutrition program, 10, 291, 311

NYNEX, 381

Obesity, 311
Objectives, 126–128, 408
Objectivity, 279, 379
Observation, direct. *See* Direct observation
Occupational choice, 334, 325, 340
Occupational Safety and Health Act (OSHA), 247–248
OCIPS. *See* Officer Career Information and Planning System (OCIPS)
OD intervention, 11. *See also* Organization development (OD); Intervention strategy
OFCCP. *See* Office of Federal Contract Compliance Programs (OFCCP)
Office of Federal Contract Compliance Programs (OFCCP), 464
Office of Personnel Management (OPM), 380, 382–385
Office of Technology Assessment, 238
Officer Career Information and Planning System (OCIPS), 342
Ohio Edison, 281
OJT. *See* On-the-job training (OJT)
One-group pre-test/post-test design, 181, 183
On-line approach, 393
On-the-job experiences, 371, 373, 390, 392–396
On-the-job training (OJT), 133, 138–140, 159, 380
    apprenticeship and, 244
    classroom instruction combined with, 246–247
    implementing, 159–160
    one-on-one, 160
Open-ended questions, 142, 279, 280
Openness to experience, 59
Operations analysis, 99. *See also* Task analysis
OPM. *See* Office of Personnel Management (OPM)
Opportunism, 393, 400
Ordering information (in learning strategy), 76
Organization
    employee behavior model and, 25
    as environmental influence, 46–47
Organizational analysis, 94, 95–99
    sources of data for, 100–101
Organizational change
    career development and, 325
    quality training and, 249
    team building as part of, 254
    See also Change
Organizational charts, 12, 141, 250
Organizational choice, 340, 342
Organizational climate. *See* Climate, organizational
Organizational culture, 417, 418

affirmative action and, 466
career development and, 335
changing labor market and, 454–455
cultural diversity and, 452, 468
defined, 453–454
large systems change and, 441, 442
See also Multicultural organization
Organizational development (OD),
10–11, 413–448
attitudes and, 40
change process theory of, 415–416
college/university courses in, 18
coaching and, 267
cultural diversity and, 468
defined, 414
HRD programs and, 446
implementation theory of, 416–419
job design, 47
lack of fundamental research in,
419–420
model of planned change and,
420–422
team building and, 254
unions and, 428
Organizational goals, 95, 97
career paths and, 348
enrichment and, 359
global managers and, 385
large systems change and, 418
organization development (OD) and,
414
orientation and, 223
team building and, 430
See also Strategic goals
Organizational learning strategies, 76
Organizational outcomes, 43
Organizational paradigm, 421, 442
Organizational psychology, 18
Organizational resources, 95, 96
Organizational roles, 205–207
orientation and, 222, 223
Organizational socialization. *See* Socialization
Organizational structure
cultural diversity and, 468
orientation and, 223
self-directed teams (SDTs) and,
439
See also Strategic change
Organizational transformation (OT), 421
Organizing, 388
Orientation, 10, 204–233, 222–229
at Apple Training Support, 229–231
at Corning, 224, 226, 227, 228–229
cultural diversity and, 468, 477–478
designing programs for, 228–229,
232
human processual intervention and,
446
problems in, 227–228
role, custodial, and innovative,
206–207, 215, 216
supervisors and, 11

at Texas Instruments, 227
OSHA. *See* Occupational Safety and
Health Act (OSHA)
Ostracism, 44
OT. *See* Organizational transformation
(OT)
Outcomes, 43–45
Outdoor leadership programs, 257
Outgroup, 46, 402, 461
Outlines (for HRD program), 156–157
Outlining (in learning), 76
Outplacement, 341, 346
Outreach, for employee
counseling/EAPs, 293, 310
Overhead projectors/transparencies,
132, 143
Overlearning, 61–62, 63
"Ownership," 416

Pacific Bell, 256
Pacific Gas & Electric (PG&E), 466, 469
Palo Verde Nuclear Generating Station,
240
Paraphrasing
coaching and, 279, 280
in learning, 76
Pareto chart, 250
Participation
change theory and, 417
self-directed teams (SDTs) and,
439
total quality management (TQM) and,
439
Participation rate (employment), 455
Participative management, 417
coaching and, 265, 277
See also Employee participation
Partnership, coaching and, 278
Paternalism, 400
Path-goal theory, 46
Pay. *See also* Compensation; Salary
Pay raises/increases, 44, 47, 460
PC. *See* Computers; Process consulta-
tion (PC)
PDT. *See* Performance dimension
training (PDT)
Pedagogy, andragogy vs., 68, 69
Peer-intergroup model, 429
Peers, 379, 429
Penney. *See* JCPenney
People processing strategies, 213–216
"People skills," 388
Perception
career plateaus and, 356
learning and, 57, 59, 77
organizational roles and, 206
of outcomes, 44
self-fulfilling prophecy and, 45
Performance
alcoholism and, 300, 314–315
analysis, 271
career plateaus and, 356, 357
change theory and, 417

Performance (continued)
coaching for effective or superior, 273–274, 277–278
deficiency, 94, 115
employee behavior model and, 25
expectations and, 45, 207
health promotion and, 309
HRD evaluation by various indexes of, 191
job enrichment and, 432
leadership and, 45–46
motivation and, 26
objectives in, 126–127
organization development (OD) and, 417, 422
organizational roles and, 206
poor. See Poor performance
quality circles and, 434
rating. See Rater training; Rating errors
rewards and, 47
self-directed teams (SDTs) and, 439
skills and, 42
social learning theory and, 36
task analysis for optimum, 99
test for HRD evaluation, 177
variability, 103, 104
Performance appraisal/evaluation, 111–115, 177
career development and, 340, 342, 365
career plateaus and, 356
coaching and, 280–281
of minorities, 459, 461
rating from, 459
Performance dimension training (PDT), 403–404
Performance goals
attribution theory and, 37
coaching and, 277, 281, 282
See also Goal setting
Performance management systems, 8
Performance standard training (PST), 403–404
Performance standards, 102, 103–104
absolute vs. relative, 269
change theory and, 416
cultural diversity and, 477
poor performance and, 269
total quality management (TQM) and, 435–436
See also Standards and measures
Peripheral behaviors, 207
Persistence, motivation and, 26
Person analysis, 94, 110–119
Personal impact, 379
Personal outcomes, 43
Personality, learning and, 59–60
Personnel psychology, 18
Physical environment, training and, 159–160
Physical exercise, 309–310

stress and, 302, 304
See also Fitness
Physical fidelity, 65
PIC. See Private industry council (PIC)
Pillsbury, 140, 467, 469, 471
Pilot programs, 360, 362, 473
Pivotal behaviors, 207
Planned change
cultural diversity and, 470
vs. forced change, 421
model of, 420–422
Planned interventions, 414, 416, 421, 422
Planning
coaching and, 279
management and, 374, 378, 388
reflective, 374
self-directed teams and, 438
See also Human resource planning
Planters LifeSavers Company (PLC), 53, 82–83
Plaques, 47
Platform skills, 160
Pluralism, 469
Polaroid, 239, 444
"Political correctness," 469
Political environment, 96
Politics, in orientation, 230–231
Poor performance, 268–277, 356, 357
and alcoholism, 300, 314–315
Porter-Lawler model, 39, 211
Position power, 397
Positive reinforcement, 38
Positive transfer, 63
Potential assessments, 349–350
Poverty, 460
Power, 397, 458
Practicality (in HRD evaluation), 178–179
Practice, 55, 56
conditions of, 60–62
in JIT, 139
massed vs. spaced, 60–61, 63
in rater training, 404
Preemployment drug screening, 299, 300
Preretirement counseling, 330, 341, 344, 346–347
President's Commission on Mental Health, 294
Primerica, 444
Printed materials (for training), 143
Private industry council (PIC), 241
Problem analysis, 388
Problem solving
change theory and, 416
convergent learning and, 75
cultural diversity and, 474
glass ceiling and, 458
groups for, 254
learning and, 57, 78
self-directed teams and, 438, 439

total quality management (TQM) and, 436, 439
Procedural knowledge, 78, 80
Process consultation (PC), 416, 430
Process flow analysis, 250
Process skills, 249, 254–255
Process specialists, 424, 425
Procter & Gamble, 385, 480
Productivity
    alternative work schedules vs. job redesign and, 433
    career development and, 336
    downsizing and, 444
    employee counseling and, 288, 293
    health promotion and, 309
    leader-member exchange (LMX) and, 402
    organization development (OD) and, 417, 422
    quality circles and, 434
    self-directed teams (SDTs) and, 439
    team building and, 429, 430
    technostructural interventions and, 433
Products, 223, 249
Professional associations, 256–257
Professional meetings, 257, 258
Professionals, 20, 255–258. See also HRD professionals
Profitability, organization development (OD) and, 422
Program designer, 14
Promotability, 341, 349, 350. See also Potential assessment
Promotions, 47
    career plateaus and, 357
    discrimination in, 460, 477
PST. See Performance standard training (PST)
Psychological fidelity, 65
Psychological testing, in career development, 341
Psychomotor activities, 42
Public Employees Federation, 256
Punishment, 39
Pygmalion effect, 45

QC. See Quality circle (QC)
Quality
    Deming's principles regarding, 417, 418
    quality circles and, 434
    predictions for year 2000 regarding, 19
    product, 249
    self-directed teams (SDTs) and, 439
    skills, 249
    sociotechnical intervention and, 446
    total quality management (TQM) and, 436, 439
    training, 248–251
Quality circles (QC), 254, 417, 434–435

total quality management (TQM) and, 436
Quality of work life, 47, 417
Quasi-experimental designs, 186–187
Questionnaires, 112
    compared with other methods, 177
    cultural diversity and, 470
    job inventory, 105
    participant reaction, 174, 175
    writing effective, 176
Questions, types of, 142

Race, career development and, 461
Racial minorities. See Minorities
Racism/racial discrimination, 452, 454, 480
    affirmative action and, 466
    cultural diversity and, 468, 471, 477
    See also Discrimination
Random assignment, 183, 184, 186
"Rapid response teams," 243
Rater training, 403–405
Rating error training (RET), 403–404
Rating errors, 349, 403
Rating scales, 109, 113. See also Self-rating
Reaction, coaching and, 276
Reactive arrangements, 187
Realistic job preview (RJP), 205, 217–222
Reasoning, 57, 75
Recession, 96
Reciprocal teaching, 79
Recognition, 44, 47
    total quality management (TQM) and, 436
    at Xerox, 447
Recruiting, 6–7
    affirmative action and, 465, 479
    career development and, 340, 342
    cultural diversity and, 452, 479
    discrimination in, 459
    employee counseling and, 288, 289
    expectations and, 208
    "flypaper approach" to, 217
    glass ceiling and, 459
    job posting for, 348
    videos for, 220
    See also Realistic job preview (RJP)
Referral
    career development and, 340
    in employee counseling/EAPs, 290–291, 297
Reflection of feeling, 279, 280
Reflective observation (RO), 74, 75
Reflective planning, 374
Reflective questions, 142
Reflector, 424, 425
Refreezing, 415, 416
Regression, in HRD evaluation, 187
Rehabilitation Act, 314–315
Rehearsal learning strategies, 76

Rehearsal phase of modeling, 405
Reinforcement theory, 27, 38–39
    change theory and, 416
    learning and, 55, 56, 80
    rewards and, 47
Relational research, 181, 183
Relaxation, learning and, 76
Relaxation exercises, 303
Relevant behaviors, 207
Reliability, 177–178
Remedial activities/training, 115, 238
Reorganization. See Large systems
    change
Reports, orientation and, 223
Representative STS programs, 440
Rescheduling. See Alternative work
    schedules (AWS)
Research, 8, 14
    HRD evaluation and, 180–189
    organization development (OD), lack
    of, 419–420
Resource exchange, 402
Resource library, cultural diversity and,
    467, 468
Respect, coaching and, 279
Response shift bias, 180
Responsibility
    job design and, 47
    job enrichment and, 431
    self-directed teams and, 437
Restraining forces, 415, 426
RET. See Rating error training (RET)
Retention, 61–63, 80
    feedback and, 62
    See also Memory
Retention phase (of modeling), 405
Retirement, 336
    incentives for, and career plateaus,
    357
    mentoring and adjustment to, 351
    See also Preretirement counseling
Retraining, 359
Retrieval, learning and, 57
Reverse discrimination, 465
Review boards, 189
Rewards, 44
    career development and, 356, 357,
    365
    co-workers and, 47
    large systems change and, 417
    leader-member exchange (LMX) and,
    402
    organization development (OD) and,
    414
    total quality management (TQM) and,
    436
    for trainees, 97
    at Xerox, 447
Risk-taking, 379
RJP. See Realistic job preview (RJP)
RJR-Nabisco Corporation, 53
RO. See Reflective observation (RO)

Robotics, 238
Rocco Enterprises, 240
Rockwell Tactical Systems, 437
Role clarification, 416
Role conflict, career plateaus and, 357
Role innovation orientation, 215, 216.
    See also Innovative orientation
Role models, 457–458, 478
Role orientation, 207. See also Organi-
    zational roles
Role play, 65, 74, 113, 151–152
    for behavior modeling, 405, 407
    coaching and, 280
    employee counseling/EAPs and, 289
    videotape used for, 144
Roles. See Organizational roles
Run chart, 250
Russians, 475

Sabbaticals/education leaves, 257, 258,
    357
"Safe landing" program, 48–49
Safety training, 247–248
Salary, 459. See also Compensation;
    Pay
Sales training, 252
SANE, 288, 318–319
Satellite broadcasts (in training),
    144–145
Satisfaction. See Job satisfaction
Saturn division (of General Motors),
    215, 235–236, 252
    self-directed teams at, 255
Saturn Training and Partnership
    (STEP), 258–259
Scandinavian Airlines Systems, 253
Scanning, 385
Scattergram, 250
Scheduling, work. See Alternative work
    schedules (AWS)
Schein's socialization model, 211, 213
Schein's change model, 415–416
School-to-work program, 245
Scientific management, 4
Scott Paper Company, 87–88
Scott Worldwide Foodservice (SWF),
    87–88
Screening, 308, 312. See also Preem-
    ployment screening
Scripted situation data, 178
SDTs. See Self-directed teams (SDTs)
Seasons, 330–331
Selection, 6–7
    assessment centers for, 349–350
    career development and, 340, 342
    career plateaus and, 356
    HRD evaluation and, 187
    job posting and, 348
    realistic job preview and, 217, 219
    self-, 217, 220
Self-assessment, 341–346
    information needed for, 347

Self-awareness, 337, 339, 340
  assessment center and, 350
  of baby boom generation, 359, 360,
    361
  in career development, 344–346
  career plateaus and, 356
Self-concept, change theory and, 416
Self-confidence, learning and, 72
Self-diagnosis, 70
Self-directed, 68
Self-Directed Search, The, 342
Self-directed teams (SDTs), 254, 417,
    437–439, 446
  total quality management (TQM)
    compared with, 439–440, 441
Self-discovery, 152
Self-efficacy, 36, 406
  attribution theory and, 37, 38
Self-esteem
  affirmative action and, 466
  career development and, 336
  enrichment and, 359
  fundamental attribution error and,
    270
Self-fulfilling prophecy, 45, 46–47, 350
Self-image, 335
Self-knowledge, management develop-
    ment and, 371
Self-managed teams, 254. See also
    Self-directed teams (SDTs)
Self-questioning, 76
Self-rating, 115
Self-regulation and control, 79
Self-report data, 179–180, 349
Self-selection, 217, 220
Self-study modules, 259
Semiautonomous groups, 417, 439
Seminars, 10, 20, 258
  career development and, 341, 358
  sabbaticals and, 258
  at Saturn, 259
  for skills training, 242
Semiskilled workers, 4–5, 20
Senior Executive Service (SES), 382
Senior management. See Top/senior
    management
Sensor, manager as, 385
Service quality, 249. See also Customer
    service training
SES. See Senior Executive Service
    (SES)
Sexism/gender-based discrimination,
    452, 454, 480
  affirmative action and, 466
  cultural diversity and, 468, 471, 477
Sexual harassment, 18, 96, 454
"Show, tell, do, and check," 5
SHRM. See Society for Human
    Resource Management (SHRM)
Simulation training, 65, 150–151
  for HRD evaluation, 177, 180
  or potential assessment, 350

"Skill stretching," 278
Skill variety, 356, 431
Skill-acquisition interventions, 303–304
Skilled employees, vs. unskilled, 236,
    289
Skills
  career development and, 326, 359
  career plateaus and, 355, 356
  cultural diversity and, 473, 474
  defined, 42
  leadership and learning new, 46
  process vs. quality, 249
  task analysis and, 105, 107
  task vs. process, 254–255
  See also KSAs (knowledge, skills,
    and abilities)
Skills and technical training, 10
Skills assessment feedback, 40
Skills gap, 19, 237–238
Skills inventory, 97, 101, 341, 349
  developmental needs and, 115
Skills training, 235–260
  methods of, 242
  at Saturn division, 235–236, 258–259
  self-directed teams and, 438
  technostructural intervention and,
    446
  See also Basic skills/literacy educa-
    tion; Nontechnical training; Techni-
    cal training
SKILLWARE, 153
Slides, 143
Smile sheet, 174
SMIs. See Stress management inter-
    ventions (SMIs)
Smith-Hughes Act, 4
Smoking, 10, 257, 310–311
  policy at Central States Life & Health
    Company, 318–319
Social environment, 96
Social learning theory, 27, 36–37, 39,
    405
  behavior modeling and, 152
Social loafing, 48
Social needs
  mentoring and, 351
  training and, 160
Social pressure, 40
Social reinforcement, 37
Social security, 336
Socialization, 204–217
  anticipatory, 210–211, 218
  career development and, 334
  cultural diversity and, 477–478, 480
  defined, 205
  hazing and bonding in, 226
  human processual intervention and,
    446
  institutionalized vs. individualized,
    215–216
  mentoring and, 351, 457
  organizational culture and, 454

Socialization *(continued)*
  orientation roles and, 223, 225
  outcomes of, 209–213
  people-processing tactics in, 213–216
  stage models of, 210–213
  strategies of, 215
Society for Human Resource Management (SHRM), 469
Sociopolitical culture, 452, 453
Sociotechnical systems (STS) designs, 417, 433–440, 446
Software, 153–154
Solomon four-group design, 185
Southwest Airlines, 144
Spaced practice, 60–61, 62, 63
Spanish-speaking workers, 240
  See also English-as-a-second language (ESL)
SPC. *See* Statistical process control (SPC) techniques
Stability, 325, 333, 334
  balancing change and, 419
Staff authority, 8
Staff survey, 109
Stagnation, 333, 336
Standards and measures, 435–436, 447. *See also* Performance standards
Stanley-Bostitch, Inc., 246–247
Static media, 143
Statistical power, 185
Statistical process control (SPC) techniques, 249, 250, 436
Status, 325, 358
STEAMER, 154
Steering committee, 361, 434
STEP. *See* Saturn Training and Partnership (STEP)
Stereotyping, 452
  cultural diversity backlash and, 469
  mentoring and, 352
  minorities, 463
  women, 459
Stigmatizing, 465–466
Stimulus variability, 64, 65
Stimulus-response-feedback method, 104
Storyboarding, 144
Strategic change, 442–444
Strategic goals
  career development and, 348, 359, 360
  cultural diversity and, 471, 478
  enrichment and, 359
  management development and, 408
  organizational analysis linked to, 97, 98
  See also Organizational goals
Stress
  career plateaus and, 357
  counseling for, 10

defined, 302
  employee counseling/EAPs and, 288, 296, 301–305, 313
  job design and, 47
  organizational roles and, 206
  orientation and, 222
  preretirement, 330
Stress management
  career plateaus and, 357
  counseling on, 346
  cultural diversity and, 474, 475, 477
  human processual intervention and, 446
  training, 257
Stress management interventions (SMIs), 301–307
  defined, 302
  evaluating, 313–314
  legal issues regarding, 315
Stressors, organizational, 303
STS. *See* Sociotechnical systems (STS) designs
Subcultures, 452
Subjective norms, 40
Subject-matter expert (SME), 131, 438, 440
  at Alexander Consulting Group, 123–124, 161–162
Subordinates, 379, 380, 393
  leader-member exchange theory regarding, 402
  position power and, 397
  survey feedback and, 429
Substance abuse, 10
  behavior patterns of, 298, 300
  employee counseling/EAPs and, 198, 288, 289, 293–294
  preemployment screening for, 299, 300
  See also Cocaine addiction
Succession planning, 88, 327, 341, 350
Summarizing, in learning, 76
Summary person analysis, 110
Superiors, 379, 380, 429
Supervisors
  as career counselors, 338–340, 341, 347
  coaching by. *See* Coaching
  employee behavior model and, 25
  employee counseling/EAPs and, 293, 295–297, 316, 317
  as environmental influence, 45–46
  HRD role of, 11
  job rotation and, 140
  leader-member exchange theory regarding, 402
  learning tasks of, 61
  observation of job behavior by, 175
  orientation and, 225–226
  quality circles and, 435
  support for learning from, 66
  See also Superiors

Supervisory training, 10
Supportiveness/support, 64, 66
    coaching and, 281–282
    large systems change and, 444
    mentoring and, 351, 353
Survey feedback, 416, 428–429
Suspension, job, 275
Synergistic learning, 385, 386
System, 425

T&D. *See* Training and development
    (T&D)
Taco Bell, 143
Talent scout, manager as, 385
Tardiness, employee counseling and,
    288
Targets, in management, 376, 379
Task analysis, 56, 60, 94, 99–110
  example of, 108–110
Task forces, 373, 380, 381
Task identification, 99, 103–106
Task identity, 356, 431
Task sequencing, 56, 62
Task significance, 356, 431
Task skills, 254–255
Task structure, 397
Taxonomies, 42–43, 79–80
Teams/team building, 131, 401,
    429–430
    career development and, 364
    change theory and, 416
    human processual intervention and,
      446
    self-directed, 417
    training and, 251, 254–255
    See also Self-directed teams (SDTs)
Team Management, 400
Technical HRD competencies, 15
Technical specialist, 424
Technical training, 237, 243–251
    defined, 237
    technostructural intervention and,
      446
Technology
    artifacts and, 454
    change theory and, 417, 418–419
    enrichment and, 359
    large systems change and, 418–419
Technostructural intervention, 416–417,
    430–433, 446
Telecommunication, 144–148
Teleconferencing, 20, 145, 147
Television (in training), 144–145, 146
Tenant Company, 435
Tenneco, 309
Tension, 27
Termination, job
    alcohol abuse and, 314–315
    coaching and, 275, 277
    counseling for, 346
Test anxiety, 76
Tests, 76, 112

aptitude, 240
drug/urine, 293, 314
for HRD evaluation, 177, 180, 187
for potential assessment, 350
psychological, for career develop-
    ment, 341
Texas Instruments Corporation (TI),
    108–110, 145, 227
Textbooks (for training), 143, 157
Thai culture, 463
Theoretical models/thinking, 74, 75
Theory Y, 267
Thinking (as learning style), 74, 75
"Thought transmission," 279
Time management, 257
    stress and, 302, 303
Time series design, 186–187
Time/work sampling, 102, 104, 112
Tokenism/tokens, 457, 459, 478
Top/senior management
    career development and, 360, 362
    employee counseling/EAPs and, 293
    HRD professionals and, 13
    management development and, 408
    managing diversity and, 467–468, 471
    quality circles and, 435
    self-directed teams and, 437
    total quality management (TQM) and,
      435, 447
    training programs and, 99
Total quality management (TQM),
    248–251, 417, 435–437
    self-directed teams (SDTs) compared
    with, 439–440, 441
    seven basic tools for, 250
    sociotechnical intervention and, 446
    at Xerox, 446–447
Towers/Perrin survey, 468–469
TQM. *See* Total quality management
    (TQM)
Tradition, socialization and, 213
Trainability, 57–59
Trainers, 160–161, 424, 425
    audiovisual aids and, 144
    lectures by, 141
    in role play, 152
    selecting, 130–132
    "training the," 466
Training and development (T&D), 6, 10,
    11, 18
Training and Development, 161
Training competency, 131, 160
Training design, 60–62
Training Within Industry (TWI), 5–6
Training/HRD programs, 2–21, 87–121
    attitudes and, 40–43
    attribute-treatment interaction (ATI)
      and, 68, 72
    attribution theory and, 38
    business games in, 65, 113, 150
    career development and, 325,
      340–342, 350–353, 362–363

Training/HRD programs (continued)
  career plateaus and, 356
  case study method of, 65, 113,
    148–150
  coaching and, 271, 273
  cognitive theories of motivation and,
    28
  computer-based. See Computer-
    based training
  costs of, 190–197
  cultural diversity and, 451–481,
    466–468, 473–479
  data collection for, 168, 174–180
  delivery of, 130, 140
  design/implementation phase in. See
    Design/implementation phase
  discrimination in, 460–461
  early programs, 4–5
  employee counseling/EAPs as, 289,
    293
  evaluating, 90–91, 165–200
  feedback in, 62
  four-dimensional management model
    and, 378
  fraud in, 190
  group dynamics and, 48
  and HRD process model, 89, 125,
    166
  HRD professionals and, 14
  HRM and, 6–8
  implementing, 159–161
  interference in, 63
  job design and, 47
  journals relating to, 161
  leadership and, 46, 402–403. See
    also Leadership training
  learning and, 53–84
  learning principles and, 56–59
  lesson plan for, 132–136
  management development and,
    370–371. See also Management
    development
  methods, 133–155
  minorities and, 463
  modeling and, 37
  models for evaluating, 170–173
  motivation and, 26, 39, 43
  needs assessment in. See Needs
    assessment
  older workers, 68–70, 72–73
  organization development (OD) and,
    446
  organizational structure of, 11
  orientation and, 222–229
  outcomes and, 44–45
  phases of, 88–91
  pre-purchase evaluation of, 169
  predictions for year 2000 regarding,
    18–19
  preparing materials for, 156–157
  prioritizing needs in, 108, 119, 124,
    108, 119, 124

  professionals. See HRD profes-
    sionals
  purchasing programs for, 128–130
  reinforcement theory and, 39, 39
  retention in, 62–63
  rewards and, 47
  at RJR Nabisco, 53–54
  role play in, 65, 74, 113, 151–152
  scheduling, 90, 157–158
  selecting, 155–156
  self-directed teams and, 438
  self-assessment and, 342
  simulation in, 65, 150–151
  skills gap and, 19
  skills. See Skills training
  social learning theory and, 36–37
  supplemental materials for, 128
  technical. See Technical training
  term approved by ASTD, 6
  total quality management (TQM) and,
    436
  "train the trainer" and, 128, 131–132
  "transfer of training" and, 63–66
  women and, 459
  at Xerox, 447
  See also Education; Learning
Training magazine, 133, 161
Transfer (of training/learning), 63–66,
  80
Transfer of training/learning
  for behavior modeling, 406
  in classroom method, 140
  on-the-job methods and, 133, 138
  role play and, 152
  mentoring and, 351
Transfers (job), 44, 275, 359, 380
Transition and adaption, 385, 386
Transition state (in large systems
  change), 441–442, 445
Transnational managers, 385–387
Travelers, The, 144
Treatment discrimination, 459, 460–461
"Triangulation approach," 473
"True score" ratings, 404
Trust, coaching and, 279
TRW, 444
Tuition reimbursement, 257–258, 341,
  349
  nonexempt employees and, 358
Turnover
  employee counseling/EAPs and, 198,
    288, 293, 318
  health promotion and, 309, 310
  leader-member exchange (LMX) and,
    402
  leadership and, 46
  mentoring and, 351
  organizational roles and, 206
  orientation and, 222, 225, 225
  realistic job preview and, 219, 220,
    221
  self-directed teams (SDTs) and, 439

stress and, 302
Tutoring, 241, 242
TWI. *See* Training Within Industry (TWI)
Two factor theory. *See* Herzberg's two factor theory
Two-group post-test-only design, 181, 184–185
Two-group pre-test/post-test design, 181, 184

Unemployment
    employee counseling/EAPs and, 293
    minorities and, 460
Unfreezing, 415
Unions, 7
    affirmative action and, 465
    employee counseling/EAPs and, 293, 296, 315–316
    job design/enlargement and, 431
    organization development (OD) and, 428
    quality circles and, 435
    self-directed teams (SDTs) and, 439
    skills training and, 240, 245, 247, 256
    Xerox and, 414, 447
    See also Labor relations
United Auto Workers, 240
United Kingdom, 294
United States v. the National Association for the Advancement of Colored People, Inc,. 465
University courses. *See* College/university courses
University of Michigan, 390
Unskilled workers, 4, 236
US WEST, 466
Utility analysis, 191, 195–196

Vaccination (against expectations), 217, 220
Valence, 44
Valid information, 416
Validity (in HRD evaluation), 178, 188
    internal, 181, 182
    quasi-experimental designs and, 186–187
Value shaping, 278
Valued outcomes, 62
Values
    artifacts and, 454
    baby boom generation and, 359, 361
    career development and organizational, 364
    career plateaus and, 356
    change theory and, 416
    coaching and, 278
    cultural diversity and, 468, 470
    divergent learning and, 75
    human processual intervention and, 446
    large systems change and, 417, 418
    orientation and, 222, 230

socialization and, 217
women and, 459
Valuing differences, 18, 442, 466–467, 473, 478
    See also Cultural diversity
VDL. *See* Vertical dyad Linkage (VDL) theory
Verbal information, 80–82
Vertical dyad linkage (VDL) theory, 46, 402
Vertical loading, 356
Vickers AMD, 255
Videos
    for behavior modeling, 405, 406, 407
    for career development, 358
    realistic job preview and, 220
    in training, 74, 132, 143–144, 146, 242
Vietnamese, 463, 475
Vision, 362, 421
Visual aids, 141. *See also* Audio-visual aids
Vocational education, 3–4, 19, 245

Wallace Company, 437
Wanous's socialization model, 211, 213
WARN. *See* Worker Adjustment and Retraining Notification Act (WARN)
Warning letters, 275
Watching, 74, 75
Weber v. Kaiser Aluminum and Chemicals, 465
Weight control, 10
Well-being, employee, 414, 422, 429
Wellness programs
    at Central States Health & Life Company, 287–288, 318–319
    evaluating, 313–314
    legal issues regarding, 315
    See also Fitness programs; Health promotion programs (HPPs)
Western Electric, 4
Westinghouse, 4, 444
Weyerhauser Company, 280
Wharton School at the University of Pennsylvania, 388, 389, 390
What Color Is Your Parachute?, 342
WMS and Company, Inc., 120
Women, 18, 479
    affirmative action and, 465, 479
    glass ceiling and, 456–459, 463, 474
    organizational culture and, 455–459
    as percentage of new workers, 452, 454–455
Word processing, 153
Work Force 2000, 18, 454. *See also* Hudson Institute
Work force, 8, 18
Work habits, 416, 422
Work planning and review system, 113

Workbooks, in career development, 341, 342–344
Worker Adjustment and Retraining Notification Act (WARN), 243
Worker's compensation, 288, 318
Workplace competencies, 237–238. *See also* Basic skills
Workshops, 289, 358
Written test, 177

Xerox Corporation, 20, 153
  basic skills/literacy program at, 239
  change at, 413–414, 446–447
  coaching at, 264–265, 283–284
  company academy/college at, 391, 392
  cultural diversity at, 468
  health promotion at, 309, 313

Zero transfer, 63